Human–Computer Interaction

Human–Computer Interaction

JENNY PREECE

Yvonne Rogers
Helen Sharp
David Benyon
Simon Holland
Tom Carey

ADDISON-WESLEY PUBLISHING COMPANY

Wokingham, England · Reading, Massachusetts · Menlo Park, California · New York
Don Mills, Ontario · Amsterdam · Bonn · Sydney · Singapore
Tokyo · Madrid · San Juan · Milan · Paris · Mexico City · Seoul · Taipei

EDITOR-IN-CHIEF: Simon Plumtree
PRODUCTION MANAGER: Stephen Bishop
PRODUCTION EDITOR: Susan Keany
PRODUCTION CONTROLLER: Jim Allman
TEXT DESIGNER: Valerie O'Donnell
ILLUSTRATIONS: Chartwell Illustrators
TYPESETTERS: CRB Associates, Norwich
COVER DESIGNERS: Designers & Partners, Oxford
PRINTER: R.R. Donnelley & Sons Co.

First printed 1994. Reprinted 1994 and 1995 (twice).

British Library Cataloguing in Publication Data
A catalogue record for this book is available from the British Library.

Library of Congress Cataloging in Publication Data
Preece, Jenny,
    Human-computer interaction / Jenny Preece [with] Yvonne Rogers ...
[et al.].
        p. cm.
    Includes bibliographical references and index.
    ISBN 0-201-62769-8
    1. Human-computer interaction. I. Title.
QA76.9.H85P74   1994
004'.01'9--dc20   94-16158
                                                           CIP

Trademark notice
MacPaint, QuickTime, MacDraw, HyperCard and Macintosh are trademarks of Apple Computer Inc.
Excel, Word, Microsoft and Windows for Workgroups are trademarks of Microsoft Corporation
Post-it is a trademark of 3M
UNIX is a trademark of UNIX System Laboratories Inc.
VODIS is a trademark of British Telecom, Logica (Cambridge) Ltd, Cambridge University
Private Eye is a trademark of Reflection Technology
SuperBook is a trademark of AT&T
Telstar is a trademark of British Telecom
DataView is a trademark of VI Corp.
PARTS Workbench is a trademark of Digitalk Inc.
X11 Windows System is a trademark of Massachusetts Institute of Technology
Prograph is a trademark of Gunakara Sun Systems Ltd
UIM/X is a trademark of Visual Edge Software Ltd
Etchasketch is a trademark of Peter Pan Playthings Ltd
MacroMind Director is a trademark of Macromedia
Data Glove is a trademark of VPL

Foreword

The growth of interest in human–computer interaction (HCI) in the past 20 years has been extraordinary. It is one of the most rapidly developing subjects in computer science on both sides of the Atlantic. What was a fascinating research subject is now recognized as a vital component of successful computer applications. It is not hard to see why.

In the last decade the power of computing has risen dramatically and costs have dropped in an equally spectacular fashion. Computers were the province of the specialist but are now a mass consumer product. The majority of the population in the developed world now encounter computer applications as part of their daily routine; in the high street, embedded in domestic products, in school, at work and so on. As a result, the average user of a computer system is now less likely to understand the technology and also less likely to spend much time learning about a particular system. The developers of computer systems now have to deliver beneficial services to the user, *and* deliver them in a usable way. Many of these users cannot be trained and systems have to be designed so that they can simply walk up to the device and use it successfully first time.

Interaction with computers has come a long way since punched cards and binary codes. We know a great deal about how to support successful interaction by different kinds of people. There is now a very considerable research literature on HCI. What has been missing is a substantial textbook on the subject, and this is why this volume is such a landmark for the discipline.

HCI is inherently a multidisciplinary subject. The student has to embrace theories of human behaviour as well as the principles of computer systems design. This textbook introduces us to the separate disciplines and then shows us how to combine them. The authors first take us on a tour of the many human characteristics that have to be understood before we can judge what would make a system easy to use and easy to learn. I am particularly pleased to note that the book also explores the social and organizational context of the user, since this can have a very powerful effect upon whether we find a computer system acceptable and usable.

The book then offers us a guide to the increasingly wide array of means by which humans can interact with the technology. To the ubiquitous keyboard we can now add the mouse, the tracker ball, speech recognizers and the headset by which we can enter the world of virtual reality. With so many options to choose from, it is no wonder that it is now a major task to determine which form of interaction is best for which user and which task.

The richness of the human condition and the growing richness of technological opportunities means there is no panacea for HCI, no single right answer. It is appropriate that the bulk of this textbook addresses the design process by which we can develop the right system to fit a specific purpose. We need to know how to study users and their tasks and how to relate this information to design styles, human factors theories, guidelines and standards in order to select and build an appropriate form of interaction. We also need to know how to evaluate whether systems are in fact usable by the target user population.

One of the strengths of this textbook is that it has been developed by a group of people who are experts in both HCI and in the preparation of teaching materials. The Open University distance learning course on HCI has been rightly acclaimed and has proved a very sound basis upon which to build this ambitious textbook. There is a rich variety of exercises, illustrations and examples to support the text which brings the subject to life and bridges the gap from theory to practice. The interviews with the leading figures in the field also serve to convey the sense of excitement and mission which pervades the subject. It is my hope that the many students who study this text – whether from a computing or human science background – will come to share the excitement of those of us who have helped shape the discipline. Good HCI will not result from the work of a few specialists. It needs the informed work of the multitude of people involved in the design of the products and services that reach the mass of the public. I believe this book provides the basis for everybody who is now or will in the future be involved in design to improve the quality of interaction between people and computers.

Ken Eason
Loughborough
March, 1994

Preface

Dramatic advances in technology have revolutionized the way that people now interact with computers. Bigger and faster machines, in conjunction with ISDN and satellites, make it possible not only to process and transmit combinations of video and live images, as well as text, sound and graphics, but also to interact with this data. Virtual reality and intelligent agents also promise, or maybe we should say threaten, to blur reality and science in ways that many of us have associated only with science fiction.

In parallel with these technical advances, our understanding of Human–Computer Interaction (HCI) has also advanced phenomenally over the last ten years. Research into all aspects of HCI has extended our understanding of what it means to interact with technology and how to put this understanding to practical use in the design and evaluation of products. Much of this knowledge has found and is finding its way into university courses.

Despite this growth of knowledge, technology will always lead the way. The speed of advance in research and development makes it difficult to prevent the gap between research and development and the uptake of key ideas in education from broadening. However, sound principles and basic knowledge provide a good basis from which to consider the implications of new technology. In this book we try to provide these and to relate them to some state-of-the-art applications as well as to systems that have become commonplace.

Several key themes are developed in the book:

- Balanced coverage: HCI is a multidisciplinary subject that draws on concepts and skills mainly from computer science, psychology, sociology, anthropology and industrial design. We have tried to give a representative coverage of the important issues from each.
- Design methods: We do not believe that there is a single solution to the problem of how to do interaction design, so we do not strongly advocate a single method. Our solution has been to pick those methods that we have found successful and to include brief coverage of some of the more well-known alternatives.

- State-of-the-art applications: Computer supported cooperative working (CSCW), hyper- and multimedia and virtual reality are discussed in appropriate chapters throughout the book and not in separate chapters on their own. CSCW and multimedia, for example, are becoming so pervasive that we prefer to discuss them where they relate to concepts or issues under discussion. New research and development issues, such as distributed cognition, participative design and evaluation, are covered in a similar way.
- Ethical issues: these issues are important and we urge instructors to introduce them as discussion topics in classes. Unfortunately, space constraints have not permitted us to give much coverage of these issues.

Readership

This book is intended for students in both undergraduate and graduate courses in computer science, psychology and social sciences. It will also be useful to students with a professional background who work in developer or user organizations.

How to use this book

HCI in the curriculum

Our book is designed to be flexible so that it can be used for teaching a variety of different courses. It has the following components:

- An introduction to HCI that describes what HCI is and why it is important (Part I).
- Two parts that consider the human (Part II) and technological (Part III) aspects of HCI. Part II discusses cognitive and organizational psychology and related subjects and Part III examines the selection of devices and interaction styles drawing on their use in particular exemplar systems when appropriate.
- Parts IV, V and VI teach the design process. Part IV covers the techniques and methods used in interaction design. Part V discusses the various forms of design support available for designers and Part VI describes a range of evaluation methods.

There are many cross-references between the chapters within the different parts. The human aspects (Part II) and technology aspects (Part III) provide the basic knowledge that is needed for interaction design: design methods, design support and evaluation (Parts IV, V and VI, respectively). However, in order to make sense of many of the issues relating to the technology it will be necessary to understand the human aspects. Furthermore, as we explain in the introduction and reaffirm many times throughout the text, design, design support and evaluation are closely interwoven. Indeed the important role of evaluation throughout design is stressed by adopting the star life cycle (Hix and Hartson, 1993) in which its central role is made obvious. Consequently, we expect readers to regularly switch between different parts.

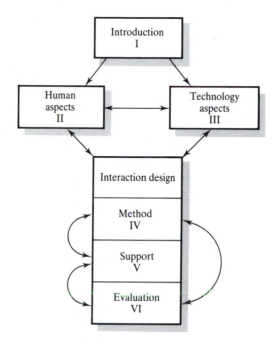

Figure 1 The relationship between the parts of this book.

We see the relationship and use of the different parts of our book as illustrated in Figure 1.

We recognize that there are marked differences in educational structure in different countries – a workshop at INTERACT'90 made this point apparent (see Mantei *et al.*, 1991 for further discussion). Through Tom Carey and Jenny Preece we have knowledge of the ACM SIGCHI Curriculum Group's Curricula for Human–Computer Interaction,[†] chaired by Tom Hewett (ACM SIGCHI, 1992), and also with the HCI Education and Curriculum Group of the British Computer Society.

The ACM SIGCHI Curriculum is now being adopted by many countries outside of North America who are tailoring it to national and local needs. Germany, Australia and Britain, for example, are following this route and others are likely to follow. Although there are many courses that could be given, each with a different bias reflecting its own particular aims, the SIGCHI Curriculum document recognizes four generic courses and we shall adopt these as representative of many 'typical' courses in HCI. Two of the courses are technology oriented (User Interface Design and Development (CS1) and Phenomena and Theories of Human–Computer Interaction (CS2)) and would fit well in software engineering and more general computer

---

† Copies of the ACM SIGCHI Curricula for Human–Computer Interaction may be ordered prepaid from:
ACM Order Department
PO Box 64145
Baltimore, MD 21264 USA
Telephone + 1-800-342-6626, + 1-410-528-4261

ACM Order Number: 608920
ISBN 0-89791-474-0

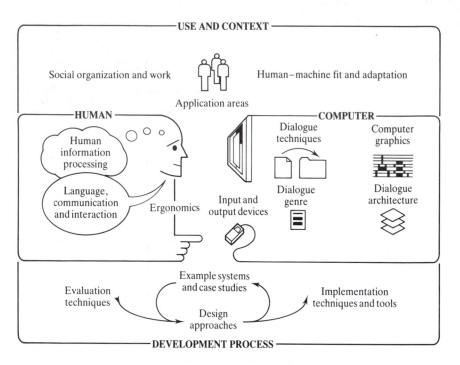

Figure 2 Human–Computer Interaction as described by the SIGCHI Committee (ACM SIGCHI, 1992).

science programs. The other two courses have a human orientation (Psychology of Human–Computer Interaction (PSY1) and Human Aspects of Information Systems (MSI)) and would fit in psychology programmes. CS2 and PSY1 also provide a basis for moving into more specialized and research-oriented programmes of study. You will notice that the relationship of topics suggested in the SIGCHI Curriculum, shown in Figure 2, is quite similar to the plan of our book.

The following general suggestions are intended to help those planning to use this text with the SIGCHI Curricula.

User Interface Design and Development (CS1)
This course stresses practical software development and it would be a natural complement to software engineering. Suggested parts of this book that might be useful include:

Introduction (Part I)
Human Aspects (Part II, Chapters 4–7 are the most relevant)
Technology Aspects (Part III)
Design (Part IV)
Design Support (Part V)
Evaluation (Part VI)

Phenomena and Theories of Human–Computer Interaction (CS2)
This course looks at HCI in a broader context and it is intended for students with a good background in computer science who wish to specialize in HCI.

> Introduction (Part I)
> Human Aspects (Part II, Chapters 4–7 and overview of the other chapters)
> Design (Part IV)
> Design Support (Part V, overview of Chapters 23–26)
> Evaluation (Part VI)

Psychology of Human–Computer Interaction (PSY1)
This course would most likely be offered in psychology or social sciences departments, where it is considered important to stress the theoretical and empirical foundations of the field. These students are assumed to have knowledge of human information processing, empirical methods and applied statistics. The main emphasis of this course is, therefore, to take this knowledge and help students to apply it to system design and evaluation.

> Introduction (Part I)
> Human Aspects (Part II, focus on Chapters 7–10)
> Technology Aspects (Part III, focus on Chapters 13, 15, 16 and overview of the other chapters)
> Design (Part IV, Chapter 21 may not be needed)
> Design Support (Part V, Chapters 23, 26 and 27 are the most relevant)
> Evaluation (Part VI)

Human Aspects of Information Systems (MISI)
This course is designed to give professional non-technically oriented people a better understanding of the HCI issues in the systems with which they interact. The suggested syllabus is based on the premise that many of these people will need to make decisions about what technology to buy and how to integrate it into organizations.

> Introduction (Part I)
> Human Aspects (Part II, Chapters 7 and 10 are particularly relevant and an overview of Chapters 4–6 will be useful)
> Technology Aspects (Part III, Chapters 13, 15 and 16 are the most relevant)
> Design (Part IV, Chapter 17 and knowledge of Chapter 22 may be useful if working with developers)
> Evaluation (Part VI, an overview)

If you wish to obtain the ACM SIGCHI Curriculum the address is given on p. ix.

How to study with this book

Most chapters are quite short so that they are convenient to study and can be worked through easily in an evening. Each chapter also has a number of special features to help you study more effectively. These include:

- **Aims and objectives** are listed at the beginning of each chapter to tell you what you should be able to do after studying the chapter.
- **Key points** are listed at the end of the chapter so that you can check the main things that you should know after studying the chapter.
- **An overview and mini-contents list** are provided at the beginning of each chapter to give you a preview of what to expect in the chapter.
- **Exercises and questions** are included in the text to help you study effectively. The aim of the exercises is to encourage you to apply the concepts that have just been taught to a particular example or they may just ask you to reflect. Comments are provided after the exercises. These exercises are an important part of your learning and you should not omit them, because they often contribute key ideas to the flow of the text. Questions are different. There are fewer questions and they are there to encourage you to revise important concepts as you study to ensure that you have learnt these concepts before proceeding through the text. The answers to questions are placed at the end of the book.
- **Boxes** contain additional information and examples. They are an important part of the book but they can be omitted on first reading. However, we don't recommend you to make this your usual practice.
- **An annotated list of suggested further reading** is included at the end of each chapter so that you can find more material on aspects of interest.
- **Terms** that are important are shown in bold and defined when they are first introduced and a definition of most of them is included in the glossary at the end of the book for easy reference.
- **References** are listed at the end of the book in the normal way.
- **Part introductions** provide an overview of the part.
- **Interviews** with some well known researchers in the field are included so that you can read about their ideas and see the faces that belong with some of the frequently cited references.

Whether you are using this book as a main text for an undergraduate course or to dip into during your graduate studies we hope that these features will help to make it easy and enjoyable to study.

Contents

About the Authors

David Benyon

After graduating in 1974 David worked as a systems analyst in a software house before becoming a senior systems analyst/designer at a large Leicester-based knitwear company. He left in 1980 and joined Leicester Polytechnic (now De Montfort University) as a lecturer in systems analysis and design. In 1983 he obtained an MSc in computing and psychology and began to concentrate on the human aspects of computer systems. He joined the Open University in 1987 where he has developed distance learning courses on database systems, software engineering and human–computer interaction. He has published over twenty research articles, authored *Information and Data Modelling* (Blackwell Scientific Publishers, 1990) and co-authored *A Guide to Usability* (originally published by the DTI, now available from Addison-Wesley) and *Automating Systems Development* (Plenum Press, 1988). David's research interests centre on human–computer system design and the application of knowledge-based techniques to HCI design. David led the authoring of Part IV on design methods.

Tom Carey

Tom is a professor in the Computing and Information Science Department at the University of Guelph in Canada, where he developed the first HCI course at Guelph in 1982. Currently he directs the university's human–computer interaction laboratory. He was a member of the ACM SIGCHI Curriculum Development Group, and was also education editor of the SIGCHI Bulletin from 1989 to 1992. Tom was co-organizer of a tutorial on Teaching HCI at CHI'91 and a workshop on the same theme at CHI'92, and was Tutorials Chair for INTERCHI'93. Tom's research interests focus on design approaches for HCI and on representation aids for exploring on-line information spaces. Tom is also a research consultant with IF InterFace Consulting in Ottawa and with a variety of government agencies and companies in North America and Europe, including IBM Canada, Eastman Kodak and Northern Telecom. Tom contributed to the authoring of Part III on the technology aspects and commented upon all parts of the book during the final stages of authoring.

Simon Holland

Simon is a lecturer in the Computing Department at the Open University. He was co-director of the NATO Advanced Study Workshop in 1989 on multimedia interface design in education, and was co-editor of a resulting book on multimedia interface design. He gave an invited talk jointly with Jim Alty at INTERCHI'93. Simon has developed new courses in HCI, virtual reality and education, intelligent tutoring systems and computing for humanities students at the University of Aberdeen. He is now part of a team developing a course on object technology and Smalltalk at the Open University. Simon's research interests focus on the design of highly empowering tools for open-ended tasks. He uses music composition, virtual reality and visual programming as driving domains. He has acted as research consultant in hypermedia for Shell Exploration and Production UK, and on Computing in the Arts for the Open University. Simon led the authoring of Part III on the technology aspects.

Jenny Preece

In 1994 Jenny Preece became Professor of Information Systems at South Bank University, London, Prior to this Jenny was a senior lecturer in the computing department of the Open University. She chaired the team that produced the OU masters course in HCI and various spin-off projects, which include *Guide to Usability* for British Industry funded by the UK Department of Trade and Industry; *A Guide to Usability* (1993, Addison-Wesley); *Human–Computer Interaction: Selected Readings* (1990, Prentice-Hall); this book project; and a European Consortium who are producing hypermedia modules for training about HCI. She currently chairs the OU's HCI and Software Engineering Research Group and the British Computer Society's HCI Education and Curriculum Group. Jenny has a number of externally funded research projects, including HCI methodology in safety-critical software design, internationalization of software, hypermedia development and the use of technology in teaching and learning. Jenny coordinated the authoring of this book and led the authoring of Part I, Introduction, and Part VI, Interaction Design: Evaluation, and contributed to Parts III, Humans and Technology: Technology, and IV, Interaction Design: Methods and Techniques. She also conducted the interviews and edited the entire book.

Yvonne Rogers

Yvonne has been teaching and researching in the field of HCI since the mid-eighties, when she completed her PhD on representation and the design of graphical interfaces. She is currently a lecturer in the School of Cognitive and Computing Sciences at Sussex University, UK, where she teaches undergraduate and masters courses in HCI and CSCW. Prior to this she was a lecturer in the Computing Department of the Open University, where she was a founder member of the course team that set up the distance education master's course in HCI. Yvonne has also worked in industry as a human factors researcher for Alcatel, a telecommunications company. Her current research interests are in the fields of computer supported cooperative work and distributed cognition. In particular, she is concerned with the implementation of new networking technologies in work practices. Yvonne's other research interests include social and cognitive aspects of HCI, mental models, graphical interfaces, distributed artificial intelligence, intelligent tutoring systems, explanation and expert systems and collaborative learning. Yvonne led the authoring of Part II on the human aspects and also contributed to the introduction and wrote the chapter on direct manipulation in Part III. Yvonne has made a major contribution to this project since 1988.

Helen Sharp

Helen graduated in mathematics in 1981 and gained her masters in computer science the following year. She worked in industry as an analyst/programmer before returning to academia in 1984 to start her PhD studies. Her PhD concentrated on the design of knowledge-based support for software designers. Helen joined the Computing Department of the Open University in 1987. Most of her teaching has been concerned with software engineering, but she has always had a keen interest in the human side of software development. In particular, her research has concentrated on providing appropriate support for designers in the field of engineering, with particular emphasis on software engineering. Her publications are in the fields of software engineering project management, knowledge-based systems and designer studies. Helen led the authoring of Part V on software support.

The Story of this Book and Acknowledgements

In 1987 a team from the British and Dutch Open Universities, chaired by Jenny Preece, got together to collaboratively develop a distance learning course in Human–Computer Interaction (HCI) for study by students at the two Universities. The course consisted of eight specially prepared topic booklets, a course guide, a 75 minute video, a book of published readings, assessment material and practical exercises. Within the terminology of the Open Universities this package of material is referred to as being 'multimedia' because of the integration of these different media. However, now that this term is more commonly used to refer to material delivered through a single workstation, it seems more accurate to describe it as 'multiple media'. This development effort took two years and involved academics from the two institutions, an editor, graphic designer, illustrator, educational technologist and a video production team from BBC OU Productions. Two external assessors oversaw this production and commented upon the academic content of the materials and their industrial and educational relevance, as is common practice in the development of Open University courses. We also employed a number of critical readers who commented upon the material at various stages of development and a small group of students who 'developmentally tested' the materials by working through them and providing us with feedback.

Many people contributed to this course, which provided the foundations for this book and we would like to thank them: Jill Alger, Stef Blom, Sue Dobson, Felicity Head, Laurie Keller (author), Paul Kirschner (educational technologist), Rob Lyon, Jenny Preece (chair and author), Yvonne Rogers (author), David Saunders, Hans Stolk (chair for the Dutch OU), Christine Tucker.

The following people acted as consultants: Gilbert Cockton (University of Glasgow), Stephen Draper (University of Glasgow), Claire O'Malley (University of Nottingham), Simon Richardson (University of Loughborough), Brian Sharratt (Logica, Cambridge), Michael Tauber (Universität-Gesamthochschüle, Paderborn, Austria). Some of the ideas underlying these contributions have been helpful in formulating the structure of this book and fragments of their work are included in this text. Gilbert's work on design guidelines is represented in Chapter 24, Claire's and

Steve's work on mental models is in Chapter 6 and Brian's work on evaluation is in Part VI. Brian also devised the Eurobank system which is used throughout the interaction design parts. Ken Eason (Loughborough University of Technology), Pat Endacott (McDonnell Douglas Computer Systems Co.) and Gerrit van der Veer (Vrije Universiteit, Amsterdam, The Netherlands) were external assessors. I would also like to thank the students who tested the material and the critical readers.

In 1992 we accepted a contract to produce this book. We used the course materials as the basis but, of course, we have updated them and revised them considerably. We have worked as a team writing outlines, drafting sections and commenting upon each other's work.

The manuscript of this book was reviewed by Allan MacLean (Xerox EuroPARC Ltd), William Newman (Xerox EuroPARC Ltd), Ken Eason (Loughborough University of Technology), Andrew McGettrick (University of Strathclyde), Margaret Christensen (Drexel University), John Long (University College, London) and two anonymous reviewers from the USA. I would like to thank all the reviewers for their many insightful comments that have helped us to improve the quality of this book. Many other people have either allowed us to include excerpts from their work or have facilitated our understanding and interpretation of it. When possible we have acknowledged this in the text and cleared the rights but I would also like to personally thank Dan Crow, Ken Eason, Alistair Edwards, Allan MacLean, Diane McKerlie, William Newman, Steve Scrivener and Cathleen Wharton.

Students are fascinated by the leaders of a field. They want to know what they do; what they look like; what kind of people they are and why they are so successful and well known. The interviews in this book provide a small glimpse of answers to some of these questions and I am very grateful to the following people for giving their time to be interviewed: Deborah Hix (Virginia Tech, USA), Roy Kawalsky (British Aerospace and University of Hull, UK), Marilyn Mantei (University of Toronto, Canada), Tom Moran (Xerox PARC, USA), Donald Norman (University of California, San Diego, USA and Apple, Inc.), Brian Shackel (Loughborough University of Technology, UK), Ben Shneiderman (University of Maryland, USA), Terry Winograd (University of Stanford, USA) and Bill Verplank (Interval Co. and University of Stanford, USA).

Working at the Open University has made me crucially aware of the importance of good publishing support and technical publishing expertise. Giles Clark from the OU Book Trade Department has given both in abundance and I am grateful to him for his help and support. Addison-Wesley have an impressive publishing record and have published the work of many of the most well-known people in HCI. It has been a pleasure to work with Simon Plumtree and his colleagues Alan Grove, Stephen Bishop, Peter Gordon, Bob Woodbury and Susan Keany. Simon's concern over content as well as the details of the publishing process, together with his enthusiasm and patience, are a rare and much valued combination of skills for which we are very grateful. Susan has been a patient and fastidious production editor and we are grateful for her help.

Special thanks are due to Mark Treglown and Simon J. Holland IV for their help providing pictures.

I would be pleased to receive feedback to help us improve the next edition of this book. Please email all comments to me at South Bank University, London: preecej@vax.sbu.ac.uk

Finally, my special thanks go to Tom Carey and Ken Eason, who both have the wonderful talent of always being there with help and friendship when it is most needed. We were fortunate to have Tom Carey as a Visiting Professor at the OU during the summer of 1993, when he joined our authoring team. Ken has been involved with our work since 1987, first as external course assessor and then as external examiner, and he has contributed much to our understanding of HCI and to teaching students. He has helped us with sound advice, enthusiasm and sparks of humour through difficult as well as good times. Ken is a much valued colleague and friend and I am immensely grateful to him.

Jenny Preece
Milton Keynes
March, 1994

I would like to thank everyone who has sent us comments about the book. Some inaccuracies, missing references and typographical errors have been corrected for the second printing. The more substantive comments will be useful when we write the second edition. In particular, my thanks go to Jonas Lowgren and Gary Perlman, who each read the book so thoroughly that it took me a whole weekend to work through their comments!

Jenny Preece
London
October, 1994

Acknowledgements

Chapter 1

Figure 1.1: Open University Human–Computer Interaction Course PMT 607 Unit 1; Figure 1.3: Eason K.D. (1984), Towards the experimental study of usability, *Behaviour and Information Technology*, 3(2), pp. 133–43. London: Taylor & Francis, Copyright © Taylor & Francis; Figure 1.4: SIGCHI (1992), p. 16 New York: ACM; Figures 1.5, 1.7, 1.8: Eason K.D. (1988), *Information Technology and Organisational Change*, London: Taylor & Francis. Copyright © K.D. Eason; Figure 1.6: Bjørn-Anderson N. (1986), Understanding the nature of the office for the design of third wave office systems. In M.D. Harrison and A.F. Monks (eds) *People and Computers: Designing for Usability*, Cambridge: Cambridge University Press.

Quote: Kay A. and Goldberg A. (1977), Personal Dynamic Media, *IEEE Computer*, 10(3), pp. 31–44. Reproduced with permission; Quote: Eason K.D. (1988), *Information Technology and Organisational Change*, p. 107 London: Taylor & Francis, Copyright © K.D. Eason; Box 1.2: Open University Human–Computer Interaction Course PMT 607 Unit 1; Box 1.3: Anonymous quote from *Human Factors Society Bulletin* (1981), 24(10), p. 8; Box 1.5: Lee L. (1992), *The Day the Phones Stopped*, New York: Primus, Donald I. Fine Inc., Copyright © 1992 Leonard Lee; Table 1.2: adapted from Eason K.D. (1984), Work Organisation Implications of Word Processing, report.

Chapter 2

Figures 2.1, 2.3: Open University Human–Computer Interaction Course PMT 607 Unit 1; Figure 2.2 and Box 2.1: Johnson W. *et al.* (1993), Bridging the paper and electronic worlds: the paper user interface. In S. Ashlund *et al.* (eds) *Bridges Between Worlds INTERCHI '93 Conference Proceedings*, New York: ACM; Figure 2.4: Eason K.D. (1991), Figure from Ergonomic perspectives on advances in human–computer interaction, *Ergonomics*, 34(6), pp. 721–41. London: Taylor & Francis. Copyright © Taylor & Francis; Figure 2.5 and Quote: Carroll J.M. (1990), Infinite detail and emulation in an ontologically minimized HCI. In J.C. Chew and J. Whiteside (eds) *Empowering People, CHI '90 Conference Proceedings*, New York: ACM; Figure 2.6 and Quote: Sommerville I. (1992), *Software Engineering* 4/e, Wokingham: Addison-Wesley; Figure 2.7: Open University Human–Computer Interaction Course PMT 607 Unit 1; Figure 2.8: Hix D. and Hartson H.R. (1993), *Developing User Interfaces: Ensuring Usability Through Product and Process*, Copyright © 1994 John Wiley. Reprinted by permission of John Wiley & Sons Inc.

Tables 2.1 and 2.2 Open University Human–Computer Interaction Course PMT 607 Unit 1; Cartoon: Penhill R. (1987), From Malik R. *The World's Best Computer Jokes*, London: HarperCollins Publishers Ltd.

Chapter 3

Figures 3.1, 3.2: Barber P. (1988), *Applied Cognitive Psychology*, London: Methuen & Co; Figure 3.3: Atkinson R.C. and Shiffrin R.M. (1968), Human memory: a proposed system and its control processes. In K.W. Spence and J.T. Spence (eds) *The Psychology of Learning and Motivation: Advances and Theory* Vol. 2, New York: Academic Press; Figure 3.4: Card S.K., Moran T.P. and Newell A. (1983), *The Psychology of Human–Computer Interaction*, Hillsdale, NJ: Lawrence Erlbaum Associates, Inc. Copyright © Xerox Corporation.

Quote: Winograd T. and Flores F. (1986), *Understanding Computers and Cognition*, Norwood NJ: Ablex Publishing Corp. Copyright © Ablex Publishing Corporation.

Chapter 4

Figure 4.1: Gleitman H. (1991), *Psychology* 3rd edn, New York: W.W. Norton & Company, Inc. Photograph by R.C. James; Figure 4.2: Selfridge O.G. (1955), Pattern recognition and modern computers. In *Proceedings of the Western Joint Computer Conference*, New York: IEEE; Figure 4.4: Easterby R.S. (1970), The perception of symbols for machine displays, *Ergonomics* 13, pp. 149–58. London: Taylor & Francis. Copyright © Taylor & Francis Ltd; Figure 4.5: Gaver W. (1991), Technology affordances. In S.P. Robertson, G.M. Olson and J.S. Olson (eds) *Human Factors in Computing Systems, CHI '91 Conference Proceedings*, New York: ACM, pp. 79–84; Figure 4.6c: Mueller C.G. (1965), *Sensory Psychology*, Englewood Cliffs, NJ: Prentice-Hall Inc. Photograph by Ansel Adams. Copyright © 1994 by the trustees of The Ansel Adams Publishing Rights Trust. All rights reserved; Figure 4.6d: Gregory R. (1966), *Eye and Brain*, World University Library, London. Courtesy of Weidenfeld and Nicolson Archives. Copyright © Weidenfeld & Nicolson Ltd; Figure 4.6e: Brown R. and Herrnstein R.J. (1975), *Psychology*, Methuen & Co, London. Photographs by C. Manos and E. Hartmann by permission of Magnum Photos Ltd; Figure 4.7: Gleitman H. (1991), Reprinted from *Psychology* third edition by Henry Gleitman with the permission of W.W. Norton & Company, Inc. Copyright © 1991, 1986, 1981 by W.W. Norton & Company, Inc.; Figure 4.8: Boissonnat J.D. (1988), Shape reconstruction from planar cross-sections, *Computer Visions Graphics and Image Processing*, 44(1), p. 27, Fig 27, New York: Academic Press; Figure 4.9: Edward R. Tufte (1990), *Envisioning Information*, Cheshire, Connecticut: Graphics Press; Figures 4.10, 4.11: Keller T.L. (1986) *Space M + A + X Operators Manual*, Final Frontier Software; Figures 4.12, 4.13, 4.14: Travis D. (1991), *Effective Colour Displays*, London: Academic Press; Figure 4.15: courtesy of Apple Computer UK Ltd.

Table 4.1: Reprinted from *Computer and Graphics* 9(3), Maguire M.C. (1985), A review of human factors guidelines and techniques for the design of graphical human–computer interfaces, pp. 221–35. © 1985 with kind permission from Pergamon Press Ltd, Headington Hall, Oxford OX3 0BW, UK; Table 4.2: Adapted from Tullis T.S. (1988), Screen Design. In M. Helander (ed.) *Handbook of Human–Computer Interaction*, Amsterdam: North-Holland, Elsevier Science Publishers BV, Academic Publishing Division; Quote: Gregory R. (1978), *Eye and Brain* 3rd edn. London: Weidenfeld and Nicolson.

Chapter 5

Figure 5.1: Tullis T.S. (1988) Screen Design. In M. Helander (ed.) *Handbook of Human–Computer Interaction*, Amsterdam: North-Holland, Elsevier Science Publishers BV, Academic Publishing Division; Figures 5.2, 5.10: Screenshot copyright © 1983–1992 Microsoft

Corporation. All rights reserved. Reprinted with permission from Microsoft Corporation; Figure 5.3: Gleitman H. (1991), Reprinted from *Psychology* third edition by Henry Gleitman with the permission of W.W. Norton & Company, Inc. Copyright © 1991, 1986, 1981 by W.W. Norton & Company, Inc.; Figures 5.4, 5.5: Maguire M.C. (1985), Reprinted from *Computer and Graphics* 9(3), Maguire M.C. (1985), A review of human factors guidelines and techniques for the design of graphical human–computer interfaces, pp. 221–35. © 1985 with kind permission from Pergamon Press Ltd, Headington Hall, Oxford OX3 0BW, UK; Figure 5.6: International Business Machines Corporation. Copyright © International Business Machines Corporation; Figure 5.8: Rogers Y. (1989), Icons at the interface: their usefulness, *Interacting with Computers* 1(1) p. 110. By permission of the publishers, Copyright © Butterworth-Heinemann Ltd; Figure 5.9: Baecker R.M. *et al.* (1991), Bringing icons to life. In S.P. Robertson, G.M. Olson and J.S. Olson (eds) *Human Factors in Computing Systems, CHI '91 Conference Proceedings*, New York: ACM.

Table 5.2: Rogers Y. (1989), Icons at the interface: their usefulness, *Interacting with Computers* 1(1), p. 109. By permission of the publishers, Copyright © Butterworth-Heinemann Ltd; Table 5.3: Norman D.A. (1988), *The Psychology of Everyday Things*, New York: Basic Books. Copyright © Donald A. Norman. Reprinted by permission of Basic Books, a division of HarperCollins Publishers, Inc.

Chapter 6

Figure 6.1: Shepard R.N. and Metzler J. (1971), Mental rotation of three dimensional objects, *Science*, Vol. 171, Fig 1, p. 702. Copyright © 1971 American Association for the Advancement of Science; Figure 6.2: Martindale C. (1991) adapted from McClelland (1981), *Cognitive Psychology: A Neural-network Approach*, Pacific Grove, CA: Brooks/Cole Publishing Co. Copyright © 1991; Figure 6.3: Schank R.C. and Abelson R. (1977), *Scripts, Plans, Goals and Understanding*, Hillsdale NJ: Lawrence Erlbaum Associates, Inc.; Figure 6.4: London Underground Map. London Regional Transport. LRT Registered User No. 93/1964; Quote: Craik K.J.W. (1943), *The Nature of Explanation*, Copyright © Cambridge University Press, Cambridge p. 7.

Chapter 7

Figure 7.1: Smith D.C. *et al.* (1982), Designing the Star user interface, *Byte* 7(4) pp. 242–82; Figure 7.2: Weiser M. (1991), The Computer for the 21st Century, *Scientific American*, September, Photograph copyright © Matthew Mulbry Photography; Figure 7.3: Norman D.A. and Draper S. (1986), *User-Centred System Design*, Hillsdale, NJ: Lawrence Erlbaum Associates, Inc.; Cartoon: Koren, Copyright © 1979 The New Yorker Magazine, Inc.; Quote: Norman D.A. and Draper S. (1986), *User-Centred System Design*, Hillsdale, NJ: Lawrence Erlbaum Associates, Inc.

Chapter 8

Figure 8. 1: Tognazzini B. (1992), *Tog on Interface*, Reading, MA: Addison-Wesley: © 1992 Apple Computer, Inc.; Figure 8.2: Glinert E.P. and Tanimoto S.L. (1984), Pict: An interactive graphical programming environment, *IEEE Computer*, 17, pp. 7–25. Copyright © 1984 IEEE; Table 8.1: Mack R.L. *et al.* (1983), Learning to use word processors: problems and prospects, *TOOIS*, July '83 New York: ACM: © 1983, Association for Computing Machinery, Inc. reprinted with permission; Table 8.2: Mayer R.E. (1988), From novice to expert. In M. Helander (ed.) *Handbook of Human–Computer Interaction*, Amsterdam: North-Holland, Elsevier Science Publishers BV, Academic Publishing Division, pp. 569–80; Cartoon: Breathed B. (1993), Copyright Washington Post Writers Group. Reprinted with permission.

Chapter 9

Figure 9.1: Winograd T. and F. Flores (1986), *Understanding Computers and Cognition*, Norwood NJ: Ablex Publishing Corp. Copyright © Ablex Publishing Corporation; Figure 9.2: Flores F. *et al.* (1987) *The Coordinator Workgroup Productivity System 1 (Computer program). Version I.* Action Technologies, Emeryville CA; Figure 9.3: Winograd T. (1988), Where the action is, *Byte*, December pp. 256–8. McGraw-Hill.

Chapter 10

Figure 10.1: Bødker S. (1991), *Through the Interface: A Human Activity Approach to User Interface Design*, Hillsdale NJ: Lawrence Erlbaum Associates, Inc.; Figure 10.2: Fish R.S, Kraut R.E. and Chalfonte B.L. (1990), The Video window system in informal communication. In *Proceedings of the Conference on Computer Supported Cooperative Work (CSCW '90)*, New York: ACM, pp. 1–12; Quote: Button G. (ed.) (1993), *Technology in Working Order: Studies of Work, Interaction and Technology.* London: Routledge; Box 10.1: Mumford E. (1987), Sociotechnical systems design: evolving theory and practice in G.F. Bjerknes *et al.* (eds) *Computers and Democracy*, Aldershot: Avebury, pp. 59–77, © E. Mumford.

Chapter 11

Figure 11.1: Norman D.A. (1988), *The Psychology of Everyday Things*, New York: Basic Books. Copyright © Donald A. Norman. Reprinted by permission of Basic Books, a division of HarperCollins Publishers Inc.; Figure 11.2: M. Helander (ed.) (1988), *Handbook of Human–Computer Interaction*, Amsterdam: North-Holland, Elsevier Science Publishers, Academic Publishing Division, p. 490; Figures 11.3, 11.7, 11.8, 11.9 and Quote: Buxton W. (1986), There's more to interaction than meets the eye: some issues in manual input. In D.A. Norman and S. Draper (1986), *User-Centred System Design*, Hillsdale, NJ: Lawrence Erlbaum Associates, Inc.; Figures 11.4, 11.5: Open University Human–Computer Interaction Course PMT 607 Unit 2; Figure 11.6: Kalawsky R. (1993), *The Science of Virtual Realities and Virtual Environments*, Wokingham: Addison-Wesley. Copyright © British Aerospace Defence Ltd; Figure 11.10: Calhoun G.L. *et al.* (1986), Use of eye control to select switches. Adapted with permission from *Proceedings of the Human Factors Society 30th Annual Meeting*, Copyright © 1986 by the Human Factors and Ergonomics Society, Inc. All rights reserved; Figure 11.11: Edwards A.D.N. (1991), *Speech Synthesis: Technology for Disabled People*, London: Paul Chapman Publishing; Figure 11.12: Technology in Education, *Communications of the ACM*, May 1993, 36(5) p. 58; Figure 11.13: Core penpoint gestures. *Byte*, Feb 1991, p. 213, McGraw-Hill; Figure 11.14: Blissmer R.H. (1992), *Introducing Computers*, Copyright © 1992 John Wiley, reprinted by permission of John Wiley & Sons, Inc. Photograph courtesy of GO Corporation; Figure 11.15: Greenstein J.S. and Arnaut Y. (1988), In M. Helander (ed.) *Handbook of Human–Computer Interaction*, Amsterdam: North-Holland, Elsevier Science Publishers BV, Academic Publishing Division.

Cartoon: Copyright © 1986 United Feature Syndicate, Inc. Reprinted with permission; Cartoon: Universal Press Syndicate. Copyright 1993 G.B. Trudeau.

Chapter 12

Figure 12.1 Harmony Space © Simon Holland; Figure 12.2: Open University Course PMT 607 Unit 2; Figure 12.3: Card S.K. *et al.* (1991), The Information Visualiser, an Information Workspace, *Proceedings of CHI '91*. Copyright © New York: ACM; Figure 12.4: Buxton W. *et al.* (1989), Use of non-speech audio at the interface, Tutorial notes, *CHI '89*, New York: ACM;

Figure 12.5: *Computer Weekly* 23 July 1992, p. 24. Reed Business Publishing. Copyright © Solo Syndication; Figure 12.6: Yavelow C. (1992), *MacWorld Music and Sound Bible*, San Mateo, CA: IDG Books © Christopher Yavelow; Figure 12.7: Edwards A.D.N. (1988), Design of auditory interfaces for visually disabled users. In E. Soloway *et al.* (eds) *Human Factors in Computing Systems, CHI '88 Proceedings*, New York: ACM; Cartoon: Copyright © 1986 by Newspaper Enterprise Association. Reprinted by permission.

Chapter 13

Figure 13.2: Open University Human–Computer Interaction Course PMT 607 Unit 2. Screenshot copyright © 1983–1992 Microsoft Corporation. All rights reserved. Reprinted with permission of Microsoft Corporation; Figure 13.3: Callahan J. *et al.* (1988). An empirical comparison of pie vs linear menus. In E. Soloway *et al.* (eds), *Human Factors in Computing Systems, CHI '88 Proceedings*, New York: ACM; Figure 13.4: Ben Shneiderman (1992) *Designing the User Interface: Strategies for Effective HCI* 2nd edition, Reading, MA: Addison-Wesley; Figure 13.5: From the book *Using Excel 4 for the Mac.* by Christopher Van Buren, Copyright © 1992. Que Corporation, a division of Prentice-Hall Computer Publishing. Used by permission of the publisher; Figure 13.6: Open University Course PMT 607 Unit 2; Figure 13.7: Norman D.A. and Draper S. (1986), *User-Centred System Design*, Hillsdale, NJ: Lawrence Erlbaum Associates, Inc.; Figures 13.8, 13.9: Open University Human–Computer Interaction Course PMT 607 Unit 4; Figure 13.10, 13.11: Norman D.A. (1988), *The Psychology of Everyday Things*, New York: Basic Books. Copyright © Donald A. Norman. Reprinted by permission of Basic Books, a division of HarperCollins Publishers Inc.

Cartoon: Breathed B. Copyright © 1993, The Washington Post Writers Group. Reprinted with permission; Cartoon: Shenton D. *The Guardian* 18 August 1989.

Chapter 14

Figure 14.1: Henderson D.A. and Card S.K. (1986), Rooms: the use of multiple virtual workspaces to reduce space contention in a window-based graphical user interface, *Transactions on Graphics*, 5(3), July, New York: ACM; Figure 14.2: Shneiderman B. (1992), *Designing the User Interface: Strategies for Effective HCI* 2nd edn, Reading MA: Addison-Wesley. Reproduced with permission from Hewlett-Packard; Figures 14.3, 14.4, 14.7, 14.8, 14.9, 14.10: Marcus A. (1992), *Graphic Design for Electronic Documents and User Interfaces*, Reading, MA: Addison-Wesley. © 1991, Association for Computing Machinery, Inc.; Figures 14.5, 14.11, 14.12, 14.13, 14.14: Shneiderman B. (1992), *Designing the User Interface: Strategies for Effective HCI* 2nd edn, Reading, MA: Addison-Wesley; Figures 14.6, 14.13: Screenshot copyright © 1983–1992 Microsoft Corporation. All rights reserved. Reprinted with permission of Microsoft Corporation.

Quote Box 14.3: Newman W. *et al.* (1985), A window manager with a modular user interface. In P. Johnson and S. Cook (eds) *Proceedings of the British Computer Society, HCI Conference*, September 1985. Cambridge: Cambridge University Press; Cartoon: Open University (1990) *A Guide to Usability*.

Chapter 15

Figures 15.1, 15.2: Carroll J.M. (1992), *The Nurnberg Funnel: Designing Minimalist Instruction for Practical Computer Skill*, Cambridge MA: The MIT Press; Figure 15.3: Shneiderman B. (1992), *Designing the User Interface: Strategies for Effective HCI* 2nd edn, Reading MA: Addison-Wesley; Figure 15.4,: Woodhead N. (1990), *Hypertext and Hypermedia: Theory and Applications*, Wokingham: Addison-Wesley. © Apple Computer Inc.; Figure 15.5: Reproduced by permission of D. Egan; Figures 15.6, 15.7: Thomas C.G. and Krogsoeter M. (1993), An adaptive environment for the user interface of Excel. In W.D. Gray, W.E. Hefley and D. Murray (eds) *Proceedings of the 1993 International Workshop on Intelligent User Interfaces*, New York: ACM. pp. 123–130; Figures 15.8, 15.9: Woodhead N. (1990) *Hypertext and Hypermedia: Theory and Applications*, Wokingham: Addison-Wesley. Copyright © 1990 Office Work-stations Limited.

Cartoon: Honeysett M. (1982), *MicroPhobia*, London: Hutchinson.

Chapter 16

Figure 16.1: Weiser M. (1991) The Computer for the 21st Century, *Scientific American*, September 1991. Photograph © Matthew Mulbry Photography; Figure 16.2: Watabe K. *et al.* (1990), Distributed multiparty desktop conferencing system: MERMAID in *Proceedings of the Conference on Computer-Supported Cooperative Work (CSCW '90)*, pp. 27–38. New York: ACM; Figure 16.3: Shneiderman B. (1992), *Designing the User Interface: Strategies for Effective HCI* 2nd edn, Reading MA: Addison-Wesley. Photograph © Marilyn Mantei; Figure 16.4: Buxton W. and Moran T. (1990), EuroPARC's integrated interactive intermedia facility (IIIF): early experience. In S. Gibbs and A.A. Verrijn-Stuart (eds) *Multi-user Interfaces and Applications, Proceedings of the IFIP WG 8.4 Conference on Multi-user Interfaces and Applications*, Heraklion, Crete. Amsterdam: Elsevier Science BV (North-Holland). Copyright © IFIP; Figure 16.5 reproduced courtesy of W. Buxton; Figure 16.6: Brooks F.P. Jr. *et al.* (1990), Project GROPE – Haptic displays for scientific visualisation, *Computer Graphics*, 24(4), August, pp. 177–85. New York: ACM; Figure 16.7: Reprinted from *Computer Music Journal*, 13(4) p. 81, by permission of The MIT Press, Cambridge, Massachusetts, Copyright © 1989; Figure 16.8: *The One*, September 1991, p. 37; Figure 16.9: Iwata H. (1990), *Computer Graphics*, 24(4), August. New York: ACM.

Table 16.1: Adapted from Shneiderman B. (1992), *Designing the User Interface: Strategies for Effective HCI* 2nd edn, Reading MA: Addison-Wesley; Cartoon: *Private Eye* (1993); Quote: Scrivener S.A.R. and Clark S. Computer Supported Co-operative Work. The publisher would like to thank the following for permission to reproduce the material: Unicom Seminars Ltd, Cleveland Road, Brunel Science Park, Uxbridge, Middlesex UB8 3PH.

Chapter 17

Figure 17.2: Boehm B. (1988), The Spiral model of software development and enhancement. *IEEE Computer*, 21(5), May, pp. 61–72.Copyright © 1988 IEEE; Figures 17.4, 17.5: Gould J.D. *et al.* (1987), The 1984 Olympic Message System: A test of behavioural principles of system design. From *Communications of the ACM*, 30(9), September, pp. 758–69. New York: ACM; Figures 17.6, 17.7: CAA Central Library.

Chapter 18

Figure 18.1: Eason K.D. (1992), Presentation given at DTI seminar, 24 June 1992, London; Figure 18.3: Eason K.D. (1988), *Information Technology and Organisational Change*, London: Taylor & Francis. © K.D. Eason; Figure 18.4: Avison D. and Wood-Harper T. (1990), *Multiview Methodology*, Oxford: Blackwell Scientific; Figure 18.5: Hix D. and Hartson, H.R. (1993), *Developing User Interfaces: Ensuring Usability Through Product and Process*, Copyright © 1994 John Wiley. Reprinted by permission of John Wiley & Sons Inc.

Chapter 19

Table 19.2: Catterall B.J. *et al.* (1991), The HUFIT planning analysis and specification toolset: human factors as a normal part of the IT product design processing. In J. Karat (ed.) *Taking Software Design Seriously*, London: Academic Press; Table 19.3: Tyldesley D.A. (1988), Employing usability engineering in the development of office products, *Computer Journal*, 31(5), pp. 431–6. By permission of Oxford University Press; Table 19.4: Whiteside J. *et al.* (1988), Usability engineering: our experience and evolution. In M. Helander (ed.) *Handbook of Human–Computer Interaction*, Amsterdam: North-Holland, Elsevier Science Publishers BV, Academic Publishing Division; Cartoon: Honeysett M. (1982), Microphobia, London: Hutchison.

Box 19.1: Adapted from Benyon D.R. (1990), *Information and Data Modelling*, Oxford: Blackwell Scientific; Box 19.2, 19.3: Benyon D.R. (1990), *Information and Data Modelling*, Oxford: Blackwell Scientific.

Chapter 20

Figure 20.2: Shepherd A. (1989), Analysis and training in information tasks. In D. Diaper (ed.) *Task Analysis for Human–Computer Interaction*, Chichester: Ellis Horwood; Figure 20.3 and Question 20.5: Kieras D. (1993), The GOMS model methodology for user interface design and analysis. In S. Ashlund *et al.* (eds) *Bridges Between Worlds, INTERCHI '93*, New York: ACM, Tutorial Notes 5; Box 20.3: Johnson P. (1992), *Human–Computer Interaction Psychology, Task Analysis and Software Engineering*, Maidenhead: McGraw-Hill; Question 20.2: Eriksen Brown G. in Avila K. (ed) *Take Six More Cooks*, London: Little, Brown.

Chapter 21

Figure 21.7: Open University Human–Computer Interaction Course PMT 607 Unit 7.

Chapter 22

Figure 22.1: Ehn P. and Sjögren D. (1991), From system descriptions to scripts for action. In J. Greenbaum and M. Kyng (eds) *Design at Work: Cooperative Design of Computer Systems*, Hillsdale, NJ: Lawrence Erlbaum Associates, Inc.; Figures 22.2, 22.3, 22.5: Verplank W. (1989), *CHI '89 Tutorial Notes: Graphical Invention for User Interfaces*, San Francisco: ID Two; Figure 22.4: Verplank W. and Kim S. (1986), Graphic invention for user interfaces: an experimental course in user interface design. *SIGCHI Bulletin*, 18(3) pp. 50–67.

Cartoon: Honeysett M. (1982), *MicroPhobia*. London: Hutchinson.

Chapter 23

Figure 23.1: Brest J. *et al.* (1991), *The NeXTstep Advantage*. NeXT Computer Inc., 900 Chesapeake Drive, Redwood City, CA 94063; Figures 23.2, 23.3: Karat J. and Bennett J.L. (1991), Using Scenarios in Design Meetings. In J. Karat (ed.) *Taking Software Design Seriously*. London: Academic Press.

Quote: Brooks F.P. Jr. (1975), *The Mythical Man-Month: Essays on Software Engineering*, pp. 30, 66–67. Reading MA: Addison-Wesley; Quote: Curtis B. *et al.* (1988), A field study of the software design process for large systems. From *Communications of the ACM*, 31(11), pp. 1279–80. New York: ACM; Table 23.1: Rosson M.B. *et al.* (1988), The designer as user: building requirements for design tools from design practice. From *Communications of the ACM*, 31(11), New York: ACM.

Chapter 24

Figure 24.1 and Table 24.1: Shneiderman B. (1992), *Designing the User Interface: Strategies for Effective HCI* 2nd edn, Reading MA: Addison-Wesley; Figures 24.2, 24.3: Open University Human–Computer Interaction Course PMT 607 Unit 8.

Cartoon: Dedini E. (1985). *A much much better world.* Bellevue WA: Microsoft Press Copyright © E. Dedini; Quote: Durrett J. and Trezona J. (1982) How to use colour displays effectively, *Byte*, April 1982, p. 53. Copyright © McGraw-Hill, Inc.; Quote: Smith S. L. and Mosier J.N. (1986), *Guidelines for Designing User Interface Software*, ESD-TR-86-278, Bedford MA: MITRE Corporation; Quote: ISO International Standard 9241 has been reproduced with the permission of the International Organization for Standardization. The complete standards can be obtained from any ISO member or from the ISO Central Secretariat, Case Postal 56, 1211 Geneva 20, Switzerland. Copyright remains with ISO. (Draft International Standard) Part 14; Quote: EC Council Directive 90/270/EEC, 29 May 1990; Quote: DeMarco T. (1982). *Controlling Software Projects*, New York and Englewood Cliffs: Yourdon Press; Quote: Porteous M.A., Kirakowski J. and Corbett M. (1993), *Software Usability Measurement Inventory Handbook*, Human Factors Research Group, University College Cork, Ireland. The Software Usability Measurement Inventory is copyright © 1993 by Human Factors Research Group, University College Cork, Ireland.

Table 24.2: Brooks F.P. Jr. (1988), Grasping reality through illusion: interactive graphics serving science. In E. Soloway *et al.* (eds) *Human Factors in Computing Systems, CHI '88 Proceedings*, New York: ACM; Box 24.1: Gaines B.R. and Shaw M.L.G. (1984). *The Art of Computer Conversation: A New Medium for Communication*, pp. 56, 120. Englewood Cliffs NJ: Prentice-Hall.

Chapter 25

Figure 25.1: IBM, United Kingdon Limited Corporation (1991), *Common User Access Guide to User Interface Design*. Extract from style guide; Figure 25.2: Apple Computer Inc. (1985), Inside Macintosh, Vol. V, p. 18. Reading MA: Addison-Wesley; Figure 25.3: Microsoft (1992) *The Windows Interface: an Application Design Guide*, Bellevue WA: Microsoft Press; Figures 25.4, 25.5: Screenshots copyright © 1983–1992 Microsoft Corporation. All rights reserved. Reprinted with permission of Microsoft Corporation; Figure 25.5 reproduced courtesy of Apple Computer UK Ltd.

Box 25.2, Quote: Rengger R. *et al.* (1993), *MUSiC Performance Measurement Handbook*. ESPRIT Project 5429. MUSiC, National Physical Laboratory, UK Crown Copyright; Exercise: adapted from Arent M. *et al.* (1989), Three characters in search of an interface: a case study in interface design process. In B. Laurel (ed.) *Inventing the Interface*, Reading MA: Addison-Wesley.

Chapter 26

Figure 26.1: Fischer G. *et al.* (1991), Making argumentation serve design, *Human–Computer Interaction*, Lawrence Erlbaum Associates, Inc., Vol. 6, pp. 393–419; Figure 26.2, 26.3, 26.5: Maclean A. *et al.* (1991), Questions, options and criteria: Elements of design space analysis, *Human–Computer Interaction*, Lawrence Erlbaum Associates, Inc., Vol. 6, pp. 201–50; Box 26.2: *Computers in Context*, videotape published by Copyright © California Newsreel, 149 9th Street, Suite 420, San Francisco, CA 94103, USA.

Chapter 27

Figure 27.1 (a–j): Copyright © MacroMedia Europe; Figure 27.2 and quote: Wulff W., Evenson S. and Rheinfrank J, (1990), Animating interfaces. In *Proceedings of the Conference on Computer-Supported Cooperative Work (CSCW '90)*, New York: ACM. pp. 241–54; Figure 27.3: Miller-Jacobs H.H. (1991), Rapid prototyping: an effective technique for system development. In Karat J. (ed.) *Taking Software Design Seriously*, London: Academic Press; Figures 27.4, 27.5: Wasserman A.I. and Shewmake D.T. (1985), The role of prototypes in the user software engineering (USE) methodology. In H.R. Hartson (ed.) *Advances in Human–Computer Interaction*, Vol. 1, Norwood NJ: Ablex Publishing Corp. pp. 191–210; Figures 27.6, 27.7, 27.8, 27.9 and 27.10 courtesy of Apple Computer UK Ltd; Cartoon: Honeysett M. (1982) *MicroPhobia*, London: Hutchinson.

Chapter 28

Figure 28.2: The Gunakara Sun Systems Ltd; Figure 28.3: Part of the user interface toolkit for the NeXT computer. NeXT Computer Inc., 900 Chesapeake Drive, Redwood City, CA 94063; Figure 28.4: Visual Edge Software Ltd, (1992), Build it and reap. *UNIXWorld Magazine*. May 1992. Copyright © McGraw-Hill, Inc.; Figures 28.5, 28.6: Myers B. A. *et al.* (1990), Garnet: Comprehensive support for graphical, highly-interactive user interfaces, *IEEE Computer*, 23(11), pp. 71–85; Figure 28.7: The Design Research Centre, Derby University, UK.

Tables 28.1, 28.2 and 28.3: Open University (1990) *A Guide to Usability*; Cartoon: Honeysett M. (1982) *MicroPhobia*, London: Hutchinson; Box 28.3: *UNIXWorld*, 1992, McGraw-Hill Inc.; Box 28.4: Eason K.D. *HCI Tools and Methods Handbook*, DTI. Copyright © HCI Services.

Chapter 29

Figure 29.1: DTI (1991), *Case Studies: Usability Now!* From IBM Consulting Group; Cartoon: Auth and Szep, Copyright © 1983 The Washington Post Co. In R. Rubinstein and H. Hersh (1984), *The Human Factor: Designing Computer Systems for People*, Burlington MA: Digital Press.

Box 29.1: DTI (1991) *Case Studies: Usability Now!* © Open University.

Chapter 30

Figures 30.1–30.6: Open University Human–Computer Interaction Course PMT 607 Unit 7; Figure 30.7: Open University Undergraduate Computing Survey; Cartoon: Honeysett M. (1982), *MicroPhobia*, London: Hutchinson; Quote: Diaper D. (1989), Task observation for Human–Computer Interaction. In D. Diaper (ed.) *Task Analysis for Human–Computer Interaction*, Chichester: Ellis Horwood. p. 221; Quote: Carroll J.M. and Mack R. (1984), Learning to use a word processor: by doing, by thinking and by knowing. In J. Thomas and M. Schneider (eds) *Human Factors in Computing Systems*, Norwood, NJ: Ablex Publishing Corp. pp. 13–52. Copyright © Ablex Publishing Corporation; Quote: Nielsen J. *et al.* (1986), Integrated software usage in the professional work environment; evidence from questionnaires and interviews. In M. Mantei and P. Oberton (eds) *Human Factors in Computing Systems, CHI '86 Proceedings*, Special issue of *SIGCHI Bulletin*, New York: ACM. pp. 162–7.

Chapter 31

Figure 31.1: NPL (1993), *Counting on IT*, Summer, Issue 1. p. 7. National Physical Laboratory, UK Crown Copyright; Quote: Robinson C. (1990), Designing and Interpreting Psychological Experiments. In J. Preece and L. Keller (eds) *Human–Computer Interaction*, pp. 357–67, Hemel Hempstead: Prentice-Hall. © Open University; Quote: Good M. *et al.* (1986), User-derived impact analysis as a tool for usability engineering. In M. Mantei and P. Oberton (eds) *Human Factors in Computing Systems, CHI '86 Proceedings*, special issue of *SIGCHI Bulletin*, New York: ACM. pp. 241–6.

Table 31.3: Whiteside J. *et al.* (1988), Usability engineering: our experience and evolution. In M. Helander (ed) *Handbook of Human–Computer Interaction*, Amsterdam: North-Holland, Elsevier Science Publishers BV, Academic Publishing Division; Box 31.1: Bewley W.L. *et al.* (1983), Human factors testing in the design of Xerox's 8010 Star office workstation, *SIGCHI Proceedings*, New York: ACM.

Chapter 32

Figure 32.1 and Quote: Suchman L.A. and Trigg R.H. (1991), Understanding practice: video as a medium for reflection and design. In J. Greenbaum and M. Kyng (eds) *Design at Work: Cooperative Design of Computer Systems*, Hillsdale, NJ: Lawrence Erlbaum Associates, Inc.; Cartoon: Honeysett M. (1982) *Microphobia*, London: Hutchison.

Quote: Walsham G. (1993), *Interpreting Information Systems in Organizations*, p. 5, p. 166. Reprinted by permission of John Wiley & Sons Ltd, Chichester.

Quote: Whiteside J. *et al.* (1988). Usability engineering: our experience and evolution. In M. Helander (ed) *Handbook of Human–Computer Interaction*, Amsterdam: North-Holland, Elsevier Science Publishers BV, Academic Publishing Division; Box 32.1: Monk A. *et al.* (1993), *Improving your Human–Computer Interface A Practical Technique*, Englewood Cliffs, NJ: Prentice-Hall; Box 32.2: Murray D. and Hewitt B. (1992), *TMPI Project report*, Capturing Interactions: requirements for CSCW, Social & Computer Sciences Research Group, University of Surrey.

Chapter 33

Figure 33.1: Nielsen J. (1993), Usability evaluation and inspection methods. In S. Ashlund *et al.* (eds) *Bridges Between Worlds, INTERCHI '93* Tutorial notes, New York: ACM; Box 33.2: Lewis C, Polson P. Rieman J. and Wharton C, (1991), personal communication.

Chapter 34

Case Study 1, Tables 34.5, 34.6: Jeffries R. *et al.* (1991), User interface evaluation in the real world: a comparison of four techniques. In S.P. Robertson *et al.* (eds) *Human Factors in Computing Systems, CHI '91 Conference Proceedings*, pp. 119–24 New York: ACM; Case Study 2, Tables 34.7, 34.8, 34.9: Karat C-M. *et al.* (1992), Comparison of empirical testing and walkthrough methods in user interface evaluation. In P. Bauersfield *et al.* (eds) *Human Factors in Computing Systems, CHI '92 Conference Proceedings*, New York: ACM. pp. 397–404.

The publisher has made every attempt to obtain permission to reproduce material in this book from the appropriate source. If there are any errors or omissions please contact the publisher who will make suitable acknowledgement on the reprint.

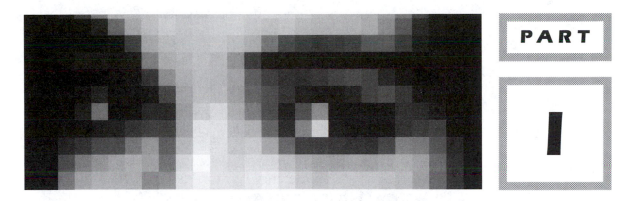

INTRODUCTION

Human–Computer Interaction (HCI) is about designing computer systems that support people so that they can carry out their activities productively and safely. HCI has a role in the design and development of all kinds of systems, ranging from those like air traffic control and nuclear processing, where safety is extremely important, to office systems, where productivity and job satisfaction are paramount, to computer games, which must excite and engage users.

The general aim of Part I is to provide an introduction and overview of HCI. When you have completed it, you will understand:

- how to make a case for the importance of HCI in systems development,
- how the interdisciplinary nature of HCI makes it different from other disciplinary areas you may have studied,
- how the various underlying disciplines of HCI contribute to design,
- how HCI has evolved as a separate area of study,
- the nature of the HCI design process.

We will also be introducing you to the way of thinking about HCI that we apply in our own design work and which forms the framework for this book.

Throughout the book, there are interviews with key figures in HCI. The first is with Terry Winograd, a professor at Stanford University, who is best known for his work in artificial intelligence, including pioneering the use of natural languages for interacting with computers. According to Terry, although advances in technology tend to drive advances in the field, technology needs to be usable as well as functional:

'Except for special things like computer games, people don't use computers because they want to use computers. They use computers because they want to write papers; they want to communicate with people; they want to design bridges and so on. Whatever they're doing, the computer is an enabling device that can help them to do it.'

In order to capitalize on the potential that technology has to offer,

'you always have to have one eye open to the question: what can the technology do? ... And one eye open to the question: what are people doing and how would this fit in? What would they do with it?'

(interview with Terry Winograd, see p. 53)

The first chapter traces how the rise in interest in HCI has followed the technological developments that have enabled computers to pervade most aspects of human life. It also discusses how good HCI design can have profound influences on the productivity of both individuals and organizations, and how lack of attention to HCI can endanger life in safety-critical situations. In the second chapter you will read about the disciplines that contribute to HCI and find out about the nature of the HCI design process.

You will also see why studying HCI is likely to be different from anything you have studied so far, and how the interdisciplinary nature of HCI makes it an exciting and challenging field, which we hope you will enjoy.

1

What is HCI?

Aims and objectives

The aim of this chapter is to introduce you to the study of Human–Computer Interaction (HCI), so that after studying it you are able to:

- describe what HCI is,
- discuss and argue about why HCI is important with reference to the way in which technology has developed during the past thirty years,
- describe some of the goals of HCI that are concerned with improving productivity and designing safe systems,
- describe how HCI has evolved to ensure that the needs of different kinds of users are taken into account in computer system design,
- outline the quantifiable benefits of good HCI design for both individuals and organizations,
- describe the role of HCI in the design of safety critical systems.

Overview

During the past twenty years technology has advanced to such an extent that almost everyone comes into contact with computers in one way or other. Unlike in the early days of computing, when only highly skilled technical people used computers, nowadays the range of knowledge and experience of different users is very broad. So, it is important that the way in which people interact with computers is intuitive and clear. However, designing appropriate HCI is not always straightforward, as the many poorly designed computer systems testify. One of the challenges of HCI design is to keep abreast of technological developments and to ensure that they are harnessed for maximum human benefit.

The main reason why many people in the business community are interested in finding out about HCI is because they want to increase the efficiency of their staff and, hence, make more money. Another important factor is safety; some kinds of computer systems can endanger life if they do not have good HCI.

When computers first appeared on the commercial scene in the 1950s, they were extremely difficult to use, cumbersome and at times unpredictable. There were a number of reasons for this:

- They were very large and expensive machines, so that by comparison human labour (that is, 'people time') was an inexpensive resource.
- They were used only by technical specialists – scientists and engineers – who were familiar with the intricacies of off-line programming using punch cards.
- Little was known about how to make them easier to use.

None of these conditions holds today: computers have become much less expensive, users come from every walk of life, and we understand a great deal more about how to fit the machines to people's needs and their work.

Dramatic decreases in the cost of computing resources have resulted from new technological advances, the most significant being the development of the silicon chip. The ability not only to miniaturize circuits but also to pack large numbers of them on to tiny, individual chips paved the way for the development of powerful computers with large storage capacity. In less than thirty years computers changed from being huge machines housed in large, air-conditioned rooms to much smaller machines, including some that can easily be carried around by children. Computers have also become more reliable and today's machines do not suffer from overheating like their ancestors. Computing has entered a new era and is becoming ubiquitous.

The development of the first personal computers in the 1970s was a major landmark because these machines provided interactive computing power for individual users at low cost. Consequently, instead of just a handful of highly experienced programmers being the only users, people from all walks of life – commerce, farming, education, retailing, defence, manufacturing and entertainment – began using computer systems.

These changes in the technology have opened up a wide range of new possibilities for the way in which computers can be used. The sheer costliness and time required to run programs on the early machines dictated the kinds of commercial application in which computers could be used. Businesses such as banking and accounting, with large-scale record keeping activities, were the first to take up computing technology. Companies that were involved in activities with 'fast' cycles, such as transaction processing for airlines and retailing, could not make use of these machines. They were not sufficiently fast or responsive, but this is not a problem with modern computers.

Computers have also found a place in many private homes. In fact, such has been their pervasiveness that now just about everyone, young or old, able or disabled, skilled or unskilled, is using or is directly affected by computers in one way or another.

1.1   Technological change: different design needs

For computers to be widely accepted and used effectively they need to be well designed. This is not to say that all systems have to be designed to accommodate everyone, but that computers should be designed for the needs and capabilities of the people for whom they are intended. Ultimately, users should not even have to think about the intricacies of how to use a computer. Just as knowledge of how the actual mechanics of steering an automobile is transmitted from the steering wheel to the wheels is of little concern to most motorists, so too should knowledge of the internal workings of a computer be of little consequence to its users. However, just as the shape and position of the steering wheel and its effect when turned has an enormous impact on the driver, so too will the design of the computer system have an effect on its user. The format of the input and the style of feedback affect the success with which any artefact is used.

Donald Norman (1988, 1992), author of *The Psychology of Everyday Things*, and *Turn Signals are the Facial Expressions of Automobiles*, catalogues many examples of everyday things that do not present a clear and obvious image to their users. If you think about the complexity of most computer systems you can see that the potential for poorly designed HCI is very high. However, Norman identifies two key principles that help to ensure good HCI: **visibility** and **affordance**. Controls need to be visible, with good mapping with their effects, and their design should also suggest (that is, afford) their functionality. Box 1.1 contains more information about visibility and affordance.

Box 1.1 Visibility and affordance

In cars things are generally visible. There are good mappings between the controls and their effects, between the driver's goals and needs and the functions available. A control often has just one function. There is good feedback and the system is understandable. In general, the relationships between the user's goals, the required actions and the results are sensible, meaningful and not arbitrary. With many video recorders, however, there is no visible structure. Mappings between controls and their effects are arbitrary, there is no correspondence between the user's goals and the buttons and displays that make up the interface. Several of the controls have multiple functions. There is very poor feedback, so a user is often unsure whether the desired result has been obtained. In general, the system is not easily understandable.

Norman (1992, p. 19) defines **affordance** as a 'technical term that refers to the properties of objects – what sorts of operations and manipulations can be done to a particular object'. Doors, for example, afford opening, whereas a chair affords support. Affordances play a large part in the design of objects but what is important is 'perceived affordance' – what a person thinks can be done with the object. For example, does the design of the door suggest that it should be pushed open or pulled? Unfortunately, aesthetics sometimes conflict with good affordance and the appearance of the object takes precedence over its use.

EXERCISE

The management of British Rail were trying to decide which material to use for a partition on one of their platforms. Should it be glass or very thin plywood? Both were about the same cost. Thinking that glass would be the more attractive, they selected toughened glass. However, even toughened glass was not strong enough to deter the vandals in that area, and after replacing the smashed glass twice they eventually opted for the plywood. Although no stronger, the plywood remained intact but there were other problems. Can you think what they were? What kind of actions did the glass afford and what did the plywood afford?

COMMENT

Within a very short time the plywood was covered with all kinds of graffiti, but despite being thin it was not smashed. The glass afforded smashing and the plywood afforded drawing and writing. Section 13.7 discusses affordance in more detail and contains more examples.

Visibility and affordance, therefore, are very important principles in HCI design. (See Norman (1988, 1992) for further examples.)

Producing computer systems that are straightforward to use means that system designers have to think beyond merely what capabilities the system should have. They also need to consider the interaction that goes on between users and a computer system. During the technology explosion of the 1970s the notion of the **user interface**, also known as the **Man–Machine Interface** (MMI), became a general concern to both system designers and researchers. Moran defined this term as 'those aspects of the system that the user comes in contact with' (1981, p. 4), which in turn means 'an input language for the user, an output language for the machine, and a protocol for interaction' (Chi, 1985, p. 671).

Computer companies became aware that if they could somehow improve the physical aspects of the user interface they would stand a better chance of being successful in the market-place. To exploit this new dimension, a greatly overused cliché evolved – calling a system 'user-friendly'. In practice, this often simply meant tidying up the screen displays to make them more aesthetically pleasing. While this was an improvement on earlier interfaces (which wasn't that difficult), many companies – unfortunately – used the term simply as a marketing ploy, paying lip service to the real issues surrounding HCI. Most systems were still not designed to match users' needs and still required users to cope with what seemed more like 'user-hostile' interfaces. Academic researchers, in contrast, were concerned about how the use of computers might enrich the work and personal lives of people. In particular, they focused on the capabilities and limitations of human users, that is, understanding the 'people side' of the interaction with computer systems. At that time this primarily meant understanding people's psychological processes when interacting with computers. However, as the field began to develop it soon became clear that other aspects impinge on users and that these, too, should be included. For example, training issues, working practices, management and organizational issues and health hazards are all important factors contributing to the success or failure of using computer systems.

The term **human–computer interaction** (HCI) was adopted in the mid-1980s as a means of describing this new field of study. This term acknowledged that the focus of interest was broader than just the design of the interface and was concerned with all those aspects that relate to the interaction between users and computers. Also, unlike the term man–machine studies, it did not imply gender bias. Although there are still no currently agreed definitions of HCI, the following definition embodies the spirit at that time: '[a] set of processes, dialogues, and actions through which a human user employs and interacts with a computer' (Baecker and Buxton, 1987, p. 40). A more recent and broader characterization is provided by the following definition: 'human–computer interaction is a discipline concerned with the design, evaluation and implementation of interactive computing systems for human use and with the study of major phenomena surrounding them' (ACM SIGCHI, 1992, p. 6).

Question 1.1

What is the difference between the terms 'user interface' *and* ' human–computer interaction'*?*

1.2 The challenge of HCI

A decade ago, when our understanding of HCI was more limited, many systems developers might have felt that good intentions were the major requirement for producing an effective HCI design. Now we know that HCI design is a rich challenge, partly because of the rapid change in the underlying technology, partly because of inherent conflicts and trade-offs among design goals and partly because of the many different components (and supporting areas of study) that make up HCI. The development of the silicon chip has changed the world so that many people use or come into contact with computers. Furthermore, the speed of innovation is not diminishing. The development of faster and larger (in terms of processing power) machines continues. In addition new improved hardware and software technologies are opening up new possibilities for HCI. Special devices enable users to grab and move virtual objects in a virtual space, or even to move through that space in virtual reality. Multimedia applications, in which sound, dynamic and static graphics, video and text are intermingled, are now common. Recent developments in telecommunications, such as the Integrated Services Digital Network (ISDN) and high-definition TV, are enabling increasingly large amounts of different types of information to be channelled through networks. Images, video, sound and text can all be transmitted with minimum loss of efficiency and quality. Information held in databases across the world is becoming accessible to people in their own homes. These changes bring two important challenges to HCI designers:

- How to keep abreast of changes in technology.
- How to ensure that their designs offer good HCI as well as harnessing the potential functionality of the new technology.

These challenges become apparent in the design of everyday appliances like telephones. Consider the design of a standard telephone that you use. The general procedure for using most push button or dial phones is broadly the same in all countries, although the details often vary. If you try to ring someone using a British phone you have first to pick up the handset, then listen to find out if there is a dialling tone, press a series of buttons (or dial numbers on the old type of telephone), listen to the clicks and various noises that tell you that the call is being connected, and finally wait for a ringing tone. If nothing happens for a while except odd clicks you know that you are unlikely to get through, and so you put the receiver down or press the redial button to repeat the dialling. If you get a rapid series of tones then you know the person you are calling is engaged with another call, and so you put the receiver down and try again intermittently. When you get a normal ringing tone you wait for a while until you get an answer or if there is no reply you put the telephone down.

Although it may seem like stating the obvious, this series of user actions and system feedback is an example of a simple user interface whereby information is passed between a person and a system. Figure 1.1 shows this interaction. At the physical level, on the machine's side, are the keypad or dial and the receiver, while

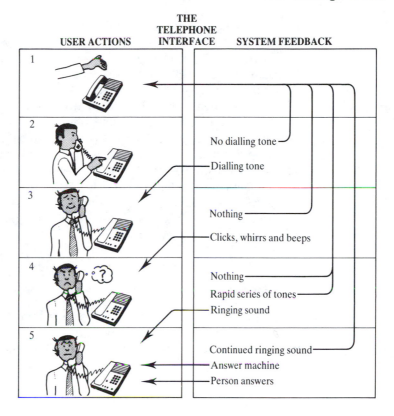

Figure 1.1 The interface between a person and a telephone.

on the person's side are primarily ears, eyes and fingers. The information that is passed from human to machine by means of these physical aspects is the keying or dialling of a number in order to contact someone. The machine (through the telephone exchange, which is invisible to the user) informs the person whether an attempt has been successful or not at various stages of the process.

The basic telephone interface creates few problems for most people who are familiar with its use. This is because the operating parts of the telephone system are visible and the implications of how to use them and what happens are relatively clear. For now, at least, assume that the design of the numbered buttons or holes means that the way they are to be used is obvious. Pressing the button with a 1 on it, or inserting a finger into the hole with a 1 in it and turning the dial, maps directly on to the task of ringing a number that begins with 1. Likewise, the auditory clues are intuitively meaningful in that they give you direct feedback as to the success of your interaction: they tell you whether the call has been connected, the line is busy, the receiver is engaged, and so on. It is as if the interface has become invisible in the sense that people seem to know how to use a telephone without really having to think much about how to use it. It has become an everyday activity.

Now consider two changes to this scenario. Firstly, assume that you are a visitor to Britain from another country, say North America, where the phones appear very similar but have different dialling tones. At first you will probably wonder what the dialling tones mean when the call connects. The fluency with which you used a telephone in North America has gone; even quite a small change from the expected form of feedback causes you confusion temporarily. Secondly, consider what it would be like to use one of the modern types of telephone interface with added facilities that allow the user to have three-way or more conversations, call-back facilities, automatic redial and so on. Using this kind of phone is an entirely different matter. Here the existing telephone interface maps poorly on to the telephone's increased functionality, and very often people have problems when trying to operate these functions; many give up.

EXERCISE

Think about the new functionality available with modern telephones. Try to identify what tasks someone would like to perform using the telephone. Then make a note of the controls and the sorts of feedback provided by the telephone when the controls are activated. How do these map on to your initial list of user actions? What are the main weaknesses in the design?

COMMENT

In the new-style telephone example you might try to achieve the following:

- Forward your calls to another extension while you are out of the office.
- Ask for a colleague's calls to be forwarded to your extension because the colleague will be working with you in your office all day.
- Redial a telephone number which has been engaged or where there has been no answer.
- 'Remember' a list of commonly called numbers and substitute shortened codes for them.

(There are others, but this will suffice for discussion.)

How would the user break the first task down into a series of actions? There is no button on the telephone labelled 'redirect calls'. In fact, the list of actions might begin with 'look up how to redirect incoming calls in the telephone handbook'!

On our new-style office phones, for example, there are five additional buttons labelled *, #, S, LR and R. There are no obvious controls for redirecting calls, unless R happens to stand for 'redirect' (and it doesn't!). If I pick up the handset and listen, I hear the dialling tone. If I press any of the above buttons except LR there is no change in the tone; pressing LR results in tones that indicate dialling – probably the last number dialled from my telephone. But what was that number? It may have been several days since I last dialled out, or I may have made several different calls recently and can't remember the most recent. There is almost no feedback from the system.

In fact, on my telephone I need to press * followed by 8 and then the extension to which I wish to redirect my calls. If I do this correctly, I hear an intermittent plain tone. However, if I have misdialled the extension number, some stranger will receive my telephone calls, not my secretary! The mapping between redirecting calls, the procedure for doing so, and the feedback from the system for key items such as the number to which I have actually redirected the calls is very, very poor. The same comments apply to the other tasks listed above.

In the case of my office phone there is a blatant conflict between ease of use and the functionality that the designers wanted to provide. Could this conflict be resolved by the use of sounds or voice, I wonder? For example, if I could just give my secretary's extension a special tone then I would at least be able to distinguish her phone from others. What might be the advantages and the problems of using video phones? How would you deal with issues of privacy? For instance, imagine that you like to take a bath after work, where you soak and chat to your friends on the phone while recovering from the day's chores. Will you have to change your habits or will designers think to cater for such behaviour in their designs?

Now think for a minute about other household devices. Can you think of similar problems concerning the way user actions map on to the design of the gadgets that you have in your house? One well-known gadget that causes lots of users problems is the video recorder, like the one described in Box 1.2.

Box 1.2   Using a video recorder

While most people find it relatively easy to work out how to insert a video cassette, get it to play or record, rewind and fast forward, they often do not find it easy to set the timer to record a programme at some time in the future. Setting the timer is usually not so straightforward. For most video recorders it is not obvious from the interface between the person and the machine how information should be specified to the system, nor is the feedback information from the system obvious. You usually only find out whether or not you have been successful when it is too late!

TIMER RECORDING

ALL YOU HAVE TO DO IS TO SET THE TIMER CORRECTLY AND YOU CAN LEAVE THE HOUSE WITHOUT MISSING VITAL PROGRAMMES

This function makes it possible to automatically turn the unit on and start recording on a preset day and time, and turn the unit off after another preset time.

CHECK THE FOLLOWING ITEMS BEFORE SETTING TIMER RECORDING

1   Day of the week required
2   Start and stop times
3   Channel
4   Length of cassette

PREPARATION

- Load a blank cassette which has not had the tab removed.
- Make sure that the TIMER SWITCH is OFF.
- Make sure that the TIMER DISPLAY shows the correct present time.

NOTE

- The cassette cannot be removed during timer recording. Remove after turning off the TIMER SWITCH.
- Start automatic recording at least 20 seconds before the desired time, then stop automatic recording at desired stop time.
- Set the TIMER SWITCH to OFF if you wish to stop the timer recording or after the timer recording is finished. If stopped, in this way, the TIMER mode will be retained in memory.
- After setting the TIMER switch to ON, the unit is automatically turned off.
- To turn the unit on, set the TIMER button to OFF. If a cassette without tab is inserted, the cassette will be automatically ejected.
- When the tape comes to its end during OTR the VCR will turn itself off. The tape will not automatically rewind.

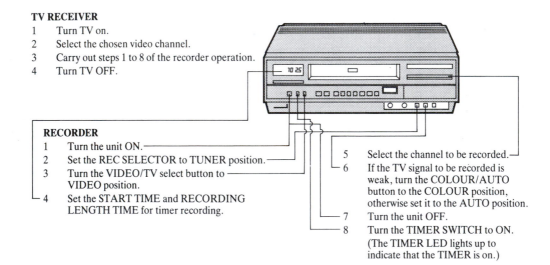

TV RECEIVER

1   Turn TV on.
2   Select the chosen video channel.
3   Carry out steps 1 to 8 of the recorder operation.
4   Turn TV OFF.

RECORDER

1   Turn the unit ON.
2   Set the REC SELECTOR to TUNER position.
3   Turn the VIDEO/TV select button to VIDEO position.
4   Set the START TIME and RECORDING LENGTH TIME for timer recording.

5   Select the channel to be recorded.
6   If the TV signal to be recorded is weak, turn the COLOUR/AUTO button to the COLOUR position, otherwise set it to the AUTO position.
7   Turn the unit OFF.
8   Turn the TIMER SWITCH to ON. (The TIMER LED lights up to indicate that the TIMER is on.)

Figure 1.2   Typical set of instructions plus a schematic diagram of the interface of a VCR.

EXERCISE

Table 1.1 provides a list of the tasks that an average user might consider when trying to record a programme at some time in the future. Figure 1.2 provides a typical set of instructions and a schematic diagram of the interface of an early video recorder interface. Try to map what you would do to record a programme with the way the system appears to operate. It may help you to draw a dynamic flow diagram like the one in Figure 1.1, mapping out the controls, the user's actions and the system feedback, if any. (No comment is provided for this exercise.)

Table 1.1 A possible sequence of tasks for recording a programme on a VCR.

Before setting the timer	Find a tape
	Make sure it is OK to record over it
	Make sure there is enough space on the tape to record the programme
	Make sure it is rewound
	Insert the tape in the correct position
Setting the timer	Set the start time
	Set the finish time
	Set the date
	Check that the video time is correct
	Set the channel

There can be no denying that many computing systems have been designed with very poor interfaces. The point that needs to be understood, however, is that increased functionality should not to be used as an *excuse* for poor design. It is possible to design good interfaces whose controls have relatively obvious operations and effects and that also provide useful and immediate feedback. Such systems result from a good knowledge of HCI. As Norman (1988) points out, in the case of a car, for example, we find that it is increasingly common for new cars to have over 100 controls – ten or so for the radio, five to ten or so for the heating and ventilation system, five or more for the windows, about ten for windscreen wipers, washers, turn indicators and lights, several for locking and opening the doors, some for driving the car, and so on. Most people, with a little trial and error (often when in the process of driving) or after a quick look at the manual, have little trouble mastering the whole range of functions very rapidly. Why is it, then, that the car, with its diversity of functions and numerous controls, is so much easier to use than, say, the video recorder, with its much smaller set of functions and controls? What makes the car interface so good and the video interface so poor? One reason is that feedback in cars is usually immediate and is more obvious. Also, people who have driven a car before know the kinds of things to expect. Although cars differ, the position of many controls is the same or similar, and similar symbols are used to indicate their functions.

1.3 The goals of HCI

The goals of HCI are to produce usable and safe systems, as well as functional systems. These goals can be summarized as 'to develop or improve the safety, utility, effectiveness, efficiency, and usability of systems that include computers' (*Interacting with Computers*, 1989, p. 3). In this context the term 'system' derives from systems theory and it refers not just to the hardware and software but to the entire environment – be it an organization of people at work, at home or engaged in leisure pursuits – that uses or is affected by the computer technology in question. 'Utility' refers to the functionality of a system or, in other words, the things it can do. Improving 'effectiveness' and 'efficiency' are self-evident and ubiquitous objectives. The promotion of safety in relation to computer systems is of paramount importance in the design of safety-critical systems. **Usability**, a key concept in HCI, is concerned with making systems easy to learn and easy to use. Poorly designed computer systems can be extremely annoying to users, as the anecdote in Box 1.3 suggests.

Box 1.3 Who shot the terminal?

The National Electronics Council (1983, p. 13) reports the following anecdote from *Human Factors Society Bulletin* (1981). The manager of a system installation for police and sheriff departments reported that one day he received the call: 'your terminal is dead. Come and get it.' He suggested that the repair service should be contacted but the caller insisted that he go out and visit it. The terminal had two bullet holes in it. Apparently an officer got 'Do not understand' on the screen one time too many, so he stepped back and shot it!

Contrary to what some people may think, providing lots of different kinds of functions is not necessarily the way to ensure good usability. Eason (1984), for example, did a field study of a banking system that provided staff with 36 different ways of extracting

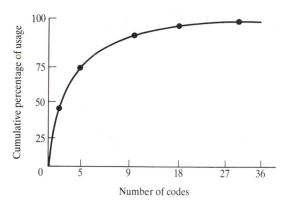

Figure 1.3 The pattern of usage in Eason's (1984) study of a banking system.

information from a customer's account. After examining the usage logs he found that just four codes accounted for 75% of the usage and that many codes were virtually unused despite being designed specially for banking tasks, as indicated in Figure 1.3. As often happens, the full flexibility of this system was not being exploited because users did not invest effort in learning to use extra search strategies unless absolutely necessary.

In order to produce computer systems with good usability, HCI specialists strive to:

- **understand** the factors (such as psychological, ergonomic, organizational and social factors) that determine how people operate and make use of computer technology effectively, and to translate that understanding into the
- **development** of tools and techniques to help designers ensure that computer systems are suitable for the activities for which people will use them, in order to
- **achieve** efficient, effective and safe interaction both in terms of individual human–computer interaction and group interactions.

Underlying all HCI research and design is the belief that the people using a computer system should come first. Their needs, capabilities and preferences for performing various activities should inform the ways in which systems are designed and implemented. People should *not* have to change radically to 'fit in with the system', the system should be designed to match their requirements.

Question 1.2

What kind of conflicts might designers face when designing computer systems?

Good HCI depends upon HCI designers and design teams having a wide range of knowledge about both humans and technology and about how they relate to each other. For this reason HCI is multidisciplinary, and we shall discuss what this means in Section 1.4 and then in more detail in Chapter 2.

1.4 HCI and its evolution

Figure 1.4 shows the main topics that make up the discipline of HCI. All HCI takes place within a social and organizational context. Different kinds of applications are required for different purposes and care is needed to divide tasks between humans and machines, making sure that those activities that are creative and non-routine are given to people and those that are repetitive and routine are allocated to machines. Knowledge of human psychological and physiological abilities and, more important still, their limitations is important. As Figure 1.4 shows this involves knowing about such things as human information processing, language, communication, interaction and ergonomics. Similarly, it is essential to know about the range of possibilities offered by computer hardware and software so that knowledge about humans can be mapped on to the technology appropriately (remember Terry Winograd's comments in the introductory section). The main issues for consideration on the technology side involve input and output techniques, dialogue techniques, dialogue genre or style, computer graphics and dialogue architecture. This knowledge has to be brought together somehow into the design and development of computer systems with good HCI, as shown at the bottom of the figure. Tools and techniques are

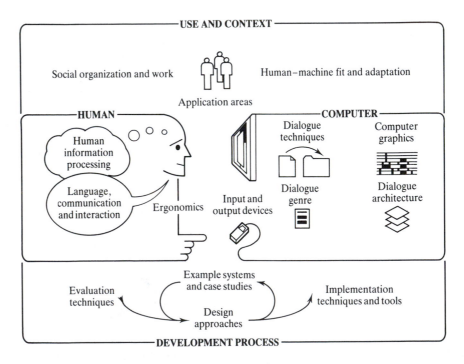

Figure 1.4 The discipline of human–computer interaction (ACM SIGCHI, 1992, p. 16: © 1992, Association for Computing Machinery, Inc. reprinted by permission).

needed to realize systems. Evaluation also plays an important role in this process by enabling designers to check that their ideas really are what users want.

Although most of these topics have been recognized as part of HCI for some time, the balance of interest in various topics has shifted over the years, largely in response to the technological developments described earlier. In the 1970s and early 1980s, for example, there was considerable interest from psychologists in the information processing aspects of computer system design. Topics such as the menu names and depth versus breadth in menu design were popular areas of study. The early and mid-1980s also tended to be dominated by the 'usability' of single-user computer systems in response to the PC explosion. In the late 1980s and 1990s the trend has been towards very powerful multi-user workstations and more powerful PCs, improved communications, multimedia, multitasking machines and virtual reality. In response, the HCI community was quick to realize that although it was important to understand the interaction of one user with one machine across an interface there were other topics that needed to be considered in order to capitalize upon the new technology. The kind of issues that needed to be studied included: group working, integration and interaction of media, and the impact of such technologies in the workplace, in the home and in society in general.

Three systems that provide landmarks along this evolutionary path are the Dynabook, the Star and the Apple Lisa, predecessor of today's Apple Macintosh machines. A brief history of these three systems is contained in Box 1.4. An important unifying theme present in all three computer systems is that they provided a form of interaction that proved effective and easy for novices and experts alike. They were also easy to learn, and provided a visual–spatial interface whereby, in general, objects could be directly manipulated, while the system gave immediate feedback. In the words of Kay and Goldberg, 'There should be no discernible pause between cause and effect. One of the metaphors we used when designing such a system was that of a musical instrument, such as a flute, which is owned by its user and responds instantly and consistently to its owner's wishes. Imagine the absurdity of a one-second delay between blowing a note and hearing it!' (1977, p. 32).

Box 1.4   The Dynabook, the Star and the Lisa

Dynabook was the brainchild of Alan Kay and his associates at Xerox's Palo Alto Research Centre in California in the early 1970s. The original intention was to develop a highly responsive book-sized personal computer with a high-resolution colour display and a radio link to a worldwide computer network that could function as secretary, mailbox, reference library, telephone centre and amusement centre. Although still a vision, these early ideas had a major influence on the design of computing systems. In the late 1970s the same group developed a personal workstation known as the Star which, although desk-sized rather than book-sized and with much less computing power than had been hoped for, was a very powerful machine. The Star workstation was designed to be used by one individual. This meant that the problems associated with time-sharing, such as unreliable response times and terminals in fixed locations, were effectively eliminated. Most significantly, the system was designed with a large, bit-mapped, high-resolution display, capable of fast and high-quality graphic imagery. With such good graphics and computer power, the scope was there for far more sophisticated interactions than had previously been possible. A mouse was installed, making it possible to point to options on a menu displayed on the screen instead of typing commands. By moving the mouse over a flat work surface a corresponding cursor or arrow moved across the screen. In later versions icons on the screen were used to represent objects and functions. These could be moved around the screen and selected or opened by manipulating the mouse.

The seeds were sown for a new type of interaction. Although Xerox was slow to capitalize on its invention, it paved the way for another computer company – Apple – to exploit the discovery. In the early 1980s the Apple Lisa was developed. This was superseded by a smaller, cheaper and more powerful version, the Macintosh. Its success was astounding. Moreover, in the late 1980s almost all new operating systems for graphically oriented computers were based on the Star–Macintosh style of interface. The importance of graphics and graphical metaphors has continued into the 1990s and Graphical User Interfaces (GUIs) now look as though they are here to stay.

While giving credit to the workers at Xerox it should also be mentioned that much of the groundwork was done in the 1960s and early 1970s. One influential researcher was Licklider (1960), who visualized a symbiotic relationship between humans and computers. He envisaged computers that would be able to do more than simply handle information: the partnership of computer and human brain would greatly enhance thinking processes and lead to more creative achievements. Another influential development was the pioneering work of Sutherland (1963), who developed the Sketchpad system at MIT. The Sketchpad system introduced a number of powerful new ideas, including the ability to display, manipulate and copy pictures represented on the screen and the use of new input devices such as the light pen.

Alongside developments in interactive graphic interfaces, interactive text processing systems were also evolving at a rapid rate. Following in the footsteps of line and display editors was the development of systems that allowed users to create and edit documents that were represented fully on the screen. The underlying philosophy of these systems is captured by the term WYSIWYG, which stands for 'what you see is what you get' (pronounced 'whizzee-wig'!). In other words, the documents were displayed on the screen exactly as they would look in printed form. This was in stark contrast to earlier document editors, where commands were embedded in the text and it was impossible to see what a document would look like without printing it.

Interestingly, a difference in research and development interests could be discerned on the two sides of the Atlantic. Pioneers of HCI in the USA were primarily concerned with how the computer could enrich our lives and make them easier. They foresaw it as a tool that could facilitate creativity and problem solving. During the late 1970s and 1980s several research groups were established in major computer companies as well as in universities. Their work involved building models of the interface, carrying out empirical evaluation and examining the psychology of programming. In Europe early research focused on hardware aspects such as terminal and keyboard design. In the 1980s researchers began to be more concerned with constructing theories of HCI and developing methods of design which would ensure that the needs of users and their tasks were taken into account. One of the major contributions from the European side was an attempt to formalize more fully the concept of usability (originally developed in the USA) and to show how it could be applied to the design of computer systems (Shackel, 1981). The principal direction of the work was the development of operational criteria and assessment metrics.

1.5 The importance of HCI: productivity

Productivity and individuals

One way of demonstrating the importance of HCI is by showing tangible benefits that can be talked of in cash terms. In turn, this means providing clear-cut examples of case studies where, for example, costs have been reduced, work levels improved and absenteeism reduced. For many aspects of HCI, however, benefits are largely hidden, intangible and unquantifiable. As you will see later in this chapter, it is not difficult to provide examples of when things go wrong – such as major disasters, people complaining of health problems and gross underuse or even non-use of expensive computer technology in industry. Showing the financial benefits of HCI can be more difficult because invariably many factors are involved, which make it difficult to attribute success directly to good HCI design.

The most commonly used tool to have infiltrated office environments is the word processor, although spreadsheets and various planning applications are also popular. Table 1.2 reports some of the main findings of a study (Eason *et al.*, 1984) conducted in the early 1980s, which examined the benefits that organizations were aiming to achieve by introducing word processing software into 92 different individual installations. As the table shows, the most significant benefits were improved turnover, greater flexibility and better use of staff.

In another study by Chapanis (reported in Shackel, 1990), HCI was shown to be directly responsible for the improvements in installing IBM systems. The main problems associated with installation resulted from it being a labour-intensive activity that took a long time and consequently caused severe disruption to customer services. The indirect benefit of including HCI specialists in the team was an

Table 1.2 Expected benefits in 92 word processing installations (adapted from Eason *et al.*, 1984).

Benefit	Percentage of cases	Percentage of expected improvement achieved
Improved turnover	86	91
Greater flexibility	75	90
Better use of staff	67	68
Service to authors	54	74
Reduced workforce	49	71
Other cost savings	13	

improvement in productivity and customer satisfaction. A further benefit was the satisfaction that the customer and engineers felt because of the reduction in hard physical tasks. During one year the net savings for IBM attributable to these changes were estimated as $554,840. Similarly, Wixon and Jones (1991) reported that DEC increased its sales of the second release of an applications generator software product as a result of the development team's commitment to improving the usability of the product. The recorded benefits (Karat, 1993, p. 20) were:

- revenue increased 80 % over first release,
- revenues were 30–60 % greater than optimistic projections,
- customers cited improved usability as the second most important aspect of version 2,
- usability helped to increase product sales and provided excellent return on investment.

Organizational productivity

Most work and, for that matter, play or any social interaction involves groups of people interacting with each other, with various natural and man-made objects and with the environment in which they are placed. Computer Supported Cooperative Work (CSCW) is now an important research topic and there are many projects examining the way in which people use electronic mail, video conferencing and other forms of collaborative systems (see Chapter 16, for example). If these systems are to be successful researchers and developers need to understand such issues as the kinds of activities that people wish to do, and how the technology will fit in and support individuals, groups and the organization as a whole. As Eason (1988) and Bjørn-Anderson (1986) have pointed out, these issues need to be considered in relation to any organization that introduces new technology if the benefits shown in Figure 1.5 are to be gained. In a competitive world cost is a significant factor. While hardware costs are decreasing significantly, the organizational costs of implementing new technology can be very high, as shown in Figure 1.6, so it is essential that significant benefits result from the investment. For example, in a study described by

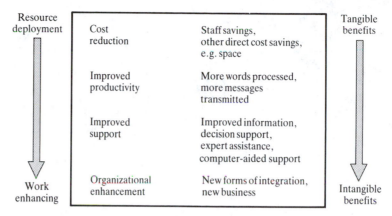

Resource deployment → Work enhancing

Cost reduction	Staff savings, other direct cost savings, e.g. space	Tangible benefits
Improved productivity	More words processed, more messages transmitted	
Improved support	Improved information, decision support, expert assistance, computer-aided support	
Organizational enhancement	New forms of integration, new business	Intangible benefits

Figure 1.5 Information technology benefits in the office (Eason, 1988).

Eason (1988), which was carried out in North America, only 20% of the systems introduced into organizations achieved their intended benefits, as Figure 1.7 shows.

Ignoring the effects of new technology can result in financial loss and stress among staff, which may result in unhappy staff, high staff turnover and reduced productivity. The introduction of new technology inevitably leads to changes in the structure of jobs and the organization itself, which can be problematic:

> 'Frequently these matters are dealt with in an *ad hoc* way as problems arise and constitute a piecemeal and unsystematic way of changing from one form of organisation to another. It is a strange counterpoint to the planning of the technical system which is often highly structured and rational.'
>
> (Eason, 1988, p. 107)

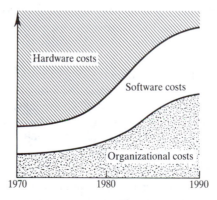

Figure 1.6 Costs of implementing new systems (Bjørn-Anderson, 1986).

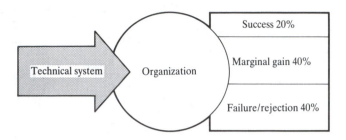

Figure 1.7 Success rates in information technology (Eason, 1988).

The type of management to which Eason refers often leads to frustration and under-utilization of the new system. However, technology itself does not improve or degrade people's jobs; it is the way that it is used that matters. Figure 1.8 shows how technology can have either a positive or negative effect. Depending upon whether the technology becomes a tool or simply exerts control, it can change the nature of jobs and the way people feel, increase productivity and in general have an enormous impact on the organization. For example, some of the ways in which working practices may change as a result of introducing new technology include:

- **Job content** who does what, when, how and how much (computers often make things more formal rather than less formal).
- **Personnel policies** probably as a result of changes to job content (confidentiality of information, for example).
- **Job satisfaction** motivation, control, financial and other rewards, learning new skills.
- **Power and influence** this may shift between individuals or groups.
- **Working environment** changes in space and equipment allocation.

An example of a positive outcome is job enrichment through more variation and learning new skills, for instance a clerical worker who does word processing and telephone follow-up for a group of customers, instead of performing only one task for a much larger group of customers.

An example of a negative outcome is that jobs become more routine and the volume of work increases. For instance, Eason (1988) found that doctors were able to make laboratory test requests in batches after the introduction of a new system, which was much easier and quicker for them than when using the old procedure. However, the result was that the laboratory was overrun with test requests. The laboratory had not been provided with any additional resources to cope with this unpredicted extra load and hence could not maintain the service that the doctors relied on.

In order to understand and plan for the introduction of new technology it is important to learn from existing knowledge about organizational theories. Sociotechnical theory, for example, embodies the philosophy that to be most

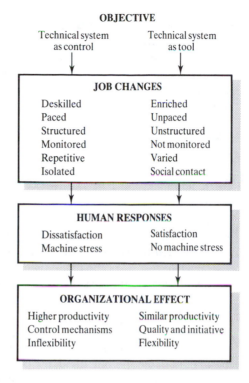

Figure 1.8 The impact of information technology on jobs (Eason, 1988).

effective for the organizations and people that use information technology, systems should be designed and implemented in parallel with the design or redesign of the social and organizational structures of the company. This social design process considers allocation and grouping of jobs and their boundaries, rewards and how people should relate to one another. Sociotechnical and other organizational theories are discussed in more detail in Chapters 10 and 18.

Question 1.3

What are some of the ways that working practices may change as a result of introducing new technology?

1.6 | When things go wrong

A more sensational way of convincing the unconverted of the benefits of applying HCI knowledge to system design is to use the 'told you so' tactic. One of the most talked-about issues during the early 1980s was the Three Mile Island nuclear power plant disaster, which nearly resulted in a meltdown of the nuclear reactor. The cause of the incident was never agreed but experts, official bodies and the media all blamed a combination of operator error and bad interface design. In particular, much media attention and several official reports focused on the design of the control panels in the process plant. The incident could have been prevented if the control panels had been designed to provide the operators with the necessary information to enable them to perform their tasks efficiently and correctly. Some of the interface problems identified were:

- A light indicated that a valve had been closed when in fact it had not.
- The light indicator was obscured by a caution tag attached to another valve controller.
- The control room alarm system provided audible and visual indication for more than 1500 alarm conditions. Evidently this number of alarms was intended to facilitate control of the entire plant during normal operating conditions. A single acknowledge button silenced *all* the alarms at the same time, but was not used because the operators knew they would lose information if they silenced some of the alarms.

The root of the problem, therefore, seemed to be that the control panels misinformed the operators. On the one hand, the control panels did not indicate to the operators the true state of affairs in the reactor plant, while on the other they did not provide the necessary information in a form that the operators could understand and use to rectify the situation.

Misinformation can also breed rumours and fear. One issue in particular, which has been the focus of considerable media attention, is health hazards and the use of VDUs. All sorts of claims have been made about the potentially dangerous physical effects of prolonged use of VDUs. The most scaremongering have included the inducement of epileptic fits, spontaneous abortions and radiation sickness, and the development of cataracts and skin diseases. Those more commonly reported include complaints of eye strain, headaches and muscular fatigue. Clearly, this is a very sensitive issue where the application of HCI knowledge and research can clarify the nature of the problems. The situation, however, is by no means clear-cut and there is considerable conflicting evidence. With regard to radiation-induced effects, it appears that these should be minimal since the emission level of radiation from VDUs is no higher than natural background levels (Terrana *et al.*, 1980). But there may still be cause for concern in particular circumstances, such as long-term exposure and low level emissions from other equipment components. In contrast, there is considerable evidence to suggest that using VDUs can cause a number of visual, skeletal and muscular strains, the most common symptoms of which are burning, itching and watering eyes, blurred vision, aching shoulders and backache.

Further scare-stories are provided for those that still need to be convinced of the importance of HCI in systems design in Leonard Lee's very readable book entitled *The Day the Phones Stopped* (1992). Box 1.5 provides a few snippets.

Box 1.5 *The Day the Phones Stopped*

In 1990 Indian Airlines Flight 605 airbus 320 crashed, killing 98 people. *Flight International* magazine reported: 'this undoubtedly derives from poor understanding between the machine and the pilot, and here the aircraft builders have to do something'. Airbus Industrie Officials agreed that there was indeed a problem: 'the company maintains the problem is the pilots failing to adapt to the automation, rather than acknowledging the need for the software to work smoothly with the humans' (Lee, 1992, p. 42).

After China Airlines Flight 006 plunged thirty thousand feet towards the Pacific Ocean for two minutes while the pilot tried frantically to regain control, which in the process resulted in huge chunks of the tail and landing gear being ripped off, veteran pilot Peter Garrison commented on the design of airline software as follows: 'the crew's role is reduced to one of monitoring the performance of boringly reliable systems. Humans make bad monitors, however. To perform well, they need to be ... giving commands or control inputs and then feeling ... the result' (Lee, 1992, p. 65).

'The Pentagon issues a statement that the *Vincennes* has downed an Iranian F-14 fighter. The Navy dismisses Iranian reports that an unarmed civilian jetliner has been shot down. Minutes later, the Navy issues a correction: they have indeed shot down, by mistake, Iran Air 655. Two hundred and ninety people were aboard. There were no survivors' (Lee, 1992, p. 233). 'In his final report on the incident, Fogarty [the Navy investigator] concluded that Aegis [a sophisticated onboard computer] had provided accurate information. The crew had somehow misinterpreted the data. ... The operators had fallen victim to the one major flaw of the Aegis ... [a] "seemingly trivial design decision."'

'The radar image of the Airbus on one of the giant computer screens displayed the airplane's position and heading. But critical information about the plane's altitude was omitted, and instead displayed on different consoles. Correlating the two pieces of information proved difficult at best'. In the final summing-up of the investigation, 'Joint Chiefs of Staff chairman Adm. William Crowe stated, "I recommend that some additional human engineering be done on the display systems of the Aegis. It seemed to our inexperienced eyes that the Commanding Officer should have some way of separating crucial information from other data. The vital data should be displayed in some fashion so that the CO and his main assistants do not have to shift their attention back and forth between displays"' (Lee, 1992, pp. 234–5).

Remember the discussions earlier about feedback? We rest our case; you decide – is HCI important?

Key points

- Computers are used by a wide variety of different kinds of people and not just technical specialists as in the past, so it is important to design HCI that supports the needs, knowledge and skills of the intended users.
- A user interface is those aspects of the system that the user comes in contact with (Moran, 1981, p. 671).
- Usability is a key concept in HCI. It is concerned with making systems safe, easy to learn and easy to use.
- HCI is concerned with understanding, designing, evaluating and implementing interactive computing systems for human use.
- The goals of HCI are 'to develop or improve the safety, utility, effectiveness, efficiency, and usability of systems that include computers' (*Interacting with Computers*, 1989, p. 3).
- The importance of HCI is demonstrated by evidence of increased productivity and improved safety.
- Organizational issues that need to be taken into account include the way different people's activities interrelate within an organization and how technology impacts upon these activities.
- The introduction of, or change in a technical system can influence people's job content, working practices and job satisfaction, personnel policies, power and influence and also physical aspects of the working environment such as space.

Further reading

EASON K.D. (1988). *Information Technology and Organisational Change*. London: Taylor & Francis.
This book provides an excellent account of the organizational issues that need to be considered in the design and introduction of computer systems into organizations.

LEE L. (1992). *The Day the Phones Stopped: How People Get Hurt When Computers Go Wrong*. New York: Primus Donald I. Fine, Inc.
Lee catalogues a wide range of dangerous and potentially dangerous events in safety-critical systems, including air traffic control, as well as examples from medical practice and an account of the famous day when the phones stopped at AT&T. This breakdown brought chaos to the business community, resulting in huge loss of revenue to many companies, not to mention the losses incurred by AT&T themselves. Although Lee does not distinguish between software bugs and poor HCI design, you will find plenty of both to alarm you for a long time!

NORMAN D.A. (1988). *The Psychology of Everyday Things*. New York: Basic Books.
In this, the first of Donald Norman's books, he describes a wide range of everyday artefacts that are poorly designed. This book challenges us to consider design and to ask 'why doesn't this work?' It is both thought-provoking and amusing.

NORMAN D.A. (1992). *Turn Signals are the Facial Expressions of Automobiles*. Reading, MA: Addison-Wesley.
This book followed *The Psychology of Everyday Things* and is written in similar style. Throughout the book, Norman draws our attention to the need to humanize modern technology in all ways and provides a series of examples to support his argument.

2

Components of HCI

Aims and objectives

The aim of this chapter is to examine the multidisciplinary nature of HCI and to review the process of HCI design. After studying this chapter you should be able to:

- describe the components of HCI in a way that informs HCI design,
- assess the contributions of different disciplines to HCI,
- realize what a mix of skills and disciplines will be needed, in terms of HCI, to promote good HCI design,
- apply an integrated perspective to the design process.

Overview

As we said in Chapter 1, the underlying aim of work in HCI is 'to develop or improve the safety, utility, effectiveness, efficiency, and usability of systems that include computers' (*Interacting with Computers*, 1989, p. 3) and to ensure that they integrate well in the organizational settings in which they are used. The difficult part is knowing how best to achieve this goal. Those involved in HCI attempt this from a multidisciplinary perspective. In other words, they attempt to address the problems of HCI design by analysing them from different perspectives, which in turn means considering a range of factors. For example, health and safety issues will be addressed, efficiency and productivity will be considered, and social and organizational issues will be taken into account. To tackle all these issues a clear understanding is needed of how different disciplines can contribute to resolving them.

2.1 HCI as interdisciplinary practice

The main factors that should be taken into account in HCI design are shown in Figure 2.1. Primarily, these relate directly to users, such as comfort and health, or are concerned with users' work, the work environment or the technology being used. What makes the analysis even more complex is that many factors invariably interact with each other. For example, if changes are made to improve productivity, this may have an undesirable effect on users' motivations and levels of satisfaction because issues relating to job design and work organization are ignored. So, instead of considering the factors in our case studies independently we will accept that several factors are interrelated and consider them together. The first case study is of a ticketing system for travel agents and it is a typical example from the 1970s and early 1980s. The second example is concerned with automating a checkout in a supermarket – a common feature of the 1980s. The third is a state-of-the-art 1990s example, in which the notion of 'paper user interfaces' is being explored at Xerox PARC in California.

The travel agency needs a new ticketing system

Consider the following scenario:

A small travel agency with a number of shops distributed throughout the country decides that, in order to survive in the travel industry, it needs to install an efficient ticketing system. Current practice involves sales staff in a lengthy procedure for issuing tickets to customers. First they have to call an airline to check if there are any vacant seats for the time when the customer wishes to fly. Then they have to check with the customer which of the available seats is suitable before making a reservation with the airline. The ticket is then written out by hand. In addition, the customer needs a receipt and an itinerary, which are also written by hand. One of

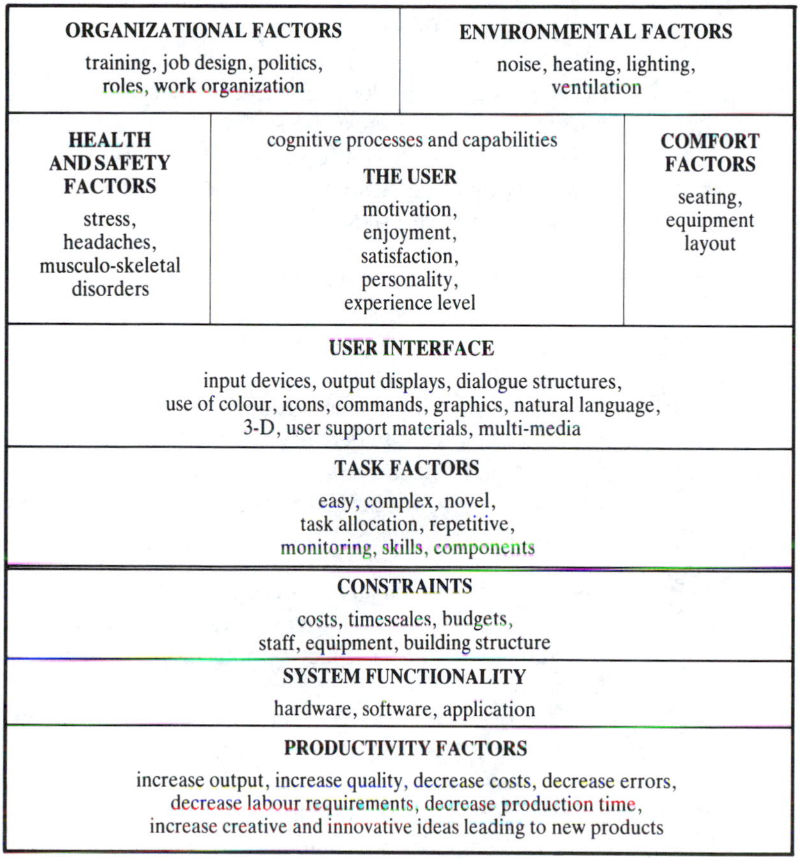

ORGANIZATIONAL FACTORS training, job design, politics, roles, work organization		ENVIRONMENTAL FACTORS noise, heating, lighting, ventilation
HEALTH AND SAFETY FACTORS stress, headaches, musculo-skeletal disorders	cognitive processes and capabilities **THE USER** motivation, enjoyment, satisfaction, personality, experience level	COMFORT FACTORS seating, equipment layout

USER INTERFACE

input devices, output displays, dialogue structures,
use of colour, icons, commands, graphics, natural language,
3-D, user support materials, multi-media

TASK FACTORS

easy, complex, novel,
task allocation, repetitive,
monitoring, skills, components

CONSTRAINTS

costs, timescales, budgets,
staff, equipment, building structure

SYSTEM FUNCTIONALITY

hardware, software, application

PRODUCTIVITY FACTORS

increase output, increase quality, decrease costs, decrease errors,
decrease labour requirements, decrease production time,
increase creative and innovative ideas leading to new products

Figure 2.1 Factors in HCI.

the biggest problems with this practice is getting a telephone connection to the airline. This means that customers often have to wait while a frustrated sales assistant keeps trying in vain. To overcome this problem it is common practice to ask the customers to come back later in the hope that the sales staff will manage to get through to the airline in the meantime. Another time-consuming job is accounting for each ticket that has been issued, and the sales staff have to do this by hand every two weeks.

Before deciding to get a new system the branch manager does some background research into how the agency really functions. She starts by visiting branches in a sister company that is using a computerized ticketing system. After talking to the staff for just a short time she discovers that there are problems. The sales staff complain that the computer is always going wrong and that they don't trust it. Furthermore, they can't understand some of the messages that it produces when they make errors. In fact, they wish that they could go back to the old uncomputerized way of working. Sales figures since the new system was installed are also disappointing and a large number of staff have left the office. Not surprisingly, the manager is concerned by this information so she seeks advice from a consultancy firm. The consultants examine the users' needs and how they currently go about their work in detail and also find out exactly what the goals of the company are. They then recommend a system with the following characteristics:

- immediate ticket booking via a computer connection (alleviating the problem of engaged phone lines),
- automatic print-out of tickets, itineraries and receipts (eliminating the need to write these by hand and thereby reducing the possibility of errors and illegibility while speeding up the process),
- direct connection between the booking system and accounting (speeding up the process of accounting),
- elimination of booking forms (reducing overheads as less paper and time are used).

The consultants suggest making the interface to the system mimic the non-computerized task, so menus and forms are used, which means that the sales assistant only has to select options and fill in the resulting forms by typing at a keyboard.

The consultants are optimistic that customer satisfaction will improve because customers will get their tickets on the spot. They point out to the manager, however, that in order to get the most out of the new system the layout of the agency needs to be changed to make it comfortable for the sales staff to operate the computer, while still providing scope for direct contact with customers. Staff will also need training, and some careful changes to existing jobs are needed too – job design. In particular, the reluctance that older members of staff may feel about having to learn to use new technology means that they will need support during the period of change. Staff will also need to know how to cope when an airline's computer malfunctions. Changes in employment conditions must also be examined. For instance, if staff are expected to carry out more transactions in less time, are they going to be rewarded for this extra activity? Staff relations with other staff in the company who will not be using the computerized system must also be taken into account. For example, problems associated with 'technology power', such as feelings of élitism among staff who know how to use the new technology, will need to be resolved.

EXERCISE

Table 2.1 is a partially completed summary table of the main HCI factors that are important in the travel agency case study. Look through Figure 2.1 again andcomplete the description for the factors that have been left out. While you do this try to consider what the effects of each particular factor might be on the other factors.

Table 2.1 Some of the HCI factors identified in the travel agency scenario.

Category	Factors
User: staff	Motivation, experience level and cognitive capabilities, fear of new technology, coping strategies
User: customer	Faster and more efficient service
User interface	
Work activity	
Organization	
Comfort	
Productivity	

COMMENT

Some of the missing HCI factors are shown in Table 2.2.

Table 2.2 Completed version of Table 2.1.

Category	Factors
User: staff	Motivation, experience level and cognitive capabilities, fear of new technology, coping strategies
User: customer	Faster and more efficient service
User interface	Keyboard input, menu- and form-based system, form of any feedback, presentation and form of output
Work activity	Similarity to previous ways of working, ease of use, minimum occurrence of errors likely, combination of previously separate tasks
Organization	Training needs, restructuring reward system, job redesign, staff relations
Comfort	Equipment layout, restructuring office for optimizing staff–client contact as well as giving easy access to the system
Productivity	Immediate booking with computerized records, faster transaction time, less paper and no forms needed, linking booking and accounts together

Now try the following exercise for the supermarket example.

EXERCISE

A supermarket chain decides to implement a computerized system to automate checkout because it will improve customer services as well as provide automated stock-keeping. The system will have the following features:

'…This one's thin line, thin line, space, thick line, thin line, space, thin line, thick line, space, thin line, thin line…'

(*Source*: Malik)

- a bar code reader for use at the checkout counter which provides a record of all the goods sold as well as an itemized receipt for the customer,
- a bar code reader with a digital display which is installed on the front of each trolley, providing the shopper with the potential for a constant update of how much all the items in the trolley will cost,
- a cashless paying system where only credit cards and direct debit cheque cards are allowed.

Using the previous case study as a guide, try to determine the important factors that need to be taken into account when considering the implementation of the computerized system. In your analysis think about the advantages and disadvantages of introducing this new technology.

COMMENT

You should consider the different types of user: the customers, the sales staff, shelf fillers, stock-keepers. How will the computerized system affect them and how easy will it be for them to use it? You also need to consider changes in roles and work practices. In particular, think about the checkout attendant, who will be required simply to move so many kilograms of food across a bar code reader and may suffer from boredom, backache and so on, but will have the advantage of being face-to-face with the customers, so she will at least be able to chat to them. Also, what about bottlenecks in such a system? What happens when there is no bar code fixed on the item of food as in the case of fresh fruit and vegetables? How do you facilitate the flow of goods being removed from a trolley, checked in and then packed into bags for the customer to take away? How easy will it be for the shopper to read the digital display given the very bright lighting that generally occurs in supermarkets? What happens if shoppers decide they don't want items any more; how will these items be deducted from the running total? The list of possibilities is endless. It is up to you to decide on the important factors and work out a solution that optimizes the use of the new system for the various people who will be affected by it. This will mean making trade-offs and making judgements as to which are the most important factors.

An essential point to note when you carry out any such analysis is that users are not homogeneous either in terms of their personal characteristics or their requirements. While all humans may share certain physical and psychological characteristics, they are heterogeneous in terms of qualities like size, shape, cognitive abilities and motivation. Such individual differences have important consequences for design. Consider the design of car seats, for example. If we were all the same shape then a designer would have no difficulty in arriving, theoretically, at the perfect seat. Compared with psychological differences physical differences seem quite straightforward. One way in which designers can deal with this variation is to provide flexible systems that can be 'customized' or 'tailored' to meet individual needs. For example, returning to the design of car seats, it will come as no surprise to you to note that car seats now offer significantly more ways of adjustment than they did even ten years ago. Similarly, many application packages, such as word processing packages, offer a range of different options to match the level of expertise and preferences of users.

Question 2.1

Recall the main factors that need to be considered when analysing an HCI problem.

Box 2.1 contains the last case study, a state-of-the-art example from the 1990s about a 'paper user interface', in which the characteristics of paper are combined with those of computer technology.

Box 2.1   Xerox PARC's paper user interface

'Since its invention millennia ago, paper has served as one of our primary communications media. Its inherent physical properties make it easy to use, transport and store and cheap to manufacture. Despite these advantages paper remains a second class citizen in the electronic world.'

(Johnson *et al.*, 1993, p. 507)

Researchers at Xerox PARC have developed a paper user interface which brings together the many advantages of paper with those offered by desktop computer

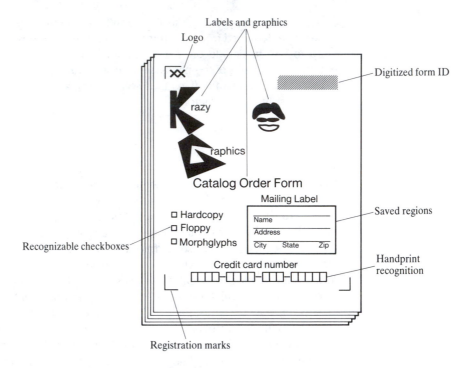

Figure 2.2 A paper user interface (Johnson *et al.*, 1993: © 1993, Association for Computing Machinery, Inc. reprinted by permission).

software such as the ability to manipulate, communicate, file and process information (Johnson *et al.*, 1993). Using paper as the user interface has many advantages because everyone knows how to use paper. The characteristics of the paper user interface are:

- the user can interact with the system via paper through the paper user interface (or electronically),
- a form, like the one in Figure 2.2, is presented to the user to complete and the user's details (entered via this form) provide instructions for processing documents,
- it has many uses, including electronic filing.

Tests with users reveal that the primary advantage of the paper user interface over existing systems is that the task is made much easier. Tasks like document entry and retrieval, for example, were simplified by avoiding cumbersome workstation interfaces.

EXERCISE

Briefly consider what kinds of factors might be important in the introduction of paper interfaces into offices. Try to complete Table 2.3.

Table 2.3 Some of the HCI factors identified in the paper user interface case study.

Category	Factors
User: staff	
User: customer	
User interface	
Work activity	
Organization	
Comfort	
Productivity	

(No comment is provided for this exercise.)

If you haven't analysed examples like the Travel Agency, the Supermarket Checkout and the Paper Interface case studies before you may be surprised by the variety of different kinds of knowledge that are brought into play in the analysis. You probably guessed that a knowledge of computer science and cognitive psychology would be needed in HCI but did you think about social psychology, organizational psychology, ergonomics or even physiology? And this is not an exhaustive list; if you go back to the examples you may think of other kinds of knowledge that would be useful.

2.2 Disciplines contributing to HCI

Figure 2.3 shows the different disciplines that contribute to HCI together with their shared and distinct areas of interest. In Figure 2.3, the major areas that have contributed to HCI are represented by large circles. They are: computer science, cognitive psychology, social and organization psychology, ergonomics (a European term) and its sister discipline human factors (a North American term). Other areas of interest include: artificial intelligence, linguistics, philosophy, sociology, anthropology, engineering and design.

Computer science

'The discipline of computing is the systematic study of algorithmic processes that describe and transform information: their theory, analysis, design, efficiency, implementation and application. The fundamental question underlying all of computing is: "what can be (efficiently) automated?"'

(Denning *et al.*, 1989, p. 12)

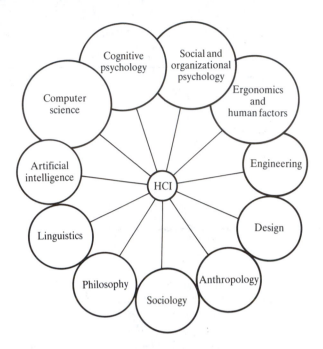

Figure 2.3 The disciplines that contribute to HCI.

One of the main contributions of computer science to HCI is to provide knowledge about the capability of technology and ideas about how this potential can be harnessed. In addition, computer scientists have been concerned about developing various kinds of techniques to support software design, development and maintenance. In particular, there has been a strong interest in automating design and development when feasible. Notable developments during the past ten years include: high-level programming languages (for example, object-oriented and fourth and fifth generation programming languages – 4GLs, 5GLs), User Interface Management Systems (UIMS) and User Interface Design Environments (UIDEs), and debugging and other tools (discussed in Chapter 28). Prototyping tools have also been produced for the purpose of mocking up interfaces and testing systems, which is discussed fully in Parts IV, V and VI. Some effort has also been directed at theoretical developments, which include system architectures, abstractions and notations that provide rigorous methods of analysing the way in which HCI is designed and incorporated within a system. Recently, video compression data structures like Apple's QuickTime have been developed to support multimedia development. Reuse and reverse engineering concepts are also being applied to HCI design. In particular, work is being done to enable novice designers to reuse the work of more experienced colleagues so that they can make better use of, for example, widget libraries. The sophisticated graphics used in visualization and virtual reality systems are also the work of computer scientists (see Parts II and III).

Cognitive psychology

Psychology is concerned primarily with understanding human behaviour and the mental processes that underlie it. To account for human behaviour, cognitive psychology has adopted the notion of information processing. Everything we see, feel, touch, taste, smell and do is couched in terms of information processing. As you will discover in Part II some important topics for HCI design are: perception, attention, memory, learning, thinking and problem solving. The objective of cognitive psychology has been to characterize these processes in terms of their capabilities and limitations. For example, one of the major preoccupations of cognitive psychologists in the 1960s and 1970s was identifying the amount of information that could be processed and remembered at any one time. Recently, alternative psychological frameworks have been sought which more adequately characterize the way people work with each other and with the various artefacts, including computers, that they have to use. The most notable of these is distributed cognition, which is discussed in Chapter 3. Cognitive psychologists have attempted to apply relevant psychological principles to HCI by using a variety of methods, including development of guidelines, the use of models to predict human performance and the use of empirical methods for testing computer systems.

Social and organizational psychology

Social psychology is concerned with studying the nature and causes of human behaviour in a social context. Vaske and Grantham (1990) identify the four core concerns of social psychology as:

- the influence of one individual on another person's attitudes and behaviour,
- the impact of a group on its members' attitudes and behaviour,
- the impact of a member on a group's activities and structure,
- the relationship between the structure and activities of different groups.

The role of social and organizational psychology is to inform designers about social and organizational structures and about how the introduction of computers will influence working practices. In large organizations, for example, computers have a role in everything ranging from the electronic exchange of memos, to paying salaries, to controlling the heating and lighting in the building. This involves understanding the structure and function of organizations in terms of authority and power, size and complexity, efficiency and effectiveness, information flow, technology, working practices, the work environment and social context. Models of organizational change can be helpful in providing this understanding. These and other related aspects are discussed further in Chapters 9 and 10.

Ergonomics or human factors

Ergonomics, or human factors, developed from the interests of a number of different disciplines primarily during World War II. Its purpose is to define and design tools and various artefacts for different work, leisure and domestic environments to suit the capacities and capabilities of users.

The role of the ergonomist is to translate information from the above sciences into the context of design, whether for a car seat or a computer system. The objective is to maximize an operator's safety, efficiency and reliability of performance, to make a task easier, and to increase feelings of comfort and satisfaction. Some of the prime concerns from ergonomists and human factors specialists for HCI include workstation and any kind of hardware design and those aspects of software design that may have adverse physiological effects on humans, such as the readability of information on visual display units. Radiation from visual display units has also been a key concern in recent years, as has the physiological effects of workstation design. There have been several instances, and indeed court cases, concerning repetitive strain injury in the workplace.

Question 2.2

What are the main contributions from cognitive psychology, social psychology, ergonomics and computer science to the study of HCI?

Linguistics

Linguistics is the scientific study of language (Lyons, 1970). From the point of view of HCI there are several issues that may be better understood by applying knowledge and theories from linguistics. For example, in the early days of command languages there was some debate about whether or not the object to which a command applied should come before or after the command itself. When deleting a file called 'fred', for example, should you type *delete 'fred'* or *'fred' delete*. A field closely related to HCI that has benefited from linguistic theory is AI. Within HCI itself understanding the structure (syntax) and meaning (semantics) is important in developing natural language interfaces, which are discussed in Part III, and more recently conversational analysis (Chapter 9), which is being used to understand how individuals and groups interact with computers in natural environments. As communications across the world improve through advanced network technologies, and as more databases of information and applications are shared, linguistics will have an increasingly important role to play in internationalization and localization of software. Internationalization focuses on isolating the cultural aspects of the product, such as text and dates, from the rest of the product, which can then be culturally generic. Localization, on the other hand, is about infusing a specific cultural context into a previously internationalized product (Russo and Boor, 1993).

Artificial intelligence

Artificial Intelligence (AI) is concerned with the design of intelligent computer programs which simulate different aspects of intelligent human behaviour. In particular, the focus has been on representing knowledge structures that are utilized in human problem-solving. AI knowledge and methods, such as the use of production rules, have been applied to HCI in connection with the development of tutoring and expert systems with intelligent user interfaces. However, the relationship of AI to HCI is mainly concerned with users' needs when interacting with an intelligent interface. These include, for example, the use of natural language and speech as a way of communicating with a system and the need for the system to explain and justify its advice. The development of intelligent agents to support users' navigation and to reduce the menial tasks that many users encounter when using computer systems is a fairly recent challenge in hypermedia and multimedia development.

Philosophy, sociology and anthropology

Although it is probably unjust to lump these three subjects together, it has been done because their contribution to HCI has historically been from a 'soft sciences' perspective. By this it is meant that traditionally they have not been directly involved with the actual design of computer systems in the same way as 'hard sciences', but rather with the consequences of developments in Information Technology (IT) and technology transfer. A major concern of these disciplines until relatively recently, therefore, has been to consider the implications of the introduction of IT to society. More recently, attempts are being made to apply methods developed in the social sciences to the design and evaluation of systems. One such technique is that of *ethnomethodology* where the basic premise is to assume no *a priori* model of what is going on when people use computer systems and, instead, to analyse behaviour by observing events as they occur in practice in their natural context (see Chapter 32). Hence the emphasis is on how to make sense of what is going on when people communicate with each other or with machines during and after the event rather than to model and predict beforehand as cognitive psychology has tended to do.

The reasons for applying social science methods of analysis to HCI, it is argued, are that a more accurate description of the interaction between users, their work, the technology that they use and the environment in which they are situated can be obtained. One application of social science methods has been to characterize computer supported cooperative writing (CSCW), which is concerned with sharing software and hardware among groups of people working together (see Chapters 10 and 16). The aim is to design tools and ways of working which optimize the shared technology so that maximum benefit can be obtained by all those who use or are affected by it. For example, a study might be carried out in a workplace to assess how existing computer systems and software are used. The results may then point out areas where changes to work practices could increase the use of the systems. In addition it might suggest the implementation of new, emerging types of *groupware*, which is software specifically designed to be used by more than one person.

Engineering and design

Engineering is an applied science which relies heavily on model building and empirical testing. Engineering essentially takes the findings of science and utilizes them in the production of artefacts. Design contributes creative skills and knowledge to this process. In many respects the greatest influence of engineering on HCI and subsequently on interface and system development is through software engineering. Design too is a well-established discipline in its own right which has potential benefits when applied to HCI problems. An obvious example is graphic design. The increasing technological potential available for producing high-quality two-dimensional and three-dimensional graphics provides the stimulus for capitalizing on graphic information display. Until relatively recently, computer programmers and software designers tended to assume that their own intuitions about what constituted good graphic design were adequate. However, raised awareness brought about partly by the development of HCI as a field of study and partly by increased interest and involvement of graphic designers themselves in screen design has meant that 'professional graphic design' has gained importance in computer system design. As well as graphics, typographic issues are also a major concern. Graphic design practice has also started to influence the way that HCI design is done. For example, sketching techniques can be used for initial brainstorming and the studio approach of putting work on display for critique by peers is starting to be used by some designers (see Chapter 22 and the interview with Bill Verplank in Part V). The relationship between engineering, design and HCI is much more a two-way process than is the case with some of the other disciplines. Not only do engineering and design contribute to HCI practices and knowledge, but they also derive considerable benefit from HCI work. For example, it is now very common for engineers and designers to make use of various computerized design tools, computer-aided design and computer-aided engineering packages for designing anything from aircraft to the architecture of a new shopping precinct.

Having reviewed the contributions of the various disciplines to HCI you may now be asking yourself how this knowledge and these skills can be brought together to bear on HCI design. In Terry Winograd's view:

> 'Human–computer interaction is the kind of discipline which is neither the study of humans, nor the study of technology, but rather the bridging between those two. So you always have to have one eye open to the question: what can the technology do? How can you build it? What are the possibilities? And one eye open to the question: what are people doing and how would this fit in? What would they do with it? If you lose sight of either of those, you fail to design well. ... I think the challenge is

to really keep knowledge of both the technology and the people playing off against each other in order to develop new things.'

(interview with Terry Winograd, see p. 53)

2.3 A conceptual model for HCI

It should now be clear that the role of HCI in system design is to enhance the quality of the interaction between humans and computer systems. To achieve this, we need systematically to apply knowledge about human goals, human capabilities and limitations together with knowledge about computer capabilities and limitations. Furthermore, we must also relate this knowledge to understanding the social, organizational and physical aspects of the users' work environment. The challenge for system designers, human factors specialists and anyone interested in designing 'computers for people to use' is knowing how to make the transition from what can be done (that is, the functionality) to how it should be done in order to match users' needs (that is, usability) in the natural work environment. At the 'nuts and bolts' level (that is, the physical level) this means selecting the most appropriate input devices (such as keyboards, mice, pens and so on) for the task and likewise the most appropriate output devices (such as video, speech, text, graphics and so on). It also means deciding on the best style of interaction (such as forms, natural language, GUIs, multimedia, virtual reality and so on). As well as knowing the characteristics of the technology it is also essential to understand human psychology and the particular characteristics of the users, such as expertise and age. Such decisions also need to take account of the environment in which the system will be used in terms of physical attributes such as space and light; social aspects to do with how people interact or share tasks; and organizational aspects like hierarchies and different working roles.

Figure 2.4 shows how we can view these different issues in terms of a model (Eason, 1991) of HCI. There are four components in this model – people, work, the environment and technology – and the following assumptions are made about them:

- people can mean one or more people,
- work can mean narrowly or broadly defined activities including tasks or more loosely defined activities,
- environment refers to the physical, organizational and social aspects of the environment,
- technology can be any technological artefact including any kind of computer or workstation.

The model can be viewed in terms of levels. The first level is concerned with the user interacting with the computer in order to achieve a particular task within a particular environment, shown as the second level. The third level shows that the activity takes

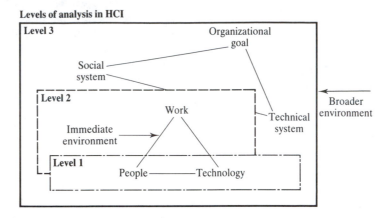

Figure 2.4 A model of HCI (adapted from Eason, 1991).

place within a much broader setting, in which a number of people interact to create a social and organizational setting. Furthermore, the organization itself has a goal which also influences the way individuals behave. Each component within the model interacts with the others and, in turn, contributes to the design requirements of any artefact that will be used within that social and work system. Conversely, the artefact will change some aspects of the system, such as the way people work. So there is constant interplay between the components of the model, and if anything changes then the other components change in response. Introducing or changing the technology, for example, will change the way people work and it will change the environment in physical, social and organizational ways. Carroll (1990) illustrates this argument in his task–artefact cycle, which is concerned with understanding how work and the design of artefacts such as computer systems cyclically influence each other.

> 'A task implicitly sets requirements for the development of artifacts, and the use of an artifact often redefines the task for which the artifact was originally developed [Figure 2.5]. For example, typewriting altered office tasks, word processors altered them again, desktop publishing systems altered them still more. In each case, changed tasks themselves suggested new needs and opportunities for further change.'
>
> (Carroll, 1990, p. 323)

In order to design better systems we need a better understanding of the tasks that people do or want to do so that we can use this knowledge to influence design. Much of this understanding comes directly from observation in the field, and operationalizing it has implications for the nature of the design process.

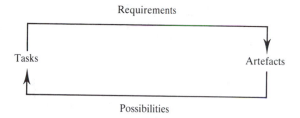

Figure 2.5 The task–artefact cycle (Carroll, 1990: © 1990, Association for Computing Machinery, Inc. reprinted by permission).

2.4 | Designing HCI

Computer systems can be extremely complex so it is not surprising that the design process which results in their creation may also be complex and long. The design and development of large systems, for example, may involve over a hundred people in one way or another over several years. The design process, like any creative activity, can vary from team to team depending on the resources and personalities involved and the kind of product that is being developed. Designing a brand-new product, for example, is different from updating or maintaining an already existing product. Similarly, designing a generic product, such as a word processing system like Microsoft Word, which will be used by a wide range of people for a variety of tasks is different from designing a product to meet the specific needs of a narrow range of users in a single company. (In the UK the latter is often referred to as 'bespoke design', a term derived from tailoring meaning 'made to measure' – hence 'bespoke suits'.) Some of these differences are explored in more detail in later chapters. In this introduction we shall attempt to take a more general and cursory overview of design in order give you enough background to study Parts II and III. In particular we shall try to answer the questions:

● What is HCI design and how does it differ from the software engineering 'waterfall model'?
● Who gets involved in design?
● What is creative design?

In Figure 2.6 you can see a representation of the standard software engineering waterfall model of design. Notice particularly that it is quite linear, the implication being that requirements for the system are collected at the beginning, this information is processed and converted into a design, which is coded and tested, and then the product is completed, tested and maintained for the rest of its life. Of course, this view is very simplistic, and software engineers readily accept that although the design is guided and regulated by this top-down, somewhat linear model, in practice there are many migrations up and down between stages. Sommerville, for example, says:

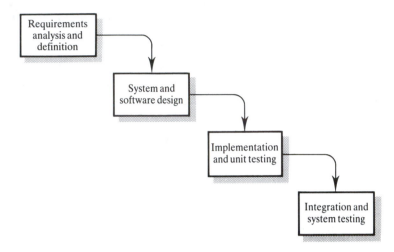

Figure 2.6 A simplified version of the waterfall model of software design and development (Sommerville, 1992).

'In practice, however, the development stages overlap and feed information to each other. During design, problems with requirements are identified; during coding, design problems are found; and so on. The software process is not a simple linear model but involves a sequence of iterations of the development activities.'

(Sommerville, 1992, p. 7)

The essential difference between this and the HCI design model that we will use in this book is that the latter is based on the premises that design should:

● be **user-centred** and involve users as much as possible so that they can influence it,
● **integrate** knowledge and expertise from the different disciplines that contribute to HCI design,
● be highly **iterative** so that testing can be done to check that the design does indeed meet users' requirements.

We shall now consider each of these points briefly.

Involving users

One way of being user-centred is by involving users, which can mean a variety of things from simply observing users' working practices as part of collecting system requirements, to using psychologically based user modelling techniques, to including user representatives on the design team. In the case of the latter we need to ask the question: who are the users? They can be the people who actually use the technology, that is the end users, or they may be other people within the user organization who have a 'stake' of some kind in the development of the system, such as management at all levels and trade unions. End users want to feel confident that the system will offer the right facilities to ensure that their work is carried out at least as effectively as with previous methods. Managers want to be sure that the organization's effectiveness is not impaired by the introduction of the new system, and that the final solution is cost-effective, is not a threat to efficiency, and is safe and reliable. The trade unions want to make sure that union agreements are not broken and that workers' rights are protected.

As well as users, design team managers, marketing personnel, software engineers and designers, programmers, graphic designers, systems analysts, HCI specialists and other research and development staff are all involved in design and development. A software engineer, for example, may provide advice about optimal configurations of system architecture to meet a particular work activity or to comply with ergonomic or other human factors standards. A graphic designer may wish to establish whether graphics are appropriate to all application areas or whether there are any potential problems in selecting iconic representations in certain situations. Marketing people want to sell products on time and as cost-effectively as possible.

Integrating different kinds of knowledge and expertise

Essentially, there are three avenues from which expertise comes:

● directly from a knowledge source,
● from tools developed by researchers and consultants,
● from experts themselves.

Figure 2.7 shows how knowledge from the different disciplines is translated into HCI expertise, which may be packaged into methods for design and evaluation, guidelines, software development and prototyping tools. This expertise and these tools are available for members of a design team to use or they can be applied by HCI consultants. Alternatively, a company may have its own in-house HCI group who will customize the tools for the development of their company's products.

Making the design process iterative

Making the design process iterative is a way of ensuring that users can get involved in design and that different kinds of knowledge and expertise can be brought into play as needed. Various design models have been proposed (as discussed in Chapter 18). We shall use one adapted from a model proposed by Hix and Hartson (1993), known as the 'star life cycle' for obvious reasons, as you can see from Figure 2.8. This life cycle encourages iteration. Firstly, you will notice that the central and most focal point of the star is evaluation, which is viewed as being relevant at all stages in the life cycle and not just at the end of product development as the waterfall model tends to suggest. Not surprisingly, a whole host of different evaluation techniques (discussed

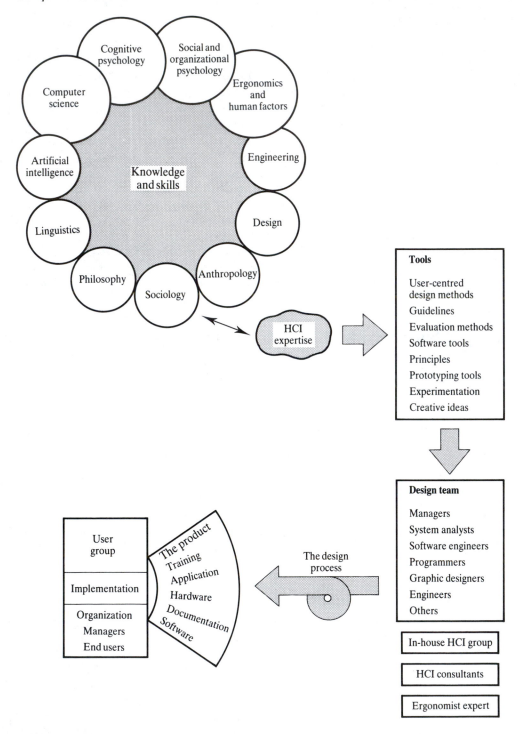

Figure 2.7 Who and what are involved in the design cycle?

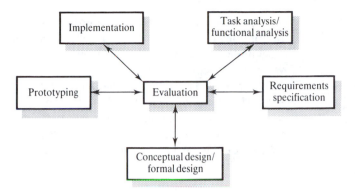

Figure 2.8 The star life cycle (adapted from Hix and Hartson, 1993).

in Part VI) are needed to support the different stages of design and to reflect the design needs of different kinds of products. Secondly, the star life cycle is 'intended to be equally supportive of both top-down and bottom-up development, plus inside-out and outside-in development' (Hix and Hartson, 1993).

As well as evaluation, the following design activities are also important:

- User, work, task and environment analyses – the human aspects of requirements analysis.
- Technical analysis, which aims to match the user requirements with the technology.
- Requirements specification.
- Design and design representation, including coding.
- Prototyping and use of other design support tools and techniques.
- Coding or implementation.

You may also have noticed that this model of design to some extent resembles the way in which topics are presented in this book. Unfortunately, information in books has to be presented sequentially, so it will be important to keep this star model in your mind and to remember that design is highly iterative: appropriate knowledge, tools and methods are drawn upon as they are needed. Exactly what is involved at any moment in doing design is a somewhat philosophical question. However, at the practical level researchers are seeking to understand all aspects of the design process in order to improve design techniques and develop support tools, which will ultimately produce better products. As you do more and more design you too may question the fundamental nature of the activity in which you are involved. Elucidating the processes involved in any creative pursuit is difficult. Schön (1991), in his book *The Reflective Practitioner: How Professionals Think in Action*, attempts to describe how practitioners carry out their practice. Based on many observations, Schön describes how 'practitioners themselves often reveal a capacity for reflection on their intuitive knowing in the midst of action' (Schön, 1991, p. viii).

So while iterative design approaches, such as the star life cycle, provide opportunity for reflection on the results of user testing and consideration of what the design alternatives could be that would provide improved HCI, Schön suggests that we also reflect 'in the midst of action' when actually doing design. This means considering and reflecting on alternatives during designing. This is difficult, especially for novice designers, but the optimistic view is that with more practice and a greater knowledge of possible alternatives you can become a better designer. One aim of this book is to provide some of that knowledge and experience and in Part II, we start by considering the 'human aspects' that need to be taken into account in HCI design.

Key points

- HCI is concerned with designing computer systems to match the needs of people.
- HCI draws from the knowledge and methods of many different disciplines, chiefly computer science, cognitive psychology, social science and ergonomics or human factors.
- Computer science provides knowledge about technology and a wide assortment of software tools and methods for facilitating design and development.
- Cognitive psychology provides knowledge about the capabilities and limitations of users. Recent work on distributed cognition aims to model the way groups of users interact with the artefacts that they use and each other in their natural environments.
- Social psychology helps to explain the structure and functions of organizations through the use of techniques like ethnomethodology.
- Ergonomics and human factors knowledge ensures that hardware and software is designed so that it does not damage users physiologically.
- HCI can be viewed as a model in which people, activities (often concerned with work), technology and the environment (social, organization and physical) are closely interrelated.
- HCI design should be user-centred, integrate knowledge from different disciplines and be highly iterative.
- Evaluation forms the focal point in the star model of design, which assumes that design calls upon a variety of knowledge and methods when necessary.

Further reading

General

PREECE J.J., ed. (1992). *A Guide to Usability: Human Factors in Computing*. Wokingham: Addison-Wesley.

This book provides a broad and concise introduction to HCI. It is a summary of the field.

RUBINSTEIN R. and HERSH H.M. (1984). *The Human Factor: Designing Computer Systems for People*. Bedford, MA: Digital Press.
Although now quite old, this readable little book discusses many issues that are still important for good HCI design.

More specialist

BAECKER R., GRUDIN J., BUXTON W. and GREENBERG S., eds (1995). *Readings in Human–Computer Interaction: Toward the Year 2000*. San Mateo, CA: Morgan Kaufmann.
This book contains a collection of readings.

CARROLL J.M., KELLOG W.A. and ROSSON M.B. (1991). The task–artifact cycle. In *Designing Interaction: Psychology at the Human–Computer Interface* (CARROLL J.M., ed.). Cambridge: Cambridge University Press.
This paper discusses the rationale for the task–artefact cycle. It also examines the evolution of tasks in HCI and the psychology of tasks.

INTERVIEW WITH **TERRY WINOGRAD**

Terry Winograd is a professor of computing at Stanford University in California, where he developed one of the first courses in HCI. In 1990 he gave a keynote address at the ACM CHI conference (the largest conference on HCI) in Seattle about HCI education. He is also internationally known for his research on computing and natural languages. In this interview he describes his view of HCI and gives some hints about possible future trends in the field.

Terry, you've been involved in human–computer interaction for a long time. What is it and what makes it so important?

The name 'human–computer interaction' is in some ways a misnomer because it focuses on the fact that you have a person using a computer. The fact that the person is trying to do something means it's really 'human–work interaction' with the computer as an intermediary. So I think for me the focus isn't on interacting with the computer, but interacting *through* the computer.

What do you think are the exciting areas of research that we are going to see developing through the 1990s?

There are a lot of directions that we're developing in human–computer interaction. It is being driven by the technology. There is more power to do more computing, more realistic visual things, and for different kinds of input and output. I think advances in technology are always going to drive the field by triggering the imagination. No particular piece of technology is

an end in itself, but then somebody sees it and says 'here's something new we can do with this technology that we couldn't have done before'. We are also really trying to bring people back into view and to see human–computer interaction as a kind of conduit for human–human interaction. One of the things that we're able to do now with networks and with interfaces that have a more personal stamp to them is to contextualize information. In computing there is a notion of 'information', you have information banks, information transmission and so on. It's kind of a detached idea that the 'information' is the bits and the bytes of the words when, in fact, everything that is in the computer came from somebody in some context with some purpose

and some meaning. I think that human–computer interfaces are going to move in the direction of letting us see through the information to the underlying context and meaning much better.

Are you suggesting that in the past we weren't facilitating people as fully as we could? Is that going to change during the 1990s?

Yes. I think that what's happened in this last decade is really a shift in thinking. First there was the mainframe, and then there was your own personal computer and you could swap disks with somebody. Now 'connectivity' is going to be taken for granted. There'll be no point in having a computer and not bothering to connect it to other computers and devices because the cost will be low enough and the benefit will be high. Consequently, we're going to rethink how we can interact at every level. For example, if I discover a problem while I'm using a piece of software, I should be able to communicate that to the people who

53

designed it. The feedback loop will be much shorter.

Finally, have you any particular messages that you would like to give to students starting off in HCI?

Human–computer interaction is the kind of discipline which is neither the study of humans, nor the study of technology, but rather the bridging between those two. So you always have to have one eye open to the question: what can the technology do? How can you build it? What are the possibilities? And one eye open to the question: what are people doing and how would this fit in? What would they do with it? If you lose sight of either of those, you fail to design well. And of course they require different ways of thinking. So I think the challenge is to really keep knowledge of both the technology and the people playing off against each other in order to develop new things.

If you build something you need to consider not just 'I'm building something because I need to build it', but 'what effect is it going to have on the way people work and the way people live?' So when you are looking at the 'human side', it's not just one person, it's looking at the whole social structure of what's going on and how technology can both make that better and help solve problems.

HUMANS AND TECHNOLOGY: HUMANS

Human beings are highly variable: they are often subject to lapses of concentration, changes in mood, motivation and emotion, have prejudices and fears, make errors and misjudgements. At the same time, they are capable of remarkable feats: they can perceive and respond rapidly to external stimuli, solve complex problems, create masterpieces and coordinate their actions with others so that they can play symphonies, make films and fly planes. In the past, system designers paid little attention to this 'human element'. They tended to assume that somehow, given enough effort, users could learn and make use of the systems and applications that were developed. However, as you probably know from your own experience, systems are often difficult, awkward and frustrating to use. Try asking people about the problems they have had with a computer system and it is highly likely that they will reel off a number of pet horror stories.

We should not have to be battling constantly with computer technology. More and more system designers, users and managers are questioning this situation and asking how it can be changed. One answer is to spend more time trying to understand the 'human aspects' of computing. By doing this it is possible to develop much more usable and useful systems that may also be a joy to use. In addition, it is important to consider how to make systems reliable and safe to use by humans. By considering the way people act and react in their environment, systems can be designed to support their needs as well as to provide powerful functionality. This can be achieved by examining and learning about cognitive, social and organizational aspects of human behaviour.

Cognitive psychology can help to improve the design of systems by:

- providing knowledge about what users can and cannot be expected to do,
- identifying and explaining the nature and causes of the problems users encounter,
- supplying modelling tools and methods to help build interfaces that are easier to use.

Social knowledge (derived from social psychology, sociology, anthropology, linguistics and philosophy) can help to improve the design of systems by:

- providing knowledge about the context of use,
- identifying and explaining how people work together and what sorts of computer systems are needed to support collaborative working,
- supplying frameworks of social interaction and conversation that can form the basis of HCI frameworks.

Organizational knowledge (derived from organizational psychology, social psychology, sociology and management science) can help to improve the design of systems by:

- providing models of the processes and structures of organizations,
- identifying 'trouble spots' in organizations that are preventing computer systems from being used optimally and people from obtaining satisfaction from their work,
- supplying organizational methods for the design and evaluation of new technologies that are being introduced into work settings.

Most research has until now focused on the cognitive aspects of HCI. The reason is that the dominant framework in HCI has been based on the needs of a single user interacting with a single interface. Recent developments in system and software design, however, have begun to provide much more scope for supporting group working and multitasking. HCI research has since widened to cover these concerns by looking at social and organizational aspects. This part of the book covers all three aspects, but more attention is given to the cognitive issues because much more research has been done in this area. Rather than try to cover all aspects, the intention of this part of the book has been to select theories, frameworks and methods from cognitive psychology and the social sciences that are relevant to HCI and, where possible, to show how they have been applied to system design.

After studying this part of the book you should:

- have a good understanding of the range of established and emerging theories, conceptual frameworks and methods of the human aspects of HCI,
- be able to see how this knowledge has been applied to HCI and system design and to apply the knowledge to your own design problems,
- be aware of the difficulties and pitfalls of translating theory and principles, derived from research findings, into practical advice on system design,
- be able to think about how to develop new ways of understanding and applying knowledge of human aspects to system design.

INTERVIEW WITH **DONALD NORMAN**

Donald Norman is currently a research fellow at Apple Cupertino Inc. He was formerly professor and founding chairman of the Department of Cognitive Science at the University of California, San Diego. He is well known for his theoretical contributions to cognitive psychology and for his inspiring books on product design, two of which are mentioned below. In this interview he cites a few examples of designers not being aware of people's cognitive needs and cultural conditioning; issues that are addressed in Part II.

What are the big challenges for people working in human computer interaction?

I'll talk about the challenges and then I'll discuss the role of psychology. The challenges are social and attitudinal. In fact, I was triggered to write *The Psychology of Everyday Things* when I spent six months living in England. I was especially struck by the relative insensitivity of people to the difficulties that everyone had in getting around the environment. The attitude seemed to be, 'Why are you so dumb that you can't work a water tap?' I found that the water taps in England were not even standardized – that sometimes hot water would come from the left tap, and sometimes from the right tap. Sometimes I had to turn it counter-clockwise and sometimes clockwise. Many of the things I encountered were very frustrating because I was an outsider to the culture. I would notice frustrations more than if I were British. In England, I became very sensitive to the fact that the world was conspiring against me to make life difficult, and worst of all,

nobody seemed to care. Of course, when I went back to the United States, I found an equally large number of problems there.

Most industrial accidents today are blamed on human error. We blame the person, and we fire or retrain them. 'Blame and train' I call it. But if most accidents are caused by humans then maybe it's not the humans, maybe it's that we aren't designing things appropriately for people to use. If you designed an electronic circuit and it got too hot so it malfunctioned, or if there was an electrical problem triggering errors in the circuit, you wouldn't blame the

circuit. What you would do is redesign it so that it wouldn't be affected by the heat, or add a cooling system, or you'd redesign it with error-correcting codes so that it could find any errors and correct them itself. We should do the same for people. We know that people make errors, so we should design systems so that either people no longer make errors, or the systems are insensitive to the errors. The real challenge is to raise designers' sensitivities so that we design things that people can use.

In my book *Turn Signals*, I have an essay called 'Coffee cups in the cockpit', in which I worry about the fact that even in our most expensive aeroplanes, pilots remember details of what they're doing by improvising such schemes as taking an empty coffee cup and putting it over the flap handles, so that when they come to use the flaps, the coffee cup will be in the way and they'll remember: 'Ah yes, before I lower the flaps I'd better turn off the excess electrical load'. It's a strange world we live in where penny coffee cups provide our safety backup!

3

Cognitive Frameworks for HCI

Aims and objectives

The aim of this chapter is to introduce two cognitive frameworks: (i) human information processing, which has formed the basis of much understanding in HCI, and (ii) an alternative cognitive framework that is currently being developed, known as distributed cognition.
   After studying this chapter you should be able to:

- characterize HCI in terms of cognitive processes,
- describe how information processing has been used as the basis for a model of user interaction,
- explain why there is growing dissatisfaction with such models and what alternative cognitive approaches are attempting to do,
- decide whether you think it is important to have a cognitive framework when designing systems.

Overview

The notion of information processing has played a fundamental role in HCI by providing a theoretical basis for cognitive models of users. However, there are a number of problems with the information processing approach and several researchers have begun to reconceptualize the cognitive aspects of HCI, from other perspectives, with the aim of developing an alternative approach which overcomes these problems. One alternative is distributed cognition, in which the central concern is to re-embody cognitive processes in a real-world context. Instead of conceptualizing an individual's cognitive tasks when interacting with an individual computer, the distributed cognition approach attempts to characterize the computer-mediated, cognitive activities of a group of people working together in a given setting.

3.1 A cognitive perspective

The dominant framework that has characterized HCI has been cognitive. In general, **cognition** refers to the processes by which we become acquainted with things or, in other words, how we gain knowledge. These include understanding, remembering, reasoning, attending, being aware, acquiring skills and creating new ideas. The main objective in HCI has been to understand and represent how humans interact with computers in terms of how knowledge is transmitted between the two. The theoretical grounding for this approach stems from cognitive psychology: it is to explain how human beings achieve the goals they set. Such goal-oriented activity is comprised of performing cognitive tasks that involve processing information.

Human information processing

During the 1960s and 1970s the main paradigm in cognitive psychology was to characterize humans as information processors; everything that is sensed (sight, hearing, touch, smell and taste) was considered to be information which the mind processes. The basic idea was that information enters and exits the human mind through a series of ordered processing stages (Lindsay and Norman, 1977), as summarized in Figure 3.1. Stage 1 encodes information from the environment into some form of internal representation. In stage 2, the internal representation of the stimulus is compared with memorized representations that are stored in the brain. Stage 3 is concerned with deciding on a response to the encoded stimulus. When an appropriate match is made the process passes on to stage 4, which deals with the organization of the response and the necessary action. The model assumes that information is unidirectional and sequential and that each of the stages takes a certain amount of time, generally thought to depend on the complexity of the operations performed.

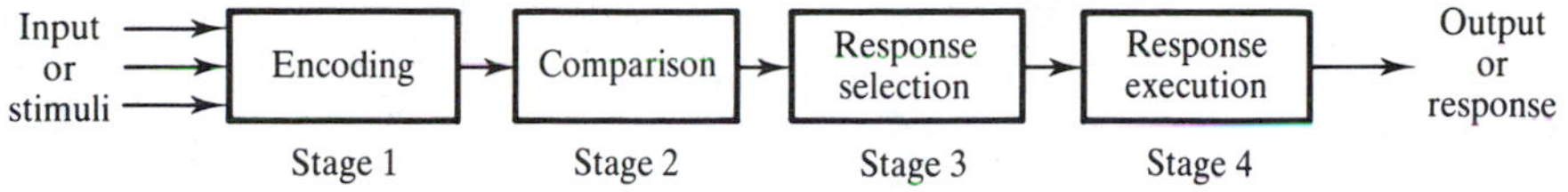

Figure 3.1 Human information processing stages (adapted from Barber, 1988).

To illustrate the relationship between the different stages of information processing, consider the sequencing involved in sending mail (Anderson, 1990). First, letters are posted in a mailbox. Next, a postman empties the letters from the mailbox and takes them to the central sorting office. The letters are then sorted according to area and sent via rail, road, air or ship to their destination. On reaching their destination, the letters are further sorted into particular areas and then into street locations and so on. A major aspect of an information processing analysis, likewise, is tracing the mental operations and their outcomes for a particular cognitive task.

EXERCISE

Carry out an information processing analysis for the cognitive task of determining the phone number of a friend.

COMMENT

Firstly, you must identify the words used in the exercise. Then you must retrieve their meaning. Next you must understand the meaning of the set of words given in the exercise. The next stage involves searching your memory for the solution to the problem. When you have retrieved the number in memory, you need to generate a plan and formulate the answer into a representation that can be translated into a verbal form. Then you would need to recite the digits or write them down.

Question 3.1

What are the four stages of the human information processing model?

Extending the human information processing model

Two main extensions of the basic information processing model are the inclusion of the processes of attention and memory. Figure 3.2 shows the relationship between the different processes. In the extended model, cognition is viewed in terms of:

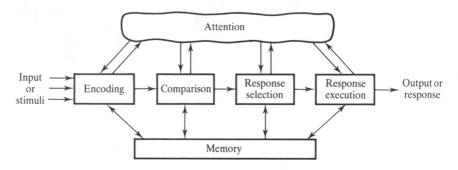

Figure 3.2 Extended stages of the information processing model (adapted from Barber, 1988).

(1) how information is *perceived* by the perceptual processors (see Chapter 4),
(2) how that information is *attended* to (see Chapter 5), and
(3) how that information is processed and stored in *memory* (see Chapter 5).

The multi-store model of memory, outlined in Box 3.1, describes more explicitly how the three processes are connected.

Box 3.1   The multi-store model of memory

The main characteristic of the multi-store model of memory (Atkinson and Shiffrin, 1968) are the various types of memory stores. These are:

* **sensory store**   modality-specific, holds information for a very brief period of time (a few tenths of a second),
* **short-term memory store**   holds limited information for a short period of time (a few seconds),
* **permanent long-term memory store**   holds information indefinitely.

Figure 3.3 shows a simplified adaptation of the multi-store model.

Sensory stores

Information from the external world is initially registered by the modality-specific sensory stores (there are different stores for visual, auditory and tactile material), where it persists for a few tenths of a second. The modality-specific stores can be regarded as input buffers holding a direct representation of sensory information. Only a small fraction of all the information entering the sensory stores is attended to and selected for further processing in the short-term store. The rest is lost by being 'written over' by successive information or through the process of decay.

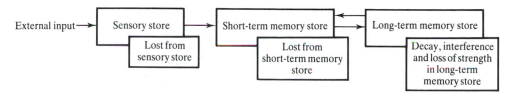

Figure 3.3 The multi-store model of memory (adapted from Atkinson and Shiffrin, 1968).

Short-term memory

Information reaching the short-term memory store is actively processed and may then be transferred into a long-term memory store. Nowadays, the expression 'short-term memory' has been replaced by the term **working memory** (Baddeley and Hitch, 1974), because it is a working area in which information is held temporarily for another processing activity such as handling inputs, selecting, retrieving, storing, planning and preparing outputs. The two main characteristics of working memory are that its capacity to hold information is limited in amount and time. At most, the number of items or 'chunks' we can remember at any one time, be they digits, names, letters or any type of complex concept for which we have a label of any kind, is about seven. This phenomenon, now classically known as 'the magic number 7 ± 2' was identified by Miller in 1956.

Long-term memory

Information entering the long-term memory is assumed to be permanent, and in Chapter 6 we discuss how the knowledge is represented and retrieved.

Information processing and HCI

The information processing model has been highly influential in shaping the development of cognitive models of the user in HCI. In particular, the theoretical framework has provided a means of conceptualizing user behaviour that enables predictions to be made about user performance. One of the earliest models of the user was the model human processor, which, as the name suggests, was based on an abridged version of the human information processing model (Card *et al.*, 1983). The model human processor consists of three interacting systems: the perceptual system, the motor system and the cognitive system. Each has its own memory and processor. Similar to the notions of human information processing, human performance is viewed as a series of processing stages, whereby the different processors and memories are organized in a particular way. Figure 3.4 shows the

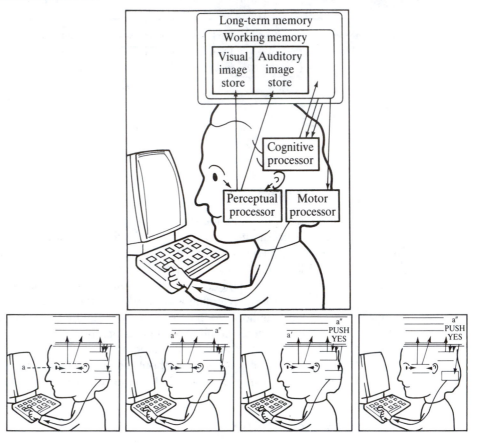

Figure 3.4 The human processor model (adapted from Card *et al.*, 1983).

processing stages involved when someone presses a key in response to seeing a character on a screen.

The model human processor provides a means of characterizing the various cognitive processes that are assumed to underlie the performance of a task. From this conceptual model, Card *et al.* (1983) have abstracted a further family of models, known as GOMS (Goals, Operations, Methods and Selection rules), that translate the qualitative descriptions into quantitative measures. The reason for developing a family of models is that it enables various qualitative and quantitative predictions to be made about user performance; these are discussed further in Chapters 20 and 33.

One of the problems of abstracting a quantitative model from a qualitative description of user performance is ensuring that the two are connected. In particular, it has been noted that the form and content of the GOMS family of models are relatively unrelated to the form and content of the model human processor (Barnard, 1987) and it also oversimplified human behaviour. More recently, attention has focused on explaining:

- how knowledge is represented (Chapter 6),
- how mental models (these refer to representations people construct in their minds of themselves, others, objects and the environment to help them know what to do in current and future situations) develop and are used in HCI (Chapter 6),
- how users learn to interact and become experienced in using computer systems (Chapter 8).

With respect to applying this knowledge to HCI design, there has been considerable research in developing:

- interface metaphors (these are GUIs that consist of electronic counterparts to physical objects in the real world) to match the knowledge requirements of users (Chapter 7),
- conceptual models (these are the various ways in which systems are understood by different people) to help designers develop appropriate interfaces (Chapter 7).

Question 3.2

What is the main use and problem of the model human processor?

Recent developments in cognitive psychology

With the development of computing, the activity of the brain have been characterized as a series of programmed steps using the computer as a metaphor. Concepts such as buffers, memory stores and storage systems, together with the types of process that act upon them (such as parallel versus serial, top-down versus bottom-up) provided psychologists with a means of developing more advanced models of information processing, which was appealing because such models could be tested. However, since the 1980s there has been a move away from the information processing framework within cognitive psychology. This has occurred in parallel with the reduced importance of the model human processor within HCI and the development of other theoretical approaches. Primarily, these are the computational and the connectionist approaches. More recently other alternative approaches have been developed that have situated cognitive activities in the context in which they occur (for example, distributed cognition, which is discussed below).

Computational approaches continue to adopt the computer metaphor as a theoretical framework, but they no longer adhere to the information processing framework. Instead, the emphasis is on modelling human performance in terms of what is involved when information is processed rather than when and how much. Primarily, computational models conceptualize the cognitive system in terms of the goals, planning and action that are involved in task performance. These aspects include modelling: how information is organized and classified, how relevant stored information is retrieved, what decisions are made and how this information is re-assembled. Thus tasks are analysed not in terms of the *amount* of information processed *per se* in the various stages but in terms of *how* the system deals with new information (see Chapter 6).

Connectionist approaches, otherwise known as neural networks or Parallel Distributed Processing (PDP), simulate behaviour through using programming models. However, they differ from computational approaches in that they reject the computer metaphor as a theoretical framework. Instead, they adopt the **brain metaphor**, in which cognition is represented at the level of neural networks consisting of interconnected nodes (Rumelhart *et al.*, 1986). Hence, all cognitive processes are viewed as activations of the nodes in the network and the connections between them rather than the processing and manipulation of information (see Chapter 6).

Question 3.3

What is the difference between the information processing approach and the computational approach to cognition?

3.2 **Broadening the cognitive framework**

It is becoming increasingly recognized that a cognitive perspective of the individual user performing various tasks at the interface is an inadequate conceptual framework for HCI. Specifically, the traditional cognitive approach has neglected the importance of how people work in the *real* world when using computer systems. Moreover, there has been a lack of consideration of other aspects of behaviour besides how users process information at the interface – namely, how people interact with each other, and other objects besides computer systems, in the environment they are in.

There is a growing concern that if computer systems are to be designed to match users' needs then it is necessary to consider the context in which they are to be used, as aptly stated by Landauer (1987): 'There is no sense in which we can study cognition meaningfully divorced from the task contexts in which it finds itself in the world'. Hence, a central focus of research in HCI must be the work setting where users carry out their tasks. This requires considering the social, organizational and political aspects of HCI. In turn, this requires viewing HCI from multifaceted perspectives, as mentioned in Chapter 2, drawing from a diversity of disciplines. These include sociology and social psychology (see Chapter 9), and organizational psychology and management science (see Chapter 10).

Another important concern is the emergence of alternative and interdisciplinary frameworks that are intended to inform the design of *real* systems for *real* people to carry out *real* work activities in *real* organizational settings.

'It is clear that (and has been widely recognized) that one cannot understand a technology without having a functional understanding of how it is used. Furthermore, that understanding must incorporate a holistic view of the network of technologies and activities into which it fits, rather than treating the technological devices in isolation.'

(Winograd and Flores, 1986)

From human factors to human actors

Bannon (1991), in a recent paper on the role of psychology in computer system design, has outlined a new approach to understanding and conceptualizing the relationship between people, work, technology and organizational constraints. He argues that a fundamental shift that is needed is to replace the term 'human factors' (an ergonomics term) with 'human actors'. The reason for this is that the former term has tended to be associated with a 'passive, depersonalized' person while the latter implies an 'active, controlling' one. By changing terms it is suggested that 'emphasis is placed on the person as an autonomous agent that has the capacity to regulate and coordinate his or her behaviour, rather than being a simple passive element in a human–machine system' (Bannon, 1991, p. 28). Hence, instead of viewing the human as an information processor it focuses on the way people act in real work settings.

Question 3.4

From the discussion in Chapters 2 and 3:
(a)   What is the traditional cognitive perspective of HCI?
(b)   How can this framework be broadened to take into account the context of HCI?

Distributed cognition

Distributed cognition is an emerging theoretical framework whose goal is to provide an explanation that goes beyond the individual, to conceptualizing cognitive activities as embodied and situated within the work context in which they occur (Hutchins, 1990; Hutchins and Klausen, 1992). Primarily, this involves describing cognition as it is distributed across individuals and the setting in which it takes place. The collection of actors (more generally referred to just as 'people' in other parts of the text), computer systems and other technology (sometimes referred to as cognitive artefacts by psychologists) and their relations to each other in the environmental setting in which they are situated are referred to as **functional systems**. Functional systems that have been studied include ship navigation, air traffic control, computer programmer teams and civil engineering practices.

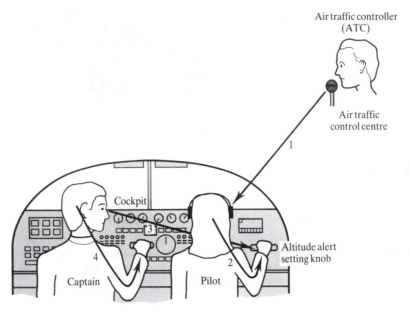

Propagation of representational states:

1 ATC gives clearance to pilot to fly to higher altitude (verbal)
2 Pilot changes altitude meter (mental and physical)
3 Captain observes pilot (visual)
4 Captain flies to higher altitude (mental and physical)

Figure 3.5 An illustration of how information is propagated through the functional system.

A main goal of the distributed cognition approach is to analyse how the different components of the functional system are coordinated. This involves analysing how information is propagated through the functional system in terms of technological, cognitive, social and organizational aspects. To achieve this, the analysis focuses on the way information moves and transforms between different representational states of the objects (media) in the functional system and the consequences of these for subsequent actions. For instance, when someone (for example, an air traffic controller) verbally passes on a piece of information (for example, giving clearance to fly to a higher altitude) to another person (for example, a pilot) a verbal representational state is propagated through the system. On receiving this information, that person may respond by transforming the representational state of a computer system (for example, changing the setting of a control on a flight instrument) within the functional system. This may then have consequences for someone else (for example, the captain), who carries out a further action (see Figure 3.5), and so on.

This example of how information is propagated through the functional system is oversimplified for the purpose of illustrating the way in which distributed activities are coordinated. In contrast, a detailed analysis of any small snippet of distributed activity will reveal a much more complex web of propagations. Moreover, an essential property of distributed cognition that is often discovered through such micro-level analysis is the importance of **situation awareness** (Norman, 1993). By this is meant the silent and intersubjective communication that is shared among the group. When a team is working closely together, they will monitor each other to keep abreast of what each member is doing. This is essential for the coordination and synchronization of distributed tasks. However, rather than explicitly stating to each other what tasks each one is carrying out, they observe each other through largely implicit glancing and overhearing.

A main concern of the distributed cognition approach, therefore, is to map out how the various representational states of the functional system are coordinated across time, location and objects. In many settings, the coordination of distributed cognitive activities is able to be maintained. However, there are also many situations when this coordination breaks down. Often the breakdowns are very subtle. In the aviation example, the pilot may misunderstand the significance of a glance of the captain and subsequently carry out an inappropriate action. In turn, this could have a knock-on effect, propagating the faulty representational state through the functional system. The effect can range from having minimal impact on the group's working activities to creating a catastrophe. It could result in a few minutes of wasted time or end up as a disaster on the scale of the now classic Three Mile Island incident, where there was almost a meltdown of a nuclear reactor plant (see Section 1.6).

The other main goal of the distributed cognition approach, therefore, is to analyse and explain the breakdowns in coordination that emerge in work settings (Rogers, 1993). The term **breakdowns** is used to describe the various incidents, problems, inefficiencies, mishaps and accidents that arise in the work setting. Rather than view the breakdowns in terms of any one particular cause or one individual's fault, their causes are analysed in terms of the interactions between the multiple components of the functional system (cf. Perrow, 1984). In turn, various solutions can be postulated. The underlying philosophy is that instead of just focusing on improving the technical system to match the cognitive requirements of an individual user, ways of improving the whole functional system are considered.

Question 3.5

What are the two main goals of the distributed cognition approach?

EXERCISE

Consider the following scenario. In further automating the control of an electricity power plant, the designers have developed a system that displays information about the process control plant via individual workstations. The new system has been designed to replace the old system, which consisted of a display panel that covered the length of the wall, and which was positioned in front of the team of operators. A significant difference between the two displays is that whereas the old system allowed the team of operators to see the same information at a glance, the new system only allows individual operators to access certain kinds of information via their workstations. One of the goals of introducing the new control system was to make the running of the power plant more efficient. In doing so, it means that only one operator is required to supervise the automated system. However, because of government regulations, it is still necessary for the company to maintain a small team of two or three operators to control the power plant at all times. The new system is installed and the operators have been able to adjust to their new role as system supervisors. Initially, there are few problems and the system works smoothly, but one day the power plant unexpectedly begins to overheat and dangerous gases begin to escape into the plant. There is pandemonium in the control room. The team of three operators have great difficulty locating the source of the problem and deciding what to do. In particular, they find it difficult to coordinate their actions.

Based on the brief description above, explain why you think the operators are unable to coordinate their actions and suggest from a distributed cognition perspective how this might be resolved.

COMMENT

From a distributed cognition analysis (which in real life would be based on a detailed analysis of the operators' actions, their interaction with each other and the system, the way in which information is represented and changes at the individual workstations, and the operators perception of it), a key problem that might be identified is the interaction between the lack of shared information available to the operators and their inability to keep each other informed of their current knowledge of the system. For example, whereas one operator will be accessing certain information about the power plant via her individual workstation, the other operators might be accessing completely different information on their workstations. Instead of all the operators being able to update themselves, at the same time, of any changes or anomalies in the processes of the power plant (which the old wall display panel was able to provide) they each have separate 'windows' onto the functioning of the power plant. The operators, therefore, are having to spend valuable time explicitly communicating with each other about their current understanding of the state of the power plant – which previously would have been largely determined between them subjectively. Hence, the operators are having to spend far more time trying to coordinate their understanding of what is wrong with the power plant and subsequently how to deal with it, than with the previous system.

Another problem that would be considered is how limiting the new screens are in providing the necessary information (in contrast to the old system where all the system process information was displayed continuously and simultaneously on the panel display). This would be viewed in terms of the extra cognitive effort required to access the same information. To overcome the problem of not having shared information available it is likely that the operators would crowd around one workstation, allocating one operator to take control. A more optimal solution might be to consider developing an electronic display that allows all the operators to share the same information. This could be through having an enlarged screen and controls that could be operated by two or three operators. Another solution might be to network the workstations and applications running on the system, and provide a shared workspace such as a communal electronic whiteboard (see Chapters 9, 10 and 16 on group working). This would allow the operators to work collaboratively using the same information. Both solutions are intended to take into account cognitive and social requirements (that is, supporting communication and the sharing of knowledge).

Distributed cognition is attempting to provide a method of analysis and a theoretical framework that enables researchers to conceptualize 'cognition in the wild' in a way that can inform system design. It does this by examining the coordination and breakdowns of interdependent activities and their implications for future technological developments.

Key points

- The human information processing model was the basis of early cognitive frameworks for HCI.
- For a given cognitive task, information was assumed to be processed as a series of ordered stages.
- An example of a cognitive model of the user, which was developed from the information processing approach, is the model human processor.
- Cognitive models provide a theoretical basis from which to make predictions about task performance.
- Whereas early cognitive models tended to oversimplify user behaviour, more recently distributed cognition has broadened the theoretical basis to take into account how users carry out their work activities when using computer systems in work settings.

Further reading

Introductory textbooks on cognitive psychology

ANDERSON J.R. (1990). *Cognitive Psychology and its Implications* 3rd edn. New York: W.H. Freeman and Co.
    This classic textbook, now in its third edition, is well written, thought-provoking and provides concrete examples and illustrations.

Eysenck M.W. and Keane M.T. (1990). *Cognitive Psychology: A Student's Handbook*. Hove: Lawrence Erlbaum Associates.

This is another highly readable introductory textbook to cognitive psychology, which gives a good coverage of the different cognitive theoretical frameworks.

Application of cognitive theory to user interface design

Card S.K., Moran T.P. and Newell A. (1983). *The Psychology of Human–Computer Interaction*. Hillsdale, New Jersey: Lawrence Erlbaum Associates.

This is the original source of the model human processor and its extended family of models. It is quite heavy going in places but provides a comprehensive description of the models and a number of empirical studies that were carried out to validate them.

Carroll J.M., ed. (1987). *Interfacing Thought*. Cambridge, MA: MIT Press.

Carroll J.M., ed. (1991). *Designing Interaction: Psychology at the Human–Computer Interface*. New York: Cambridge University Press.

These two collections of polemic papers, edited by Jack Carroll, include some sceptical critiques of attempts to apply basic cognitive research to HCI. Most notable are papers by Thomas Landauer (1987, 1991) and Liam Bannon and Susanne Bødker (1991).

Gardiner M.M. and Christie B., eds (1987). *Applying Cognitive Psychology in User-interface Design*. London: John Wiley.

An interesting collection of papers that attempts to bridge the gap between the body of knowledge in cognitive psychology and interface design.

Alternative perspectives on cognition

Hutchins E. (1995). *Distributed Cognition*. Cambridge, MA: MIT Press.

This book provides an excellent introduction to distributed cognition, together with several detailed case studies that analyse the coordination and breakdowns that occur in various functional systems.

Lave J. (1988). *Cognition in Practice*. Cambridge: Cambridge University Press.

Suchman L. (1987). *Plans and Situated Actions: The Problem of Human–Machine Communication*. Cambridge: Cambridge University Press.

These two books are highly recommended for those who are interested in reading in-depth critiques of the traditional cognitive framework. Both challenge many of the basic assumptions and tenets of cognitive psychology.

Perception and Representation

Aims and objectives

The aim of this chapter is to introduce you to perception as it relates to the representation of objects and events at the interface. After studying this chapter you should:

- understand why it is important to consider how people perceive interfaces,
- understand what some of the problems are when trying to represent objects on a two-dimensional screen,
- understand how to represent three-dimensional models on a flat screen or in a virtual environment,
- know what the different forms of graphical coding are, and know how to make the most of them when designing user interfaces, for example, how to use colour most appropriately.

Overview

Perception is fundamental to interacting with computers. To be able to use a computer, you need to perceive the information that is presented at and through the interface. If you want to design computer systems, then it is important to understand how theories of perception can influence interface design. Two important but opposing theories are the constructivist and the ecological approaches. Information needs to be represented in a way that makes it unambiguous to perceive and understand.

Most of the research on perception and interface design has been in terms of what we can see at the interface. With the emergence of multimedia and virtual reality, however, the notion of the interface as a screen is beginning to change. Other perceptual modalities of sound and touch are being incorporated into the newly emerging technologies, which are discussed in Part III.

4.1   Visual perception

The visual system is remarkable. It is capable of perceiving objects in the brightest of sunlight and in the darkest of night. It can also perceive and follow rapidly moving objects (such as darting insects) and rapidly decaying events (for example, lightning). At the same time there are many things it does not perceive (a bullet being shot, a plant growing, infra-red light). This means that, on the one hand, we are capable of obtaining information from displays varying considerably in quality, size and other characteristics but, on the other, we do not do so with uniform efficiency across the whole spectrum and at all speeds.

There are several competing theories that have attempted to explain the way we see. They can be roughly categorized into two classes: constructivist and ecological approaches. **Constructivist theorists** believe that the process of seeing is an active one in which our view of the world is constructed both from information in the environment and from previously stored knowledge (for example, Gregory, 1970; Marr, 1982). **Ecological theorists** believe that perception involves the process of 'picking up' information from the environment and does not require any processes of construction or elaboration (for example, Gibson, 1979).

EXERCISE

Look at Figure 4.1 and try to work out what the scene is of without looking at the figure caption.

COMMENT

Did you recognize the scene as a picture of a Dalmation sniffing leaves in a park? How long did it take? Or were you able to recognize the dog only after you knew what to look for? Having recognized the scene as a picture of a Dalmatian, can you see it as anything else? Our interpretation of the scene is made possible by the fact that we have prior knowledge of what Dalmatians look like. The use of such knowledge, in trying to make sense of the black shapes, is considered to entail a process of active construction of the image. Without the prior knowledge, we would not be able to make sense of the picture.

Figure 4.1   Photograph of a Dalmatian dog (by R.C. James).

The constructivist approach

The main assumption behind the constructivist approach is that perception involves the intervention of representations and memories. What we see is *not* a replica or copy of the world such as the image that a camera would produce. Instead the visual system constructs a model of the world by transforming, enhancing, distorting and discarding information. But why does the perceptual system need to do this? It seems a lot of cognitive processing is required just to enable us to see. As Gregory (1978) points out, there is a very good reason:

'We are so familiar with seeing, that it takes a leap of imagination to realize that there are problems to be solved. But consider it. We are given tiny distorted up-side-down images in the eyes, and we see separate solid objects in surrounding space. From the patterns of stimulation in the retinas, we perceive the world of objects, and this is nothing short of a miracle.' (Gregory, 1978, p. 9)

The effect of construction is to provide us with a more constant view of the world than if we were merely to 'see' the images that impinge on our retinas. Hence, when we walk down the street we 'see' buildings as being stationary and people as being approximately the same size and shape, despite the fact that the images that our retinas receive may have radically different positions and shapes. Similarly, our ability to perceive objects on a screen – be they text, graphics, two-dimensional or three-dimensional representations – is a result of our prior knowledge and expectations as to what should appear and the images that fall on our retinas.

Context and *Gestalt*

EXERCISE

Look at Figure 4.2 and read what it says. Do you notice anything strange about the middle letter of each word?

TAE CAT

Figure 4.2   The effect of context on perception. The same stimulus is perceived as being an H in one word and an A in the other (Selfridge, 1955: © 1984 IEEE).

COMMENT

The stimuli in Figure 4.2 are usually read as the words 'the cat'. The middle letter is exactly the same in both words although it is seen as an H in the first word and an A in the second. This is an effect of **context**. We interpret the letters as two meaningful words that go together ('the cat') rather than two meaningless syllables ('tae cht'). The context of the other characters together with our prior knowledge enables us to interpret the 'H' as being two different characters. Hence, when presented with ambiguous stimuli, our prior knowledge of the world helps us to make sense of it. The same is true of ambiguous information displayed on computer screens.

Another aspect of the constructive process involves decomposing or partitioning images into separate entities that are readily recognizable. The object (the **figure**) is distinguished from the rest of the information (the **background**). A number of general principles have been identified that underlie this process. These were first described by the *Gestalt* psychologists (for example, Koffka, 1935; Köhler, 1947), who believed that our ability to interpret the meaning of scenes and objects was based on us having innate laws of organization, as discussed in Box 4.1.

Box 4.1 The *Gestalt* laws of perceptual organization

EXERCISE

Figure 4.3 shows examples of the laws of perceptual organization. Look at each of the stimuli (a)–(e) and describe in your own words what 'patterns' or organizing principles are displayed.

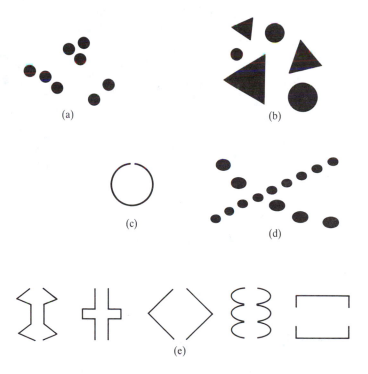

Figure 4.3 The *Gestalt* laws of perceptual organization.

COMMENT

The organizing principles which enable us to perceive the patterns of stimuli as meaningful wholes are defined as (a) proximity, (b) similarity, (c) closure, (d) good continuation and (e) symmetry.

(a) **Proximity** the dots appear as groups rather than a random cluster of elements.
(b) **Similarity** there is a tendency for elements of the same shape or colour to be seen as belonging together.
(c) **Closure** missing parts of the figure are filled in to complete it, so that it appears as a whole circle.
(d) **Continuity** the stimulus appears to be made of two lines of dots, traversing each other, rather than a random set of dots.
(e) **Symmetry** regions bounded by symmetrical borders tend to be perceived as coherent figures.

In terms of their utility for guiding information design, Easterby (1970) has outlined a number of useful principles for the organization of components. Figure 4.4 shows examples of the main ones.

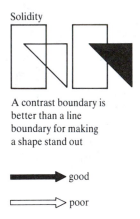

Solidity

A contrast boundary is better than a line boundary for making a shape stand out

good

poor

Figure 4.4 The importance of *Gestalt* principles in symbol design (Easterby, 1970).

The ecological approach

The ecological approach argues that perception is a direct process, in which information is simply detected rather than being constructed (Gibson, 1979). The primary concern is understanding what we do when we perceive. Rather than trying to understand how we can make sense of a scene (like the Dalmatian picture) or how we recognize an object, the ecological approach is concerned with how we deal with continuous events over time (Michaels and Carello, 1981). It asks what we need to know about our environment to carry out our activities (for example, finding a file in a cluttered screen of windows) and how it might be known. Users will actively engage in activities that provide the necessary information. In the above example, this includes flicking through the windows, by bringing to the front windows that were previously occluded.

It is important to note that both ecological and constructivist approaches argue that we are *active* perceivers. However, they mean quite different things. Whereas the constructivists suggest that we actively perceive in the sense of embellishing and elaborating retinal images, the ecologists propose that we actively explore the objects in our environments (by seeing, smelling, listening to, tasting and touching).

A central concept of the ecological approach is the notion of affordances (see also Chapters 1 and 13). What we see as the behaviour of a system, object or event is that which is afforded or permitted by the system, object or event. When the affordances of an object are perceptually obvious, it is easy for us to know how to interact with it. Conversely, when the affordances are less obvious or ambiguous, it is easy for us to make mistakes when trying to interact with the object.

EXERCISE

Describe the different affordances of the objects represented in Figure 4.5(a). Which of the two scroll bars in Figure 4.5(b) has a more obvious affordance?

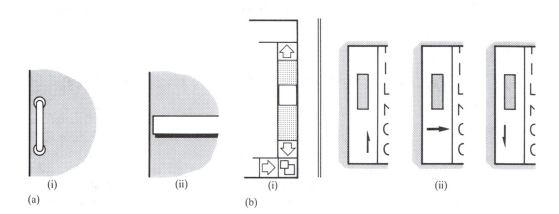

Figure 4.5 The affordance of objects (Gaver, 1991). (a) Door handles; (b) scroll bars (© 1991, Association for Computing Machinery, Inc. reprinted by permission).

COMMENT

The representations of the two door handles in Figure 4.5(a) afford opening and closing. In (i) the thin vertical door handle affords grasping, which in turn affords pulling. Alternatively, the flat horizontal plate in (ii) affords a pushing action rather than a grasping action.

The two scroll bars represented at the interface show the difference between one that has been designed to afford more obviously scrolling than the other. Whilst both representations have a box which initially affords the property of 'touching' through mouse clicking, it is more obvious what to do next from (i). Specifically, the scroll bar in (i) affords the property of moving the box up and down the shaft, while in (ii) the box appears to be floating in space and so it is not obvious what to do with the box once it has been selected. Instead the action of scrolling requires moving the cursor over the scroll bar, which changes the cursor into an arrow pointing up, down or sideways. Hence, the object must be acted upon in a non-obvious way, and signs (in the form of arrows) are required to guide the user.

The ecological approach has been influential in developing theoretical accounts of interface design. Most notable is the work of Norman (1988) and Gaver (1991), who have identified a number of specific properties of the affordances of objects, devices and computer interfaces (see Chapter 7). They argue that a knowledge of affordances can be very beneficial when designing direct manipulation interfaces. In particular, making affordances of interface objects perceptible can help to make systems easy to use.

Question 4.1

(a) What are the main differences between the constructivist and ecological approaches to perception?
(b) How have the two approaches been useful in understanding the design of information at the interface?

4.2 | Graphical representation at the interface

Ideally, it may seem desirable to present information on the screen that has characteristics similar to the objects we perceive in the environment. The visual system could then use the same processes that it uses when perceiving objects in the environment. In particular, design and manufacturing applications might benefit from the use of realistic images in helping the users design and create objects. The problem with this approach, however, is the high cost of real-time image generation. Moreover, when considered against the actual needs of an application, such a degree of realism is often unnecessary. For example, in a flight simulator it is less important to deceive pilots into believing that they are flying through real terrain than it is to provide all the necessary information in the right form to allow them to function as if they were in a plane. Furthermore, as you will discover in Chapter 6, the visual system can perform certain mental visual tasks such as rotating an imaginary object; this means that high fidelity real-time image generation is not critical for tasks where mental simulation of events can be constructed.

In this section the main methods that have been used to represent information at the interface are described and compared. These are classified in terms of (i) the various kinds of graphical modelling techniques used to represent three-dimensional objects and scenes, and (ii) the various forms of graphical coding used to represent different types of system information at the interface. The focus is on the efficacy of the different representational forms in terms of the function they are intended to provide, their perceptual discriminability and ease of recognition. More specific details about screen design in terms of windowing systems and interaction styles (menus and spreadsheets, for example) can be found in Chapters 13 and 14. The way that textual information should be structured at the interface is discussed in Chapter 5 with respect to attentional constraints.

Graphical modelling and three-dimensional representation

Graphical models, developed for use with a conventional computer display, have to be represented on a two-dimensional surface. To make the objects appear as three-dimensional, monocular depth cues are used.

EXERCISE

Figure 4.6 shows five examples (a)–(e) of how monocular depth cues have been used to make objects appear as three-dimensional. Can you describe what they are?

COMMENT

The perceptual depth cues that have been used in Figure 4.6 are:

(a) **Size** the larger of two otherwise identical objects appears to be closer than the smaller one.
(b) **Interposition** if one object partially obscures a second object then the blocked object is perceived to be behind and beyond the blocking object.
(c) **Contrast, clarity and brightness** sharper and more distinct objects appear to be nearer, and duller objects appear to be further away. In Figure 4.6(c) the sharper rocks appear closer and the duller mountains further away.
(d) **Shadow** shadows cast by an object provide some cues to the relative position of objects.
(e) **Texture** as the apparent distance increases, the texture of a detailed surface becomes less grainy.

Figure 4.6 Examples of apparent three-dimensional images created through the use of perceptual depth (Mueller, 1965; Gregory, 1966; Brown and Herrnstein, 1975).

(e)

Figure 4.6 *(cont.)*   Examples of apparent three-dimensional images created through the use of perceptual depth (Mueller, 1965; Gregory, 1966; Brown and Herrnstein, 1975).

Another important depth cue is **motion parallax**. When moving one's head from side to side the objects one sees are displaced at different rates (see Figure 4.7). Objects that are further away appear to move more slowly than objects that are closer. This effect is one of the most important cues that enable us to perceive distances and depth. In screen design, the trick is to move the standpoint of the 'camera' so that the image on the screen moves according to the principles of motion parallax.

Three-dimensional models can also be constructed by using **stereoscopic** or binocular depth cues, in which two images of the same object, from slightly different angles, are presented separately to each eye. This is equivalent to how we perceive in real life, since because of the position of our eyes being slightly apart in our head we receive slightly different images of the world. The visual apparatus in the brain puts these two images together to recreate a three-dimensional image. This technique alone is sufficient to induce perceived depth, although the monocular perceptual depth cues play a significant part. For example, it is still possible for you to perceive three-dimensions, even if you remove binocular depth cues by closing one eye.

Objective
motion

Figure 4.7 Illustration of motion parallax. When an observer moves relative to a stationary environment, the objects in that environment will be displaced (and will therefore seem to move) relative to him. The rate of relative displacement is indicated by the length of the arrows. The longer the arrows, the more quickly the objects seem to move. The observer's movement is indicated by the arrow at the bottom of the figure (Gleitman, 1991).

The stereoscopic technique is used in head-mounted displays developed for virtual reality applications. Two tiny TV screens are enclosed in a headset so that the computer-generated images projected on to the two screens fill the viewer's field of vision. Up to 30 frames per second are generated, allowing for the images to update in coordination with the person's head and limb movements. Hence, as the person moves, the virtual perspective images that are presented to the eyes also move (see Chapter 16 for more on virtual reality).

For the images to appear to move smoothly in relation to the background that is part of the virtual reality environment, the objects must move according to the principles of motion parallax. In addition, various mathematical modelling techniques have been developed, such as the use of fractal geometry, for creating simulations of moving through landscapes and vegetation. Sometimes problems arise, however, when implementing perceptual depth cues while trying to make an object appear as real. For example, as the complexity of the displayed image increases, the effectiveness of using brightness as a depth cue decreases. It may therefore be necessary to make compromises depending on the level of realism required.

Two of the most commonly used techniques of three-dimensional computer modelling are solid-object modelling and wireframe modelling. Solid-object modelling attempts to obtain a high level of fidelity (in which the object displayed is designed to resemble the object modelled) by using colour and shading, whereas wireframe modelling simply consists of schematic line drawings. Figure 4.8 provides an example of each.

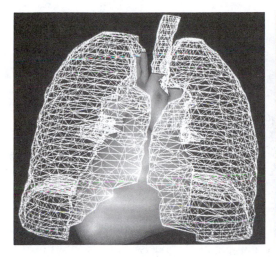 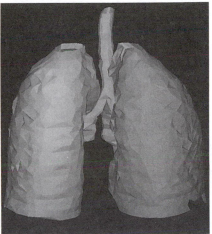

Figure 4.8 Examples of wireframe and solid-object model computer graphics (Boissonnat, 1988).

Both methods have advantages and disadvantages. Solid-object modelling provides more information about the form of the object and is necessary for resolving ambiguities about its shape and surface. For example, solid-object models enable the viewer to distinguish between the inside and outside of objects while wireframe models do not. There is less risk of misinterpreting solid modelling, but it can be very costly and time-consuming in terms of computing resources. In contrast, wireframe models require much less computing power. They can be most useful for tasks in which surface structure is not important, but internal structure is. For example, in engineering applications such as bridge construction an engineer may need to perceive the mechanical structure of an object and its transformations when various stresses are applied.

The need to work with three-dimensional representations is most prevalent in design tasks. In particular, they can allow designers to view the model they are working on – be it a building, car or aircraft – from different viewpoints. The use of virtual reality for such design tasks has the further advantage of 'bringing alive' the domain by providing a means of interacting dynamically with the objects being designed. Applications developed for using with virtual reality systems include architecture and scientific modelling. For example, *Walkthrough* (Brooks, 1986) has been designed to allow the architect and/or client to 'walk through' a virtual building that has been specified by two-dimensional plans and elevations. A number of applications have also been developed to allow biochemists to explore the structure of molecules by 'walking through' them. The advantage is that this allows active exploration of the molecules, thereby facilitating a better understanding of the forces between the different structures in them. Within medicine, the use of virtual reality could also prove to be very valuable in transforming two-dimensional X-rays into virtual 'bodies' that provide a means of allowing critical surgery to be simulated on a virtual representation of the patient prior to the actual operation.

Question 4.2

(a) What are the main perceptual depth cues that can be used to represent three-dimensional objects on a two-dimensional screen?

(b) What are the advantages and disadvantages of solid-object and wireframe modelling?

Graphical coding

In addition to using graphical models to represent three-dimensional objects and scenes, graphical representations can be used as a form of coding at the interface. Abstract system processes, data objects and other features of the interface can be represented by different forms of graphical coding. These can consist of arbitrary mappings, where there is no relation, other than an established convention (for example, the use of red in warning signals in western cultures to represent danger) between the represented object and the representing form. Examples include the use of:

● abstract codes to represent files,
● reverse video to represent the current status of files,
● abstract shapes to represent different objects,
● colour to represent different options,
● alphanumerics to represent data objects.

More direct mappings exist where there is some correspondence between the objects being represented and the form of representation that is used. One form of correspondence is the relative differences between the objects displayed on the screen and the relative differences in the underlying objects that are being represented. Examples include the use of:

● different sizes to reflect different file sizes (for example, small, medium, large),
● different line widths to represent the increasing sizes of pencil width available in a drawing package,
● bar charts to show trends in numerical data.

The most direct mappings include various types of icons that are designed to resemble the objects they are portraying at the interface. Examples include a picture of:

● a wastebin to represent the place to dispose of unwanted files,
● a paper file to represent a file.

A comparison of the advantages and disadvantages of the various coding methods is presented in Table 4.1.

Table 4.1 Comparison of coding methods (Maguire, 1985).

Coding method	Maximum number of codes	Comments
Alphanumerics	Unlimited	Highly versatile. Meaning can be self-evident. Location time may be longer than for graphic coding
Shapes	10–20	Very effective if code matches object or operation represented
Colour	4–11	Attractive and efficient. Excessive use confusing. Limited value for the colour-blind
Line angle	8–11	Good in special cases, for example, wind direction
Line length	3–4	Good. Can clutter display if many codes displayed
Line width	2–3	Good
Line style	5–9	Good
Object size	3–5	Fair. Can take up considerable space. Location time longer than for shape and colour
Brightness	2–4	Can be fatiguing, especially if screen contrast is poor
Blink	2–4	Good for getting attention but should be suppressible afterwards. Annoying if overused. Limit to small fields
Reverse video	No data	Effective for making data stand out. If large area is in reverse video, flicker is more easily perceived
Underlining	No data	Useful but can reduce text legibility
Combinations of codes	Unlimited	Can reinforce coding but complex combinations can be confusing

Graphical coding for quantitative data

Graphical coding also provides a powerful way of displaying quantitative data (see Table 4.2). In particular, graphs are able to abstract salient relational information from quantitative data. The main advantages of using graphical representations are that it can be easier to perceive:

(1) the relationships between multidimensional data,
(2) the trends in data that is constantly changing,
(3) defects in patterns of real-time data (for example, process control output).

Colour coding

Colour coding provides many opportunities for coding and structuring information at the interface as well as making it pleasant and enjoyable to look at. However, excessive use of colour can result in **colour pollution**, particularly when highly saturated colours, such as a 'full' red and a 'deep' blue are used. This can result in garish, difficult to interpret and confusing interfaces, as illustrated in Figure 4.9.

Table 4.2 Graphic techniques for representing numeric data (adapted from Tullis, 1988).

Graphic technique	Example	Usage notes
Scatterplots		Show how two continuous variables are correlated (or not), or show the distribution of points in two-dimensional space. Lines or curves may be superimposed to indicate trends.
Line graphs or curves	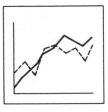	Show how two continuous variables are related to each other, especially changes in one variable over time. If time is included, it is typically plotted on the horizontal axis. A third, discrete, variable can be included using line-type or colour coding. Some designers recommend using no more than four lines (curves) per graph. When using multiple lines, each line should have an adjacent label.
Area, band, strata or surface charts	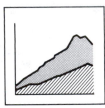	Special type of graph that can be used when several line graphs or curves represent all the portions of a whole. The shaded areas stacked on top of each other represent each category's contribution to the whole. Least variable curves should be on the bottom and most variable on top to prevent 'propagation' of irregularities throughout stacked curves. Label the categories within the shaded areas.
Bar graphs, column charts or histograms	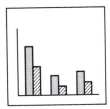	Show values of a single continuous variable for multiple separate entities, or for a variable sampled at discrete intervals. Adopt a consistent orientation (horizontal or vertical) for related graphs. Spacing between adjacent bars should typically be less than the bar width to facilitate comparisons between bars. A useful variation is the deviation bar chart, in which bars are constructed so that, under normal conditions, the bar ends lie in a straight line.
Pie charts		Show the relative distribution of data among parts that make up a whole. However, a bar or column chart will usually permit more accurate interpretation. If pie charts are used, some designers recommend using no more than five segments. Label the segments directly, and include the numeric values associated with the segments.

Table 4.2 *(cont.)* Graphic techniques for representing numeric data (adapted from Tullis, 1988).

Graphic technique	Example	Usage notes
Simulated meters		Show one value of one continuous variable. When showing multiple values (that is, multiple meters) that must be compared to each other, it is probably more effective to use other techniques, such as bar or column charts to show values for separate entities, or line graphs to show values changing over time.
Star, circular or pattern charts		Show values of a continuous variable for multiple related entities. Values are displayed along spokes emanating from the origin. Different continuous variables may be represented if they are indexed so that the normal values of each variable can be connected to form an easily recognized polygon. Useful for detecting patterns, but not for determining precise values or making accurate comparisons among values.

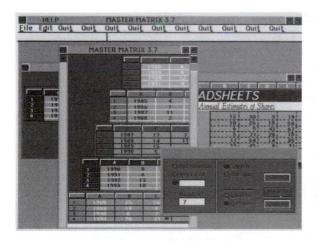

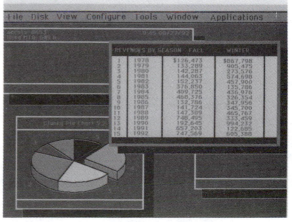

Figure 4.9 Colour pollution (Tufte, 1990). See colour plate 1.

A number of psychological experiments have been carried out to determine the effectiveness of using colour coding in cognitive tasks. These include searching and identifying target stimuli from crowded displays. Davidoff (1987) has summarized the main findings and their implications:

- **Segmentation**   colour is a very powerful way of dividing a display into separate regions. Hence segmentation of a display for detection and search tasks is very useful. In particular, areas that need to be seen as belonging together should have the same colour.
- **Amount of colour**   too many colours in a display will increase search times, so they should always be used conservatively.
- **Task demands**   colour is most powerful for search tasks and of less use in tasks requiring categorization and memorization of objects.
- **Experience of user**   in comparison with achromatic (black and white) coding, colour has been shown to be of more use in search tasks for inexperienced than for experienced users.

More specifically, Travis (1991) suggests the following guidelines for using colour at the interface:

- Based on the principle of colour being a useful coding mechanism for grouping, use different colours to distinguish layers, for example, front and back layers of a circuit board.
- Based on the principle that colour makes things stand out, use colour to make features prominent, for example, currently active files could be coloured in orange.
- Based on the principle of figure/background, dark or dim backgrounds should be used, such as deep blue, and bright colours for the foreground.

EXERCISE

Look at Figures 4.10 and 4.11, which are displays taken from Space M + A + X, a space station construction simulator game and educational aid. How has information been structured on the two screens? How effective is the use of colour?

Note that the displays are segmented and that the colours act as **redundant coding** (on both screens the crew status information is in yellow on brown, for example). Textual segmentation places the user message, prompt and input space at the bottom centre of the screen for all screens which require these. However, the large graphical display in Figure 4.11 has displaced the crew status information to a different part of the screen from where it appears in Figure 4.10, despite the designer's efforts to use a standard layout for all screens. Figure 4.10 shows one problem in colour use: the display showing consumables at the bottom centre uses highly saturated blue on red – a combination that is difficult to read.

Colour can also be used to make text stand out. Figure 4.12 shows how white text that is not separated by spaces is very difficult to read. Figure 4.13 shows how

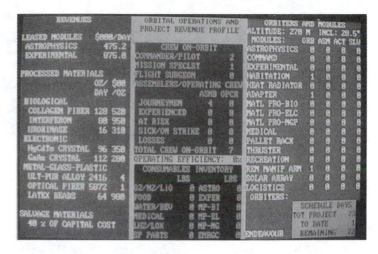

Figure 4.10 A colour screen display consisting primarily of text (courtesy of Final Frontier Software). See colour plate 2.

the same text can be made significantly more legible by using colour to separate the boundaries of the words. Figure 4.14 shows an example of **colour stereoscopy** or 'fluttering hearts' – an illusion whereby red and blue words appear to lie in different depth planes. The effect can be used to attract attention, such as making certain messages stand out. However, if used unwittingly it can hinder the reading of text.

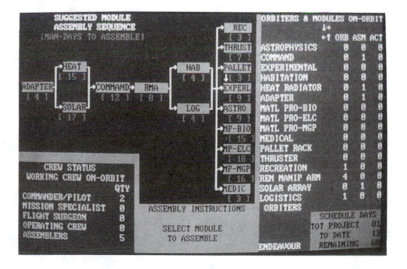

Figure 4.11 A colour screen display showing some graphics (courtesy of Final Frontier Software). See colour plate 3.

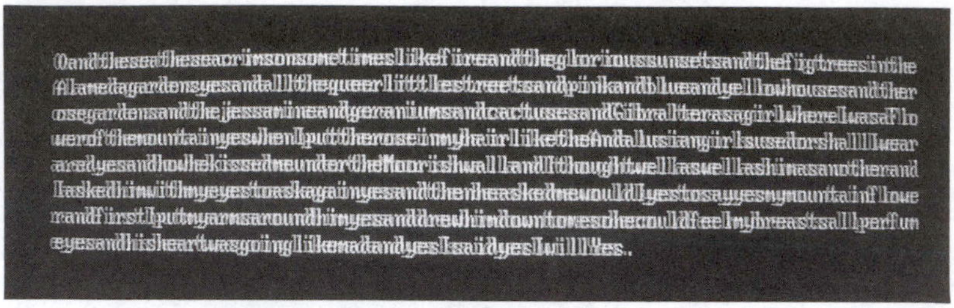

Figure 4.12 An example of text that is difficult to read (Travis, 1991). See colour plate 4.

Colour versus monochrome coding

A number of studies have shown that for certain types of tasks colour has no advantage over a monochromatic display. For example, in an extensive review of the literature Christ (1975) reported that alphanumeric coding was superior to colour coding for identification tasks. Similarly, Luder and Barber (1984) found that colour coding was no more helpful than achromatic coding for a task that required subjects to identify the state of a component at a known location on an aircraft cockpit display unit. Other studies have also shown that there is no difference in response time or accuracy for the identification of simple black and white line drawings compared with fully coloured photographic images of the same objects (for example, Biederman and Ju, 1988).

The implication is that using black and white – particularly for alphanumerics – may be sufficient for the purpose of many identification tasks. However, colour can be effective as a form of redundant coding. For example, it can provide a further means of alerting the user to a message on a screen which has already been designed to blink when it needs attention. Combining colour with other coding methods, therefore, can facilitate recognition of an object on a screen. It can also be used as a way of cueing the user to look at certain parts of a textual display that are important (similar to the way in which highlight felt pens are used). However, it should also be remembered that about 8% of the male population are colour-blind,

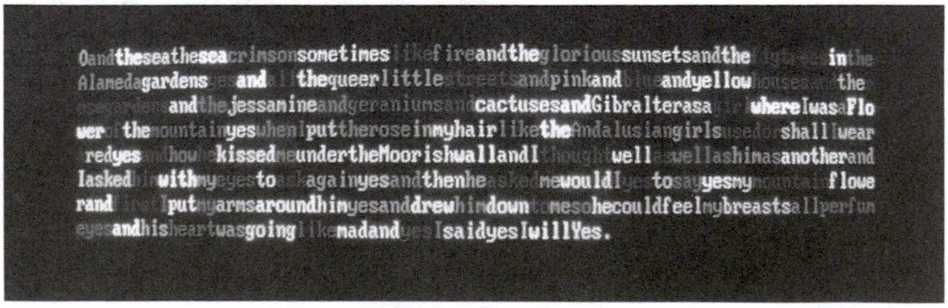

Figure 4.13 The same text as in Figure 4.12 made more legible through the use of colour (Travis, 1991). See colour plate 5.

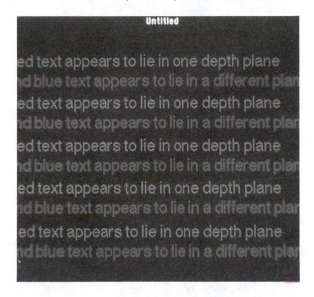

Figure 4.14 An example of colour stereoscopy or 'fluttering hearts' (Travis, 1991). See colour plate 6.

that is, unable to distinguish between various colours. In addition, therefore, other forms of redundancy such as brightness contrast should be used.

Question 4.3

(a) For what types of tasks may colour have no advantage or be disadvantageous compared with monochrome displays?
(b) In what types of task is colour more useful?

Icons

Icons are small pictorial images that are used to represent system objects, application tools such as those for drawing, and utilities and commands (such as PRINT or MOVE). For example, as part of the desktop metaphor (see Chapter 7) objects associated with working at an office desk (such as files, folders, printers) are depicted as icons (see Figure 4.15). Increasingly, icons are being used at the interface for a range of systems. One of the main reasons for their increased popularity is the assumption that they can reduce the complexity of the system, making it easier to learn and use (see Chapter 5 on designing meaningful icons).

When a large number of icons are used for an application it can become problematic to distinguish between them. This is particularly so if the underlying concepts are very similar to each other. For instance, a designer may have to design icons for a set of graphic tools, many of which are similar to each other. In an architectural Computer Aided Design (CAD) setting these tools might include many different types of technical drawing instrument. In order that the different tools can

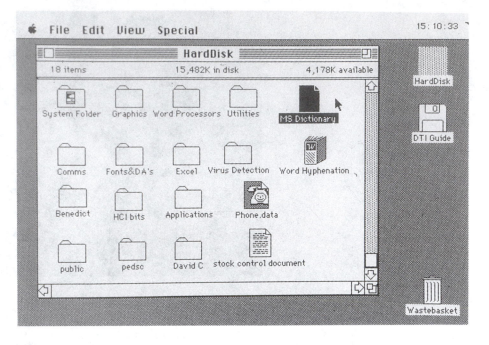

Figure 4.15 Macintosh screen showing different desktop icons (courtesy of Apple Computer UK Ltd).

be readily identified, maximum perceptual discriminability is required between the representational forms. However, as it is often the case that icons can be of only a limited size and resolution it may not be possible to develop a set of icons that resemble the different tools. Many of the tools would look the same at low resolution and therefore would be very difficult to discriminate. One solution would be to use additional (redundant) coding such as colour, shape and size. For example, one type of drawing instrument could be coded in red, another in blue, and so on.

Key points

- Perception is an active process.
- There are two main theories of perception: the constructivist approach and the ecological approach.
- The constructivist approach has been used to inform the design of information displays to make information stand out and be readily perceivable.
- The ecological approach has been used to inform the design of interface objects in terms of how they afford the actions that are intended to be performed on them.

- The main methods that have been used to represent information at the interface are graphical modelling and graphical coding.
- Graphical coding can provide a powerful way of displaying quantitative data.
- Colour is most useful for identification tasks and as a form of redundant coding.

Further reading

Perception

GLEITMAN H. (1991). *Psychology* 3rd edn. New York: W.W. Norton & Co.
This introductory textbook on psychology has an excellent section on perception, with many illustrations and examples of perceptual phenomena.

WATT R. (1991). *Understanding Vision*. London: Academic Press.
A more advanced book, which brings together the disparate techniques, approaches and theoretical perspectives on human and computer vision.

Colour

TRAVIS D. (1991). *Effective Colour Displays*. London: Academic Press.
There are a number of books on the use of colour. This one, which was used as a source for writing this chapter, provides a good balance between the physical, psychological and human factors aspects.

Representational issues

NORMAN D.A. (1993). *Things that Make Us Smart*. Reading, MA: Addison-Wesley.
This is an engaging and easy-to-read book that challenges you to think about the design and effectiveness of graphical representations used in everyday life, such as maps and timetables.

TUFTE E.R. (1990). *Envisioning Information*. Cheshire, CT: Graphics Press.
This is a beautiful and aesthetic book, which follows its own principles on how to design effective graphical displays.

Attention and Memory Constraints

Aims and objectives

The human brain is limited in its capacity. The aim of this chapter is to explain why this is so in terms of attention and memory constraints. After studying this chapter you should:

- know the importance of designing for attentional and memory constraints,
- know what are meaningful and memorable interfaces,
- be able to apply some of the techniques to structuring interfaces that are attention-grabbing and require minimal effort to learn and remember.

Overview

Our senses are constantly bombarded with images, sounds, smells, tastes and touch. The problem confronting us is how to deal with all this information in such a way as to make sense out of it. Furthermore, we need to avoid getting overloaded with information. So how do we achieve this?

The answer is by employing the selective process of attention. As Williams James, a famous psychologist, noted:

'Everyone knows what attention is. It is the taking possession of mind, in clear and vivid form, of one out of what seem several simultaneously possible objects or trains of thought. ... It requires withdrawal from some things in order to deal effectively with others.'

(W. James, 1890, pp. 403–4)

Similarly, why is it that we remember some things and not others? Why, for example, do some icons tend to be easier to remember than command names and what it is about graphical interfaces that makes them much easier to use compared with command-based systems?

5.1 Focusing attention

EXERCISE

Can you remember the last time you were at a party or in a crowd and all around you were a sea of faces and a babble of voices? How long was it before you found yourself turning your attention to one specific conversation? What happened to the other voices and faces? Did they simply become a blur? While being involved in the one conversation did you find yourself overhearing anyone else's conversation? Perhaps it was a piece of gossip to which you could not resist listening. What happened when you tuned in to this other conversation? Were you able to carry on with your conversation or did you find you became distracted?

COMMENT

This everyday experience of focusing on one particular activity while switching between others is what has come to be generally known as the **cocktail party phenomenon** (Cherry, 1953). You probably found that, after the initial impression of chaos, you found yourself attracted to one group and one conversation, and the others 'faded'. But, for example, if you heard your own or a familiar name mentioned elsewhere in the room, you may have found that your attention switched in this new direction, and that you then lost the thread of the former conversation.

Focused and divided attention

Our ability to attend to one event from what amounts to a mass of competing stimuli in the environment has been psychologically termed as **focused attention**. The streams of information we choose to attend to will tend to be relevant to the activities and intentions that we have at that time. For example, when engaged in a conversation it is usual to attend to what the other person is saying. If something catches our eye in the periphery of our vision, for example another person we want to talk to suddenly appears, we may divert our attention to what she is doing. We may then get distracted from the conversation we are having and as a consequence have to ask the person we are conversing with to repeat themselves. On the other hand, we may be skilled at carrying on the conversation while intermittently observing what the person we want to talk to is doing. When we attempt to attend to more than one thing at a time, as in the above example, it is called **divided attention**. Another example that is often used to illustrate this attentional phenomenon is being able to drive while holding a conversation with a passenger. A further property of attention is that it is either voluntary, as when we make a conscious effort to change our attention, or involuntary, as when the salient characteristics of the competing stimuli grab our attention. An everyday example of an involuntary act is being distracted from working when we can hear music or voices in the next room.

Question 5.1

What is the difference between focused and divided attention?

Focusing attention at the interface

What is the significance of attention for HCI? How can an understanding of attentional phenomena be usefully applied to interface design? Clearly, the manner in which we deploy our attention has a tremendous bearing on how effectively we can interact with a system. If we know that people are distracted, often involuntarily, how is it possible to get their attention again without allowing them to miss the 'window of opportunity'? Moreover, how can we focus people's attention on what they need to be looking at or listening to for any given stage of a task? How can we guide their attention to the relevant information on a display?

Structuring information

One way in which interfaces can be designed to help users find the information they need is to structure the interface so that it is easy to navigate through. Firstly, this requires presenting not too much information and not too little on a screen, as in both cases the user will have to spend considerable time scanning through either a cluttered screen or numerous screens of information. Secondly, instead of arbitrarily presenting data on the screen it should be grouped and ordered into meaningful parts. By capitalizing on the perceptual laws of grouping (see Chapter 4), information can be meaningfully structured so that it is easier to perceive and able to guide attention readily to the appropriate information.

EXERCISE

If possible, arrange for someone else to help you with this exercise by timing you using a watch with a second hand.

Figure 5.1 shows two different screen displays. Looking at the one labelled (a), see how long it takes you to (1) find the phone number of Howard Johnsons in Columbia and (2) the name of the hotel that offers a double room for $46.

For screen (b) see how long it takes you to find (1) the phone number of Holiday House and (2) the name of the hotel that offers a double room for $27.

Which one takes the longer? Can you think why?

COMMENT

As you have discovered from the exercise, the way information is structured determines how quickly an item of information can be found. You should have taken longer to find the pieces of information in the second screen than in the first. In the original study (Tullis, 1984) average search times for a single item were 3.2 seconds for the first screen and 5.5 seconds for the second screen. Even though the two screens have approximately the same level of overall density (that is the proportion of character spaces that are occupied) the characters in the first screen have been grouped into categories. Hence, all the hotel names are listed in one column, the phone numbers in another and so on. Furthermore, the space between these columns facilitates the perceptual processes involved in searching for an item. In the second screen, the lack of such structuring and spacing makes it much more difficult to find particular items.

Other techniques for guiding attention

Other techniques for presenting information at the interface to guide attention include the use of:

- spatial and temporal cues,
- colour (see Chapter 4),
- alerting techniques such as flashing and reverse video and auditory warnings.

Windows are another useful way of partitioning the computer screen into discrete or overlapping sections, to enable different types of information to be separated (see Chapter 14). For example, a word processor may display the working text in one

City	Motel/Hotel	Area Code	Phone	Rates Single	Double
Charleston	Best Western	883	747-8961	$26	$38
Charleston	Days Inn	883	881-1888	$18	$24
Charleston	Holiday Inn N	883	744-1621	$36	$46
Charleston	Holiday Inn SW	883	556-7188	$33	$47
Charleston	Howard Johnsons	883	524-4140	$31	$36
Charleston	Ramada Inn	883	774-8281	$33	$48
Charleston	Sheraton Inn	883	744-2401	$34	$42
Columbia	Best Western	883	796-9400	$29	$34
Columbia	Carolina Inn	883	799-8200	$42	$48
Columbia	Days Inn	883	736-0828	$23	$27
Columbia	Holiday Inn NW	883	794-9448	$32	$39
Columbia	Howard Johnsons	883	772-7288	$25	$27
Columbia	Quality Inn	883	772-8278	$34	$41
Columbia	Ramada Inn	883	796-2700	$36	$44
Columbia	Vagabond Inn	883	796-6240	$27	$38

(a)

Pennsylvania
Bedford Motel/Hotel: Crinoline Courts
   (814) 623-9511 S: $18 D: $28
Bedford Motel/Hotel: Holiday Inn
   (814) 623-9006 S: $29 D: $36
Bedford Motel/Hotel: Midway
   (814) 623-8107 S: $21 D: $26
Bedford Motel/Hotel: Penn Manor
   (814) 623-8177 S: $18 D: $25
Bedford Motel/Hotel: Quality Inn
   (814) 623-5188 S: $23 D: $28
Bedford Motel /Hotel: Terrace
   (814) 623-5111 S: $22 D: $24
Bradley Motel/Hotel: De Soto
   (814) 326-3567 S: $28 D: $24
Bradley Motel/Hotel: Holiday House
   (814) 362-4511 S: $22 D: $25
Bradley Motel/Hotel: Holiday Inn
   (814) 362-4581 S: $32 D: $40
Breezewood Motel/Hotel: Best Western Plaza
   (814) 735-4352 S: $28 D: $27
Breezewood Motel/Hotel: Motel 78
   (814) 735-4385 S: $16 D: $18

(b)

Figure 5.1 The structuring of text (Tullis, 1988).

window, footnotes in another and a set of available commands in a temporarily overlapping pull-down menu as shown in Figure 5.2.

In using the various methods it should be noted that:

● important information which needs immediate attention should always be displayed in a prominent place to catch the user's eye (e.g. alarm and warning messages);

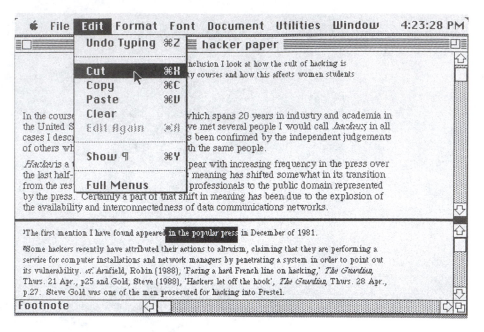

Figure 5.2 Microsoft Word window with multiple windows and a pull-down menu (courtesy of Microsoft Corporation).

- less urgent information should be allocated to less prominent but specific areas of the screen so that the user will know where to look when this information is required (e.g. reports and reference material);
- information that is not needed very often (e.g. help facilities) should not be displayed but should be made available on request.

As it may have become apparent to you, the above guidelines on designing information at the interface are as much geared towards facilitating perception of the information as they are for guiding attention. In this context, the two cognitive processes are considered interdependent: in order to attend to something the user needs to be able to perceive it. Hence, it is useful to consider attentional issues at the interface in relation to perceptual issues.

Question 5.2

(a) *How can information be structured at the interface to guide attention and perception?*

(b) *What other techniques can be used to guide the user's attention to important information at the interface?*

Multitasking and interruptions

When carrying out tasks using computer systems in a work setting, people are continually interrupted by the moment to moment demands of the situation. This could be the phone ringing, the signalling of electronic mail arriving, someone else knocking on the door and asking a question and so on. In addition it is common for people to do **multitasking** – that is, carry out a number of tasks during the same period of time by alternating between them. Hence, someone may switch between writing a letter, arranging a meeting, and doing the accounts. More often than not we are continually switching between different activities rather than performing and completing tasks in a serial manner.

In complex environments, such as the cockpit, operators are required to manage a multitude of overlapping tasks. In particular, they need to be able to switch between **primary** and **secondary** tasks, the former being the most important task at that time. For example, pilots have to switch rapidly between attending to air traffic control communications and monitoring various flight instruments while having to deal with any system malfunctions that might have arisen, such as a fuel leak. When an activity is attended to it is said to be foregrounded, while the other activities are momentarily suspended.

While most people show great flexibility in coping with multitasking, they are also prone to distraction. On returning to a suspended activity, it is possible for them to have forgotten where they were in the activity. As a result they may not restart from where they left off, but will recommence at a different point of entry. For example, pilots may think they have completed part of a procedure (such as a checklist) but in fact they have not done so. Alternatively, they may forget that they have already done something and repeat it. This most frequently occurs for routine procedures where knowledge for carrying out the various tasks has become largely automated. An everyday analogy is forgetting to salt the potatoes or adding the salt twice, if our routine procedures when cooking are interrupted by having to answer the phone.

People have developed various strategies to remind themselves of the actions they need to perform at a later stage. The most common include writing lists, using Post-it notes and tying knots in a handkerchief. Norman (1992) describes these reminders as **cognitive aids** – external representations that are intended to gain our attention at a time relevant to the task that needs to be performed. In the cockpit, pilots have been observed to use a number of such makeshift reminders. For example, remember the interview with Donald Norman in which he describes the practice adopted by pilots of placing an empty coffee cup over the flap handle to remind them to reduce the electrical load before lowering the flaps on the wings of the plane!

Ideally, systems should be designed to provide information systematically about the status of an activity in terms of what has been done and what currently needs to be carried out. If users are distracted from the activity at hand, the system should then be able to inform them of where they were in that activity when they return to it. In addition, routine background tasks that are prone to being forgotten, especially when users are distracted, such as saving files, should be brought to the users' attention by displaying reminder prompts at the interface.

Automatic processing

Many activities that we carry out in our everyday lives have become automated. We simply do them without thinking about them. For example, the activities of reading, writing, speaking in a native language, riding a bike and reciting multiplication tables are relatively effortless for most of us.

It is well known that the more we practise, the more our performance improves to the point that we become skilled and our performance is automatic. This is especially so for sensory–motor tasks, like skiing, typing and riding a bike. With prolonged practise, cognitive processes can also become fully automatic. **Automatic cognitive processes** are identified as:

- fast,
- demanding minimal attention and hence not interfering with other activities,
- unavailable to consciousness (Eysenck and Keane, 1990).

The classic example used to demonstrate the nature of an automatic cognitive process is the Stroop effect. To understand what is meant by this, it is best to try Exercise 5.3 in Box 5.1.

Box 5.1   Automatic processing

EXERCISE

If possible, arrange for someone else to help you with this exercise by timing you using a watch with a second hand. Now, see how long it takes you to name the colours of the items in the two lists of words in Figure 5.3. Try to say them as quickly as possible.

COMMENT

You should have found that it took you longer to say the colour names in the second list than in the first. When asked to name the colours of a list of nonsense syllables that are written in coloured ink we have little problem. However, when asked to do the same for a list of colour names that are printed in conflicting colours (for example, the word BLUE printed in red) our performance slows down. This is because the automatic process of reading the word conflicts with the automatic process of perceiving the colour.

A	B
ZYP	RED
QLEKF	BLACK
SUWRG	YELLOW
XCIDB	BLUE
WOPR	RED
ZYP	GREEN
QLEKF	YELLOW
XCIDB	BLACK
SUWRG	BLUE
WOPR	BLACK
SUWRG	RED
ZYP	YELLOW
XCIDB	GREEN
QLEKF	BLUE
WOPR	GREEN
QLEKF	BLUE
WOPR	RED
ZYP	YELLOW
XCIDB	BLACK
SWRG	GREEN

Figure 5.3 The Stroop effect (Gleitman, 1991). See colour plate 7.

An important distinction that is made in psychology is between these types of automatic cognitive processes and those that are non-automatic (known as **controlled processes**). An example of a controlled cognitive process is performing mental arithmetic where the person has to consciously work through the different parts of the sum.

The main distinction between the two kinds of processes is:

● automatic processes are not affected by the limited capacity of the brain and do not require attention,
● controlled processes have limited capacity and require attention and conscious control (Shiffrin and Shneider, 1977).

Another difference is that automatic processes are very difficult to change after they have been learned whereas controlled processes can be changed relatively easily. An everyday example is driving an unfamiliar car where the indicator is on the opposite side of the steering wheel to the one that you are used to. Instead of turning on the indicator you end up turning on the windscreen wipers or the lights!

What are the implications of automatic processing for interface design? Consider the following example. Having learned a set of computer commands for a word processing application, such as pressing the <ctrl> key with the <p> character key to print a file, to the extent that they are performed automatically it can be very difficult to *unlearn* them. When confronted with a new version of the software, in which some of the commands have been changed to mean something else, it is likely that experienced users will have problems remembering the change. For example, the <ctrl> key with the <p> character key combination may have been changed to issue the command to display the page layout on the screen, while the shift key in combination with the <ctrl> key and the <p> character key now need to be pressed simultaneously to issue the print command.

Typically, experienced users will continue for some time to press the <ctrl> key with the <p> character key whenever they want to print. The reason is that the cognitive process of associating the combination of keys with the commands has become automatic. Only after considerable relearning is it possible to change this. However, even after learning the new combinations it is common for people in times of stress to revert to the automatic processes that were previously learned. While the effect may just be frustrating when using different versions or types of software it can have much more catastrophic effects in work settings like process control plants.

Question 5.3

What are the advantages and disadvantages of automatic processes compared with controlled processes?

5.2 Memory constraints

Memory is involved in all our everyday activities (as are perception and attention). Talking, reading, writing, using the telephone – all need memory. Without memory we would not be able to perform the simplest of actions, such as brushing our teeth, since we would not remember where to find the brush or what to do with it.

The human memory system is very versatile. It can record detailed sensory images that enable us to identify and classify sights, sounds, tastes, smells and feelings. It can record facts about the world and details of how to perform tasks. And it can also record experiences for use throughout our lives. Human memory, however, is by no means infallible. Although we can remember all sorts of obscure facts, we are often faced with very embarrassing situations where we can't remember the name of someone we have just been introduced to. It seems we find some things relatively easy to remember, while others are very difficult to remember.

The same is true when we try to remember how to interact with a computer system. Some operations are straightforward and take minimal effort to memorize while others take forever to learn – and often drop out of memory soon after they have been used. For example, most people find it relatively easy to remember how to use cursor keys, whereas they find it more difficult to remember commands that require combinations of keys to be pressed.

Levels of processing theory

The extent to which new material can be remembered depends on its **meaningfulness**. In psychology, the **level of processing theory** has been developed to account for this (Craik and Lockhart, 1972). According to this theory, information can be processed at different levels, ranging from a shallow analysis of a stimulus (for example, processing the physical features of a word such as its sound) to a deep or semantic analysis. It is this depth that determines how well an item can be remembered over a period of time, and it is the meaningfulness of an item that determines the depth at which it is processed. In other words, the more meaningful a piece of information, the deeper the level at which it is processed when first encountered and the more likely it is to be remembered over time.

Within psychological research a number of factors have been found to contribute towards the meaningfulness of a stimulus. These include attributes such as the **familiarity** of an item and its associated **imagery**. The familiarity of a word refers to the frequency with which it occurs in everyday language. Examples of highly familiar words are 'door', 'read' and 'stop', while examples of unfamiliar words include 'compile', 'substitute' and 'scan'. By imagery is meant the ability with which the word can elicit images in one's mind. Examples of high imagery words are 'ride', 'sleep' and 'eat', while examples of low imagery words are 'begin', 'increase' and 'evaluate'. Words found to be the easiest to remember are those that are both highly familiar and highly 'imageable'.

Question 5.4

What is the main factor that determines our ability to remember stimuli?

Meaningful interfaces

The fact that certain items are more meaningful than others and are thus more memorable has obvious implications for interface design. In particular, it suggests that items that need to be remembered at the interface should be as meaningful as possible. For example, command names and icons should be selected on the basis of their meaningfulness. One of the problems, however, is determining what exactly is a meaningful name or icon. An obvious conclusion from the psychological findings is to assume that they should be selected on the basis of how familiar or imageable they are.

However, it is not as simple as that. One of the problems with using highly familiar words or images is that they can be confusing when used in the (less familiar) computing domain. Specifically, users may find it difficult to dissociate their normal understanding of a word or image from the way it is being used in an interface. For example, the normal meaning of the verb 'to cut' is to sever with some form of instrument. As a command name it has often been used to represent the operation of removing a piece of text or graphics from the screen and placing it in a buffer for future use. This has quite a different meaning, and therefore initially 'cut' can be confusing. Simply selecting familiar and imageable names or icons, therefore, is not necessarily the most effective design strategy.

Designing meaningful command names

In contrast, the trend within computer science has been to select names that are highly abstract and, at times, quite arbitrary. Most designers, however, have not deliberately selected names to be obscure and difficult to learn but have chosen them because of their efficiency. For example, a common technique is to use abbreviations or combinations of control keys. While these are quick to use, they have their drawbacks. One of the problems is that it can be difficult for novices to learn and subsequently remember the abbreviations or control key combinations – particularly if there are a large number of commands. Furthermore, having learned a command set, users often experience difficulty in remembering which command names or abbreviations relate to which system functions and vice versa. This is particularly so for infrequent users or users who use several systems with different command names or abbreviations for the same functions. Box 5.2 contains examples of some ambiguous command names.

Box 5.2   Command names that are ambiguous

EXERCISE

Table 5.1 lists some command names from UNIX. Try to remember or work out the meaning of these commands. Can you think of some other examples from any system of command names whose meaning you have found difficult to remember?

Table 5.1   Some UNIX commands.

UNIX commands
cat
grep
lint
mv
pr
lpr

COMMENT

The meanings of the UNIX commands are as follows:

- The **cat** command is mainly used to display the contents of files on an output device, usually a screen. The name is an abbreviation of 'catenate and print', though the documentation on many UNIX systems mistakenly claim that it is a shorthand for 'concatenate and print'.
- **grep** is a pattern searching tool. It is used to search files or the standard input for arbitrary sequences of characters. In UNIX jargon, the search patterns are called 'regular expressions'. Hence this tool was called **grep**: an abbreviation of 'global regular expression and print'.
- The **lint** command is used to analyse programs written in C. It performs extra consistency checks on the program that would not normally be done by the C compiler. These checks include common programmer errors such as using uninitialized variables, non-portable language constructs and so on. These errors may cause problems when a program is executed even though the C code is syntactically correct. This utility was considered to pick out 'fluff' from C programs. Its author called the program 'lint' since its purpose was analogous to using a piece of lint to rmove bits of fluff from cloth.
- The **mv** command is used to move a file. This actually renames the file and does not normally cause the file to be physically copied. In essence, the file's contents are not moved and the name of the file is changed by modifying directory entries. Although modern UNIX systems now have a rename primitive (system call), the **mv** command has not been retitled for historical reasons to preserve backwards compatibility with older UNIX systems and existing shell scripts.
- **pr** formats a file for printing but does not print it.
- Printing on an output device in UNIX is commonly done by the **lpr** (line printer spooler) command, which submits requests to the line printer subsystem.

See Donald A. Norman, The trouble with UNIX: the user interface is horrid. *Datamation*, **27** (12), 139–50, November 1981 for an extended critique of UNIX commands.

A general guideline for the selection of command names is to consider the contextual, cultural and user characteristics. For example, if a particular application is to be used in a specific design culture, then the selection of names that are already used in the design world may be appropriate. An editing tool developed for use by children should also try to select names that the children already understand. Another alternative is to design meaningful icons.

Designing meaningful icons

EXERCISE

Try to work out the meaning of the icons in Figures 5.4 and 5.5. Which ones are the easiest to work out? Why do you think it is easier to guess the meanings of some than others?

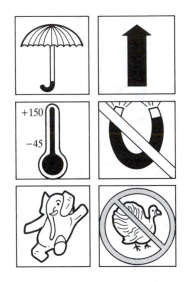

Figure 5.4 Various icons designed as warning symbols on a packing case (Maguire, 1984).

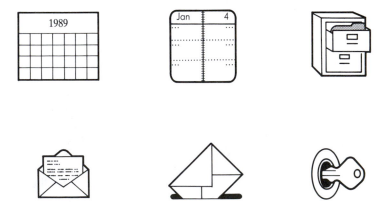

Figure 5.5 Various icons designed to represent office objects (Maguire, 1984).

COMMENT

You probably found the icons shown in Figure 5.5 quite simple to understand, especially if you have worked in an office. However, the icons in Figure 5.4 on the packing case can be confusing. What, for example, is meant by the dancing elephant? Even something so simple as the arrow (for 'this way up') can be confusing in some contexts.

As with command names, there are several factors that determine the meaningfulness of icons. These include the **context** in which the icon is being used; the **task** for which it is being used; the surface **form of the representation**; and the nature of the **underlying concept** that is being represented.

Context

In parts of Europe the public toilets for men and women are signified by icons of a typical man's shoe and a woman's high-heeled shoe. When seen on two doors in a restaurant, it is relatively easy to determine what they signify. On the other hand, when displayed on a public information sign in a shopping mall they could easily be misinterpreted as signifying the place where you can buy men's and women's shoes.

The significance of this example is that it illustrates the importance of **context** when understanding the meaning of icons. If they are being used at an interface and not on road signs, for instance, their possible interpretations are narrowed. When used in more specific contexts, such as in the Apple Macintosh desktop metaphor example, the possible set of meanings can be narrowed still further. However, when icons are used in more general contexts their meanings can be ambiguous.

Function

Increasingly, icons are being used for a range of functions, as indicated in Table 5.1. The type of task for which they are being used is also an important factor in determining their meaningfulness. For tasks that require the user to specify and retrieve textual information, it is generally more compatible for the domain to be

Table 5.1 Range of functions underlying interface icons (Rogers, 1989b).

Function	Example
Labelling	Menu item
Indicating	System state
Warning	Error message
Identifying	File storage
Manipulating	Tool for zooming and shrinking
Container	Object for placing discarded objects
Gestalt pattern (detection)	Structure in programming language

represented at the interface in a textual form. To represent verbal information in an iconic form could actually make the task of retrieving information more difficult, since it might be cognitively more demanding for a user to have to associate visual forms with verbal forms that may not have much in common. For example, if people want to access specific bibliographic records, it is more natural and efficient for them to do so by asking the system in 'natural' language, rather than searching for an icon that refers to the material in which they are interested.

However, the use of graphic images for other types of information retrieval task can sometimes be helpful. For instance, when users are unsure of the precise nature of the information wanted, icons can be very useful as cues to guide their search. An example is a restaurant reservation system developed for the 1992 Universal Exposition in Spain, which used icons to represent the various kinds of cuisines, places to eat and ways of booking, as shown in Figure 5.6. This task involves recognition of information rather than recall (which is discussed more fully below).

Where recognition plays a major part in the task, therefore, the use of iconic interfacing can be very beneficial. In particular, icons can act as mnemonic tags for tasks where large amounts of information have to be readily identified (such as personal filing systems). Iconic interfacing may also be effective for tasks that require a diversity of manipulative operations to be performed. For example, the range of drawing and painting techniques necessary for graphic design tasks may best be represented as iconic tools, where each icon refers to a specific drawing process.

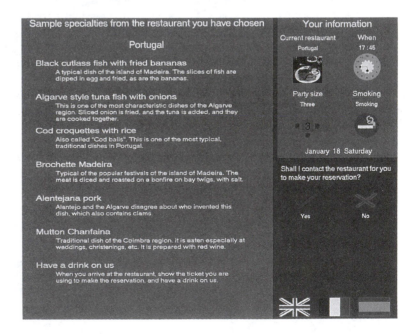

Figure 5.6 Restaurant reservation system using icons to represent information (courtesy of IBM Corporation). See colour plate 8.

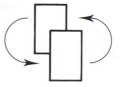

Figure 5.7 An example of an icon using a combination of concrete objects and arrows.

Representational form

The extent to which the meaning of an icon can be understood will depend a lot on how it is represented. Essentially there are three forms: (i) the use of concrete objects (ii) the use of abstract symbols (such as arrows, circles, dots, lines), and (iii) a combination of the two. In general, icons that are the most meaningful are those that use a combined form of representation, provided the users are familiar with the conventions depicted by the abstract symbols (Rogers, 1989a). In particular, the combination of objects and symbols can portray specific messages that, once learnt, become highly memorable. The use of arrows, dashes and various lines provides dynamic or specific information about the status of an object or the actions that can be done with it. The example in Figure 5.7, taken from the drawing application within Microsoft Word, shows an icon for switching two objects that are superimposed, so that the one at the back appears at the front and the one at the front moves to the back. The arrows used in this context portray the sense of movement involved in the switching operation.

The representational form can be categorized further into the particular type of mapping that is used to represent the underlying concept. These can be classified as resemblance, being an exemplar, being symbolic or by being arbitrary.

- **Resemblance icons** depict the underlying concept through an analogous image. A good example is the road sign for 'rocks falling' (see Figure 5.8(a)).
- **Exemplar icons** serve as a typical example, such as the man's and woman's shoe as described above, or the knife and fork used in the public information sign to represent 'restaurant services' (see Figure 5.8(b)).The latter is a better exemplar icon (for western cultures), in the sense that it has a most salient attribute associated with what one does in a restaurant – eating with utensils. The depiction of the shoes, on the other hand, is less directly related to the referent it is intended to represent.
- **Symbolic icons** used to convey an underlying referent that is at a higher level of abstraction than the image itself. For example, the picture of the wine glass with a fracture in it is intended to convey the concept of 'fragility' (see Figure 5.8(c)).
- **Arbitrary icons** bear no relation to the underlying concept and hence the association has to be learned (see Figure 5.8(d)). In this sense, it is a completely arbitrary form of coding.

(a)   (b)   (c)   (d)

Figure 5.8 Different mappings that icons can take. (a) Resemblance, (b) exemplar, (c) symbolic and (d) arbitrary (Rogers, 1989b).

Underlying concept

The extent to which any form will be meaningful also depends on the type of concept that is being represented. The easiest types to represent are concrete objects such as files and folders, where icons can be drawn to have a physical resemblance to the actual object. Because of the resemblance between the form and visual characteristics of the underlying object type the meaning of the icons is likely to be intuitive (able to be inferred without prior learning). For more abstract concepts, such as warning signs and operations, it is much more difficult to design icons that have such mapping. Icons can be designed to represent the concept only through less direct means, such as by indirect analogy (like the elephant used in Figure 5.4 to represent the concept 'heavy'). This means that in most cases the meaning of the icons will initially need to be learned. These ideas are also discussed in Chapter 7, which is about interface metaphors and conceptual models.

EXERCISE

Try to design icons for the following interface concepts listed below and then ask a friend to tell you what they mean. Try not to take too long; just draw the first thing that comes to mind.

(a) A place to discard files
(b) To open
(c) To copy
(d) A place to store files

Which was the easiest to draw and understand?

COMMENT

You probably found (a) and (d) the easiest to draw. Probably, also, your friend found (a) and (d) the easiest to infer the meaning of. This is because they can be represented as concrete objects whereas the other two have to be represented through analogy or abstraction.

Question 5.5

(a)   What are the main factors that contribute to the meaningfulness of icons?
(b)   What are the four main mapping types?

The best of both worlds: Combination and animated icons

The use of icons is often favoured as an alternative to command names. One of the main advantages is that, whereas it is quite common for users, especially those who use a system infrequently, to forget the meaning of command names, it is less so with icons. It seems that once users have learned the meaning of a set of icons they are much less likely to forget them than they would if they were just names (Rogers, 1989b). However, many designers have sidestepped this issue by going for a redundant form of representation. It is now a common practice for interface icons to be displayed in conjunction with the names of the command. The advantage of having a combination of pictorial images with names is that it reduces the problems of the meaning of icons being confusing. Textual labels can provide the necessary disambiguating information. This may be particularly useful if the underlying concept is abstract, the context vague, the set of icons large and the representational form ambiguous. The obvious disadvantage of combining labels with icons is that it takes up more space on the screen.

Animated icons are a recent development aimed at 'bringing icons to life' (Baecker *et al.*, 1991). By animating the underlying function of the icons it is proposed that complex and abstract processes can be more effectively portrayed (see Figure 5.9). In doing so, it is suggested that animated icons should be easier to recall and be more meaningful. In some ways, the development of animated icons can be viewed as an extension of the use of static icons portraying abstract symbols, such as arrows in combination with concrete objects. The main difference is that instead of letting the user imagine what dynamic actions the abstract symbols are conveying, the animation does it for them. To be effective, however, the animations

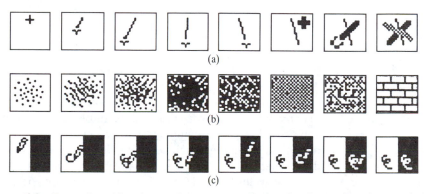

Figure 5.9   Examples of key frames from prototype animation icons (Baecker *et al.*, 1991: © 1991, Association for Computing Machinery, Inc. reprinted by permission).

have to be designed to focus on the key aspects of the function. Otherwise the animation may prove to be counterproductive and result in a confusing set of moving elements being displayed. Another constraint is the small size of icons on the screen. Given that only a limited number of elements can be animated at any one time, the effect can be to make the action appear disjointed and jerky. Another problem is the cursor getting in the way and obscuring the animation, since to select an icon requires covering it with the cursor. There is also a related mode problem of knowing how to access an icon for application and knowing how to access it to provide an animation.

It may be the case, therefore, that well-designed static icons are easier to comprehend than animated ones because they are less busy and can more effectively capture the essence of the meaning of the underlying referents – in the same way as caricatures and cartoons do.

Recognition versus recall: Knowledge in the head and in the world

One of the most well-established findings in memory research is that we can recognize material far more easily than we can recall it from memory. The superiority that the phenomenon of **recognition** has over **recall** has obvious ramifications for interface design. Indeed, during the last decade there has been a shift towards designing interfaces where the amount of information users are required to recall has been reduced in favour of requiring them to *recognize* the information that is needed to perform a task. For example, many user interfaces now employ an extensive range of menus containing text or iconic lists of operations, options, files and so on. Instead of having to recall a name or a particular combination of function keys to perform an operation – as is the case with command-based systems (discussed in Chapter 13) – the users only have to scan through the menu until they recognize the name or icon representing the object that is required. Norman (1988) has since developed the notion of recognition and recall in terms of knowledge in the head and knowledge in the world. The basic idea is that when we carry out our everyday tasks we combine information that is stored in memory with information in the world. Examples of knowledge in the world include the use of various types of cognitive aids, as described earlier.

Since people are bad at remembering what, when and where they have to do something, they will structure their environment to provide the necessary information that will remind them of what has to be done. What people actually remember in their heads also depends on how much they can rely on using knowledge in the world. Furthermore, people tend to remember information that is necessary for them to carry out their everyday tasks. For example, try to describe the details of a coin that you use every day. Even though such objects are very familiar to us, most of us find it difficult to remember much about the details of the coin. It is likely we will remember the shape, size and colour and that it has a head on one side but not whose head, which way the head is pointing, or what writing is inscribed on the coin. One explanation is that we only remember knowledge that is important; incidental details that are not functional are either not learned or are easily forgotten.

Table 5.2 The trade-off between knowledge in the head and knowledge in the world. (Norman, 1988.)

Property	Knowledge in the world	Knowledge in the head
Retrievability	Retrievable whenever visible or audible	Not readily retrievable. Requires memory search or reminding
Learning	Learning not required. Interpretation substitutes for learning. How easy it is to interpret information in the world depends upon how well it exploits natural mappings and restraints	Requires learning, which can be considerable. Learning is made easier if there is meaning or structure to the material (or if there is a good enough model)
Efficiency of use	Tends to be slowed up by the need to find and interpret the external information	Can be very efficient
Ease of use at first encounter	High	Low
Aesthetics	Can be unaesthetic and inelegant, especially if there is a need to maintain a lot of information. This can lead to clutter. In the end, aesthetic appeal depends upon the skill of the designer	Nothing need be visible, which gives more freedom to the designer, which in turn can lead to better aesthetics

In addition to using cognitive aids, people have developed various **cognitive mnemonics** to help them remember things. These can be especially useful when needing to remember the ordering of objects. For example, I always have to recite the mnemonic 'Never Eat Shredded Wheat' when trying to identify in clockwise order the (N)orth, (E)ast, (S)outh and (W)est points of the compass.

There are obvious advantages and disadvantages of using either knowledge in the head or knowledge in the world, as described in Table 5.2. In most cases people will utilize a combination of the two. People who know they have a poor memory will often rely more heavily on cognitive aids and mnemonics.

Question 5.6

(a) What is the difference between knowledge in the head and knowledge in the world?

(b) What is the difference between a cognitive aid and a cognitive mnemonic?

Knowledge in the world and user interfaces

The use of graphical interfaces has resulted in a substantial reduction in the amount of mental effort that is required to interact with systems. In many situations the intuitive direct feel of the interface means that users do not have to think about what they're doing or remember sequences of commands. Instead users need primarily to learn how to interact with the simulated world of objects. In the case of graphical interfaces they need to know how to find items on menus, how to select an icon and so on. Much of the information about the system's structure and functionality is available at the interface, meaning that the users do not have to remember much. Instead they can let the interface do the 'remembering' for them.

In addition, people continually use each other as knowledge resources. If I cannot remember the obscure command string required to copy a file from someone else's file on the UNIX system, I seek out one of the 'local' experts who can effortlessly carry out the command sequence for me. However, they may not be able to recite the command sequence so easily off the top of their head. For example, in a study of the number of commands experts remembered for the UNIX system, Draper (1985) found that they were able to recall very few. He proposed that the reason for this was because the experts were experts in discovering information as and when they needed it. In this sense, the expert's knowledge is in the skill of remembering where to find the information in the outside world.

A number of other studies have examined the knowledge people use when interacting with Macintosh systems (e.g. Mayes *et al.*, 1988; O'Malley and Draper, 1992; Payne, 1991; Young *et al.*, 1990). Similarly, they found that experienced users have great difficulty in recalling details about the interface, such as what options are available in the menus. Nevertheless, the users were very efficient at knowing how to find information at the interface. The 'knowledge in the head' that they did possess is suggested as:

- knowledge of how to access and interpret information that is displayed on the screen,
- knowledge of the information that is not displayed on the screen.

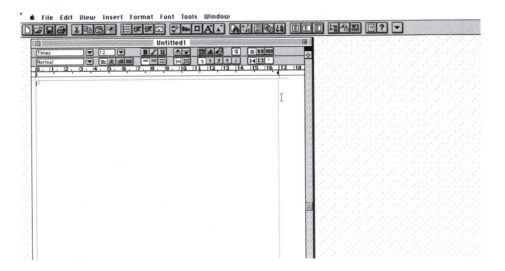

Figure 5.10 Word 5 screen showing menu headers (courtesy of Microsoft Corporation).

An example of how knowledge is accessed is knowing something about the semantics of a menu header that enables you to know which menu to select. So, if I want to check the spelling of a word, I know roughly which menu header to select – that is the 'Tools' header in Word 5. However, I am unlikely to be able to recall specifically the name of the header (see Figure 5.10).

An example of knowledge not displayed on the screen is understanding how to copy text by using the 'cut' and 'paste' operations in Word. When the text is cut it disappears off the screen into a hidden buffer and only reappears when the users paste it back in or if they specifically request the buffer (known as the clipboard on some machines) to be displayed.

In general, knowledge that is stored in the head is typically in the form of facts, rules, images and experiences. When certain information is needed it is retrieved by searching through memory; this is known as **episodic memory**. We also build up throughout our lives a large body of general knowledge, which is known as **semantic memory**. In Chapter 6 we examine how this knowledge is represented and organized.

Key points

- Attention can be focused or divided: the events that we attend to in the world are filtered so that we can make sense of the world.
- Cognitive processes can be controlled or automatic.
- Memory is limited: the more information is processed, the more likely it will be remembered.
- The more meaningful names and icons are, the more likely they will be remembered.
- Material is far more easily recognized than recalled.
- When we carry out our everyday tasks we combine knowledge in the head with knowledge in the world.
- The use of graphical interfaces substantially reduces the amount of knowledge people have to remember about an interface.
- Memory of events and occurrences that are experienced is called episodic; memory of facts and general knowledge is called semantic.

Further reading

Memory

There are several good introductory textbooks on memory.

BADDELEY A. (1982). *Your Memory: A User's Guide*. Harmondsworth: Penguin.
    This is an excellent beginner's guide to memory that is very engaging. It is full of illustrations and tests to challenge your memory.

PARKIN A.J. (1993). *Memory*. Oxford: Blackwell.

This is a more extensive introductory text that focuses on the 'classic' theories and experimental research that has been carried out in this vast field.

Memory in the everyday world

NORMAN D.A. (1988). *The Psychology of Everyday Things*. New York: Basic Books.

NORMAN D.A. (1992). *Turn Signals are the Facial Expressions of Automobiles*. Reading, MA: Addison-Wesley.

NORMAN D.A. (1993). *Things that Make Us Smart*. Reading, MA: Addison-Wesley.

Donald Norman's series of three books provides many interesting and thought-provoking examples of the different ways in which we use knowledge in the world and knowledge in the head.

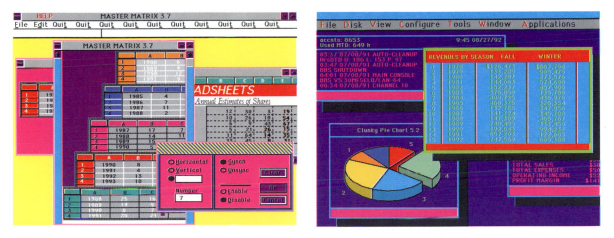

1 Colour pollution (Tufte, 1990). See p. 91.

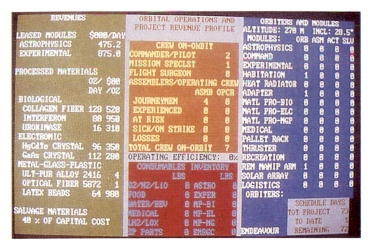

2 A colour screen display consisting primarily of text (courtesy of Final Frontier Software). See p. 93.

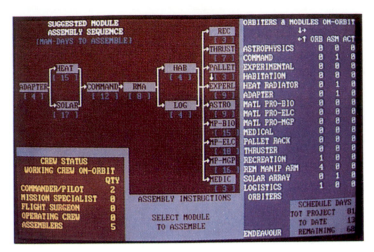

3 A colour screen display showing some graphics (courtesy of Final Frontier Software). See p. 93.

4 An example of text that is difficult to read (Travis, 1991). See p. 94.

5 The same text as in colour plate 4 made more legible through the use of colour (Travis, 1991). See p. 94.

Untitled

Red text appears to lie in one depth plane
and blue text appears to lie in a different plane
Red text appears to lie in one depth plane
and blue text appears to lie in a different plane
Red text appears to lie in one depth plane
and blue text appears to lie in a different plane
Red text appears to lie in one depth plane
and blue text appears to lie in a different plane
Red text appears to lie in one depth plane
and blue text appears to lie in a different plane

6 An example of colour stereoscopy or 'fluttering hearts' (Travis, 1991). See p. 95.

A	B
ZYP	RED
QLEKF	BLACK
SUWRG	YELLOW
XCIDB	BLUE
WOPR	RED
ZYP	GREEN
QLEKF	YELLOW
XCIDB	BLACK
SUWRG	BLUE
WOPR	BLACK
SUWRG	RED
ZYP	YELLOW
XCIDB	GREEN
QLEKF	BLUE
WOPR	GREEN
QLEKF	BLUE
WOPR	RED
ZYP	YELLOW
XCIDB	BLACK
SWRG	GREEN

7 The Stroop effect (Gleitman, 1991). See p. 107.

8 Restaurant reservation system using icons to represent information (courtesy of IBM Corporation). See p. 114.

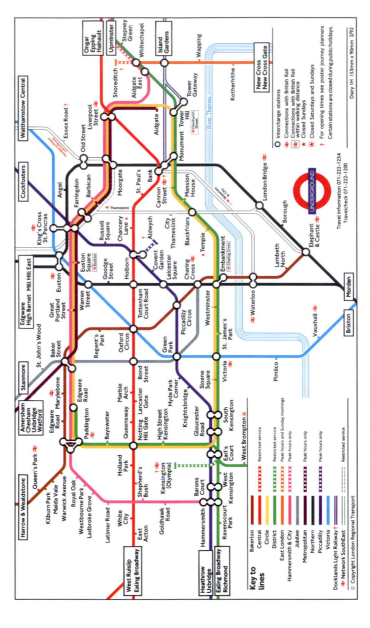

9 A schematic map of the London Underground (LRT registered user no. 93/1964). See p. 135.

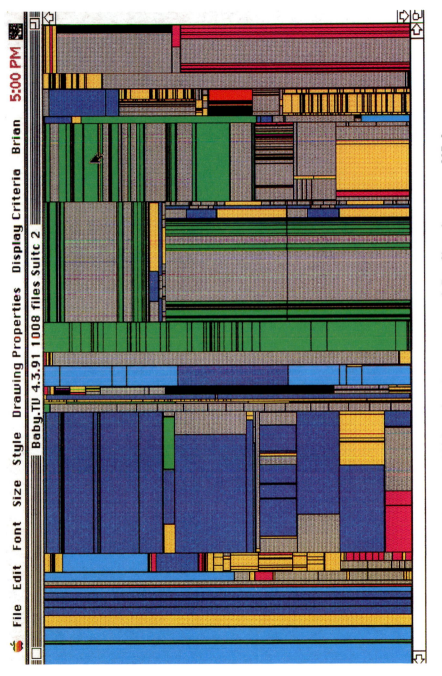

10 Tree-map screen snapshot with 1000 files. See the interview with Ben Shneiderman pp. 207–9.

Windspeed and direction —

Windspeed —

Database page —

Runway

Time

Instrument runway

11 Multitasking workstation for air traffic controllers. See p. 366.

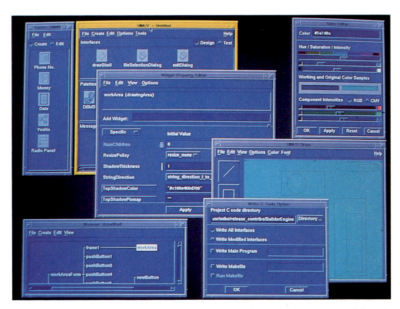

12 UIM/X gives you the tools to simplify the creation of graphical interfaces for new applications and existing character programs (*UNIXWorld*, May 1992). See p. 578.

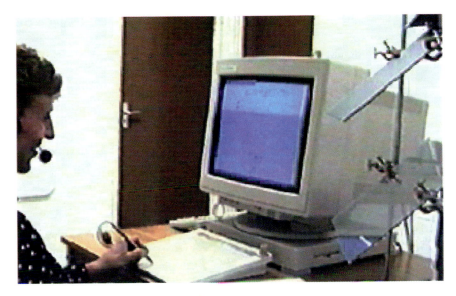

13 The ROCOCO Station. See p. 585.

14 The IBM usability laboratory set up to resemble an FT reception area (DTI, 1991: courtesy of IBM Consulting Group). See p. 607.

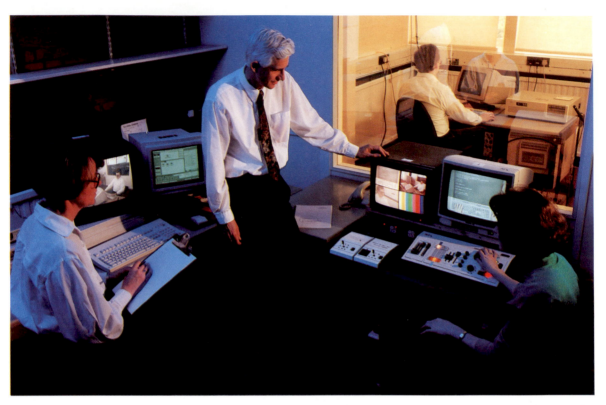

15 The usability laboratory at the National Physical Laboratory, showing the evaluators' room and a subject working in the room behind separated by a partition of one-way glass (National Physical Laboratory, 1993). See p. 652.

6

Knowledge and Mental Models

Aims and objectives

The aim of this chapter is to introduce you to the area of knowledge representation and mental models. After studying this chapter you should:

- know the difference between the main types of knowledge representation and knowledge structures,
- understand why the concept of mental models has been so appealing to HCI research and yet at the same time poorly understood,
- know the difference between structural and functional models,
- be able to think of ways of applying the concept of mental models to interface design.

Overview

Interest in knowledge and mental models from an HCI perspective is based on the idea that, by discovering what users know about systems and how they reason about how the systems function, it may be possible to predict learning time, likely errors and the relative ease with which users can perform their tasks (see also Section 20.3, on cognitive task analysis).

Moreover, by analysing the process through which users acquire beliefs, correct or otherwise, about a system, it is hoped that interfaces can be designed that support the acquisition of appropriate user mental models. Of all the theoretical concepts of how knowledge is organized, it is the notion of mental models that has been explored and developed the most in HCI.

6.1 | Knowledge representation and organization

The way knowledge is structured in memory is assumed to be highly organized, as we said at the end of Chapter 5. Before looking in more detail at the way such knowledge is used when carrying out cognitive tasks like thinking and problem solving, however, it is important to understand how knowledge is represented in memory.

Representational form

Knowledge is represented in memory as three main types:

- analogical representations
- propositional representations
- distributed representations

Analogical representations are picture-like images, such as an image of an apple, for example. **Propositional representations** are abstract and language-like statements that make assertions, like 'the book is on the table'. **Distributed representations** are networks of nodes where knowledge is implicit in the connections between the nodes. The first two are generally viewed as **symbolic** representations, while the latter are considered as **sub-symbolic** (Eysenck and Keane, 1990). The main difference between symbolic and sub-symbolic levels is that the former subscribe to the view that cognition depends on manipulating symbolic structures through using rule-like structures, while the latter do not.

One of the main controversies in cognitive science is the different functions played by propositions, images and distributed representations in cognitive processing. Part of this debate is deciding whether the three are distinct forms of mental representation. One school of thought – the **imagists** – believe that images are distinct and play an important role in thinking and reasoning. An opposing school of thought – the **propositionalists** – believe that images are a by-product, of no purpose to cognitive functioning and that, alternatively, propositional representations underlie all mental processing.

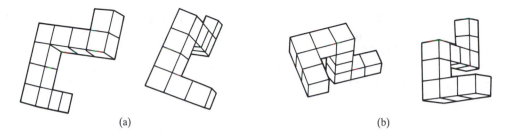

(a)   (b)

Figure 6.1   Objects for mental rotation (Shepard and Metzler, 1971: © 1971, by the AAAS).

To shed light on this issue investigations have been carried out which make different predictions for the two positions. A well-known paradigm requires subjects mentally to rotate different shapes in memory. Subjects are given two shapes and asked to judge whether they are the same object which has been oriented differently, or whether the two shapes are different (see Figure 6.1). To do the task subjects have to change mentally the orientation of one picture and then match it up with the other. The imagists predict that the larger the rotation, the more time is required to perform the task. The assumption is that the process of mental rotation is similar to the physical action of doing the same thing with a piece of paper of the same shape on a desk. The more the object has to be moved to match up with the other shape the more time it will take. Conversely, the propositionalists argue that it is the complexity, in terms of the number of propositions that have to be transformed, that affects the time to rotate an object mentally and not the angular disparity. Hence objects that are physically more complex (have many projections) will take longer to rotate and match than objects that are relatively simple (have fewer projections).

EXERCISE

Figure 6.1 shows two sets of shapes. Can you say whether they are the same or different? Which one took the longer to work out and which was the more difficult to perform?

COMMENT

These two-dimensional drawings of three-dimensional objects demonstrate the human ability to rotate such objects mentally. The two objects in (a) are different: this can be determined by 'rotating' the object on the left into the same orientation as the object on the right and then comparing them. The two objects in (b) are the same: again, one must be rotated and compared to the other. You probably found the set in (a) was more difficult and took longer. This is because, when one 'rotation' does not result in a match, it is necessary to look at other 'rotations' in order to be certain that the two objects differ.

The debate is by no means clear, because some studies have found that the amount of movement required affects the time to perform the task (for example, Shepard and Metzler, 1971), while others have shown that it is the complexity of the shape that is the determining factor (for example, Yuille and Steiger, 1982). Barfield *et al.* (1988), on the other hand, have found that when using wireframed modelling on a high-resolution computer-aided design screen, both the complexity and the angular disparity affected the time to complete the task.

It seems likely that people use both images and propositions in thinking and problem solving. Indeed, more recently, the **connectionists** have argued that the two are complementary: images and propositions can co-exist at a higher level of representation. However, they argue that at a sub-symbolic level of representation, the two should be viewed as emergent properties of a neural network of nodes. An analogy is the difference between high level programming languages such as Pascal and Prolog and low-level languages like machine language. The former describes what has to be done and the other how it is to be done. Box 6.1 contains more information about connectionist networks.

Box 6.1   Connectionist networks

EXERCISE

The connectionist network in Figure 6.2 concerns knowledge about five people, in terms of their name, profession, race, sex, car owned and favourite cheese. The various attributes are represented by nodes in the various circles. The nodes are connected by two-way excitatory connections represented by the arrows. The nodes in each circle inhibit each other while exciting other nodes that they are connected to in other circles. The effect of the activation and inhibition process is that some nodes are maximally excited while others are inhibited. Knowledge, therefore, is represented in terms of patterns of activation and inhibition of nodes. For example, asking the network about Joe automatically activates the nodes that contain information about him. Following the arrows you can see that the network 'knows' (it is implicit in the connections between the nodes) that Joe is a white, male professor who drives a Subaru and likes Brie cheese. What are the networks of knowledge for the other people?

Solution

Fred has the same attributes as Joe. Harold and Frank are both black male stockbrokers who drive Maseratis. The difference between them is that Frank likes Cheese Whiz while Harold likes Brie. Claudia is a black female professor who drives a Maserati but the network does not know her favourite cheese.

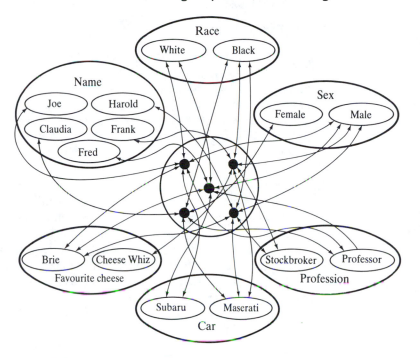

Figure 6.2 A connectionist network for storing knowledge about people (Martindale, 1991, adapted from McClelland, 1981: © 1991 Brooks/Cole Publishing Co.).

Question 6.1

What is the difference between images, propositions and distributed representations?

A question for HCI is: to what extent does the form of representation used at the interface affect the way users think about solving problems? Furthermore, is it possible to develop interfaces that facilitate thinking and problem solving? Consider again the example of programming languages: one that is inherently propositional, like Prolog, may be easier to use than one that is low level, like machine code. This is because it enables the users to construct programs in terms of more language-like procedures, which is a preferable mode of thinking for most people. Alternatively, a programming language that is visually-based and consisting of images rather than propositions may be even easier to use because it provides a more 'natural' way of thinking about problems in terms of images. For example, Clarisse and Chang (1986) claim that graphical programming uses information in a format that is closer to the user's mental representation of the problem than other formats (see Chapter 8 for more on facilitating learning through visual programming).

Knowledge organization

One of the main characteristics of knowledge is that it is highly organized. This can be demonstrated quite simply. Even though we have millions of facts and pieces of information stored in memory, we are able to answer questions about that information very rapidly. For example, see how quickly you can name the president of the US, a vegetable beginning with C and the capital of France. In most cases it is likely that you could answer such questions in just a fraction of a second. Such fast response would seem highly unlikely if semantic memory were not organized in some way.

Exactly how knowledge is organized and used in memory has been a major debate in cognitive science. One of the most influential approaches has been to assume that knowledge is organized as some form of network. Concepts are arranged so that those that have something in common are linked in some way. For example, the names of countries and their capitals would be stored in close connection to each other rather than distributed randomly. **Semantic networks** (Collins and Loftus, 1975) are represented as nodes and links. Nodes correspond to objects, such as cat, dog, horse, or classes of objects, such as animals, whereas links correspond to the relationships between the objects. These can be simple links like 'a cat is an animal' or 'a dog can bite'.

Another theory views knowledge as consisting of numerous **schemata**. Essentially, a **schema** is a network of general knowledge based on previous experience. Its function is to facilitate our understanding of commonplace events. In turn, this is what enables us to behave appropriately in different situations. The most well-cited example of a schema is Schank and Abelson's (1977) restaurant **script**. (A script is a special subcase of a schema which describes a characteristic scenario of behaviour in a particular setting.) The underlying assumption is that people develop a script by repeatedly carrying out the same set of actions for a given setting. The restaurant script contains various knowledge components about the typical sequence of events involved in going to a restaurant to have a meal. At a general level these are classified in terms of the default actions of entering, ordering, eating and leaving, as shown in Figure 6.3. More specific actions are slotted into these components, such as sitting down, looking at the menu, eating the food and paying the bill.

Similarly, when we interact with computers, schemata can be viewed as guiding our behaviour. For example, when learning how to use a computer system we may develop a specific script for creating documents, another for editing and an overall schema for using the computer, such as switching the computer on and off, inserting and removing disks.

The significance of schemata is that they allow us to carry out everyday activities with minimum effort and to capitalize on the regularities of events and situations. When confronted with new but similar situations, they help us to know how to behave appropriately and what to look for. For example, when we go into an unfamiliar building we can use schema-based knowledge to help us to locate the room we are looking for. By activating a 'building schema', we know that if we find the reception desk then someone will be able to help us find our location. We also know that the reception desk is most likely to be in front of us on the ground floor.

Script name	Component	Specific action
Eating at a restaurant	Entering	Walk into restaurant Look for table Decide where to sit Go to table Sit down
	Ordering	Get menu Look at menu Choose food Waiter arrives Give order to waiter Waiter takes order to cook Wait, talk Cook prepares food
	Eating	Cook gives food to waiter Waiter delivers food to customer Customer eats Talk
	Leaving	Waiter writes bill Waiter delivers bill to customer Customer examines bill Calculate tip Leave tip Gather belongings Pay bill Leave restaurant

Figure 6.3 Components and features of the restaurant script (Schank and Abelson, 1977 cited in Eysenck and Keane, 1989).

While this may all seem fairly obvious, it does have implications for interface design. For instance, if computer systems could be designed such that they were based on culturally accepted conventions as to how to print a file, save a disk, and so on, it would be possible for users to develop a 'how to use a computer' schema which enabled them to switch between systems, effortlessly and without fear of making errors. When encountering a new system, users could activate the schema – similar to the 'new building' schema – which would enable them to know how to get into the system, where to find help and so on.

The problem, however, is that as yet there appears to be no universally accepted conventions for coping with problems when encountering new systems (Norman, 1988). Instead, a diversity of computer systems and interfaces have evolved that each have their own methods for performing tasks. To print a file on one system requires one set of commands or menu selections while a different repertoire of actions is needed for another machine. Furthermore, similar commands may have totally different effects. For example, carrying out a 'quitting' procedure learnt from one system, on another system, could result in files being deleted. The physical location of objects on the hardware can also vary. For instance, the position of the on/off switch on an upgraded version of the same computer may be quite different.

Likewise, function keys on a keyboard can be in different positions. Applying an existing script learnt from one machine to a novel system, therefore, can be dangerous or simply frustrating – as you may have witnessed.

On the other hand, many aspects of computer interfaces are becoming increasingly standardized. For example, we are currently witnessing a universal trend towards the development of applications that are window-based, be they PC, Macintosh, UNIX or other system. Likewise, in-house style guidelines are being used more by different designers for developing applications that have the same 'look and feel' as, for example, in Macintosh programs. The evolution of standardized interfaces and ways of interacting with computers is discussed in Chapter 25.

Question 6.2

What is the difference between a schema and a script?

6.2   Mental models

One of the main criticisms of schema-based theories of knowledge is that they are too inflexible. While it can be very useful to have a large set of scripts to deal with typical everyday situations, like going to restaurants, meeting people for the first time, going shopping and so on, we are also very good at coping with situations where our scripts are inappropriate. For example, when we enter a self-service style restaurant, such as a burger joint, we wait in line, order, pay for the food, collect the food, sit down, eat, clear up and then leave. The restaurant script described by Schank and Abelson (1977) clearly does not match this sequence of actions and yet we have little problem in adapting our behaviour.

Furthermore, we can make inferences in complex situations, predict future states and comprehend situations we have never personally experienced. Schema theory has not been able adequately to explain this kind of flexible behaviour. An alternative, but related, theoretical concept, which has been developed to account for these more dynamic aspects of cognitive activity, is **mental models**. In relation to schemata, mental models are assumed to be dynamically constructed – as creations of the moment – by activating stored schemata.

The concept of mental models has manifested itself in psychological theorizing and HCI research in a multitude of ways. It is difficult to provide a definitive description, because different assumptions and constraints are brought to bear on the different phenomena it has been used to explain. A well-known definition, in the context of HCI, is provided by Donald Norman: 'the model people have of themselves, others, the environment, and the things with which they interact. People form mental models through experience, training and instruction' (1988, p. 17).

It should be noted that in fact the term 'mental model' was first developed in the early 1940s by Kenneth Craik. He proposed that thinking ' . . . models, or parallels reality':

'If the organism carries a "small-scale model" of external reality and of its own possible actions within its head, it is able to try out various alternatives, conclude which is the best of them, react to future situations before they arise, utilise the knowledge of past events in dealing with the present and future, and in every way to react in a much fuller, safer, and more competent manner to emergencies which face it.'

(Craik, 1943, p. 57)

Just as an engineer will build scale models of a bridge, in order to test out certain stresses prior to building the real thing, so, too, do we build mental models of the world in order to make predictions about an external event before carrying out an action. Although, our construction and use of mental models may not be as extensive or as complete as Craik's hypothesis suggests, it is likely that most of us can probably recall using a form of mental simulation at some time or other. An important observation of these types of mental models is that they are invariably incomplete, unstable, easily confusable and are often based on superstition rather than scientific fact (Norman, 1983a).

Question 6.3

What is a mental model?

Within cognitive psychology, the term 'mental models' has since been explicated by Johnson-Laird (1983, 1988) with respect to its structure and function in human reasoning and language understanding. In terms of the structure of mental models, Johnson-Laird argues that mental models are either analogical representations or a combination of analogical and propositional representations. They are distinct from, but related to, images. A mental model represents the relative position of a set of objects in an analogical manner that parallels the structure of the state of objects in the world. An image also does this, but more specifically in terms of a *view* of a particular model.

An important difference between images and mental models is in terms of their function. Mental models are usually constructed when we are required to make an inference or a prediction about a particular state of affairs. In constructing the mental model a conscious mental simulation may be 'run' from which conclusions about the predicted state of affairs can be deduced. An image, on the other hand, is considered to be a one-off representation. A simplified analogy is to consider an image to be like a frame in a movie while a mental model is more like a short snippet of a movie.

But perhaps the best way of understanding the dynamic aspect of a mental model is for you to construct one yourself.

EXERCISE

Without going outside to check, calculate how many windows there are in your house. If you find this exercise too easy, try doing the same for the building in which you work. Then go outside and check whether or not you were right.

COMMENT

You might be surprised to get one or two of the windows wrong. It is unlikely that you have any specific knowledge stored about how many windows there are in your house. What you probably did was imagine going through all of the rooms and counting the number of windows in each room, or walking around the outside and looking. This is a simple example of running a mental model.

The fact that we can 'run' a model means that we can derive new predictions without having to test them out in the real world. Even if no specific memories are stored, remembering the model and running it enables us to derive inferences or reconstruct procedures. This is a distinct advantage when faced with unfamiliar situations.

Question 6.4

(a)   What is the difference between a mental model and an image?
(b)   What does 'running a mental model' mean?

EXERCISE

Now consider the following question and try to answer it.

Your house is centrally heated. You arrive home from holiday on a cold February afternoon. You have a small baby and you need to get the heating up to about 21°C as quickly as possible. Should you set the thermostat higher than 21°C or set it to 21°C?

COMMENT

The correct answer is to set the thermostat to 21°C. The house will not get warmer any faster by setting the thermostat higher than that. Surprisingly, many people get this wrong, even if they think they know how a thermostat works. Many people have a mental model of their central heating that is drawn from experience with other types of heating such as older gas fires, where the more you turn the gas tap, the more gas comes out and the more heat is produced. In other words, the tap acts as a valve. Many people with electric cookers still think in this way, not realizing that electric ovens work on the principle of a thermostat. Most gas ovens nowadays are also fitted with a thermostat. The correct model for a thermostat is that it operates by setting a threshold, above which the system cuts out.

The examples presented above show the importance of a person's mental models in deciding how to operate even simple devices such as thermostats. In general, if mental models are sufficiently accurate then it is possible to solve unexpected problems, but inappropriate models can lead to difficulties.

EXERCISE

Can you think of any examples of inappropriate mental models that you or someone else you know has developed when using a computer system?

COMMENT

An example of a computer system that often elicits an incorrect mental model is voice mail (Erikson, 1990). The voice mail system provides mailboxes for each user where messages can be left. When callers reach the voice mail system, a recorded message tells them that the person they are trying to contact is not available and invites them to leave a message. The voice mail system will then pass on any message that is left to that person. If the voice mail system is busy, it can take up to half an hour for the message to reach its destination. The problem is that most people's mental model of voice mail is based on a model of a conventional answering machine. Hence, they assume that messages are recorded directly on the phone machine that sits on each person's desk, in the same way as an answer machine works. However, this is not the case, since all messages are recorded on a central machine and then delivered to the individual mailboxes. When the system is busy, a queuing mechanism operates, whereby messages have to wait their turn before being sent to their destination. This system works well provided that the message left on the system does not need attending to immediately or soon after. However, a problem can arise when someone leaves a message on a colleague's machine saying, 'see you in five minutes in my office', and assumes that the person has popped out of his office for a minute or so and will receive the message when he returns. So, while the person may return to his office after a couple of minutes, he may not receive the message for half an hour, because the system is busy, and so he misses the appointment.

Erikson (1990) notes how most people do not understand how voice mail works, and even those who do still present the wrong model. A more appropriate model would be one based on an answering or reception service model where messages are left with an intermediary whose job it is to forward them on and furthermore, where it is known that there can be a delay if the receptionist is busy or cannot reach the person for whom the message is intended.

Structural versus functional models

In the early 1980s two main types of mental models that users employ when interacting with devices were identified: these are categorized as **structural** and **functional** models. A structural model is one where it is assumed that the user has internalized the structure of how the device or system works in memory, while a functional model assumes that the user has internalized procedural knowledge about how to use the device or system. Consider the London Underground map shown in Figure 6.4, which provides a representation of the station locations and the lines that connect them. The schematic form used provides a structure that regular commuters learn to internalize. This is then used as the basis from which to work out how to go from A to B. As a model of how to use the underground system, the schematic map is less useful. Instead, a functional model is needed to enable people to know how to get the right sort of ticket from an automatic ticket machine, what to do with the ticket, how to get on and off trains and so on. This is developed through using prior knowledge of underground train systems such as the Métro in Paris or the subway in New York, observing others and activating general schemata about how to use public transport.

A simple distinction is to consider structural models as models of 'how-it-works' and functional models as models of 'how-to-use it'.

Structural models

In HCI, structural models are used to describe the internal mechanics of a device, in terms of its component parts. Another way of describing them is as **surrogates** because they can act as substitutes for the real thing (Young, 1983). Typically, surrogate or structural models are simplified models that enable the person using the model to make predictions about the behaviour of the device it represents.

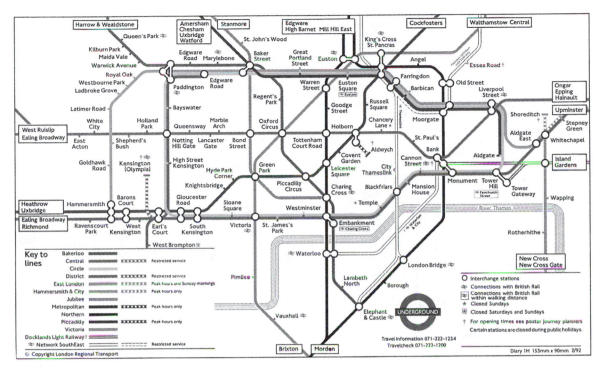

Figure 6.4 A schematic map of the London Underground (LRT registered user no. 93/1964). See colour plate 9.

A key question is to determine whether users actually develop these kinds of models, and if so the extent to which they help them understand and make predictions about a device or system. In general, it is assumed that such models are highly limited in their applicability because they do not account for how the users are going to perform their actions (this is what the functional models are assumed to do). The advantage of structural models is that by explaining how a device works, they allow a user to predict the effects of any possible sequence of actions, and hence to work out (eventually) how to achieve most tasks possible with the device. The disadvantage is that constructing a structural model in one's mind often requires a great deal of effort, both in learning the model and in using it to work out what to do.

Structural models may be most useful when a device breaks down and it is necessary to work out how to mend it. In certain domains, like electronics and engineering, the use of such models may also be essential for understanding how circuit boards and the like work. Various types of instructional material have been developed with the aim of instilling an appropriate structural model in the user.

However, in the everyday world of technological devices people seem to get by without using structural models. Most of us quite happily operate the phone, the TV, the cooker, the car and so on without ever thinking about the insides of the machine and how it might work. Moreover, as Miyake (1986) points out, trying to infer a structural model is extremely difficult, if not impossible, for even the simplest of devices. Even experienced users get by without having a detailed model of how a system works. For example, she found that people who had years of experience in using a sewing machine did not use structural models. Instead, their understanding is largely based on functional models.

Question 6.5

What are the advantages and disadvantages of structural models?

Functional models

In general, most people use a calculator in the same way as they learnt to do algebra at school. It is rarely the case, unless they have read the manual explaining the underlying mechanism of the device, that anyone would develop a structural model. They simply employ a model of how to do it.

This type of model is called a **functional** model. More specifically, Young (1983) has called it a **task–action mapping model**, which distinguishes between the task domain and the action domain. Designers try to describe the connection between the two so that there is a simple and direct mapping between them. From this it may then be possible to help design better task domains such that they match the user's knowledge of the action domain (see also Section 20.5).

In terms of helping users to learn how to use and understand new systems, existing knowledge of another domain or system is accessed. Functional models, therefore, develop from past knowledge of a similar domain and *not* – like structural models – from a model of how the device works. Another major difference between structural models and functional models is that whereas the former can answer unexpected questions and make predictions, the latter are structured around a set of tasks. Furthermore, functional models are context-dependent, whereas structural models are largely context-free. The advantage of being context dependent is that it makes the model easier to use. On the other hand, the advantage of a context-free model is that it is easier to extend and integrate with other knowledge.

Question 6.6

What are the three main differences between structural and functional models?

EXERCISE

Consider the choke in a car – a manual choke, not an automatic one. Think about how it works in starting the car under several conditions, such as when it is cold or when the engine has just stalled. Think about trying to construct a structural model to capture the essential features of how it works. Then do the same with a functional model. Which type of model do you find more difficult to construct? What do you think are the relative advantages and disadvantages of the two types of model?

COMMENT

You probably found that generating a structural model of a manual choke was difficult. It depends, for one thing, on you having detailed knowledge of the air intake, the carburettor, and so on. A functional model would include describing the task of pulling the choke out before starting the engine on a cold day. If the car was suddenly to stall soon after you had started it, the functional model would allow you to decide that more choke was needed. If the car was to stall when the engine had warmed up you could use the same functional model to decide that in this situation the choke was not needed to restart the engine. A structural model would not be needed in either case and would be of use only if you needed to repair the choke.

6.3 The utility of mental models in HCI

Numerous studies have been carried out in an attempt to discover whether people actually have and use mental models when interacting with devices and systems (see Rogers *et al.*, 1992). The general assumption is that people do use some type of model, but that it is often incomplete and vague. Empirical evidence of actual mental models of systems is difficult to find (Wilson and Rutherford, 1989). In many cases, what tends to get described is a combination of different knowledge structures (e.g. Bainbridge, 1992).

This is in sharp contrast with the prescriptive advice in HCI, that interfaces need to be designed to help users 'grow' productive mental models of relevant aspects of the system. Much has been written about why designers need to develop interfaces that will shape a user's mental model, but there are very few suggestions as to how to achieve this. Part of the problem is that we simply do not know enough about how people construct and use models of computer systems. It is one thing to conjecture putative models; it is another to prove their existence. Accordingly, much research effort has been spent on developing and evaluating methods for eliciting mental models. Less attention has been paid to prescribing *how* to design interfaces that will ensure the appropriate user mental model.

The utility of conceptualizing users' knowledge in terms of assumed mental models, however, should not be underestimated. It can be very productive for helping designers to construct an appropriate model of the system (see Chapter 8). Moreover, it can provide a valuable heuristic tool that, arguably, has greater flexibility than more formal modelling techniques that are based on idealized knowledge (for example, see Chapter 33). Hence, focusing on the methods by which to elicit mental models is a very fruitful avenue for HCI.

Mental models in process control

In a related field, that of complex systems such as process control, the utility of the concept of mental models was evident as far back as the 1960s and 1970s. One of the leading figures in the field, who did much in the way of developing a theoretical framework of mental models for complex systems, was Jens Rasmussen (1979, 1986). Primarily, he was concerned with how to reduce human error in the control of complex systems, and in doing so characterized process control operators' knowledge in terms of three levels: **Skill-based**, **Rule-based** and **Knowledge-based** (SRK). Briefly, these are defined as:

- The **skill-based level**, which refers to the normal way of interacting with the system. This consists of automated routines (see Chapter 5).
- The **rule-based level**, which refers to situations of the process plant that are familiar to the controllers and that can be resolved by applying learned routines.
- The **knowledge-based level**, which refers to the conscious and analytic processes that occur when the operators are confronted with novel and unexpected situations. It is at this level that operators must evaluate the unexpected problems by using mental models.

The function of mental models at the knowledge-based level is to predict future events, find causes of observed events and determine appropriate actions to cause changes. Rasmussen also suggested that a number of different types of mental models are used for answering the various questions about the process control plant. In addition to structural and functional models, there are models of why the system exists and what it looks like.

Orthogonal to the three levels of knowledge is the idea that people understand complex systems at a multitude of levels, varying in function, structure, generality and form. When thinking about the system in terms of what it does, most of the details are lost. At a lower level, the details of the physical structures of the system are entailed.

The SRK framework (for a more detailed review and account of the framework, see Sanderson and Harwood, 1988) has been received most favourably by people working with complex systems. In particular, it has provided 'understandable, usable and extendible concepts for classifying the behaviour of humans in their interaction with the world ... a market standard within the systems reliability community' (Goodstein *et al.*, 1988, p. 1). The aspiration in HCI is also to produce a conceptual framework, mapping out the important characteristics of mental models, that is robust, useful and clear to understand for researchers and designers alike. The development of such a framework is still in its infancy, but significant strides are currently under way (see Chapter 7).

Key points

- There are three types of mental representations: analogical, propositional and distributed.
- General knowledge is stored as schemata, which, when activated, can be used to construct mental models.
- Mental models enable people to generate descriptions and explanations about systems and to make predictions about future events.
- Structural models describe how devices and systems work.
- Functional models describe how to use a device or system.
- Most people's understandings of devices or systems is functional.
- Conceptualizing users' knowledge in terms of mental models can help designers to develop appropriate user interfaces.

Further reading

Mental models from a cognitive science perspective

JOHNSON-LAIRD P.N. (1989). Mental models. In *Foundations of Cognitive Science* (POSNER M.I., ed.), pp. 469–93. Cambridge, MA: MIT Press.
Johnson-Laird is one of the leading experts on mental models and has written a number of books on mental models and reasoning. This is a good introductory chapter.

Mental models from an HCI perspective

CARROLL J.M. and OLSON J.M. (1988). Mental models in human–computer interaction. In *Handbook of Human–Computer Interaction* (HELANDER M., ed.), pp. 45–65. Amsterdam: North-Holland.
This is a very good overview of the various characterizations of users' knowledge, contrasting the GOMS modelling approach with the mental models approach. It also provides an interesting set of recommendations on how to go about researching and applying mental models.

ROGERS Y., RUTHERFORD A. and BIBBY P., eds (1992). *Models in the Mind: Theory, Perspective and Application*. London: Academic Press.
This is a collection of papers and adjoining in-depth discussions of the various perspectives and criticisms that currently exist in the mental models literature. It includes chapters on mental models and reasoning, HCI, process control, instruction, elicitation methods and social and pragmatic factors.

Interface Metaphors and Conceptual Models

Aims and objectives

The aim of this chapter is to describe how the cognitive principle of metaphorical reasoning – that we use prior knowledge to understand new situations – has been applied to user interface design. After working through this chapter you should be able to:

- describe the difference between verbal and virtual interface metaphors,
- explain why the development of composite interface metaphors has been necessary,
- discuss the problems and advantages of using metaphors at the interface,
- decide whether you think the interfaces that you use or develop should model some aspect of the world (that is, metaphor-based) or that it be invisible to the user (that is, ubiquitous computing).
- understand the different ways in which the term 'conceptual model' is used in HCI.

Overview

The term 'metaphor' is traditionally associated with language use. When we want to convey an abstract concept in a more familiar and accessible form we frequently resort to using metaphoric expressions. For example, we tend to talk about time, which is a very abstract concept, in terms of money (Lakoff and Johnson, 1980). We save it, spend it, waste it, give someone our time, live on borrowed time and so on. In fact, the whole of language is based on these types of metaphorical abstractions.

When we consider how system interfaces have been designed, we can also see how metaphors play an important role. The objects on the screen, the types of user interactions we perform, the way the system responds, the names given to command names, tend to be based on familiar terms. Desktops, icons, menus, windows, cutting, pasting, copying are either system objects or actions that are part of a virtual interface metaphor. In fact, it is difficult to think of a system that is not based on some form of metaphor. We need to ask ourselves, therefore, to what extent and how they help users interact with computer systems.

7.1 Verbal metaphors

When confronted with a new piece of technology, such as a computer, for the first time people will often compare it to a machine with which they are familiar in a metaphorical way. The classic example is of people who use a word processor for the first time; it occurs to them how similar it is to a typewriter. Having activated the typewriter schema (see Chapter 6), they are then able to interpret and predict more readily how the word processor functions. On seeing that the computer has a keyboard the obvious inference is that it behaves like the qwerty keyboard on a typewriter. Hence, an obvious assumption is that the character keys should act in the same way as they do for the typewriter.

These links provide the basic foundation from which users develop their mental models of computer systems. Knowledge about a familiar domain in terms of elements and their relation to each other is mapped on to elements and their relations in the unfamiliar domain. **Elements** include the keyboard, the spacebar and the return key. **Relations** between the elements include 'only one character key can be hit at any one time' and 'hitting a character key will result in a letter being displayed on a visible medium'. By drawing on this prior knowledge a learner can develop an understanding of the new domain more readily.

As well as similarities between a new and familiar domain, however, there are obviously going to be many dissimilarities. Two examples are the spacebar and backspace key, which are both present on the typewriter and word processor keyboards but which perform different functions. Whereas the backspace key on the typewriter physically moves the carriage (this is the mechanism that holds the paper feed rollers and travels across the top of the machine) one space back and the spacebar moves the carriage one space forward, the backspace key on the word processor *deletes* the character marked by the cursor on the screen while the spacebar inserts a blank character. Moreover, if users want to move backwards or forwards, as they would do when using a typewriter, then they have to use another set of cursor control keys (or move the cursor on the screen via a mouse). The effect of changing the function played by the spacebar and return key, together with introducing a different way of doing spacing, often causes problems for learners because it contravenes their expectations about how the elements and their relations should behave. However, it should also be noted that once users become aware of the discrepancies and differences between the old and new systems, they can develop a new mental model, accordingly.

EXERCISE

Can you think of any other similarities or mismatches between the typewriter and the word processor domains?

COMMENT

Other similarities include the tab key, which moves the carriage/cursor to a pre-set point and the shift key, which when used in combination with a character key has the effect of changing the character to upper case or to one of the expressions displayed on the 'dual character' keys (for example, the & symbol on the '7' key). A mismatch is the lock key. On the typewriter keyboard the shift key can be locked to enable continous typing of upper case and the upper expressions on dual keys whereas on most word processor keyboards there is a 'caps' lock key which allows the continous typing of upper case but not the upper expressions on the dual keys.

A number of studies have been carried out that have investigated the effects of providing verbal metaphors in the form of written or spoken instructions. For example, Foss *et al.* (1982) looked at the effects of providing an 'advance organizer' on learning to use a word processor. The advance organizer described how files were created, stored and retrieved in terms of a filing cabinet metaphor. The results showed that subjects who had been presented with the verbal metaphor before using the word processor showed better performance in terms of making fewer errors and

Drawing by Koren; © 1979 The New Yorker Magazine, Inc.

faster times to complete the tasks. Other studies have also shown similar improvements (e.g. Borgman, 1986).

In general, the results suggest that verbal metaphors can be useful tools to help users begin to understand the new system. However, it must be remembered that computer systems are much more complex and have different ways of doing things. For example, in the typewriter analogy there are clearly a number of properties about the word processing domain that do not map on to existing features in the typewriter domain. The most obvious include the ability to save text and manipulate it in a number of ways (such as copying sections and formatting). Here there are no obvious links with the typewriter domain, so users have to develop a new understanding. In addition, it is important that users understand how the new system works *as a computer system*. Accordingly, instructions and descriptions of the system need to be developed that also describe aspects of the structure and function of the system (see Halasz and Moran, 1982).

Question 7.1

What knowledge types are mapped between the familiar and unfamiliar domains of metaphors?

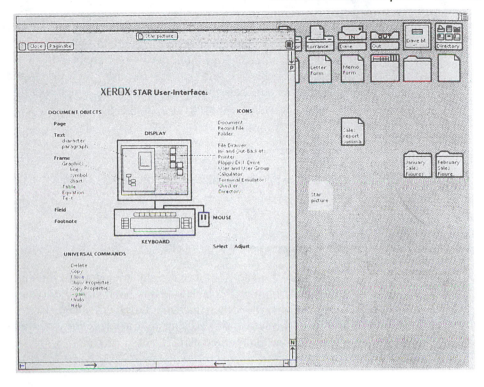

Figure 7.1 The desktop metaphor as it originally appeared on the Star screen (Smith *et al.*, 1982).

7.2 | Virtual interface metaphors

One of the first computer companies to realize the enormous potential of designing interfaces to be more like the physical concrete world that people are familiar with was Xerox (see Box 1.4). Instead of developing verbal metaphors as ways of helping users to understand the interface, they went one step further and designed an **interface metaphor** that was based on the physical office. The outcome was the 'Star user interface' (Smith *et al.*, 1982) discussed in Chapter 1. The core aspect of the interface metaphor was to create electronic counterparts to the physical objects in an office. This involved representing office objects as icons on the screen. These included paper, folders, filing cabinets and in and out trays, as shown in Figure 7.1. The overall organizing metaphor that was presented on the screen was of a desktop, resembling the top of a typical office desk.

Instead of being abstract entities, having arbitrary names, files were transformed into pictorial representations, which everyone could easily identify and understand (see Chapter 5 for more on icons). Moreover, having this basic understanding would provide the basis from which users would know how to interact with the icons. Just as one opens, closes, copies and trashes paper files in the physical world, the interface was designed so that equivalent actions could be done on the electronic versions. The trick was to design an input device that enabled such electronic actions to be performed intuitively. And so the 'mouse' was developed to enable actions equivalent to physically handling documents, which were achieved by 'clicking', 'pointing', 'selecting', 'moving' and 'dragging'.

EXERCISE

What are the physical equivalent actions for (i) clicking, (ii) pointing, (iii) selecting and (iv) dragging?

COMMENT

The physical actions are not directly analogous to the electronic counterparts but consist of (i) placing one's hand on the object and grasping it, (ii) scanning the office, locating the object and making physical movements towards the object, (iii) picking up the object and (iv) holding the object and moving it to another location.

A difference between virtual interface metaphors and verbal metaphors is that the former are part of the interface. Whereas verbal metaphors invite the user to 'see' the similarities and dissimilarities between the system and the familiar domain, interface metaphors combine the system and familiar domains into one entity. Instead of imagining parts of the computer system to be like a typewriter, the interface metaphor conflates the familiar domain and the new system domain into one model. In other words, the desktop metaphor *is like* an office desktop but *it is* also the system interface. The effect is that users will develop mental models of the system that are more like the metaphor world rather than how the underlying system works. When they place an icon of a file into an icon of a folder they will assume that the system is doing just that (rather than it changing the pointer to the file).

Hence, instead of using the metaphor as a basis from which to develop a *new* mental model of the *new* domain, the metaphor is the model that is learned. This means that users will tend to develop functional-based mental models of the system and be largely unaware of the structural aspects of the system (see Chapter 6 on the difference between structural and functional models).

Question 7.2

What is the difference between a verbal metaphor and a virtual interface metaphor?

A design problem with the 'metaphor as model' approach is working out ways in which to incorporate additional functionality, which is not part of the interface metaphor, but which enables the computer application to be more powerful than non-electronic means. For example, how has it been possible to represent in familiar terms the manipulation of documents, like copying, moving, formatting and so on that could not have be done with the older technology?

Composite metaphors and multiple mental models

Designers have got round this problem by developing **composite metaphors** at the interface (Carroll, *et al.*, 1988a). The desktop metaphor has been combined with other metaphors to allow users the flexibility of carrying out a range of computer-based actions. One example is the scroll bar. Such objects do not exist in real life but they are metaphorical in the sense that they have been designed to capitalize on the main feature of the concept of a scroll – that is, a rolled-up document that has to be unrolled to be read. In the same way, files can be 'unrolled' by moving a box up and down a bar adjacent to the text file.

Other examples of interface metaphors based on objects that have been combined with the desktop metaphor are menus and windows. Both have their own metaphorical basis that is distinct from the concept of an office or a desk. Another type of metaphor that has been used is based on a prototypical activity associated with a professional practice. For example, the 'cut' and 'paste' actions used for moving and copying text is based on the process used in page layout in the printing profession.

From a cognitive perspective, it might be assumed that people would have difficulties with interpreting composite metaphors. In most instances, though, it seems that people can readily assimilate differing concepts and develop **multiple mental models**. The idea of moving around in a file, by scrolling through a window and selecting items from a menu attached to the top of the window by a bar, appears to create few conceptual problems. In fact, most people do not actually think about what they're doing in terms of the various metaphors (Tognazzini, 1992). Instead, they just interact with the system, thinking in terms of windows, menus, icons, scroll bars and so on as if they were everyday terms.

Needless to say, there are some poorly designed composite metaphors that can cause conceptual problems to their users. One of the main problems is the mismatch between the user's expectation of what an interface object should and should not do, based on their previous knowledge, and what the interface object actually does.

Question 7.3

What is a composite metaphor?

EXERCISE

As part of the desktop metaphor it is common practice to have an icon of a waste basket that serves other functions besides those for which it is conventionally used (as a container for discarded objects). One of these is to represent the place where disk icons are put in order to eject the corresponding disk from the disk drive. This implies that one has to 'throw away' a disk in order to retrieve it. Do you think that these contradictions can cause conceptual problems, and if so can you suggest another way of representing this operation at the interface?

COMMENT

Certainly on first encountering the waste basket, it is not intuitive that this action will eject the disk and that no harm will result from trying this. In fact many first-time users have been too frightened to do such an action. Some manufacturers have tried to alleviate the problem by allowing users to eject disks by selecting a menu option. Another solution might be to have another icon on the desktop, just for ejecting disks. For example, it could represent a Macintosh-shaped computer with an arrow pointing out from the disk drive.

A counter-argument against conceptual confusion is to treat such problems as actual learning experiences. For example, Carroll *et al.* (1988a) describe how they observed a user trying to tear off a sheet of paper from a stationery pad icon by dragging the cursor across an icon representing the stationery pad. The interface had not been designed to allow this action; sheets of paper could only be selected from a menu option. However, what Carroll *et al.* noted was that the invalid action enabled the user to understand better the difference between menu-based and mouse-based operations. Accordingly, she developed a more elaborate mental model of the interface.

Paradoxically, it could be the case that the more unexpected and the more bizarre the interface metaphor is, the more likely the user will develop a better understanding of the system. By carrying out inappropriate actions the user is enlightened as to what are the appropriate and permissable operations. Provided the user is able to experience the 'ah-ha' phenomenon relatively easily, and not be humiliated or frustrated in the process, such a strategy may be very effective. However, where the interface metaphor contravenes deep-rooted expectations (cf. the voice mail system and the central heating control models discussed in Chapter 6) users may find it difficult to switch their models and adapt to the new way of understanding how an object works. Furthermore, if the interface metaphor elicits inappropriate actions that have undesirable consequences, such as unexpectedly deleting files, the users may be reluctant to experiment further with the interface and hence never learn the full functionality of the system.

The dividing line between what consititutes a good or a poor interface metaphor is by no means clear cut. But by being aware of users' expectations about different objects' behaviour in conjunction with having a thorough understanding of the system's functionality and what aspects users are unlikely to understand about the system, designers can begin to have a better understanding of what metaphors are most appropriate (Erikson, 1990).

7.3 Classification of interface metaphors for applications

The desktop metaphor and its composites have been the most successful and pervasive of all interface metaphors. There are other metaphors, however, which have been developed for applications other than information systems (see Chapter 22). Table 7.1 presents some examples with their associated applications.

An important consideration when searching for interface metaphors is the appropriate effect. This is the subjective and emotional impact that different graphical representations can convey (Verplank, 1988). The kinds of metaphors like spreadsheets and multi-agents may be very appealing to adults working in office environments, but may be inappropriate for schoolchildren. Imaginary characters like demons and wizards might be far more attractive. Some sketching techniques for helping you to explore different metaphors by brainstorming are discussed in Chapter 22.

Table 7.1 Examples of applications and associated metaphors.

Application area	Metaphor	Familiar knowledge
Operating environment	The desktop	Office tasks, file management
Spreadsheets	Ledger sheet	Columnar tables
Object-oriented environments	Physical world	Real-world behaviour
Hypertext	Notecards	Flexible organization of structured text
Learning environments	Travel	Tours, guides, navigation
File storage	Piles	Categorizing objects in terms of urgency, projects and so on
Multimedia environments	Rooms (each associated with a different medium/task)	Spatial structure of buildings
Computer supported cooperative work	Multi-agents	Travel agents, butlers and other serving roles

7.4 Ubiquitous computing

Ubiquitous computing is a term coined by Weiser (1991) for 'invisibly enhancing the world that already exists' (p. 61). The ultimate aim of ubiquitous computing is to make the interface metaphor invisible to the user in the same way as computer

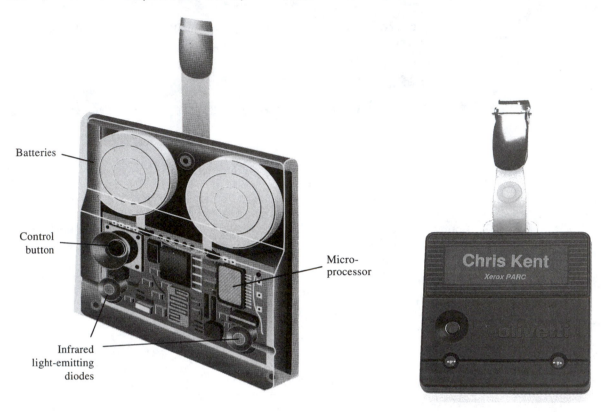

Batteries

Control
button

Micro-
processor

Infrared
light-emitting
diodes

Chris Kent
Xerox PARC

Figure 7.2 An example of ubiquitous computing: the 'tab' with an invisible interface metaphor (*Scientific American*, September 1991, p. 69: photograph by courtesy of Matthew Mulbry).

systems are invisible in home appliances, such as the VCR, the microwave oven and the washing machine. Just as we use these tools unconsciously and effortlessly to accomplish our everyday tasks (with the exception of the VCR, whose interface has generally been all too visible and difficult to use) it is envisaged that ubiquitous computing systems will be effortless to use.

An example of a ubiquitous system is the 'tab' which is a tiny networked computer that is intended to be worn by the user, shown in Figure 7.2. The tab or 'active badge' can identify itself throughout a building, making it possible to keep track of the person it is attached to. This can be very useful for buildings with high security areas in so far as the person wearing the tab can enter secure areas without having to remember a password and then key it in, as the tab does it automatically. Among other opportunities such automaticity affords are: on entering a room people can be greeted by name, telephone calls can be automatically forwarded and computer terminals can change to the customization specified by the person sitting at it.

Negreponte (1989) also discusses the idea of invisible computers that intercommunicate with each other with the purpose of doing all the chores in life.

Instead of you having to decide that you need to buy some more milk, or that the heating needs turning up or the trash needs emptying, a 'society of objects' in the form of virtual butlers, secretaries and housekeepers will organize and manage everything for you! However, a problem with such extensive anthropomorphism is that users may assume that the system is more intelligent than it is. When the virtual agents fail to behave as expected users may get frustrated. There is also the danger that designers could mislead users in undesirable ways.

Question 7.4

What is ubiquitous computing?

7.5 | Conceptual models

Conceptual models is the generic term that describes the various ways in which systems are understood by different people. Primarily these consist of (i) the way users conceptualize and understand the system and (ii) the way designers conceptualize and view the system.

As we said in Chapter 6, whether interacting with devices, machines, computers, people or the physical world, people use their prior knowledge to develop mental models to enable them to understand and predict their behaviour. A highly successful approach in interface design is to capitalize on users' existing knowledge and the use of metaphors. However, the problem confronting designers who follow this approach is finding a suitable metaphor. The aim for designers is to help users to develop accurate mental models of the system. As Donald Norman (1986, p. 46) puts it, 'The problem is to design the system so that, first, it follows a consistent, coherent conceptualisation – a design model – and, second, so that the user can develop a mental model of that system – a user model – consistent with the design model'.

Users' models, design models and the system image

An important consideration of conceptual models is the relationship between designers' models – the design model – and users' mental models – the user's model shown in Figure 7.3. As most designers work in teams, it is more accurate to consider the design model as the product of a collection of individuals rather than the outcome of any one individual. Ideally, the user model should map onto the design model. That way the users will be able to use the system's full capability as intended by the designer. However, in the real world this does not often happen. More often, users only develop a partial mental model of the design model. Their understanding and ability to use the system, therefore, is limited. Another problem is that the design model may be inappropriate for what the user wants to achieve. In this situation the

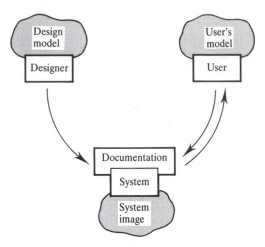

Figure 7.3 The design model, the user's model and the system image (Norman and Draper, 1986, p. 46).

users are forced to develop a mental model that is unfamiliar to them. A mismatch can also arise if the design model is ambiguous, inconsistent or obscure.

Generally, the way users get to find out about the design model is through the interface, its behaviour and the documentation. Collectively, these are called the **system image** as shown in Figure 7.3. A large part of the accessible system image comprises the physical interface (that is, the knobs and dials or images on a screen). It is important to bear in mind, however, that the system image also includes the system's behaviour, that is, the way it is used (for example by pressing keys, moving a mouse, and so on). The sequences of operations required in using the system (such as commands or menu selections) and the resulting events are all part of the system's image, and users learn not just from looking at the system, but also from their experience of using it.

If the system image is not able to convey to the users the design model in a clear and obvious way, then it is likely that the users will develop incorrect mental models. Consequently, they will experience great difficulties in understanding the system, using the system and knowing what to do when the system doesn't behave in the way they assumed it would. Much frustration, time-wasting and error-making can result. In Section 13.7, we shall extend these concepts further in relation to the design of direct manipulation systems. In particular, we shall consider what happens when the user's model does not match the designers' model well, creating 'gulfs' between the two, and how designers can help to prevent this happening.

Question 7.5

(a)   What is the difference between a design model and a user model?
(b)   What is the system image?
(c)   Why do mismatches occur between the design model and the user's model?

Key points

- Verbal metaphors are analogies based on familiar knowledge, spontaneously elicited or used in written or spoken instructions, which help users begin to understand new systems.
- Interface metaphors combine a familiar domain with the system structure to make a concrete system image.
- Composite interface metaphors are a combination of multiple and partial models of familiar domains.
- There are several kinds of interface metaphors, although the most common one is the desktop.
- Users and designers both have conceptual models of the system; Norman has called these the user and the design model, respectively.
- A main goal in interface design is to develop a system image that maps the design model onto the user model.
- Ubiquitous computing systems have invisible interfaces, are interconnected and intended to be effortless to use.
- A conceptual model provides a framework from which to consider how to design appropriate interface metaphors.

Further reading

Metaphors and language

LAKOFF G. and JOHNSON M. (1980). *Metaphors We Live By*. Chicago: University of Chicago Press.
A wealth of books are available in the linguistic, psychological and philosophical literature, but this is one of the most readable, lively and thought-provoking books, which has now become a 'classic'.

Interface metaphors

CARROLL J.M., MACK R.L. and KELLOGG W.A. (1988). Interface metaphors and user interface design. In *Handbook of Human–Computer Interaction* (HELANDER M., ed.), pp. 67–85. Amsterdam: North-Holland.

ERICKSON T.D. (1990). Working with interface metaphors. In *The Art of Human–Computer Interface Design* (LAUREL B., ed.). Reading, MA: Addison-Wesley.
These two chapters provide several useful suggestions on how to generate and design interface metaphors.

Conceptual models

NORMAN D. (1986). Cognitive engineering. In *User-Centred System Design* (NORMAN D. and DRAPER S., eds), pp. 31–61. Hillsdale, NJ: Lawrence Erlbaum Associates. Although dated and rather general, Norman's introductory chapter on cognitive ergonomics includes an account of his original framework of conceptual models.

Learning in Context

Aims and objectives

The success of any computer system depends on the extent to which the intended users can learn and make use of it. The main objective of this chapter is to discuss how we can facilitate learning. After studying this chapter you should:

- understand the difficulties in learning to use a computer system,
- know the different strategies people use when learning,
- be able to suggest ways of helping learners to use computer systems,
- be able to describe why the context of learning is important.

Overview

How we learn is a complex process involving a number of interdependent factors. It can be viewed as both an active process and a collaborative process. To this end, it is important to understand the individual cognitive processes and the social processes that are involved in learning. The first part of this chapter considers the various ways novices actively learn to use computer systems and some of the methods that have been developed to help them. However, people do not generally remain as novices but gradually become more experienced, and this has implications for system design. In addition to learning how to use a computer application, many people need to learn how to program. This is a difficult skill but current research is looking for ways of making it easier for learners. The context in which users learn is also important.

8.1 Learning as an active process

When people encounter a computer for the first time their most common reaction is one of fear and trepidation. In contrast, when we sit behind the steering wheel of a car for the first time most of us are highly motivated and very excited with the prospect of learning to drive. Why, then, is there such a discrepancy between our attitudes to learning these different skills?

One of the main differences between the two domains is the way they are taught. At the end of the first driving lesson, a pupil will have usually learned how to drive through actually *doing*. This includes performing a number of complex tasks such as clutch control, gear changing, learning to use the controls and knowing what they are. Furthermore, the instructors are keen to let their pupils try things out and get started. Verbal instruction initially is kept to a minimum and usually interjected only when necessary.

In contrast, someone who sits in front of a computer system for the first time may only have a very large manual, which may be difficult to understand and poorly presented. Often training and reference materials are written as a series of ordered explanations together with step-by-step exercises, which may cause the learner to feel overloaded with information or frustrated at not being able to find information that she wants. One of the main problems with learning to use computer systems is the lack of effort put into developing usable training materials and help facilities. There is a general assumption that having read something in the manual users can immediately match it to what is happening at the interface and respond accordingly. But, as you may have experienced, trying to put into action even simple descriptions can sometimes be difficult. For example, trying to construct DIY furniture from the manufacturers' instruction sheets can cause much grief. Often the instructions are poorly described, using diagrammatic representations which do not map onto the parts of the device. This means that in addition to trying to understand the real system or device, the person initially has to understand the instructions. Ironically, it can be the device or system that helps the user to understand the instructions.

It seems we find it difficult, and at times impossible, to master a set of procedures for operating a piece of equipment simply by following a manual. Reducing the gap between the system and the users by improving the system image

(© 1993 Washington Post Writers Group.)

(the instructions, on-line help and the interface) is clearly important (see Chapters 7, 13 and 15). However, it is also necessary to consider the more 'natural' way in which people learn. Many people learn by watching others or by simply getting on with it themselves. Just as we are keen to put the key into the ignition and then our foot on the accelerator so that we can get a feel for the car and its controls, so too do new users of computer systems like to get going and do something that will give them a feel of interacting with the system.

For example, after studying the plight of first-time users of word processing systems over a period of two years, Carroll and his colleagues (Carroll *et al.*, 1988b; Carroll and Ray, 1988) found that new users tended to 'jump the gun' whenever they were introduced to new topics. More often than not they would plunge straight into the new subject without really looking at the manual. Interestingly, the few new users who tried to be methodical and follow the manual ended up committing a number of small errors that often resulted in them becoming sidetracked.

Experienced users also appear to be reluctant to learn new methods and operations from manuals. When new situations arise that could be handled more effectively by new procedures, experienced users are more likely to continue to use the procedures they already know rather than try to follow the advanced procedures outlined in a manual, even if the former course takes much longer and is less effective. For example, once experienced users have established a means of getting to a certain destination or option within a database they will tend always to use that route even though, if they were to look through the manual, they would find that there are quicker routes.

On the basis of their findings Mack *et al.* (1984) have classified some of the major problems confronting users when trying to learn (see Table 8.1).

EXERCISE

Try to remember the first time you used a computing system and what problems you encountered. Do they resemble any of those in Mack *et al.*'s classification in Table 8.1? Can you think of any other categories of learning difficulties that are not included. In Chapter 30 we discuss how this data was collected and analysed. (No comment is provided for this exercise.)

Table 8.1 Summary of Mack *et al.*'s classification of learning difficulties (Mack *et al.*, 1984).

(1) Learning is difficult
Learners experience frustration and blame themselves
Learning takes longer than expected, and learners have trouble applying what they know after training

(2) Learners lack basic knowledge
Learners are naïve about how computers work (for example, they do not understand computer jargon)
Learners do not know what is relevant to understanding and solving problems

(3) Learners make *ad hoc* interpretations
Learners try to construct interpretations for what they do or for what happens to them
Learners' interpretations can prevent them from seeing that they have a problem

(4) Learners generalize from what they know
Learners assume that some aspects of text editors will work like typewriting (especially functions that simply move the typing point on a typewriter)
Learners assume that text editing operations will work consistently

(5) Learners have trouble following directions
Learners do not always read or follow directions
Learners do not always understand or correctly follow directions even when they do try

(6) Problems interact
Learners have trouble understanding that one problem can create another

(7) Interface features may not be obvious
Learners can be confused by prerequisites and side effects of procedures
Learners can be confused by feedback messages and the outcome of procedures

(8) Help facilities do not always help
Learners do not always know what to ask for
Help information is not always focused on the learner's specific problem

Learning through analogy

When confronted with a new system, learners often invoke prior knowledge in order to interpret and predict the behaviour of the system when they try out operations. Confronted with a word processor for the first time, novices often think of it in terms of their experiences with typewriters and office routines (see Chapter 7 for a discussion on analogical reasoning). Besides providing users with a preliminary conceptual basis on which to formulate their understanding of the new system, the use of such analogies provides a means of bridging the old ways of doing things with the new ways. As discussed in Chapter 7, the development of interface metaphors has enabled designers to capitalize on this. However, the design of mainstream instructional and training material has yet to exploit this knowledge in any substantial way.

Question 8.1

What type of learning strategy do novice users of computer systems adopt?

Fathoming things out: Explanations

Just as users are active when learning, they are also active when understanding a system's behaviour. Since it is a natural instinct for us to make sense of our experience, new users are curious to understand what is happening when interacting with a computer, especially when unexpected events occur. As they often have little knowledge about the way the system operates, they will try to understand by developing explanations based on incomplete notions and implicit beliefs (see Turkle, 1984). These can entail a degree of magic and anthropomorphism in which the user will explain a system's behaviour as something that happened because 'it just did' or 'the computer knew and did it deliberately'. In contrast, other types of explanation can be quite elaborate, although inaccurate. One example in Carroll *et al.*'s study was that of a user trying to understand cursor control functions. For the system that she used, one set of functions moved the cursor in the menu display while another set moved it in the text area. She reconciled this discrepancy by reasoning that the structure of the two displays was different. The point is that because we have limited information to begin with, we need to make up our own hypotheses. Unable to use more systematic forms of reasoning behaviour such as inductive and deductive methods, we tend to rely on *ad hoc* reasoning.

Fathoming things out: Errors

Whenever we try to learn a new skill, be it skiing, typing, cooking or playing chess, we are bound to make mistakes. In most situations it is not such a bad thing because the feedback from making errors can help us to learn and understand an activity. When learning to use a computer system, however, learners are often frightened of making errors because, as well as making them feel stupid, they think it can result in catastrophe. Hence, the anticipation of making an error and its consequences can hinder a user's interaction with a system. Box 8.1 discusses errors.

Box 8.1   A classification of errors: Slips and mistakes

There are various types of errors. Norman (1981) has categorized them into two main types, slips and mistakes:

(1) **Mistakes** occur through conscious deliberation. An incorrect action is taken based on an incorrect decision. For example, trying to throw the icon of the hard disk into the waste basket, in the desktop metaphor, as a way of removing all existing files from the disk is a mistake. A menu option to erase the disk is the appropriate action.

(2) **Slips** are unintentional. They happen by accident, such as making typos by pressing the wrong key or selecting the wrong menu item by overshooting.

The most frequent errors are slips, especially in well learned behaviour. Slips can be further classified into six types: capture errors, description errors, data-driven errors, associative–activation errors, loss-of-activation errors and mode errors:

- A **capture error** is a frequently done activity which takes over (captures) the intended action. For example, in the UNIX text editor VI, the command for saving or writing a file to disk is W, and the command for quitting the editor is Q. Experienced users overlearn (see Chapter 5 on automatic processes) the sequence WQ for writing and quitting, and frequently make the mistake of using WQ when they really mean to save the file and continue editing (entering the command W by itself).

- A **description error** is when the correct action is carried out on the wrong object. It tends to occur when one is distracted. For example, (i) putting the salad in the oven and the casserole in the fridge, (ii) clicking in the zoom box at the top of the window when trying to close the window instead of clicking in the close box. The close box is in the left-hand corner and the zoom box is in the right-hand corner. Both look very similar.

- A **data-driven error** is when unconscious processing of external data interferes with what you had intended to do. For example, saving a file with the name of the file that is displayed in the adjacent window instead of the name you intended.

- An **associative–activation error** is when internal thoughts interfere with what you are supposed to be doing. For example, saving a file with the name of the person you were thinking about rather than the name you had intended.

- A **loss-of-activation error** is when you forget to do something in mid-flow of an activity. For example, searching through a database and realizing that you have forgotten what it is you were looking for.

- A **mode error** is when you think you are in one state but in fact you are in another. For example, you think you are entering a command but in fact you are typing in text.

Question 8.2

What is the difference between a slip and a mistake?

EXERCISE

How would you classify the following types of errors? Can you suggest ways of helping to reduce the occurrence of such errors?

(a) In the UNIX system the command for listing files in a directory is LS, and the command for listing headers in the mail system is HA (for 'Headers of All messages'). A very common type of error is for the user to type LS in the mail system.

(b) On being asked to save a file, the user types the name of a file she has been working on previously and inadvertently overwrites the contents of that file with the new file.

(c) The phone rings and the user gets distracted from the task of checking the data on a spreadsheet. She forgets where she had got to and so starts again.

(d) When trying to copy a file from a hard disk onto a floppy disk, it has been known for users instead to inadvertently copy the floppy disk file onto the hard disk file.

COMMENT

(a) This could be either a mode error or a description error. It is more likely to be a mode error, in which case, what might you do as a designer to help the user avoid this type of error? You could display the mode clearly on the screen, remembering that users often do not read relevant signs. Another solution might be to try to make the commands in the two modes more consistent with each other, for example by changing the command HA to LS.

(b) This could be a data-driven error or an associative–activation error. One way of helping to reduce this type of error is to alert the user to the fact that she already has a file under that name.

(c) This is a loss-of-activation error. The spreadsheet could be designed to show a message of where the user was at if the cursor is left idle for more than five minutes.

(d) This could be a description error or a mode error. To help reduce this type of error, System 7 (which runs on the Macintosh) has now installed a confirmation box that appears every time a user wants to copy a file, specifying whether an older version is to be written over the newer version and asking if that is what the user wants:

'A newer item named "HCI book" already exists in this location. Are you sure you want to replace the newer item with the one you're moving?'

Reducing and recognizing user errors

Lewis and Norman (1986) discuss several ways of minimizing errors through good design. One method of avoiding error is to design an appropriate representation. For example, if files are represented by icons or names, then they only have to be selected rather than specified through typing (which is when it is easy to make typos). Menus also make it less likely that the user will make a mistake in specifying a file. Mode errors can be minimized by providing clear feedback about what state the system is in. For example, changing the cursor from an arrow to an insertion bar in text editing (the arrow cursor indicates selection mode, or is used in selecting commands, and the insertion bar indicates the mode of entering text in, for example, the Macintosh system).

Since we are prone to making errors, it would be unrealistic to prevent users making errors altogether. Also, since making errors can facilitate learning, an error-free situation would seem equally undesirable. An alternative strategy is to make it easier for users to detect errors once they have been made and to enable them to recover relatively painlessly from them. In recognition of the fact that people make errors, several systems now provide easy to use 'undo' facilities.

System errors

It is unlikely that we will ever have complex systems that are bug-free, especially when new software is being continually launched. Currently, if a system makes an identifiable error it will relay a message informing the user of what has happened. In many cases, however, the content of the message is only decipherable by the software designers or dedicated hackers. For the average user, the messages issued can be quite baffling and totally unhelpful. For example, one message that now appears when the System 7 software crashes is 'a Type 1 error has occurred'. For those with a statistical background such a message has a very specific meaning: you have accepted the alternative hypothesis when in fact the null hypothesis is true, that is, you accepted something when you shouldn't have. In terms of System 7, however, I'm sure it means something totally different. System error messages, therefore, should be designed to be as informative and as honest (!) as possible, like the one in Figure 8.1. A good guideline from Tognazzini (1992) is 'system-level error messages should state the assumed problem, then offer the alternative possibility that the message-giver has gone berserk' (p. 241).

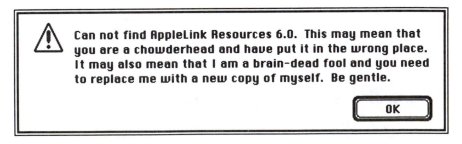

Figure 8.1   The all-eventualities system error message (Tognazzini, 1992).

Question 8.3

(a) List the six kinds of slip that people can make.

(b) What techniques can be used to help users better deal with their errors and system errors?

Other ways of supporting learning and providing user support are discussed in Chapter 15.

8.2 Gaining expertise

On reaching a certain level of expertise, it is likely that users will want different interface styles. For example, they may find that a menu-based interface is too restricting and that they would prefer to use a faster method of issuing commands. To determine what types of interfaces are best suited to users of differing levels of experience, however, it is important to understand how expertise develops.

Novice to expert continuum

When learning a skill for the first time we are called novices. As we become more experienced we reach various levels of competence. After much practice and when we can perform the task automatically without consciously having to think about each move, as we use our native language, we are considered experts.

One of the main differences between novices and experts is the way knowledge about the skill is structured in memory. A classic study by Chase and Simon (1973) found significant differences between chess players with different abilities. Specifically, they found that chess masters typically store in memory between 50 000 and 100 000 board positions, but rather than simply being random positions, they are remembered as meaningful 'chunks'. For example, rather than remembering a board position as a pawn on one square, the king on another and so on, the pieces are remembered in terms of their relation to each other as an organized whole. These are then assigned a particular name, according to the configuration, such as 'castle–king' position. They also found that experts develop a repertoire of sequences of moves. Novice players, on the other hand, can only recognize a few positions and have not developed any such sequences. Hence, the main difference between the two is in terms of the way their knowledge is structured in long-term memory; experts have meaningful chunks of knowledge, while novices do not.

Skill acquisition

There are many kinds of skill and several ways in which we can develop expertise. At one level a skill can be classified as perceptual and sensory-motor – in the sense that it is largely changes in perception and sensory-motor control that enable us to select relevant information from the world and perform actions smoothly. For example, after a few times of using a menu-based interface with mouse-driven input we usually find that we can physically select an option much more quickly with fewer errors.

At a more cognitive level, skill acquisition involves changes in the knowledge structures stored in memory. As you should recall, when you learn a new skill you access prior knowledge. Information about a new domain is combined with existing knowledge and reorganized to form new knowledge structures. For example, when learning to use an interface based on the desktop metaphor, our knowledge about desktops and office behaviour is accessed and combined with knowledge about the new domain, to result in new knowledge structures. In this way we 'make the connection' that, for example, the icon displayed on the screen is a representation of a file, which is a document about some subject matter. As we learn more about a system these structures are modified and extended, enabling us to integrate more new information, such as that a number of editing operations can be performed on files using the command operations provided by the system.

In cognitive psychology one of the most influential explanations of skill acquisition is Anderson's theory (1983) based on Fitts and Posner (1967). Essentially, Anderson characterizes the learning of a skill in relation to two different types of knowledge: declarative and procedural.

- **Declarative knowledge**   consists of facts about the world which can be put into words (for example, the computer keyboard consists of a set of alphanumeric and function keys).
- **Procedural knowledge**   refers to how we do things (for example, how to use the keyboard).

Anderson suggests that the first **cognitive stage** of learning involves acquiring declarative knowledge that is relevant to the skill. Applied to learning to use a computer, this includes memorizing things like 'to select an option from a menu move the cursor to the required option using the mouse and then click twice rapidly in succession on the mouse button'.

Following the acquisition of declarative knowledge, an **associative stage** occurs in which the connections between the various elements required for successful performance are strengthened. In the above example this would include things like learning how to move and 'double-click' the mouse as a smooth action for selecting an option. With increasing practice procedural knowledge develops. We also comprehend and eliminate errors during this process.

The final stage is known as the **autonomous stage**. The skill becomes more and more automated and rapid. The declarative knowledge used during the earlier stages of learning becomes secondary to the performance of the task, often disappearing altogether. For example, a highly skilled typist or musician often finds it impossible to know consciously which characters or notes were pressed while performing the task.

Learning to use a computer system, therefore, can be viewed in terms of the acquisition of a skill in which declarative knowledge changes into a skill. In this respect, the difficulties new users face when learning to use a system can be explained in terms of a 'bottleneck' occurring during the initial stages of acquiring declarative knowledge. In particular, the types of problem that arise when learning to use a system such as a word processor can be related to the learner's inability to absorb and put into action declarative instructions.

Question 8.4

What is the difference between procedural and declarative knowledge?

Facilitating the acquisition of computer interaction skills

One way of facilitating learning is to make sure that users have very few options so that the declarative knowledge they have to apply is kept small. (This notion forms the basis of a minimalist approach, Carroll *et al.* (1988b), discussed in Chapter 15.) Another way is to allow for the rapid development of procedures. Rather than expect the user to learn how to perform tasks and what the commands mean through rote learning, which requires much practice, an interface should be designed to encourage the user to acquire the various skills of interaction as quickly as possible. Menu-based mouse-driven interfaces are a good example of this approach since all a learner needs to know initially is how to use the mouse and select an option. In fact, this action in itself requires minimal declarative information since much can be learned simply by moving the mouse and exploring its effect on the screen. It also enables the user to take advantage of 'knowledge in the world', as discussed in Chapter 5.

Once users become more experienced with using a system, they may want to move on to use quicker and more efficient means of performing tasks – especially those which need repetitive sequences of operations. For example, copying an object from a library in a CAD menu-based system often requires going through a series of menus until the required option is reached. Alternatively, with a command-based system the same option can be selected by keying one or two commands. Switching from using menus to commands, however, requires consolidating more declarative knowledge. This may not be as problematic for experienced users as it would be for novices, since they already have a body of proceduralized knowledge for interacting with the system. This means that they will have more cognitive resources available to learn the new command keying sequences.

In relation to interface design, therefore, it is desirable to provide a means of interaction that can facilitate rapid learning as well as one that is compatible with the needs of more experienced users.

8.3 The psychology of programming

One area of skill acquisition that has received considerable attention within HCI is the psychology of programming. One of the main reasons for this is that conventional programming has proved to be a very difficult skill to learn. Psychologists have been interested in trying, initially, to understand why this is so and, secondly, to develop various tools and alternative languages that can make the skill of programming easier.

Following the research strategy used to investigate chess playing skills, a number of studies on the psychology of programming have focused on the differences between novice and expert programmers. Similar results have also been reported. For example, McKeithen *et al.* (1981) found that while expert programmers were very good at remembering meaningful computer programs, novices were very bad. Both groups were equally poor when presented with meaningless 'scrambled' code. The results suggest, therefore, that experts organize their knowledge of programming into meaningful chunks of code that reflect the relationships and routines between the words in the language (for example, the words 'for', 'step', 'do' and 'while' would be remembered in the logical sequence of 'while', 'do', 'for' and 'step') while novices would not organize their knowledge in this way.

Mayer (1988) has since developed a framework of programmer's knowledge that characterizes in more detail the main differences between novices and experts. These are classified into four types: syntactic, semantic, schematic and strategic knowledge (see Table 8.2).

Table 8.2 Classification of the different kinds of programming knowledge experts and novices have (Mayer, 1988).

Knowledge	Definition	Example
Syntactic	Language units and rules for combining language units	Distinction between $X = Y + Z$ as acceptable and $A + B = C$ as unacceptable
Semantic	Mental model of the major locations, objects and actions in the system	Concept of the pipes and files in UNIX
Schematic	Categories of routines based on function	Distinction among looping structures, DO-WHILE, DO-UNTIL, IF-THEN-ELSE
Strategic	Techniques for devising and monitoring plans	Breadth-first and top-down search in debugging

The main differences between novices and experts are:

- **Syntactic**   experts have automated their syntactic knowledge to a greater degree than novices.
- **Semantic**   experts have a more integrated model of the programming knowledge than novices.

- **Schematic**   experts have a much larger repertoire of categories for types of routines than novices.
- **Strategies**   experts are much better at decomposing their programming goals into plans and exploring more solution alternatives.

Positive and negative transfer

When beginning to learn a programming language, there is a tendency to understand and organize the new knowledge according to natural language associations rather than in terms meaningful to the programming language. This can be viewed as an example of **negative transfer**. The novices are appropriating their knowledge of natural language in an attempt to understand how the programming language works (see Section 7.2). While this can be very useful at the very beginning of learning to program, the natural language meaning can persist, causing problems of confusion later on. For example, the words 'if' and 'while' have similar meanings in natural and programming languages. The differences are quite subtle: 'while' in programming language entails a specific sequence of test and action, and 'if' in natural language is often interpreted as 'whenever' (diSessa, 1991). The outcome is that novices can have difficulties switching from their understanding of the words in natural language to their more precise meaning in programming languages.

Positive transfer occurs when users are faced with a task similar to one that has been done before. Programmers are able to use this knowledge and solve the problem more easily than if they had not had that experience. For example, having learnt how to program in one language (for example, Pascal), it may be easier to learn a similar type of programming language (for example, C). However, negative transfer can also occur when learning different types of languages (for example, functional and procedural).

Facilitating programming skills

It is a well-known problem that only those with the tenacity and willingness to spend hundreds of hours mastering the difficult skill of programming succeed in becoming expert programmers. To help programmers through some of the hurdles, from getting started to writing efficient program design, a number of techniques have been developed. These include:

- extending the minimalist approach (discussed in Chapter 15),
- the use of software visualization,
- the construction of visual programming languages,
- the development of intelligent tutoring systems.

The minimalist instruction approach

Rosson *et al.* (1990) have applied the minimalist approach to teach users to learn to use Smalltalk, an object-oriented programming language. By streamlining the amount of information in the manuals and making it more task-oriented, they have been able to develop a curriculum that enables programmers to get started more quickly on the tasks that interest them.

Software visualization

Software visualization is a graphical method of representing the different aspects of programming. Primarily these include algorithms, data and code. A main aim is to help computer science students understand the function and structure of programming languages. Various kinds of static and dynamic graphics, in the form of icons, flow charts and other diagrams have been used. The idea is that by providing such visual aids, the novice programmer can visualize, and thus learn to understand more easily, the various parts of the program.

One of the first software visualizations, which animated how various *algorithms* worked, was developed by Baecker (1981). He created a film, called *Sorting out Sorting*, which showed how nine different sorting algorithms manipulated their data. The video has been highly successful as a teaching aid and is still shown today in computer science classes. The first widely used software visualization system developed to illustrate *data* structures in action was BALSA (Brown and Sedgewick, 1984). The system works by highlighting the current contents of the data structures in the programming language Pascal. A software visualization system developed to facilitate the tracing and debugging of *code* on-line was the Transparent Prolog Machine (TPM) (Eisenstadt and Brayshaw, 1988). This works by allowing programmers to monitor the execution of their programs. The idea is that TPM can help the novice programmer to 'see' what is going on rather than having to infer what their program is doing.

The most effective kinds of software visualization provide high level abstractions that match the way the person thinks about problems (Eisenstadt *et al.*, 1992). Hence, instead of having to continually switch between conceptualizing the program at differing levels, the programmer can work at a high level of abstraction while debugging. This can greatly reduce the cognitive load. TPM is also discussed in Chapter 12.

Visual programming

Visual programming differs from software visualization in the sense that it *is* a graphical programming language rather than an animation of a program. Users program via selecting various graphical components, like icons, and compile them together. For example, one of the earlier visual programs, Pict/D (Glinert and Tanimoto, 1984), allowed users to create sequential flow charts from combining various iconic representations (see Figure 8.2). An advantage of this form of programming is that it can be easier for novice programmers to understand and generate programs, with little training (Myers, 1990) (see also Chapter 12).

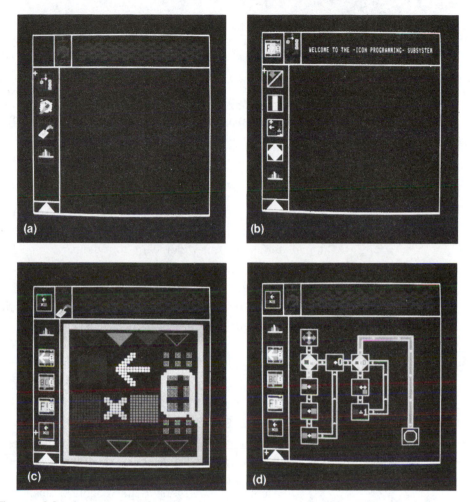

Figure 8.2 Example of a visual programming language, Pict/D (Glinert and Tanimoto, 1984; © 1984, IEEE). (a) The initial display screen with four main icons representing programming (flow chart), erasing (a hand holding an eraser), editing (a hand holding a pen) and a user library (a shelf of books). The library icon is selected and a new screen appears in (b), showing the elements in the library. The icon representing the last routine of a subprogram for natural number multiplication has been selected and shows up as enlarged on the editor's easel in (c); (d) shows the whole routine.

Intelligent tutoring systems

Another approach for helping the development of programming skills is intelligent tutoring systems (ITSs). These are computer systems that have been designed to tutor the student while they are developing a program and decide on what the student should learn given their current state of knowledge. One of the most advanced and successful tutors is Anderson's LISP tutor (Anderson *et al.*, 1984). The tutor has been developed to lead the complete novice by the hand through the first few hours of an extended LISP lesson. This is comprised of a set of problems that gradually increase in difficulty. The student works on each of the problems. Based on the student's input and its representation of the knowledge domain, the tutor works out whether the student has got the correct solution. If the student has, then the next problem is presented, and so on. If the student gets it wrong the tutor immediately responds by displaying an appropriate error message. Should the student attempt to veer from the in-built ordering of problems, then the tutor displays an immediate message of words to this effect.

The underlying theory behind the teaching methods used by the LISP tutor is to let the students know immediately when they have made a mistake. This philosophy is what is also advocated by Lewis and Norman (1986) for helping users learn in general how to use computer systems. Rather than let mistakes go undetected, the interventionalist approach focuses the students' attention on their mistakes immediately, so that they can learn from them.

Question 8.5

List the four main techniques that have been developed to facilitate the development of programming skills.

8.4 Collaborative and situated learning

Besides thinking about the individual learning of computer skills, it is important to consider the context in which learning takes place. Much learning that goes on in the 'real' world occurs through interacting and collaborating with others.

An alternative framework to the cognitive science view of conceptualizing learning – as the acquisition of knowledge structures – is to view it as **collaborative** and **situated learning**: collaborative in the sense that we learn together by observing and talking with each other, and situated in the sense that it always occurs in a context, which is forever changing.

Collaborative learning

The main advantage of collaborative learning is that it encourages co-learners to engage in social interactions, which can facilitate learning and conceptual change. The co-learners are able to articulate their ideas, ask each other questions and discuss and negotiate solutions. In doing so, more ways of viewing the problem can be gained than if the learners just follow a manual or training routine, by themselves. In addition, the presence of others, who are also struggling to learn, can be highly motivating.

Collaborative settings, in which a computer system is shared, can also facilitate children's learning. It is often the case that children need to justify, explain and expand their ideas to the others co-present. For example, if there is an input device that has to be shared, like a mouse, it can force the children to articulate their ideas and learn how to negotiate over the time-sharing of interacting with the computer system (Singer *et al.*, 1988). A disadvantage of collaborative learning, however, is that only one of the group of learners may actually benefit. In particular, if one of the members is very assertive and dominating, the other learners may take a passive role and let the dominant person do most of the work.

Situated learning

In many situations learning takes place through a form of apprenticeship, whereby novices learn a skill through a gradual process of interacting and watching experts and those more experienced than themselves perform (Lave and Wenger, 1991). The learners acquire a skill to perform through 'limited doing' under the watchful eye of the experts in the field. Lave and Wenger describe this as **legitimate peripheral participation**, in which novices learn how to take an increasing role in a practice. As novices become more experienced, they are allowed to take more responsibility for the work activities. When they become fully competent, they are acknowledged as full members of the community.

The community knowledge is maintained through various forms of social interaction. For example, technical engineers whose job it is to diagnose and repair photocopier machines often tell each other 'war' stories of their latest success in sorting out a copier problem (Orr, 1990). This form of technical gossiping enables the other technicians to file away the idiosyncratic knowledge in memory for future reference, which can then be accessed should they come across a similar problem.

More generally, the various types of people that constitute an organization – the secretaries, administrative staff, management and so on – are continually transmitting knowledge between each other. In many situations, they use each other as resources to obtain valuable information that enables them to carry out their work. In this sense, situated learning is continually taking place in work settings. The dynamic process of exchanging knowledge is particularly evident for tasks and work activities that have changed or are changing through becoming computerized.

When developing methods to facilitate the learning of computing systems, therefore, it is important to consider the social situation in which the system is to be used. In particular, the nature of the social interactions that facilitate learning within social and organizational settings is critical (see Chapters 9 and 10). Systems that support communication and social interaction will be more effective in enabling the various members of the community to continue to learn about the functions of the system than those designed to isolate individuals. Moreover, if systems are designed to encourage collaborative learning and working, it is highly likely that new users will feel less intimidated and find it much easier and more enjoyable to become competent users of the technology, as well as succeeding as masters of their own profession.

Question 8.6

What is the main difference between individual, collaborative and situated learning?

Key points

- Learning is an active process; we learn most naturally by doing and following examples.
- Active learning involves using analogies, making errors and trying to explain the system's behaviour.
- Active learning methods include minimalist instruction and encouraging novices to explore the interface by reducing the chance of making errors, through restricting the availability of advanced facilities.
- Experts have both *more* knowledge and *different kinds* of knowledge compared with novices.
- The learning of a skill consists of initially acquiring declarative knowledge and then procedural knowledge.
- Users with different levels of knowledge are likely to have different interface requirements.
- Learning to program can be facilitated by the use of minimalist instruction, software visualization, visual programming and intelligent tutoring systems.
- Learning takes place in a context; it can be collaborative and situated.

Further reading

Learning and skill acquisition

ANDERSON J.R. (1983). *The Architecture of Cognition*. Cambridge, MA: Harvard University Press.
  Anderson provides a detailed and historic description of his computational theory of how we acquire knowledge and learn cognitive skills.

Learning how to use computer systems

CARROLL J.M. (1990). *The Nurnberg Funnel*. Cambridge, MA: MIT Press.
  This book is a culmination of ten years of research on how people learn how to use new technology. An extensive number of empirical studies, together with theoretical discussions and practical implications for training strategies, are presented.

9

Social Aspects

Aims and objectives

The main aim of this chapter is to describe the communicative and interactive processes in which people engage when interacting with each other and with computer systems. After reading this chapter you should be able to:

- describe how our understanding of conversation has been used as the basis for a communication application,
- begin to compare the implications and principles derived from social and cognitive analyses of user behaviour,
- think about the problems of communication and interaction facing designers of CSCW systems.

Overview

Until recently, theoretical frameworks in HCI have been dominated by cognitive theories (see Chapter 3). It is becoming increasingly recognized, however, that the social aspects of HCI have been much neglected, a situation that needs to be redressed. Researchers from various backgrounds in social science are now studying the social aspects of human–computer interactions. This involves analysing how people communicate with each other and how they interact with the variety of artefacts that constitute their work environment.

A main assumption behind considering social aspects instead of or in conjunction with cognitive aspects is that since most work occurs in a social setting, computer systems that are designed on the basis of organizational and social knowledge will be more successful in supporting it (Grudin, 1990). Designing computer systems to support group working, therefore, may be more effective if different perspectives from those used for single-user interfaces are adopted. In addition, it has been argued that socially-oriented perspectives of HCI can be very informative in terms of accounting for the context in which computers are used, be they individual or multi-user. This chapter cannot do justice to the emergent field but instead introduces three of the main aspects of concern.

9.1 Analysing conversation

In contrast to modelling individual cognitive acts, social approaches aim to elucidate the invariant structures and patterns in the organization of people's interactions. Sociologists, linguists, anthropologists, philosophers and social psychologists have developed theoretical frameworks in which to study such patterns and structures. Of these, the language/action perspective has been the most influential in HCI.

The language/action approach

The **language/action approach** views language as a means by which people act (Winograd, 1988a). The approach is based on the theory of 'speech acts' derived from the philosophy of language (Austin, 1962; Searle, 1969). The basic premise is to assume that when we make an utterance we are performing an action. For example, when we make a request we are 'doing' an action. Likewise, in response to the speaker's utterance, the listener performs an action by either promising to do what was requested, declining the request or making a counter-offer (suggesting an alternative). Each of these acts leads to a new state which, in turn, presents options available to the listener. Having accepted to do something the listener will generally report that the request has been fulfilled. In turn, the first speaker can accept the report or reject it. If satisfied, the conversation is completed. Alternative strategies include withdrawing or cancelling the promise. Box 9.1 provides further details.

Box 9.1 **The model of conversation that forms the basis of the language/action approach**

Figure 9.1 represents the range of possible speech acts available in any conversation. The circles represent possible states in the conversation and the arrows represent the speech acts that can be taken by the initial speaker (A) or the hearer (B). The model characterizes the possible options available after the initial request as:

- the hearer can accept the conditions (promising to satisfy them),
- she can reject them,
- she can ask to renegotiate a change in the conditions requested (counter),
- the original speaker can withdraw his request or
- he can modify its conditions.

EXERCISE

Look at Figure 9.1 and flesh out the speech acts with imaginary conversations, for the 'dances' that go through the following states: 1-2-6-2-8 and 1-2-3-4-5.

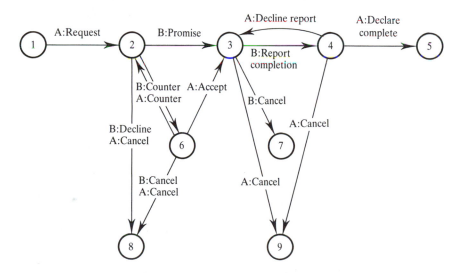

Figure 9.1 The basic conversation for action diagram (Winograd and Flores, 1986).

COMMENT

An example conversation for dance 1-2-6-2-8 might be: (1) Request: A asks 'can you switch on the light?' (2) Counter: B replies 'What for, it's a waste of energy?' (6, 2) Counter: A responds, 'Oh go on, just this time. My eyes are hurting and I can't read my book.' (8) Reject and withdraw: B replies 'No, you've been reading for far too long. You should go and do some exercise.' A turns her nose up at B. Conversation complete.

Using the same example, a dance for the sequence 1-2-3-4-5 might be: (1) Request: A asks 'can you switch on the light?' (2) Promise: B answers, 'Yes, sure, in a minute when I've finished this.' (3) Assert: B says, 'You see I've done it for you.' (4) Declare: A replies, 'Oh thanks very much, that was most kind of you.' (5) Conversation complete.

Winograd and Flores (1986) claim that an advantage of the model is its clarity and simplicity. The basic model can also be extended to show the temporal relations between speech acts and the linking of conversations. From an applied perspective, it has been used as a model for developing systems whose dialogue is in the form of explicit speech acts, in particular, the 'Coordinator' (Flores *et al.*, 1988), which is a computer-mediated communication system. The aim of developing this system was to facilitate more efficient interaction between people. Specifically, the Coordinator was designed to be a general-purpose communication application for use in sales, finance, general management and planning in organizations.

A problem with face-to-face conversations is that they are sometimes vague, resulting in misunderstandings and promises not being carried out. The Coordinator was designed to overcome this weakness in communication by making people aware of the nature of their transactions. In doing so, Flores *et al.* (1988) claim that people would be better at communicating with each other if the types of commitments that are made during conversations were made explicit to all parties involved. The Coordinator attempts to do this. It functions by providing the user with a menu of 'action' options whenever a request is made, as shown in Figure 9.2.

SPEAKING IN A CONVERSATION FOR ACTION

Acknowledge	Promise
Free-form	Counter-offer
Commit-to-commit	Decline
Interim-report	Report-completion

Figure 9.2 Screen menu for responding to request (Flores *et al.*, 1987, cited in Winograd, 1988b).

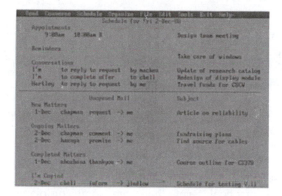

(a) The screen that faces me when I begin work for the day. Notice that my work is organized around the conversations in which I am currently engaged.

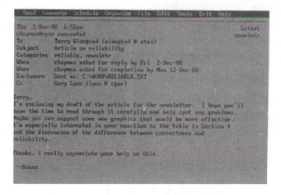

(b) A new message. Notice the expressed conversational action, in this case, "Chapman@cpsr requested ..." and explicit dates for completion or reply.

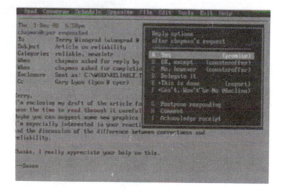

(c) The response menu. This contains the different kinds of responses I may select. Notice that they include promise, counteroffer, report, and decline responses.

Figure 9.3 Screen dumps from a typical interaction using the Coordinator (Winograd, 1988b).

The first three options in the right-hand column are the actions available to the responder so they can make a promise, a counter-offer or decline. The fourth choice – report completion – is an action available to the respondent after having made the initial response. The options in the left-hand column are concerned with the management of the conversation and do not advance the 'action' like the other options do. For example, 'acknowledge' lets the requester know that the message has been received, while 'free-form' allows conversations that do not fit into any of the categories, such as notes and questions. Figure 9.3 shows three screen interfaces of a typical interaction, from the default set up (Figure 9.3(a)), the receipt of a message from a requester (Figure 9.3(b)) and the menu of options available to the responder (Figure 9.3(c)).

The Coordinator, however, has received mixed reviews. At a theoretical level, there is little evidence of any empirical evaluation of the model to support the hypothesis that making speech acts explicit should make conversations more efficient. Most evaluations have been informal, varying in their response from outright hostility to the system to favourable usage (see Robinson, 1991, for a review). Organizations where the system has been found to work best are stable, hierarchical and authoritarian. Conversely, organizations that found the tool unnatural and restrictive were those where the norm was for conversation to be free-flowing and largely spontaneous.

At a practical level, there are some problems with the language/action approach. Extra effort and time is required to determine how to label an interaction. It can also be difficult to decide how to label a message, especially if it does not fit neatly into either the request or promise categories. From a designer's perspective, Rodden (1991) has also noted how even the diagrams required to represent the simplest of conversations are highly complex. Furthermore, the modelling of conversations in terms of actions between requester and responder is based on pairs of users rather than on more general patterns of interaction, involving a number of people.

Question 9.1

(a) *What are the main types of speech acts?*
(b) *In which organizations has the Coordinator proved to be (i) most and (ii) least effective?*

9.2 Group communication

Most of the analysis of conversation patterns has been based on two people communicating. While the knowledge gained from this approach can be informative for designing systems for single-user interactions it is inappropriate for applying to computer systems that mediate conversations involving more than two individuals. Formal meetings, informal gatherings and multi-party communications have different properties and coordination patterns from conversation pairs.

Hence, in relation to developing computer systems that support group communications it is necessary to identify the key aspects of multi-party communication with and without technology mediation. One main finding is that the extent to which we can understand and communicate with people varies considerably depending on the presence and type of media that is used. For example, in face-to-face meetings people can see each other, whereas they cannot do so when communicating through the use of various technological media such as multi-party telephone and computer conferencing. In the former, control and sequencing of conversation is facilitated through the use of non-verbal communication such as gaze, nodding, gesture and pointing, whereas in the latter such cues are not available (Clark and Brennan, 1991). This can lead to less optimal forms of communication and the potential for misunderstandings. Conversely, it can alleviate some of the social pressures of speaking in a group of people. For example, people who find it difficult to talk in face-to-face meetings can find a computer conferencing system less threatening.

Face-to-face, multi-party conversations

A main observation of face-to-face, multi-party conversations is that communication decreases in efficiency. One of the problems is that humans find it difficult to manage the increased amount of coordination that is required when multiple participants are involved. Instead of having to manage the turn-taking sequences with just one other person, participants in multi-party conversations are required to manage multi-turn-taking, openings, closings and so on. Within formal meetings **social protocols** have been established to enable participants to cope better. These include having a pre-set agenda, hand-raising to take a turn and having a chair to control the conversation. These kinds of formalized procedures impose a structure on the conversation, which can improve the efficiency of the multi-party communication (Novick and Walpole, 1990).

The problems of group communication can also be reduced depending on the type of communication network that is established in the group. In a classic social psychology study, Leavitt (1951) found that a 'wheel' arrangement (see Figure 9.4(b)), whereby communication was channelled through a central 'spoke' person, was the most efficient set-up. In the study, five people were seated around a table separated by wooden partitions. The partitions had slots in them to allow for written messages to be passed between the participants. The slots were closed or opened depending on the configuration in the group. Figure 9.4 shows two of the main configurations: the circle and the wheel. The circle allows each person to pass a message to his or her left or right, whereas the wheel only allows the four 'outside' people to pass messages to the central person. However, that person can send

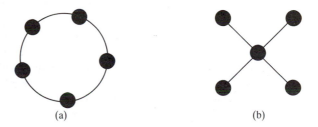

(a)   (b)

Figure 9.4   (a) Circle and (b) wheel communication networks.

messages to all the others. The task that was set was a problem solving one: each participant was given a card with various symbols on it and the group was required to find out which symbol they all had in common. The wheel group worked much faster and made fewer errors than the other set-ups.

The difference between the wheel and circle groups disappears, however, if the group is given sufficient time to organize itself (Guetzkow and Simon, 1955). This is because the more open network groups develop their own operating structure by selecting the one best suited to the problem rather than having an enforced structure imposed upon them.

Computer-mediated multi-party communication

Multi-party communication can be mediated by various forms of technology. Current systems include multi-party telephone conversations, computer conferencing, video conferencing, electronic mail and networked communication via on-line typed 'chat' and other asynchronous text-based talk tools. One of the main advantages of these systems is that they offer the potential for allowing communication for participants who are not able to be face-to-face, that is, they are not co-present. For example, if a company is geographically dispersed with one team in California and another in Paris it can be more convenient and more economic if the teams can meet in virtual rooms rather than travelling to one or other destination. (See also the interview with Marilyn Mantei at the end of Part II, in which she discusses some important issues in computer supported communication, and Chapter 16.) Another advantage for participants who *are* face-to-face, is that electronic meeting rooms can provide facilities to enhance group working, such as co-authoring and brainstorming tools, and in doing so, encourage both talking and 'doing' in the same meeting.

However, there are a number of disadvantages. Besides having initially to adapt to more 'unnatural' ways of communicating (for example, multi-party telephone calls can feel quite strange and inhibiting when first experienced) there are various obstacles and bottlenecks that prevent the free flow of computer-mediated group communication. One problem is the restrictive nature of having to converse via the interface language that the system affords; most computer networked systems currently have only text and graphic capabilities, so users are forced to talk to each other via their fingers.

For computer-mediated communication systems that include video images, such as video conferencing, the constraints imposed by the amount of information that can be sent across the telephone lines can mean that fewer images are shown per minute than are usually shown on TV, causing them to appear static and have shadows. A number of social psychological problems with using video communication have also been identified. These include a lack of mutual knowing. For example, even though one person may be able to see on their video screen all the other people in the other location, they might not be able to see that person on their screen. The person may be unaware that they are out of sight of the camera. Maintaining eye contact is also difficult, if not impossible, because in order to appear to be gazing at someone's eyes each person has to look directly at the camera, which is usually positioned above the monitor. When looking at the screen to see if the other person is looking at them, that person's gaze automatically changes to appear as if they are looking away.

Likewise, when making a gesture, like pointing or shaking one's head, it is done towards the appearance of the other people on the screen rather than directly at them. It is difficult for that person, therefore, to know how the other people perceive the gesture. Furthermore, the cameras may distort the gestures so that subtle movements may go unnoticed while more emphatic ones appear larger than life, filling up the screen (Heath and Luff, 1991a).

Another problem is coordinating control. In face-to-face meetings, gaze and head-turning are well established methods for keeping the floor, taking the floor, avoiding having to take the floor (ask a question and all eyes look to the floor) and to suggest who should speak next (when all heads turn towards one person). Such cues are largely eliminated in video communication and, moreover, it can often be the case that someone thinks he has made eye contact, and in doing so assumes he is signalling to that person to take over the conversation, but in actual fact he has not. Consequently, people find it more difficult to take control of the conversation in video communication (Sellen, 1992). New protocols, therefore, need to emerge for the computer-mediated communication technologies. For example, in computer supported meeting environments, the inclusion of a human facilitator or leader can greatly reduce control and coordination problems.

Question 9.2

(a) *What are the main differences in turn-taking between two-way and multi-party conversations?*

(b) *How can computer-mediated communication facilitate or hinder conversations?*

9.3   Group working in context

In addition to considering how computers can mediate communication, it is important to look at how they mediate group working. Very little is known, however, about the processes involved in coordinating work practices. Several researchers have, therefore, begun to carry out ethnographic and detailed observational studies of group working in the social and cultural settings in which they occur (Section 32.3 describes some techniques that are used in ethnography). A main aim of this research is to characterize the informal processes and properties that are critical to the success and adaptation of groups working together.

A general observation concerns the instrumental role played by cultural and technological artefacts in mediating group activities. For example, in a study of an airline operations room, Suchman and Trigg (1991) discuss the multiple roles played by both paper documents and on-line computer information displays in coordinating the work of the operators. Similarly, Bentley *et al.* (1992) note how air traffic controllers organize the paper strips, which have information about the planes they are controlling, to schedule their work tasks. Rogers (1993) also discusses the important communicative role played by a shared information display, in the form of a whiteboard, to coordinate the activities of a group of engineers working closely together.

Another finding is that groups are quite flexible at changing their division of labour to cope with unexpected situations. Hutchins (1991) notes how a ship's navigation team was able to restructure the group's activities in a systematic way when a piece of the navigational equipment failed. Similarly, in a study of a London Underground control room, Heath and Luff (1991b) found that when a crisis arose the controllers were able to manage the problems by developing the practice of overhearing each other's conversations in conjunction with overseeing each other's actions, while simultaneously engaged in distinct and apparently unrelated tasks.

These preliminary studies show the important role of informal working practices and shared artefacts in coordinating work activities. The findings are intended at this stage to act as pointers, highlighting problems and issues that need to be considered in the design and redesign of systems. As more studies are carried out, it may be possible to make further generalizations that are of direct relevance to system design.

The findings also have important bearing on issues surrounding the introduction of more automated systems and CSCW systems to support group working (see also Chapter 10). Replacing old technology with new can have dramatic effects on the social interactions and dynamics of the group. The question is how and whether it is possible to design systems that support change. If care is not taken to consider the informal practices of group working, detrimental effects on work productivity and employee well-being could result. Conversely, if the nature of the working practices that are undergoing change is taken into account in the design of new systems to support group working, then it is more likely that improved quality of work will ensue.

Key points

- Social aspects of HCI focus primarily on communicative and interactive processes.
- The language/action model is a 'social' approach that has been applied to the design of computer-mediated conversations for people interacting with other people.
- Group communication has different properties and processes than paired conversations.
- Computer-mediated communication is impoverished compared with face-to-face communication, and so new social protocols need to be established to compensate.
- Computer systems designed to support group working need to consider the importance of informal group working practices.

Further reading

Communication and interaction in relation to CSCW

There are a number of collections of papers that have been published on CSCW, covering a range of aspects. Two recent ones that include sections on computer- and video-mediated communication and group working are:

BAECKER R.M., ed. (1993). *Readings in Groupware and Computer Supported Cooperative Work*. San Mateo, CA: Morgan Kaufmann.

GREENBERG S., ed. (1991). *Computer-Supported Cooperative Work and Groupware*. London: Academic Press.

The Greenberg collection also includes a very good annotated bibliography of CSCW articles and books, together with a cross-referencing table of CSCW concepts.

10

Organizational Aspects

Aims and objectives

The aim of this chapter is to make you think about organizational issues in relation to HCI. After studying this chapter you should:

- know what the main organizational approaches are,
- understand how technology impacts organizations,
- be able to describe the advantages and disadvantages of the key methods that social scientists have proposed to improve the quality of work in organizations,
- be able to explain why it is important to consider organizational aspects in relation to HCI,
- know what the problems are of trying to incorporate this knowledge within HCI and system design.

Overview

The difference between the social aspects just discussed and the organizational aspects of HCI is not a clear division but is more a question of focus. Whereas the social analyses have tended to look at 'local' aspects of work, such as communication and coordination, in relation to HCI, approaches concerned with organizational issues have generally adopted a more 'global' framework in which to analyse the nature of work and society at large in relation to technology.

For computer systems to be useful they need to be integrated within an existing network of humans and other technological artefacts. If little or no attention is paid to the organizational structure, the working practices and the culture of the organization, then it is likely that the introduction of any new computing system will be used sub-optimally, or at worse discarded, as the poor success rate discussed in Chapter 1 shows. However, the study of organizations and how they change is complex. In this chapter, we provide an overview of the main approaches that have been influential and also introduce the alternative frameworks of ethno-methodology and activity theory.

10.1 The nature of organizations

Organizations come in all shapes and sizes. They are highly complex, ambiguous entities consisting of a multitude of interacting factors. These include:

- **The people in them** each having differing roles, expectations, motivations, and so on.
- **The technology used and created** each having different functions, histories, reliabilities, dependencies.
- **The work organization** the way the organization is structured, the work is allocated and the number and types of groups.
- **The organizational culture** often summarized as the 'way we do things around here', includes stories, myths, rituals, ways of behaving, codes of practice and ways of talking.

When coordinated, the various components and mechanisms enable the organization to perform efficiently and effectively, producing the desired outcome, be it a product, service or other commodity. However, when the parts become uncoordinated the organization becomes inefficient and unproductive. As described by Chandrasekaran (1981), an organization is a distributed system of subdivisions which 'when successful, mesh together in a miracle of purposefulness, but when the overall structure strays too far from the changing environment, it resembles a maladaptive dinosaur' (p. 3).

The issue is how to design and implement computer systems into an organization so that they have a positive effect. This requires understanding the dynamic and complex nature of organizations which are themselves part of an ever-changing environment.

The metaphorical perspective

One way of understanding how organizations work, is to conceptualize them in terms of metaphors (Morgan, 1986). As discussed in Chapter 7, metaphors provide a powerful means of understanding abstract, complex and unfamiliar domains. Used in the context of organizations, they can provide a useful framework in which to conceptualize the nature of the processes and structures of organizations. Metaphors that are commonly used are to consider the organization as a machine (see Section 10.3 on scientific management) and as an information processor (Cyert and March, 1963; Galbraith, 1974). Similar to the information processing model of cognition (see Chapter 3), the information processing metaphor characterizes organizations in terms of how information is processed and transmitted. For example, the introduction of new forms of communication such as electronic mail is analysed in terms of how they facilitate or hinder the flow of information in an organization.

With respect to future developments of organizational structures, several metaphorical notions have been proposed. The main ones are:

- **The paperless office**   where all information, be it newspapers, books, memos or other documents, is handled, manipulated, processed and read by people electronically.
- **The automated office**   where factories are operated by robots and remote controlled equipment.
- **The electronic cottage**   where people work from terminals at home.
- **The global village**   where the convergence of computing and telecommunications has brought about an interconnected worldwide society.

The participants' perspective

Another approach to characterizing organizations is to look at how the members of the organizations themselves interpret the structures and processes present in the organization in which they work. For example, Bowers and Middleton (1991) describe a conversation that occurs in a child development clinic, where a nursing sister and physiotherapist informally discuss a discrepancy in work practices that has arisen. The problem confronting them is deciding whether the 'private' or the 'team' way of doing things is best. Eventually the sister gives her opinion that the 'correct' way of doing things is the team way, which concurs with that of the physiotherapist and provides her with support for a previously uncertain position on which course of action to take. From the participants' perspective, the informal conversation is considered as creating a new **organizational form**. In other words, a previously disputed course of action has since become established as the correct way of doing something in the particular practice. In this sense, the organization is constructed in terms of the outcomes of informal discussions between the participants of the organization, rather than as attributes of a formal model constructed by researchers.

Question 10.1

What is an organization?

10.2 The impact of information technology on organizations

In addition to attempting to describe the different types of organizations and the various healthy/unhealthy states they can be in, social scientists and social commentators have been concerned with the impact of technology and more specifically, computerization, on organizations. At one level, there is general concern over whether computerization is revolutionizing society, while at another, there are those concerned with explaining the relationship between the introduction of technology and the way an organization changes (see Chapter 1). In both cases, there is a strong motivation to chart the various changes so that cause–effect relations can be identified, which would enable system designers and policy makers to predict the kinds of systems that will be most beneficial.

EXERCISE

Spend a couple of minutes writing down the advantages that you think computers have provided to people and organizations (some suggestions were made in Chapter 1). Then beside it write a second list of the various social, ethical and political problems that computerization has brought.

COMMENT

Both lists are endless. You might have included in the first list: reduction of monotonous jobs, the increase in flexibility and type of services (for example, 24-hour banking facilities), the ability to keep electronic records, increased productivity, reduced costs, safer systems, and global communication allowing instant access to vast information resources. For the other list, you might have included increase in unemployment, the development of hi-tech weapons and control systems, more alienation, infringements on privacy through increased data surveillance, greater reliance on fallible computer systems resulting in erroneous information being created (for example, unaccounted bills on your bank statement), and so on.

The question of how computers are changing our lives has fuelled a big debate. On the one hand, there are visionaries that believe that an information revolution is in our midst, whereby new opportunities, enabled by emerging technologies, such as hypermedia, artificial intelligence and virtual reality, will allow people to create and develop intellectually in innovative and exciting new ways (for example, Feigenbaum and McCorduck, 1983). On the other hand, there are the pessimists, who believe that undesirable, radical changes are occurring to society through the introduction of new technology. For example, Weizenbaum (1976) warns of the dangers of society's increasing reliance on computer systems to do more and more of its thinking and reasoning.

One of the major concerns has been the impact of technology upon jobs (see also Chapter 1). Again, two views have been most prominent (Eason, 1988):

(1)   Technical system as control – IT is deskilling, taking work from people and reducing the remainder to tedious and repetitive work.
(2)   Technical system as tool – IT is enriching, whereby the routine and boring jobs are allocated to the computers, which also provide tools to allow people to be creative and handle information in diverse and powerful ways

In relation to evaluating the impact of IT on jobs, organizational theorists have sought to identify the process by which benefits or problems evolve. Again, two main theoretical approaches have been identified: technological determinism and social action.

The **technological determinist** school of thought believes that technology is the single most important factor in determining the success of an organization (for example, Woodward, 1965). Investing in the latest technology is considered the only way to survive. Notions like 'automate or liquidate' and fear of being 'left behind' exemplify this view.

In contrast, the **social action** approach proposes that technology is enabling rather than deterministic. Moreover, it is the strategic choices, made by management, as to how technology is to be used that determine how the organization is structured (for example, Child, 1972). Hence, within an organization, changes are assumed to be caused by decisions made by managers, which can include adopting IT, but this is considered only as one resource of many.

In reality, it is likely to be the case that both technology and the decisions made in an organization bring about change. For example, in an extensive study of the introduction of computing systems into a large number of diverse industries in Scotland, Buchanan and Boddy (1983) found that both management goals and technological factors caused changes to the organization. Similarly, the impact on jobs will vary within any organization. Some will be deskilled, while others are enriched. Different conditions will produce different changes and interactions, making it impossible to predict the outcome of introducing new systems or organizational structures. Nevertheless, the desire to change organizations to increase productivity is all-pervasive within industrial societies. Methods have even been developed with this aim in mind. These range from adopting the 'system as control' framework and trying to get the maximum out of both machinery and workers, by reducing jobs to simple tasks, to the 'system as tool' framework, where the involvement of workers is encouraged as much as possible in deciding how to select and design new technology to match their work needs. Examples of both approaches are presented in Section 10.3.

10.3 Methods for organizational change

A number of different approaches have been proposed for changing organizations in order to improve them. The main goals have been either to attain greater efficiency or to enhance working conditions and support social needs.

Scientific management

Frederick Taylor (1911), an American engineer, pioneered **scientific management**. The underlying assumption was that work obeys scientific laws and can therefore be analysed using scientific methods. The organization was viewed as a rational system that should operate as efficiently as possible towards some goal, typically to maximize profit. Taylor proposed a set of simple, scientific principles for maximizing efficiency. These are summarized as:

(1) Separation of planning and working. All responsibility for the planning and design of work should be delegated to management. The implementation of these plans should be carried out by the workers.
(2) Choose the best person for the jobs that have been planned and designed.
(3) Determine how a task can be performed the most efficiently. To do this use scientific methods.
(4) Train the workers to perform the tasks in the manner outlined.
(5) Determine the best form of reward for the different tasks.
(6) Monitor worker performance to ensure that the prescribed methods are followed and the set goals achieved.

Taylor proposed that these principles could be applied through the use of **time and motion studies**. Essentially, this entailed carrying out detailed observational studies and taking precise measurements of the workers performing various tasks. The goal was to use the assessment to determine how the work could be decomposed into the optimal number of small tasks that could be done by one person for which there could be found one best method. Having collected such measures, it was assumed that time spent on a given task could be accurately predicted.

Taylor's influence on the management of work in organizations has been enormous. In particular, it has been responsible for increased productivity while dramatically replacing skilled crafts people with unskilled workers (Morgan, 1986). It has also been claimed that the scientific management perspective brought about major improvements in American business, making the Americans world leaders in manufacturing until the 1970s (Denning, 1991). Furthermore, during the past 40 years or so, many Americans have viewed scientific management as the best approach to running organizations. In place of time and motion studies, contemporary managers have developed ways of formalizing and assessing working activities through rule books, job descriptions, sets of procedures, checklists and in-depth personnel assessment schemes.

At the same time as being highly influential, Taylor's scientific management approach has been the most maligned and criticized. One of the major objections to his approach is that it assumes that workers are like machines, who will reliably and efficiently perform simple, repetitive jobs if motivated and rewarded sufficiently. In doing so it fails to recognize the human qualities of people, and as a consequence has the effect of dehumanizing and alienating the workforce. As a method of management, it has been argued that it is inflexible and unable to cope with rapid change, unexpected developments and competition.

Scientific management, therefore, can be effective where work can be mechanized and the people working accept the separation of the 'thinking' management and the 'doing' workforce. However, in work organizations where the nature of work is changing, concomitantly with the installation of emerging technologies, the method seems most inappropriate. An approach is needed that optimizes both the technology and the workforce. The sociotechnical systems approach attempts to achieve this.

Question 10.2

(a) Why has the scientific management approach been so influential?
(b) What are the main problems with the approach?

Sociotechnical systems approach

The notion of a **sociotechnical** system was developed initially at the Tavistock Institute of Human Relations to show how the social and technical subsystems of an organization interact with each other. The design of a technical system (be it a computer system or style of management) always has effects on the human aspects and vice versa. A study carried out by Trist and Bamforth (1951), from the Tavistock Institute, on mechanization in coal mines clearly demonstrated this relation. The problem identified was that the organizational changes that were brought about considerably upset the existing practices. Prior to mechanization, the miners had worked in small independent units (typically pairs), deciding for themselves who they worked with and setting their own goals and pace of working. Post-mechanization, these working practices were replaced with the 'longwall' method, in which the small groups were reorganized into much larger groups with less autonomy over how to organize their work. Furthermore, the tasks were fractionized, making it much more difficult for the miners to maintain good working relationships.

The sociotechnical approach came about through a growing awareness of the need to match technical and social systems in the most appropriate way. A number of principles have been outlined. For example, Cherns (1986) proposed that work groups should be largely autonomous, possessing the necessary equipment and computers to allow a part of the work activity to be completed by one group. In contrast to the scientific management approach, the autonomous work group should have responsibility for its work, sharing among itself much of the decision making concerned with the planning and execution of the work. In this context, the managers and supervisors would be seen more as coordinators that provide the resources. In order to enable the individual workers within the autonomous groups to participate in the decision making a set of design principles were outlined. These are summarized in Box 10.1.

Box 10.1 The sociotechnical design principles aimed at achieving autonomous group working

Step 1. Initial scanning briefing

Describe the main characteristics of the production system and its environment. Determine where the problems lie and where the emphasis of the analysis needs to be placed. The description of the existing system should cover – the geographical layout of the production system, the existing organizational structure, the main inputs and outputs, the main transformations and variances, the objectives of the system, both production and social.[†]

Step 2. Identification of unit operations

Identify the main phases in the production process which convert materials into products. Each unit operation will be relatively self contained and will effect some transformation of the raw material.

Step 3. Identification of variances

Identify all variances and note key variances. Key variances are those that significantly affect the ability of the production system to pursue its objectives. A variance is considered key if it affects the quantity or quality of production, or operating or social costs.

Step 4. Analysis of the social system

Identify the main characteristics of the existing social system. This requires the following:

(i)   a brief review of the organizational structure

[†]   A variance is a potential problem area – a weak part of the system where deviation from some desired or expected norm can occur.

(ii)   a table of variance control, noting:
- where the variance occurs
- where it is observed
- where it is controlled
- by whom
- what tasks are performed to control it
- what information is needed for control

(iii)   a note of ancillary activities unconnected with the control of variances
(iv)   a description of the relationships between workers (over time or in geographical space)
(v)   a note on flexibility (the extent to which workers share a knowledge of each other's roles)
(vi)   a description of pay relationships
(vii)   a description of the workers' psychological needs.

Step 5. Workers' perception of their roles

An assessment of the extent to which the workers believe that their roles meet psychological needs.

Step 6. The maintenance system

An assessment of the extent to which this impacts on, and affects, the production system.

Step 7. The supply and user systems

A description of the way in which these environmental systems impact on the production system.

Step 8. The corporate environment and development plans

An assessment of the extent to which these affect the production system's ability to achieve its objectives.

Step 9. Proposals for change

Finally, all the hypotheses and proposals considered during the process of analysis must be gathered together, considered and turned into an action programme. Proposals for action must contribute to both the production and the social objectives of the system.

(*Source*   Mumford, 1987.)

One of the problems with the sociotechnical systems approach is that it has been difficult to put into practice. In particular, the sociotechnical principles have proved very difficult to operationalize and apply by designers (Blacker and Brown, 1986). A further criticism is that the approach has failed to address the technical systems aspects adequately; in particular there was never any advice on how to design new technology (Blacker and Brown, 1986; Mumford, 1987). An extensive review by Pasmore *et al.* (1982) found that the most typical solution that was initiated in over a hundred sociotechnical studies was the introduction of autonomous working groups. Only 16% of the studies accomplished any technological changes.

It would seem, therefore, that the sociotechnical approach has tended to focus heavily on the 'socio' aspects, taking the technology as a 'given' around which work is reorganized (Clegg and Symon, 1989). However, more recently, there have been some attempts to rectify the various weaknesses of the sociotechnical approach by developing more practical methods and considering the design of the technological aspects more. For example, Eason and Harker's **open systems task analysis** (cited in Eason, 1988) has been geared more towards the analysis of the user and task requirements of sociotechnical systems. A set of detailed principles of system design is also provided. The intention is to provide a more detailed analysis of the overall sociotechnical system that will be most affected by the proposed change (see Section 18.2 for more on these and other methods that have evolved within the sociotechnical tradition).

In Scandinavia there have also been various developments, such as the **collective resource approach**, which focuses more on how to involve the trade unions in the decision making activities of the workforce and the design of new technology (Ehn and Kyng, 1987). The emphasis, therefore, is on more participation by the workers, rather than just social scientists doing the analysis and research. This idea of user involvement has since become very popular in mainstream HCI thinking (see Chapters 2, 17 and 18).

Activity theory

An evolving theoretical framework, which is used to inform the analysis and implementation of systems that are used in the workplace, is **activity theory**. Originating from ideas developed in the former Soviet Union (Marx, Engels, Vygotsky, Leont'ev and Luria) it has since been developed as a method to analyse user interfaces (Bødker, 1991) and CSCW systems (Kuutti, 1991).

The basic tenet of activity theory is human (work) activity. Activity is driven by various needs, in which people want to achieve a certain purpose (or goal). The activity is usually mediated by one or more tools or artefacts (for example, hammers, pens, computer systems, telephones, language). Work activities are carried out by a community of people in a praxis (for example, banking, architecture, software design, teaching). The design and usefulness of artefacts is viewed in terms of the way they are used in the praxis. Importantly, artefacts are used in a work activity and

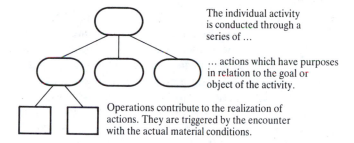

The individual activity is conducted through a series of ...

... actions which have purposes in relation to the goal or object of the activity.

Operations contribute to the realization of actions. They are triggered by the encounter with the actual material conditions.

Figure 10.1 The relationship between individual human activity, actions and operations (Bødker, 1991).

also are products of an activity. As such they are viewed as continuously in a state of flux. The significance of this conceptualization is that artefacts need to be studied in terms of how they mediate group activities rather than as objects that are acted upon by individual users. Hence, studying word processing should be in terms of how word processors are used in a particular practice, for example, as secretaries use them (Bannon and Bødker, 1991).

A core conceptual distinction that is made is between activities, actions and operations:

- **Activities** refers to the collective venture of various groups (for example, the production of engineering plans using a networked CAD system).
- **Actions** refers to the conscious acts of an individual in view of specific intentions (for example, the placing of a symbol of a drain on a drawing plan).
- **Operations** are the individual's means of realizing an action that are carried out relatively unconsciously (for example, the selection of a drain element from a CAD library).

The distinction between the different levels is illustrated in Figure 10.1. Ideally, artefacts (including computer systems) should be designed to allow users to direct their operations towards the artefact in order to proceed with their work smoothly. They should not have to perform operations at a conscious level, as it is assumed that this will detract from the action at hand.

A common starting point for an activity theory analysis is from a company or organization's recognition that there is a need for change. This might be a manager of a hospital or process control plant wanting to automate a particular processor or wanting to improve a procedure by introducing a new computer application. With this in mind, activity theory analysts seek to identify 'breakdowns' and 'contradictions' present at the level of the work activity, that are preventing the organization from utilizing existing technology effectively.

Breakdowns occur when there is a conflict between what is assumed to happen and what actually happens. (See also p. 71 on the use of breakdowns in the distributed cognition approach.) For example, a group of users who have been taught to issue a set of commands for printing files on a printer find that the commands do not always work. There is a discrepancy between what they assume should happen when issuing the commands and what actually happens. **Contradictions** occur when vicious circles develop that prevent the workers from breaking out of inefficient and undesirable situations that have developed in a community practice. For example, in hospitals contradictions can arise when there is pressure on doctors to give speedy consultations while at the same time there is a demand by patients for quality care (Cole and Engeström, 1993).

To resolve breakdowns and contradictions, activity theory proposes that the users and practitioners themselves need to understand the nature of the conflict and work out a way of overcoming it. To do this requires thinking about the object of the activity. In turn, the activity needs to be considered in terms of the work relations in the praxis, for example, why is there pressure on doctors to give speedy consultations at the expense of the patients' care? By reflecting and articulating the conditions of the problematic activity and actions, the users and practitioners can reconceptualize the object of their work.

Ethnomethodology

Ethnomethodology is a sociological approach that has been used recently to study how new technologies have been introduced into various work settings. In ethnomethodological terms, the interest is in 'the details of the work of technology as a social achievement and in the social practices through which participants recognizably and accountably orientate themselves to the technology in the course of its design, construction, development, and use, and in talking and writing about it' (Button, 1993, p. 1).

A main issue under consideration is how well new technologies, ranging from computer systems to video links, support existing working practices, and the nature of the mismatches that arise. For example, a study of how video and audio links have been introduced into an office environment showed that the new form of communication severely disrupted the 'normal' communicative practices of the administrative staff in the building (Heath and Luff, 1993). Other ethnomethodological studies have also shown how lack of concern with the way new technology has been introduced into the workplace has resulted in various disruptions. A problem that this highlights is that organizations may think twice about introducing any further new technology on the grounds that 'once bitten twice shy' (Button, 1993). Clearly, this is an undesirable situation since it is very likely that benefits would ensue if only the technology was designed and implemented to support the work practices in the first place. Although, in general, ethnomethodology has not been directly concerned with design practice and implementation issues, it may prove particularly valuable in the development and introduction of systems concerned with supporting group working, that is, CSCW.

10.4 | CSCW and organizational considerations

In Section 10.3 the instrumental role of informal working practices and shared technologies in mediating group working was outlined. Fish *et al.* (1990) have also compared informal communicative processes with formal ones (see Figure 10.2). Significantly, they point out that informal conversations, held in corridors and around coffee machines, were often more effective than formal ones. Another aspect of organizational structure that needs to be considered in relation to the use of CSCW systems is the relative contributions and benefits each member of the organization obtains from the groupware. Ideally, everyone should benefit but the reality of current CSCW systems is quite different. For example, managers may benefit more from the introduction of multi-user computer systems than the users of it, because the users are required to do extra work that they would not have done otherwise (Grudin, 1988). For example, consider how an automatic meeting schedule, designed to be used by all the organization, might work. To schedule a meeting requires someone to send a message to a distribution list to check each person's calendar on the list, in order to find a time convenient for all, which requires everyone to update their electronic calendar. However, this requires extra effort by everyone. The manager benefits most because she will request most of the meetings and also have a secretary to do the additional work of maintaining her calendar. It is little wonder that this application has not been liked except by managers.

On the other hand, if CSCW systems are designed to take into account how the additional workload and benefits are to be shared, then it is possible for it to be seen as a means by which to share power. Crowston and Malone (1988), for example, suggest that a networked computer system can lead to greater data sharing, which can equalize the share of power between individuals. The redistribution of power can lead to more coordination within the organization, which, in turn, leads to improved performance. Being aware of the nature of these disparities is important for the design and introduction of distributed systems. Detailed analyses are needed of how people work together in organizations in relation to how CSCW applications are actually going to be used. In the interview with Marilyn Mantei the behaviour of people in meetings is discussed in relation to design issues in computer supported cooperative meetings. CSCW is also discussed in Chapter 16.

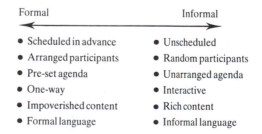

Figure 10.2 The informal and formal dimensions of communication (Fish *et al.*, 1990: © 1990, Association for Computing Machinery, Inc. reprinted by permission).

Key points

- Organizations are complex, dynamic entities, consisting of a multitude of interdependent factors.
- The impact of technology on society and organizations has been both positive and negative; on the one hand, it has resulted in deskilling and increased control over workers, and on the other, it has provided tools for enriching work.
- A well-known method developed to improve the efficiency of organizations is scientific management.
- The sociotechnical approach attempts to match the needs of both the social and technical systems when reorganizing work.
- Activity theory focuses on the activities, actions and operations that occur in the workplace and encourages the workers to resolve any breakdowns that emerge in their work practices.
- Ethnomethodology is a sociological approach that considers how well new technologies support existing working practices.
- It is important that organizational issues, such as the distribution of work and who benefits from the introduction of new technology, are taken into account in the design and implementation of CSCW systems. Otherwise, disparities can arise, resulting in systems not being used and maintained effectively.

Further reading

Models of organizations

MORGAN G. (1986). *Images of Organizations* Newbury Park, CA: Sage.

This is an excellent introduction to the analysis of organizations. It adopts a multi-perspective approach, elucidating the complexity of organizations through the use of a number of different metaphors.

Technological change and work

BUTTON G., ed. (1993). *Technology in Working Order: Studies of Work, Interaction and Technology*. London: Routledge.

This volume brings together a body of sociological research that addresses the problem of introducing new technology into a variety of work settings, including air traffic control and the police. It is recommended for those who have a background in sociology and are interested in knowing more about ethnomethodology and work studies.

DUNLOP C. and KLING R., eds (1991). *Computerization and Controversy*. San Diego: Academic Press.

This is a collection of 'classic' papers on the effects of computers on society. Topics covered include computerization and the transformation of work, economic and organizational aspects, the visionaries versus sceptics debate, social control, privacy, security and reliability.

EASON K.D. (1988). *Information Technology and Organisational Change*. London: Taylor & Francis.

This is a comprehensive and practical guide on how best to harness and use IT in organizations. Its approach is both user-centred and sociotechnical. A number of concepts, methods and tools are described for introducing technology into organizations.

Business applications of computing

It has not been possible to cover the business perspective of organizations. However, for those interested we recommend the following two books.

HIRSCHHEIM R.A. (1985). *Office Automation: A Social and Organizational Perspective*. Chichester: John Wiley.

This book explores the social and organizational implications of office automation and provides a comprehensive classification of the many techniques available for analysing business functions, designing appropriate technical systems and implementing change.

WALTON R.E. (1989). *Up and Running: Integrating Information Technology and the Organization*. Boston, MA: Harvard Business School Press.

Drawing on nineteen case studies in which organizations have made strategic implementations of information technology, this book concludes that successful use of the technology depends upon integration, involvement and competence. The central theme is the need to integrate technical development and organizational change in pursuit of organizational goals. The methods by which it is done involve user participation at all stages to gain the commitment of future users and to develop their competence to work effectively in the new work environment.

CSCW and organizational concerns

BAECKER R.M. (1993). *Readings in Groupware and Computer-Supported Cooperative Work*. San Mateo, CA: Morgan Kaufmann.

This was recommended in the previous chapter. There is a whole section on human behaviour in groups and organizations, together with chapters on the current adoption, deployment and use of groupware.

GALEGHER J., KRAUT R.E. and EGIDO C., eds (1990). *Intellectual Teamwork: Social and Technical Bases of Collaborative Work*. Hillsdale, NJ: Lawrence Erlbaum Associates.
This is a diverse collection of papers that address the question of how the new technologies (for example, electronic mail, computer conferencing, hypermedia) can be employed to overcome the problems of communication and coordination in collaborative work.

INTERVIEW WITH **MARILYN MANTEI**

Marilyn Mantei is associate professor of computer science and of library and information science at the University of Toronto. Marilyn headed the CAVECAT project, a 3-year video desktop conferencing research initiative, and she is currently co-investigator on the Telepresence Project, to develop communication technology for tomorrow's workplace. In this interview Marilyn discusses issues of concern for the design of computer supported cooperative work (CSCW) systems.

What are the key issues in CSCW research?

One of the biggest ones is 'what shall we do?' We know from using electronic mail that computers can facilitate communication. But who invented electronic mail? Is there a name? Did somebody create it? Do we invite this person to be a plenary speaker at conferences? We don't know who it is because electronic mail was a grassroots phenomenon. Many people all over the world created electronic mail, and they did it when we started connecting computers. People in different cities would agree that 'this is a file that you can read' and they just put them in the same place in the database. Then people said: 'this is clumsy so let's build a mail system'. Then they said: 'this mail system is awkward so let's build a better one'. This gave the sense that computers can do a lot more because after all, they're just moving information around and when people communicate what they're trying to do is to move information back and forth between themselves. Now we can get computers to move all sorts of information, for example, we can

digitize video images of people and we can ship them back and forth. We can use computers to create a sense of presence with each other even though people are some distance away.

Might CSCW make managers feel that their power is reduced?

Well I've certainly seen it in face-to-face meeting rooms supported by computers. The 'power seat' is a place where people sit that gives them a fair amount of control over the meeting. There are a couple of reasons for this. One is that they face the other people in the meeting; they tend to have the most obvious position in the meeting. They just

look stronger because of where they're sitting. Second, they control the communication. They sit near an easel or a board so that they control who goes up there, often it's them themselves or if somebody else is there, they're right next to that person. They also control the access to the meeting. They sit facing the door so they can see whoever enters. There is a lot of power in a seat that's sitting close to the front of the room, facing the rest of the people at the table, facing the door and sitting close to the place where people write. People who don't sit in those positions can take power in other ways by drawing attention to themselves. For example, you may see managers who aren't in that seat roll their seat back so everybody is forced to turn their seats, including the people sitting next to them and face them when they start to talk.

A lot of people believe that CSCW systems are somehow going to make meetings equal and they're going to take away some of the problems of people dominating meetings, but those structures are there for other reasons. They developed as a result of a need and CSCW should not take them away. If people within the group want those things to go away, they should manage them away and there should be a consensus in the group.

There are a variety of different kinds of meetings. Sometimes one person is powerful in one meeting, but does not take power in another. And one of the reasons it's so easy to do this is because we've developed all sorts of non-verbal signalling as social cues for passing power back and forth. It is hard to achieve this with a computer in a way that is as quick, accurate and as recognizable as the ways we have developed since being children.

What other aspects of CSCW are being studied?

We've been talking mostly about CSCW as a meeting environment and CSCW is a lot more than that. A lot of hypertext systems are considered as CSCW systems. Studies in anthropology which are concerned with how people culturally handle meetings and handle communication are also part of it. There's even an AI component where people have intelligent agents that pass messages back and forth and help with the meeting. I'm only working on face-to-face communication, but there are long distance meeting environments. The idea is to bring people together as working groups but not necessarily just in formal meetings. Serendipitous meetings where people happen to see each other and decide to talk are also important. Researchers and developers are trying to understand and support all these kinds of communication.

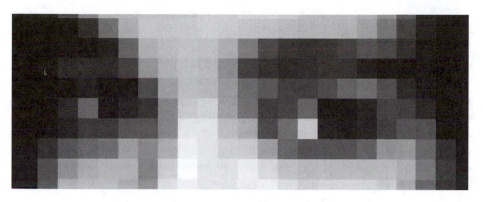

HUMANS AND TECHNOLOGY: TECHNOLOGY

Many kinds of work are now supported by interactive computer systems that either automate tasks or aid people in carrying them out. In some cases, like process control, the computer has largely automated the tasks, while in others, like document creation by word processing, it has introduced more flexibility or power. The computer can change the nature of human work from complex to routine and vice versa. When designing a computer system, it is important, therefore, to take into account both how the work is currently carried out and how the resulting system will change it. Characteristics that need to be considered include:

- to what extent tasks vary from one occasion to the next,
- whether the tasks will be carried out regularly, infrequently or only once,
- what kinds of skills and knowledge are required to perform tasks,
- how much the work is affected by changes in the environment,
- whether time is critical for the work,
- whether there are safety hazards,
- whether the user will do the work alone or with others,
- whether the user will normally be switching between several tasks.

Repetitive tasks in particular may require simple and straightforward methods of input, such as pressing only one or two keys. Long messages about how users should input data will not be needed and, in fact, would be very annoying. More 'open-ended' work such as document creation will require a flexible system with good help facilities, which can assist any user who may not have carried out a particular task or operation for some time. In cases where users are required to carry out several tasks simultaneously and safely, as occurs in air traffic control work, they will need carefully designed screen displays that take account of the cognitive issues mentioned in Part II, such as memory load, focusing attention and so on.

It is important to have a good understanding of human *psychological* processes to ensure that systems are designed to match users' capabilities. Similarly, it is important to consider human *physiological* capabilities. Individual differences concerned with gender, age, culture, educational background and physical abilities and disabilities also need to be accommodated by designers. One way of overcoming the problem of individual differences is to develop specialized interfaces such as electronic braille keyboards for visually impaired people. Experience also needs to be taken into account. For example, trained typists who use word processing for a limited range of document preparation tasks will have different requirements to authors who type with two fingers but explore and employ a much wider range of the system's functions. Learners having no knowledge of a system will need to know how to get started. Carefully designed documentation and good tuition can alleviate many of the problems of the novice. As users become more experienced, however, their requirements from the system will differ.

The general aim of Part III is to introduce you to a range of input and output devices and interaction styles in the first three chapters and then to look at some higher level system design issues, taking a primarily techno-logical perspective, in the last three chapters. After working through Part III you should:

- know about a range of different devices and interaction styles and how they can be selected to meet the needs of users, their work and work environments,
- be aware of the kinds of technical trade-offs that occur in system design,
- have the confidence to make some of your own technical judgements.

In the last three chapters we consider more composite system design issues that involve technological choices and trade-offs. The first of these deals with designing windowing systems in shared systems. The next is concerned with user support, on-line information and the design of hypermedia training modules. The last chapter considers some design issues in CSCW and virtual reality systems. Taking a technological perspective does not imply that cognitive issues are unimportant, and in Chapter 13 we consider direct manipulation from a cognitive point of view as well as a technological one and also look in more detail at the cognitive issues underlying affordances. There are also interviews with two well-known experts in the field. Ben Shneiderman talks about how he characterized the concept of direct manipulation and about the role of visualization in various applications. Roy Kalawsky, a scientist from British Aerospace, talks about virtual reality and its role in training pilots. You may also be interested to compare the views of these two experts towards virtual reality immersion systems.

INTERVIEW WITH **BEN SHNEIDERMAN**

Ben Shneiderman is a professor in the Department of Computer Science, Head of the Human–Computer Interaction Laboratory, and member of the Institute for Systems Research, all at the University of Maryland at College Park. His technical interests include user interface design, information visualization and applying educational technology. Ben is author of several books including *Designing the User Interface: Strategies for Effective Human–Computer Interaction* (1992). In this interview Ben recalls his early ideas about direct manipulation and then discusses his recent work on visualization.

I'd like to talk to you about direct manipulation, Ben. You coined the term some years ago. What does it mean and how is it being applied in modern systems?

Around 1980 I began listening carefully to users who were enthusiastic about their systems. These systems were very different from the ones that most of us were thinking about; they included video games, air traffic control systems and the new WYSIWYG editors (What You See Is What You Get). Some educational games also captured the imagination of the users.

In trying to understand the commonalities across these diverse interfaces, I began to notice a certain pattern. The first was a visual representation of the world of action. The objects of interest and the actions of interest were shown on the screen, so for example, you could see a cursor in a word processor and if you pressed backspace, the previous character would be deleted. This was in stark contrast to the earlier systems where you had to type a command like 'change/old string/new string/' and then issue another command to see the results. These new systems showed the objects of interest, and when actions were taken the results were also shown immediately and continuously on the screen. A second set of principles that also seemed important were that the actions were rapidly executed, incrementally described and reversible. Furthermore, in direct manipulation systems, pointing, selecting and dragging replace the need to type commands. For example, you could drag an icon towards a folder or you could bring it back.

These principles seemed to be important, and as I looked at other successful technologies, such as automobiles, I found confirmation. In an automobile, for instance, you see the world of action in front of you and you can turn the wheel slightly to the left and adjust it if you wish, and you continuously have feedback about where you're going. Imagine trying to drive a car by typing 'left 37 degrees' and then issuing a command to find out where you are, and waiting for the screen to repaint, and then having to type 'undo' or some other operation. I tried to characterize these principles in an article that was first published in the *IEEE Computer*, 1983. I think my contribution was to enable others to more rapidly discover these principles and apply them. During the past decade, to my pleasure, we've seen the emergence and the refinement of many systems, including graphical user interfaces, which embody successful application of these principles.

Let me clarify one point, it's not that a system is direct or not direct; there are degrees of directness. There are no specific metrics; directness is a guiding principle that designers have to interpret in terms of the application domain, the users and their tasks. I think we'll find that as the technology improves to give higher resolution and more rapid displays, there will be many more ways to apply these principles.

I feel that direct manipulation systems are a grand success because they engage our strong skills of perceptual recognition. Our eyes provide us with enormous amounts of information and they are a very effective way of understanding and learning about the world. For me the computer is appropriately a visual delivery machine. Mega-pixel displays can show a great deal of information. We humans can recognize patterns in remarkable ways which we have not yet been able to reproduce in machines, so it seems to me that the natural mechanism for humans to operate machines is by having a visual display and then pointing and selecting.

I think that the future of computing will be more like flight simulators or video games; users will fly through, swim through, drive through, large amounts of information, be able to select and filter information, combine components and create meaningful results. Although we have great discussions about the speed of chips and parallel processing, we still need hardware parallelism at the front end; maybe one CPU per pixel would be a goal for the future, so that we could have rapid visual displays that can be animated and flown through. For example, if I show a globe of the earth on the screen, there is no computer today that will allow me to zoom in on one part of the globe and get a close-up view of that country and then go into a particular city, and into a particular building. The systems that have attempted such things do it by jumps, and I want a smooth and continuous view.

How do these sorts of ideas relate to virtual reality immersion systems?

Virtual reality (VR) is a lively new direction for those who seek the immersion experience, where they block the real world out by having goggles on their heads. There'll be some interesting applications in entertainment, architectural walkthroughs and other applications. But I find VR a replay of a frequent theme in the emergence of technology. For example, in 1905 the Victorian stereographs provided 3D images and goggles to block the world and keep users immersed as best as possible. In the 1950s Cinerama was invented. Then, in the 1960s there was the phenomenon of the total immersion experience – the 'be-in'. There are times when that is enjoyable and maybe even useful but I think higher resolution 'look at', where several people can look at, talk and see each other's expressions and reactions, is more important when we're looking at art objects in a museum, or when physicians discuss an X-ray, or when computer scientists look at a screen display or demo. The importance of the human connection is strong and the desire to 'look at' is strong. I think you'll find that even many developers of virtual reality systems use a high resolution display that they point at, rather than wearing the head garments.

What I am interested in is 'visual reality', which maybe sounds more practical and that's my intention. We talk about 'visualizing reality' and 'realizing virtuosity'. The point is to support experts, virtuosos, in doing the jobs that they have to do. There may be times where 'flying through' is appropriate, but I think we'll find there are more situations where

'looking at' objects will be more acceptable. Let me add a little spice to this. Our efforts in information visualization have focused on trying to enable people to see relationships and patterns in complex information. For example, a common problem we face, and so do many people, is that the hard disk on a computer fills up. In our laboratory we have an 80 megabyte disk with 14 users, 3200 files and 300 folders, and we couldn't even tell who was using the largest fraction, or if there were unneeded applications, somewhere three or four levels deep. There were no tools available for us to explore that space in any orderly way, which led me to try to make a visual representation of the information hierarchy, so that I could find the space hogs. I managed to get a space filling representation, a sort of tiled mosaic approach, which enabled me, in one glance, to see all 3200 files. So the tree-map idea was generated by that particular practical situation, and it shows nested rectangles where the area of each rectangle is proportional to the number of bytes occupied by the file as shown in Figure 1.

The application that we built on the Macintosh enables us to see three or four thousand files pretty conveniently on a display, and pointing at any one of them produces a dialogue box that gives the full information about that file. As we do this, we invariably find duplicate files and duplicate folders on people's systems. I think of it as X-ray vision into this hierarchy! Of course, directories on a hard disk are only one example of hierarchies. We have also used this idea with people at General Electric to study sales information. It enables them to study the relative profit and loss, and sales, of hundreds of products at a time. Currently we are applying this concept to a stock market portfolio

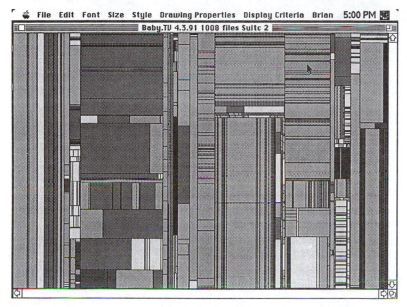

Figure 1 Tree-map screen snapshot with 1000 files. See colour plate 10.

browser, so that you can see thousands of holdings at once.

So what you're capitalizing on is the fact that hierarchical tree structures are very common and can provide a visualization tool to help people.

Exactly! We're also capitalizing on the remarkable human skill to see patterns. It would be hard to write a computer program to find 'interesting' patterns but you can see them right away. So these tree-maps are, as you point out, good because hierarchies are often used to represent information, and also because human perceptual skills are so great.

Tree Viz is distributed for a small fee by the Office of Technology Liaison at the University of Maryland, 4312 Knox Road College Park, MD20742 (phone: (301) 405 4210).

Photograph of Ben Shneiderman © Nick Wass.

11

Input

Aims and objectives

The aim of this chapter is to introduce you to various kinds of input devices and discuss some of the factors that need to be considered when selecting an input device. After studying this chapter you should be able to:

- discuss the properties of different input devices in relation to different design needs,
- apply your understanding of user, work and environment characteristics to select appropriate input devices and techniques,
- envision the design impacts of emerging input technologies.

Overview

Environmental conditions, safety hazards, the variation in tasks and their relationship to other work all have to be taken into account when selecting devices in system design. Similarly, you also need to consider variation in user characteristics. For example, users can vary in knowledge, skills, abilities or disabilities and experience, as well as in more subtle characteristics like culture and gender. Knowing the scope of different kinds of devices is important too, because ultimately you have to match the technology with the user and work needs, not forgetting the work environment.

11.1 Input devices

Input is concerned with recording and entering data into the computer system and issuing instructions to the computer. In order to interact with computer systems effectively, users must be able to communicate their intentions in such a way that the machine can interpret them. Therefore, we can define an input device as: a device that, together with appropriate software, transforms information from the user into data that a computer application can process.

One of the key aims in selecting an input device and deciding how it will be used to control events in the system is to help users to carry out their work safely, effectively, efficiently and, if possible, to also make it enjoyable. The choice of input device should contribute as positively as possible to the usability of the system. In general, the most appropriate input device will be the one that:

- matches the physiological and psychological characteristics of users, their training and their expertise. For example, older adults may be hampered by conditions such as arthritis and may be unable to type; inexperienced users may be unfamiliar with keyboard layout.
- is appropriate for the tasks that are to be performed. For example, a drawing task requires an input device that allows continuous movement; selecting an option from a list requires an input device that permits discrete movement.
- is suitable for the intended work and environment. For example, speech input is useful where there is no surface on which to put a keyboard but is unsuitable in noisy conditions; automatic scanning is suitable if there is a large amount of data to be gathered.

Frequently the demands on the input device are conflicting, and no single optimal device can be identified: trade-offs usually have to be made between desirable and undesirable features in any given situation. Furthermore, many systems will use two or more input devices together, such as a keyboard and a mouse, so the devices must be complementary and well coordinated. This means that not only must an

'Darn these hooves! I hit the wrong switch again!
Who designs these instrument panels, raccoons?'

(© 1986 United Feature Syndicate, Inc. Reprinted by permission.)

input device be easy to use and the form of input be straightforward, there must also be adequate and appropriate **system feedback** (Norman, 1988) to guide, reassure, inform and, if necessary, correct users' errors. This feedback can take various forms. It can be a visual display on a screen: a piece of text appears, an icon expands into a window, a cursor moves across the screen or a complete change of screen presentation occurs. It can be auditory: an alarm warning, a spoken comment or some other audible clue such as the sound of keys clicking when hit. It can be tactile: the feel of a button being depressed, or a change in pressure, such as occurs when using a joystick. In many cases feedback from input can be a combination of visual, auditory and tactile responses. For example, when selecting an icon on a screen, the tactile feedback from the mouse button or function keys will tell users that they instructed the system to activate the icon. Simultaneously, visual feedback will show the icon changing shape on the screen. This is coordinated with the sound of the button clicking or the feel of the key resisting further pressure. In this chapter the various types of device are discussed in terms of their common characteristics and the factors that need to be considered when selecting an input device. In Chapter 12 we return to the issue of feedback.

11.2 A sample of input issues: Keyboards

The most common method of entering information into the computer is through a keyboard. Since you have probably used them a lot without perhaps thinking about the related design issues, thinking about keyboards is a convenient starting point for considering input design issues. Broadly defined, a **keyboard** is a group of on–off push buttons, which are used either in combination or separately. Such a device is a **discrete entry device**. These devices involve sensing essentially one of two or more discrete positions (for example, keys on keyboards, touch-sensitive switches and buttons) which are either on or off, whereas others (for example, pens with digitizing tablets, moving joysticks, rollerballs and sliders) involve sensing in a continuous range. Devices in this second category are, therefore, known as **continuous entry devices**.

When considering the design of keyboards, both individual keys and grouping arrangements need to be considered. The physical design of keys is obviously important. For example, if keys are too small this may cause difficulty in locating and hitting chosen keys accurately. Some calculators seeking extreme miniaturization and some modern telephones suffer from this. Some keyboards use electro-mechanical switches, while others use sealed, flat membrane keyboards. When pressing a key on a membrane keyboard, unless appropriate feedback is given on screen, or using sound, it may be difficult to tell which key, if any, has been pressed. On the other hand, membrane keyboards can typically withstand grease, dirt and liquids that would soon clog up typical electromechanical switches. This can be an important consideration in environments such as production floors, farms and public places.

Alterations in the arrangement of the keys can affect a user's speed and accuracy. Various studies have shown that typing involves a great deal of anticipation, with fingers hovering over the keys that are to be struck next. Finger analyses of trained typists suggest that typing is not a sequential act, with each key being sought out and pressed as the letters occur in the words to be typed. Rather, the typist looks ahead, processes text in 'chunks' (a meaningful group of words), and then types it in chunks. For alphabetic text these chunks are about two to three words long and for numerical material they are three to four characters long. The effect is to increase the typing speed significantly.

Most people are quite familiar with the layout of the standard alphanumeric keyboard, often called the qwerty keyboard, the name being derived from the first letters in the uppermost row from left to centre. This design first became a commercial success when used for typewriters in the USA in 1874, after many different prototypes had been tested. The arrangement of keys was chosen in order to reduce the incidence of keys jamming in the manual typewriters of the time rather than because of any optimal arrangement for typing. For example, the letters 's', 't' and 'h' are far apart even though they are frequently used together. With the advent of electric and electronic keyboards and the elimination of levered hammers (replaced by golfballs and daisy wheels) such considerations are no longer necessary. Attempts at designing alternative keyboards that are more efficient and

Figure 11.1 Simplified Dvorak keyboard (Norman, 1988).

quicker to use have produced, among others, the Dvorak and Alphabetic boards. The **Dvorak** board, first patented in 1932, was designed using the following principles:

- Layout is arranged on the basis of frequency of usage of letters and the frequency of letter patterns and sequences in the English language.
- All vowels and the most frequently used consonants are on the second or 'home' row, so that something like 70% of common words are typed on this row alone.
- Faster operation is made possible by tapping with fingers on alternate hands (particularly the index fingers) rather than by repetitive tapping with one finger and having the majority of keying assigned to one hand, as in the qwerty keyboard, which favours left-handers. Since the probability of vowels and consonants alternating is very high, all vowels are typed with the left hand and frequent 'home' row consonants with the right.

The improvements made by such an ergonomic design are a significant reduction in finger travel and consequent fatigue and a probable increase in accuracy. Dvorak also claimed that this arrangement reduces the between-row movement by 90% and allows 35% of all words normally used to be typed on the home row. Despite its significant benefits, the Dvorak layout, shown in Figure 11.1, has never been commercially successful. The possible gain in input speed has to be weighed against the cost of replacing existing keyboards and retraining millions of people who have learned the qwerty keyboard. There are also chord keyboards, which are discussed in Box 11.1.

Box 11.1   Chord keyboards

In **chord keyboards** several keys must be pressed at once in order to enter a single character. This is a bit like playing a flute, where several keys must be pressed to produce a single note. Since many combinations can be produced with a small number of keys, few keys are required, so chord keyboards can be very small, and many can be operated with just one hand. One commercially available

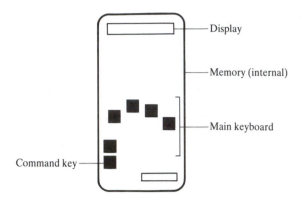

Figure 11.2 Microwriter (Potosnak, 1988).

chord keyboard is the Microwriter, shown in Figure 11.2. Training is required to learn the finger combinations required to use a chord keyboard. They can be very useful where space is very limited, or where one hand is involved in some other task. Chord keyboards are also used for mail sorting and a form of keyboard is used for recording transcripts of proceedings in law courts.

Question 11.1

Think about the key characteristics of the keyboards listed in Table 11.1 and complete the table.

Table 11.1 Types of keyboard.

Device	Description	Key characteristics
Qwerty keyboard	Uses the most common arrangement of alphabetic keys.	Required when the data to be input are highly variable. Many people are trained for using it. Very slow for those not trained.
Dvorak keyboard	Similar to the qwerty keyboard but the arrangement of the keys allows for more efficient input.	
Chord keyboard	Various arrangements. To form words (usually in a shorthand type notation), several keys are pressed simultaneously.	

11.3   Pointing devices

Pointing devices are input devices that can be used to specify a point or path in a one-, two- or three-dimensional space and, like keyboards, their characteristics have to be considered in relation to design needs. Example pointing devices include joysticks, trackballs and mice. Pointing devices are typically continuous entry devices, although a device like a mouse uses both continuous movement and (with its button) discrete movement.

Cursor controls: Mice, trackballs, joysticks and cursor keys

Joysticks, like the one in Figure 11.3, operate in two dimensions and are often used for tasks where a direction and speed is to be indicated, rather than a location. A trackball, such as the one in Figure 11.4, is a ball that a user can rotate in any direction within a fixed socket. It can be moved by drawing the fingers or the palm of the hand over the surface or by flicking. An important design consideration is, therefore, how large to make the accessible surface area of the ball. The mouse is similar to the trackball but it is not fixed and the user can move it around on a flat surface. Cursor control keys can also be used to move a cursor, but the other devices enable the user actually to drag objects around the screen as well as just pointing, which is difficult to accomplish using cursor keys. The user also has a sense of being able to manipulate objects. This is an important principle in the design of many of today's interfaces, which will be discussed further in later sections and in Chapter 13.

Figure 11.3   Joystick
(Norman and Draper, 1986).

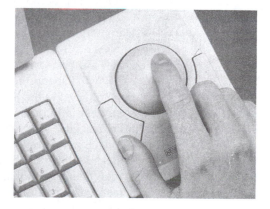

Figure 11.4   Trackball
(courtesy of Kensington Microware, New York).

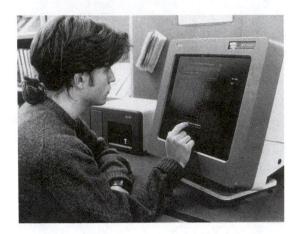

Figure 11.5 Touch screen (photographed in Milton Keynes central library).

Touch screens

Touch displays allow the user to input information into the computer simply by touching an appropriate part of the screen or a touch-sensitive pad near to the screen. In this way the screen of the computer becomes a bidirectional instrument in that it both receives information from a user and displays output from a system. Using appropriate software, different parts of a screen can represent different responses as different displays are presented to a user. For example, a system giving directions to visitors at a large exhibition may first present an overview of the exhibition layout in the form of a general map. A user may then be requested to touch the hall that he wishes to visit and the system will present a list of exhibits. Having selected the exhibit of his choice by touching it, the user may then be presented with a more detailed map of the chosen hall.

The advantages of touch screens, as in Figure 11.5, are that they are easy to learn, require no extra workspace, have no moving parts and are durable. They can provide a very direct interaction. Ease of learning makes them ideal for domains in which use by a particular user may occur only once or twice, and users cannot be expected to spend time learning to use the system. (In Chapters 21 and 22 you will be introduced to the Eurochange system in which a touch screen is used.) However, some less favourable reports claim lack of precision, high error rates, arm fatigue from reaching to the screen, fingers obscuring detail on the screen and screen smudging. A survey by Muratore (1987) implied that, of various cursor control devices studied, touch screen was the fastest but least accurate. Problems with arm fatigue and fingers obscuring the screen can be eased by the use of a remote off-screen touch pad, which can be positioned horizontally. In general, touch screens are thought to be good for large targets and untrained users, but inappropriate for frequent high resolution tasks or expert users. For recent developments in touch screens, see Section 11.7.

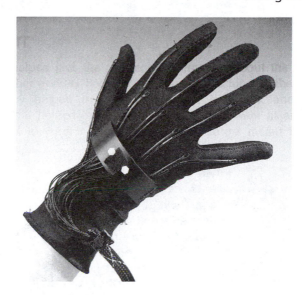

Figure 11.6 Dataglove (Kalawsky, 1993).

Question 11.2

What advantages are claimed for touch screens? What disadvantages do they appear to have? In what kinds of environment might they be beneficial?

3D trackers

There are various devices known as 3D trackers that can measure the absolute position and orientation of a sensor in free space in three dimensions. Currently, high accuracy 3D trackers typically employ a small lightweight magnetic sensor cube attached to a wire, and one or two transmitters a few feet away. Coordinates for x, y and z position as well as for yaw, pitch and roll, that is to say, rotation in various directions, of the sensor are calculated with respect to the transmitters by comparing signal strengths. Different versions of such devices differ in price, range, number of measurements per second and susceptibility to interference. Less expensive versions of 3D trackers use ultrasound in place of magnetic techniques. Resolution, speed of update and range are typically less with ultrasonic systems than with magnetic systems. 3D trackers can be mounted on gloves to act as hand trackers, on helmets to act as head position trackers, or on other parts of the body to track limbs. By combining one or more 3D trackers with flexion sensors woven into a glove so that they detect finger bending and finger separation, it is possible to construct datagloves, like the one in Figure 11.6, and datasuits that track the movement of an entire hand or body in detail.

In the case of datagloves, cables from the sensors are connected to an interface board near to the wrist, which in turn is connected to the computer. When worn, datagloves provide the user with the apparent ability to grasp and move computer-generated objects as though they were in three-dimensional space. The glove is wired in such a way that, with appropriate software, an image of the hand is presented on a display which mimics the user's own movements. The effect is to enable the user to use the precision, control and agility of the human hand for input purposes. The use of datagloves is still relatively rare, but of great interest, because of the potential 'naturalness' of the interaction.

Datagloves are also sometimes used in collaboration with output devices such as head-mounted displays that give three-dimensional visual feedback (see Chapter 12). When gloves are used with ordinary computer monitors that give only a two-dimensional view, perspective problems can arise from not having sufficient information about depth. For example, it is possible to put a hand right through an object represented on the screen. To some extent this can be addressed by using auditory cues to replace tactile and visual cues, for example, making appropriate sounds when a virtual object is 'touched'. This is generally found to be helpful by users, but is not adequate for many tasks. (See Chapter 16 for some recent developments in touch and force feedback for datagloves.) Perhaps a more serious problem is that of the rather cumbersome nature of this technology, which is not always comfortable or convenient to wear, especially for long periods. (Chapter 16 studies some issues in the use of virtual reality technology in detail.)

Question 11.3

Think about the key characteristics of the pointing devices listed in Table 11.2 and complete the table.

Table 11.2 Other input devices.

Device	Description	Key features
Dataglove	Glove that communicates hand and finger position to a computer.	Used for manipulating virtual objects, specifying paths and positions, and issuing commands in the form of gestures.
3D tracker	Device that relays its position and orientation to a receiver.	
Joystick	Small stick that can be moved in any direction within a fixed socket.	
Mouse	Continuous input device that has one or more buttons for discrete input. Unlike the trackball or joystick it is not fixed, so the user can move it around on a flat surface.	
Touch screen	Special screen that detects the position of a finger touching it.	
Trackball	Rotatable ball embedded in a surface in a fixed socket.	

11.4 | Matching devices with work

Rather than reviewing all the input devices (which are well covered in Shneiderman, 1992), we will now consider some of the issues that you need to take into account when selecting them for a design. We shall start with work issues and then go on to consider issues concerned with users and the environment in which the system will be used.

Buxton (1986) uses a series of three situations or 'scenarios' to demonstrate how, by judicious choice of task, almost any arbitrarily chosen property of any input device can constitute an advantage in one situation, but a disadvantage in another. Consider, for example, the following three task settings, and match them with the most appropriate pointing device. The first situation involves 'panning' over a large graphical surface such as a Very Large-Scale Integration (VLSI) layout, too large to be seen in detail as a whole. Using a trackball, panning is accomplished by rolling. With a joystick, direction of pan can be arranged to correspond to direction of displacement from the centre position and speed of pan to amount of displacement. Dealing with the large graphical surface also involves zooming in on detail at points of interest. We will assume that the joystick and trackball are designed like the ones in Figures 11.3 and 11.4, so that in either case this can be accomplished by using a twisting movement.

Buxton's analysis is that the trackball is better suited to this situation as a whole than the joystick. There is no obvious advantage to either device for the zooming task, but panning is easier with the trackball, since motion of the ball is mapped directly to motion over the surface. This contrasts favourably with the joystick, where position is mapped to motion, which is less direct and requires learning. Both devices are adequate to express the desired messages, but in one case the mapping is more natural.

In the second scenario, one task requirement is added. Suppose that *simultaneous* zooming and panning are absolute requirements of some task. This totally reverses the conclusion just reached. Zooming and panning at the same time is physically possible with the joystick (just displace and twist), but in the case of the trackball, simultaneous rolling and twisting is difficult, if not impossible (try doing it on an imaginary trackball). Given the expanded task requirement, the joystick appears to have the advantage. This argument starts with a task requirement (for simultaneous zooming and panning), moves through expressiveness considerations (that is, what manipulations are required on each device to produce the desired result), and then ends up with a usability conclusion (based on what is easy or feasible for people).

Another subtle change in the task requirements produces a third scenario. Suppose that objects must be located by panning, and then operated by twisting without letting the *xy* position drift, as for example, when operating valves in a simulated production plant. This would be difficult with the spring-loaded joystick but easy with the trackball (by the simple expedient of resting the fingertips on the trackball bezel, and then rotating – the recommended technique for rotation on this device).

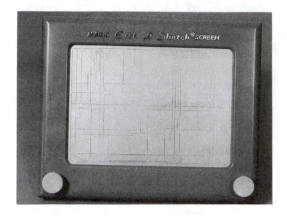

Figure 11.7 Etchasketch: a drawing toy with an instructive interface (Buxton, 1986).

Figure 11.8 Skedoodle: another drawing toy with an interesting interface (Buxton, 1986).

What lessons can be drawn from Buxton's three hypothetical scenarios? Firstly, it is important to take into account the particular manipulations that would have to be carried out to perform required tasks. As we have just seen, some required manipulations may be inconvenient or impossible with a particular device interfaced to a particular program in a particular way. Adaptations in the device or in the way it controls the program may be called for. Secondly, it is important to try to set up natural mappings between the ways in which the device can be manipulated, the feedback given by the program, and the meaning of the result in terms of the user's mental model (see Chapter 6). Mapping is a technical term describing relationships or correspondences between the structure of two things. Norman (1988) defines 'natural' in this context as taking advantage of human propensities, physical analogies and cultural standards. For example, the motion of the trackball corresponds directly to motion over a plane, making a good natural mapping, whereas displacement of the joystick, also used to control motion over a plane, does not correspond nearly so directly. Deciding how natural a particular mapping might be in any particular case comes down, in part, to judgements about the extent to which 'like actions produce like responses'. At the same time, the three scenarios demonstrate that it is necessary to take into account how natural any particular manipulation or mapping is for the people who will have to carry it out, and we will discuss this in Section 11.5.

EXERCISE

It is vital for the interface designer to realize that although two devices may belong to the same class of logical devices, their usability for given tasks may be quite different. Consider the following challenge, formulated by Bill Buxton (1986). You have a choice of two drawing devices (both children's toys): the Etchasketch shown in Figure 11.7 and the Skedoodle shown in Figure 11.8. Both allow you to draw on a screen. In the case of the Skedoodle, the movement of the drawing point is controlled by a joystick. In the case of the Etchasketch, it is controlled by two knobs. One knob moves the drawing point along the *x*-axis and the other along the *y*-axis. To make a curve with the Etchasketch, you have to turn the two knobs at once in the appropriate direction at the appropriate relative speeds. The first challenge is to identify the 'best' device for drawing. Try this challenge now and give reasons for your choice.

COMMENT

If you haven't already guessed, the point of the challenge is to demonstrate that there is no such thing as a best device: it all depends on the task in question. If you chose the Etchasketch, try the task of drawing a perfect circle. If you chose the Skedoodle try to draw a horizontally aligned square instead.

Interestingly, the Skedoodle is sold with 'templates' that make it easy to draw a horizontally aligned square (as long as you have a template of the size required), as shown in Figure 11.9. To see a related idea on a computer, consider a drawing package such as MacDraw on the Macintosh, which allows line drawing using a mouse. It is arranged so that if the 'option' key on the keyboard is depressed before drawing a line, then the result will be a straight line, enforced by software, displayed horizontally or vertically aligned or at 45 degrees. To some extent, this kind of use of added constraints can make an input device suitable for a task for which it would otherwise be unsuited.

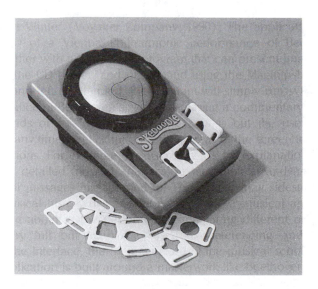

Figure 11.9 Templates for a Skedoodle – useful constraints on an interaction (Buxton, 1986).

Buxton sums up his approach to designing and selecting input devices as follows:

'My thesis is that we can achieve user interfaces that are more natural, easier to learn, easier to use and less prone to error if we pay more attention to the 'body language' of human–computer dialogues. I believe that the quality of human input can be greatly improved through the use of *appropriate gestures*. In order to achieve such benefits, however, we must learn to match human physiology, skills, and expectations with our physical ergonomics, control structures and functional organization.'

(Buxton, 1990, p. 120)

Question 11.4

(a) *On the basis of the analysis of Buxton's three scenarios, what differences might there be for the user between two apparently similar input devices and, conversely, what similarities might there be between two different devices?*
(b) *Which task is easier to do with (i) the trackball and (ii) the joystick?*
(c) *What is the problem with analysing in isolation only one of the tasks that a system is designed for?*

11.5 Matching devices with users: Input for the disabled

Computers can enable disabled people to communicate with others or undertake paid employment where this would otherwise be difficult or impossible. For example, speech synthesizers, word processors and other technology can be operated via a keyboard or special input device by severely disabled people. Legislation in the United States (section 508 of the Rehabilitation Amendments Act, 1986) now *requires* that office automation products bought or rented by government must conform to guidelines regarding accessibility for disabled people (Edwards, 1991). Depending on the exact needs of the person and the task involved, special input devices may be required for a disabled person to use a computer system effectively. More recently, the Americans have extended similar demands to employers more generally with the Disabilities Act, 1990.

Eye and head movement input

The use of eye and head movement as input can be beneficial where a user's hands are disabled or otherwise occupied. If the computer can determine where the user is looking at any given time, it can present an input menu and then let the user select items by making a sound, blowing or pressing a foot pedal to signal a selection.

There are two main ways for recording eye movement and converting it into input data. The first method is electrophysiological and records the movements of the muscles that control the eye. The second uses photoelectric reflection to record movements in reflected light from the eye. A major problem with the first, older technique, is that electrodes have to be secured to the skin to detect muscle

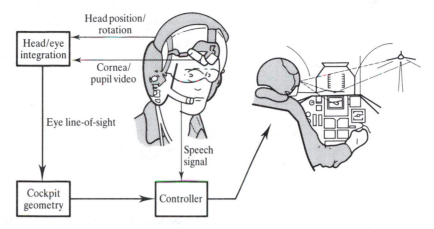

Figure 11.10 Gaze-driven system for aircraft pilots. This system combines a helmet containing a sensor for magnetic position and orientation with a helmet-mounted oculometer for detecting the relative direction of eye gaze (Adapted with permission from *Proceedings of the Human Factors Society 30th Annual Meeting*, 1986. Copyright 1986 by the Human Factors and Ergonomics Society, Inc. All rights reserved).

movement and are therefore subject to general body movement. With the second technique, a user is required to track an object on the screen by moving his eyes to maintain a stable image on the central part of the retina where vision is most acute. This is not easy to achieve because eyes do not move in a sufficiently smooth fashion, which has obvious implications for the success of this technique. For example, this form of input is not well suited to the tracking of very small targets because of the number of involuntary movements that occur when the eye is attempting to fix on a point. Body movement can also be a problem with this second technique. It has, however, been investigated for use by aircraft pilots (see Figure 11.10), in conjunction with helmets containing devices that sense head orientation (as discussed in Section 11.3 and in Chapter 12). Details of some other devices for disabled people are discussed in Box 11.2.

Box 11.2   Other devices for disabled people

Another device that has been developed for people with severe motor impairment is the eye typer. This device has letters displayed on a panel in the familiar qwerty keyboard layout with the numerals in a row beneath. Each letter and number has a light embedded in it. A camera in the centre of the display catches the reflection from the user's eye of the particular letter or number as it is looked at. This is converted into a character that appears in a liquid crystal display at the bottom of the panel. Hence, the user 'types' by scanning the keyboard and fixing momentarily on each character that is wanted.

Table 11.3 Eye and head movement methods of input.

Method	Description	Key features
Electrophysiological sensing of movement	Records muscle movement.	Electrodes have to be secured to the skin to detect muscle movement and are subject to general body movement. May be uncomfortable and confining. Not well suited to tracking very small targets or to fine control.
Photoelectric reflection to track movement	Records movements in reflected light from the eye.	User must maintain a stable image on the central part of the retina, which is not easy. Not well suited to the tracking of very small targets or to fine control.
Head movement tracking	Lightweight headset transmits ultrasonic signals to a measurement unit on top of the computer.	The 'keyboard' is a display on the screen. The system detects slight movements of the user's head and moves the cursor accordingly. To operate a key, the user locates the cursor on the key and then blows on a blow switch. This device can be used even by severely disabled users.

Methods of input using eye or head movement are summarized in Table 11.3. Provided a severely disabled person has more or less any kind of movement under voluntary control, then one of these methods for detecting eye or muscle movement should, in principle, allow an input device adapted to the individual to be found or devised. Another promising general-purpose input technique for severely disabled people is to attach a 3D tracker to whichever limb or part of the body can be voluntarily moved (Pausch, 1990). Whatever method is adopted, it is a prerequisite that input is coordinated with appropriate system feedback in a form suitable to the person in question.

The equalizer system is an example of a system that is technically fairly simple but that is closely tailored to the needs of its user. The user in this case is Professor Stephen Hawking, the celebrated physicist, who suffers from motor neuron disease. This system employs a standard personal computer with specialized hardware and software to enable users to control a speech synthesizer and a word processor using just a single switch. The input system uses a series of menus arranged on a screen, shown in Figure 11.11. Different parts of the screen are automatically highlighted in turn by the system in a repeating pattern. The user selects the portion of the screen currently of interest by clicking when that area is highlighted. Many ingenious strategies are used in different parts of the system to minimize the number of clicks required for common speaking and writing tasks. For example, in one area of the top level display, the thirty-six most commonly used words in the English language, as measured in empirical studies, are arranged according to frequency of use. Another

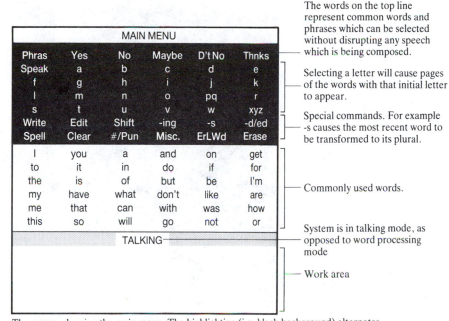

The words on the top line represent common words and phrases which can be selected without disrupting any speech which is being composed.

Selecting a letter will cause pages of the words with that initial letter to appear.

Special commands. For example -s causes the most recent word to be transformed to its plural.

Commonly used words.

System is in talking mode, as opposed to word processing mode

Work area

The screen, showing the main menu. The highlighting (i.e. black background) alternates between the two topmost areas. By pressing the switch the user selects the currently highlighted area.

Figure 11.11 Top menu of the Equalizer, Stephen Hawking's personal input device (Edwards, 1991).

part of the top level screen allows less common words to be spelt out letter by letter, or gives access to a carefully laid out dictionary list from which complete words may be chosen. When a complete word has been spelt out or chosen by whatever means, the system displays a row of up to six predictions about what the next word is likely to be. These guesses may be ignored, or one of them may be chosen. The Equalizer uses more or less every known technique to speed up text input where the input device is a single switch. It is described in detail in Edwards (1991) and Woltosz (1988).

11.6 Matching devices with environments of use

Figure 11.12 shows a user in a work environment with special needs. While the user, who is a telephone installer, and the specifics of the tasks (entering and receiving order information) are not particularly unusual, the work environment has some unusual characteristics. The environment requires a mobile, compact tool, with different properties than standard office workstations might allow.

Figure 11.12 A work environment with special needs. The radio-linked computer system was improvised by attaching a radio frequency modem to a standard pen-based computer (*Communications of the ACM*, 1993, **36**(5), p. 58: © 1993, Association for Computing Machinery, Inc. reprinted by permission).

Pen systems are typically small, notebook-sized computers that allow the user to write directly on the screen using a special pen that the screen is programmed to sense. Handwriting recognition software translates handwritten characters (letters, numbers, punctuation marks and so on) into ASCII text which can be displayed instantly on screen as printed characters. It is intended in such systems that the pen should replace both the keyboard and the mouse. Commands can typically be issued to pen systems in the form of traditional editing marks and gestures such as carets, circles, crossings out and so on. So, for example, to insert a word between two words, a caret might be used, and to delete a word, an X might be drawn through it, as shown in Figure 11.13.

One of the first problems is to decide where one character ends and another character begins. This problem (**symbol segmentation**) is not quite as difficult as the corresponding problem in speech recognition (speech segmentation, which we discuss later), but it is nonetheless a serious problem. Most current systems use one or more strategies to make the task as a whole more tractable. Some systems avoid the problem of symbol segmentation by constraining the writer to write in a grid of boxes, one character to a box, as shown in Figure 11.14. One disadvantage of this approach is that it inhibits the natural flow of writing. Many systems are restricted to dealing with limited symbol vocabularies, such as upper case letters only. At present, due to limitations in the speed and accuracy of character recognition software, pen systems are used mainly for filling in forms and other applications requiring input in small quantities or of limited kinds. If recognition software improves, pen-based systems could become much more widely used.

CORE PENPOINT GESTURES		
Tap	·	Select, Invoke
Press-hold	●	Initiate drag (move, wipe through)
Tap-hold	· ●	Initiate drag (copy)
Flick (four directions)	|	Scroll, Browse
Cross out	X	Delete
Scratch out	=	Delete
Circle	O	Edit
Check	✓	Options
Caret	∧	Insert
Brackets	[ ]	Select object, adjust selection
Pigtail (vertical)	℘	Delete character
Down-right	L	Insert space

Figure 11.13 Basic pen gestures recognized by the penpoint operating system (*Byte*, February 1991, p. 213).

Question 11.5

What advantages are claimed for handwriting recognition systems? What are the current limitations? For what kind of task might they be advantageous?

Figure 11.14 An experimental pen system that recognizes hand-printed characters (courtesy of Go Corporation).

11.7 Developments in input

The examples in the previous sections illustrated how to match input technologies with various characteristics of tasks, users and work environments. Designers must also keep in mind potential technologies that might dramatically improve HCI. We review here some current developments in input technologies, including speech recognition, touch screens, datagloves and handwriting recognition. We should sound a word of caution: just because something is new does not mean that it will be better; you will still need to judge it critically by examining the characteristics of the task, user and environment of usage.

Speech recognition

Speech input (Booth, 1989) suggests a number of advantages over other input methods:

- Since speech is a natural form of communication, training new users is much easier than with other input devices.
- Since speech input does not require the use of hands or other limbs, it enables operators to carry out other actions and to move around more freely.
- Speech input offers disabled people such as the blind and those with severe motor impairment the opportunities to use new technology.

However, speech input suffers from a number of problems:

- Speech input has been applied only in very specialized and highly constrained tasks.
- Speech recognizers have severe limitations. Whereas a human would have little problem distinguishing between similar sounding words or phrases, speech recognition systems are likely to make mistakes.
- Speech recognizers are also subject to interference from background noise, although the use of a telephone-style handset or a headset may overcome this.
- Even if the speech can be recognized, the natural form of language used by people is very difficult for a computer to interpret.

The development of speech input systems can be regarded as a continuum, with devices that have a limited vocabulary and recognize only single words at one end of the spectrum and systems that attempt to understand natural speech at the other. **Isolated word recognition systems** typically require pauses between words to be longer than in natural speech and they also tend to have a limited vocabulary from which to recognize words, requiring the user to be quite careful about how she speaks. **Continuous speech recognition systems** are capable, up to a point, of recognizing single words within strings of words. This means increased programming problems and system complexity. Although these systems still operate by recognizing a restricted number of words, the advantage is that they allow much faster data entry and are more natural to use.

One way of reducing the possible confusion between words is to reduce the number of people who use the system. This can overcome some of the problems caused by variations in accent and intonation. **Speaker-dependent systems** require each user to train a system to recognize her voice by repeating all the words in the desired vocabulary one or more times. However, individual variability in voice can be a problem, particularly when a user has a cold. It is not uncommon for such systems to confuse words like 'three' and 'repeat'. **Speaker-independent systems**, as the name suggests, do not have this training requirement; they attempt to accommodate a large range of speaking characteristics and vocabulary. However, the problems of individual variability mean that these types of system are less reliable, or have a smaller vocabulary than speaker-dependent systems.

The perfect system would be one that would understand natural speech to such an extent that it could not only distinguish differences in speech presentation but also have the 'intelligence' to resolve any conflicts in meaning by interpreting speech in relation to the context of the conversation, as a human being does. This is a deep unsolved problem in Artificial Intelligence (AI), and progress is likely to be slow.

EXERCISE

Given the current technological constraints, make a list of some of the applications for which speech input systems might be most useful.

COMMENT

Possible applications include:

- automated handling of materials
- quality control and inspection
- security
- limited command input for interactive computer systems
- communication for blind and physically disabled people.

A number of specialized speech input devices have been developed for people with disabilities. One example is a control device that responds to vocalized requests made anywhere within a house, such as using voice commands to dim the lights or raise the temperature, and also to commands made over a telephone line. Box 11.3 contains a description of the VODIS system.

EXERCISE

Two applications where speech input could be used are for controlling various functions in a car for a physically disabled person and to assist visitors to obtain information in an exhibition hall. What are the main differences in conditions that a system designer would need to take into account in designing these applications?

COMMENT

In the first application, the system would need to recognize only one speaker (that is, be speaker-dependent) and a limited set of simple one- or two-word commands like 'left', 'right', 'windscreen wipers'. In the second application, the system would need to be able to recognize a variety of speakers (that is, be speaker-independent), who may have different accents, and cope with continuous messages varying in vocabulary, grammatical construction and complexity.

Box 11.3 Voice-Operated Database Inquiry System (VODIS)

Another interesting example of speech input is the Voice-Operated Database Inquiry System (VODIS), developed by British Telecom, Logica (Cambridge) Ltd and the University of Cambridge. The objective was to design a prototype that could eventually be used by ordinary telephone users to obtain train timetable information about the departure and arrival times of specific trains suitable for their personal travel requirements. Before building a prototype, studies of actual enquiries about rail travel were carried out and a model of an enquiry dialogue was developed. Constraints imposed by voice input and output technologies also had to be taken into account. Subsequently, the dialogue was structured with two conversation stages: the first is concerned with the enquirer specifying travel requirements, the second is the delivery of appropriate train timetable information from the system. VODIS uses a continuous speech recognizer that accepts naturally spoken words and phrases and passes them to a dialogue controller, which interprets the received speech using knowledge of the application domain.

Erroneous matches have occurred when users respond with more than one word at a time. To overcome this problem the questioning was worded so that people were constrained to respond in a restricted way from the outset. Another line of research has been to investigate ways of incorporating visual cues from lip movement to facilitate word recognition.

EXERCISE

What kind of problem do you think users could experience when using VODIS?

Question 11.6

In what kinds of work environments might speech input be beneficial?

Advances in other input devices

High-precision touch screens

Recent touch screens have addressed some of the problems of lack of precision by offering single-pixel accuracy. Experiments by Sears and Shneiderman (1991) with early experimental high-resolution touch screens showed that single-pixel accuracy was achievable, but suggested that such screens were not pleasant to use for tasks that required extreme accuracy. This may change as designs for high-precision touch screens continue to improve. One important consequence of the recent improvement in accuracy is that while older touch screens were too inaccurate to permit anything much more than the equivalent of button pressing, modern high-precision touch screens allow actions such as line drawing, dragging, sliding, typing, direction sensing and velocity sensing (Shneiderman, 1993). For this reason, new generation touch screens are now suitable for use in a direct manipulation interaction style (see Sections 13.6 and 13.7 on direct manipulation for definitions

Doonesbury   BY GARRY TRUDEAU

(*Source*   Universal Press Syndicate © 1993 G.B. Trudeau.)

and examples). This means that they are much more widely applicable than older touch screens. If cheap, flat high-precision touch screens are developed, especially ones that can be manufactured in curved shapes, they could proliferate (Shneiderman, 1993). Examples could include information and control panels for vehicles, tools, telephones, clocks, thermostats, door locks and consumer goods of all kinds.

Handwriting recognition

Claims are made for accuracy of around 90 % in handwriting recognition, but the accuracy depends greatly on who is writing what, and under what limitations and restrictions. Current techniques work only if severe constraints are accepted, not for unrestricted general applications. One increasingly used technique for handwriting recognition is **neural network** recognition, which involves training a program known as a 'neural net' by feeding it with samples of handwriting together with the correct ASCII translation. Training continues until it fails to produce significant improvement. Many neural-based systems require retraining for each new user (Tappert *et al.*, 1988). Some important uses of this technology include inputting characters in languages like Japanese, Chinese and Korean (see also Section 11.6).

Input devices using other parts of the body

Increasingly, it is being recognized that human beings can use their feet, gesture and make facial expressions, and employ a combination of touch and movement to initiate input into computer systems. This raises the issue of why few systems have as yet been designed that can be controlled by the feet or other parts of the body. One obvious advantage would be that using other parts of the body can free the hands to perform other tasks, in the way that feet and hands are used to control different tasks

Figure 11.15   A footmouse or 'mole' (Greenstein and Arnaut, 1988).

when sewing using a foot-operated sewing machine and when driving a car. The footmouse, or 'mole', as it is sometimes called, is one attempt at delegating control to the feet. In one version, its rubberized surface, shown in Figure 11.15, pivots so that a foot can drive a cursor up or down, left or right, depending upon which edge is depressed. Continued depression causes the cursor to continue moving.

Question 11.7

What are the main strengths of the following input technologies, and what are their chief limitations?

(a) *High-precision touch screens*
(b) *Datagloves*
(c) *Handwriting recognition*
(d) *Footmice*

Key points

- An input device is a device that, together with appropriate software, transforms information from the user into data that a computer application can process.
- Choice and method of use of input device should contribute as positively as possible to the usability of the system as a whole: that is, help users to carry out tasks safely, effectively, efficiently and enjoyably.
- The usability of an input device depends greatly on the provision of appropriate feedback.
- Many types of keyboards are available to suit different situations. If an unusual keyboard is to be used, any requirements for special training should be carefully weighed against potential advantages.
- A variety of pointing and tracking devices are available but many are experimental. These have various characteristics and features, which may suit different users or tasks.
- Eyes, heads and feet can be used to control computers as well as hands.
- Handwriting recognition and pen-based systems may become increasingly important for some tasks and users, but currently it is important to understand their limitations and the trade-offs that must be made in any given situation.
- Speech recognition systems are very well suited to some tasks and environments, but for effective use, their strengths and weaknesses must be understood. Speech recognition is becoming increasingly important.
- Various input techniques and systems exist that can allow disabled people to control computer systems provided they can make some movements and perceive the system feedback. For the system to be effective, careful consideration of the person and the task involved is required.

Further reading

Input devices

BAECKER R.M. and BUXTON W.A.S., eds (1987). *Readings in Human–Computer Interaction: A Multi-disciplinary Approach*. San Mateo, CA: Morgan Kaufmann.
This book contains an excellent collection of papers with good coverage of the issues underlying the selection of input devices. An updated version is being released in 1994 entitled *Readings in Human–Computer Interaction: Towards the Year 2000* by Baecker R., Grudin J., Buxton W. and Greenberg S.

BOOTH P. (1989). *An Introduction to Human–Computer Interaction*. Hove: Lawrence Erlbaum Associates.
This book contains a section on speech input.

MACKINLAY J.D., CARD S.K. and ROBINSON G.G. (1990). A semantic analysis of the design space of input devices. *Human–Computer Interaction*, **5**(2, 3).
These papers provide a theoretical approach to the classification of input devices.

SHNEIDERMAN B. (1992). *Designing the User Interface: Strategies for Effective Human–Computer Interaction* 2nd edn. Reading, MA: Addison-Wesley.
This book provides excellent general coverage of a wide range of devices, and is also well illustrated.

SHNEIDERMAN B., ed. (1993). *Sparks of Innovation in Human–Computer Interaction*. Norwood, NJ: Ablex.
This book comprises an edited collection of research papers. Section 4 provides in-depth discussion of research into high-precision touch screens, as well as papers on the usability and usage of this technology.

Input devices for users with special needs

EDWARDS A.D.N. (1991). *Speech Synthesis: Technology for Disabled People*. London: Paul Chapman Publishing.

HAWKRIDGE D. and VINCENT T. (1992). *Learning Difficulties and Computers*. London: Jessica Kingsley Publishers.
The first of these two books focuses mainly on output devices but both books are excellent sources of information on computer technology for people with special needs.

PAUSCH R. (1990). Tailor and the UserVerse: Two approaches to multimodal input, Technical Report, Computer Science Department, University of Virginia.
This describes the use of 3D position trackers as input devices for people with limited voluntary movement.

WOLTOSZ W. (1988). Stephen Hawking's communications system, *Communication Outlook*, **10**(1), 8–11.
Contains detailed information on Stephen Hawking's personal communication system.

12

Output

Aims and objectives

The aim of this chapter is to introduce you to various types of output and to consider some of the factors that influence the most appropriate way of using output devices for particular systems, situations and users. After studying this chapter you should:

- be aware of basic issues in visual feedback,
- be able to identify characteristics of good and poor visualizations and discuss the role of visualization in applications such as program debugging and information display,
- be able to identify applications in which sound could have a significant role and be aware of its strengths and weaknesses,
- be able to describe how speech is generated and identify where different kinds of speech could be used in interaction design.

Overview

A well-designed presentation is a **perceptualization** (Grinstein and Smith, 1990), which can make clear relationships that might otherwise be slow to tease out. For example, good presentation can turn a heavy cognitive load of interpreting numbers into a light perceptual load of comparing lengths. Any presentation, whether it involves diagrams, animation, sound etc. that in a similar way transforms a cognitive load into a perceptual load is a perceptualization. In Chapters 4 and 5 we discussed the psychological issues concerned with perception, attention and memory constraints in relation to various representations. In this chapter we shall take a more technological perspective and also consider examples of the usage of different kinds of output.

When studying this chapter it is important to remember that there are many emerging techniques that take us far beyond traditional text-based displays, and that output can be non-visual (for example, auditory and tactile) as well as visual.

12.1 Devices and output

Output devices are those devices that convert information coming from an electronic, internal representation in a computer system into some form perceptible by a human, which is known as **output**. Until recently almost all computer output was visual and two-dimensional; it was presented on a screen or as hard copy from a printer. These are, and are likely to remain for some time, two of the most common

ARLO AND JANIS ® by Jimmy Johnson

(© 1986 by Newspaper Enterprise Association. Reprinted by permission.)

output devices. However, recently, various new trends and possibilities in the managing of output have started to emerge:

- Graphical user interfaces (GUIs) and multi-window systems have become commonplace.
- Output devices that can fit in laptop and pocket computers are becoming commonplace.
- Vision, moving pictures, sound and, in some cases, touch are being combined in hypermedia (and, in extreme cases, virtual reality) systems.
- Various forms of three-dimensional output are available for specialized purposes.
- The use of both speech and non-speech audio output has become more common, with facilities for synthesized speech and synthesized or sampled sound now standard on many machines.
- Specialized forms of output that stimulate the sense of touch are available. Many of these are experimental, or for use in specialized markets, or aimed at people with particular disabilities (for example, braille pads).

Designers are also realizing that more effort must be made to present output in ways that take into account the needs of disabled users. Disabilities such as blindness, colour-blindness, partial sight and hearing impairment involve a substantial number of people. Physical aspects, such as brightness, which is a subjective description of the illumination that enters the eye from an object (its luminance), need to be considered. The contrast between the luminance of the characters and the background upon which they are displayed is important: if the contrast is too high a user will suffer from glare, and if it is too low there will be a problem distinguishing characters from one another. Suitable contrast between characters and their background is important. Research suggests that dark characters on a light background produce the optimum contrast. Furthermore, having a light background reduces the possibility of glaring reflections on a screen. Resolution and flicker are other important factors that are determined by the technical design of the display. For example, if resolution is poor it is difficult to differentiate between certain characters and objects on the screen. A '0' may be mistaken for an '8' and a 'g' for a '9'. There is a large body of literature on all these aspects (for example, Osborne, 1985).

12.2 Visual output

Visual display of text or data is the most common form of output. We expect to see output displays in most interfaces, except for tasks where visual attention has to be focused elsewhere, such as operating a machine or driving a vehicle. The key design considerations are that the information displayed be legible and that it be easy for a user to locate and process, as discussed in Chapters 4 and 5. Poor lighting, eye fatigue, screen flicker and the quality of the displayed characters can all have a detrimental effect on visual output.

Three important aspects relating to a user's needs in terms of visual displays are: physical aspects for perception (for example, brightness, colour combinations and the selection of colours with regard to colour-blindness); the way the information is displayed (for example, the size of the text, the order of items on a menu and the way icons are designed) and the way the information is used. The psychology underlying these issues is discussed in Chapters 4 and 5, and information display is well covered by Tufte (1990), so after discussing the need for visual feedback we will focus on task-related aspects.

Visual feedback on user actions

Users need to know what is happening on the computer's side of an interaction. In particular, a system needs to provide high quality, timely responses to keep users well informed and feeling in control. This includes providing both information about normal processes and warnings if there is a problem. For example, in a way similar to the manner in which human communication progresses (taking turns, clarifying, confirming), where possible, a system should be able to:

- tell the user where he is in a file or process,
- indicate how much progress through a process has occurred (that is, confirm that some processing has taken place since the last exchange with the user),
- signify that it is the user's turn to provide some input,
- confirm that input has been received,
- tell the user that input just received is unsuitable.

If feedback is not current, correct or clearly expressed a user may think or do the wrong thing. Moreover, if there is no feedback the user will be left wondering what is happening and may feel that he is not in control.

As a commonplace example, many word processing systems provide some indication of where a user is in the document on which he is working. In using Microsoft Word on the Apple Macintosh, for instance, the position of the box in the scroll bar on the right-hand side of the screen indicates the position of the text in the screen relative to the whole document. The page number in the bottom left-hand corner of the screen tells the user on which page of the document he is currently working. If, with the mouse, the user positions the pointer somewhere in the text and then clicks the button on the mouse to mark a point at which to insert a few words, a flashing cursor bar will appear at that position. This indicates to the user exactly where he positioned the cursor and if he now types, the text will be inserted at that position. When the user issues the appropriate command to save the file, he will be given a report on the system's progress. As the system saves the file the proportion saved will be shown as an increasing percentage at the bottom of the screen. If the user wishes to search for the occurrence of a particular string of text, a small wristwatch symbol will appear on the screen to indicate that the system is searching through the file.

EXERCISE

Consider a system that you use, for example, a word processing or graphics package.

(a) What kind of visual feedback, if any, does it give to indicate (i) when the system is processing and cannot accept any input at that time, (ii) when the system requires you to input some information in a particular form, and (iii) when the system does not understand your input?

(b) What other types of visual feedback could be useful, especially for people new to the system?

COMMENT

(a) While your answer may contain variations, the following are things to watch for in assessing visual feedback.

    (i) In several systems a small icon, for example, a wristwatch, a bee, a cup and saucer, is used to indicate that the system is active and to request you to wait. When the system has completed that activity the icon disappears, indicating that it is ready to receive more input.

    (ii) In some systems a dialogue box is displayed with specific fields that need to be entered. A flashing cursor is often used to indicate the field that needs to be entered. When all the data has been entered the user initiates the input by clicking on an 'OK' button or simply by pressing the <return> key.

    (iii) The most common form of feedback is to provide a message saying that some kind of error has occurred.

(b) Other types of visual feedback that might be useful include: something that suggests what actions to take if you make an error; disabling of advanced features or commands that cannot be performed at a particular time by distinguishing them (such as by the use of shading); and on-line explanations as to what all the various control devices do (such as scroll bars).

Chapter 15 discusses other forms of user support.

12.3   Dynamic visualizations

> 'If mathematics is Queen of the Sciences, Computer Graphics is the royal interpreter.'
>
>   (Frederick Brooks, quoted in Rheingold, 1991, p. 43)

In the last few decades, the possibilities of graphical communication have been greatly extended by video and moving pictures. For example, techniques such as animation, speeded up changes over time, zooms, pans, edited sequences and many others can be used as powerful means of communicating information. More recently, the development of computer-controlled visualization driven by computer models and electronic sensors has extended yet again the possibilities of graphical communication. Computer-based visualizations can be divided loosely into the following two categories:

- Model-based visualizations, where the subject is some underlying computer-based model, program or simulation directly under the user's control. One example is Mathematica-based visualizations, which allow mathematical relationships to be visualized.
- Visualization of external data, which comes from a process beyond direct computer control, such as stock market data.

Many situations, such as some industrial process control applications, involve characteristics of both categories.

Visualization is currently applied in a number of areas, including the visualization of data, programs, algorithms, scientific phenomena, musical relationships, statistics and financial patterns. In principle, computer-based visualizations have at least three advantages over other kinds of visualization, such as video recordings, for communicating information:

- Once a mapping has been established between some underlying computer model and the way in which it is to be displayed, visualizations of totally new situations can be produced instantly, or at least quickly.
- Computer visualization can often be controlled in minute detail interactively by the user: thus feedback can be used to guide the user's exploration.
- It is easy, at least in principle, to change the mappings used to generate a computer visualization. For example, someone who is colour-blind might want to change colour assignments, or a statistician exploring data might try arranging or filtering information in various different combinations to try to find an underlying pattern.

Computer visualization allows data or processes to be visualized in any desired form. However, from the designer's point of view it is at least as difficult to devise a dynamic visualization that gets the salient details across well as it is to design an effective diagram or video animation. Frequently the design challenge is compounded by the potentially unlimited variations in data that may be used in a computer visualization. Few tested guidelines are available for the production of effective computer visualizations. Ultimately, whether any particular visualization makes a given task easier for a specified set of users in given circumstances is a question for empirical testing. (See also Section 8.3.) However, case studies of existing computer-generated visualizations can act as useful starting points and sources of inspiration, and in Box 12.1 we examine two case studies that highlight some basic issues for the designer. Each takes account of two key considerations:

- to find a mapping from elements and relationships in the chosen domain into display elements and relationships that will make *perceptually* prominent those things that we wish to be *conceptually* prominent;

- to make the mapping in a principled, consistent way, rather than in a piecemeal, *ad hoc* fashion.

Box 12.1 Visualization case studies

Harmony Space

Harmony Space, shown in Figure 12.1, is a tool designed to allow both beginners and experts to explore aspects of musical harmony rapidly and effectively. Harmony Space (Holland, 1992, 1994) uses an unusual mapping both to visualize and control harmonic sequences. This mapping translates the basic elements of musical harmony in a principled, consistent way into a visual form that is simple

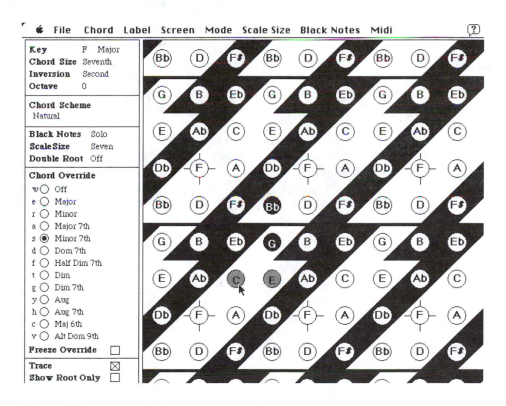

Figure 12.1 Harmony Space, an interactive visualization with a consistent mapping. (© Simon Holland).

for people to use. The mapping converts diverse basic technical tasks in music into simple perceptual–motor tasks such as:

- making straight lines,
- distinguishing between different points of the compass,
- judging when objects are close to each other,
- finding the central object from a collection,
- judging similarity of shape relationships,
- keeping within a marked territory,
- conforming the shape of objects to the shape of a container.

The mapping used in this visualization works well because it translates an entire set of musical relationships consistently into perceptual–motor relationships. Harmony Space can be used both as a model-based visualization, where the student creates and has complete control of her own musical sequences, or as an external data-driven visualization, where it is used to analyse existing pieces.

Transparent Prolog Machine (TPM)

A good example of a model-based computer-based animation for software visualization is the Transparent Prolog Machine (TPM) (Brayshaw and Eisenstadt, 1991), also discussed in Section 8.3. TPM, shown in Figure 12.2, is a debugger used to animate and visualize the execution of Prolog programs. Here, the computer-based model being visualized is the Prolog program and its interpretations by the Prolog system.

Prolog is a powerful programming language related to predicate calculus. It allows beginners to write programs very quickly to solve substantial problems, while ignoring details about how their programs work. This is fine, until less simple, less ideal cases are encountered, where details of how the program will actually be executed must be taken into account. The TPM takes an abstract model of the way Prolog executes (based on structures called AND/OR trees) and makes this abstract model perceptually concrete as visual trees. The entire execution history of a program can be displayed as a single static diagram, or it can be shown in whole or in part as an animation. To focus on different levels of detail, TPM has many different display options and refinements that reflect variations on the same representational theme. The form of the different displays has been carefully designed to meet the following two design constraints, which apply generally to all visualizations where there is a lot of complex data:

- **Scalability**   a visualization that works well for a small process or collection of data may not work well for industrial-sized collections of data. The TPM makes use of views at various levels of detail that make it fully scalable.
- **Navigational aids**   if a machine makes use of different views there must be some way for the user to understand where she is and how they relate to each other.

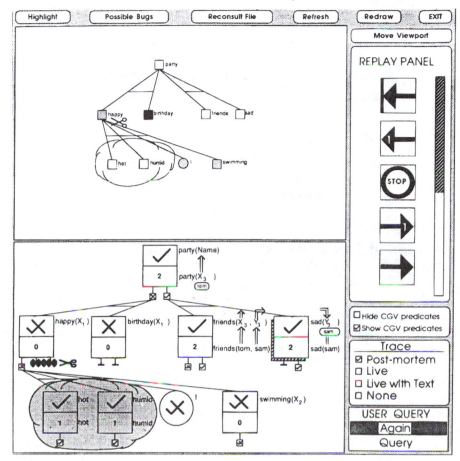

Figure 12.2 The Transparent Prolog Machine (Brayshaw and Eisenstadt, 1991).

In order to meet these two constraints, the designers of TPM refined its design by iterating many times over the following design steps (Eisenstadt *et al.*, 1993), which can be applied to the design of any computer visualization:

- consider a large range of tasks the visualization can be used for, such as programming education, debugging, program development and so on,
- work with pencil and paper mock-ups and implemented prototypes,
- test a large range of example data, in this case, programs,
- carry out test studies on a large number of real users.

Question 12.1

(a) When data is being mapped into display elements in a dynamic visualization (for example, numbers into varying line lengths) does it matter what data element is mapped into what display element?

(b)   What principles apply to choosing an appropriate mapping for a
      visualization?
(c)   What design constraint must be considered when designing a visualization
      where there are very large quantities of data?

Question 12.2

*What advantages do computer-based visualizations have over other kinds of
visualization such as video recordings from the point of view of communication of
information?*

Three-dimensional interactive animation

One key facility for high quality three-dimensional animation is a sufficiently powerful
graphics processing system. Given an internally represented model of, say a house or
a protein molecule, such a computer can render it in real time from any viewpoint.
Such systems can calculate a perspective view from any angle, and in some cases
may take into account the interplay of multiple light sources, shadows and textures.
This allows the user to rotate, spin, zoom and translate three-dimensional images on
a high resolution screen in real time using a controller such as a mouse. Such
facilities may be used, for example, to examine the structure of molecular models
from different angles, or to 'fly' around and inspect the rooms of an unbuilt house.
Factors such as perspective, shadows and lighting effects, together with parallax
effects as the image is moved or rotated, can generate perceptual cues that give a
strong subjective impression of three dimensions. (See Section 4.2 for a discussion of
the cognitive issues involved in representing depth.)

One interesting existing contribution towards general purpose three-dimensional interfaces is the Camtree, a kind of display forming part of the Xerox PARC
Information Visualizer (Figure 12.3) (Clarkson, 1991; Card *et al.*, 1991). To see how
this works, try to recall everyday collections of information that are arranged as
hierarchies or trees, for example, a computer manual or book, which has parts,
chapters, sections, paragraphs, and so on. A frequently recurring problem is to locate
quickly information relevant to a given problem from such a collection of
information. The Camtree, shown in Figure 12.3, is a highly flexible, animated
three-dimensional tree, somewhat like a cone on its side, which can be rotated,
pruned and expanded selectively in various different ways. The hierarchy runs from
left to right. A Camtree containing, for example, the first 600 nodes from an 80-page
Xerox organization chart can be displayed and manipulated without any great
difficulty. A Camtree allows the user to make areas of interest more perceptually
salient and other areas less so (though still visible), simply by rotating the tree. The
Information Visualizer, of which the Camtree is only a small part, is one of an
increasing number of tools (Holland, 1991b) that use three-dimensional animation
to display commonplace information structures.

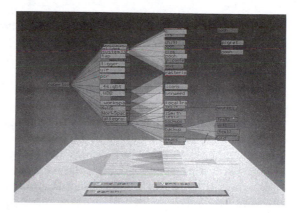

Figure 12.3 A Camtree, one of the three-dimensional animations provided by the Xerox PARC Information Visualizer (Card *et al.*, 1991: © 1991, Association for Computing Machinery, Inc. reprinted by permission).

EXERCISE

If you know a procedural programming language such as Pascal, and if you know any simple general algorithms or data structures, such as sorting algorithms or stacks, see if you can think of a way in which a three-dimensional animation could help a beginner understand how they work. Specify your animation as a sequence of diagrams showing successive stages of the animation. (No comment is provided for this exercise.)

12.4 Sound output

Current uses of sound at the interface are largely for alerting and feedback purposes. For example, various forms of beeps and bells are used to indicate that an incorrect command has been issued or that a process needs attending to. The use of sounds as warning indicators has also been extensive in process control plants. Until recently few computers could generate deliberately designed sounds other than beeps, but this has changed in the last few years. Different kinds of sound, each of which can be either synthesized or sampled (that is, digitally recorded and replayed), include the following:

- speech (see Section 12.5)
- musical sounds
- natural sounds

Some researchers, such as Buxton *et al.* (1989) have suggested that sound can be used in more information-rich ways to show what is happening in a system. In particular, it can be used as a coding method for augmenting graphical representations. They suggest that complex systems might benefit by using sounds that have a direct form of mapping to the processes they represent. Given that we have a highly evolved hearing system capable of gathering very detailed information about our environment, there should be a great potential to improve interfaces by exploiting this capability. To consider a simple illustration, Buxton *et al.* note that in computer games with well-designed sound, scores improve when the sound is turned on. It is sometimes argued that increased use of sound would make computers too noisy. Buxton *et al.* argue that in practical cases, quiet sounds are not perceived as intrusive if their use is well designed and if they provide useful information. In cases where noise pollution is a critical problem, earphones or quiet directional speakers close to the ear could be used.

Sound is of particular value where the eyes are engaged in some other task, or where a complete situation of interest cannot be visually scanned at one time. Sound can be useful for monitoring continuous background processes that are normally not important until something out of the ordinary happens, like hearing an unusual car engine note, or for drawing attention to an unusual one-off event, such as an object hitting a car from the outside. Sound can also be useful for drawing attention when expected background events fail to happen, for example, lack of disk access noise when intending to save a file to disk. These strengths of sound as a means of feedback are reflected in the following list of areas in which sound output has already proved valuable:

- Applications where sound complements a standard visual interface.
- Applications where the eyes and attention are required away from the screen; for example, flight decks, medical applications, industrial machinery, transport and farms.
- Applications involving process control in which alarms must be dealt with, or continuous monitoring is required.
- Applications addressing the needs of blind or partially sighted users.
- Data sonification. That is to say, situations where data can be explored by listening to it (given an appropriate direct mapping).
- Algorithm animation, in which understanding how an algorithm executes can be explored by listening to an appropriate mapping of its operation into sound, sometimes as a complement to visual animation.

Natural sounds

One interesting way of using sound in computer interfaces is to make use of natural sounds, either synthesized or digitally recorded. Gaver (1989) argues that evolution has adapted the human hearing system to be capable of extracting large quantities of information effortlessly from natural sounds such as rustles, thumps, hits, scrapes, tinkles, creaks, patters, reverberations, and so on.

EXERCISE

How might you use sound in an electronic mail system? Think about such things as the length and kinds of message, who they are from and so on.

COMMENT

You may have several suggestions. Bill Gaver (1989), a researcher into the use of sound in interaction design, points out that it might be useful if it were arranged for incoming electronic mail to make a sound something like a letter falling into a real mail box. Such a sound could be interpreted easily by a user concentrating on some other task. So, for example, a lengthy electronic mail message might produce a heavy thud, whereas a short message might produce a light rustle. The degree of reverberation might indicate the extent to which the mailbox was full or empty, with a nearly empty mailbox reverberating most. A metallic clang might indicate the mailing of machine code, whereas a gentler quality of impact might indicate a text file. Different mappings into sound might be preferred by individual users, for example, a deep thud could be set to indicate mail from one's boss, a brief signature tune to herald a mailing from a particular mail group (although this is taking us away from Gaver's ideas, which centre on purely natural sounds), and so forth. Box 12.2 contains another example of the use of sound to provide feedback in the Sonic Finder.

Experiments by Gaver and others (Gaver *et al.*, 1991) have also indicated that sound can be particularly useful in helping a team of users to collaborate on a process control task. For example, in a program that simulated a soft drinks bottling factory (ARKola) implemented in the collaborative SharedARK computer environment, sound was generated from a digital sampler to represent a variety of information. This included the sound of clanking bottles to represent the bottle dispenser and a splashing sound to indicate that liquid was being spilt. The rhythm of the sounds was intended to reflect the rate at which the machine was running, while the rapidity at

Box 12.2 Sonic Finder

A device called the Sonic Finder (Gaver, 1989) has been used experimentally on the Macintosh (see Figure 12.4) to add sounds to actions such as opening windows, moving, copying and deleting files and so forth. In our experience this program was very useful because the sound cues helped to avoid some common errors, such as intending to drop a file in the trash can but missing.

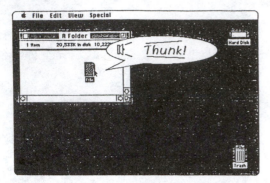 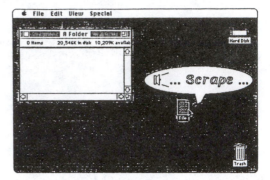

Figure 12.4 The Sonic Finder, which adds sound to interactions on the Macintosh desktop. Interactions shown (in cartoon style) include selecting an object, dragging an object, dragging an object over the trashcan ready for deletion, and dropping an object into the trashcan (deleting it). Most sounds vary according to the parameters of the objects involved (Buxton *et al.*, 1989: © 1989, Association for Computing Machinery, Inc. reprinted by permission).

which sounds changed was designed to convey a sense of urgency. Small teams of operators had to work together to ensure the safe running of the plant. Each operator could see only a part of the plant at a time. The sound of events in the factory (for example, bottles breaking and boilers overheating) helped to draw the operators' attention to malfunctions when they were looking at other parts of the factory, and to monitor the status of the plant as a whole.

EXERCISE

What other information might be usefully conveyed by sound in this example and what kinds of sounds could be used?

EXERCISE

What problems might occur with the use of sounds in this application?

A strong feature of natural sounds is that they can carry a lot of information that is easy to interpret. On the other hand, in situations where there are many sounds that could easily be confused, or where there are complicated relationships that need to be communicated, for example in exploring data structures, the use of temporal patterns and musical notes may be required instead of or in addition to natural sounds.

Musical sounds

The use of musical sounds in general-purpose computer interfaces is still at an early stage. Its value in particular cases can depend greatly on the individual user: for example, not all users will always be able to tell if one note is higher or lower in pitch than another. However, musical sounds have been used successfully to communicate for some time in many cultures (Blattner and Greenberg, 1992), for example: signature tunes, clock chimes, the 'V for victory' signal of World War II, alarms, church bells, street vendor cries, talking drums, etc. Uses of these kinds of sounds in interfaces are likely to be found increasingly. Some blind users may find such interfaces particularly useful. A colleague, who is blind, implemented a computer game played entirely using tones. For example, to catch an enemy before shooting it down, a rising and falling tone, indicating a moving target, had to be matched in pitch with a 'chase' tone.

Musical sounds are also starting to appear as a channel of feedback on computer interfaces for some specialized applications (Di Giano *et al.*, 1993). For example, Brown and Hershberger (1991, 1992) and Alty and Holland (1993) independently added sounds to sorting algorithms to help users grasp how the algorithms work. Experiences by Alty and Holland (1993) demonstrate that in some cases, bugs in sort algorithms could be located by listening to the sound of a sort alone. Franconi *et al.* (1992) added sounds to parallel programs to help debugging. It emerged that certain bugs in the pattern of message sending were much more easily spotted when mapped into sound than when mapped in the standard graphical diagrammatic form for these patterns. One important aspect of designing musical sounds to use in interfaces is that it is easy for beginners to produce mappings that do not have the intended perceptual effect. For example, tones that one might expect to sound distant may sound close if they are exactly an octave apart. There are many other similar effects. It is too early for detailed guidelines to have been published, but such pitfalls can be anticipated by working with musicians and music psychologists.

For other uses of non-speech sounds in interfaces, see Section 11.5 on disabled users and Section 12.6 on the uses of external computer-controlled sound sources.

12.5 Speech output

Speech output is one of the most obvious means of using sound for providing users with feedback about a system's current state. The value of speech as a natural means of communication was stressed earlier. However, as with speech recognition, speech generation is a complex process. For speech output to be successful it is important to understand the various aspects of natural speech production, such as grammatical structure, context and its effect on tone and intonation, and how a listener is able to understand a speaker's intentions by interpreting clues such as changes in tone. In this section you will be introduced to a subset of the design issues raised by speech output. The section is based on Edwards (1991), which should be consulted for fuller detail.

Speech synthesis technology

Speech is generated using one of two basic methods: concatenation or synthesis-by-rule. The essential idea behind **concatenation** is that digital recordings of real human speech are stored by the computer. These may be stored as sentence, phrase, or word segments. Later, these may be played back under computer control.

New sentences can be constructed by arranging words in the right order. Most people have heard this kind of speech synthesis when using the telephone system. For example, with current directory enquiry systems in many countries, after having made an enquiry of a human operator, a voice says something like 'The number you require is 273148'. The first part of this computer-generated message is smooth and flowing (having been recorded by a human speaker all as a piece). The number itself is then spoken in a rather jerky, stilted fashion, as digital recordings of the individual digits are played back in concatenation (some telephone systems use more sophisticated variants of this technique that give human-like intonation).

Smooth delivery and intonation, which are important elements of natural speech, are a problem with concatenation. The speech produced by this method often sounds artificial. The method has, however, been used successfully in cases where few phrases are used to produce a large number of varied but similar messages. Apart from telephone directory enquiries, other examples include the speaking clock and British Telecom's star services, which provide routine information such as details about changed telephone numbers and call diversions. Other telephone companies, like AT&T in the USA, provide similar services. The method has also been used with various industrial warning systems. Concatenation tends to be limited to applications requiring small vocabularies of fewer than 200 words.

Synthesis-by-rule does not use recorded human speech directly. The synthesis of words and sentences is controlled by rules of phonemics and rules that relate to the context of a sentence or phrase (see below). Used in conjunction with a database, this method has the potential of producing a much larger range of responses than speech produced by concatenation. It also allows for pitch and tone to be varied. Even so, the speech produced can sound somewhat synthetic. Synthesis-by-rule is useful where larger vocabularies are required.

If one cannot be certain in advance which words may be needed, a finer building block of speech is required than the word. The basic building block of the spoken word is the **phoneme**. By using phonemes as the building block, a system can, in principle, articulate an indefinite range of words. The phoneme is defined as the smallest unit of sound such that if a single phoneme is changed in a word, the meaning may be changed. For example, the spoken words 'banned' and 'hand' differ only in their initial phoneme. The English language is usually taken to have some forty phonemes.

EXERCISE

The disadvantages of artificial-sounding speech are that it can be annoying and sometimes unintelligible. Can you think what might be its advantages?

COMMENT

In certain circumstances mechanical-sounding speech can have the advantage of attracting people's attention. In other cases, it can imply to the listener that the speaker (the computer system) is not very intelligent. This may be desirable in that it can prevent people giving long and complicated requests to a system that cannot cope with them.

Question 12.3

Where might a user:

(a) benefit from receiving both auditory and visual information?
(b) find it difficult to receive both visual displays and speech output?

Box 12.3 illustrates how different kinds of devices can be coordinated in a single work environment.

Box 12.3 Easy Writer

One freelance writer and consultant, Steve Roberts, claims that he finds it much easier to write on the move than sitting in an office. He does most of his writing while riding a specially equipped bicycle, with several on-board computers, using a chord writer on the handlebars. Roberts uses an array of input and output devices to let him write, design and run a business effectively in his chosen work environment, as shown in Figure 12.5. A Macintosh fitted under the windshield is

Figure 12.5 HCI on the move: Steve Roberts' computerized place of work (*Computer Weekly*, 23 July 1992, p. 24).

operated using a helmet-operated mouse. A Private Eye (an eye level display fitted to the helmet) gives access to one of his PCs. A speech synthesizer replays electronic mail messages. A helmet microphone is used to issue voice commands to computers, and talk on CB radio and mobile telephone. The trailer includes a satellite link, keeping him in contact with his office and the Internet.

12.6 Developments in output

Other output techniques include use of touch as a medium. For example, aviation simulators have been developed to provide tactile feedback when interacting with the various input devices (such as the throttle providing a sense of torque when pulled forward). Providing tactile feedback in general-purpose virtual environments, however, is much more difficult. We will return to this issue in Chapter 16.

While we have treated various output media in isolation, it is clear that interesting issues (Edwards and Holland, 1992) emerge as they are combined in what is termed **multimedia**. In this sense, any computer application that employs a video disk, images from a CD-ROM, uses high quality sound, or uses high quality video images on screen may be termed a multimedia application. Such interfaces are often aesthetically appealing and, where high capacity storage devices such as CD-ROM are used, can provide effective interactions for the user, by acting as very large databases or storehouses of information with dense but easy-to-use cross-referencing and indexing.

One exemplary multimedia application is the interactive CD-ROM of Beethoven's Ninth Symphony in collaboration with the music scholar and educator, Robert Winter (Voyager Company, 1990). The application comprises a conventional CD of a Vienna Philharmonic performance of Beethoven's Ninth Symphony, together with a HyperCard program that can present images and text on screen, control the CD player, and play sound using the Macintosh internal sound chip. If started and left unattended, the program will simply run synchronized with the CD performance of Beethoven's Ninth, displaying a commentary which changes every five seconds or so. This is interesting as it is but the user may stop the performance at any time by clicking on various areas of the screen to explore in any of various directions. For example, the user may ask for explanations, examples of technical terms, detailed musical analyses, or may look at and hear Beethoven's early sketches of passages just listened to. The listener may sidestep into relevant cultural and musical history of the period, or pursue a musical analysis in depth, perhaps jumping about in the performance comparing different occurrences of a theme. The very full but simple to use cross-referencing and indexing, the consistency of the interface, the high standard of the musical scholarship, and the fact that the application is built around a masterwork like Beethoven's Ninth help to make this an inspiration for designers of hypermedia. Winter has also produced a second interactive CD-ROM based around Stravinsky's *Rite of Spring*, shown in Figure 12.6. (For another example of use of multiple media, see Sections 15.3 and 15.4.)

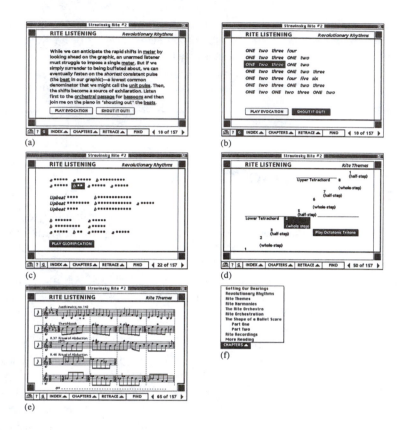

Figure 12.6 One of the many varied displays of the interactive CD-ROM *Rite of Spring* (Yavelow, 1992).

Some interaction designers using diverse forms of presentation (for example, sound, touch, moving pictures) and input (for example, gesture, sound, body movement), who want to emphasize the need to make the most appropriate possible use of the human sensory and effector channels in combination, refer to **multimodal** interface design (although the term can have other meanings). Several interesting multimodal interfaces have been built for blind or partially sighted users which use a combination of speech generation, gesture and sound. Edwards (1991) describes an experimental word processing system, Soundtrack, in which all the interactions that a sighted person would see between the mouse, the cursor and the objects on the screen are replaced by sounds. Edwards called these interactions between the mouse and the program 'auditory objects' and they take the form of either musical tones or synthetic speech. The screen is termed the auditory screen, and it is divided into four windows of equal size, as shown in Figure 12.7. Each window has its own tone and any area off-screen is delimited by another tone. The role of any one window never changes, although its contents do, and at any time

File menu	Edit menu	Speech menu	Format menu
Alerts	Dialogues	Document 1	Document 2

Figure 12.7 A diagram of the auditory screen used in Edwards' word processing system for blind and partially sighted users (Edwards, 1988: © 1988 Association for Computing Machinery, Inc. reprinted by permission).

only one window can be active. As the mouse moves from one window to another, a tone is sounded. Using these kinds of techniques, Edwards provided menus and command keys similar to those of a visual system.

Question 12.4

What factors can enable CD-ROM multimedia applications to act as potent sources of information for users?

Key points

- Output devices provide information or feedback in a form perceptible by a human.
- Visual output using a screen or VDU is by far the most common form of output today but other forms are becoming increasingly popular.
- Dynamic visualization is becoming increasingly important in particular application areas, such as the visualization of data, programs, algorithms, industrial processes, scientific phenomena, financial data and many other areas.
- A key issue in visualization is to find consistent mappings that make perceptually salient those things that should be conceptually salient.
- The more general term 'perceptualization' covers the use of sound and touch feedback as well.
- Three-dimensional animation is likely to come to form an important part of general-purpose interfaces.

- Sounds can complement a visual interface where attention is focused away from the screen, there is a glut of visual information, multiple processes must be continuously monitored, or background events can become important at any time in unpredictable ways.
- An important use of sound is to give information about background processes.
- Concatenation involves digitally recording human speech in large 'chunks' such as words or short sentences and then reassembling and playing it back.
- Synthesis-by-rule involves synthesizing speech according to prescribed rules of sound formation, tone, volume and intonation and has the potential to generate a much larger range of words and to sound less artificial than concatenation.
- Multimedia applications can act as very large databases or storehouses of information with very dense but easy to use cross-referencing and indexing.

Further reading

Information presentation

TUFTE E.R. (1990). *Envisioning Information*. Cheshire, CT: Graphics Press.
   This book is a *tour de force* on graphical presentation and includes many wonderful examples drawn from best practice over several centuries.

For detailed information about the use of colour in HCI see Christ (1975) and Doney and Seton (1988).

Dynamic visualization

CLARKSON M.A. (1991). An easier interface. *Byte*, February 1991, pp. 277–82.
   This provides an excellent general introduction to the Xerox Information Visualizer.

For detailed information about the use of colour in HCI see Christ (1975) and Doney and Seton (1988).

Sound output

BUXTON B., GAVER W. and BLY S. (1989). Uses of non-speech audio at the interface, tutorial notes, in *Nonspeech Audio*, CHI '89 Conference Proceedings. New York: ACM Press.
   These authors also have a book in preparation at the time of writing on non-speech audio.

EDWARDS A.D.N. (1991). *Speech Synthesis: Technology for Disabled People*. London: Paul Chapman Publishing.
   This contains a very clear exposition on speech output and its uses.

Much work has been carried out on the redesigning of aircraft flight deck alarm sounds to make the information carried easier to decipher when under stress or when several alarms sound at once. This research is very relevant to the use of sound in interfaces. See, for example:

EDWORTHY J. and PATTERSON R.D. (1985). Ergonomic factors in auditory systems. In *Proceedings of Ergonomics International 1985* (BROWN I.D., ed.). London: Taylor & Francis.

Human–Computer Interaction (1989). **4**(1).
A special issue on non-speech audio.

Interactive multimedia

BLATTNER M.M. and DANNENBERG R.B., eds (1992). *Multimedia Interface Design*. New York: ACM Press.

EDWARDS A.D.N. and HOLLAND S., eds (1992). *Multimedia Interface Design in Education*. Heidelberg: Springer Verlag.

WATERWORTH J.A. (1992). *Multimedia Interaction with Computers: Human Factors Issues*. Chichester: Ellis Horwood.
These are three excellent collections of papers on interactive multimedia interface design.

HOLLAND S. (1992). Interface design for empowerment: A case study from music. In *Multimedia Interface Design in Education* (EDWARDS A. and HOLLAND S., eds). Heidelberg: Springer Verlag.
Harmony Space, a highly interactive interface for learning about, visualizing, playing and composing harmonic sequences, is described and analysed.

VOYAGER COMPANY (1990). *Beethoven's Ninth Symphony*. Santa Monica, CA: Voyager Company CD Companion series.

YAVELOW C. (1992). *Macworld Music and Sound Bible*. San Mateo, CA: IDG Books.
Programs written by musicians to help them compose, perform, produce, teach and learn music form an endlessly rich source of case studies, expertise and inspiration on all matters multimedia. This book is highly recommended.

Feedback

OBORNE D. (1985). *Computers at Work: A Behavioural Approach*. Chichester: John Wiley.
A detailed account of the ergonomics, physiological and psychological aspects of computer system design with reference to a number of industrial examples.

RUBINSTEIN R. and HERSH H. (1984). *The Human Factor: Designing Computer Systems for People*. Burlington, MA: Digital Press.
Although now rather old, this book contains a useful chapter on 'responding to users'.

13

Interaction Styles

Aims and objectives

The aim of this chapter is to examine some of the factors that need to be considered when selecting an interaction style. After studying this chapter you should be able to:

- assess critically the design trade-offs of using different interaction styles,
- make decisions about which interaction styles to use in different applications,
- understand how cognitive issues influence design of interaction styles.

Overview

A range of different terms has been used in HCI for describing the communication that occurs between users and computers. Until recently, most interactions with a computer involved strictly defined turn-taking, in which text was typed in and responses were displayed on a screen. This is still a widespread and important way of interacting with a computer. For this kind of interaction, it makes sense to use the term **dialogue** to refer to the exchange of instructions and information that takes place between a user and a computer system. From a user's point of view, a typical if idealized dialogue can be broken down into the following stages. First of all, instructions are specified in some form to a computer. This may involve speaking, pointing, typing, gesturing and so on. The user hopes that her intentions were correctly specified and that the computer has carried them out as required. Then the system, if it has been thoughtfully and well programmed, will provide some feedback. The user hopes for the desired result but, failing this, a message explaining what has happened is displayed.

As you have seen in Chapters 11 and 12, richer styles of communications between a user and a computer have now become commonplace. Human–computer communication often takes non-verbal forms, such as the manipulation of objects and tools, the indication of points, paths and areas, and various types of gesturing, so it is necessary to have a wider perspective. Many authors (such as Baecker and Buxton, 1987) view the exchanges that occur between users and computers more generally and describe them as **interactions** rather than as dialogue. In this book we shall use the term **interaction styles** as a generic term to include all the ways in which users communicate or interact with computer systems.

13.1 Interaction styles

To make sense of different interaction styles, it is useful to take a historical perspective. Consider, for example, early command-driven applications and form-fill applications. They matched the user and task requirements at the time relatively well. The early command-driven applications tended to be used by expert users or at least technical, knowledgeable people who were not afraid of computers and could be expected to overcome any obstacles by sheer perseverance. The development of the form-fill mode of interaction was aimed at a completely different set of users and tasks. This type of interface was designed for clerical workers who had little, if any, experience with computers, to enable them to carry out repetitive clerical data collection tasks. These interfaces mimicked paper forms, with the aim of retaining as far as possible the characteristics of entering data that are part of the manual task, while benefiting from the data processing power of a computer system. In addition,

(© 1993, The Washington Post Writers Group. Reprinted with permission.)

the two kinds of interface were designed with specific task characteristics in mind. The command-driven form was general and could be used for a variety of different applications, whereas the form-fill mode was designed for a specific type of task.

Gradually the design of games and general word processing systems gained increasing importance, and more and more non-specialists became computer users. Designers then had to start catering for a much wider range of users, some of whom would be experts and others complete novices, with all levels of ability in between. The tasks became much more varied too. More supportive communication styles, such as question and answer sequences and menus, were developed. However, these were often found to be frustrating for experienced users who wanted the speed and flexibility of command-driven systems. Thus, there was a need for hybrid systems that catered for different user preferences.

While we will now describe various styles separately, they are not mutually exclusive. Many systems use styles in combination; for example, mixing direct manipulation and menus.

13.2 Command entry

How impoverished human–computer communication can be, compared with human-to-human communication! In fact, unless a person knows the protocol that has to be followed, no dialogue may be possible. Consider Figure 13.1, which shows a command-driven system, typical of early microcomputers. The message is particularly cryptic. The '>' symbol indicates that the system is waiting to receive a command to tell it what to do next, for example, 'DIR' – list the file directory, 'TYPE' – display a file on the screen, 'B:' – set the 'B' disk drive to 'current' and, therefore, to refer to it by default. Then look at Figure 13.2(a), which shows a menu-driven

Figure 13.1 An MS-DOS system after the power has been switched on.

system. Users also need some basic knowledge to use this system. They must know that they have to use the mouse to position the cursor on one of the words in the title bar and then click to obtain a menu, which 'pulls down' to offer more choices, as shown in Figure 13.2(b).

Question 13.1

What are the main differences between the command-driven system shown in Figure 13.1 and the kind of menu system shown in Figure 13.2(a) and (b)?

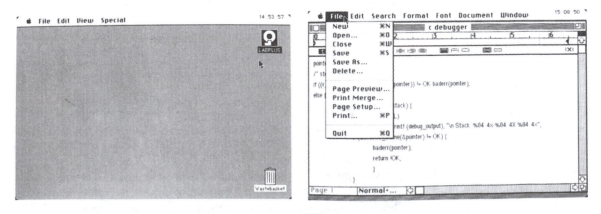

Figure 13.2 Pull-down menus and alternative commands for Microsoft Word on the Apple Macintosh (courtesy of Microsoft Corporation).

Commands provide a way of expressing instructions to the computer directly. They can take the form of function keys, single characters, short abbreviations, whole words or a combination of the first two (for example, using the <control> key together with the letter 'e' to mean EXIT). The advantage of using single characters or function keys is that only one or two keystrokes are required to execute the command compared with two or more when using a combination such as a word or an abbreviation (for example, having to type 'EXIT'). The disadvantage with using single characters is that it is generally more difficult to remember an arbitrary letter than a well-chosen command name or abbreviation, especially if there are a large number of them. Giving commands appropriate names is important because it helps users to remember what the commands refer to (see Section 5.2).

13.3 | Menus and navigation

A **menu** is a set of options displayed on the screen where the selection and execution of one (or more) of the options results in a change in the state of the interface (Paap and Roske-Hofstrand, 1988). Unlike command-driven systems, menus have the advantage that users do not have to remember the item they want, they only need to recognize it (see Section 5.2 for more information on the psychological advantages). This means that for menus to be effective, the names or icons selected have to be self-explanatory (see Chapter 5), which is not always the case.

In the past one of the problems with using menus is that they take up a lot of space on the screen. Two solutions are the use of **pull-down** or **pop-up** menus. In the former the menu is dragged down from a single title from the top of the screen, an item is selected and the menu automatically returns back to its original title. Pop-up menus (see Figure 13.2) appear when a particular area of screen, which may be designated by an icon, is clicked on and the menu remains in position until the user instructs it to disappear again, usually by clicking on a 'close box' in the border of the menu's window. When there are a number of menus each with a set of options a user needs to know where to look to find the desired option. There are various strategies for achieving this. The fastest and simplest form of search occurs when the task matches one of the options displayed; this is called an **entity match**. An example of this is when the user knows that he wants to number the pages of a document and an option called 'NUMBERING' is provided.

Designers have to decide the best way of displaying menus so that they are comprehensible and natural to use. In the majority of cases it is useful to organize the commands in a hierarchical way. The problem is deciding which items to include at various levels and which items to group together at different levels. Empirical evidence suggests that there are four reasonable alternatives for ordering menu items: alphabetical, categorical, conventional and frequency forms of organization. Alphabetical is self-explanatory. Categorical organization relies on the selection of suitable categories, which can be quite difficult. Conventional menus are neither alphabetical nor categorical but can have a temporal order such as the days of the week or the months of the year; they do not occur very often. Frequency of use is another way of organizing a menu if the number of options is small.

EXERCISE

Suggest ways of ordering lists of menu items for the following applications and give reasons for your answers:

(a) an index to a filing system for doctors' patients
(b) the months and days of the year
(c) text processing and editing commands

If possible, look at a menu-based system with which you are familiar and make notes about the way the menus are organized.

COMMENT

(a) The most likely organization would be alphabetical. However, various forms of categorical organization might also be appropriate, for example, geographical location of patients' homes, age, gender, type of illness or form of treatment.
(b) A chronologically ordered and hierarchical menu in which the months were ordered in the first-level menu and days in the next level of the menu would be most likely.
(c) Some form of categorical organization in which similar operations were grouped together is most likely, for example, grouping formatting operations, editing operations, file operations.

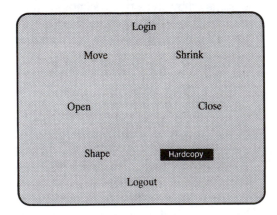

Figure 13.3 An example of a pie menu (Callahan *et al.*, 1988: © 1988, Association for Computing Machinery, Inc. reprinted by permission).

A more recent innovation is the pie menu. In these menus the list of choices is presented as a pie graph, as shown in Figure 13.3. Compared with linear menus it has been found that error rates and search times can be lower when searching a pie menu.

EXERCISE

Why might a pie menu produce better performance for some tasks?

COMMENT

One of the reasons why pie menus have these advantages is that all the items are placed at equal radial distances from the centre of the menu; therefore a user need only move the cursor a short distance in some direction for the system to recognize the intended selection. In contrast, it can often be the case that the item required on a linear menu is towards the end of the menu, or the cursor is 'dragged' too quickly, increasing the chances of selecting a wrong option. Another reason for the advantages of a pie menu is that the area that can be selected is much larger than for a linear menu so the probability of accidentally selecting a wrong option is reduced.

Question 13.2

Which of the following applications would be best suited to having pop-up pie menus, pull-down categorical menus or fixed-matrix menus?

(a)   a word processing system
(b)   a radar warning system

See also Section 14.2, which discusses menus in relation to windowing systems.

Question and answer dialogues

The term 'question and answer dialogues' can refer to a rudimentary type of menu system where each interaction (consisting of a question, set of choices and response from the user) typically takes up just one or two lines of a display. The questions are asked one at a time and the next question to be asked may depend on the previous answer given. This type of communication can be used when the expected input is constrained, for both user and computer, by the domain. For example, the reply might be a part number, an amount of money, a person's name or the name of a book. Question and answer dialogues of this sort are often used in tasks where information is elicited from users in a prescribed and limited form, such as in automatic bank tellers, library catalogues and scheduling applications. In either form, question and answer dialogues are system-driven dialogues, which protect the user from any considerations of navigation. Therefore, they are suitable for novice users, but can be very frustrating for experienced users who know what they want to do.

13.4 Form-fills and spreadsheets

When several different categories of data are fed into a system using a keyboard it is often helpful to design the screen as though it is a form (**form-fill**), particularly if the same type of data has to be entered repeatedly, as occurs in retailing (type, number, price, stock, delivery) and personnel records. The advantage of having fill-in forms is that they can help users to position data in the correct place, thereby reducing the need to watch the screen too carefully. As one part of the form is completed the cursor usually moves directly to the position where the next item of data should be entered. This means that users do not have to bother to position the cursor themselves; they only have to press a <return> key or make a mouse click. As with any form, it is possible to make life difficult for users by designing it poorly. Forms need to be designed so that they enable users to know which kinds of data are permissible in each field. It should also be obvious to users how to make corrections. One way of making forms easy to use is to design them so that they are similar to well-designed paper forms in the way they look and are filled in (see Figure 13.4).

```
Type in the information below,
pressing TAB to move the cursor, and
press ENTER when done.

Name: _____     Phone:( ____ ) ____ - ____
Address: _____

_____

City: _____ State: _____ Zip code: _____
Charge number:  __ __ __ __ __

Catalog                          Catalog
Number      Quantity             Number      Quantity

_____      _____               _____      _____
_____      _____               _____      _____
_____      _____               _____      _____
_____      _____               _____      _____
_____      _____               _____      _____
```

Figure 13.4 A form-fill design for a department store (Shneiderman, 1992).

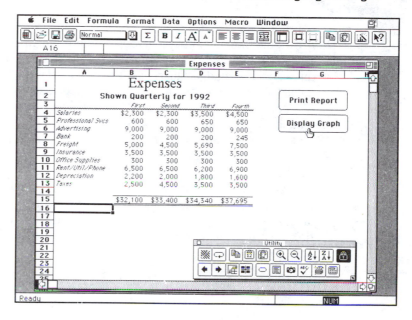

Figure 13.5 An example of a screen from the Excel 4 spreadsheet system. Two user-defined buttons are shown on the right-hand side (Van Buren, 1992).

Spreadsheet programs have also been designed using the principle of electronically mimicking a familiar paper predecessor. In the case of spreadsheets, however, the electronic versions provide much more functionality (and are now typically combined with elements of direct manipulation style, as described in Section 13.6). For example, they often enable various calculations, such as sums, percentages and ratios, to be performed automatically on data that have been entered on the screen. The advantage of this is that users can try out alternative plans and see the results instantly. Figure 13.5 shows an example of a screen from Excel.

Question 13.3

What human factors considerations have made form-fill and spreadsheet systems so successful?

13.5 Natural language dialogue

As discussed in Chapters 11 and 12, the use of language as a means of communicating with a computer has been considered highly desirable because of its naturalness. This includes typing in natural language at a keyboard. The system needs to be able to cope with the same vagueness, ambiguity and ungrammatical constructions associated with speech recognition. Typing eliminates problems of accent and intonation but it introduces the problem of spelling variations, mistakes and keying errors. While it may not yet be possible to develop systems that can understand natural language as it is typed, several kinds of expert system and intelligent tutoring system have been developed using some form of structured subset of a natural language. A user is required to learn how to use such a subset language unambiguously and to phrase sentences in a way that the target system can understand. Another problem with natural language interaction is the amount of typing that has to be undertaken. For a user who is a novice at the keyboard it can be quicker to use a menu-driven system. For an expert computer user, a command language that requires minimum key-pressing may also be quicker. Although natural language promises flexible and easy communication with computers, most natural language systems developed in the foreseeable future will be limited to well-defined domains with a limited vocabulary.

13.6 Direct manipulation

As you should remember from reading the interview with Ben Shneiderman, the term **direct manipulation** describes systems that have the following features:

- visibility of the objects of interest,
- rapid, reversible, incremental actions,
- replacement of complex command language syntax by direct manipulation of the object of interest.

Typically, direct manipulation systems have icons representing objects, which can be moved around the screen and manipulated by controlling a cursor with a mouse. The Apple Macintosh was the first widely successful general-purpose commercial system to include direct manipulation features. It is based on the metaphor of a desktop, in which icons representing objects commonly associated with desktops are used. Files, for example, are displayed as small box-like icons which can be grouped together into another icon of a folder. There is also a 'clipboard' on which information can be 'pasted' (that is, kept in a temporary file). A 'waste basket' is available for disposing of documents (that is, erasing files). Many CAD systems for automotive engineering, electronic circuitry, architecture, newspaper layout and aircraft manufacture now also use some of the principles of direct manipulation. For example, a CAD system used for circuit layout can be designed such that it enables a user to capture a schematic diagram on the screen by placing and removing resistors or capacitors with a light pen. Another form of direct manipulation occurs in the programming of some industrial robots. An operator holds the robot 'hand' and guides it through a spray-painting or welding task while the controlling computer records every action. The controlling computer can then operate the robot automatically and repeat the precise actions whenever necessary. Video games

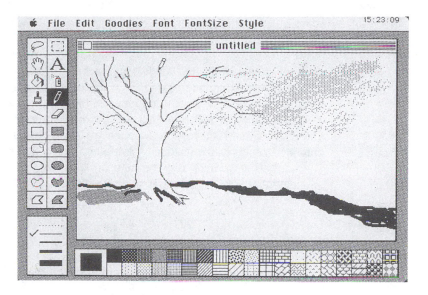

Figure 13.6 An early and influential example of a direct manipulation system for drawing, the original MacPaint (courtesy of Apple Computer UK Ltd).

also provide examples of well-engineered and commercially successful systems based on the principles of direct manipulation. Figure 13.6 shows a screen from MacPaint, an early drawing system developed by Apple.

Well-designed direct manipulation systems may also engender enthusiasm and elicit enjoyment from their users. Shneiderman (1983a) believes that this is owing to the following factors:

- novices can learn the basic functionality quickly,
- experienced users can work extremely rapidly to carry out a wide range of tasks, even defining new functions and features,
- knowledgeable intermittent users can retain operational concepts. Error messages are rarely needed,
- users can immediately see if their actions are furthering their goals and, if they are not, can simply change the direction of their activity,
- users experience less anxiety because the system is comprehensible and because actions are so easily reversible,
- users gain confidence and mastery because they initiate an action, feel in control and can predict system responses.

One of the problems with direct manipulation, however, is that not all tasks can be described by concrete objects and not all actions can be performed directly. For example, one of the early problems in graphical interfaces was finding a way to make concrete the concept of a buffer. On the Apple Macintosh this was overcome through the use of 'cutting' and 'pasting' operations and a hidden 'clipboard', which caused conceptual problems for some early users. Nevertheless, direct manipulation has been much heralded within HCI as the way forward in interface design. Note, however, that the term 'direct manipulation' describes the style by its interaction features rather than the underlying technology required. Sometimes the term 'graphical user interface' is used as a loosely equivalent label. This term originally arose to describe interfaces that required bitmapped displays rather than character displays, although some of their interaction techniques such as pull-down menus have since been successfully applied in interfaces on character displays. These interfaces, such as the historically important Xerox Star system described in Chapter 1, required *graphical* displays and mouse tracking to support selection and movement of screen objects as part of a direct manipulation interaction style.

EXERCISE

How would you set about designing an interface that suited all levels of users?

COMMENT

One solution is to provide a hybrid of communication styles. For example, a direct manipulation interface could be designed such that it is possible to convert icons of objects into textual lists and to perform operations on the icons by typing in commands. In this way both users who like to perform operations using a mouse and those who prefer the speed of command-based operations are catered for. It also allows for users who like to carry out some actions by mouse movements and some through key presses. For example, a user may find it easier to carry out selecting operations with a mouse and editing operations with a keyboard rather than through selecting a command from a menu.

Question 13.4

What are the main advantages of direct manipulation interfaces in comparison with command-driven systems? What are the comparative disadvantages?

Question 13.5

Complete Table 13.1, which lists the various interaction styles with a column for their key features. You should include comments on the tasks to be carried out and the types of user to which they are most suited.

Table 13.1   Communication styles.

Communication style	Key features
Command languages	Versatile and quick if the syntax and names are learned. Good for tasks where the user has to carry out operations that require the input of repeated commands. Best for experienced, regular users.
Menus	
Natural language	
Query language	
Question and answer	
Form-filling	
Spreadsheet	
Direct manipulation	

13.7   Cognitive issues in direct manipulation

Part II reviewed many aspects of user interfaces from the perspective of the behavioural and social sciences. In this section we show how you can apply such insights, by considering direct manipulation interaction from a cognitive science perspective. While studying this section, think back to the discussion in Chapters 6 and 7 on interface metaphors, mental models and conceptual models.

A detailed attempt to analyse the notion of directness has been made by Hutchins *et al.* (1986). They developed a framework that characterized directness in terms of two 'gulfs' which describe the gap between the users' goals and the system image. The degree of directness in direct manipulation interfaces can be considered as the discrepancy or distance between two gulfs: the gulf of execution and the gulf of evaluation (see Figure 13.7). The distance relates to the potential mismatch that can occur between the way a person thinks about a task and the way it is represented by the system. The **gulf of execution** refers to the distance between the user's goals and the means of achieving them through the system. The **gulf of evaluation** refers to the distance between the system's behaviour and the user's goals. Both gulfs are related; the point of representing the gap as two gulfs between the user and system is

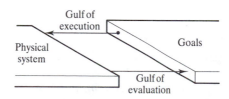

Figure 13.7   The gulfs of execution and evaluation (Norman and Draper, 1986).

that it shows the bidirectional relationship between the system and the users. The key concern is finding ways to reduce the discrepancy between the users' goals and the system's physical state and form. By reducing the gap, the mismatch between the users' way of thinking about their tasks and the system's representation is reduced, thereby making it easier for users to carry out their tasks. This is achieved by bridging the two gulfs, either by changing the users' goals and interpretation of the system or by changing the input or output aspects of the system image, as suggested in Box 13.1.

Box 13.1   Bridging the gulfs

The users can *bridge the gulf of execution* through changing the way they currently think and carry out the task towards the way the system requires it to be done.

The designers can *bridge the gulf of execution* by designing the input characteristics to match the users' psychological capabilities. This can include reducing both the physical actions needed and the effort of deriving them mentally through planning.

The gulf of evaluation can also be bridged by either the users or the designers.

The users can *bridge the gulf of evaluation* by changing their interpretation of the system image and evaluating it with respect to their goals.

The designers can *bridge the gulf of evaluation* by changing the output characteristics of the system.

Hutchins *et al.* (1986) argue that the major burden of bridging the gulfs should be carried by changing the system image and that the onus should be on the designers. However, one problem with focusing too much on changing the properties of the system image to match the users' current articulated needs and existing tasks is that it can thwart future innovative design (Gaver, 1991). It is important, therefore, to develop bridges that can be adapted, enabling innovative design while accommodating existing users' needs.

Question 13.6

(a)   What is the difference between the gulf of execution and the gulf of evaluation?
(b)   Why is it important to bridge the gulfs?
(c)   How can the users bridge the gulfs?
(d)   How can the designers bridge the gulfs?

As we mentioned in Box 13.1, to attain a degree of directness requires reducing the distance between users and the system. To explain how the directness of engagement works the nature of the gulfs is further distinguished in terms of:

(1)   how meaningful the types of objects and representations used at the interface are to the user,

(2)   the relationship between the objects and representations used.

These are described in more detail in Box 13.2.

Box 13.2   Expanding the notion of directness – the feeling that one is operating directly in the world of interest

The first part of the relationship between the user and the interface refers to the semantic directness and the other to the articulatory directness.

Semantic directness concerns the relation between what the user wants to express and the meaning of the expressions available at the interface. The problem is whether the expressions provided at the interface enable users to say what they want to say and, if so, whether it can be said in a concise manner. For example, if users want to create a document that includes pictures, text and cartoons, does the system provide the means by which they can alternate between writing, drawing and sketching in the same document? If so, then the semantic directness is considered to be good. Alternatively, if the expressions require the user to reconceptualize their task as creating separate documents using different applications, which subsequently have to be combined using a set of expressions never encountered before, then the semantic directness is considered to be poor.

Articulatory directness concerns the relation between the meanings of expressions and their physical form. This is more than mere syntax; it includes the sensory-motor aspects of processing – hence the term 'articulatory'. An example of articulatory directness is the turn indicator switch on the handlebar of a moped (often located on the left handlebar): pulling the switch back towards the rider indicates the intention to turn left and maps on to the action of pulling the left handlebar back to turn; pushing the turn indicator switch forward indicates an intention to turn right, and maps on to the action of pushing the left handlebar forward to turn right.

Question 13.7

What is the difference between articulatory directness and semantic directness?

EXERCISE

Describe in terms of semantic directness a word processing application that:

(a) allows users to move text around in a file by marking the beginning and end of the section to be moved and then issuing a move command; and

(b) uses 'drag-and-drop' editing.

Describe how drawing packages can be analysed in terms of semantic directness.

COMMENT

The operations in (a) are semantically indirect, because the goal of moving a section will have to be translated initially into the goal of issuing commands to mark the beginning and the end of the section and then a further command to move the marked section.

The operations in (b) are more semantically direct in the sense that dragging and dropping does not require the user to have to reconceptualize the task into a new set of goals, but simply to learn how to move text directly through selecting the text to be moved and then holding the mouse button down, to drag it to the desired location.

EXERCISE

Current direct manipulation systems that have incorporated interface metaphors possess only partial direct engagement. For example, most systems depend heavily on the use of a cursor for indicating to a user where they are in the interface. Can you think of how existing interfaces could be made more engaging?

COMMENT

Rather than selecting items by pointing, clicking and dragging it may be possible to do away with the mouse and cursor coordination altogether. Instead, direct manipulation of objects could take place by the users pointing to the object with their fingers or through eye movements (also see Chapters 11 and 12, and Sections 16.2 and 16.3, covering virtual environments).

'Floppy Jumpers' by David Shenton

Affordances, constraints, mappings and feedback

In addition to developing a theoretical framework for understanding the principles of direct manipulation, there has also been an attempt to define more practically-oriented principles of design that relate to direct manipulation interfaces. An excellent source of inspiration is Norman's (1988, 1992) set of design principles for everyday objects. Besides being enlightening on what makes a good design, they are an invaluable aid to fleshing out a direct manipulation interface in terms of the behaviour of the objects and their relation to each other. The primary design principles are affordances, constraints, mappings and feedback.

Affordances

The notion of affordances was first introduced in Chapter 1 and its theoretical underpinning explained in Chapter 4. An example of two contrasting scroll bars was given, illustrating how the affordance of one was more obvious than that of the other.

EXERCISE

Figure 13.8 shows two icons that are meant to represent two different actions on the part of the user. Examine it and try to work out what you would do with a mouse to operate the functions represented. Then do the same for Figure 13.9.

COMMENT

It has been suggested that Figure 13.9 should give you more obvious clues, the reason being that the representation of the cursor as a pointing hand suggests the operation of the slider and button in terms of simulating the action your

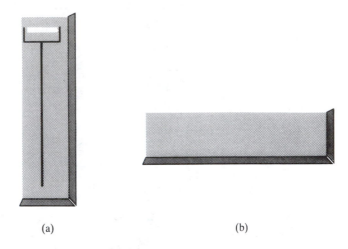

(a)   (b)

Figure 13.8   Do these icons suggest how you use them?

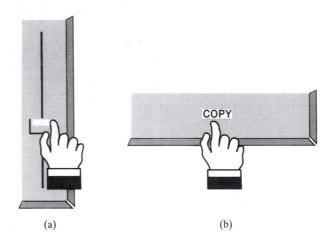

(a)   (b)

Figure 13.9   (a) Slider and (b) button icons.

finger would make if pressing a real button or pushing a slider. On the other hand, it could be argued that the same affordance could be achieved by representing the cursor as an arrow pointing at the slider or button. Empirical testing would need to be carried out to determine which provides the most obvious visual cues as to its operation.

When designing interface objects, like buttons, sliders and files, it is important that the actions meant to be performed on them are obvious. But what about complex actions? Is it possible to represent interface objects that are capable of affording more elaborate actions? What types of physical properties are needed? Gaver (1991) suggests that there are various techniques. One is to use combinations of **perceptual affordances**, as described above. Another is to design interface objects using **sequential affordances**, whereby acting on one perceptual affordance leads to information indicating new affordances. An example is the Macintosh scroll bar, described in Chapter 4, whereby after clicking on the box, the feedback provided immediately shows the box in an animated state. This then provides the affordance of moving up or down the shaft of the scroll bar. Hence, the first affordance lends itself to grabbing and the second to dragging. (The third technique described by Gaver is to use **sound affordances**, as outlined in Chapter 12.)

Question 13.8

(a) What does it mean to say that an object has an affordance?
(b) What are the main types of affordances? Give an example of each to illustrate your answer.

Constraints

Whereas affordances suggest the scope of an object in terms of what it can do and how we can interact with it or move it, **constraints** limit the number of possibilities of what can be done with it. Norman (1988) suggests that there are four main types of constraints: physical, semantic, cultural and logical.

Physical constraints restrict the possible operations of an object. As the saying goes, a square peg will not fit into a round hole. In the example of the scroll bar, the constraints of the shaft restrict movement of the scroll box to one of two alternatives; up or down (for vertical bars) or left or right (for horizontal bars). As we said above, the visual appearance can afford these constraints.

Semantic constraints depend on the semantics or the meaningfulness of the situation, which the users know about. They depend upon the user's knowledge of the world and the situation in which the computer system is being used. The icon of a wastebasket is semantically constrained in so far as it is represented upright on the desktop. It could, of course, be represented on its side or upside-down but this would contravene our knowledge of how wastebaskets are used. However, the spatial position of the wastebasket icon relative to the desktop is semantically inconsistent with our knowledge of the world; no-one has a bin on her table. Bins are always placed outside of buildings or under desks. But where else could the bin be placed at the interface? If it is hidden under the desktop then it would not be visible. (Remember the discussion of visibility and transparency in Chapter 1.) The problem with metaphoric interfaces, therefore, is that some aspects of the semantic mapping cannot be faithfully represented, and so semantic distortions have to be introduced. Provided users can understand why such semantic distortions have been introduced and that they don't contravene 'hard-wired' expectations about how objects should behave, few problems are created.

Cultural constraints, similar to the schemata discussed in Chapter 6, consist of information and rules that allow us to behave and know what to do in social settings (remember the discussion about pictorial signs on toilet doors!). Likewise, many icons have been designed to capitalize on cultural conventions. For example, the Macintosh has a warning icon that consists of a bold outlined icon with an exclamation mark in it. A balloon with a question mark in it is another icon that has been designed to represent help facilities.

Logical constraints work through constraining the order, position or location of objects. The order in which items are displayed in menus is logically constrained by appearing as lists of horizontal items. It would seem illogical if the items were randomly displayed across the screen in any direction.

Mappings

We have already mentioned the importance of good mappings in which the spatial and conceptual relations between different parts of a system relate to their controls and their outcomes. Mappings are said to be good if they appear natural and intuitive to the users. Bad mappings exist when the relations are inconsistent or incompatible – like pushing a car indicator upwards when wanting to turn left and pushing it down when wanting to turn right.

To illustrate why designers have problems getting the mappings of controls to be compatible with the users' expectations, consider the layout of cooker rings (stove burners in North America). Norman (1988) suggests a natural mapping is to have a semicircular arrangement of rings with an inner semicircle of controls. In this set-up the mappings are one-to-one, as shown in Figure 13.10. In Britain, however, most cookers are designed to be compact, presumably because most British kitchens are very small. The engineering solution has been to take up minimal space by placing the rings in a rectangular pattern. This has meant, however, that the control knobs have had to be placed away from the objects they control. A common configuration

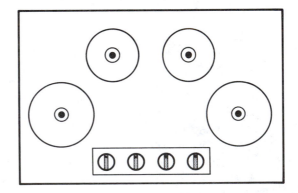

Figure 13.10 A natural mapping for the layout of cooker rings and controls (Norman, 1988).

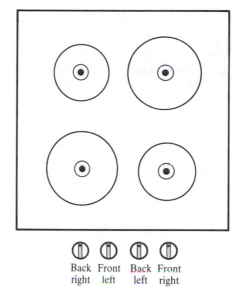

Back Front Back Front
right left left right

Figure 13.11 A design for the layout of cooker rings and controls (Norman, 1988).

is to have them positioned as a linear strip at the front of the oven, as shown in Figure 13.11. Hence, there is no obvious 'natural' solution for the rectangular–linear strip combination. It is arbitrary as to which controls should be associated with either the back or front rings.

EXERCISE

Can you work out an alternative solution for the cooker ring/control mappings?

COMMENT

One solution might be to use colour coding; a red control for a red ring, a blue control for a blue ring, and so on (Barber, 1988). However, problems would arise as soon as a pan was placed on a ring because it would no longer be visible.

Feedback

We have already discussed feedback in various places because it is such an important and fundamental design concept. **Feedback** is defined as the 'sending back to the user information about what action has actually been done [and] what result has been accomplished' (Norman, 1988, p. 27). In the light of the foregoing discussion, it should now be clear that a key principle of the design of system images is to provide visual (and if appropriate, auditory and tactile) feedback compatible with the principles of direct manipulation.

Question 13.9

We have already discussed numerous examples of feedback. Try to list some of them.

Key points

- In general, menus are considered to be more useful for novices than commands because users do not have to remember so much, but commands are usually quicker and are preferred by experienced users.
- Question and answer type dialogues are also fairly rigid, but generally require single key presses or one-word answers.
- Natural language dialogues, while promising the most flexibility, power and ease of use, are fairly restricted at present.
- Form-fills and spreadsheets require a specified form of input. Spreadsheets are more powerful than form-fills in that they provide built-in or specifiable calculating facilities.
- The key principles of direct manipulation interfaces are visibility of the objects of interest and rapid, reversible, incremental actions. Well-designed direct manipulation interfaces can benefit learners, novices, experts and occasional users. Advantages can include speed, ease of recovering from unintended effects, a feeling of confidence and an ability to predict system responses. Direct manipulation interfaces can be expensive in terms of computing resources, and can be difficult to design and program well.
- A main goal in interface design is to develop a system image which maps the design model onto the user model.
- The system image consists of the physical interface, the system's behaviour and external documentation.
- The relationship between the user and the system can be conceptualized in terms of the gulf of execution and the gulf of evaluation, which need to be bridged.
- The four main design principles of good direct manipulation interface design are affordances, constraints, mappings and feedback.

Further reading

NORMAN D.A. (1988). *The Psychology of Everyday Things*. New York: Basic Books.
This book provides a range of good examples of designs in which the principles of direct manipulation and affordance are used, and Norman discusses the underlying psychological concepts. Now published as *The Design of Everyday Things*.

SHNEIDERMAN B. (1992). *Designing the User Interface: Strategies for Effective Human–Computer Interaction* 2nd edn. Reading, MA: Addison-Wesley.
This book is an excellent source of further information on all the topics discussed in this chapter. The chapter on direct manipulation is particularly good, with lots of examples, ranging from icons, home automation, programming environments and telepresence to virtual reality.

HUTCHINS E.L., HOLLAN J.D. and NORMAN D. (1986). Direct manipulation interfaces. In *User-Centred System Design* (NORMAN D. and DRAPER S., eds), pp. 87–124. Hillsdale, NJ: Lawrence Erlbaum Associates.

ZIEGLER J.E. and FÄHNRICH K.P. (1988). Direct manipulation. In *Handbook of Human–Computer Interaction* (HELANDER M., ed.), pp. 123–33. Amsterdam: North-Holland.
These two articles provide more detailed psychological treatment of direct manipulation.

14

Designing Windowing Systems

Aims and objectives

The aim of this chapter is to illustrate some of the range of technical detail presented by HCI design. As a study-in-depth, we examine the trade-offs required when designing windowing systems. After studying this chapter you should:

- be able to identify the key elements of windowing systems,
- be able to assess the technical trade-offs in the design of windowing systems,
- be aware of the range of technical decisions required for HCI design.

Overview

One very important factor that must be taken into account when displaying information on a screen is the limitation imposed by the size of the display. Various methods have been developed to overcome this problem, most notably the use of windowing techniques. **Windows** are areas of a visual display, usually (though not always) rectangular, which divide the physical display area into several virtual displays. Windows can display data or actions from different host computers, different applications, different files in the same application, or different views of the same file. Windows also allow multiple processes (each typically represented by a different window) to share a single set of physical input and output devices, such as a keyboard and mouse. Time spent in creating a new document can be greatly reduced if the user can copy selected material from other windows in view, such as sections of text, tables, spreadsheet figures, pictures and so on. This minimizes time spent searching and retyping. However, there are many technical trade-offs to be taken into account in the design of windowing systems.

(The material in this chapter is based on work by Marcus (1992) and Shneiderman (1986, 1992).)

14.1 | General issues

In general, a windowing system may be viewed as managing input and output resources, such as the screen display and input devices, in much the same way that an operating system manages disk space and processor time. Windowing systems typically contain mechanisms to help the user move, resize, scroll, transfer data between, and generally manage multiple windows. They provide window facilities for application programs to enhance user interaction. Potential benefits of windowing systems and windowed applications include the following:

- use of limited display space can be optimized,
- users can use multiple sources on screen at once to carry out a task,

- users may be able to interact with any one of several multiple views of one item of interest on screen at the same time,
- the use of one set of input devices for various different purposes can be coordinated in a uniform way,
- mouse actions that cause different actions in different contexts are easier for users to understand due to each window giving a visual and textual context for the different kinds of interaction,
- users are shielded from complicated command languages, and allowed to specify objects and actions by pointing and selecting,
- the way in which the interface works can be more easily standardized across many applications, making it easy to learn how to operate new ones, once the first one has been learned.

Box 14.1 contains a brief history of windowing systems.

Box 14.1   A brief history of windowing systems

The invention of windows (along with the mouse and hypertext) is usually ascribed to Doug Engelbart, as part of his work during the 1960s at the Stanford Research Institute (Engelbart, 1988; Shneiderman, 1992). Windows that could overlap and be moved easily appeared in the Smalltalk environment (Shneiderman, 1992), developed by Alan Kay and others at Xerox PARC during the 1970s as part of the Dynabook project. The first high resolution, mouse-based computer system with a graphical user interface to be commercially successful in the mass market was the Apple Macintosh, in 1984, based on the earlier Apple Lisa. Development of the Lisa and Macintosh was apparently inspired by a visit to Xerox PARC made by Apple founder Steve Jobs in 1979 (Levy, 1994). Windowing systems were successfully introduced to an even wider mass market some years later when Microsoft's windowing environment, Microsoft Windows, for IBM PC compatible computers, was refined from the early rudimentary versions 1 and 2 to more sophisticated later versions, such as version 3 and beyond.

Usage

Windowing systems can be very useful to users using a single display whose work involves working with more than one document or application at a time. Example tasks using multiple sources are within most people's everyday work experience: they include creating a new draft document from a previous draft, looking up items in a database for inclusion in a letter, consulting electronic mail to write a memo, using a diary and calculator to make a work plan, and countless other tasks. Even if more than one display is available, Shneiderman (1992) notes that a single, large, high-resolution display is often preferable to multiple banks of monitors, due to distracting gaps between physical monitors. More generally, the effectiveness of a windowing system depends partly on the size, imaging model (see later in this section), speed and resolution of the display screen. With very small, slow or low resolution screens, the amount of time spent scrolling and re-ordering windows may make a windowing system counterproductive. The effectiveness of a windowing system also depends on ways in which the task and the system design minimize time spent finding, opening, closing, resizing, arranging, organizing, and generally manipulating windows, as we will now investigate.

In order to analyse the organizational overhead placed on users in managing windows, Card *et al.* (1984) introduced the idea of a **window working set**, which is defined as the set of windows needed to carry out a particular task effectively. Card argued that if the window working set cannot be fitted unobscured onto the physical screen at once, much time is likely to be wasted searching for, manipulating and reorganizing screens. This appears to be substantiated by an empirical test with eight experienced users, in which the windowed version of a system produced longer task-completion times than the non-windowed (full screen) environment (Bury *et al.*, 1985). Multiple smaller screens led to more time arranging information on the display and more scrolling activities to bring necessary information into view. However, after the time taken to arrange the display was eliminated, the task solution times were shorter for the windowed environment and fewer errors were made. These results suggest that there are advantages to using windows, but these advantages may be compromised unless good aids to window arrangement are provided. Note that these empirical results do not necessarily apply generally, since they might be different if the task or the windowing environment was different.

One way of making windows easier for users to control is to arrange for the relevant application program automatically to open the appropriate set of windows for each stage of the relevant tasks. This is a sensible solution for tasks for which the window working set can be reliably specified in advance. Even so, it is normally important that the user be given the means to adjust windows manually, to allow for the unexpected.

An alternative approach, proposed and explored by Henderson and Card (1987), is known as the Rooms model. Henderson and Card gathered data on the way in which people actually used windows. They found that different users would open different but recurring configurations for different kinds of task. To help automate the window management involved, Henderson and Card built a system that allowed particular arrangements of windows (and connections to appropriate documents and application programs) to be stored by users as a 'room'. Each complete room is displayed as a single icon. By clicking on the icon for a given room, the entire context of associated windows can be restored. Just one room can be selected and made active at any one time. The user can customize a series of rooms, one to suit each kind of task, and arrange the rooms in a collection, known as a 'building'. A study comparing users with and without the room systems found that rooms enabled users to handle comfortably about three times as many windows than they otherwise could (Bass and Coutaz, 1991). (See Figures 14.1 and 14.2.)

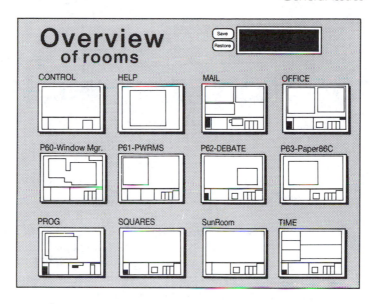

Figure 14.1 A rooms map (Henderson and Card, 1986 cited in Bass and Coutaz, 1991: © 1986, Association for Computing Machinery, Inc. reprinted with permission).

Figure 14.2 Hewlett-Packard's HP-VUE system, which offers the essence of the rooms idea. Any one of six workspaces can be selected from the strip on the lower part of the display. One workspace, which includes an image of a computer, is shown expanded (Shneiderman, 1992. Courtesy of Hewlett-Packard Company. Reproduced with permission).

Question 14.1

(a) What is a window working set?
(b) What is the relationship between windowing systems like rooms and the concept of the window working set?
(c) Give two advantages of a rooms-type approach for the user.

Software issues

There are a number of software engineering issues for windowing systems, which can affect design decisions in user interfaces that make use of them. One particularly important one that we shall consider is concerned with different imaging models; other issues are examined in Bass and Coutaz (1991).

Every windowing system must offer application programs a scheme or language for displaying graphical images via the windows. Such a scheme is known as an **imaging model**. Two important kinds of imaging model are **bitmaps** and **mathematical descriptions of curves**. Bitmaps are a system whereby, for example, the letter 'A' in a particular font is described as an array of dots, each of which may be turned on or off or assigned a colour. Bitmaps, irrespective of their contents, are very quick to draw, but tend to be difficult to enlarge or reduce. Images represented as bitmaps are not easily displayed in magnified or reduced form, or rotated at arbitrary angles (except in certain special cases, or subject to a severe loss of image quality). Mathematical descriptions of curves, areas or shapes, such as the widely used PostScript system, are imaging models whereby curves and other graphical objects are described by mathematical formulae. For example, in the case of PostScript, the letter 'A' is specified as a collection of mathematical curves, known as spline curves, each of which may be filled in with a colour, texture or image. Mathematical descriptions can be scaled to any size or rotated at arbitrary angles, in principle, without loss of image quality. Imaging systems that depend on mathematical descriptions may take a noticeable time to render a complex image. Rendering time will depend on the complexity of the image. Bitmap-based models, by contrast, can render images with a speed independent of the contents.

Question 14.2

(a) What are the main advantages and disadvantages of bitmaps as an imaging model?
(b) What are the main advantages and disadvantages of imaging models that use mathematical descriptions of curves (such as PostScript)?

14.2 Basic window components

When thinking of an input or output device, we normally think of a physical device, constructed from physical components, that exists whether or not the system is turned on. Virtual devices can be just as important as physical input devices, but they have no existence except when the system is operating. A **virtual device** is a device that exists only by virtue of the operation of a computer system. Some virtual devices are input devices (for example, buttons and touch-sensitive areas), some are output devices (for example, dials, lights and passive gauges) and others are both (for example, sliders, control panels, calculators, and mouse-driven 'rubber bands'). One special case of a virtual device is an **interface component**, sometimes known as a **widget**. Check boxes, sliders, menus and buttons are all examples of interface components. It is possible to identify basic interface components that nearly all windowing systems have in common. Figure 14.3 illustrates the standard components that appear in nearly all windowing systems:

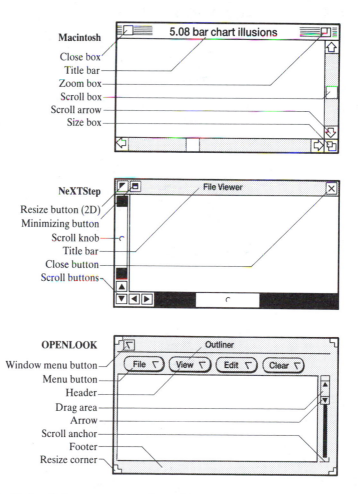

Figure 14.3 Basic window components from six common systems (Marcus, 1992).

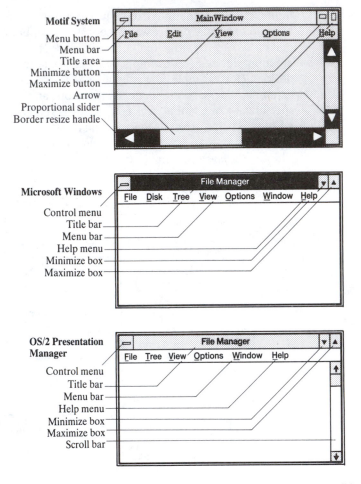

Figure 14.3 *(cont.)* Basic window components from six common systems (Marcus, 1992).

- windows
- menus
- controls and control panels
- dialogue boxes
- cursors

Windows

Windows are typically rectangular areas of the display that can be moved, sized and rendered independently on the display screen. Typically, the view of their contents can be changed using scrolling or editing. Most windowing systems provide standard

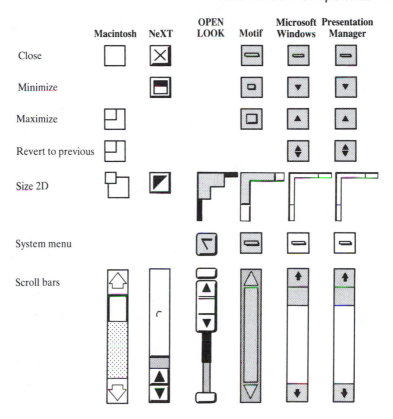

Figure 14.4 Standard window controls (Marcus, 1992).

windows with a border area for controlling the window itself, and a content area to allow the user to interact with the contents. The content area typically handles both input and output between user and an application program. Note that the effect of interaction components in the content area is determined not by the windowing system but by the application program in question. Most windowing systems provide a number of standard window types; for example, document windows for displaying and editing documents, and graphics windows for displaying and editing graphics. Figure 14.4 shows standard window controls for six different windowing systems. Sometimes a single window is divided up into **subpanes**, which occupy a fixed position in their parent window and cannot be moved independently, although their contents areas may be resizable and scrollable. Most windows can have a **title bar** at the top or bottom of the window, or a title in a tab to one side, as you can see in Figure 14.5. The tab approach can ease sorting of overlapping windows (Shneiderman, 1992). When a new window is opened or closed, animation effects such as an expanding window outline are often used to visually pinpoint the file that is the origin of the window's contents.

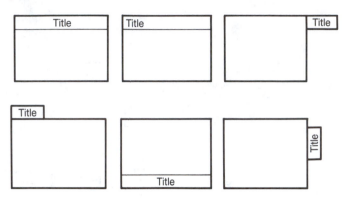

Figure 14.5 Windows with title tabs (Shneiderman, 1992).

Menus

Most windowing systems provide a system of menus (see also Section 13.3) consisting of **implicit** or **explicit pop-up menus** (Marcus, 1992). Explicit pop-up menus are triggered by clicking on appropriate interface components such as icons, menu bars, window controls and so on. Implicit pop-up menus can be made to appear without having to take the cursor to any particular labelled object. Implicit menus appear when a user clicks anywhere on the screen, or on a particular area of the screen, depending on the system, and they usually remain in position until the user instructs them to disappear by, for example, clicking on a 'close box' or selecting a close command. A special case of the explicit pop-up menu is the pull-down menu (Figure 14.6).

The menu systems used in windowing systems are predominantly operated by selecting an object or set of objects first, and then subsequently selecting an action from an appropriate menu. Visual feedback is typically given by some kind of visual emphasis, such as highlighting the entry. Elaborations of the basic menu idea are often provided, such as in the form of a **submenu** associated with some choices. The existence of a submenu is usually visibly indicated by a marker against the corresponding entries. If one of these entries is selected, then the submenu pops up to one side of the original menu, as shown in Figure 14.7. In systems with **hierarchical pop-up menus**, the facility to make a series of selections and subselections with a single extended gesture is often offered. Single-level menu selections can typically be made using one of two **gestural syntaxes**. The first syntax can be summarized as 'press–drag–release', and the second as 'click–position–click'. Press–drag–release means 'press to pop the menu up, drag to traverse the menu and release to make a selection'. Click–position–click means 'click to pop the menu up, position to traverse the menu, and click to make a selection'. Some menu selections are not complete in themselves, but require subsequent interaction with a **dialogue box**. This is typically indicated against the menu entry using a repeated dot symbol. Most menu systems show the currently selected state of any group of entries by displaying them in bold or by a tick. Entries that are

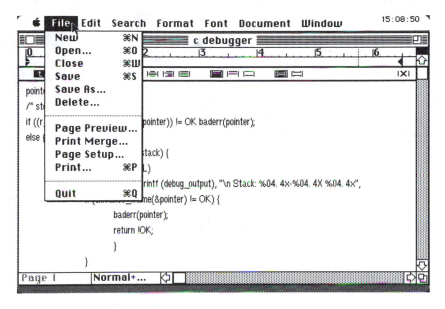

Figure 14.6 Pull-down menu (courtesy of Microsoft Corporation).

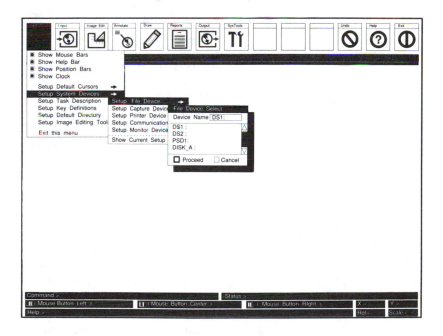

Figure 14.7 Hierarchical submenus (Marcus, 1992).

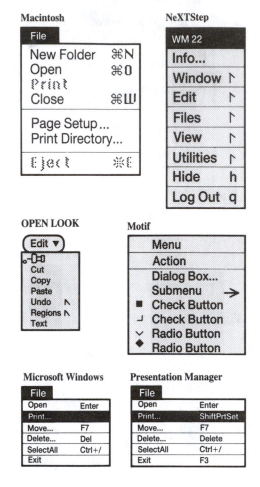

Figure 14.8 Standard menu entries for six windowing systems (Marcus, 1992).

disallowed in the current context are often shown in a dimmed font. Many menu systems list keyboard equivalents for menu selections (keyboard actions that have the same effect) next to each menu entry (Figure 14.8).

Controls and control panels

'Controls' is a general term for interface components such as sliders, buttons, check boxes and so on. Windowing systems typically provide standard controls for operations such as moving, resizing and scrolling (described in Section 14.3). Many of the controls provided by windowing systems allow users to master unfamiliar systems by using their everyday knowledge of how buttons and switches work on physical objects (remember the discussion of affordances in Section 13.7). **Control**

panels typically consist of a collection of controls and displays in an assembly that show the user the state of some object or objects of interest, and allow various parameters to be altered interactively (see Figure 12.1 for an example).

Box 14.2 contains details of some common control widgets.

Box 14.2   Control widgets

Buttons, sliders and gauges and dials

Buttons are used to select items or options. In many situations, exactly one item must always be selected from some set at all times. To help make this immediately obvious, buttons mimicking the station change buttons on a car radio are often used, as shown in Figure 14.9. Sliders are used to set quantities that vary

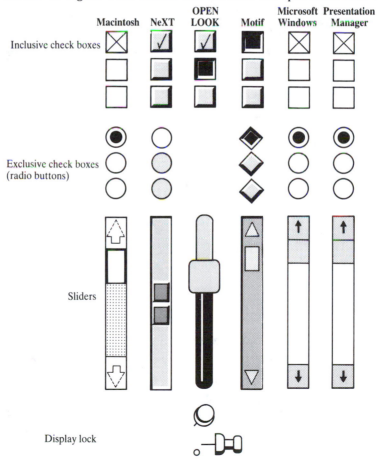

Figure 14.9   Standard widgets from various window systems (Marcus, 1992).

continuously within given limits, or to allow choices to be made between large numbers of options. Gauges and dials are sometimes used to present the same information passively.

Text fields

Text fields allow the user to input textual data. The value is typically not accepted until some confirming button on the control panel or the 'enter' key on the keyboard is pressed. This allows the entry to be edited using simple text editing facilities, which are often provided, until correct.

Dynamic menus

Dynamic menus are menus whose entries need not be fixed when the program is coded, but can be chosen by the program (or user) at runtime. These often act as alternatives to text fields, in that names of items can be selected instead of being typed in.

Immediate controls and controls subject to confirmation

Some controls take immediate effect. However, when a control panel is part of a dialogue box (see below) with a confirmatory button, the action typically does not take place until the button is pressed. Similarly, when a control panel is part of a dialogue box with a cancel button, any changes made since the dialogue box appeared may usually be cancelled by pressing the cancel button. Where control panels are part of dialogue boxes (see below), default values are often provided for all appropriate controls, including text fields. The **default value** is usually the most frequently used or safest option, indicated by a thickened border around a button, or some similar visual device.

Dialogue boxes

Dialogue boxes are on-screen controls that the system displays to provide contextual information. They may ask the user to:

- make a related set of choices,
- type in some information,
- choose from a set of options that may change depending on context,
- acknowledge a piece of information before proceeding.

Dialogue boxes may be divided into various types but in practice there is considerable overlap between them. **Modal dialogue boxes** force the user to respond to some question before any other action can be taken, because all other controls are frozen.

Modal dialogue boxes are useful when the system must force the user to take a decision to avoid an irreversible but possibly unwanted or dangerous situation. **Modeless dialogue boxes** offer information and request some action, but do not restrict the actions of the user. Typically they can be moved, resized, dealt with or ignored while other interactions continue. **Query boxes** are a particular kind of dialogue box (modal or modeless) initiated by the system rather than by the user. **Message boxes** are another special kind of dialogue box initiated by the system rather than the user. Typically, they do not allow the action that led to their appearing to be reversed. They often only allow a yes/no answer or a simple acknowledgement. They usually signal the occurrence of some event that the user cannot control, such as an external event like the arrival of a message or the occurrence of an error.

Question 14.3

What will a modeless dialogue box let the user do that a modal dialogue box prevents?

Cursors

At least two different kinds of cursor are normally provided by a windowing system, the mouse cursor and the text cursor. The mouse cursor shows the user where the current position of the mouse is considered to be with respect to the windows on screen. In most windowing systems the shape of the mouse cursor can be changed by application programs or by the window system to give the user feedback on what the system is doing or on what the user is expected to do at any given time. Windows that are specialized to deal with text typically have an additional cursor, the **text cursor**, which shows where input will be directed from the keyboard. Figure 14.10 shows various standard cursor shapes.

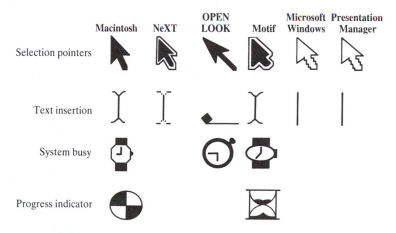

Figure 14.10 Standard mouse pointer and cursor shapes (Marcus, 1992).

14.3 Common tasks in windowing systems

Not all windowing systems allow exactly the same tasks to be performed, but there is a core of common tasks that more or less all windowing systems permit. These deal with input management, changing window focus, the management of single windows and the management of multiple windows (Marcus, 1992). We will look at each of these areas in turn.

Managing input

Most common modern windowing systems allow mouse and keyboard to be used in combination to control both the windowing system and application programs. In general, mice have one, two or three buttons. When more than one button is provided, the user must remember which button performs which action in any given context. This problem, the button overload problem (Bass and Coutaz, 1991) can confuse untrained users but the problem can be alleviated to some extent by assigning each button a standard role. There are typically just five primitive actions that can be carried out with any mouse button, irrespective of how many buttons are provided. These are point, click, press, drag and double click. The variety and convenience of tasks that can be carried out with a mouse can be greatly extended by the use of various modifier keys (shift, control and so on), particularly when there is only one mouse button. If modifier keys are used, their function must be assigned in a consistent way if the user is to remember how they are to be used.

Changing window focus

A windowing system must make it easy for the user to direct output to any desired window, and must provide visual feedback to show the user which window output is currently being directed to. The active window is indicated in most windowing systems by some alteration in the appearance of the title bar, as shown in Figure 14.11. There are two common systems for allowing the user to direct input to a chosen window, click to focus and mouse focus (Bass and Coutaz, 1991). In **click to focus**, the user's input is not directed to a new window until the user clicks anywhere within the borders of that window. In **mouse focus**, the user's input is directed to whichever window within whose borders the cursor is currently located (without any need for a mouse click). With either system, it is possible for users to shift their attention to a new window but forget, or fail to carry out correctly, the action needed to change the focus to a new window. There must also be some mechanism for controlling which window receives focus in overlayed windows. In some systems it is always the top window, which is easy for untrained users, but at a possible cost of needing to bring windows to the top frequently. In other systems, the keyboard focus may be changed to any of the stack of overlayed windows using keys on the

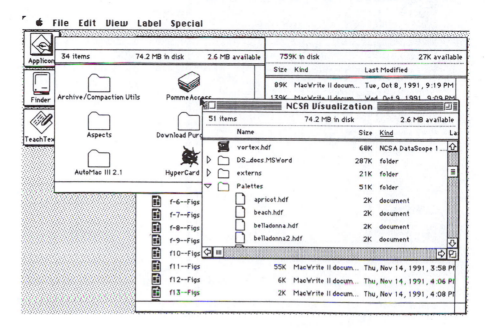

Figure 14.11 Distinguishing the active window. In this set of overlapping windows under Macintosh System 7, the active window is the one with stripes in the title bar (Shneiderman, 1992. Reproduced by courtesy of Apple Computer UK Ltd).

alphanumeric keyboard. Under this scheme, it is possible to leave the window receiving focus in an obscured position within the pile. This may be confusing for the untrained user, but it can help the experienced user save time in some circumstances.

Managing single windows

Most windowing systems permit the user to move windows by selecting in the title bar area and dragging. Some also allow windows to be moved by dragging on either side border, or by using a keyboard and menu combination. Frequently, the information available to be shown by a window takes up more space than is available in the window at one time. Scrolling is a way to give the user control over which part of the information is shown. Typically, scroll arrows are clicked on to scroll the window just one line (or other suitable small increment) in either direction, and held down to cause continuous scrolling. Shneiderman (1992) notes several ways in which scrolling mechanisms could be improved, for example, by showing page numbers in the scroll handle, and allowing users to place selectable 'bookmarks' on the scroll track (see Figure 14.12).

Figure 14.12 A proposed scroll bar innovation (Shneiderman, 1992).

Question 14.4

What actions can the scroll bar shown in Figure 14.12 support that are not supported by conventional scroll bars?

Most windowing systems allow the size of windows to be changed by means of a sizing control situated in one or more corners of each window. Often this is achieved by the user dragging on the control with the mouse, which causes the two adjacent borders to follow, shrinking or expanding depending on the direction of drag.

Managing multiple windows

Very often, not all windows in use will fit on the screen at once. For this reason, facilities are generally provided to iconify, tile or overlap windows.

- **Iconification**   occurs in some systems, which allows screen space to be saved by shrinking windows down into window icons, which may be re-expanded at will. The icons then act as a visual reminder of the window.
- **Tiling**   usually refers to systems with no overlapping that use all available space, by analogy with tiling a wall. There are many variations on the basic idea. Some simple systems use a fixed number of tiles, such as four, six or eight, in unvarying positions. Some systems allow variable numbers of tiles, and when tiles are opened or closed, they cause neighbouring tiles to grow or shrink automatically. Other systems allow tiles to be 'stacked on top of' each other, and allow users to bring tiles to the top of the pile by various mechanisms. Evidence on the effectiveness of tiling systems is inconclusive (Bass and Coutaz, 1991; Bly and Rosenberg, 1986).

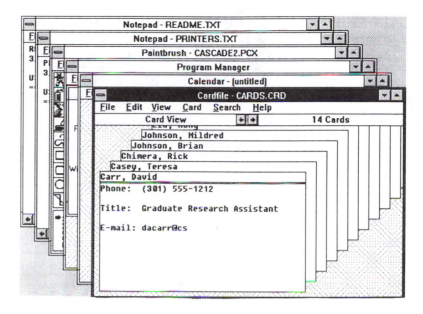

Figure 14.13 Cascaded windows. An automatically arranged cascade of windows produced in MS Word 3 by a user command from the menu (Shneiderman, 1992. Reproduced by courtesy of Microsoft Corporation).

- **Overlapping** is probably now the most popular form of window management. Windows are allowed to partially obscure each other like overlapping papers arranged on a desk. In some systems, windows must fit within the display, but in others, windows may be partially 'slid off' the display, and may even be bigger than the display (though not entirely visible at once). An overlapping system can be very flexible (and can be aesthetically attractive), but can lead to problems of clutter and disorganization. The cascade (Figure 14.13) is a version of overlapping that can be particularly helpful if a large number of windows must be opened at the same time. The windows are automatically arranged fanned out, usually in a diagonal line so that the title and one other border of each window can be seen. In this way, many windows can be displayed in a small space. Often, cascading is provided to the user as one option.

One recurring problem concerns how the system should decide where windows should be sized and placed when they are opened. Possible strategies include new windows being opened in the same way every time; each document or data object having its window opened in the same position that it was previously open or last left; or having each new window opened in a position slightly offset from the position where a similar object was last opened. Several windowing systems provide an in-built system for giving help with this and other aspects of their functioning.

Windowing systems illustrate how interface design issues interact with design issues in the underlying software, and how designers inevitably face trade-offs among their design goals. Box 14.3 contains some reflections from William Newman about his experience of designing a window system manager and its user interface (adapted from Newman *et al.*, 1985).

Box 14.3 William Newman's experiences of designing a window system manager and its user interface

William Newman, the co-author of one of the first textbooks on computer graphics, was an interface designer on a large variety of industrial projects, and is currently a researcher at Rank Xerox EuroPARC in Cambridge, UK.

'We were concerned that the designer of an application program would be relatively unconstrained in the design of the program's user interface. ... We recognised that programs would make different demands on the window manager for scrolling, subdivision of windows, etc.'

'It was important that the user should understand the underlying model of window management, so that windows did not get lost.'

'We recognised that the application program's user interface might adopt different conventions for the window control interface. We wished to minimise the danger that these conventions would clash in awkward ways.'

'We wanted to provide the user with a convenient set of controls over screen layout. ... We wanted to ensure that the user wasted as little time as possible in screen management operations.'

You can see that these goals may conflict with each other. You will often face similar trade-offs; for example, between providing maximal functionality (in this case, most flexibility for applications using the windowing system) and simplicity for users.

'One requirement for which we found little in the way of existing solutions was flexibility in providing different levels of window control. We wished to allow programs to provide scrolling and window-splitting controls to the degree required by the application, but retain consistency in operations like window moving and resizing.'

'We found it easiest to meet this requirement through a modular design. Certain controls are provided on every window: they include controls for moving, resizing, bringing windows to the "top of the heap" and sending them to the bottom. ... We also provided standard controls for shrinking windows into small icons. ... The remaining window controls – scrolling, splitting, etc. – are not constrained to a standard form, although it is expected that application programmers will take advantage of the basic set of controls provided with the window manager. In the case of applications requiring very specialized controls for these operations, the basic set may be replaced by others.'

EXERCISE

Compare the design outlined in Box 14.3 with the user interface and application program interface for the window manager system you most frequently encounter. Have the designers made different choices? What considerations do you think influenced their decisions? (No comment is provided for this exercise.)

14.4 Issues in windowing systems for CSCW

Our discussion of windowing systems has so far followed the conventional 'desktop on a workstation' perspective. Windowing systems will change as our technology evolves. As an example of issues that are now beginning to emerge, in this section we consider support for shared windows, based on work by Marilyn Mantei (1992).

Imagine a situation in which two people are each using their own workstation to communicate with each other via a shared voice channel and desktop window. It is essential that these two media be kept synchronized, so that as one person comments on objects and points to them there is no lag while the desktop window catches up with the voice. The user making the comments and carrying out the manipulations must also experience immediate feedback on actions.

As more media channels are added, the issues can become even more complex because of the compression and transmission properties of the media. For example, many voice channels do not permit more than one participant to speak at once, and some form of feedback about who is speaking may be required. Where video is used, it is often compressed using algorithms that depend on relatively stable images to be effective. When the images change dramatically, the compression rates drop and it can take longer for the video image to be available. When more than one user can be performing activities on shared objects, other coordination issues arise. How can we prevent one user from deleting or modifying an object that another user is just about to select (and will this occur often enough to be problematic?). Does one user provide 'floor control' to coordinate shared activity, or can this be done effectively with the voice channel? What kind of 'undo' facility will be required to support multiple users?

Key points

- Use of limited display space can be optimized using windows.
- Users can use multiple sources on screen at once to carry out a task.

- The use of one set of input devices for various different purposes is easily coordinated using windows.
- Standard windowing systems can allow the way in which interfaces work to be more easily standardized across many applications, making it easy to learn how to operate new ones, once the first one has been learned.
- The usefulness of windows is limited by size and resolution of display screen: if too small, too much time may be spent rearranging windows.
- Automatic facilities for organizing window working sets can save time and make large collections of windows easier to manage.
- Most windowing systems offer a set of basic interface components including title bars, windows, menus, dialogue boxes control panels, mouse cursors and fonts.
- Common tasks in windowing systems include moving windows, scrolling, resizing and changing window depth.
- Techniques for managing multiple windows include overlapping, tiling, cascading and iconification.

Further reading

BASS L. and COUTAZ J. (1991). *Developing Software for the User Interface*. Reading, MA: Addison-Wesley.
This book is strongly recommended for a software engineering perspective.

MARCUS A. (1992). *Graphic Design for Electronic Documents and User Interfaces*. Reading, MA: Addison-Wesley.
This book is strongly recommended for a designer's perspective.

SHNEIDERMAN B. (1992). *Designing the User Interface: Strategies for Effective Human–Computer Interaction*, 2nd edn. Reading, MA: Addison-Wesley.
This book gives an inspired and detailed overview from a practitioner's viewpoint.

15

User Support and On-Line Information

Aims and objectives

The aim of this chapter is to explore some of the design issues faced in the provision of on-line help and other user support systems. After studying this chapter you should:

- be aware of some approaches to supporting training, such as minimalist instruction, training wheels and scenario-driven instruction, and their advantages and disadvantages,
- be familiar with the various different kinds of on-line help offered and their strengths and shortcomings,
- be aware of the different kinds of questions users typically ask, and the kinds of problems that lead to requests for help,
- be familiar with the basic concepts involved in hypertext and hypermedia, the kind of problems users experience with hypermedia and some design approaches to solving these problems.

Overview

At some time or other, we all experience problems using computer systems. Good design of the system and system image will reduce the number of problems that users experience. However, providing information so that users can learn to use the system effectively, correct their errors and find other kinds of functionality is an important part of the design of many systems. In this chapter we consider some approaches to information design, including manuals, tutorials, on-line help, hypertext and hypermedia.

15.1 Active learning with minimalist manuals

To capitalize on more active ways of learning for computer systems, Carroll and colleagues (Carroll, 1992) have developed a number of innovative training methods, which take account of the psychological considerations discussed in Sections 8.1 and 8.2. These include minimalist instruction, which attempts to support novice behaviour, the Training Wheels word processor and the Scenario Machine, which both attempt to provide a training interface that supports novice learning strategies. (Readers interested in other forms of documentation design should consult Horton (1990, 1991), which are described in the further reading section at the end of this chapter.)

'And I bought this one to explain the manual of the first one.'

(*Source* Honeysett)

MOVING THE CURSOR   Topic 4: 2

> The four cursor-movement keys have arrows on them (they are located on the right of the keyboard).

PRESS THE ↓ CURSOR KEY SEVERAL TIMES AND WATCH THE CURSOR MOVE DOWN THE SCREEN.

> The ↑, ←, and → cursor keys work analogously. Try them and see.
>
> If you move the cursor all the way to the bottom of the screen, or all the way to the right, the display "shifts" so that you see more of your document. By moving the cursor all the way up and to the left, you can bring the document back to where it started.

DELETING TEXT

USE THE CURSOR KEYS TO MOVE THE CURSOR UNDER THE FIRST r IN THE WORD regular.

PRESS THE DEL KEY

> The DEL key is located up and to the right of the keyboard keys.
>
> Is the Displaywriter prompting you?: Delete what?
>
> ▶ If you make a mistake at this point, use CODE + CANCL and start the deletion again.

USING THE → KEY, MOVE THE CURSOR THROUGH THE MATERIAL TO BE DELETED, THE WORD regular.

> The word is highlighted: you can see exactly what is going to be deleted before it actually is deleted.
>
> ▶ If the wrong characters are highlighted use CODE + CANCL and start the deletion again.

Figure 15.1 A page from the minimalist manual encouraging the user to try things out (Carroll, 1992).

Minimalist instruction

Minimalist instruction entails removing many of the obstacles that make learning difficult. Specifically, the 'minimal manual' (Figure 15.1) was designed primarily to reduce the amount of information that a learner needs to read in order to learn to use a word processor. This was achieved by eliminating all repetition, summaries, reviews, exercises and the index. In addition, many of the explanations that were not related to doing things were drastically reduced. The manual was also designed to be

You are now ready to use the Displaywriter. The list of items you see on the screen is called the TASK SELECTION menu. It lists the major things the Displaywriter can do. From this list of selections (called a "menu"), you can choose the particular task you want to accomplish using the Displaywriter.

The majority of these tasks will be involved with letters (and other sorts of documents) -- typing or creating them, revising them, and printing them out on paper. Therefore, most of the time when you are working with the Displaywriter, you will be choosing the first item on the Task Selection menu -- TYPING TASKS.

WHAT IF I GET STUCK?

Everyone makes mistakes -- and learning to use a word processor is difficult enough to cause many mistakes. When you do make a mistake try to just correct it and go on -- you don't have to do everything perfectly. If you really do get so stuck that you can't continue, there is a general remedy you should keep in mind.

▶ **Press the END key, located to the left of the keyboard.**
▶ **Now remove all diskettes from the diskette unit to avoid damaging them, and then turn the system off.**

You must now start all over again, by re-loading your programmes from the programme diskettes.

ON YOUR OWN

Check your understanding so far: remove the Vol.1 diskette, turn the Displaywriter off, and then start it up again. Remember that any time you turn the power off, you must always first remove the diskettes. If you run into any trouble, just go on to Topic 2 .

Figure 15.2 A page from the minimalist manual showing the information that is provided on how to recover from errors (Carroll, 1992).

more task-oriented. Instead of including a series of rote exercises based on system tasks, the topics included were directed at real work activities. One category of information which is often under-represented in commercial manuals is how to recover from errors, so the minimal manual greatly increased the amount of information on this topic, as Figure 15.2 indicates. After a series of iterative design processes, user testing revealed that for a number of basic word processing activities, learning was substantially faster with the minimal manual than with conventionally available manuals (Carroll, 1992).

The Training Wheels word processor

The **Training Wheels** word processor follows the same philosophy as the minimal manual and limits the learner to simple functions by making advanced functions unavailable, so protecting the user from potentially drastic errors. The system allows a new user only to type in documents, edit and print them. Other functions such as spelling aids, format changing and menu-skipping are 'blocked', and if the user tries to access them the system provides a message saying that they are not available. The aim of this approach is to encourage users to try things out with the knowledge that nothing drastic can go wrong.

The Scenario Machine

One of the problems with the Training Wheels interface is that it can actually be detrimental to a friendly learning environment. For example, can you imagine the effects of being told 'option not available' every time you select a menu item that has been classified as an advanced function? For most of us such barriers can be quite frustrating. One way of overcoming this problem is to provide additional information explaining why these options are not available and what options the user could try instead. The **Scenario Machine** is a system for training novices that has been designed with this strategy in mind: it has been adapted from the Training Wheels interface to give more guidance to a user in the initial stages of learning. Evaluation of the Scenario Machine has shown that this enhancement to the Training Wheels interface enabled learners to type and print out simple documents more successfully than without the enhancement (Carroll and Ray, 1988).

15.2 User assistance and on-line help

When you use any tool to help you accomplish something, you are engaged in two tasks: the **primary task** is what led you to use the tool, but there is a **secondary task** of mastering enough of the tool to accomplish the primary task. So every on-line computer system has to support both tasks. The functional requirements for the system spell out the primary task, and the interaction or usability requirements define what the system must do to support you. However, in a complex tool like an interactive computer system, this secondary task can be substantial: the tool is not always 'ready-to-hand' as a natural extension of your own abilities and thought processes.

When people ask for help, they know they are missing some information, which may be about the task itself, primary or secondary, or about the semantics of one or more task functions and the state change they must achieve, or to do with the operations needed to invoke the desired state, or about the particular actions

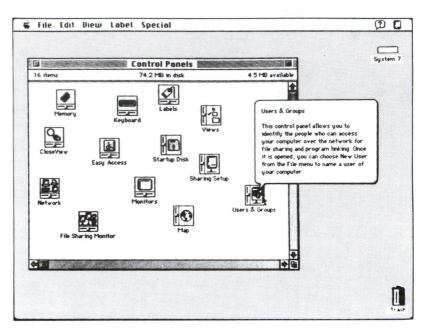

Figure 15.3 System 7.0 for the Macintosh has an option called 'Balloon Help'. When this is switched on, touching an object or feature with the cursor displays a balloon explaining that item. Application developers can buy kits to let them exploit this feature in their own applications (Shneiderman, 1992. Reproduced by courtesy of Apple Computer UK Ltd).

required, and so on. If they are missing such information about frequently used or key functions, we should suspect a design flaw, such as an inappropriate dialogue style or an internal inconsistency. But every complex system has infrequently used parts, and may have some unavoidable error-prone sections; for example, where internal consistency and consistency with natural language are in conflict. For example, studies of the Symbolic Document Examiner information revealed that after two years of intensive use people were still accessing new parts of the documentation (Walker, 1988).

Question 15.1

If users need help for a frequently used interface function what does this suggest about the system?

Most contemporary user interfaces provide at least some of the following on-line information for user assistance:

- help messages generated by selecting a desired object; for example, the Shift + F1 keys for help on menu bar options in Windows, or balloon help (Figure 15.3) in Macintosh System 7,

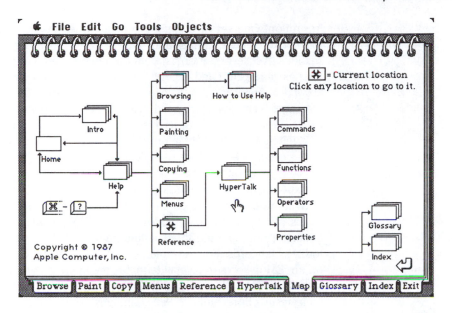

Figure 15.4 Help and tutorial information available from Apple's HyperCard (Woodhead, 1990: courtesy of Apple Computer UK Ltd).

- context-sensitive help built into application system states or dialogue boxes,
- generic help text, usually limited in length, available through a help command, menu bar item, function key or icon; for example, OS/2 Presentation Manager provides a Master Help Index icon and a keyboard Help key, F1,
- extended help screens, accessible through a 'More' button, an Index or Table of Contents. These help items can be linked together to form a hypertext (see Section 15.3 and Figure 15.4),
- extensive written documentation available on-line. This is typically authored so that it can be read like a book.

You might well ask whether such an extensive array of aids is necessary, an issue we examine next. But be wary of generalizing too much from your own experience: not all users will have your learning style, your set of companions from whom to seek assistance, or the particular costs and benefits of your working environment.

What do we know about on-line help systems?

The effectiveness of particular help systems and features is difficult to study. For one thing, it takes more user sessions to obtain data about help use: only 5% to 20% of user interactions typically involve help, but although this reflects a small percentage in terms of data collection it can be a very substantial one in terms of effort and frustration! One set of quantitative data comes from an empirical study of help in IBM's CMS system (Senay and Stabler, 1987). The data records over 52,000 help sessions over several months, from both experienced and inexperienced users. Help queries were generated in a command language format, with topics as parameters. Several interesting facts emerged from this study. For example, 15% of the help messages were never accessed, and 10% of the messages accounted for 90% of the usage. When a sample of users was asked how successful their help sessions were, 35% felt they got the right information, 16% felt they did not, and the remainder (half of the users) weren't sure whether they found what they needed.

Early laboratory studies employed a traditional cognitive psychology paradigm of experimental and control groups to compare kinds of assistance. Most of these only showed that poor on-line help was no match for good printed documents. Relles (1979) and Cohill and Williges (1984) showed that printed manuals worked better for novices than their on-line helps, but the on-line helps were primitive by today's standards. For example, the aid provided by Cohill and Williges was based on an IBM full screen display terminal, so the help completely obscured the primary task. They noted that this disadvantage alone probably accounted for a large part of their result. Borenstein (1985) similarly found that faster access to poor help messages did not improve user performance. More recent studies try to document problem areas rather than comparative advantages. For example, Campagnoni and Ehrlich (1990) collected detailed protocols that demonstrate various navigational problems and strategies with the Sun 386i help system. Other research has examined the questions in users' minds that prompt use of on-line help (O'Malley, 1986; Sellen and Nicol, 1990). Typical users' questions appear to focus on:

- goal exploration: What can I do with this program?
- definition and description: What is this? What is it for?
- task achievement: How do I do this?
- diagnostic: How did that happen?
- state identification: Where am I?

Help information usually works more effectively when the particular user question is answered, without extraneous information.

EXERCISE

Think of an application you know. Think of at least one way in which help information of the following kinds could be provided better than at present.

- goal exploration: What can I do with this program?
- task achievement: How do I do this?
- diagnostic: How did that happen?
- state identification: Where am I?

COMMENT

A good answer to this exercise could make a substantial contribution to research and scholarship, and make you a lot of money. Your answer may depend greatly on the particular application program, set of users and work context you chose. Choosing the program Harmony Space (see Chapter 12) by way of illustration, one might come up with the following ideas. (Your answers may vary considerably.)

Goal exploration: What can I do with this program?

Provide short looped video clips (micons) or static cartoons accessed by icons to dramatize the possibilities. Or simply provide a list of sample tasks as part of an indexed help message.

Task achievement: How do I do this?

Possibly supply a video to be distributed with the program. Or provide a set of animated cartoons, for example as part of a HyperCard stack. Another possibility would be to devise and supply a set of indexed instructions, in the form of minimalist instruction. Such instructions might be better delivered in the form of a printed book that can be read in bed.

Diagnostic: How did that happen?

This is a very difficult question for the chosen application. A simple expert system might be worth considering.

State identification: Where am I?

Provide a state transition diagram as a map to show where one can 'go' in the program and how to get there. Also provide a dynamic map of the last few steps just made at any given time using little screen shots and a record of the command that made each transition.

Current status of on-line assistance

Well-written, generally accessible on-line help works effectively to meet requests for operational ('what does this do?') and definitional ('what is X?') information. It is not as effective for tactical ('when should I choose X rather than Y?') information. More extensive documentation is required when users need prerequisite conceptual information. Context-sensitive help has both benefits and shortcomings. In an intensive study of 24 users of a CAD system (Moll and Sauder, 1987), researchers found that their context-sensitive help system worked well when users were seeking information on what they should do in their current state, but did not help people who didn't want to be in the state where they found themselves. The context dependency can become a trap for users seeking help if they have lost their way in the dialogue, gone astray while solving their problem, or if several input steps are unknown to them.

The most difficult situation for users occurs when they are unable to conceptualize their information needs in terms that allow them access to the information. This could result from either a lack of prerequisite knowledge or a misconception about the cause of an error situation. A study by Bagnara and Rizzo (1989) revealed five different patterns of user behaviour when recovering from errors:

- **Immediate correction**   users verbalize only correct solution.
- **Automatic causal analysis**   users verbalize correct cause and solution.
- **Conscious causal analysis**   users evaluate the outcome obtained and previous operations, then hypothesize how and why the error occurred and how to recover.
- **Explorative causal analysis**   users recognize where the problem occurred, but not how. Various hypotheses are explored, often by backward analysis. The correct causal chain is discovered (rather than merely identified or checked as in the previous case). This is the most frequent setting for access to on-line help information.
- **Conceptual mismatch**   users do not understand enough to correct, and either seek more information from extended documentation, bypass the problem or search for an alternate strategy to achieve the desired intentions.

When extensive documentation is required and provided, book-like formats may work better than hypertext networks (see Section 15.3) with less apparent overall structure. One mechanism for enhancing on-line information is to make reference and user guide information available on-line. The SuperBook system has demonstrated that effective on-line books can provide advantages over printed books (see Box 15.1). However, authors creating material that will appear both in print and on-line must be aware of the differing demands of the two media (Hendry, 1994). On-line books can, for example, also provide additional features, such as multiple tables of contents.

Box 15.1   SuperBook

SuperBook is a presentation system for on-line books, designed and built by researchers at AT&T (Remde *et al.*, 1987). SuperBook takes an existing document in a standard formatting language and presents it in a multi-windowed display, shown in Figure 15.5. The most innovative aspect of SuperBook is the interaction between the table of contents window and the word look-up. When users request a search on a particular word, the number of occurrences is

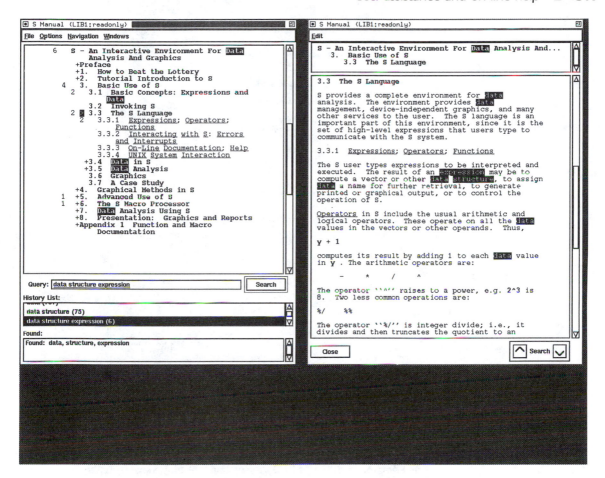

Figure 15.5 The SuperBook, a presentation system for on-line books (Egan *et al.*, 1989).

mapped onto the table of contents. This allows users to select the unit of information they wish to read. Several studies have compared performance using printed and SuperBook versions of a statistics and graphics manual (Egan *et al.*, 1989a, b, c). SuperBook users had significantly shorter search times and more correct responses than those using the printed text.

An alternative approach to improving user assistance is to maintain information about usage and provide advice based on a particular user's situation. A research project at the German National Research Centre for Computer Science has shown how to apply such knowledge within the popular spreadsheet program Excel. In one

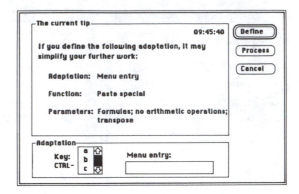

Figure 15.6 An adaptation tip from Flexcel, an adaptive interface for the spreadsheet Excel (Thomas and Krogsoeter, 1993: © 1993, Association for Computing Machinery, Inc. reprinted with permission).

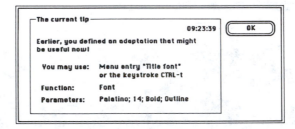

Figure 15.7 A usage tip from Flexcel, an adaptive interface for the spreadsheet Excel (Thomas and Krogsoeter, 1993: © 1993, Association for Computing Machinery, Inc. reprinted with permission).

scenario, the support system maintains a record of users' actions and compares them to a set of common plans for actions. This could enable the support system to provide customized help that reflects likely plans that the user is trying to accomplish, including those for which the user has omitted some steps (Quast, 1993) (Figure 15.6). In another scenario, the support system suggests more efficient ways of performing Excel functions, including that the user adapt the program by creating menu entries or 'hot key' shortcuts for frequent action sequences (Thomas and Krogsoeter, 1993) (Figure 15.7).

Question 15.2

Complete Table 15.1, which lists the various types of on-line help with a column for their key features. You should include comments on their strengths and weaknesses.

Table 15.1 Types of on-line help.

Types of on-line help	Key features
Help messages linked to particular objects	Help messages are linked to features that can be pointed to on the screen, such as menu bar options, icons, buttons, text windows. Good for operational information ('What does this do?'), less good for tactical information ('When to use this rather than that') and strategic information ('How do I achieve this end?').
Context-sensitive help	
Generic help text	
Extended help screens	
Extensive written documentation on-line	

15.3 Hypertext and hypermedia

The history of hypermedia systems can be traced back to the ideas of Vannevar Bush (1945), who described a conceptual system for linking pieces of information by association. During the 1960s Ted Nelson (1967) began working on the large-scale project, Xanadu, and in 1974 coined the term 'hypertext'. Doug Engelbart (1968) presented the first operational hypertext system and during the 1980s personal computer products like Guide (Figure 15.8) and Apple's HyperCard (Figure 15.9) came onto the market.

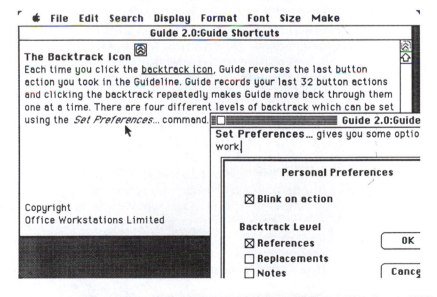

Figure 15.8 Using Guide to backtrack over a previously taken path (Woodhead, 1990).

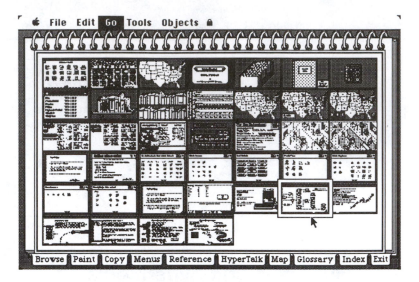

Figure 15.9 The 'recent' option in HyperCard allows direct access to any of up to 42 recently visited cards (Woodhead, 1990. Reproduced by courtesy of Apple Computer UK Ltd).

The prefix 'hyper' suggests the notions of branching and decision making, as in **hypertext**, a collection of nonlinear, text-based nodes that are linked together. When different media, such as video, sound and animations, are included as well as text in a branching structure, the system is known as **hypermedia**. Both hypertext and hypermedia can be thought of as databases containing large quantities of information which can be accessed using various specially devised navigation tools that enable users to browse and search the information. **Nodes** are the content structures of a hypermedia system; **links** are the relationship structures.

People browse the network of information by moving from one node to another, usually by following links between information items created by the author, who decides what the contents of each node will be and which nodes will link to which. As an example, consider the nodes in a literature system, which could include a best-seller list, a summary of each book, an author summary for each book's author, summaries for other books by the same authors, and character descriptions for all characters in all included books. Links could go from book list to books, books to their authors, authors to each of their books, books to appropriate character descriptions, and character descriptions to each appropriate book and so on.

Most application systems place little emphasis on giving the user a holistic picture of the information space, even though they provide extensive navigational facilities. Guide, for example (Figure 15.8), has different link types so that new information can be displayed without moving to a new place in the hypertext. HyperCard displays graphically the last few items accessed (Figure 15.9). But neither provides an overview of the hypertext. Appropriate metaphors (Chapter 7), **agents** or characters who act on behalf of the user in a virtual computer based environment

(Laurel, 1990) and good navigation tools are needed to help the user to answer such questions as: Where am I? What have I seen? What else is there to see? How can I get to see it?

15.4　Designing hypermedia for training in HCI

In the following case study we describe some design issues in the development of a hypermedia system for training, called HalClon (Preece and Crow, 1994). The HalClon system is designed to:

- motivate interest in HCI among managers,
- provide an accessible and informative resource for HCI designers.

HalClon is structured as a multimedia database of example video sequences, still images, animations, diagrams, text segments, voice-overs and sound effects. As a randomly ordered set of components, these would be of limited use to a potential user. Even if the items were linked to form a web of interconnected subjects, many users would not be motivated to explore the morass of information available to them. Therefore, efficient and rewarding ways need to be provided for users to navigate through the materials while still enabling them to determine their own paths if they so wish. One strategy is to provide several modes of access suitable for different kinds of users. Managers, for example, require concisely argued stories about the impact that HCI issues can have on their enterprise. Practitioners, however, are more interested in *how* to design better systems. They are likely to spend more time with the system and are likely to use two modes of interaction: initially they will *explore* the information available to gain a broad understanding of HCI issues; later they may require direct access to specific pieces of knowledge to aid in *problem-solving* activities. The system must, therefore, present its material in different ways so that users can follow different paths through it to achieve their particular goals.

From the user's perspective, navigating through a hypermedia system can be a daunting prospect and there are two distinct, but related, navigational problems that users are likely to encounter: conceptual navigation through the ideas the material represents and physical navigation between the different media components. The designer must, therefore, do two things: help users to build accurate mental models (Chapter 6) of the information structure, and provide appropriate tools to allow the users to navigate the conceptual space in the way they wish.

To aid user navigation, a metaphor of a 'printed magazine' has been adopted, which should be familiar to all users of the system (see Chapter 7 on the psychological issues underlying the use of metaphors). In particular, it is expected that users' expectations of a magazine will match the nature of the project well: a magazine is an information-giving artefact that is often used for both browsing (exploratory) and reference (searching and problem solving) and has an established and well-understood navigational method (page numbers combined with tables of contents, for example). The metaphor also gives natural information chunking mechanisms, such as paragraphs, stories, columns, sections and editorials, which can help to provide the management overview presentation needed. However the HalClon system also contains digital video sequences, voice-overs and interactive demonstrations of HCI techniques and practices; none of these could be present in a printed magazine, so the user may not understand how to use or conceptualize these new presentation formats – an issue for user testing.

The basic navigational technique that the magazine metaphor provides is the page numbering system, augmented by diagram and illustration numbering schemes, and possibly references at the end of articles. These are used *indirectly*, so one article refers to another by giving the page number on which the referent article resides. The contents page of a magazine is a particular form of this indirect indexing. A hypermedia system enables much more sophisticated navigation to take place, but the ability to move directly to related material breaks the magazine metaphor, and the user may become lost. Furthermore, the system allows many types of links, a concept that magazines rarely, if ever, exploit.

Question 15.3

(a) What is the difference between conceptual and physical navigation in hypermedia?

(b) What principles help the designer to decide how to provide the user with appropriate navigational aids for a particular hypermedia document?

Key points

- Different users carrying out different kinds of task in different contexts are likely to benefit from different types of help.
- The minimal instruction approach has been shown to speed learning for some tasks.
- Minimal manuals eliminate repetition, summaries, reviews, exercises and indexes. Explanations unrelated to practical action are omitted. Topics are directed at real work activities. Learners are asked to try out things and see what happens. Information on error recovery is greatly increased.
- Training Wheels interfaces to programs limit the learner to simple functions and mask other functions. This makes it impossible to commit errors, but can be very frustrating. The Scenario Machine explains why some options are unavailable, which is preferable.
- Help requests for a frequently used interface function suggest a design flaw, and possible need for a redesign.
- Typical users' questions are oriented to: goal exploration, definition and description, task achievement, diagnosis, state identification.
- Help systems are weakest when users are unable to conceptualize their questions.

- Conceptual navigation concerns navigation through the ideas represented by the material; physical navigation concerns navigation between items of information as presented.
- Tools, aids and metaphors provided in the system for physical navigation should fit the users' models of the concepts they are investigating.

Further reading

User support and on-line help

CARROLL J.M. (1992). *The Nurnberg Funnel: Designing Minimalist Instruction for Practical Computer Skill*. Boston, MA: MIT Press.
This book contains detailed information and provoking discussion about minimalist instruction.

HORTON W. (1990). *Designing and Writing On-Line Documentation: Help Files to Hypertext*. New York: John Wiley.

HORTON W. (1991). *Illustrating Computer Documentation: The Art of Presenting Information Graphically on Paper or On-Line*. Toronto: John Wiley.
Together these texts provide coverage of documentation design and on-line support.

KEARSLEY G. (1988). *On-line Help Systems*. Norwood, NJ: Ablex.
This book provides an excellent source of ideas on on-line help systems.

SHNEIDERMAN B. (1992). *Designing the User Interface: Strategies for Effective Human–Computer Interaction*, 2nd edn. Reading, MA: Addison-Wesley.
This book contains a good overview of user support and on-line help.

WENGER E. (1987). *Artificial Intelligence and Tutoring Systems*. Los Altos, CA: Morgan Kaufmann.
Many issues and ideas in adaptive interfaces and on-line help have already been explored extensively by the intelligent tutoring systems and artificial intelligence and education communities. Wenger's book is full of good ideas for training and help systems.

Hypertext and hypermedia

NELSON T. (1981). *Literary Machines*. Swathmore, PA (self-published).
A wide-reaching, inspiring, visionary book on hypermedia.

WOODHEAD N. (1990). *Hypertext and Hypermedia: Theory and Applications*. Wokingham: Addison-Wesley.
A useful introduction to hypertext and hypermedia.

16

Designing for Collaborative Work and Virtual Environments

Aims and objectives

In this chapter we consider some design issues for computer supported cooperative work (CSCW) and virtual environments. After studying this chapter you should:

- be aware of current developments and some 'classic' systems in CSCW and virtual reality,
- understand how particular aspects of these interaction styles constrain and inform design.

Overview

Most people work with other people. Organizations, by their very nature, rely on people working and cooperating together (see Chapter 10). Yet few computer systems are designed specifically to make it easy for several people to work collaboratively. The potential benefits of designing computers and their interfaces to facilitate group working appear to be huge.

Virtual environments offer one of the most powerful and natural methods of interacting with computers. There is still uncertainty about the extent to which general-purpose virtual environments will be cheap, reliable and effective enough for widespread use over the next 5 to 10 years. However, we demonstrate in this chapter how particular aspects of this interaction style can offer unique benefits already for appropriately chosen applications.

16.1 Computer supported cooperative work

Two important features of CSCW systems are the mode of interaction they support and the geographical distribution of the users. Mode of interaction can be either **asynchronous** (that is, occurring at different times) or **synchronous** (that is, occurring at the same time), and geographical distribution can be **local**, meaning that users are co-located in the same environment, or **remote**, meaning that they are in different locations (such as different rooms, buildings and so on). This leads to a four-category classification: synchronous–local, synchronous–remote, asynchronous–local and asynchronous–remote, as shown in Table 16.1.

Table 16.1   A four-category classification system for CSCW systems (adapted from Shneiderman, 1992, p. 370).

	Same time	Different times
Same place	Face-to-face (classrooms, meeting rooms)	Asynchronous interaction (project scheduling, coordination tools)
Different places	Synchronous distributed (shared editors, video windows)	Asynchronous distributed (email, bulletin boards, conferences)

The discussion that follows draws heavily on work by Scrivener (1993).

Synchronous–local: Same time, same place

An everyday example of synchronous–local group activity is a meeting. Typically, in a computer supported meeting environment, each participant has a personal computer, used for making notes, processing data and so on, which is linked to an electronic whiteboard that can be shared by all participants. One of the most successful computer supported meeting environments to date, Colab (Stefik *et al.*,

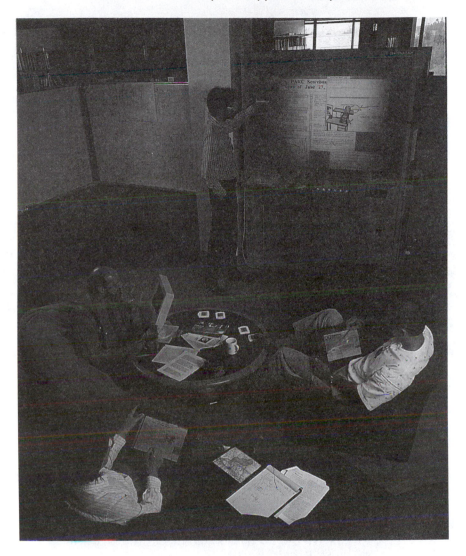

Figure 16.1 Liveboard (Weiser, 1991), a computer-based meeting system with a large-screen interactive display and individual pen systems to support brainstorming and other group activities (Shneiderman, 1992: photograph © Matthew Mulbry).

1987), drew heavily from studies of conventional face-to-face meetings. The environment was intended for use by two to six persons. Each meeting attendee was supplied with a personal computer. At the front of the room there was a large touch-sensitive screen known as the 'LiveBoard', together with a stand-up keyboard (Figure 16.1). Colab was capable of running a number of distinct meeting tools, which are discussed in Section 28.4; see also Section 10.4 for information on CSCW and organizations.

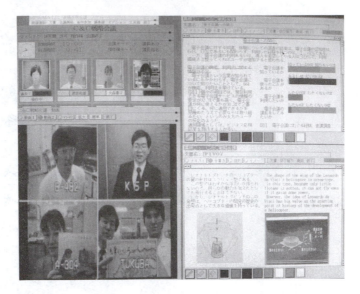

Figure 16.2 A four-party conference on the elaborate Mermaid multi-party UNIX-based desktop teleconferencing system (Watabe *et al.*, 1990: © 1990, Association for Computing Machinery, Inc. reprinted by permission). The system provides users with video images, voice, personal work surfaces, shared work surfaces and a status window (giving information on floor control, chairperson and so on).

Synchronous–remote: Same time, different place

The telephone is perhaps the most commonplace example of a medium that supports synchronous–remote group work. When compared to a face-to-face meeting the potential disadvantages of the telephone are obvious. Firstly, you cannot see your partner (or partners), neither can you show your partner pictures, gesture, or refer to information on paper. One of the main kinds of synchronous remote CSCW systems is the distributed shared workspace, designed to support groups composed of individuals at different geographical locations. A distributed shared workspace (Figure 16.2) usually provides a multimedia electronic workspace where each member can see simultaneously the drawing and writing of other group members on a shared work surface. Participants can also talk to and, in some cases, see images of other members.

In the absence of applications purpose-designed to be used by several people at once (such as those developed in Colab), **shared window systems** allow single-user applications, such as word processors, to be run on a single workstation and displayed on any number of other workstations. In order to allow users to take turns in operating the application, the shared window system may provide a mechanism for **floor control**. The floor control mechanism may be chosen by the user group (Greenberg, 1991), or it may be imposed by the system. Some mechanisms work on a first-come/first-served basis, others pass control of the application around the group in turn.

Asynchronous: Different time

Postal correspondence is perhaps the most familiar instance of asynchronous–remote group working. The electronic equivalent of postal correspondence, email, was the first widely available form of CSCW system. (Recall the interview with Marilyn Mantei at the end of Part II.) Such systems have now been extended to conferencing systems with users reading and sending articles to common repositories. Some examples of an asynchronous–local mode of group working include clerical processes in which information is passed between clerks in the same office via 'in' and 'out' trays. In practice, there tends to be little real difference between local and remote asynchronous working, so we will treat them together.

Formal versus informal groups

An increasing number of researchers believe that informal, spontaneous, communication is as important as formal communication, if not more important. For example, people at work may meet by chance in a corridor or coffee area and use the encounter as an opportunity to share information, resolve problems or identify opportunities in an unplanned way. This type of 'accidental' communication is now recognized as an important aspect of the work environment (for example, see Root, 1988; Fish *et al.*, 1991). The more physically remote co-workers are, the less likely it is that there will be opportunities for informal meetings. Therefore, some researchers are developing CSCW systems that are intended to provide opportunities for informal meetings at a distance. For example, the RAVE environment at Xerox EuroPARC (Borning and Travers, 1991) provides video and audio links between workers in different offices. Privacy can be preserved by users disabling the cameras and microphones in their offices at any time. See Figure 16.3 for an example of the related CAVECAT system for informal meetings.

EXERCISE

Consider a group situation that you know well, such as a lecture, seminar, tutorial, demonstration, planning meeting, report writing and so on. Choose the type of CSCW facilities that you think would have the most potential to help the group activity if each individual was located in a different town. Now consider and list ways in which the use of your chosen communication medium might give rise to greater misunderstanding, frustration or group friction compared with existing alternatives. As an interaction designer, can you see any way in which these problems could be alleviated by better hardware, software, services, interfaces, floor control, social processes or training?

COMMENT

Here are the comments of one computer scientist who is also a musician:

'As a musician, I would be interested in playing music live with remote colleagues. This would require good quality sound (including speech) with no appreciable time lags, and eye contact. Phone headsets and high quality phone lines could be used. Audio propagation delays should be negligible. A set of four cameras and four monitors for each participant using half silvered mirrors [Figure 16.4] could allow reciprocal eye contact, good spatial awareness, and awareness of eye contact between others (Buxton, 1991) [see Figures 16.4 and 16.5]. Video transmission over national links such as ISDN (in Britain) is likely to introduce delays of one or more seconds. This might be adequate for coarsely timed tasks such as indicating who is to play next but might be confusing for tasks requiring accurate timing such as starting and finishing together. Pilot experiments could be carried out very cheaply as follows:

(a) play together over the phone (audio only),
(b) experiment with direct video and phone links in the same building,
(c) combine (a) and (b) with a video delay.'

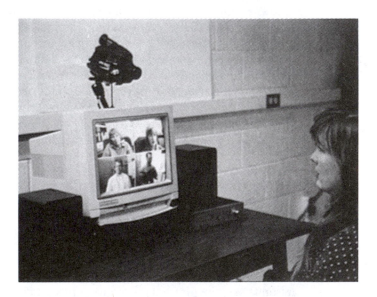

Figure 16.3 An informal video meeting system, CAVECAT at the University of Toronto. Although camera placement (above the screen) makes eye contact difficult, the system is found useful enough to be used extensively (Shneiderman, 1992).

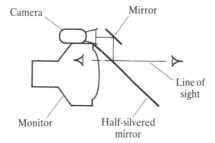

Figure 16.4 A reciprocal 'video tunnel', constructed like a teleprompter and giving mutual eye contact (Buxton, 1991). Through the combination of a mirror and half-silvered mirror, there appears to be direct eye-to-eye contact. The mirrors effectively place the camera right in the line of sight. A close approximation to reciprocal eye contact can be obtained if both parties are using such an arrangement.

Figure 16.5 The Hydra system at the University of Toronto involves separate monitors, cameras and speakers for each remote participant in a compact unit called a Hydra unit. Such an arrangement makes it easier to use natural skills that depend on awareness of who is looking at whom (Buxton, 1991).

Design issues for CSCW systems

As in the design of any computer system, the form that a CSCW system should take depends greatly on the tasks involved, the users and the environment. The following design pointers have been adapted from Sharples (1993) and emerged from the study of a system (CYCLOPS), which provided shared voice and shared drawing surfaces for Open University tutors and students working at a distance. Some issues from Scrivener (1993) have been added.

- The acceptibility of a CSCW system depends on the competing alternatives. For example, if users have the choice of walking into each other's offices rather than using the system, they may view it much less favourably than if they are separated by thousands of miles.
- Existing human conventions for working together provide a rich source of ideas for CSCW interface designers.
- If users become committed to a CSCW system, they are likely to evolve conventions and etiquette to facilitate smooth and effective use of the system. Such etiquette should be actively introduced to new users.
- Conventions and etiquette for using a CSCW system tend to arise from a given cultural and task background. When people using the same technology come from different organizational or cultural contexts, users' expectations may clash.
- Users of some CSCW systems may be in widely spaced time zones. This may require that at least one group operate outside normal working hours, or outside a normal working environment and with impoverished facilities (for example, via a car-phone).
- Synchronous systems that work well with two users may be less effective with multiple users. It may be necessary to introduce a group facilitor or some method of floor control.
- Unpredictable delays (for example, in updating video images or shared drawing surfaces) can be very frustrating. A slight but consistent delay may be preferable to an inconsistent delay, but a fast responding system is by far the best.

16.2 Virtual environments and virtual reality

The terms **virtual environment** and **virtual reality**, which we will treat more or less synonymously, are now used to refer to a variety of interaction styles, which can be hard to pin down in a precise definition. (See also Roy Kawalsky's comments in the interview at the end of Part III.) The terms are normally used to refer to interaction styles that have the following three factors in common:

- Sense of direct physical presence. Compelling sensory cues are created by the technology to give the user a strong subjective sense of 'physical presence' and 'direct experience'. These cues may be visual, aural or **haptic** (concerned with the sense of touch or force on the body), or some combination.
- Sensory cues in three dimensions. Whether the system exploits the senses of sight, sound or touch, information in at least one of these channels is usually presented in three dimensions.

- Natural interaction. Typically, virtual reality systems allow computer-generated objects to be manipulated using gestures similar to those that one would use to manipulate real objects: picking up, turning around, throwing and so on.

As you may have read in Chapter 11, one of the most common forms of present-day virtual environment requires the user to don one or more datagloves and a pair of displays built into a special headset. The displays use wide-angled miniature TV screens, one for each eye, each typically driven by a separate powerful graphics-rendering computer. Subjectively, on donning the headset of a typical system of this type, you enter a three-dimensional, colour, if rather grainy, cartoon-like world which occupies your whole field of vision. (More expensive versions are available offering, in some cases, very high resolution displays.) Typically, you can start investigating the computer-generated world in which you find yourself by turning your head and physically moving around. A disembodied skeletal hand can be seen floating where your real hand should be, which mimics every move made by your real hand, courtesy of input from the dataglove. Depending on the accuracy of the gesture recognition software, you can more or less reliably pick up virtual objects and manipulate or throw them in the virtual world (also see Chapter 11). In many systems, making a gun-like gesture in the direction that you want to go allows you to 'fly' around. Many other virtual reality styles are available, for example, three-dimensional auditory virtual interfaces. These rest on a recent and relatively cheap technique (Wenzel, 1992), which allows virtual sounds to be placed very accurately in space in three dimensions via headphones. The apparent positions of stationary sound sources remain fixed in space as you move your head. Three-dimensional

'Hi, Honey, I'm home!'

(*Source* Private Eye)

virtual sound can be very effective, particularly in combination with the helmet and glove approach already described. Tasks where virtual sound may be particularly effective include locating moving objects, using sound sources as aids to navigation and location in a virtual world, being aware of the activities of other people in a virtual world, and being aware of events in the virtual world outside of one's immediate attention. Three-dimensional virtual sound by itself can, for example, allow aircraft pilots to be directly aware of the approach of other aircraft from any direction in a sphere around their heads.

One of the few virtual environments that has been systematically used and evaluated over an extended period is the GROPE project, associated with Fred Brooks at the University of North Carolina. Unlike many better known virtual reality systems, this system centres on the haptic sense, that is, the senses related to touch. See Box 16.1 for more details.

Box 16.1 GROPE: Force feedback systems for understanding molecular interaction

GROPE allows scientists to feel directly in three dimensions (plus three rotational dimensions) the simulated electrical forces involved in trying to fit molecules into clefts in other molecules. Finding solutions to such problems can be very important in the design of new drugs and in answering questions in molecular biology. The system uses an Argonne remote manipulator force feedback arm (Figure 16.6). By grasping the handpiece, which is suspended from the ceiling, and by using shoulder, wrist and finger muscles to move it, users can manipulate computer-generated virtual objects, such as models of molecules, that can push back. In a typical interaction, the user stands in front of a large computer screen, holding the arm. On the screen, two molecules are seen, one of which, in the foreground, twists and moves with the arm. Attempts to dock the molecules may lead to repulsions and resistances, until the correct angle of approach is found. Audible clicks are used when virtual contacts are made. In later versions of the system, computer-driven headsets were worn to give a stereoscopic view of the molecules.

The technology is clearly exciting, but from our point of view a more pertinent question is what the system offers to users. The main findings from empirical studies of GROPE, as reported by Brooks and co-workers, were as follows. In cases where the visual display was already designed to be as informative as possible, adding force feedback speeded up performance on particular tasks by a factor of about two, but not much more. Serious users reported a much better general 'situation awareness'. That is to say, chemists claimed a much better understanding of the details of the receptor site and its force fields, and of why a particular drug docks well or poorly. It was not so much

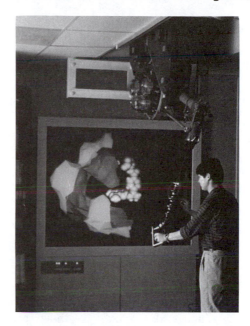

Figure 16.6 The GROPE III system provides force feedback for such tasks as trying to fit simulated molecules together, taking into account their force fields (Brooks *et al.*, 1990: © 1990, Association of Computing Machinery, Inc. reprinted by permission. Photograph by Bo Strain, reproduced courtesy of the University of North Carolina, Department of Computer Science).

that users learned whether something docked or not, more that by feeling what happened while they tried different possibilities, they got a much better appreciation of what else to try, or what might be changed to improve matters.

16.3 Design trade-offs: An environment for learning about motion

Many students, even physics graduates who are familiar with the laws of motion, have deep misconceptions about dynamics when asked to predict (without calculation) how something will move in given circumstances. For the purpose of our design case study, imagine that a psychologist postulates that if students could carry out actions directly in a simulated environment without gravity, friction and air resistance their learning would be improved. The educationalist proposes to carry out an experiment to test this hypothesis using current commercially available equipment (Whitelock and Holland, 1992).

EXERCISE

Imagine that you have been asked to itemize and analyse the extent to which current off-the-shelf virtual reality systems could generate a subjective feeling of direct experience (to some degree) of actions such as throwing projectiles in weightless or frictionless conditions. What design decisions would be involved in selecting equipment for this task, or should the proposal be rejected in advance on the grounds that current off-the-shelf virtual reality technology is too immature?

COMMENT

Immersion versus desktop systems

One of the virtues claimed for virtual reality is that the user feels subjectively 'immersed' in the computer-generated world and can interact very naturally with it using datagloves and other input devices. For marketing reasons, the virtual reality market has now split into at least two areas, desktop and immersion systems. **Immersion systems** include peripherals such as helmets and gloves, whereas desktop systems have neither. Typically, **desktop systems** use a single, large, colour screen for input and output, a three-dimensional pointing device such as a three-dimensional mouse and a keyboard. The software and controller involved make it possible, for example, to 'fly' around a model of a house, and inspect and 'turn around' to survey the rooms. Since our application aims for a subjective feeling of involvement, an immersive system is more appropriate.

Latency

Given a specification of a virtual world and sufficient computing power, it is possible in principle to render it from any point of view to an almost arbitrary level of photographic detail. However, this is very computationally intensive and can take a lot of time. In order to make it possible to carry out rendering in real-time in a virtual environment, various cartoon-like simplifications are often adopted. For example, textures and shadows may be ignored, polygons may be used in place of curves, and the number of objects may be kept very limited. Studies have tended to suggest that latency (speed of update of image in response to movement) is more important to the user's feeling of presence than high resolution or detailed rendering. Hence we would accept a medium resolution, simply rendered display in our case study if this were the price for rapid screen update. Another avoidable cause of lag (that is, slow response) is slow three-dimensional trackers. We need to insist on fast trackers. The number of trackers also matters. If more than one tracker is used, each one will slow down the system (unless expensive parallel processing is used). We will need at least two trackers: one for the headset and one for a glove.

Specifying a second dataglove or a datasuit, so that the user can see a representation of her whole body, or having facilities for more than one user at a time would add extra expense and slow the system down. Hence, unless some of our virtual physics experiments definitely demand two hands or two users, we would get a better response time using just one headset and a single glove.

Stereoscopic versus monoscopic display

Virtual reality displays come in two types: monoscopic, in which both eyes see exactly the same view, and stereoscopic, where the eyes see separately computed views to give the sensation of stereoscopic vision. One important cue in depth perception, motion parallax, can be reproduced with a monoscopic head-mounted display. This is the effect whereby moving one's head slightly makes not too distant objects move relative to each other. The closer they are, the more they move (try this with one eye closed). For our application, this cue will work reasonably well. A stereoscopic system would be very nice, but it will either cost a lot more or slow the system down. If financial constraints force a choice between a high update rate or a stereoscopic system, a high update rate is a more critical contribution so that the system will feel more natural to use.

Three-dimensional virtual sound

If we are willing to add headphones and some relatively inexpensive hardware, we can associate different sound sources with different objects in our physics world (as is possible in the system shown in Figure 16.7). Given that the visual resolution of many current systems is poor, the good quality of three-dimensional sound can greatly improve the feeling of subjective presence. Preliminary evidence suggests that three-dimensional sound makes tasks such as tracking moving objects, navigating and being aware of location easier, quicker and more pleasant to perform.

Modelling of forces and impenetrable objects

Force-based senses can be broken down into various components. Tactile perception refers to the senses of contact, pressure, pain, temperature and so on. Kinaesthetic cues give awareness of where body parts and limbs are in space, both statically and dynamically. This sense is mediated by skin, muscle and joints. Combinations of the two kinds of cues give rise to haptic perception, which includes perception of object solidity, texture, vibration, inertia, weight, elasticity, viscosity and so forth. Bearing in mind that our example is all about modelling dynamics, a major weakness using currently commercially available equipment is that the different masses, weights and solidities of different projectiles in the hand will not be directly felt.

Figure 16.7 A virtual three-dimensional sound system. Often used in conjunction with a helmet and glove, here a system is shown by itself. A positioning device is being used to place sound sources in the virtual three-dimensional auditory space (*Computer Music Journal*, **13**(4), p. 81).

Tactile and force feedback devices are starting to develop but they are mostly still experimental (see Box 16.2). Motion platforms (Figure 16.8) and vehicle simulators are able to shake people about and simulate momentary acceleration by tipping, which can be quite convincing the first few times, particularly when combined with appropriate visual cues, but controlling whole-body acceleration forces accurately for sustained periods is currently beyond the scope of any commercial system. Students will still feel the effect of gravity on their own bodies, even when they are supposed to be in weightless conditions. Impenetrable objects are not cheaply modelled in most current virtual environments; for example, sitting on a virtual chair will not suspend the user from the ground (but see Box 16.2 for an experimental system that gives force feedback to grasping gestures.). In our hypothetical study, some of these problems could be alleviated by constraining the users to sit all the time on a real chair, introducing the metaphor (see Chapter 7) that they are in a vehicle.

Summary of design choices

In summary, the virtual physics education application appears to require at least an immersion virtual reality system with high-quality wide-angled optics on a display driven by head position. Due to motion parallax, a monoscopic system might well be adequate, though a stereoscopic system would be preferable. Resolution should be as good as can be obtained, but not at the expense of total update rate. To ensure this update rate, we foresee the following requirements:

- restrict the number of trackers, probably to a single user monoscopic system with one headset and one glove,
- choose fast position trackers,
- have a fast specialized graphics computer with accelerator boards for rendering the image for each eye,
- choose a fast computer for updating the world model on the basis of signals from the sensors.

Other desirable design choices include the use of three-dimensional sound to make navigation and localization easier, and to give individual calibration of gloves and headsets for each session for each user.

Such a system would certainly allow the 'throwing' of projectiles in simulated weightless or frictionless conditions using relatively natural gestures, but the degree to which this would produce a sense of direct experience would be severely limited. Quality of rendering can be improved at a price, but problems to do with simulating touch and force present serious long-term challenges.

Figure 16.8 The Solopod, a single-person computer controlled motion platform (*The One*, September 1991, p. 37).

Box 16.2   Tactile and force feedback

Some experimental datagloves can give a sense of touching computer-generated objects.

- The experimental Teletact Glove (Stone, personal communication, 1992) uses small pockets all over the glove that may be pneumatically inflated under computer control to give tactile feedback.
- Small alloy pads called tactors (Blum and Czeiszperger, 1992) can be attached to gloves, mice, joysticks and so on. When a current is passed through them, a tactor held next to the skin changes its shape and is felt to press against it. The change may be varied by controlling the current.
- Prevention of the hand passing through a computer-generated virtual object requires force feedback. For example, the Tsukuba University table mounted system (Figure 16.9) can apply force feedback to the thumb, two fingers and the palm, in order to simulate the pressures exerted by virtual objects (Iwata, 1990). One possible application is to help designers 'feel' objects they are designing.

Figure 16.9   The Experimental Tsukuba University force feedback system can apply force feedback to the thumb, two fingers and palm to simulate pressures exerted by virtual objects (Iwata, 1990: © 1990, Association for Computing Machinery, Inc. reprinted by permission).

Roy Kalawsky also raises some important issues about virtual reality in the interview at the end of Part III, and so does Ben Shneiderman in the interview at the beginning of this Part.

Key points

- All organizations rely on people working together. The potential benefits of designing computers to facilitate group work appear to be huge.
- CSCW encompasses the study of the way people work in groups, and computer-based aids including hardware, software, services and social processes or training.
- CSCW systems can be classified as same or different place, and same or different time.
- Typical local computer supported meeting environments offer each participant a personal computer linked to an electronic whiteboard shared by all participants.
- Remote shared workspaces typically offer a multimedia electronic workspace where each member can see simultaneously the drawing and writing of other group members on a shared work surface, can talk to, and sometimes can see images of other members.
- Shared window systems typically allow single-user applications, such as word processors, to be operated in turn by more than one user at separated workstations. A floor control method to allow users to take turns may be provided. Telepointers may allow all users to 'point' at areas of the screen at any time without making alterations.
- Informal communication is an important aspect of the work environment. Some researchers are developing CSCW systems that are intended to provide opportunities for informal meetings at a distance.
- CSCW systems have to satisy groups. This makes the potential for failure of any particular CSCW system large. Extensive testing is required before committing to a particular system or design.
- Virtual environments and virtual realities typically offer a sense of direct physical presence, sensory cues in three dimensions, and a natural form of interaction (for example, interaction via natural gestures).
- Many other virtual reality styles are available, including three-dimensional sound.
- Adding force feedback can speed up performance on particular tasks by a factor of about two, but not much more (so far).
- Adding force feedback to appropriate tasks can greatly improve 'situation awareness' and awareness of possibilities; it can also dispel misconceptions, for example, about force fields.
- Different kinds of virtual environment may involve immersion or desktop systems; speed and quality of rendering may vary greatly.
- For most tasks, latency (speed of update of image) is more important than high resolution.

Further reading

CSCW

Some of the most interesting collections of papers on recent work in CSCW can be found in the following conference proceedings:

BANNON L., ROBINSON M. and SCHMIDT K., eds (1991). *Proceedings of the Second European Conference on Computer Supported Cooperative Work (EC-CSCW '91)*. Dordrecht: Kluwer.

Proceedings of the First European Conference on Computer Supported Cooperative Work (EC-CSCW '89). Slough: Computer Sciences House.

Proceedings of the Conference on Computer Supported Cooperative Work (CSCW '88). New York: ACM Press.

Proceedings of the Conference on Computer Supported Cooperative Work (CSCW '90). New York: ACM Press.

Proceedings of the Conference on Computer Supported Cooperative Work (CSCW '92). New York: ACM Press.

SCRIVENER S.A.R., ed. (1991). *Proceedings of CSCW: The Multimedia and Networking Paradigm*. Uxbridge: Unicom Seminars Ltd.

Virtual environments

EARNSHAW R.A., GIGANTE M.A. and JONES H., eds (1993). *Virtual Reality Systems*. San Diego, CA: Academic Press.

A recent edited volume of papers, that purports to restrict the 'hype' and promote the 'reality' in virtual reality. It includes a section on the human–computer interface.

KALAWSKY R.S. (1993). *The Science of Virtual Reality and Virtual Environments*. Wokingham: Addison-Wesley.

This book provides an exciting and thorough discussion of the state of the art and traces the history of this technology. Numerous example systems are discussed, several of which the author has personal experience of.

PAUSCH R. (1991). Virtual reality on five dollars a day. *CHI '91 Conference Proceedings*, pp. 265–70. New York: ACM Press.

Provides an excellent account of home-assembled, low cost systems and many usability issues.

RHEINGOLD H. (1991). *Virtual Reality*. London: Secker & Warburg.

Books on virtual reality are proliferating. This is one of the first books to be written and it is an excellent introduction to the field, written in a journalistic style.

INTERVIEW WITH **ROY KALAWSKY**

Roy Kalawsky is head of the British Aerospace Virtual Environment Laboratory, the largest facility of its kind in the UK. He is also Professor of Virtual Environments and Advanced Display Technology at the University of Hull, where he has established a centre of excellence in this field. In 1993 Roy published one of the first texts in the field entitled *The Science of Virtual Reality and Virtual Environments*. In this interview Roy discusses some provocative concerns about VR technology.

What is virtual reality, VR?

There are as many definitions of VR as there are people who try to define it. VR is the state where the level of interaction, autonomy and feeling of presence is indistinguishable from the real world. Unfortunately we are a long way from achieving really good VR today because of technology limitations and lack of human factors understanding. A more fundamental question is whether or not we need to achieve virtual reality for a particular application. Some CAD system manufacturers have been driven by the fear that VR will someday destroy their position in the market. Consequently, they have relabelled what is little more than animated CAD as 'desktop VR'. The original concept for VR has since been labelled 'immersive VR'.

Has VR been oversold? What does it offer?

This is a difficult question and requires a two part answer. In terms of advertising the concepts behind VR there are very few people who have not heard of the term. Many people will have experienced what they believe to be VR mainly in entertainment parks or through some form of advertising promotion. In this respect the concepts of VR have been successfully implanted in people's minds. The second part of the answer must deal with how well the concept matches people's perception of the capability of VR. In almost every case VR has not delivered the sort of performance that was indicated by the press and media. There are a few exceptions and these systems deliver a remarkable sense of presence. Many people will judge VR by what they have seen or experienced. I recall a meeting with Dr Steve Ellis of NASA Ames Research Center, where we purposely visited the students union at the University of Berkeley to see how well the virtual reality game was comparing with other more traditional entertainment simulator systems. It was switched off and not in use! The students had obviously voted on which systems they preferred. Even a cursory examination of these arcade-type VR systems reveals the extremely poor visual cues and total lack of realism.

The more sophisticated virtual environment systems used in defence and aerospace are significantly better, offering not only higher resolution visuals but more accurate modelling of object attributes such as motion dynamics, lighting, texture and so on. Having given countless demonstrations to people it is very gratifying to receive comments such as: 'I didn't know that it was possible to produce such a realistic system.' Human beings are used to operating in a three-dimensional spatial environment. An even greater sense of presence can be achieved if one allows part of one's own body to become part of the virtual environment. I am convinced that integration of the real world with a virtual world offers the best compromise with today's technology.

Apart from mimicking the real world, VR has the capacity to take a

343

user into abstract or otherwise impossible environments. These can be macroscopic or microscopic worlds.

What are the dangers of VR?

VR, or rather the use of VR, is not properly understood in terms of sociological and psychological issues. It must be remembered that in all current VR systems we are dealing with imperfect simulations. These will have an effect on users' performance. In some instances the user will be able to operate in hazardous environments – free from any danger. A key issue to be addressed is the level of abstraction or involvement the user gets. People tend to perform better in a simulator than in a real environment because of the low risk factor. Considerable human factors research is required to deal with the complex issues that arise from technology trade-offs.

With respect to people believing that they are still in a virtual world after a long exposure in a VR system, I don't think that they will have much chance of confusing a virtual world with a real world. Levels of realism in all aspects still fall short of the real world.

Consequently, I don't believe there will be any real dangers. However, perhaps a word of caution is needed. It is tempting to jump on the VR band-wagon but there are many alternative and probably more affordable solutions.

For what kinds of tasks does VR have most to offer?

Application areas include:

- Scientific visualization and interaction

- Training (simulators)
- Engineering design and manufacture (rapid prototyping)
- Medical (mainly training – virtual cadavers)
- Aerospace
- Architectural planning
- Operations in hazardous environments

Is it cost-effective?

This depends on the application. Applicability to large simulators is obvious where unit cost and support infrastructure can be substantially reduced by adopting a VR solution. The ability to network multiple VR systems together can be very powerful, particularly in training where people need to interact with each other.

High performance VR systems are expensive because of the computational resource and the high resolution peripherals required to interface the human into the virtual environment.

Employing a virtual design environment has the potential to allow a manufacturer to reduce the time to market, reduce development risk and assess customer acceptability much earlier on in product life cycles.

What is the future of VR?

VR or its derivatives are here to stay. Given that traditional flight simulators are a form of virtual reality it was obvious that the physical components of simulators would at some time be replaced by virtual equivalents.

The press exposure has created a market for the enabling technol-

ogies. Small companies have realized the potential and the accessibility of the technology. They will be seeking the high returns that are almost guaranteed for those that can deliver interface peripherals with the appropriate fidelity.

Today's youngsters are becoming extremely computer literate and will more readily accept new concepts such as VR or indeed any form of computer technology.

In future VR, or whatever we prefer to call it, will find application in many diverse areas, some of which have yet to be developed. Quite often the most beneficial are not always the most obvious.

When will VR deliver?

To some extent VR is already delivering a capability to designers. Obviously one has to define what is meant by VR. In terms of flight simulators (one kind of VR) then the technology is relatively mature. The same is true for desktop VR. The fidelity depends on the amount one can afford. On the other hand immersive VR systems (head-mounted display-based) are still in their infancy. As display resolution improves then the visuals will become more acceptable. For true user interaction then glove-like devices will be required that can communicate haptic and kinaesthetic forces. These devices are several years away. A total VR system could be as much as 5–10 years away. The trick will be to determine just what level of immersion and interaction is required for each task. For some tasks the VR technology available today may be acceptable.

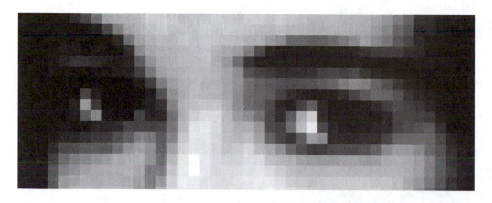

INTERACTION DESIGN: METHODS AND TECHNIQUES

Designing a computer system is no easy matter. Computer systems are complex entities, so their designers have to deal with numerous people, sources of information, tools and techniques. Selecting the most appropriate design methods requires much skill and experience. Design practice can vary considerably from organization to organization, from team to team and from individual to individual. Consequently, there are a number of different approaches concerning the nature of design and the way that it should be carried out. One school of thought, for instance, believes that computer system design should follow formal scientific and engineering practices, while another argues that it should include a strong creative element and will always be a craft rather than a science.

In this book we focus on user-centred design. Although there are various different schools of thought in HCI about what constitutes user-centred design, the common thread that links HCI design is that it should:

● be user-centred and involve users as much as possible so that they can influence the design,
● integrate knowledge and expertise from the different disciplines that contribute to HCI design,
● be highly iterative so that testing can be done to check that the design does indeed meet users' requirements.

In Parts IV–VI we will discuss the most popular design and evaluation methods and design support tools that are available to make HCI design user-centred. In Part IV you will learn about the importance of considering users and their work and how this knowledge can be used in design. In Part V you will be introduced to various techniques and tools for supporting design, and in Part VI you will learn methods for evaluating your design decisions at various stages during the design. All three parts are interdependent, and when you are designing technology you will find that you are constantly drawing on ideas and knowledge from each. For example, you will remember that in Part I we introduced the star life cycle (Hix and Hartson, 1993), which illustrates that evaluation is an essential part of the design process and not just something that happens at the end before the product is shipped.

This part begins with an overview of HCI design given by one of the most influential HCI theorists and practitioners – Tom Moran. Then we introduce the main issues and processes for designing better HCI. Firstly, we examine some methods and representations for gathering system requirements and analysing users' needs and their tasks. The process of design is covered in two chapters; the first deals with a structured approach to design and the second with approaches that emphasize envisioning the conceptual structure of the design and the situation in which the design is to operate.

When you have completed this part of the book, you will:

● understand why user-centred approaches are important,
● be able to select and apply suitable techniques for collecting users' requirements and analysing tasks,
● know how to do structured design,
● be aware of a number of methods that are becoming important for envisioning design,

- understand how user-centred design is changing, how it can be integrated with software engineering and why it is important for HCI design.

One very important aspect of design is selecting representations of the product that are suitable for the particular stage of the design that is being worked upon. Different representations are introduced in the text where appropriate, often placed in boxes so that you do not have to study them if you are already familiar with the technique from your previous studies.

INTERVIEW WITH **TOM MORAN**

Tom Moran obtained a degree in architecture before completing a PhD in computer science at Carnegie Mellon University. In 1974 he joined Xerox Palo Alto Research Center in California where he worked for a number of years before becoming the first Director of EuroPARC in Cambridge, England. Tom has worked on the design of a number of highly innovative systems including: the NoteCards idea processing hypertext system; the RAVE media space environment and the Tivoli electronic whiteboard system. Tom is well known for his early work on the theoretical foundations of HCI including *The Psychology of Human–Computer Interaction* (1983), which he wrote with Stuart Card and Allen Newell. Some of the key ideas from their book are discussed in Parts II, IV and VI of this text. In this interview Tom discusses problems related to managing design.

What would you say are the most difficult aspects of design?

I think there are several kinds of design and we lump them all together, which often leads to confusion. There is what the British call 'bespoke design' and Americans call a 'custom system', which is aimed at a particular customer or user community for use in a particular way in a particular situation. That is one kind of design. Then there's design of a generic product, in which there is no particular targeted user. There is also 'technology exploration', in which we try to understand the properties of the technology and we invent imaginary scenarios to apply it to. The emphasis is different in all these situations, so there is no single notion of 'design'. There are different demands and different things you ought to attend to in different situations.

What kinds of techniques and processes lead to good HCI design?

There isn't a fixed process. Engineering doesn't have a fixed process

either. I think you learn design by apprenticeship. There isn't a recipe we can give but there are some obvious things that everybody picks up, like figuring out what the real problem is, considering the user, the work environment, whatever it is you're trying to address, and paying attention to those factors rather than imagining what you think the problem is. I think that's the biggest thing you can do to make your design more likely to succeed.

Who should be involved in the design process?

I think you've got to be careful about the context of design. There's a context for design in terms of the developer's context. If you are in a big corporation like I am, there are organizational constraints and issues about whether designers belong in a separate organization, or whether each program maintains its own front-end designers. So there are organizational demands about who's going to be on the team. Clearly, you ought to have people who are going to develop, build, and manufacture the system, trainers and marketing people as well as people involved with the interface design.

What are the problems of large design teams?

If design is anything, it's a very highly managed activity. You're resource constrained, you've only got so many people, you've only got so many dollars, you've got deadlines. My impression when I look at big design teams is the amount of management it takes. The amount of focusing, really keeping in mind what are the difficult problems we're trying to deal with, and making sure you spend enough time on difficult problems. The routine problems, those things that you haven't solved but you know you can solve because you have the skills, will take care of themselves in the sense that you just need to leave time for them, while concentrating on the difficult problems. I'm very impressed by how much design is a management activity, an activity that really tries to sort the difficult significant problems from the routine problems. Brainstorming has to fit into the same kind of scheme. If you really want to innovate in certain kinds of ways, you have to allocate enough time for that process.

One final question. What motivates you in your own career?

I guess one particular issue that motivates me these days, and has for a long time, is the notion that perhaps computers are over-formal, and formalize our behaviour and our thinking in ways that are not necessarily productive. The kind of things that we're trying to do now involve looking for ways to make it a much less formal medium. Informal in the way that pencil and paper is informal, and yet capturable so that you can still do all the other wonderful things. There seem to be natural structures for certain kinds of activities. But a lot of activities aren't easy to structure, particularly creative activities, where I think computers haven't helped us nearly as much as I would like to see. I would like computers to aid and liberate thinking, not constrain it.

Photograph of Tom Moran: credit Brian Tramontana and Andrew Aronson of Xerox PARC. Reproduced with permission of Xerox Corporation.

17

Principles of User-Centred Design

Aims and objectives

User-centred principles are fundamental in HCI design. After studying this chapter you should be able to:

- understand the fundamentals of design,
- identify the stages involved in software development,
- understand the need for an iterative approach to design,
- explain why the principles of user-centred design are important.

Overview

This chapter discusses design and introduces you to the fundamental principles of user-centred design. You will find that designing computer systems shares some characteristics with all design activities. However, it differs in other respects. In particular, there is a wide range of factors to be considered in the design of human-computer systems. Accordingly, a variety of development methods and representations of the proposed system are required. Some of these are illustrated by the two short user-centred design case studies.

The term **design**, even when used in the context of designing a computer system, can have different meanings. In a review of general design philosophy, Jones (1981) found a number of definitions including:

> 'Finding the right physical components of a physical structure.'
> 'A goal-directed problem-solving activity.'
> 'Simulating what we want to make (or do) before we make (or do) it as many times as may be necessary to feel confident in the final result.'
> 'The imaginative jump from present facts to future possibilities.'
> 'A creative activity – it involves bringing into being something new and useful that has not existed previously.'
>
> (Jones, 1981, p. 8)

These descriptions focus on the process of design in general. On the topic of engineering design, Jones (1981) found this: 'Engineering design is the use of scientific principles, technical information and imagination in the definition of a mechanical structure, machine or system to perform pre-specified functions with the maximum economy and efficiency.'

Webster, on the other hand, stresses the relationship between design representation and design process: 'A design is an information base that describes aspects of this object, and the design process can be viewed as successive elaborations of representations, such as adding more information or even backtracking and exploring alternatives' (Webster, 1988, p. 8).

Thus, 'design' refers to both the process of developing a product, artefact or system and to the various representations (simulations or models) of the product that are produced during the design process. As you will see in the next few chapters, there are many representations, which are more or less appropriate in different circumstances. Designers need not only to be able to understand users' requirements, but also to be able to represent this understanding in different ways at different stages of the design. Selecting suitable representations is, therefore, important for exploring, testing, recording and communicating design ideas and decisions, both within the design team and with users.

17.1 Fundamentals

In order to develop any product, two major activities have to be undertaken: the designer must understand the requirements of the product, and must develop the product. Understanding requirements involves looking at similar products, discussing the needs of the people who will use the product, and analysing any existing systems to discover the problems with current designs. Development may include producing a variety of representations until a suitable artefact is produced.

Requirements for design

If you were to develop a pottery jug, you would first determine the requirements by critically examining other jugs and analysing the intended user's needs and abilities.

EXERCISE

Identify three likely requirements of a jug.

COMMENT

(i) An ability to hold liquids, (ii) it should be light enough for its intended users to lift and carry, and (iii) it should be capable of pouring liquid.

Let's say that the requirements of the jug are understood to be those identified above. Firstly, you might sketch several different shapes of jugs, which you could show to your intended users to see which they liked best. You would then develop the product by taking a piece of clay and fashioning the jug. Of course, the first attempt may not be very successful and as a result you would learn more about both the requirements and your design. For example, the first attempt may be too heavy and have an inadequate pouring mechanism. Thus, you may learn that the design did not meet requirement (ii) and that you need to refine your understanding of requirement (iii). Once you had learned more about both the requirements and how they can be met you would make another jug, trying to incorporate the new findings in the design. The process of analysing requirements and gathering information about the product would continue until the result was satisfactory.

As systems become more complex, this trial and error approach becomes less viable. It would be a serious waste of effort to build an ocean liner only to discover that it sank on its first sailing. A more measured engineering approach needs to be taken in which the design passes through several stages as more and more detailed work is done. During each stage various simplified representations may be produced which can be evaluated before more detailed work is undertaken.

Representations for design

Developing suitable representations of an artefact is fundamental to design. The representations employed may be formal or informal, precise or vague and may be used for very different purposes within the overall design activity. One of the skills of the designer is selecting an appropriate representation for the task at hand. Another is making good use of that representation.

In the design of any complex artefact a range of representations, or **models**, is needed during the design process. A model is a representation of something, constructed and used for a particular purpose. A good model is accurate enough to reflect the features of the system being modelled, but simple enough to avoid confusion. A good model adopts a style of presentation that is suitable for its purpose. Much of this part of the book is concerned with looking at different representations, the range of uses to which they can be put and how different representations link together.

In order to illustrate the role of models in design, consider the following example.

A car designer, who has been commissioned to produce a new luxury sports car, doodles a few designs on paper and shows them to the other designers. They make certain comments and criticisms, and as a result changes are made to the designs. Finally, the designer is satisfied with one of the designs and draws up detailed blueprints, which are given to the firm's model maker. Scale models of the design are produced and are sent to marketing and sales for customer reaction. The models are also subjected to wind tunnel experiments to investigate the aerodynamics of the design and the results are used in a computer program which will calculate the car's speed and fuel efficiency. The designer is using four different models in at least four different ways:

- The original models are doodles and sketches, which are used to generate new ideas, examine possibilities and prompt for questions.
- The blueprints given to the model maker and the scale model given to the marketing and sales departments are suitable models for accurately expressing ideas to others.
- The wind tunnel experiments show models being used to test ideas.
- The computer model is used to make predictions.

EXERCISE

Which models in the example above are being used to explore the problem space? Which are being used to communicate ideas?

> **COMMENT**
>
> The initial doodles are used for the purpose of exploring the problem space. The blueprints and scale model are used for communication.

This example shows that different models are suitable for different purposes. Notice that the blueprints and the scale model are both used for communication, but the blueprints are inappropriate for communicating with marketing. Marketing are interested in the physical shape of the design, but the model maker requires a more precise description of the designer's ideas in the form of blueprints. Also notice that the model must be accurate enough for its purpose, highlighting the important features but ignoring the irrelevant aspects. In the wind tunnel, the interior design of the car is unimportant, so the scale model takes no account of this.

Choosing and constructing appropriate models is a difficult but vital part of the designer's job. The designer must always bear in mind how the model is to be used and who is going to use it, and must choose a modelling technique appropriate to the required level of abstraction and intended recipient.

Within human–computer systems design there are a great many representation techniques, which can be used to focus attention on different aspects of the design. During this part we will introduce representations where they are particularly appropriate. In Chapter 18 we will discuss some different user-centred design methods.

17.2 The design of software systems

The traditional view of software engineering characterizes the development of software as consisting of a number of processes and representations that are produced in an essentially linear fashion. You will remember from Chapter 2 that this view of software production is often called the **waterfall model**, because the output of each process 'tumbles down' neatly to the next activity, as illustrated in Figure 17.1. Box 17.1 describes the main features of the waterfall model.

Although we touch on all aspects of systems development identified in Figure 17.1, our interest is primarily with processes B, C and F and with representations 2 and 3.

Question 17.1

If you were to commission a new room for your house, which specific activities would you expect to be undertaken and which representations would you expect to be produced? Who would be involved? Use the processes A–F of the waterfall model to structure your answer.

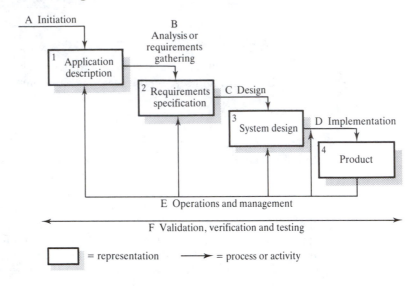

Figure 17.1 Traditional 'waterfall' model of system development.

Box 17.1 The waterfall model of software development

Following the definition of the application, the process of analysis, or requirements gathering, is undertaken, which results in a requirements specification. This is usually seen as a formal document, which is used as the basis of a contract between the product developers and the clients. Based upon this agreed specification, the process of design is undertaken, resulting in a formal representation of the system. This describes all aspects of the system at a suitable level of detail. The implementation process involves programming and testing the system, writing manuals and other documentation, implementing databases and entering data into the system. This process results in the final product, which should be verified by the clients and accepted as meeting the original specification. The operations and maintenance process involves running the system, enhancing the system and correcting any system errors discovered after the product was accepted (revising the implementation). Maintenance may result in further refinement of the application description, requirements specification or design. In theory, the contract agreed at the start of the project should make clear which changes are the responsibility of the client and which are the responsibility of the developer.

EXERCISE

Why do you think that the requirements specification often fails to clarify responsibilities?

COMMENT

There are a number of reasons, but probably the most important is that the representation of the requirements (typically a natural language description of the system) is inadequate for this purpose.

An important characteristic of this view of software development is that at each stage the progression of the product can be checked to ensure that it conforms to the clients' requirements (known as **validation**) and that it is a correct and consistent representation of the previous stage (**verification**). For example, the designer might validate that a particular system function is exactly what the users require and then verify that a specific piece of program code can meet that requirement. Because program and system testing is such an important aspect of software development, these three aspects of ensuring a quality product are often referred to together as Validation, Verification and Testing (VV & T). Another important feature of the waterfall model is that it helps in project management by providing checkpoints throughout the product development to ensure that the development can be effectively managed and that it remains on schedule.

There are a number of problems with the waterfall view of software development. Firstly, the underlying client–developer relationship – the 'contract' approach – imposes demands on the representations used that cannot be met by the available techniques. In particular, the application description and requirements specifications are often expressed in plain English, which means that they are liable to be ambiguous. Secondly, many projects are initiated at the board or corporate management level and imposed, to a greater or lesser degree, on a user department. Thirdly, maintenance is one of the most important stages and is certainly the longest in a product life cycle. (This is particularly true in larger systems, where estimates of up to 60% of effort have been observed.) This problem is further exacerbated if the development team is disbanded, as often happens. Fourthly, there is no formal recognition in traditional system design of the fact that organizational changes often result from the introduction of new systems; hence no effort is made to predict or control these.

While all of these problems are important, the first highlights the most fundamental shortcoming of this approach: it is really impossible to completely understand and express user requirements until a fair amount of design has been undertaken. This problem has sparked a number of alternative views of how the development process should be undertaken.

In the mid- to late 1970s software began to emerge which gave system designers much more power to create systems quickly and effectively. Thus, the ability to **prototype** systems, or certain aspects of systems, became available. The prototyping

Box 17.2 Some alternative views of software development

The response to the problem of management and control advocated by Barry Boehm (1988) is the spiral model of software development, shown in Figure 17.2. This characterization of the development process still uses the main processes of systems development – requirements gathering (or analysis), design, implementation – but now shows that several iterations are required. Most importantly, the model introduces the idea of prototype systems being developed in order to better

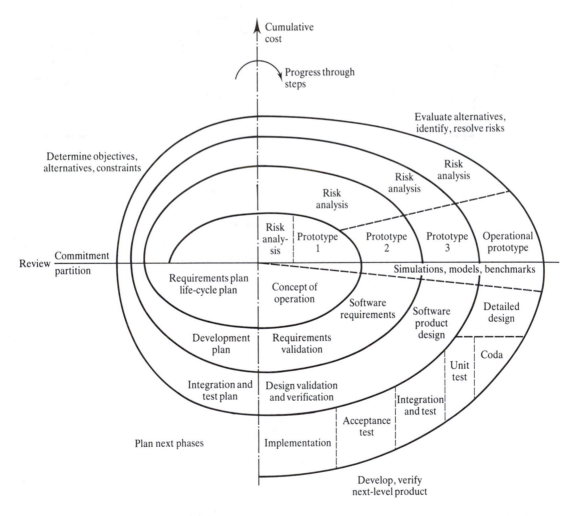

Figure 17.2 The spiral model of the software process (Boehm, 1988: © 1988 IEEE).

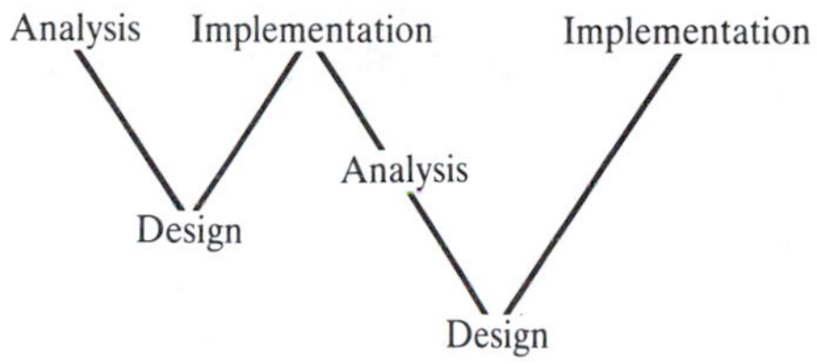

Figure 17.3 The W model of system development (from a talk by John Harrison at the Department of Trade and Industry (DTI), UK, 22 June 1992).

understand the requirements for the next stage and an explicit consideration of the risks involved – identifying those components that have the highest probability of being wrong, or the highest cost of correcting – during each cycle. Another response to the perceived problem of spiralling costs and late delivery associated with prototyping is the so-called 'W' model of software development, shown in Figure 17.3. In this model a single 'design in miniature' is undertaken and tested. Following this, the requirements are fixed and a traditional approach to development is undertaken. The advantage of this model is that it is less expensive than the spiral approach since only one iteration is undertaken. It also helps with project control and in identifying accurately user requirements.

approach to system development deals directly with the problem of needing to check that users' requirements really are being met by the design at different stages. With these new tools, designs could be created and commented on by the users before a great deal of expensive development work had been completed. Brooks sums up the situation: 'the question is not whether to build a pilot system and throw it away. You will do that. The question is whether to plan in advance to build a throwaway' (quoted in Smith *et al.*, 1991).

Prototyping helps to deal with the problem of understanding requirements, but it brings its own problems, notably a lack of management control. Developers and managers may be worried that excessive prototyping will result in systems being delivered late, or not being completed at all. Some of the solutions that have been suggested in software engineering are discussed in Box 17.2.

Although the spiral model, discussed in Box 17.2, has been applied to HCI design (James, 1991), software engineering models are primarily oriented towards the development of large software systems with a focus on system functionality. By contrast, the field of HCI has established user-centred design because it recognizes the importance of frequent user testing using informal representations as well as computer-based prototyping. Although there are different varieties of user-centred design the basic principles are derived from work by Gould *et al.* (1987) on the 1984 Olympic Messaging System, which is described in the next section.

17.3 Two examples of user-centred design

The overriding objective of user-centred system design is to produce systems that are easy to learn and use by their intended users, and that are safe and effective in facilitating the activities that people want to undertake.

Question 17.2

Recall the general principles of user-centred design that were stated in the introduction to this part.

The first example of user-centred design is the 1984 Olympic Messaging System (OMS) (see Gould *et al.*, 1987). Although this is not a 'typical' computer system, it shows how the principles of user-centred system design can be effectively utilized. The second example is of a safety critical system, which has quite different requirements to the OMS but was nevertheless developed using the same user-centred principles.

User-centred design example 1: The OMS

The OMS was developed in order to provide a message service ('voice mail') and other support for the 10,000 athletes who attended the 1984 Olympic games in Los Angeles. Kiosks (see Figure 17.4) were placed around the Olympic village which allowed the athletes to send and receive voice messages among themselves. People from around the world could also send messages of congratulations, commiserations or encouragement to the athletes and officials. Examples of an Olympian receiving and sending a message are shown in Figure 17.5. The OMS worked in 12 languages (but did not translate between them). The system proved very successful. It was well-used and well-liked.

The approach to the design of the OMS proceeded as follows. After some initial analysis of the requirements for the system, printed scenarios of the user interface were prepared (similar to Figure 17.5). These were commented on by designers, management and prospective users. As a result of this early evaluation, a number of the system functions were altered and others were dropped completely. The design team also produced brief user guides aimed at explaining what the system did and how it worked. These were tested on the main user groups (Olympians, their families and friends) and were developed iteratively (over 200 slightly modified versions were produced) before the final form was decided. Early simulations of the messaging system were also constructed and evaluated for the purpose of designing help messages. These simulations were tested with users. One thing that these tests revealed, for example, was that an 'undo' or 'backup' key was required so that users could retrieve a previous position if they made a mistake (for example, entering a valid but incorrect country code).

Question 17.3

Identify the various representations and processes that were used in the above description.

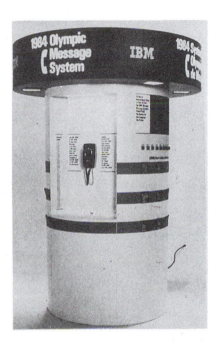

Figure 17.4   An Olympic Message System kiosk (Gould *et al.*, 1987: © 1987, Association for Computing Machinery, Inc. reprinted by permission).

Caller:	(Dials 213-888-888.)
Operator:	Irish National Olympic Committee. Can I help you?
Caller:	I want to leave a message for my son, Michael.
Operator:	Is he from Ireland?
Caller:	Yes.
Operator:	How do you spell his name?
Caller:	K-E-L-L-Y.
Operator:	Thank you. Please hold for about 30 seconds while I connect you to the Olympic Message System.
Operator:	Are you ready?
Caller:	Yes.
OMS:	When you have completed your message, hang up and it will be automatically sent to Michael Kelly. Begin talking when you are ready.
Caller:	'Michael, your Mother and I will be hoping you win. Good luck.' (Caller hangs up.)

(a)

Figure 17.5   Example messages. (a) A parent leaving a voice message for an Olympian.

```
You:      (Dial 740-4560.)
OMS:      Olympic message system.
          Please keypress your three-letter Olympic country code.
You:      U S A
OMS:      United States. Etats-Unis.
          Please keypress your last name.
You:      J O N E
OMS:      John Jones.
          Please keypress your password.
You:      4 0 5
OMS:      New messages sent by Message Center
          'John, good luck in your race. Dad.'
          End of message.
          Press 1, listen again; 2, leave a message; 3, hang up.
You:      3
OMS:      Good-bye.
```

(b)

Figure 17.5 *(cont.)* Example messages. (b) a user listening to a message.

```
You:      (Dial 740-4560.)
OMS:      Olympic Message System.
          Please keypress your three-letter Olympic country code.
You:      U S A
OMS:      United States. Etats-Unis.
          Please keypress your last name.
You:      J O N E
OMS:      John Jones.
          Please keypress your password.
You:      4 0 5
OMS:      No new messages. Press 1, leave a message; 2, listen to an old message;
          3, hang up.
You:      1
OMS:      Please keypress the country code of the person you want to leave a message for.
You:      A U S
OMS:      Australia. Australie.
          Please keypress recipient's last name.
You:      B R O W
OMS:      Jane Brown.
          Press 1 when you have completed your message.
          Begin talking when you are ready.
You:      'I'll meet you tonight at 8 : 00.'
          1
OMS:      Press 1, listen to this message; 2, send it; 3, do not send it.
You:      2
OMS:      Message sent to Jane Brown.
          Press 1, leave a message; 2, listen to an old message; 3, hang up.
You:      3
OMS:      Goodbye.
```

(c)

Figure 17.5 *(cont.)* Example messages. (c) an Olympian sending a message (Gould *et al.*, 1987: © 1987, Association for Computing Machinery, Inc. reprinted by permission).

Many other methods were used to collect information about what was needed, including tours of the Olympic village sites, early demonstrations of the system, interviews with the different people involved in the Olympics and discussions with an experienced ex-Olympian who was part of the design team. A prototype was then developed which was tested with different user groups. This resulted in many more iterations and retesting.

Other methods used included the informal 'hallway' method, which consisted of collecting opinions on the height and layout of the prototype kiosk from people who happened to be walking past, and the 'try-to-destroy-it' tests in which computer science students were invited to test the robustness of the system by trying to 'crash' it. Other details of the OMS can be found in Gould *et al.* (1987).

The design of the OMS demonstrates the importance of the three principles of user-centred design, from which our more general principles are derived. Gould and Lewis (1985) originally phrased these principles as follows:

- To focus on users and their tasks early in the design process, including user guides, help and ensuring that users' cognitive, social and attitudinal characteristics are understood and accommodated.
- To measure reactions by using prototype manuals, interfaces and other simulations of the system.
- To design iteratively because designers, no matter how good they are, cannot get it right the first few times.

The OMS team identified one additional principle:

- All usability factors must evolve together and be under the responsibility of one control group.

Gould *et al.* (1987) comment that 'the extra work these principles initially require greatly reduces work later on'. On the use of simulations, they point out that using live simulations (or prototypes) indicates how much a user must know to use the system. The approach of iterating the designs ensures that users' needs are constantly being kept central.

Over the years user-centred system design has evolved from the original definition provided by Gould and Lewis (1985) and now includes almost any approach that emphasizes methods, techniques and representations for software systems which place the user at the core of the development process.

User-centred design example 2: An air traffic control system

The combination of people, work, environment and technology determines how the principles of user-centred design should be applied. In this example (DTI case studies in HCI, 1991), the Civil Aviation Authority (CAA) in the UK employed a user-centred approach to the development of a new air traffic control system. Although it is apparently very different from the OMS, it illustrates how the principles can be applicable in a more 'traditional' environment and how the application of the principles can help to improve the usability of systems.

The CAA operates in the increasingly complex world of air traffic control, with primary responsibility for the safety of all users of UK airspace. CAA wished to integrate the disparate information systems that occupied the desks of air traffic controllers. The information needed varied by location and task.

The role of the air traffic controller is to give instruction and advice to pilots in order to maintain a safe and expeditious flow of aircraft throughout the airspace, including in and out of busy airport environments. In order to carry out their task the controllers need large amounts of data, both dynamic operational data and static information. This needs to be presented in a form that is easy to access and assimilate.

In the original system, the data needed by air traffic control staff was provided in a variety of formats, each designed to fulfil one role only. In consequence, controllers were presented with information by means of analogue and digital dials, closed circuit television and paper-based media such as order books and temporary instructions. Some were located in direct line of sight, others were inconveniently located on ceiling mountings or on other control desks outside the normal visual scan of the controller.

CAA wanted to introduce an integrated data display system to present as much information as practical on common displays. Safety aspects were a major factor and to take account of these, CAA recognized that the active involvement of the users would be crucial during the requirements specification phase of the project and again during the final stage of development to confirm their acceptance. They also recognized that the needs of the controller would change over time, and so the new system should have the capability to cope with both anticipated and unforeseen requirements. Furthermore, the system would be used at a number of different airports and the local requirements would also need to be taken into account.

The approach adopted by CAA to achieve these goals is illustrated in Figure 17.6. During the first cut design, evaluation of the controller's task demonstrated the dangers of proliferation of data processing systems. Controllers wanted to bring key information sources into a single workstation, to include windspeed and direction, time, runway use and visual range, other meteorological data, and text and graphic information such as maps and special procedures. An initial system was built for use at London City Airport and later at London Heathrow to provide an initial evaluation of the concept and, importantly, to gain early feedback from a system in actual operation. It was anticipated that future systems would grow out of the Heathrow experience.

Early feedback from controllers at Heathrow indicated that attention was needed to improve the usability of the system. Suggestions included:

● modified information requirements,
● different screen layouts for different controllers and tasks,
● greater use of colour to indicate exceptional situations, and to cater for different ambient lighting situations,
● ability to make up own pages for specific local conditions,
● simple editing facilities to allow rapid updates.

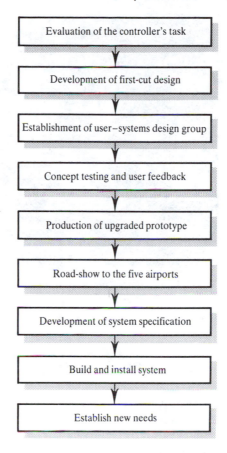

Figure 17.6 The method employed by the CAA.

At this stage it was agreed that an upgraded prototype would be constructed that incorporated the lessons learned from Heathrow. A team was established to manage the development of the new system from prototype to installation at all five airports. Importantly, as well as CAA systems designers, this team also included representatives of each airport to input local requirements. To confirm that user requirements were being met, the CAA launched a 'road-show' (a travelling demonstration of the new system) to demonstrate the upgraded prototype. This also aimed to secure further user input and commitment. CAA recognized that further changes would be needed during implementation, and that these should be capable of local introduction wherever possible. After the road-show, and taking account of its findings, the system specification was developed.

The initial system was introduced into Heathrow in early 1989. The upgraded system incorporating the improved usability features was introduced into the other airports in 1991 (Figure 17.7). Intelligent workstations have allowed the characteristics of the displays to be modified easily, and this can be achieved by a

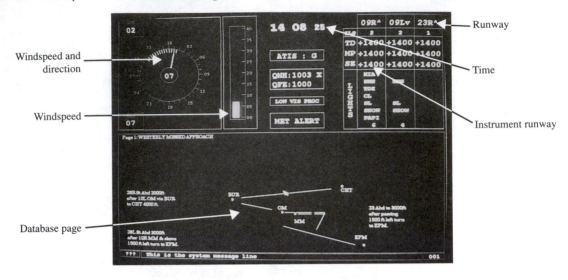

Figure 17.7 Multitasking workstation for air traffic controllers. See colour plate 11.

knowledgeable user. Automated software tools have enabled the provision of different control configurations. Resizing and repositioning of objects on screen, colour changes and highlighting can also be effected by the user.

Recognizing the advantages of prototyping so clearly demonstrated by this experience, the CAA have developed an air traffic control prototyping workstation using state of the art technology for use by air traffic controllers. Again, the early involvement of the user provided much needed and valuable research information.

17.4 The scope of human–computer system design

People, work, technology and the environment

In Chapter 2 we said that there are four key factors that need to be taken into account in interaction design: people, work, technology and the environment. The nature of these components will be different for different designs.

Question 17.4

From your experience of reading this book, make a note of the important aspects associated with the factors listed in Table 17.1 which need to be considered in the design of any technology.

Table 17.1 User and task factors and features.

Factors	Features
People	For example, age, disability
Individual characteristics	
User groups	
Frequency of usage	
Work	
Task features	
Time constraints	
Errors	
Environment	
General environment factors	
Organization	
User support	

EXERCISE

Identify the people, work and environment features in (i) the OMS and (ii) the CAA air traffic control system.

COMMENT

(i) People: users all start as novices. Many discretionary, but probably few casual users. Large range of different characteristics such as language, education, ethnic and social background. However, there were only two main user groups – Olympians, and family and friends.

Work: well-defined and specified tasks, but perhaps difficult for user to understand – not previously well-known tasks.

Environment: although sharing many of the characteristics of all walk-up-and-use systems (queues, open environment and so on), the OMS was a purpose-built system. Training was available, but no expert advice is easily available and error-recovery could not easily be supported.

(ii) People: highly trained, specialized users. Used to working with computer equipment. No discretionary or casual users.

Work: critical nature of tasks. Air traffic control tasks were well-understood, but also a need for less well-defined information retrieval activities.

Environment: busy, high-pressure situation. Expected to have good physical environment and good user support. However, later in the system, night-working and so on will mean less support is available.

Different kinds of systems

In addition to people, work and environmental factors, it is important to consider the kind of system that is to be developed. Software systems differ in many ways, including size, complexity, constraints and purpose, and this affects the design process and representations employed. One important consideration is whether a product under development is designed specially for a particular company (known as 'bespoke' in the UK) or is generic. With bespoke systems the organization that will use the final product tends to be closely involved in the design process because it has commissioned software to fulfil its own requirements. In the case of generic systems, however, the product is sold on an open market with no specific user organization in mind. This means that only general information about users can be considered during design. Thus the methods employed in the design process may be very different for these different classes of system.

A distinction also needs to be drawn between the design of a completely new system and the kind of design that occurs when updating or maintaining a system. Designers generally spend most of their time modifying and upgrading existing products; hence, much design activity is concerned with redesign. In these situations the freedom of the designer is severely restricted by decisions taken previously, either in the original design of the product or in the product line to which that product belongs. The **design space** available for taking decisions is small. On the other hand, the design space of new products starts much larger, and a product can take many different forms. The designer of a new system may be faced with the problem of having to select from among a number of options with different design outcomes.

Another important consideration is the size and complexity of the software system. Individual users who develop their own application using a standard database management system or spreadsheet need to consider the design carefully, but they do not need to go through the formal processes required by a major software development. Here a team of programmers, human factors specialists, quality assurance staff and systems analysts may be required. The staff on a project are likely to change during the lifetime of the system development and so the demands for formal representations and good methods of communication are vital. Other systems may use just one analyst/programmer who follows the system through from start to finish and who can establish a good personal rapport with the system users.

Constraints on systems must also be considered. These include features such as whether they are real-time systems (for example aircraft control systems) which have to give an almost instantaneous response or whether they are safety-critical. Safety-critical systems must employ techniques that are extremely thorough, robust, unambiguous and that can be shown to conform to safety standards.

Question 17.5

Describe the characteristics of the OMS and the CAA air traffic control system in terms of the types of systems described earlier (bespoke versus generic, and so on).

Key points

- Design is a creative process, but one that should employ engineering principles.
- Design involves the production of a number of intermediate representations of the final artefact.
- User-centred systems design focuses on people, their work and their environment, and how technology can best be deployed and designed to support them.
- User-centred systems design employs a rapid, iterative design process with comprehensive evaluations.
- User-centred design needs to employ user-centred representations.

Further reading

GOULD J.D., BOIES S.J., LEVY S., RICHARDS J.T. and SCHOONARD J. (1987). The 1984 Olympic Message System: A test of behavioural principle of system design. *Comm. ACM*, **30**(9), 758–69. Reprinted in PREECE J. and KELLER L., eds (1990). *Human–Computer Interaction: Selected Readings*. London: Prentice-Hall.

This paper provides an accessible description of the development of the OMS. The authors show how the principles of user-centred design were applied and developed during the project. It provides an excellent illustration of the points made in this chapter.

GOULD J.D. and LEWIS C. (1985). Designing for usability: Key principles and what designers think. *Comm. ACM*, **28**(3), 300–11.

This paper is the first exposition on user-centred design with the three principles spelled out in detail.

18

Methods for User-Centred Design

Aims and objectives

The aim of this chapter is to examine a number of approaches to design that are particularly applicable to HCI design. After completing this chapter you should be able to:

- identify the importance of considering the whole human–computer system,
- describe the aims of design methods discussed in this chapter,
- understand the role of the different methods within HCI design,
- understand the 'star' life cycle approach.

Overview

A central aspect of user-centred system design is the involvement of users throughout the design process. Users are not there simply to comment on a designer's ideas. They should be intimately involved in all aspects, including how the implementation of a new system will affect their jobs. This chapter looks at a number of approaches aimed at ensuring that users really do get involved in the development of a system and that systems are developed considering both the social and technical aspects of design.

As we said in Chapter 17, the essential principles of user-centred design are to make user issues central in the design process, to carry out early testing and evaluation with users and to design iteratively. However, as with any relatively complex subject, there are many variations on these themes. For example, according to Karat and Bennett (1991), 'the total system function is crafted to meet requirements for effective user learning and efficient user access ... the eventual users must see the system as useful and usable' (p. 64).

Eason takes a broader view of design and development, as illustrated in Figure 18.1, which shows the four key stages in development: planning for the system, designing it, implementing it and managing it. Various techniques and activities are listed around the four circles at approximately the points at which they are relevant. Down the right-hand side of the figure there are two methods that cover the whole of those parts of the design that they are positioned against.

At the top of the figure – Plan for systems – Eason is stressing that human, computer and human–computer systems should be developed in an ordered manner rather than in an *ad hoc* way. In particular, it is important to consider the purpose of the system under development and how it fits in with the other human and technical systems that exist or may exist. Most importantly, it is necessary to consider how a system contributes to the overall aims of the organization. The design

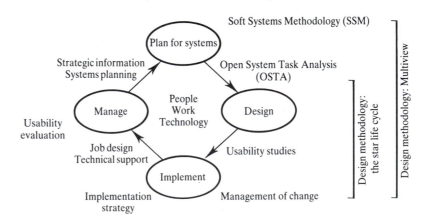

Figure 18.1 Methods for user-centred design (adapted from Eason, 1992).

process and the process of moving from design to implementation involve ensuring that the system meets its usability targets, and in Section 31.2 you will see how this can be done. Managing the change that occurs as a result of introducing a new system is also important, as we said in Chapter 10. To be successful, the system has to be implemented effectively and to gain acceptance from the user population. Job design and the management of change are covered in Eason (1988). Martin (1982) discusses strategic planning for information systems.

In this chapter we will concentrate on four approaches to system development: the Soft Systems Methodology (SSM), Open Systems Task Analysis (OSTA), Multiview and the star life cycle. These focus on different aspects of system development and are oriented to deal with the stages on the right-hand side of Figure 18.1. Soft Systems Methodology focuses on planning. OSTA is primarily concerned with the early stages of design, whereas Multiview is a complete methodology, which spans the whole of planning through to implementation. The star life cycle focuses primarily on design and, as you will remember from Chapter 2, is used as a framework within this book. In addition to discussing these methods we shall also mention a number of the techniques listed in Figure 18.1, as well as referring to other closely related ones. Before continuing to study this section you should also take note of the cyclical nature of Eason's figure, which suggests that implementation is far from the end of the story.

18.1 Soft systems methodology

All human actions take place within wider contexts, or situations. It is therefore important to understand the whole human–computer *system*. This view is recognized in many traditions, and has been stressed by Suchman (1989), Winograd and Flores (1986) and, from the world of systems theory, Checkland (1981). The essential aspect of understanding situations from a systems perspective is to consider the system as a whole. One of the most popular descriptions of this systems or holistic view is known as the Soft Systems Methodology (SSM) (Checkland, 1981; Checkland and Scholes, 1991). The emphasis of SSM is not on finding a solution to a specified problem, it is on understanding the situation in which a perceived problem is thought to lie.

SSM is illustrated in Figure 18.2. Stages 1 and 2 of the method are concerned with obtaining a rich expression of the problem situation. During these stages, meetings are held and all interested parties – the 'stakeholders' – are involved. Frequently, different stakeholders will have different views on what the purpose of the system is. For example, some people will argue that the purpose of the UK health service is to provide employment, others that it is to make people better and others that it is to operate efficiently or provide value for money. These different views will not necessarily be contradictory, but they may emphasize different aspects of the overall situation and they must be brought together if they are to be reconciled.

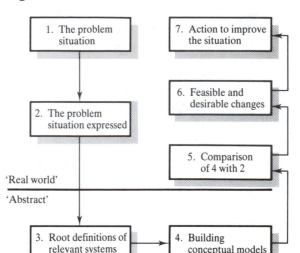

Figure 18.2 Stages in the soft systems methodology.

Question 18.1

In a drive for greater efficiency in education, the government of a small European country is considering implementing a system that will require schools to administer standard assessment tests to all pupils at ages 7, 11, 14 and 16. The results of these tests are to be published nationally so that comparisons between schools can be made.

Identify the stakeholders in this system. What is the declared purpose of the system from the government's perspective?

Stage 3 of the method demands a precise definition of the system. This is used (in stage 4) to produce conceptual models – abstract representations of the system. One of the vital aspects of the approach is that stages 3 and 4 are carried out away from the real world – this allows a representation to be produced that is not cluttered by real-world constraints. Checkland (1981) and Wilson (1984) provide a number of methods that can be used to produce a formal and comprehensive definition of what the system is. Checkland calls this the 'root definition' and provides a useful mnemonic to help designers ensure that they cover all aspects of the system and produce robust root definitions. These are the CATWOE elements: Clients (or customers), Actors, Transformation, *Weltanschauung* (that is, the world view), Owners and Environment.

The root definition should identify the various people involved in the system: who will benefit or suffer from the system (the clients), who is involved in the system (the actors) and who has commissioned the system (the owners). For example, if a new management information system was to be introduced into a hospital, we might identify the hospital managers as the system owners, the administrators as the clients (those people who will benefit from the new information) and the nurses, doctors and patients as the actors in the system. Frequently, the actors in a system derive little or no benefit, but are expected to alter their working practices in order to provide data for the clients. This can cause severe problems, as actors feel that they are being asked to do more work for no apparent benefit.

The CATWOE model also emphasizes the basic transformation, or purpose, of the system, the environmental constraints on the system and the *Weltanschauung* – the perspective from which the root definition is formulated. This last aspect is particularly important. Any system description will be biased to a particular point of view.

Question 18.2

Produce a root definition for the school system in (Question 18.1) using the CATWOE elements.

Conceptual models can be produced from this definition during stage 4. Notice how the methodology emphasizes that the modelling stages should take place away from the real world, using the root definition to drive the modelling exercises. Modelling the system will expose gaps in the root definition (stage 5) and the analyst will cycle round the processes until a well-formed root definition is agreed.

The conceptual model of the situation is compared with the original expression of the situation, and as a result feasible and desirable changes are exposed (stage 6). Stage 7 may often result in a further iteration of the process – the new problem, 'what actions are required', can be analysed using the SSM approach.

SSM has much to recommend it. Applied to human–computer systems engineering, the focus is on establishing the purpose, people, constraints and 'world view' of the human–machine system, and on developing conceptual models of that ideal system.

Question 18.3

Why does SSM stress understanding the situation and not understanding the problem? Why are designers encouraged to develop models away from the 'real world'?

18.2 Cooperative design

Several different names are used for approaches that all involve working with users to do the design. They differ primarily in the philosophy and practices that each adopts.

Participative design (sometimes known as the Scandinavian approach) accepts the importance of involving users in the design process and, indeed, argues that they have a right to be involved in the design of the systems which they will subsequently use. This strong ideological basis underpins all of participative design in Scandinavia. Users participate by analysing organizational requirements and planning appropriate social and technical structures to support both individual and organizational needs.

Sociotechnical design is a form of cooperative design that focuses on developing complete and coherent human–machine systems. The emphasis of this approach is on considering social and technical alternatives to problems. Catterall *et al.* (1991) describe the basis of sociotechnical theory:

> 'human and organizational issues cannot be considered in isolation from the technology.'
>
> (p. 256)

> 'User-centred design implies the active participation of users in the design process ... [it] should be comprehensive and not simply part of an end-process evaluation procedure.'
>
> (p. 258)

The underlying philosophy of these approaches is summarized by Greenbaum and Kyng (1991), who coined the term 'cooperative design'. They argue that the usefulness of human–computer systems depends on

> 'the fragile relationships of the person, the working environment and the computer technology.'
>
> (p. ix)

They also emphasize the social dimension of computer systems:

> 'system development is difficult, not because of the technical problems, but because of the social interaction when users and developers learn to create, develop and express their ideas and visions.'
>
> (p. viii)

In taking this stance, Greenbaum and Kyng focus on the essential difficulty of designing human–computer systems; the different models of tasks, domains and systems that are employed by users and designers (see Chapter 10). Many methodologies of system design, analysis and design techniques and evaluation methods (Part VI) have been proposed in order to deal with this problem. We discuss several of these techniques in Chapters 19–22.

The emphasis in all sociotechnical approaches to system design is on understanding both the social system and the technical system. Many methods have been proposed over the years in order to help analysts focus attention on the main issues. The most significant of these is the Open Systems Task Analysis (OSTA) method (Eason, 1988; Eason and Harker, 1989).

OSTA follows a sociotechnical systems analysis model in which technical requirements (the system's structure and functionality) are specified alongside social system requirements (that is, usability and acceptability). Its underlying aim is to provide a methodology for understanding the transformation that occurs when a computer system is introduced into a working environment. Figure 18.3 illustrates the principles of such an analysis. Systems analysis explores organizational issues, for example, goals, values and sources of job satisfaction, as well as traditional information flows and key tasks. Following systems analysis (shown above the thick line in Figure 18.3), sociotechnical solutions involving the identification of technical and social constraints are identified (shown below the thick line in Figure 18.3). The

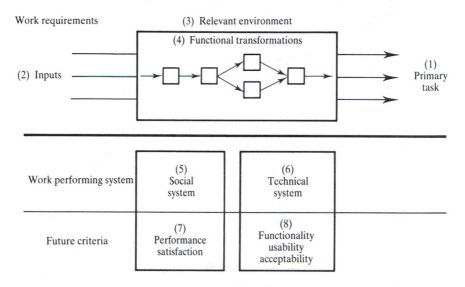

Figure 18.3 Open systems task analysis for user requirements specification (Eason, 1988).

steps involved in OSTA are shown in Box 18.1. The information collected using this technique is communicated to the design team in the form of flow charts and descriptions written in ordinary language.

Question 18.4

What types of information are collected using OSTA? Why do you think OSTA stresses the importance of establishing the criteria for the future social system before trying to establish the criteria for the technical system?

Box 18.1   Steps involved in OSTA

The steps in an OSTA are as follows:

(1)   The **primary task** of a work system is stated, in which the goals of the group of workers are identified.

(2)   **Task inputs** are identified. These usually come from outside the system. The character of these inputs can be variable (for example, customers' orders can be handwritten, telephoned or typed), which can affect the way in which the system behaves in order to achieve its primary task.

(3)   The **external environment**, including physical environment, economic and political conditions and the demand for task output, are then established. The relative importance of these factors will depend on the

extent to which the work system liaises with the outside world. For example, a work system that deals directly with the general public is likely to have to cope with a wide range of external conditions.

(4) **Transformation processes** are described. This involves describing the functions that have to be undertaken to transform the inputs into outputs such that the primary goal requirements are fulfilled. It is generally done by constructing an object/action flow chart in which the objects to be transformed and the actions that bring this about are identified. For example, in one *Weltanschauung* of a hospital, the patients are the 'objects' and the goal is to get them better through the actions of 'performing operations', 'administering drugs' and so on. The relations (that is, whether they are sequential, parallel, reciprocal and so on) between the functions are also shown. This flow chart can be annotated to provide information about time constraints, the variance in procedures and the allocation of tasks between people and machines.

(5) The **social system** is analysed; the roles of the people in an organization are assessed in relation to one another. In addition, the characteristics and qualities of the people who will ultimately become the users of the new system are detailed.

(6) The **technical system** is analysed in terms of how the new system will be integrated with other systems and what remains of the old system. The effect it will have on the nature of the work is also considered.

(7) **Performance satisfaction** refers to those requirements outlined for the new social system when the new technical system is introduced.

(8) The requirements for the **new technical system** are also derived from the task analysis. Many aspects of functionality are defined, together with usability and acceptability criteria for the technical system. The roles of technology and of people in the new system are allocated. Statements are then made about the form of the interface to the system, what changes are needed to the overall system, and the training needs of the staff.

Sociotechnical and participative design approaches focus on involving users in the design process and on considering a wide range of social and technical alternatives. Although these approaches involve users at various stages in design, they are not without their problems. One is the need for an expert to guide the design process and support users. Another is the degree to which it can be integrated with other system development processes and methods. Designers have to understand the need for this additional effort. A third problem with the methods is that they can only be used if the organizational and political climate is suitable. Finally, the issue of cost-effectiveness is sometimes raised. There must be a commitment by management to involve users and to take on board their requirements.

Alone, the methods may provide sound guidance, but they do not really tell designers *how* they can involve users. More direction is needed if such approaches really are to be usable.

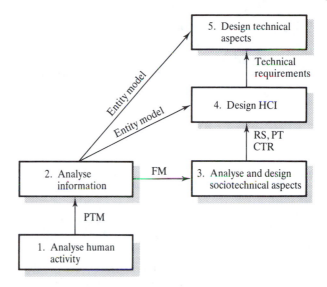

Figure 18.4 Multiview methodology (Avison and Wood-Harper, 1990).

18.3 Multiview: A user-centred methodology

A more prescriptive approach is to embed sociotechnical and soft systems into a more all-encompassing methodology. Multiview (Avison and Wood-Harper, 1990) is an information systems design methodology which combines these different approaches into a staged, controlled methodology (Figure 18.4). The primary task model (PTM) is similar to Checkland's root definition. It describes the purpose of the system, the stakeholders involved and the perspective of the system owners. Stage 2, 'analyse information', is concerned with conceptual modelling of information flows and information structure. The functional model (FM) is used in stage 3 as the basis for task allocation – designing people tasks (PT), role sets (RS) and computer task requirements (CTR). It is only then that the technical requirements are used to design the computer system. This part of the methodology includes a strong sociotechnical approach. The sociotechnical options, along with the entity model of information structure (see Chapter 19), is used to drive the design of the HCI. Only when the human system has been defined can the technical aspects of the computer system be determined.

Several aspects of this representation are worth noting. Firstly, the methodology has an explicit component devoted to HCI design. This follows a considered approach of looking at sociotechnical alternatives. Most importantly, however, it begins with an analysis of the human activities (Section 18.1), which results in the production of a PTM – a definition of the system purpose. The methodology also employs entity relationship modelling and dataflow modelling (Chapter 19) in order to develop a conceptual model before physical design decisions are taken.

Multiview provides more direction for system designers. In common with most methodologies, it emphasizes the order in which certain activities should be undertaken. This is both a strength and a weakness. Its strength lies in its ability to aid designers, ensuring that systems are developed carefully and logically. Its weakness is that it is sometimes difficult to fit specific designs into a rigid framework.

18.4 An HCI design approach

In contrast to the methodological view provided by Multiview, the star life cycle (mentioned in Section 2.4) emphasizes that an ordering of activities is inappropriate. The star model (Figure 18.5; Hartson and Hix, 1989) was derived following extensive analysis of actual design practice among HCI designers. It takes the idea of prototyping and evaluation much further than any other approach. Evaluation is central in this method. *All* aspects of systems development are subject to constant evaluation by users and by experts. The star model also promotes an 'alternating waves' approach to system development. Whereas the traditional model and most methodologies including Multiview advocate a 'top-down' or analytic method, the star model recognizes that this approach needs to be complemented by a 'bottom-up' or synthetic approach. The star life cycle also stresses rapid prototyping and an incremental development of the final product. Although the titles given to the main stages are different, they represent similar activities to the waterfall model (Figure 17.1): analysis (task analysis/functional analysis), requirements specification, design (conceptual/formal design) and implementation but the process involves considerably more iteration. Prototyping and evaluation are shown as new activities, though they can be used in any of the other stages. Evaluation extends and develops the principles of validation, verification and testing.

In the star life cycle approach, system development may begin at any stage (indicated by the entry arrows) and may be followed by any of the other stages (indicated by the double headed arrows). This may seem a strange notion, but in reality is quite common. The requirements, design and the product gradually evolve, becoming increasingly well defined. The provision of good software tools (Chapters 27 and 28) is vital in order to underpin this approach. This method is also suggested by other members of the HCI community. For example, Fischer (1989) argues that because there are no firm HCI theories and HCI problems are typically ill structured, 'we need effective exploratory programming environments and rapid prototyping tools that support iterative, evolutionary design' (p. 45).

The star life cycle (Figure 18.5) also emphasizes the important distinction between conceptual design and physical design (called formal design in Figure 18.5). **Conceptual design** concerns itself with questions of what is required; what the system should do, what data is required, what users will need to know, and so on. **Physical design** is concerned with questions of how these things can be achieved. The conceptual/physical distinction is fundamental to the provision of good systems

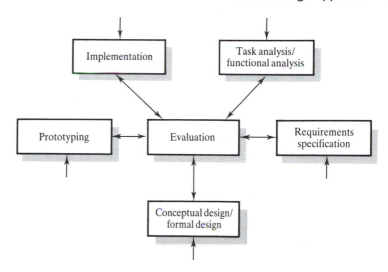

Figure 18.5 The star model (adapted from Hartson and Hix, 1989, 1993).

because it defers decisions as to who or what will ultimately perform which functions, or provide which data until late in the design process.

Question 18.5

Using the example of developing a new room for your house (Question 17.1), think of a situation where you would start the development process with

(a) an implementation
(b) a prototype
(c) a conceptual design
(d) a physical design

How might the development continue in each case?

The star life cycle (Figure 18.5) is primarily oriented to the particular demands of developing interactive systems that will be usable by people. The emphasis on rapid prototyping, alternating waves of analytic (top-down) and synthetic (bottom-up) approaches and evaluation is both realistic and user-centred. The principle that development may commence from any point in the star overcomes many of the limitations of the traditional model. Just as important as the processes of design are the representations of the system that are employed. For some purposes informal models such as sketches, scenarios and prototypes (Chapter 22) will be most apt, whereas for other purposes formal notations will be more appropriate (Chapters 19–21). Checklists, design rules and guidelines (Chapter 24) are also used to assist the designer at various stages.

Key points

- HCI design methods seek to involve users in all aspects of systems development.
- The soft systems methodology encourages a view of human–computer systems that considers the whole situation and not some identified 'problem'.
- Sociotechnical design focuses on the whole human–computer system, searching for designs that are both socially and technically feasible and desirable.
- Multiview offers a more prescriptive, user-centred methodology.
- The star life cycle reflects more accurately what designers do and stresses the central role of evaluation.
- The design of human–computer systems needs to recognize the organizational as well as local needs and to focus on the whole work situation and not on some perceived problem.

Further reading

CHECKLAND P.B. (1981). *Systems Thinking, Systems Practice*. Chichester: John Wiley.
This is one of the standard texts on the soft systems methodology.

EASON K.D. (1988). *Information Technology and Organizational Change*. London: Taylor & Francis.
This book discusses sociotechnical design and provides excellent coverage of the organizational issues of concern in design.

GREENBAUM J. and KYNG M., eds (1991). *Design at Work: Cooperative Design of Computer Systems*. Hillsdale, NJ: Lawrence Erlbaum Associates.
An excellent collection of papers coming from the 'Scandinavian' tradition. The principles and practice of participative design are laid out and illustrated with many examples.

HARTSON H.R. and HIX D. (1989). Toward empirically derived methodologies and tools for HCI development. *International Journal of Man–Machine Studies*, **31**, 477–94.
This paper lays out the rationale for and description of the star life cycle. The authors describe the results of their research and why they evolved this life cycle.

HIX D. and HARTSON H.R. (1993). *Developing User Interfaces: Ensuring Usability Through Product and Process*. New York: John Wiley.
This book provides in-depth coverage of the star life cycle and much more. It is oriented towards the design process and provides useful 'how to do it' knowledge based largely on the authors' own experience. It is a valuable aid for learning HCI design.

19

Requirements Gathering

Aims and objectives

The process of systems analysis, or requirements gathering, is a major part of any product development. After completing this chapter you should be able to:

- define the activities involved in requirements gathering,
- distinguish functional, data and usability requirements,
- use dataflow and entity relationship techniques to help analyse requirements,
- describe usability requirements.

Overview

This chapter deals with what requirements should be obtained, the importance of critical analysis in requirements gathering and techniques that are available to assist in requirements gathering. In this chapter you will see how some well-defined techniques can be used to help the designer *understand the requirements of a system. You will also find that some of the techniques are useful later on in the system development process.*

Requirements gathering or **analysis** is the process of finding out what a client (or customer) requires from a software system. Typically, the document that is produced initially by a client (called the application description or statement of requirements) describes what is wanted from the proposed new system in rather vague terms. One of the main purposes of requirements gathering is to clarify the client's needs and to identify infeasible requirements, omissions, ambiguities and vagueness.

The analyst will use a whole gamut of techniques in order to elicit the requirements. General techniques such as interviewing, observation and document analysis are used in requirements gathering (as well as in evaluation, see Chapter 30). Opinions can be sought about existing products through the use of questionnaires and interviews. In addition, the analyst should analyse user tasks using cognitive and other task analysis techniques. We shall examine some techniques for doing this in Chapter 20. HCI specialists will observe the natural work setting in order to understand its organizational and social (Chapter 10) characteristics. Prototyping can also be used to facilitate requirements gathering, and requirements animation can be used for illustrating possibilities (see Chapters 22 and 27). Analysts may also use checklists (Chapter 30) to help them remember important aspects of the situation. Matrices and other cross-referencing techniques may also be useful. Using these techniques, information can be elicited about how people go about their work, what problems they are having with the existing system, what they would like to help them with their tasks, how they think the work process could be improved, and so on.

As well as obtaining detailed information about users and their work it is important to consider the effects of the physical environment. A nice example of a potential environmental hazard is reported by Boies *et al.* (1985) from the Olympic Message System study (Chapter 17). They found that during a field study at the desert location of one of the events, insects crawled into the computer at night to keep warm. It was, therefore, necessary for them to develop some protection against possible insect damage.

This example raises another important issue. Requirements gathering is concerned with *understanding* needs. It is an analytic process in which representations of the system are produced which not only describe what is required but also help the designer to analyse situations. The result of the requirements gathering process is:

- a representation of the problems with the current system,
- a representation of the requirements of the new system.

The requirements of a system can be considered in three categories. The **functional requirements** specify what the system must do. **Data requirements** specify the structure of the system and the data that must be available for processing to be successful. **Usability requirements** specify the acceptable level of user performance and satisfaction with the system. Gathering requirements demands various analyses to be undertaken. In this chapter we discuss functional, data, user and environment analysis. Task analysis – understanding and representing what the user has to do – is discussed in Chapter 20.

19.1 Functional requirements

In line with our belief that developers should concern themselves with the whole human–computer system, when we use the term functional requirements, you should understand that it means both what the system does and what the human does. Decisions on which activities are to be carried out by human and which by computer (known as the process of **task allocation**) are deferred until after a task analysis and more design has been undertaken. Functional requirements are concerned with what the system has to be capable of doing. Alongside functional requirements, functional constraints must be identified.

The result of analysing and collecting functional requirements is a representation of the system known as the **functional specification**. This is a formal document or other representation which details what the system is to do. It is generally partitioned into separate modules, organized in a hierarchical manner. This allows the description of a system to be split up into tractable parts that can be dealt with individually. The top level of the hierarchy consists of high-level (abstract) descriptions of the functions of a system (for example, 'The system should provide monitoring facilities for the plant operators') while the bottom (most concrete) layer specifies in more detail what this should be (for example, 'The function of the "VOL" command is to display the volume of a fluid currently in a vessel designated by the operator').

EXERCISE

What possible problem can you see with the detailed functional requirement described above?

COMMENT

Detailed requirements such as this should not be specified too early in the development process. How could anyone know that there would or should be a 'VOL' *command?* There may be a requirement to display the volume of fluid, but the way that this should be implemented is a design decision.

An important part of gathering functional requirements is that they will *not* be gathered and specified all in one go. Furthermore, detailed decisions like the one in the above exercise should not be made during initial requirements gathering. Iteration and some design activities are necessary before requirements can be completely understood. Constraints must also be specified and can be expressed in terms of either the system itself or its development process. An example of a system constraint is the amount of memory that the system should fit into (for example, 256 K). An example of a constraint on the development process is the type of programming language that must be used to develop the system.

EXERCISE

The following is an extract from a hypothetical statement of requirements for a system which should provide information for staff monitoring a power plant. Can you identify the functional requirements and the constraints?

> The monitoring system should monitor and display the temperatures in a series of reactors, detect any hazard conditions from these temperatures which indicate a reactor malfunction, and periodically write temperature data to a database which is used to provide information about the day-to-day running of the reactors. Since other systems have already been implemented on the host computer only 60 K of memory is available for this system. All the file handling that the system performs should be implemented by means of calls on operating system procedures. The system should also periodically archive the temperature database to magnetic tape; otherwise the file store used for the database would become exhausted.

COMMENT

There are five system functions:

- the system should monitor the temperatures in a series of reactors,
- the system should display the temperatures in a series of reactors,
- the system should detect any hazard conditions from the temperatures which indicate a reactor malfunction,
- the system should periodically write temperature data to a database,
- the system should periodically archive the temperature database to a magnetic tape.

There are two constraints – one system and one process:
- the developer has to ensure that the system fits into 60 K of memory,
- all the file-handling that the system performs should be implemented by means of calls on operating system procedures.

Functional requirements are usually specified using some charting technique such as dataflow diagrams along with a natural or structured language description of the details of the functional components. If you are not familiar with dataflow diagrams you should study Box 19.1 before reading any further. If you just need a quick reminder then read on.

A **dataflow diagram** describes a system from the point of view of the data that is passed between processes. A dataflow diagram shows the processes (circles or bubbles) and the data flowing in and out of these processes (represented by named lines). Many processes have to access or write some more permanent data. This stored data is represented by an open rectangle. Finally, dataflow diagrams show the sources or destinations (sometimes called 'sinks') of data as boxes. An important feature of dataflow diagrams is that they represent systems as a hierarchy of functions. Each level is a correct decomposition of the level above it. The context diagram (a), level 1 (b), and some of the level 2 (c) dataflow diagrams for the functions of the reactor system are shown in Figure 19.1. Notice that the level 2

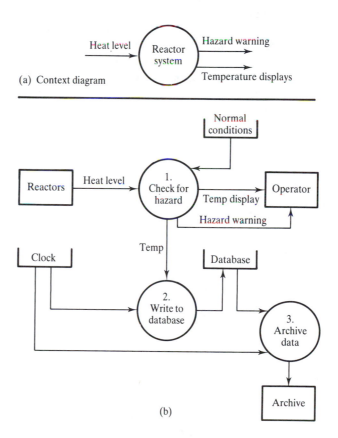

Figure 19.1 Dataflow diagram for the reactor system. (a) Context diagram, (b) level 1.

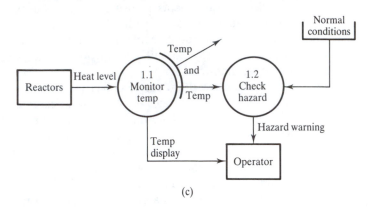

(c)

Figure 19.1 *(cont.)* Dataflow diagram for the reactor system. (c) Level 2 for process 1.

diagram is a true decomposition of process 1 at level 1 in that the data flowing into and out from the process is consistently specified.

The task of specifying the requirements for a system can become highly complex with many levels of diagrams each describing the system in more detail. All dataflows and datastores need to be described along with a specification of the processing that takes place in each bubble. These are specified in a **data dictionary**. If you are unfamiliar with this concept you will find a description in Box 19.2.

Box 19.1 Dataflow diagrams

Functional requirements are concerned with the processes that a system performs. Processes take data as input and produce (different, hopefully more useful) data as output. In order to be at all significant, therefore, every process must change the data in some way. The processes which concern us in dataflow diagrams must transform the data through some manipulation, restructure it more usefully, or relate it to other data. In order to do this, the process may need to reference a more permanent store of a 'datastore'.

For example, in an invoicing application, the process 'calculate total price' takes as its input the data elements *PartNumber* and *Quantity*, produces as its output a value in pounds and pence and uses a datastore of *PartNumbers* and *Price per part*. The process can then be checked for completeness. It must have access to enough data – either as input or from a data store – to be in a position to produce the output.

Table 19.1 Symbols for the dataflow diagram.

Symbol	Description
Name (rectangle)	The source or destination of data. Generally considered to be outside the system under investigation.
Name and number (circle)	The process which must transform the data.
Name → (arrow)	The dataflow is simply a named line. It must have a unique name.
Data (open box)	The datastore. This is a more permanent store of data than the dataflow. It is a place where data rests, sometimes only temporarily.

The basic requirements of a model of fundamental requirements are inputs, outputs, processes and stores of data. Since the output from one process may be the input to another, it is better to view all data that travels between processes as a single concept; a **dataflow**. These ideas are based on the 'structured approach' to systems analysis, which developed during the late 1970s, principally through the work of people such as DeMarco (1979) and Yourdon and Constantine (1979).

The symbols used are shown in Table 19.1, and Figure 19.2 illustrates their use in an order processing application.

Inevitably, there is some overlap between the concepts. When is a dataflow a datastore, or when is a source or destination a process? These questions can only be answered in consultation with the users of the system and so we need not worry about getting the dataflow diagrams 'right' first time. The representation is useful as a means of exploring ideas and understanding requirements as well as documenting them.

The final feature of dataflow diagrams is that they can maintain a consistency when used at different levels. At the top level is the **context diagram**. This shows the whole system as a single process with the major dataflows as inputs and outputs. The context diagram serves to define the boundary of the system. The level 1 dataflow diagram decomposes this high-level representation into its constituent subsystems or processes. A process can usually be split into several subprocesses until a level is reached that is deemed to be simple enough for the purpose. Processes at a lower level can be checked to ensure that their inputs and outputs constitute exactly the data which appears at the higher level. Dataflows and datastores are described in terms of their constituent **data elements**. This information is kept in the data dictionary (see Box 19.2).

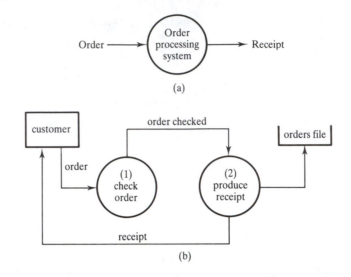

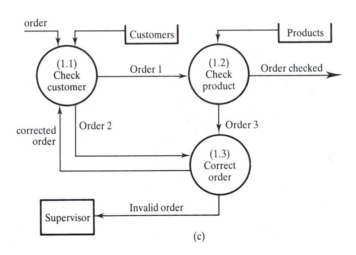

Figure 19.2 An order processing system. (a) Context diagram, (b) level 1, (c) level 2 for process 1.

In Figure 19.2 the context diagram shows that orders are processed by the order processing system to produce receipts. The level 1 diagram adds more detail and shows that a customer sends in an order, which triggers the process 'check order'. Once the order has been checked some data called 'order checked' is sent to process 2. The arrival of this data triggers the process 'produce receipt', which produces a dataflow 'Receipt' and updates a datastore called 'orders file'.

The details of process 1 are shown in the level 2 diagram, Figure 19.2(c). Process 2 would be treated similarly. Notice that process 1 is split at level 2 into processes 1.1, 1.2 and 1.3 but that the total inputs and outputs of these three processes is consistent with process 1 at level 1. This demonstrates the desirable property of consistency. Also, notice that all entities in the diagram (dataflows, data elements, processes and datastores) are described in the data dictionary (see Box 19.2).

The order processing system consists of two events, 'order' (received) and 'order checked', which trigger the processes 'check order' and 'produce receipt', respectively. These are also recorded in the data dictionary.

The diagram will take several attempts before it accurately reflects the processes involved. Where possible, the events should appear at level 1. Dataflow diagrams are abstractions of the physical world. They use the abstract idea of data to analyse and describe the functional requirements of a system.

Box 19.2 Data dictionary

The data dictionary describes all the data in a system. As with all aspects of analysis, the data dictionary evolves into its final form, helping with understanding as well as simply documenting the system. The most basic pieces of data that are of interest in the application are the **data elements**. Each should be given a useful name and accompanied by a short textual description. Many problems with computer systems are caused because the designer has attributed one meaning to a data element when the users have attributed another. For example, a data element with the name 'quantity delivered' may mean the quantity *to be* delivered as far as the users are concerned and the quantity *actually* delivered on the part of the designer. Making the meaning of data elements open and explicit helps to overcome such problems.

A **dataflow** is one or more data elements that are transferred from one process to another. The data dictionary should specify the content of dataflows in terms of their constituent data elements. This not only ensures a complete and consistent definition of the dataflow, it also facilitates checking that the processes really do transform data. If the dataflows entering and leaving a process are not different in respect of their data elements, they have not been changed by the process.

The function of each **process** is described using some high-level programming or pseudo-programming language. It is not necessary to describe *how* the processing takes place, but only *what* processing occurs. Once again, this description helps to check for consistency. The process description highlights the data elements that are required by the process so that the analyst can check that all the data is available. The processes at higher levels in the dataflow

(a) Data flows

order = *order date* + *customer#* + {*product#*s + *quantity*s}
Order1 = Order + *customer-check* (= Y)
Order checked = Order1 + *product-check* (= Y)
Order2 = Order + customer# invalid (*customer-check* = N)
Order3 = Order1 + product# invalid (*product-check* = N)
corrected order = order
receipt = *customer name, address, product#, price each, quantity* and *total, order total*

(b) Data elements

order date	date order received
customer#	our unique identification of customer
product#	unique product identification
quantity	quantity ordered
customer-check	Y = customer# valid, N = not on file
product-check	Y = product# valid, N = invalid product#
customer name	customer's initials + surname
address	customer's home address
price each	price of one product
total	price each × quantity
order total	sum of totals

(c) Datastores

customers	*(customer#, customer name, address)*
products	*(product#, product-description, price each)*
orders file	*(order#, customer#, order date, order total)*

(d) Processes

(1) check order	– triggered by event Order (received); consists of: (1.1) Check customer (1.2) Check products (1.3) Correct order
(2) produce receipt	– triggered by event Order checked; consists of: for each product retrieve *price each* calculate *total* calculate *order total* retrieve *customer name* and *address* print receipt write to orders file
(1.1) Check customer	– access Customers by *customer#*
(1.2) Check product	– access Products by *product#*
(1.3) Correct order	– examine print of Customers and/or Products to determine correct numbers. If unsuccessful refer to supervisor

Figure 19.3 The data dictionary for the order processing system (Benyon, 1990).

diagram are described in terms of the sequence of their constituent, lower level processes. Higher level processes should include a description of the **event** which triggers the process. An event is something that happens in the world, which is reflected by the arrival or change of some data in the system.

Datastores are collections of data elements that are more persistent, or more permanent, than dataflows. As the analysis and design develops, datastores will be replaced by formal definitions of the system **entities**, which are derived from the data analysis. Initially, however, it is just necessary to identify the store of data which is required by a process. Put simply, every process requires the appropriate data elements – either from a dataflow or from a datastore – to do its processing. Defining these in a data dictionary enables this consistency check to be enforced. Software systems called **data dictionary systems** are available which automate the process of defining data and processes and help the analyst perform consistency checking.

The data dictionary for the order processing system is shown in Figure 19.3.

One of the problems with traditional functional specifications is that there is often little or no mention of the user or user interaction with the system. For example, in the statement of requirements in the above exercise there is no consideration of the capabilities of users or the problem of how the system should respond to a user error (for example, overloading a reactor). In order to counter this problem, usability requirements, which are discussed in Section 19.3, should be specified alongside functional requirements. It is most important in user-centred system design that the whole system is specified using an appropriate notation such as dataflow diagrams, as this representation can then be used as the basis for a considered task allocation, as we will see in Chapter 20.

Question 19.1

A computer system is to be developed which will help users to correct the spellings in documents that have been produced. The system will contain a dictionary of words and will check each word against this dictionary. Additionally, the user may specify certain words such as proper nouns or technical terms that are not in the dictionary but that are in the 'context' of the document. If a word is discovered that is not in the dictionary or context, a decision must be taken as to whether the word is spelt correctly or not. If a correction is to be made this must be accomplished and the next word in the document checked until all words have been processed.

Draw a context diagram and level 1 dataflow diagram for the 'spell-checking' system.

The solution to Question 19.1 shows three functions. As yet these have not been allocated to human or computer (this allocation would usually follow a task analysis, see Chapter 20). However, for the purpose of this exercise let us assume that the user is to decide if a word is spelt incorrectly, that is the user performs process 2.

Question 19.2

The user must decide if a word is wrong or if it is not. If it is not wrong (for example, it may be someone's name) the user may update the store of context words. If it is wrong, the word can be looked up in the dictionary in order to determine the correct spelling. The dictionary may make a number of suggestions. The user can evaluate these and select the required correction.

Draw a dataflow diagram for this. Ensure that the levels are correct between the top level and this more detailed level diagram.

It is important to remember that when a dataflow diagram is used for specifying functional requirements it is an abstraction of the existing system and not simply a copy of the physical processes that occur at present. Constructing dataflow diagrams and using them to structure discussions with users is an effective analytic technique, which will help to expose misunderstandings and omissions. Dataflow diagrams are a complete notation and prevent exception conditions such as errors and emergencies or other non-obvious activities from being hidden, as often happens using traditional flow charting techniques. They facilitate requirements gathering because they enable the analyst to conduct structured walkthroughs with the system users (Yourdon, 1989). A **structured walkthrough** is a verbal description of the system based on the diagrammatic representation. In this way they aid understanding of the functional requirements rather than simply describing the existing processes.

Question 19.3

Produce a walkthrough for the level 2 dataflow diagram of process 1 in the reactor system (Figure 19.2). What can you say about the requirements from this? What questions does it force you to ask?

Dataflow diagrams are only one method of representing functional requirements (Benyon and Skidmore, 1987) and there are circumstances when flow charts, structure charts or other techniques may be more effective. For example, the use of scenarios is particularly appropriate in HCI because scenarios help to bring the rather abstract specification to life – situating it in terms that the user can appreciate (Chapter 22). The significant benefit of using dataflow diagrams, however, is that they demand a more abstract view to be taken. The analyst may construct a dataflow diagram of the current system as it functions physically (known as a current physical dataflow diagram), but then produce a data-centred representation (a current logical dataflow diagram), thus exposing redundant datastores, duplicated dataflows and unnecessary processes and hence widening the design space. Current, physical constraints and methods of working are suppressed, allowing the flow of data to be more clearly exposed. However, there can also be drawbacks. Dataflow diagrams tend to discourage object-centredness as in direct manipulation and additional information may be disregarded.

19.2 Data requirements

Defining the functional requirements is by no means the end of the story. In addition to representing the flow of data, the meaning and structure of the data itself must be defined and agreed with the users. Most information systems development methodologies now recognize the importance of defining the data requirements in addition to the functions. Data requirements focus attention on structure as opposed to processing. Once again, data requirements should specify the whole system and not simply the part that may be computerized. Data requirements are elicited using the same techniques (observation, document analysis, interviewing and so on) as for functional requirements (and evaluation, see Part VI). But it is just as important to analyse the meaning of this data as it is to analyse the functions. It is vital that the data elements are all understood, precisely defined and available from the system. For example, in the reactor system what should the data element *Temp display* be like? Should it be expressed in degrees centigrade or Fahrenheit? What level of precision is required? Similarly, what is the content of the data element *Hazard warning*? It may be that this has to be a very complex collection of data identifying pressures in various parts of the reactor; perhaps it needs to display a map of the reactor and show different liquids, gases and so on and their location. If this is the case, then the system will have to have access to much more information about the reactors than is currently represented on the dataflow diagram.

Question 19.4

Look again at Figure 19.2 and identify some data elements and datastores that will require precise definition.

The data dictionary is one tool to help the analyst define the meaning of data, particularly data elements. In addition to this description, data requirements seek to represent the entities and relationships that are required in an application and the constraints that apply to the data. Data elements are the basic building blocks of an information system; the most primitive parts of the system that are of interest. Data elements are grouped together into more complex objects known as entities. These entities have relationships with other entities. Data analysis is concerned with establishing exactly what data is required by the system, how it is structured and how it is logically stored.

The function of the datastore in the dataflow diagram is simply to describe what data is required by a process. An **entity**, on the other hand, is a carefully defined concept, which is concerned with expressing the semantics of data. By defining entities the analyst is understanding and describing more precisely the *meaning* of data. Logical data structure diagrams, or **Entity Relationship** (**ER**) diagrams are used, along with formal descriptions of the data elements, entities and relationships kept in a data dictionary, to describe the structure and content of the data in a system (see Box 19.3). These diagrams represent the objects of interest in the system – the entities – and the relationships they have to other objects in the system. Thus, the reactor system may have an ER diagram as illustrated in Figure 19.4. This describes

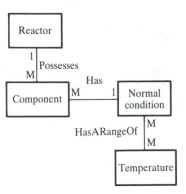

Figure 19.4 Entity relationship diagram for the reactor system. A reactor has many components. Each component has a Normal Condition, which consists of a range of temperatures. A temperature may relate to many Normal Conditions and each normal condition may relate to many components. A component is in one reactor.

the data structure of the system by showing that a reactor has many components. Each component has a normal condition, which consists of a range of temperatures. Outline entity definitions would be included in a more detailed study. They are not included here since we do not have any information on how these entities are defined in terms of their attributes (see Box 19.3 if you need detailed information on entity relationship diagrams, otherwise read on). As the system development continues these definitions are refined until they provide a precise and unambiguous description of the entities.

Although this is a very simple example, ER diagrams can become very complex and can take a long time to produce. However, they are a vital part of systems development and, when the analyst is trained in developing them, they provide a very powerful analytic technique as well as forming a part of the final system specification. As with functional and usability requirements, the data in the system must conform to operational and other constraints and these too should be recorded. For example, a constraint on the data in the reactor system would be the degree of accuracy with which it could be measured. Other constraints may relate to the allowable values for particular data elements or the relationships that are permitted to exist between entities.

Constructing ER diagrams forces analysts to be explicit about their assumptions. Users can be trained to understand ER diagrams and, as with dataflow diagrams, they can be used to 'walk-through' the system.

Box 19.3   Entity relationship diagrams

Entity relationship diagrams are graphical representations of the structure of data. An **entity** is an aggregation of a number of data elements. These data elements are known as the **attributes** of an entity. Aggregation is the process of collecting together objects or information related to an object and subsequently treating that object as a single thing. For example, the object 'person' may usefully be regarded as an aggregation of the properties 'name', 'address', 'date of birth' and so on. The object 'car' may be viewed as an aggregation of 'engine', 'tyres', 'body' and so on.

Once the properties of some object have been identified and described, it is possible to classify individual, concrete items as belonging to the class of objects sharing those properties. This process of classification allows the analyst to deal with the whole class – the **entity type** – rather than dealing with every individual instance. If a system defines an entity 'person' as consisting only of the attributes 'name', 'address', 'date of birth', then each individual person about which data is stored will have some specific **values** for those attributes. Hence we may recognize that the three individuals

Brodie	53119, East 22nd Street, Chicago	23 May 1946
Said	36, High Street, Chipping Norton	19 June 1964
Smith	Flat 2, 159, Rue des Princes, Paris	12 Oct. 1987

are all in the class 'Person'. That is, they are instances of the entity 'Person'. 'Brodie', 'Said' and 'Smith' are values of the attribute Name.

Entities have **relationships** with other entities. A relationship is an association between two or more entities which is of particular interest in the system. For example, the Person entity may have a relationship 'drives' with the Car entity. Person may have another relationship with Car such as 'owns'. An entity may have a relationship with itself (a recursive relationship). For example, Person 'is partner of' Person. Just as entities and attributes identify classes of things and properties, so a relationship expresses a class of relationship. Saying that 'Person is partner of Person' is a general statement about the entity Person. Saying 'Brodie is partner of Gonzales' is a specific statement about two individuals.

Entity relationship diagrams allow the analyst to think about and model general relationships. They express certain important constraints about the number of instances that are permitted to participate in a type of relationship. For example, in a system it may only be allowable for a person to own one car. On the other hand a person may be permitted to drive more than one car. The other side of this relationship may be that a car can be driven by many people, but may be owned by only one person. The simple distinction between whether an entity may be associated with one or many instances of another entity turns out to be a surprisingly powerful representation technique. It is expressed on the diagram by the addition of a '1' (expressing the semantics that only one instance of an entity can be involved in the relationship) or an 'M' (expressing the semantics that an arbitrary number of instances may be involved). Diagrammatically, this appears as follows:

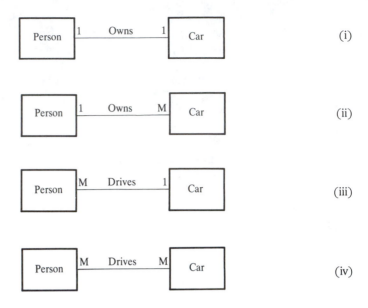

Entity A is associated with many Entity Bs. Entity B is associated with only one Entity A. This construct gives rise to four possibilities, illustrated above, showing various semantics that could be applicable in different systems.

The first model expresses the semantics that a person may own one car and a car may be owned by one person. The second expresses the fact (in the confines of a particular system) that a person may own many cars (but does not have to. A person may own just one). A car may be owned by one person. The third states that a person may drive one car and that a car may be driven by many persons. The fourth models a case in which a person may drive many cars and a car may be driven by many people.

More detail may be added to the definition of the entities and relationships by providing **entity definitions** and **relationship descriptions**. These may be included in a data dictionary or may be appended to the ER diagram. For example, the definition of a Person may be:

Person   (PersonName, Address, PhoneNumber, ...)

The attributes of the entity are shown in parentheses. The attribute(s) that are used to distinguish between entity occurrences (that is, those used to **identify** the entity) are underlined. The entity definition is very important, particularly in later stages of system development. Similarly, relationship descriptions are useful for clarifying the meaning of relationships. For example, does the Drives relationship mean 'allowed to drive' or 'has to drive'? At the requirements gathering stage entity definitions or relationship descriptions should be used if there is a danger of misunderstanding the meaning of an entity or relationship.

Other constraints can be expressed in the model, such as whether a person *must* own a car. In this case it is **mandatory** for the person entity to participate in the relationship. If this is not the case the relationship is said to be **optional**. Mandatory relationships are represented by a filled-in circle on the diagram next to the entity which must participate in the relationship. Optional participation is shown by an open circle. These semantics add to the power of the model in representing the meaning of some well-understood constraints. For the purposes of analysis, such constraints are not generally modelled.

This model expresses the semantics that a person must own at least one car and may own many. A car does not have to be owned by a person, but if it is then it can be owned by at most one person.

Entity relationship models are very powerful techniques for understanding the structure of data and are also useful for representing that structure. As with dataflow diagrams and the data dictionary, entity relationship models evolve as the analysis and design continue, providing the designer with a concise and pointed language for expressing important aspects of the system.

EXERCISE

What questions would you like to ask about the system from looking at the ER diagram in Figure 19.4?

COMMENT

For example, does a component only have one normal condition? Does it have to have one? Are all components associated with a reactor or are there some that can exist independently?

Users should be encouraged to check the diagrams and ensure that all relationships that actually exist are represented. ER diagrams also expose missing relationships. An extension of the ER diagram, known as Entity Relationship Modelling for Information Artefacts (ERMIA; Green, 1991) focuses more attention on interface issues (Chapter 21).

Question 19.5

The data requirements for the spell-checking system specify that each word is in one dictionary. The computer may make a number of suggestions for a word and each suggestion may relate to many words. A word can have a number of meanings. The system is to include a thesaurus which relates word meanings to other word meanings. A word not in the dictionary may be in the context.

Draw an ER diagram for these data requirements.

As with dataflow diagrams, ER diagrams are only one way of representing data requirements. Natural and structured languages can be used, as can object diagrams (Coad and Yourdon, 1990). For implementation as a database a relational data model can be produced. The importance of both ER and dataflow diagrams, used for requirements gathering, is that they are conceptual models of the existing system. Conceptual modelling offers many benefits. Braudes (1991) describes how conceptual models can be used for selecting an appropriate metaphor for an application, as a communication tool and for early sketching of a system in order to verify the completeness and consistency. Recall the emphasis placed on conceptual modelling by the Soft System Methodology (Section 18.1). Constructing such models away from the real world allows discrepancies, problems and misunderstandings to be exposed.

'The trouble is, it's been programmed to cut a longer lawn.'

(*Source* Honeysett)

19.3 Usability requirements

ER modelling, dataflow diagrams and data dictionaries along with structure charts (Chapter 20) form the bedrock of the structured methods of information systems design and software engineering (Yourdon and Constantine, 1979). One of the main criticisms levelled at these structured methods is that they focus too much on the system and not sufficiently on the users. In order to counter this claim, requirements gathering must also explicitly focus on the usability of the system. The notion of usability is that 'any system designed for people to use should be easy to learn (and remember), useful, that is contain functions people really need in their work, and be easy and pleasant to use' (Gould and Lewis, 1985, p. 300).

More specifically, the components of usability, which were identified by Bennett (1984) and later operationalized by Shackel (1990) so that they could be tested, can be expressed in terms of:

(1) **Learnability**   the time and effort required to reach a specified level of use performance (also described as 'ease of learning').
(2) **Throughput**   the tasks accomplished by experienced users, the speed of task execution and the errors made (also described as 'ease of use').
(3) **Flexibility**   the extent to which the system can accommodate changes to the tasks and environments beyond those first specified.
(4) **Attitude**   the positive attitude engendered in users by the system.

Usability requirements are gathered, along with functional and data requirements, using many of the same requirements gathering techniques such as interviewing and observation (Chapter 30). The activity of gathering usability requirements is often known as a **usability study** and it is closely allied to the evaluation process. Usability requirements are concerned with user satisfaction and the overall performance of the system. Determining usability requirements requires the analyst to undertake three main types of analysis. A task analysis (Chapter 20) is required to determine the characteristics, particularly the cognitive characteristics, required of the users by the system – such things as the search strategy required, the prerequisite knowledge and cognitive loading, and so on. Additionally, the analysts should conduct a user analysis. The purpose of this is to determine the scope of the user population who will utilize the system. This includes aspects such as required intellectual ability, cognitive processing ability, users' previous experience, physical capabilities and other salient characteristics of users that are variable across the user population. **User modelling** techniques have been developed in order to instantiate these models as parts of computer systems (for example, see Benyon and Murray, 1993), but as yet there are no usable conceptual user modelling techniques akin to dataflow diagrams or ER diagrams. Most user modelling relies on checklists of user characteristics. Finally, usability requirements demand an environment analysis, which focuses attention on the environments within which the system is to operate. This should include aspects of the physical environment as well as aspects of the user support environment.

Table 19.2 A line from PAS (Catterall *et al.*, 1991).

User groups	Task goals	Benefits	Costs
Unemployed member of the public over 16	To find work and therefore increase employable skills	Easier access to wide range of information	Time to learn to use system

Recently a number of paper-based 'tool-sets' have been produced which make this type of analysis available to designers. For example, the Human Factors in Information Technology (HUFIT) toolkit aims to provide human factors input into the design of IT office system products (primarily large-scale 'generic' systems). HUFIT consists of a number of related tool-sets. The Planning, Analysis and Specification (PAS) tool-set was developed in order to provide an integrated and comprehensive method for gathering human factors which did not demand human factor expertize. It is described in Catterall *et al.* (1991). The focus of PAS is to collect data about users, tasks and environment following the conception of a project. The result of this analysis is a summary of user requirements and a 'functionality matrix'. Initially, data is gathered about all stakeholders in the product, the jobs that they are intended to do and the costs and benefits associated with the proposed product. For example a single line from such an analysis for an employment benefit system might be as shown in Table 19.2. User, task and environmental characteristics are then identified and described in the functionality matrix which forms the basis of informed task allocation and evaluation. The example of a functionality matrix in Figure 19.5 shows the system features listed across the top as the column headings and the task elements listed as row headings. Specific trade-offs are recorded in the cells of the matrix. British Telecom employ a similar method, known as TELSTAR, in which human factors specialists complete forms which focus on task characteristics and defining user needs. Figure 19.6 shows a typical task description table which focuses on the characteristics of tasks (frequency, duration, fragmentation, discretion, stress and performance) and the needs deriving from such an analysis. These are prioritized (high, medium or low). Notice that this analysis demands a particular viewpoint (that is, a *Weltanschauung*) to be identified, as discussed in Section 18.1.

Usability requirements may be expressed in terms of performance measures, referred to as **usability metrics**, which are detailed in a **usability specification** (see also Chapter 31). Examples of metrics used to assess performance can include completion time for specified tasks by a specified set of users, the number of errors per task and the time spent on using documentation. Tyldesley (1988) considers many factors that could – and should – be considered in developing usability metrics and specifications. He lists 22 possible measurement criteria (Table 19.3). The selection of the most appropriate metrics will depend on the type of system being tested. For example, with information retrieval systems search time may be a key design criterion, while for a general-purpose text editing system the users' feelings of security and enjoyment when using the system might be more important than performance metrics. An overall measure of usability for an entire system may also

System features \ Task elements	Elemental system features						Compound system features			
	VDU			Keyboard	Hardcopy	Audible alarms	Relative position	Layout		
	Graphics		Technology					VDU format	Keyboard	Hardcopy printer
	Text	Symbol								
System requirements										
Information processing										
Direct access										
Navigation										
Alarm handling										
Logs										

Figure 19.5 Example of the HUFIT functionality matrix.

Task description table	Produced by *Rob Smith*	Page of
System *CTMS*	Project	Date / /

TASK IDENTITY: *One shot test*   **VIEWPOINT:** *Manager*

RESON FOR CHOICE: *New task of critical importance*

TASK CHARACTERISTICS		NEEDS	PRIORITY
Current	Proposed		
Task frequency *N/A*	10–20 times a day according to number of faults reported	Must be reliable and robust	*H*
Task duration *N/A*	No longer than 5 secs – needs to be done whilst talking to the customer	Very simple to use	*H*
Fragmentation *N/A*	Always undertaken in one go	Fast response times	*H*
Discretion *N/A*	No discretion – should always be done	Fast recovery/maintenance /support	*H*
Stress *N/A*	Should not be difficult and therefore not stressful	Ensure low stress	*M*
Performance criteria *N/A*	Error-free performance within five seconds on 90% of occasions	Monitoring capability and associated metrics	*H*

Figure 19.6 Task description table from the TELSTAR method: H = high priority; M = medium priority. (From a talk given by Chris Fowler at the Department of Trade and Industry, UK, 22 June, 1992.)

be devised if this is considered to be important. An example of a detailed specification is shown in Table 19.4. Here, the attribute of concern is the 'installability' of the system. The measure used to evaluate the system is the amount of time taken to carry out an installation. The 'worst case' is specified as one day; the 'best case' as one hour.

Table 19.3   Possible measurement criteria (Tyldesley, 1988).

(1)   Time to complete task.
(2)   Percentage of task completed.
(3)   Percentage of task completed per unit time (speed metric).
(4)   Ratio of successes to failures.
(5)   Time spent on errors.
(6)   Percentage number of errors.
(7)   Percentage or number of competitors that do this better than current product.
(8)   Number of commands used.
(9)   Frequency of help or documentation use.
(10) Time spent using help or documentation.
(11) Percentage of favourable:unfavourable user comments.
(12) Number of repetitions of failed commands.
(13) Number of runs of successes and of failures.
(14) Number of times the interface misleads the user.
(15) Number of good and bad features recalled by users.
(16) Number of available commands not invoked.
(17) Number of regressive behaviours.
(18) Number of users preferring your system.
(19) Number of times users need to work around a problem.
(20) Number of times the user is disrupted from a work task.
(21) Number of times the user loses control of the system.
(22) Number of times the user expresses frustration or satisfaction.

Table 19.4   A sample row from a usability specification (Whiteside *et al.*, 1988).

Attribute	Measuring method	Worst case	Planned level	Best case	Now level
Installability	Time to install	1 day with media	1 hour without media	10 minutes with media	Many cannot install

EXERCISE

Think of some usability metrics which may be appropriate in the reactor monitoring system.

COMMENT

There might be metrics such as:

(1)   The system should be learnable by an engineer with not more than two hours training and should be re-learnable after a period of up to one year in less than 10 minutes.

> (2) The Hazard display must be understandable by any engineer or general manager with no prior training.
> (3) The system should provide a response to any user input in not more than 2 seconds.

Chapter 31 discusses how the user testing from which usability metrics are derived is done.

19.4 Relationship between requirements and usability

Requirements gathering involves the system analyst/designer in a wide range of activities aimed at eliciting a precise description of the functional, data and usability requirements of the system under consideration. The analyst must be aware of the variety of techniques available to assist in this process – from paper-based checklists to diagrammatic techniques to prototyping, meetings and walkthroughs. Many of these same methods are used in evaluation, as you will see in Part VI. In fact, requirements gathering and evaluation are very closely related since it is essential to make sure that the requirements are properly understood by the designers. Prototyping systems, using mock-ups, games, scenarios (Chapter 22) and experimental evaluation techniques (Part VI) also contribute to establishing user-centred, but functionally feasible and structurally meaningful system requirements. Inevitably there is much overlap between data and functional requirements on one hand and usability requirements on the other. The usability criteria specify constraints on the processing and are invaluable in ensuring that the system is designed with users in mind. In Chapter 20 we will discuss task analysis, which produces vitally important design information.

Key points

- Requirements gathering is a central part of systems development.
- Requirements gathering includes analysis; trying to understand as well as simply to represent.
- Functional requirements concern the things that the system must do and the constraints under which it must operate.
- Data requirements concern the structure of the system, the data that it must have access to and the constraints on that data.
- Usability requirements are concerned with the learnability, throughput, attitude and flexibility of the system.
- Requirements gathering will almost inevitably involve some design work – requirements cannot be fully understood until some design has been completed.

Further reading

BENYON D.R. (1990). *Information and Data Modelling*. Oxford: Blackwell Scientific.
A comprehensive treatment of data modelling. This text, while primarily oriented to the needs of database design, discusses the concepts of data models, relating them to dataflow diagrams and data dictionaries.

BRAUDES R.E. (1991). Conceptual modelling: A look at system-level user interface issues. In *Taking Software Design Seriously* (KARAT J., ed.). London: Academic Press.
In this paper Braudes discusses the role of conceptual modelling in HCI. He emphasizes that conceptual consistency can be better defined and understood through the use of conceptual models, and employs ER models and a process model to illustrate this.

CATTERALL B.J., TAYLOR B.C. and GALER M.D. (1991). The HUFIT planning, analysis and specification toolset: Human factors as a normal part of the IT product design processing. In *Taking Software Design Seriously* (KARAT J., ed.). London: Academic Press.
This paper contains a description of the HUFIT method. Although few specific examples are described, the paper surveys the scope of the tools available, including the functionality matrix.

DIX A., FINLAY J., ABOWD G. and BEALE R. (1993). *Human–Computer Interaction*. Hemel Hempstead: Prentice-Hall.
Part II, design practice, contains a number of chapters that provide another perspective on design. Chapter 7 discusses task analysis and has a good section on Entity Relationship based techniques.

SHACKEL B. (1990). Human factors and usability. In *Human–Computer Interaction: Selected Readings* (PREECE J. and KELLER L., eds). Hemel Hempstead: Prentice-Hall.
A readable discussion of the idea of usability and how the term has arisen.

20

Task Analysis

Aims and objectives

The aim of this chapter is to introduce you to a range of techniques for analysing users' tasks. After completing this chapter you should be able to:

- distinguish between goals, tasks and actions,
- undertake a hierarchical task analysis,
- represent a user's 'how-to-do-it' knowledge,
- recognize the need to represent user's task knowledge.

Overview

The concept of a task is central to user-centred system design and many task analysis techniques have been developed. These techniques focus on different aspects of tasks such as the task structure, the ease of learning a task or the knowledge users require in order to accomplish a task. You will find that focusing attention on user tasks, and how tasks break down into sub-tasks, helps you to design systems which more accurately reflect what the user wants to do.

Task Analysis (TA) is a generic term for a rather bewildering range of techniques. There are techniques aimed at eliciting descriptions of what people do, representing those descriptions, predicting difficulties and evaluating systems against usability or functional requirements. Other TA techniques are concerned with predicting performance, measuring system complexity, measuring learnability or the transfer of knowledge between systems. Task analysis has arisen out of work in ergonomics, psychology and software engineering and is concerned with what people do to get things done. Although similar to the concept of a process or function, there is an important distinction between task and function. Functions are activities, processes or actions that are performed by some person or machine. Tasks are generally considered to be meaningful for the user in that users believe it to be necessary and/ or desirable to undertake tasks. The term 'task', which we shall define more formally later, embodies an intentional, or purposeful, level of description that is absent in the concept of function.

Recently it has been realized that the notion of 'task' is increasingly difficult to pin down. The shift away from the straightforward information processing perspective in HCI (Chapter 3) to approaches that emphasize the social context and distributed nature of much cognitive activity has resulted in a playing down of the importance of task analysis. In a recent short paper, Draper (1993) discusses the following various different types and meanings of task: as a function that the user wishes to perform; as a verification of the result of some previous action; as a way of finding out how to do something; as a way of finding out what a system function does; and as an insurance in case of disaster. He points out the danger of instantiating current tasks in future systems and of designing systems that are too rigid in their support of a limited number of tasks. As we said in Chapter 2, many researchers are tending to focus on the notion of 'work' or 'activities' rather than the more specific notion of 'task'. These terms acknowledge the distributed nature of real work situations. However, notwithstanding these criticisms, the idea of a task is useful in system development – as long as it is used with care.

In addition to undertaking tasks, users also perform actions or operations, such as pressing a key on a keyboard, or moving a mouse. These would not usually be considered tasks since they are devoid of any control structure; they do not require thought. The distinction between task and action is developed further in this chapter. Task analysis techniques may be grouped together in various ways, but probably the most important distinction is whether the technique aims to represent the cognition, practice or logic of the task (Payne and Green, 1989). Each of these provides an important perspective. In Section 20.2 we look at the practice of the task and in Sections 20.3 and 20.4 at cognitive task analysis. In Chapter 21 you will see how the techniques described there can be used to look at the logic of tasks.

20.1   Goals, tasks and actions

An unfortunate feature of the various task analysis techniques is that different authors use the same terms to mean different things. In particular, the terms 'goal' and 'task' are sometimes used as synonyms but on other occasions the term 'goal' is reserved for the human mental activity and the term 'task' for what the person has to do in order to accomplish a goal. Other terms such as 'operations', 'methods' and 'plans' proliferate in the literature. In order to remove some of this confusion, we will conceptualize HCI at the three levels illustrated in Figure 20.1. A **goal** (also called an **external task**) may be defined as a state of a system that the human wishes to achieve (more generally, the term 'human' can be replaced by 'agent' in the following discussion, where an agent is any autonomous, rational, creature, machine or system which formulates its own goals and seeks ways of satisfying these goals). For example, the human wants to write a letter, to go to the shops, to find out what is on television, to construct a rabbit hutch and so on. A goal must be described at a particular level of abstraction.

A goal is achieved using some instrument, method, agent, tool, technique, skill or, generally, some *device* which is able to change the system to the desired state. Typically, a goal can be accomplished using a variety of devices. For example, writing a letter can be accomplished using a device such as a typewriter, a word processor or pen and paper. A rabbit hutch can be produced by paying someone to make it for you, buying one from a shop or making it yourself using various tools. Given that the person has formed a goal, the person selects a device that will enable him or her to achieve that goal. It is only once a device has been selected that the tasks necessary to accomplish the goal may be understood. These are prescribed by the logical structure and functioning of the device, that is, by the way that it has been designed, or has evolved. Thus, we can define a **task** (or **internal task**) as the activities required, used or believed to be necessary to achieve a goal using a particular device.

A task is a structured set of activities in which actions are undertaken in some sequence. Tasks are what the human has to do (or thinks he or she has to do) in order to accomplish a goal. At some point, the human physically interacts with a device by performing an action (or operation). For example, the person types a command on a keyboard, physically moves a pointing device or speaks to another person. Actions are also known as 'simple tasks' (Payne and Green, 1989) or 'unit tasks' (Card *et al.*, 1983). An **action** is defined as a task that involves no problem solving or control structure component.

This structure is illustrated in Figure 20.1. Goals, tasks and actions will be different for different people, depending on their previous experience and

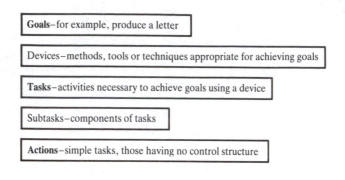

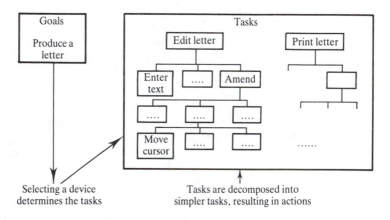

Figure 20.1 A general model for task analysis.

knowledge, and on their perception and conception of the system. In particular, actions may be different for experts and novices. Users iterate between forming goals and determining tasks based on their conceptions of the devices available. This iteration describes a **decomposition** of goals into subgoals and tasks into subtasks as the user moves downwards through a hierarchy of systems. For example, an 'edit' task is decomposed thorough the (sub)tasks of locate change, make change, verify that the change was successful and so on until we get to the level of an action such as move the cursor one character forward or type the letter 'x'. While an expert typist may consider this an action, any casual observation of novice keyboard operators will reveal that they have still to complete the complex task – locate the letter on the keyboard, type it, verify that the correct letter was entered, and so on.

Other terms commonly used in task analysis include objects and methods. A **method** (also called a **plan**) consists of a number of tasks or actions linked into a sequence. This sequence may also include the provision for tasks or actions to be repeated (called **iteration**) or for alternatives to be available at various points (**selection**). Objects (or entities, Chapter 19) are generally seen to be the focus of actions. In the above example, the focus of the edit task is the letter. At the action level, 'move' is the action, 'cursor' the object.

Question 20.1

Assume that you have the goal of listening to some music and have selected your cassette player as the device with which you will accomplish this goal. List the tasks and actions that you would have to undertake in order to achieve your goal.

Question 20.2

One of my cookery books (Kay Avila, Take Six More Cooks, *London: MacDonald and Co.) describes how to make Marrow and Coriander Soup as follows:*

(1) *Chop the marrow, potatoes and onion and boil in the water until tender.*
(2) *Liquidize the vegetables together with the Brie and herbs, then put through a coarse sieve.*
(3) *Season with salt and pepper and freshly ground nutmeg and a little lemon juice to taste.*
(4) *Serve the soup with a freestyle pattern of cream, a fresh coriander leaf and maybe a few leaves for garnish.*

Identify the tasks and actions in this description.
What are the objects in this description?

20.2 Hierarchical task analysis

Hierarchical Task Analysis (HTA), a method dating back 20 years, is one of the most well known forms of task analysis. There are many hybrid forms of HTA in use in industry. It uses as its basic construct a graphical representation of a decomposition of a high level task into its constituent subtasks and operations, or actions. This is based on the structure chart notation (Box 20.1). HTA is concerned with the logic or practice of a task. It involves an iterative process of identifying tasks, categorizing them, breaking them down into subtasks and checking the accuracy of the decomposition. Information about tasks is collected from a variety of sources including conversations with users, observation of users working, job descriptions and operating manuals. The aim of HTA is to describe the task in terms of a hierarchy of operations and plans. The goal is the desired state of the system, tasks describe the manner in which a goal may be achieved and operations are the lowest level units of behaviour. Plans are also included in the representation. These specify the conditions under which each subtask needs to be carried out. Shepherd (1989) gives a thorough description of the technique. Figure 20.2 shows an outline HTA for the Microsoft Word word processing system. From the figure it can be seen that the main task of preparing and printing a letter using a word processor is broken down into subtasks consisting of starting the word processor, entering text, and so on.

Box 20.1   Structure chart notation

A structure chart represents a hierarchical decomposition of some function into its component functions. It shows the sequencing of activities by ordering them left to right. Activities that may be repeated a number of times (iteration) are indicated by a small asterisk in the box. When one of a number of activities may be chosen (selection) a small circle is included in the box. A line in the box indicates an absence of an action. The example below shows an example of checking if a word is wrong when undertaking a spelling check. Notice that the structure chart shows flow of control. Compare this representation with the solution to Question 21.2

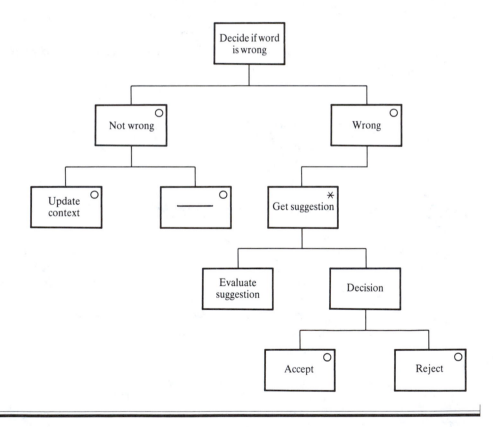

Some of the subtasks in the diagram are then decomposed into further subtasks (for example, formatting text, correcting text) and are numbered according to the order in which they are performed. These numbers constitute a plan for doing the task, which may also be described separately. A 'point' numbering system (similar to

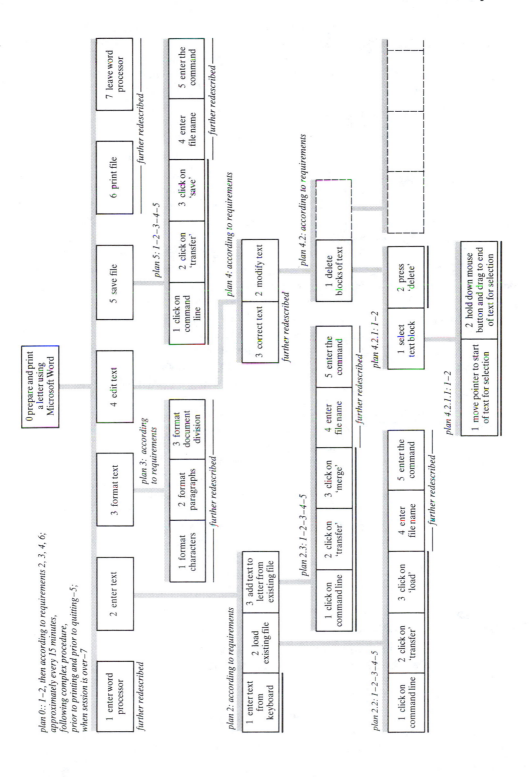

Figure 20.2 An outline HTA for a word processing system (Shepherd, 1989).

dataflow diagrams, Chapter 19) may be used, in which a point follows the number attributed to the task that has just been decomposed and then the numbering starts again. So, for example, the plan for deleting a block of text would be 4.2.1.1:1–2, shown near the lower right-hand corner of the figure.

An HTA can be described in three stages; starting, progressing and finalizing.

(1) Starting the analysis.
    (a) Firstly, the area of work or main task should be specified.
    (b) The main task should then be broken down into between four and eight subtasks. These subtasks should be specified in terms of objectives and between them should cover the whole area of interest.
    (c) Next, the subtasks should be drawn out as layered plans, ensuring that they are logically and technically correct and that none is missing.

(2) Progressing the analysis.
    (a) The next stage involves deciding upon the level of detail that is required and at what point to stop the decomposition. This can range from a very fine level of description, in which individual keystrokes (for example, 'click mouse') are outlined, to a higher level, in which basic units of activity are described (for example, 'delete a block of text'). Making a conscious decision at this stage ensures that all the subtask decompositions (that is, 'branches' in the 'tree') are treated consistently.
    (b) Following this stage of the decomposition a decision has to be made as to whether to continue by analysing each subtask in turn to the required depth (that is, a depth-first analysis) or to work on the next level along and analyse each subtask in turn (that is, a breadth-first analysis). In practice many analysts alternate between the two strategies.
    (c) The analysis is continued by using the numbering convention and the diagrammatic form shown in Figure 20.2.

(3) Finalizing the analysis.
    (a) The analysis needs to be checked to ensure that the decompositions and the numbering of the tasks are consistent. Sometimes it is helpful to produce a written account as well as the decomposition diagram.
    (b) It is good practice to present the analysis to someone else who has not been involved in the decomposition analysis but who knows the tasks well to check for consistency.

Question 20.3

Continue the task analysis for modifying text (second part of plan 4 in Figure 20.2). Process 2 under 4.2 is 'move blocks of text'.

As with all analytic and requirements gathering techniques, undertaking a task analysis is much more difficult and time consuming than we can illustrate here. If you wish to find out more you can refer to Diaper (1989a).

20.3 Cognitive task analysis

Whereas HTA is concerned with establishing an accurate description of the steps that are required in order to complete a task, the focus of this and the following sections is on techniques that capture some representation of the knowledge that people have, or that they need to have in order to complete the task. One use of the psychological theories discussed in Part II is to develop general guidelines and methods of working that are appropriate for human users of computers. But guidelines are inevitably very general (Chapter 24) and cannot assist designers in making fine-grained decisions between alternative designs. Cognitive task analysis is concerned with informing the design process through the application of cognitive theories. We have defined a task as what the person or other agent has to do (or believes is necessary) in order to accomplish some goal using some device. A task is accomplished by performing actions (or simple tasks) in some order. Cognitive task analysis recognizes that some of these actions are physical (such as pressing buttons, moving pointers or speaking) but some of them are mental, or cognitive operations. Undertakings such as deciding which button to press or where to place a pointer, recalling previously stored knowledge from memory or comparing two objects are cognitive rather than physical operations.

Johnson (1992) summarizes the rationale for cognitive task analyses:

'The task knowledge that people possess is an important subset of their total knowledge. This knowledge should be taken into account in the design and development of interactive software systems.'

(p. 156)

'In all cases [of cognitive task analysis], there is a clear belief that people structure their knowledge of tasks in a particular way. There is a further belief that this task knowledge can be analysed, modelled and predicted.'

(p. 157)

The underlying assumption of much cognitive psychology is that a human perceives the world and produces some representation of it in his or her mind (sometimes called the 'problem space'). This representation is what we would usually call 'knowledge'. It may be described in terms of the concepts that we have, the relationships between those concepts and our capacity to make use of those concepts. The human then manipulates that representation and produces some output – some behaviour – that can be observed. Cognitive task analysis seeks to model the internal representation and processing that occurs for the purpose of designing tasks that can be undertaken more effectively by humans. It is this basic characterization of human actions in terms of perceiving the world, representing it internally, manipulating it and expressing it which underlies Norman's seven-stage model and the other cognitive theories discussed in Part II. There are a number of cognitive task analysis techniques (summarized in Box 20.2) which focus on different aspects of the cognitive processing assumed to be necessary for a person to

Box 20.2 Summary of some cognitive task analysis techniques

Of the various cognitive models, historically, the most important was the model human processor (MHP; Card *et al.*, 1983), which described a psychological model of humans consisting of three interacting systems: the perceptual, motor and cognitive systems, each of which has its own memory (that is, internal representation or knowledge) and processor. This model led to the GOMS (Goals, Operations, Methods and Selection rules) and Cognitive Complexity Theory (CCT) methods of task analysis. A more 'natural' method of expressing the GOMS model is NGOMSL (Kieras, 1988), which is shown in Figure 20.3. Johnson's theory of Task Knowledge Structures (TKS; Johnson, 1992) assumes that as people learn and perform tasks, they develop knowledge structures. A method known as Knowledge Analysis of Tasks (KAT) is utilized 'to identify the elements of knowledge represented in a task knowledge structure' (Johnson, 1992, p. 165).

There are several other influential cognitive task analysis techniques which focus on different aspects of the general information processing model. Task Action Grammar (TAG; Payne and Green, 1989) is concerned with an evaluation of the learnability of systems, whereas both Moran's External Task Internal Task (ETIT; Moran, 1983) and Payne's Yoked State Space (YSS; Payne, 1987) are concerned with the mapping of tasks from the external task space to the internal task space. Moran's Command Language Grammar (CLG; Moran, 1981) is discussed in Chapter 21.

We can see where various techniques are applicable by relating them to our general model of task analysis (Figure 20.1) which consisted of three levels of description: goals, tasks and actions (see Table 20.1). Those who would like to know more about specific techniques should consult the references cited.

Table 20.1 Relating cognitive task analysis techniques to the general model.

Technique	Goal level	Task level	Action level
GOMS	Goals	(Sub)goals	Operators, methods
TAG		Tasks	Actions
ETIT	External task	Internal task	
YSS	Problem space	Device space	
CLG	Task level	Semantic level	Syntax and lexical levels
KAT/TKS	Goal, subgoal structure	Task structure	Actions, procedures

complete a task. In addition to the levels of description, most of these focus attention on the **mappings** between levels – how a description at one level is translated into a description at another level. In this chapter we focus on the two principal levels of cognitive activity that need to be undertaken: the task–action representations and mappings (Section 20.4) and the goal–task representations and mappings (Section 20.5).

20.4 Modelling 'how-to-do-it' knowledge

An important determinant of the success of any particular design is the **procedural knowledge** possessed by users – their 'how-to-do-it' knowledge. In terms of our model of task analysis, the focus here is primarily on the effectiveness of the task – action mapping. Given that the user has understood what needs to be done (in general terms) in order to accomplish his/her goal, this analysis attends to the actions that then have to be undertaken.

The best known of these representations is the GOMS (goals, operations, methods and selection rules) model (Card *et al.*, 1983), which consists of descriptions of the methods (that is, plans) needed to accomplish specified goals. The methods are a series of steps consisting of operators (or actions in our terminology) that the user performs. When there is more than one method available to accomplish a goal the GOMS model includes selection rules which choose the appropriate method depending on the context. Selection rules can be seen as another way of describing the selection of a device to accomplish a goal. For example, the goal of getting to your hotel from the airport may be accomplished by using any of the methods: walk, take a bus, take a taxi, hire a car, take a train. The 'take the bus' method consists of the operators (or actions): locate the bus stop, wait for the bus, get on the bus, pay the driver, and so on. The selection rules are used to choose between alternative methods. In this case the rules would concern 'walking is cheaper, but slower and more tiring', 'the taxi method is easy but expensive', 'the bus method may be complicated in a foreign country', and so on.

Question 20.4

Assume you have the goal of listening to some music but have not selected a particular device. List some methods (that is, think of some different devices), and selection rules that would enable you to accomplish this goal.

A GOMS analysis of human–system interaction can be applied at various levels of abstraction in much the same way that the hierarchical task analysis splits tasks into subtasks. Clearly, in the above example, 'locate the bus stop' may itself be a complex undertaking. Three broad levels of granularity determine the GOMS family of models:

- The GOMS model, which describes the general methods for accomplishing a set of tasks.

- The unit task level, which breaks users' tasks into unit tasks, and then estimates the time that it takes for the user to perform these.
- The keystroke level, which describes and predicts the time it takes to perform a task by specifying the keystrokes needed.

The way that the general GOMS model works is best illustrated by considering the 'unit task level' of how a simple task is performed using an existing system. Figure 20.3 shows a GOMS task description, expressed in the NGOMSL language, for the task of moving and deleting a file and a directory using a Macintosh computer and using a PC. The Macintosh is much more consistent and requires fewer methods than the PC.

Goals are expressed at the end of the first line of the description. For example, the first example is the method for accomplishing the goal of 'deleting a file'. The last step of a method is always 'Return with goal accomplished'. Selection rules are expressed using IF < condition > THEN accomplish goal of < goal description >, or IF ... GOTO constructs in the description. Mental operations can be included in the description. For example, there may be an operation 'think of the directory name'. David Kieras (1991 – see also Kieras, 1988) recommends that to do a useful task analysis, the analyst must make judgements about how people undertake the different tasks and construct the GOMS representation appropriately. He emphasizes that users will often tell you that they do one thing, but actually do another. It is the actual actions which are important.

GOMS models may be constructed after the design or implementation of a system or during design. As with all models (Chapter 18) a GOMS model must be appropriate for its purpose, which Kieras (1991) suggests are: producing an evaluation of the naturalness, completeness, consistency and efficiency of the design; predicting human performance with a design; providing suggestions for improving the design.

Comparison of file manipulation in PC-DOS and Macintosh finder

Illustrate how GOMS models can capture *consistency*.

While only a fragment of the systems, same pattern of results hold for larger-scale analyses.

Compare systems in terms of:
   The number of methods required to handle the set of task goals.
   The total length of the methods.
   The type of operations performed (perceptual, cognitive, motor).

User goals:
- delete a file
- move a file
- delete a directory
- move a directory

For each system list
- File manipulation methods – first level that accomplish goals
- General submethods – used like general subroutines

Figure 20.3 A GOMS task description, using the NGOMSL notation for moving and deleting a file and a directory in two different systems (Kieras, 1993).

PC-DOS

File manipulation methods – 1

Method for accomplishing goal of deleting a file
   Step 1   Retrieve-from-LTM that command verb is
            'ERASE'
   Step 2   Think of directory name and file name and make
            it the first filespec
   Step 3   Accomplish goal of entering and executing a
            command
   Step 4   Return with goal accomplished

Method for accomplishing goal of moving a file
   Step 1   Accomplish goal of copying a file
   Step 2   Accomplish goal of deleting a file
   Step 3   Return with goal accomplished

Method for accomplishing goal of copying a file
   Step 1   Retrieve-from-LTM that command verb is
            'COPY'
   Step 2   Think of source directory name and file name
            and make it the first filespec
   Step 3   Think of destination directory name and file
            name and make it the second filespec
   Step 4   Accomplish goal of entering and executing a
            command
   Step 5   Return with goal accomplished

File manipulation methods – 2

Method for accomplishing goal of deleting a directory
   Step 1   Accomplish goal of deleting all files in the
            directory
   Step 2   Accomplish goal of removing a directory
   Step 3   Return with goal accomplished

Method for accomplishing goal of deleting all files in a
directory
   Step 1   Retrieve-from-LTM that command verb is
            'ERASE'
   Step 2   Think of directory name
   Step 3   Make directory name and '*.*' the first filespec
   Step 4   Accomplish goal of entering and executing a
            command
   Step 5   Return with goal accomplished

Method for accomplishing goal of removing a directory
   Step 1   Retrieve-from-LTM that command verb is
            'RMDIR'
   Step 2   Think of directory name and make it the first
            filespec
   Step 3   Accomplish goal of entering and executing a
            command
   Step 4   Return with goal accomplished

File manipulation methods – 3

Method for accomplishing goal of moving a directory
   Step 1   Accomplish goal of copying a directory
   Step 2   Accomplish goal of deleting a directory
   Step 3   Return with goal accomplished

Macintosh

Specific file manipulation methods

Method for accomplishing goal of deleting a file
   Step 1   Accomplish goal of dragging file to trash
   Step 2   Return with goal accomplished

Method for accomplishing goal of moving a file
   Step 1   Accomplish goal of dragging file to destination
   Step 2   Return with goal accomplished

Method for accomplishing goal of deleting a directory
   Step 1   Accomplish goal of dragging directory to trash
   Step 2   Return with goal accomplished

Method for accomplishing goal of moving a directory
   Step 1   Accomplish goal of dragging directory to
            destination
   Step 2   Return with goal accomplished

Generalized file manipulation methods

Method for accomplishing goal of deleting an object
   Step 1   Accomplish goal of dragging object to trash
   Step 2   Return with goal accomplished

Method for accomplishing goal of moving an object
   Step 1   Accomplish goal of dragging object to destination
   Step 2   Return with goal accomplished

Figure 20.3 *(cont.)*   A GOMS task description, using the NGOMSL notation for moving and deleting a file and a directory in two different systems (Kieras, 1993).

PC-DOS

Method for accomplishing goal of copying a directory
    Step 1   Accomplish the goal of creating a directory
    Step 2   Accomplish the goal of copying all the files in a directory
    Step 3   Return with goal accomplished

Method for accomplishing goal of creating a directory
    Step 1   Retrieve-from-LTM that command verb is 'MKDIR'
    Step 2   Think of directory name and make it the first filespec
    Step 3   Accomplish goal of entering an executing a command
    Step 4   Return with goal accomplished

Method for accomplishing goal of copying all files in a directory
    Step 1   Retrieve-from-LTM that command verb is 'COPY'
    Step 2   Think of directory name
    Step 3   Make directory name and '*.*' the first filespec
    Step 4   Think of destination directory name
    Step 5   Make the destination directory name the second filespec
    Step 6   Accomplish goal of entering and executing a command
    Step 7   Return with goal accomplished

General submethods

Method for accomplishing goal of entering and executing a command
Entered with strings for a command verb and one or two filespecs
    Step 1   Type command verb
    Step 2   Accomplish goal of entering first filespec
    Step 3   Decide: If no second filespec, go to 5
    Step 4   Accomplish goal of entering second filespec
    Step 5   Verify command
    Step 6   Type '<CR>'
    Step 7   Return with goal accomplished

Method for accomplishing goal of entering a filespec
Entered with directory name and file name strings
    Step 1   Type space
    Step 2   Think of the drive letter for the directory and file name
    Step 3   Decide: If the drive letter is the same as shown at the prompt then go to 6
    Step 4   Type drive letter
    Step 5   Type ':'
    Step 6   Decide: If no directory name, go to 11
    Step 7   Type '\'
    Step 8   Type directory name
    Step 9   Decide: If no file name, return with goal accomplished
    Step 10   Type '\'
    Step 11   Type file name
    Step 12   Return with goal accomplished

Macintosh

General submethods

Method for accomplishing goal of dragging item to destination
    Step 1   Locate icon for item on screen
    Step 2   Move cursor to item icon location
    Step 3   Hold mouse button down
    Step 4   Locate destination icon on screen
    Step 5   Move cursor to destination icon
    Step 6   Verify that destination icon is reverse-video
    Step 7   Release mouse button
    Step 8   Return with goal accomplished

Figure 20.3 *(cont.)* A GOMS task description, using the NGOMSL notation for moving and deleting a file and a directory in two different systems (Kieras, 1993).

Comparison of PC-DOS and Macintosh goal structures

Goal structure for PC-DOS
- Starting set of user goals are in boxes
- Defined subgoals are unboxed

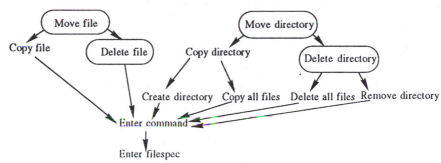

Goal structure for Macintosh – specialized methods

Goal structure for Macintosh – generalized methods

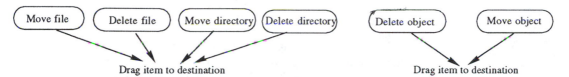

Comparison of PC-DOS and Macintosh method content

Result:
- Macintosh: 3 methods, total length of 15
  Using generalized methods
- PC-DOS: 12 methods, total length of 72

Shows how Macintosh interface is extremely consistent
  Only a few methods required to cover the same goals

Shows the essence of a direct manipulation
- Macintosh heavily uses perceptual-motor operators
  Locate icon – visual search
- Move cursor – visually guided movement

- PC-DOS uses cognitively demanding operators
  Retrieve-from-LTM command verb – memory for letter strings
  Think of name – come up with letter strings, maintain in working memory
  Method structure for entering and executing specific commands is extremely complex

Why the Mac is more 'user friendly'
  Relevant Mac advantage is the small amount of GOMS knowledge training required compared to most command language interfaces

Points to alternatives to Mac GUI interfaces
  Could we define a command language whose GOMS model was as compact as the Macintosh interface?
  If so, it would be easy to learn and use, and a lot cheaper to implement

Figure 20.3 *(cont.)* A GOMS task description, using the NGOMSL notation for moving and deleting a file and a directory in two different systems (Kieras, 1993).

Question 20.5

In a word processor, a single word can be selected by double-clicking the cursor in the middle of the word. If the user wishes to select an arbitrary string of characters, the characters must be highlighted by dragging the mouse over the text with the mouse button held down. To cut the text out of a document, the user must first highlight the text and then issue the cut command.

(a) *Write an NGOMSL description for the goal of 'cut out text'.*
(b) *Write out the selection rules for this example.*
(c) *Write out the method for selecting a word and for selecting an arbitrary string of characters.*

Once the GOMS model analysis has been completed it can then be used in a number of ways, such as:

- to predict the quality of an existing system or a prototype,
- to check for consistency of methods (to ensure that similar goals are achieved by similar methods),
- to check that the most frequent goals are achieved by relatively quick methods,
- as a quantitative evaluation technique (Chapter 33),
- to choose between alternative designs (see Chapter 33).

For simple analyses like the example above where only one unit task is described, such hierarchical notation works well. It is easy to see the relationship between methods and goals. The nesting of subgoals can get very unwieldy, however, for more complex analyses where there are a large number of unit tasks. GOMS has a number of problems, both with the ease of using the method itself and in the results it produces (see Reisner, 1987). For example, the method requires a lot of time, skill and effort to use, but despite these problems there are some strong advocates of the method for analysing the design of systems like telephones (John, 1990). Software support may alleviate practical problems associated with using GOMS but it is still not clear whether the predictions are an accurate reflection of what actually happens.

However difficult these techniques are to use on a large scale, this should not detract from the importance of considering the task–action mappings in a design, but it does illustrate that current methods of *representing* this do not scale-up well. As these methods become increasingly automated, through systems such as SOAR (Laird *et al.*, 1987), ACT* (Anderson, 1987) and the automated walkthrough (Lewis *et al.*, 1990; see also Chapter 33, where the use of this technique for evaluation is discussed), this type of analysis may become more available to designers.

20.5 Representing task knowledge

In addition to understanding people's procedural knowledge, it is important to attend to the previous knowledge that users have of both the specific task and generic tasks. For example, people may understand about a generic task such as using electronic mail and will possess knowledge of the typical objects and actions necessary for sending messages, reading messages and so on. However, they may not know how to perform the task using a particular computer system (that is, a particular device). The ease of learning a new system depends on the previous knowledge that users bring to bear. In terms of the three levels of description of HCI (Section 20.1), the focus here is on the goal–task mapping. For example, the goal of driving a car is well known to most of us and maps onto the tasks: start the car, put it in gear, release brake, accelerate, steer. These tasks map onto well-known actions: insert the key, turn the key, select a gear, press the accelerator, turn the steering wheel as appropriate.

EXERCISE

Think of a selection rule that would apply to the task of 'put in gear'.

COMMENT

If car has manual transmission, depress clutch, select first gear, release clutch. If car has automatic transmission, select drive position.

Problems may arise, however, when one of the actions, say 'insert the key', cannot be performed because the driver can't find where to put the key. An action for a driver familiar with the car becomes a task for the driver who is not. Many drivers of cars with automatic transmission will not have knowledge of the task 'select a gear' and will be unable to accomplish their goal of 'put in gear'. Indeed, some will not have the concept of a clutch in their knowledge. Hence, in some circumstances, simply examining the knowledge that users do have may not provide an appropriate type of analysis. We must also examine the knowledge that people require at the different levels of description. A number of methods have been proposed for exploring and understanding the knowledge that users bring to bear when encountering a new problem and these are described in Box 20.2.

Johnson's TKS theory assumes that people possess task knowledge structures in memory, which consist of knowledge concerned with the objects in the domain and the procedures or methods used to carry out the task (cf. the concepts of schemata discussed in Chapter 6). Certain knowledge is central to completing the task and is therefore more likely to be transferred between tasks. Other knowledge is typical of the task. Johnson also assumes that people have generic knowledge and specific knowledge and that one TKS is related to other TKSs. Johnson recognizes that certain tasks belong together and this defines a particular role. Goals have subgoals and each has conditions which define when that goal can be achievable – goal substructure includes a plan for carrying out the task.

A Knowledge Analysis of Tasks (KAT; described in Box 20.3) is a technique concerned with identifying knowledge relevant to the task. Requirements gathering techniques are used to identify the task knowledge structures possessed by users. Johnson's concept of knowledge of generic tasks is similar to the distinction that we have drawn between goals and tasks – generic task knowledge is used to evaluate the suitability of alternative devices.

Box 20.3   Undertaking a knowledge analysis of tasks

A KAT analysis requires the analyst to perform the following steps (from Johnson, 1992).

(1)   Understand the purpose of the task analysis.
(2)   Identify the person's goals, subgoals and subtasks (the goal substructure).
(3)   Consider the ordering in which the subgoals are carried out (the task plan).
(4)   Identify different task strategies.
(5)   Identify procedures.
(6)   Identify task objects and actions.
(7)   Identify representative, central and generic tasks.

Although many of the issues raised in this chapter have important consequences for HCI design, they do not tell the whole story. Frequently, the fine-grained pictures offered by the techniques described do not tackle the actual problems expressed by users. One response has been to shift from analysing interfaces with highly detailed formalisms such as GOMS towards much less detailed methods, such as claims analysis (Carroll and Kellogg, 1989), scenario analysis (Young and Barnard, 1991; Carey *et al.*, 1991), cognitive walkthroughs (Lewis *et al.*, 1990) and design rationale (Carroll and Moran, 1991; Maclean *et al.*, 1991) (see Chapter 26). One example of this move away from detailed formalisms is the 'cognitive dimensions' framework developed by Green (1989), which was designed to provide a simple vocabulary for describing the structural properties of artefacts. This should be accomplished in terms that are not too detailed and that carry clear intuitive meaning. By providing such a vocabulary the level of discourse can be raised, trade-off relationships between solutions can be discussed, solutions can be recontextualized in different domains by preserving the structure in a different presentation, and all the other virtues of a firm set of explicit concepts can be obtained. Box 20.4 provides a brief description of some cognitive dimensions.

Box 20.4   Some cognitive dimensions

Cognitive dimensions (Green, 1989) are a vocabulary for describing aspects of information structures. Much as a three-dimensional artefact can be described in terms of length, breadth, depth, weight and so on, an information artefact can be described using cognitive dimensions. Some cognitive dimensions are:

- **Viscosity**   Resistance to change. How easy is it to make changes to some aspects of the artefact (for example, changing all instances of word A to word B in a long document with no search-and-replace facility)?
- **Delayed gratification**   Effort required to meet a goal. The easiest of goals (as perceived by the user) may be difficult to achieve with a given interface.
- **Premature commitment**   The user is forced to make choices too soon. For example, a user may be required to set a limit for some aspects of the system before they know how large they want it.
- **Hidden dependencies**   Information links between items in the artefact which are not easily visible. For example, the relationships between cells in a spreadsheet are not always visible.

A technique known as ERMIA (entity relationship modelling for information artefacts; Green, 1991) employs the entity relationship notation (Chapter 19) to represent the information structure of a screen display or other artefact and allows the cognitive dimensions to be described and analysed. For example, the dimension 'Hidden Dependencies' concerns information links between conceptual entities that are not explicitly represented at the perceptual level (that is, by the interface). Thus, a modification to one entity may have unforeseen side effects. ERMIA diagrams help to expose such problems because they explicitly represent both the perceptual and the conceptual levels using the same notation. In this case, the 'UsedBy' relationship is missing at the interface. For example, a spreadsheet does not make information accessible about which cells are used by other cells (Figure 20.4).

The ERMIA diagram highlights important relationships that are missing from the perceptual information structure. Without the 'UsedBy' relationship, the only way to find out which cells depend on other cells is to exhaustively search the occurrences of 'related cell'. In a large spreadsheet this can be extremely time consuming. If the user does not do this the consequences can be significant.

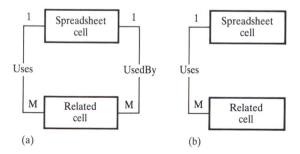

Figure 20.4   ERMIA diagram of cells in a spreadsheet. (a) Conceptual level, (b) perceptual level.

Question 20.6

Draw an ERMIA diagram similar to Figure 20.4 for the case of Word 'style sheets', based on the following description:

A style is a collection of character and paragraph formats that can be applied to paragraphs or documents as required. A style can be based on another style. For example, the styles 'List' and 'Quotation' may be based on the style 'Normal'. Changing style Normal will change all styles based upon it. The style display shows only the style which it is based upon.

20.6 Some conclusions

The recognition that users have tasks is fundamental to the grain of analysis appropriate for user-centred design. The term 'task analysis' is, however, somewhat misleading, as frequently task analysis techniques simply *describe* what happens as opposed to offering any analytic capability. The danger here is that if analysts spend too long describing current processes and task structures, they will be reluctant to abandon those designs. People interacting with a computer system will transfer knowledge from their previous experiences – of both computerized and non-computerized systems – and will make use of that knowledge to guide their behaviour. Understanding the content and structure of that knowledge can be used to inform HCI design. The structure of people's knowledge can be represented using techniques such as ER diagrams, and their knowledge of procedures can be represented using dataflow diagrams (Chapter 19). Other mechanisms such as GOMS can be used to represent people's assumed knowledge. However, rigidity in design is not to be recommended. Designers must remember that any computer system will change the tasks that people carry out in order to achieve their goals. Furthermore in any given system there is likely to be a many-to-many relationship between user goals and system functions. An understanding of task knowledge and goal–task mappings needs to be used with care.

HTA can be used in many parts of the system development process, such as to assist in designing training materials and providing documentation (Shepherd, 1989). HTA and other techniques are also useful for describing a newly designed task, but they do not focus attention on more fundamental constructs, which are offered by the data-centred techniques described in Chapter 19. Cognitive task analysis techniques aim to 'get inside the head' of the user and in so doing to reveal difficulties with specific designs, to make choices between designs or to inform the design process by removing anticipated problems. They seek to make cognitive science available to designers in a way that is more precise and focused than using guidelines. In this they offer additional tools for HCI designers, enabling them to take an 'applied science' approach to design.

All the techniques described in this chapter are still under development, and without some form of automation and integration with software engineering techniques they are unlikely to gain wide acceptance. However, even if designers do not have robust techniques for task analysis, an appreciation of the knowledge which that will bring to the system and an understanding that that knowledge involves forming goals and undertaking tasks and actions will help to improve HCI.

Key points

- Task analysis describes behaviours at three levels: goals, tasks and actions.
- Tasks are usually viewed in terms of a hierarchical decomposition of tasks into subtasks.
- HTA and related techniques focus on what actually happens, rather than on what should happen.
- Cognitive task analysis techniques aim to describe some aspect of the cognitive characteristics of users' tasks.
- Some methods (such as GOMS) concentrate on users' 'how-to-do-it' knowledge.
- Other methods focus on task knowledge.
- Many of the techniques currently available are difficult to use and do not scale up well for commercial application.
- Recent approaches are looking at a more overall picture – attempting to produce more usable tools.

Further reading

DIAPER D., ed. (1989). *Task Analysis for Human–Computer Interaction*. Chichester: Ellis Horwood.
A good book, describing a variety of task analysis techniques. It brings together some descriptions and criticisms of HTA, the TAG model and some of Johnson's work. Diaper describes his own method and gives good general advice on how to conduct a task analysis.

JOHNSON P. (1992). *Human–Computer Interaction: Psychology, Task Analysis and Software Engineering*. Maidenhead: McGraw-Hill.
A general text on HCI, but with a strong bias towards cognitive task analysis. Johnson shows how effective understanding users' cognitive processing can be in designing systems.

PAYNE S. and GREEN T.R.G. (1989). Task-Action Grammar: The model and its developments. In *Task Analysis for Human–Computer Interaction* (DIAPER D., ed.). Chichester: Ellis Horwood.
An excellent survey of task analysis, as well as describing TAG in detail.

SHEPHERD A. (1989). Analysis and training in information tasks. In *Task Analysis for Human–Computer Interaction* (DIAPER D., ed.). Chichester: Ellis Horwood.
This provides a very detailed and comprehensive description of HTA.

Structured HCI Design

Aims and objectives

The main purpose of this chapter is to produce models or representations of a design which will aid understanding and inform the design process. After studying this chapter you should be able to:

- understand the principles of structured HCI design,
- distinguish conceptual from physical design,
- understand the process of task allocation,
- appreciate that design extends to the provision of help and support, and is not simply the layout of screens,
- produce designs for simple systems.

Overview

In this chapter you will study the processes and representations involved in human–computer system design, concentrating on a structured, or formal, approach. You will see that it is desirable to use the same techniques for representing both analysis and design. As we have commented several times, these are not clear cut, separate activities and using a common notation helps to ensure a smooth transition from one activity to another and back. You will also see how cognitive analysis techniques can be used to inform the design process. This chapter could have been called 'bringing it all together' because it brings together things that you have learnt in the previous four chapters. Of course, the structured approach described in this chapter is not the only approach to HCI design. In Chapter 22 we look at some alternative approaches, which are less formal and focus on envisioning design.

We have already mentioned the interrelated nature and sometimes uneasy relationship between analysis, design and evaluation and the need – particularly in human–computer interaction design – for an iterative approach. In the discussion of task analysis techniques in Chapter 20 we suggested that there are three main layers to consider – goals, tasks and actions. It is these layers that provide us with our framework for design. This approach is similar to one of the best known design methods, the Command Language Grammar (CLG) of Tom Moran (Moran, 1981). There can be little argument concerning the impact that CLG has had on HCI. However, as with many of the early attempts at descriptions of interactions, CLG is not a technique that is easily usable by designers (Sharratt, 1987). Moran's description of CLG describes interaction from a linguistic perspective. The technique involves viewing the proposed design in four layers (six were originally proposed but only four are commonly used). Each layer provides a complete description of the system at that level. Box 21.1 provides a brief description of CLG. Since 1981, with the move away from a linguistic model of interfaces it has become increasingly difficult to distinguish the syntactic and interaction levels (see Box 21.1 for more information), particularly in graphical user interfaces (GUIs). In this text we shall consider just two types of design: conceptual and physical design. Firstly, we shall focus on **conceptual design**, which corresponds to the conceptual and semantic levels of CLG and to the goal and task levels of the generic task model (Figure 20.1) and the mappings between these levels. Our concern is with what the system has to be like if it is to meet its declared purpose, but we do not concern ourselves with *how* the structure and functions are to be realized in a physically instantiated system. We focus on function and structure first before looking in detail at the form of the interaction. The process of conceptual modelling results in a conceptual model of the whole human–computer system.

In Section 21.4 we look at the factors involved in **physical design** – the design of the physical system. You also need to remember that distinguishing between conceptual and physical design does not actually provide us with a method for the design; only guidance about what the design should be like. Analysts and designers will iterate between these two levels of description and will fix on certain physical design decisions in order to understand the conceptual level better. This iteration will involve various kinds of testing (or evaluation) with users so that we can check that the design really does meet their needs. The advantage of designing at the conceptual level before details of the physical design are fixed, however, is important as it avoids the problem of 'design fixation' and maintains a wide design space in which alternatives can be considered for as long as possible. This is vitally important, as you will see from the interview in Part V with Bill Verplank, an experienced interaction designer and international expert in HCI.

Box 21.1 Command language grammar (CLG)

CLG (Moran, 1981) is a form of grammar comprising a symbolic notation, consisting of a sequence of hierarchical levels, each being a refinement of the preceding level. Each level is itself a complete description of the system from the perspective of that level and is clearly distinguishable from the next level. Specific mappings are used to go between levels:

Component	CLG level	
Conceptual component comprises:	Task level	Semantic level
Communication component comprises:	Syntactic level	Interaction level

The task level initially involves a designer analysing users' needs in terms of the tasks to be accomplished using a system. The output from this level is a decomposition of a user's task domain into subtasks. The semantic level describes the objects and operations that a user has to employ to accomplish the tasks described in the previous level. The outcome from this level is a conceptual model which defines the functionality of a system and also maps to the task level above it and the next level below.

The syntactic level concerns embedding the conceptual model of a system in a language structure so that users can communicate with that system. The outcome from a syntactic level analysis is a syntactic specification on to which the semantic structure from the previous level is mapped, and which will in turn map on to the interaction level. The interaction level describes display actions taken by the system and dialogue conventions which ultimately must be resolved into a set of keystrokes, mouse movements or whatever is appropriate for the particular communication style selected. The outcome from an interaction level description should map to the preceding level (see Table 21.1).

Table 21.1 Summary of the main considerations for each CLG level.

CLG level	Designer considers	Designer produces	User considers
Task	What does the task analysis say that the user will want to do?	Task description	How can I use the system to do X (such as edit a letter)?
Semantic	What objects, actions and methods are needed to do each subtask?	Semantic description	How do I make the system do X (for example, delete a sentence)?
Syntactic	What should the dialogue and information displays be like?	Syntactic description	How do I mark the sentence? What is the 'DELETE' command?
Interaction	What should the exact input and output sequences be using X and Y as the input and output devices, respectively?	Interaction specification	Which keys (or mouse, buttons and so on) do I press to mark the sentence and then delete it?

21.1 A framework for design

The psychological basis of our design approach assumes that the user's knowledge is layered. Thus, a user can know something at one level but not at another. For example, the user may have a vague notion of a task (such as deleting a section of text) and the operations that need to be carried out (such as selecting a piece of text and then removing it) but not know how to do it (for example, which sequence of keys to press). In this case a user would have conceptual knowledge (know what the task involves) but would not have knowledge at the physical level (know how to do the task).

Question 21.1

Think of an example where the user may know how to do something (know the physical level) without knowing how the system works.

This description of levels considers the conceptual and physical components from both designers' and users' perspectives. Designers often fall into the trap of developing a conceptual model of a system to which the user has to adapt rather than the other way around. By analysing a design problem from the two perspectives the differences between the two can be highlighted and subsequently resolved. The conceptual level initially involves analysing users' needs in terms of the tasks to be accomplished using a system and the objects and operations a user has to employ to accomplish the tasks. The designer must define the conceptual objects – this leads to the need to make decisions about how specific or general these conceptual objects should be. In general, the designer wants to minimize conceptual complexity in the system by using familiar concepts, by having as few concepts as possible and by making methods as simple as possible. Trade-offs are likely to be involved and will need resolving. The user's view of this level is concerned with mapping a task to its associated conceptual objects and operations within the system. It is important, therefore, that the designer's conceptual model of this matches the user's mental model of the process (remember the discussion in Chapters 6 and 7).

Physical design concerns embedding the conceptual model of a system in a physical structure so that users can communicate with that system. The most basic decision for the designer is how to package conceptual operations into a dialogue – the **operational** aspects of physical design. This includes making decisions such as whether to use simple commands or operationally extensive but complex commands or graphics, whether commands should be specific or general, whether commands should allow multiple parameters or be parameterless, and so on. A major objective at this level is to simplify sequences of commands required for doing tasks. Other syntactic devices also have to be considered, for example, notations for designating objects and defaults. From the user's point of view this level consists of dialogue structure and all the information displayed on the screen including feedback. Details of exactly how to display information, such as where to position items on the screen and how to use colour, must also be considered (the **representational** aspects of design), along with the display actions taken by the system and dialogue conventions, which ultimately must be resolved into a set of keystrokes, mouse movements or whatever is appropriate for the particular communication style selected. There are many guidelines available to help designers at this level (Chapter 24). 'How-to-do-it' cognitive task analysis techniques (Chapter 20) are also useful.

Moving from the conceptual to the physical level requires the designer to decide who or what is going to undertake particular functions. This is the process of **task allocation**. The designer creates tasks for users by allocating certain logical functions to humans, to the computer or to a human–computer system. The tasks that are allocated to humans need to match the tasks that users conceive as much as possible. In addition, it is important to take account of the cognitive processing demands of any particular design. We shall return to this topic of task allocation in Section 21.3.

21.2 Conceptual design example: Eurochange

In order both to illustrate the principles of a structured design approach and to show the intermingling of analysis and design, we will consider the design of a machine that exchanges money in one European currency for another; it is like a point-of-cash (that is, autoteller) machine and it is called the Eurochange.

In the discussion that follows we may assume that you have already done the initial analysis and that you have produced the following requirements specification:

> Eurobank PLC, a mythical international bank, is designing an automatic *bureau de change* machine that resembles the autoteller machines we see in our high streets. The machine, Eurochange, is intended initially for installation in airports and railway stations and will allow travellers to obtain the main European currencies quickly without having to find the nearest bank.

Dataflow diagrams (like those described in Chapter 19) have the desirable property of representing both the computer inputs, outputs and processes and human processes using the same notation. In other words, we do not commit ourselves to a particular implementation by representing the flow of data in the system. The level 0 diagram, also known as the 'context diagram', simply represents the boundary of the system and the main inputs and outputs. The context diagram should describe the purpose of the system – the principal goal(s) that it is designed to support. In the case of Eurochange, a request for a particular kind and amount of currency is the main input and the output is the actual currency.

The level 1 diagram provides a high level description of the main system tasks. It says nothing about who or what will perform the tasks. It takes into consideration any important system constraints and highlights the major stores of data and flows of data that are conceptually or logically required if the system is to accomplish its purpose. In the case of Eurochange the system constraints include:

- the user must possess a valid card and personal identification number (PIN),
- the user must have enough credit left in order to obtain the required amount.

If these two conditions are met, the currency can be delivered and the credit card must be updated with the amount left. The task of validating the user (task 1 in Figure 21.1) must logically have access to the card, the PIN and the details of all valid users. The task of checking credit (task 2 in Figure 21.1) must have access to the amount required (*CurrencyAmount*) and know that the user has been validated. Only if tasks 1 and 2 have been completed successfully will task 3, *DeliverCurrency*, be undertaken. A necessary function of task 3 is to update the *CreditCard* and clearly this task must have access to the amount required.

The dataflow diagrams in Figure 21.1 specify the system at a level of detail which identifies the different data required (as perceived at present), as demonstrated by the different names used for the dataflows and for the datastores. At present it does not specify exactly what that data is.

The next level(s) of dataflow diagrams are used to describe the objects and actions required in order to accomplish the tasks. User and system tasks are still not distinguished. This process is only undertaken *after* the whole conceptual system has been designed. In some cases, of course, this distinction is somewhat forced. The user has to supply the credit card in this system. Almost certainly the user will supply the PIN, but how that is achieved is another matter. The design in Figure 21.2 does

Level 0–System

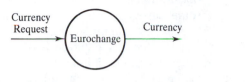

Level 1–Main Tasks

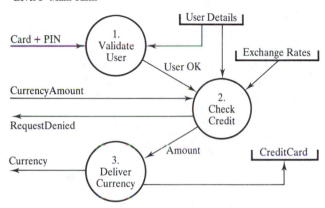

Figure 21.1 Task level description of Eurochange.

Level 2–Process 1

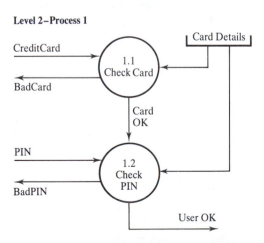

Figure 21.2 Logical level of description for Eurochange process 1.

not say that the user will type the PIN in. It may be that this data can be provided in some other way. Nor does the design specify how the system will check the card details (for example, the card itself could contain some data or the system could check a central database). These are physical, system design decisions. The processes can be further decomposed, as illustrated for processes 1.1 and 1.2 (see Figure 21.3). At the bottom level it is important to question exactly what the data is. For example, what do we mean by a credit card? Would a bank card do?

As the process of development continues, more detail can be added to the logical level of description. In real system development the analyst would, of course, discuss the emerging requirements with the users and with the other interested stakeholders, such as the credit card companies, banks and so on. However, there is more to system design than specifying processes or operations. The concepts embodied by the system must also be examined. These concepts are:

- individual data elements,
- dataflows, which may consist of several data elements,
- datastores, in which related data elements are grouped together.

The logical data structure design can be represented using ER diagrams (Chapter 19). In tandem, we define the meaning of the data elements by recording descriptions in a data dictionary (Chapter 19). Figure 21.4 shows a data model (an ER model) for the data in the Eurochange system.

The ER diagram shows all the data elements required by the system and the relationships that exist between them. The power (Benyon, 1990) of such a conceptual design is that:

- it says nothing about *how* the system will be implemented. It simply states *what* is required,
- it says nothing (yet) about *where* the data is to come from,
- it can form the basis of a robust data design following the rules of data analysis.

Question 21.2

List the conceptual operations and the conceptual objects for the Eurochange system.

Question 21.3

Write a general description of the Eurochange system from the ER model (Figure 21.4).

Level 3–Process 1.1

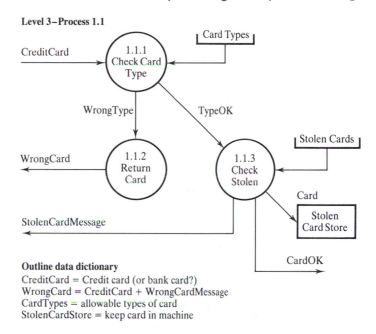

Outline data dictionary
CreditCard = Credit card (or bank card?)
WrongCard = CreditCard + WrongCardMessage
CardTypes = allowable types of card
StolenCardStore = keep card in machine

Level 3–Process 1.2

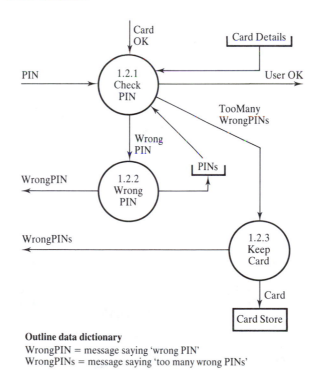

Outline data dictionary
WrongPIN = message saying 'wrong PIN'
WrongPINs = message saying 'too many wrong PINs'

Figure 21.3 Logical level of description for Eurochange processes 1.1 and 1.2.

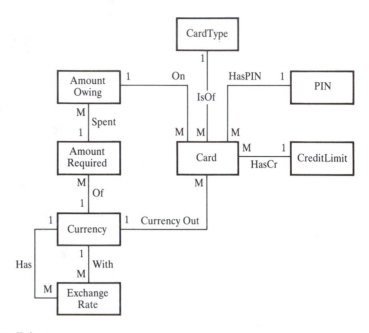

Outline data dictionary

Data descriptions

CardType	The type of card, for example, a credit card, bank card, specialist card and so on
PIN	A four-digit personal identification number
CreditLimit	The amount (in local currency) that the card is allowed to have on credit
Card	The concept of a credit card. It will have some identification number and other attributes such as an expiry date and so on
ExchangeRate	The relationship between two currencies expressing their values relative to each other
Currency	For example, Pounds, DeutschMarks, Francs and so on
Amount Required	The amount expressed in some currency which is required on a particular transaction
Amount Owing	The amount of credit already recorded against a card

Relationship descriptions

HasPIN	A Card has a PIN, though a PIN may relate to many cards
HasCr	A Card has a credit limit and a credit limit may relate to many cards
LocalCurrency	A Card uses a Currency. This is a local currency
Has	A currency has an exchange rate…
With	…with another currency
Of	The amount required is expressed in a currency
Spent	The amount required is spent against an amount already owing…
On	The amount owing is on a card

Figure 21.4 Data in the Eurochange system.

21.3 From logical to physical design: Task allocation

One of the most important decisions to be taken during the development of a human–computer system is to allocate tasks; to human, to computer or to a human–computer system. The developer needs to establish who (or what) is going to provide the data or knowledge necessary to accomplish a task and who (or what) is going to physically accomplish the task. For example, in the Eurochange example it is difficult to imagine how the computer could provide the PIN. This must be a user action in order to meet security criteria. Similarly, you would not expect the user to have to calculate the exchange amounts. The computer should do this. Many other functions that are logically required, however, can be allocated to the human, to the machine or to some combination of the two, and dataflow diagrams can be used to assist in this allocation. In order to do this, the designer needs to consider the feasibility of obtaining data from different sources and the desirability of doing so.

EXERCISE

Consider process 2 (Figure 21.1) in the Eurochange system. What will the content of the data 'CurrencyAmount' be?

COMMENT

Some possibilities are:

- the user could enter an amount in the local currency and request an equivalent amount in another currency,
- the user could request an amount in the currency required, but then would need to know what the equivalent was in local currency,
- the system could offer certain amounts in the foreign currency and restrict the user to selecting one of these.

The designer needs to produce a more detailed level of description for process 2 in order to examine the alternatives. A 'first attempt' at producing such a diagram is shown in Figure 21.5.

The processes involved in calculating the exchange are illustrated in Figure 21.5. The user could enter an amount in one currency and specify the required currency, and have the system calculate the required amount. Alternatively, the user could specify the required output amount and currency and the system would calculate the local currency equivalent. However, when considering these possibilities, we must consider how the user is to make a decision and we must also consider the constraints imposed by the machine – for example, whether it deals only with notes and if so in what denominations.

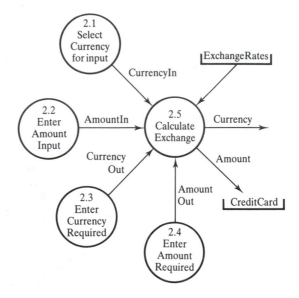

Figure 21.5 Level 2 dataflow diagram for process 2, Check Credit (first attempt).

EXERCISE

For the following two possible scenarios in Eurochange, identify the processes (from Figure 21.5) which the user would have to perform for:

(1) 'I want the equivalent of £100 in DM.'
(2) 'I want 2000 Francs.'

COMMENT

(1) User performs 2.1, 2.2 and 2.3.
(2) User performs 2.3 and 2.4.

Clearly the user has logically to perform 2.3, but there are many physical design options, all of which accomplish the same, logical process. If it is decided that the computer will support this process, then the currencies available can be pointed at by a mouse, selected from a list using cursor keys, displayed on a touch-sensitive screen or displayed using 'hard' selection keys (see Chapter 11 on input devices). The system could anticipate what the user requires either through a simple rule such as 'if the user is in France she will probably require French currency' or through more elaborate mechanisms such as inferring what the user requires from details of previous transactions which could be stored on the user's card (thus making it a 'smart card'). The designer will consider the cognitive load imposed on the user by any of the options chosen, how much learning will be required, what knowledge may

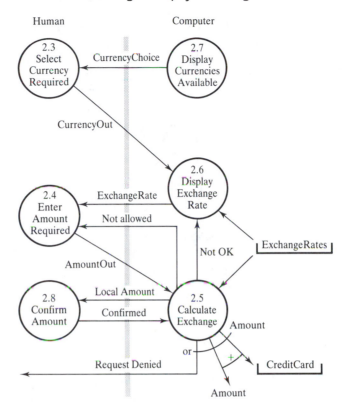

Figure 21.6 Second attempt dataflow diagram of process 2. Allocating tasks to humans and machine in the Eurochange example.

be transferred from other tasks and how best to exploit that knowledge. The simplicity of task–action mappings is also important, as is a simple conceptual–physical mapping. Task analysis techniques, particularly cognitive task analysis which focuses on the user's task knowledge, are appropriate at this stage.

There are many other considerations, which we do not have space to consider here. For example, in deciding the amount required, the user may need access to the exchange rate. We must consider the possibility of the user making errors and being able to correct them and of users changing their minds when they see how much they are asking for in the local currency. The task allocation stage of developing human–computer systems is certainly one of the most important and one which will itself involve many iterations, prototyping of options, detailed analysis and user testing (Part VI). The designer, starting off with a logical description of the whole human–computer system in the form of dataflow and ER diagrams, considers each process, bringing to bear task analysis techniques as appropriate.

Let us consider what a 'second attempt' analysis of process 2 in Eurochange might be like, and impose the human–computer boundary as illustrated in Figure 21.6. Flows across the boundary indicate the user inputs and system outputs that are required. The system will display the currencies available and the user will select the required currency. The system will display the exchange rate between the requested currency and the local currency. The user will then enter the amount of the foreign currency required. The system will display the equivalent amount in local currency and the user may then accept this or return to the start of the transaction. Amounts are only allowable in certain denominations (depending on the foreign currency). If the user enters an incorrect amount the system will request that a more appropriate amount is entered. Clearly, this solution is only one option and serves to illustrate the approach rather than defining the best design.

Task analysis techniques can be used to inform the design process at any point during system development. Clearly, in the allocation of tasks, one important consideration is the mental load demanded of the user by a particular user–system design (see Chapter 5). Indeed, we implicitly considered this in the previous section when arguing that the system should calculate the exchange amount. This is an easy task for the computer but a difficult one for the human, which is a good reason why the computer should perform it.

21.4 Physical design

Once the allocation of tasks to human and to machine has been considered, the details of the operational aspects of the system can be specified and developed. Operational aspects concern what actions the user can take and what the system responses will be: in short, what the system does (physically). The user actions can now be specified and the system responses can be itemized. In addition and in parallel to this you should consider the representational aspects; what the system will look like.

There are three main aspects to describing the operational nature of the system. Firstly, we need to consider how the system can reveal the state it is in. Secondly, the system needs to make clear what actions the user can take. Thirdly, system responses (that is, feedback) should be considered.

Essentially, there are two ways in which visual information can be used to indicate the current state of the system:

- The system's state is *visible* to users (the objects on the screen show what state the system is in).
- The system's state is not immediately visible but it is *observable*, if the user takes some action.

Usually the first of these is preferable. Various techniques are available to the designer in order to make clear what the user can do. The principal of affordance is particularly important here (Chapter 1 and Section 13.7). The design of buttons, screen displays and so on that afford certain actions such as pressing, clicking, touching and so on is important. Considerations for these aspects of design are covered in Chapters 13 and 14. Furthermore, it is also important to consider incorrect user actions. Interrupt mechanisms, such as a 'cancel' button for the Eurochange system, are also vital. The choice of input devices (Chapter 11) also needs to be made.

One method for specifying this is to use a flow chart or dataflow representation of the logical dialogue, such as Figure 21.6. Alternative representations would include state transition diagrams, structure charts and a notation called the user action notation (UAN) method (Hartson *et al.*, 1991; Hix and Hartson, 1989, 1993). Other methods based on the use of User Interface Design Environments (UIDEs) are discussed in Chapter 28. Sketches can also be used (Chapter 22) but they lack the precision of the more formal methods. The advantage of more informal methods, however, is that they can be tested with users easily. An important aspect of any notation used is that it should show the flow of control. Physical design, unlike conceptual design, needs to focus on when and where actions and decisions are taken, which actions may be iterated, which actions are optional and the sequence in which actions are undertaken.

One of the central features of the operational design is to decide on the type of interaction style (Chapter 13) that is appropriate, for example, a command language, direct manipulation, question and answer and so on. The considerations that should underpin such decisions are covered in Chapter 13. The interaction style must be appropriate for the users, the work they are doing, the system and the environment. In the case of Eurochange, the dialogue should certainly be system-controlled. Eurochange is a classic example of a 'walk-up-and-use' system which will have a wide range of users with different backgrounds, abilities and attitudes towards the system. Even if people would like to control the dialogue, the overall purpose of the system is to deliver currency quickly, securely and accurately. Both the operational and representational aspects of the design will critically depend on the characteristics of the intended users of the system.

Question 21.4

List some user attitudes and characteristics that should be considered in the physical design of Eurochange.

Question 21.5

In Chapters 4 and 5, four principles of interactive system design derived from information processing psychology were described – the perceptual, representational, memory and attentional aspects. How do these principles apply to the physical design of the Eurochange system?

The craft of design is nowhere more apparent than when specifying what the system will look like – the representational aspects of design. Details of considerations for the design of icons, text and screen displays and the importance of conforming to standards, styles and so on are discussed in detail in Parts II and III. There are also more general ergonomic concerns such as the shape and size of buttons, flicker on screens and the height and slant of the display. It is important to keep in mind the

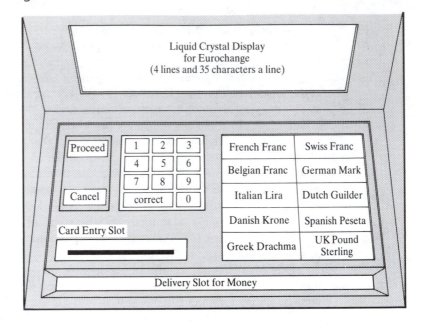

Figure 21.7 Design of Eurochange terminal.

overall context of the interaction and the need to present an appropriate coherent model of the structure and function of the machine for the intended users. Our design for the Eurochange terminal is shown in Figure 21.7.

21.5 Completing the design

In this chapter we have described a structured or layered approach to design. The conceptual layer is used to determine the logical structure and functioning of the system. This is mapped, through the task allocation stage, onto a physical design. The method employs a variety of techniques as appropriate. The Eurochange example has been used to illustrate many of the principles, but you should bear in mind that it is only one type of system and other systems may require a different kind of rigour, more intuition or the employment of other techniques. In order to complete the design process, much work still needs to be done. The designer has to reflect back upon the allocation of tasks. The tasks that humans do must be coherent and present a cogent system image for the users. Consistency has to be maintained between the different levels of interaction (see Box 21.2) and for the system as a whole. Style guides, general HCl guidelines and other material will have to be brought to bear on the system design as discussed in Part V.

Box 21.2   Consistency in the design

Physical consistency

Both operational and representational consistency are important in interaction design. Operationally, the system should support only a few ways of issuing commands. For example, in a direct manipulation system, the user usually selects an object and then specifies the action on that object. In menu systems the user usually selects the menu function and then specifies the required object through a further dialogue. Two methods are employed, but each member of the object class is treated consistently. In addition to consistency of operations, a consistent representation should be employed. For example, error messages should look the same and appear in a consistent place on the display in relation to the rest of the dialogue. In general, objects in a class should appear in the same style.

Conceptual consistency

There are a number of aspects to conceptual consistency. Firstly, a consistent metaphor should be chosen. This extends to the level of abbreviations and design of icons. Users will bring knowledge of the external world to a human–computer interaction and thus the system should be consistent with their expectations. For example, 'D' would be a poor candidate for a 'SAVE' command because it does not suggest the correct meaning, whereas 'S' would be much better for a system designed for English-speaking people. Icons should be designed to exploit an appropriate metaphor in the user interface (for example, an open door for a 'close' function would be inappropriate). Metaphorical consistency is heavily culture-dependent.

Secondly, entities within the same class, or performing a similar role, should be treated consistently. For example, deletion of a word should have the same syntactic form as deletion of a paragraph, and selecting a word should have the same form as selecting a paragraph. This means that users should be able to anticipate correctly how they should specify these operations and how the system will respond. However, it is not always easy to establish when entities do have this type of similarity.

Thirdly, we can identify task consistency; that is, the task allocation has been carried out in a consistent way so that the user has to perform similar tasks on similar objects.

Although consistency is an important goal in HCI design, it is not easily achievable. Consistency for the learner may not be consistency for the expert. Consistency for the discretionary user may not be consistency for the dedicated user. In general, since different people have different experiences to bring to the interaction, they may perceive as inconsistent what the designer perceives as consistent.

The kind of **user support** required also needs to be decided upon (see Chapter 15). Recall how in the development of the OMS (Chapter 17) user guides were developed very early in the project. These guides were an important part of the user support and were prototyped and evaluated thoroughly in tandem with the development of the system. One of the important outcomes of the task allocation stage is that the knowledge which users must have in order to use the system is made explicit. If users are not expected to have this knowledge from previous experience then it must be provided as part of the overall system design. The support required by novice users or casual users will be very different from that required by experienced or regular users.

Question 21.6

What type of user support will be required in the Eurochange example?

The combination of behaviour, look and style and consistent metaphor (Chapter 7) will ensure that the design comes close to meeting the needs of the users and that it will meet its usability criteria. In order to achieve this, the design will need to be tested with users at various stages in its development. Larger systems bring their own problems. In particular, maintaining consistency across a large number of functions introduces problems not demonstrated by Eurochange. Finally, you should remember that design is a creative activity, which can be helped by formal, structured methods, but the techniques will not do the design for you! They provide tools, which you can use to produce, verify and explore designs, but they are only ever approximations of the final product.

Key points

- The structured approach to design focuses on descriptions at the conceptual and physical levels.
- Conceptual design is concerned with what the system must do in order to achieve its purpose and the necessary structure that is required.
- Physical design is concerned with how the system does things and what it looks like.
- The move from conceptual to physical design is concerned with allocating tasks to humans and to the computer and in so doing recognizing the demands and constraints implicit in the decisions.
- The operational aspects of design are concerned with how the system controls the dialogue, with what the user must do and with system feedback.
- Representational aspects concern the display of data, the presentation of a coherent system image and the methods by which the system reveals itself.
- User support is an important and integral aspect of design.

Further reading

BENYON D.R. (1992). Task analysis and system design: the discipline of data. *Interacting with Computers*, **4**(2), 246–59.

A paper which elaborates the importance of taking a data-centred approach to the development of human–computer systems and illustrating how data models can lead to effective designs.

BENYON D.R. (1992). The role of task analysis and system design. *Interacting with Computers*, **4**(1), 102–23.

DIAPER D. and ADDISON M. (1992). Task analysis and systems analysis for software development. *Interacting with Computers*, **4**(1), 124–39.

These two papers debate the issues associated with task analysis methods and a structured approach to system design.

BRAUDES R.E. (1991). Conceptual modelling: A look at system-level user interface issues. In *Taking Software Design Seriously* (KARAT J., ed.). London: Academic Press.

This paper considers design from the perspective of building conceptual models and discusses issues of consistency in some detail. The use of ER diagrams and flow diagrams is mentioned, but not considered in any great depth.

SUTCLIFFE A.G. (1990). Integrating specification of human–computer interface with Jackson system development. *Information and Software Technology*, **32**(10).

SUTCLIFFE A.G. (1991). Integrating methods of human–computer interface design with structured systems development. *International Journal of Man–Machine Studies*, **34**, 631–55.

These two papers by Sutcliffe take a similar approach to that adopted here, but with a different motivation. He is primarily concerned with integrating HCI design with existing software engineering methods. However, he discusses the need for an explicit task allocation stage and how ER and dataflow diagrams can be used in system design.

22

Envisioning Design

Aims and objectives

The aim of this chapter is to introduce you to some approaches that will help you to conceptualize the form of your design. After studying this chapter you should be able to:

- describe the benefits of taking a holistic approach to design,
- use sketching techniques to effectively explore the design space,
- recognize the role of scenarios, snapshots and storyboards for supporting the design process,
- decide when you wish to use structured approaches and when to envision design using the techniques presented in this chapter.

Overview

In Chapter 21 we presented a structured approach to design using formal notations and this may have given the impression that HCI design is a rigorous, precise form of engineering. It is not. Considerable creativity and insight are needed to produce a good design and there are informal ways of expressing and recording design ideas as well as the structured ones that you have learnt about so far. This chapter discusses some ways of conceptualizing the form of a design at a very early stage in terms that users can understand. Bringing abstract ideas to life, as well as designing functionality, is known as **envisioning** design. As you will see, a big advantage of these approaches is that they provide a good basis for very early user testing.

HCI design is highly creative and consequently different designers use different techniques. Furthermore, as you will remember from Chapters 2 and 3, HCI design is influenced by several different disciplines, each with its own philosophies, methods and ways of viewing the world. One of the most recent impacts is from sociological approaches to system design, most notably in the area of requirements gathering. These approaches aim to place as central not just the 'user' but the whole social situation (Suchman, 1987). Designers seek to immerse themselves in the situation in which the new system will be used and through this immersion to understand how the users really work and what is important to them. This practice is known as 'ethnography' and it is discussed in more detail in Chapters 9 and 32. Although the theory offered by ethnography is important, the methods are not well understood by the HCI community and there is debate about the best way of effectively integrating the radically different views and practices of sociologists and system designers. Some approaches concern the involvement of users through meetings, game-playing and prototyping. Yet others are derived from creative design. They emphasize visualizing design and the exploration of different visual representations of the conceptual model of the system. The main thrust of this chapter is, therefore, to illustrate how system design can be undertaken in a more 'holistic' fashion using techniques that bring the system to life for the users by facilitating early user testing and by using more meaningful (for the user) design representations such as sketches.

22.1   Holistic design

Holistic approaches view design as a whole in which decisions about the way an interface should look are made in relation to how this will be physically communicated to users. Unlike a structured approach, no clear distinctions are made between different levels of the system. Design is a much less structured and constrained activity, in which there is no rigorous ordering of stages of representation. Attention is focused on the appearance and presentation of the conceptual model and then on working with manifestations of that model using actual examples. In contrast with the structured approach, which defers consideration of the physical design until late in the design process, the holistic approach focuses strongly on the visual appearance of the interface and its behaviour (that is, the system image it presents to users; see Chapter 7). There is also a strong emphasis on designers knowing how to use their creative and innovative skills in order to visualize the design problem and its solution in terms of a system image.

The holistic approach is well illustrated by considering the development of the Star user interface (see Chapter 1). Box 22.1 contains a brief description of how the Star was designed. The primary focus of this design was on getting the conceptual model in a form that could be displayed as a concrete reality to users. A key feature of the design team's philosophy was to formulate a conceptual model before writing any of the software or developing the hardware (Smith *et al.*, 1982). This meant they had a much larger design space in which to try out alternative designs and were not restricted by functional constraints. Another aspect of this design was adherence to a clearly defined set of user-centred principles (like those discussed in Chapter 17).

The Star interface is by no means typical of system development. In the first instance, the designers were developing a large and complete office information system. Secondly, they had already gathered a lot of detail about what the system should do and had prototyped parts of the system extensively. Thirdly, as it was a new, generic product they had a wide design space. The techniques described in Box 22.1 and in the rest of this chapter may not suit all design situations or all designers but in the right hands they offer promise.

Box 22.1   The Star user interface

An example of an interface that was developed using a holistic design framework is the Star user interface. The Star was the first system to employ the desktop metaphor which is now so pervasive in computer systems. Development started in the mid-1970s, with the first system launched in 1982. The Star transformed the idea of interfaces, begetting the first Apple Lisa system and changing much of the computing world from command-based systems into the familiar WIMP environments. The primary focus was on representing the user's conceptual model in a form that could be displayed on the screen. This helps to achieve the principle of 'what you see is what you get' (WYSIWYG). A key feature of the design team's philosophy was to formulate a conceptual model *before* writing any of the software or developing the hardware. This meant they had a much larger design space in which to try out alternative designs and were not restricted by functional constraints. Another aspect of this design was adherence to a clearly defined set of user-centred principles.

The designers had studied the problems of HCI and concluded that users find it difficult to comprehend concepts that are abstract, or invisible, and they find it harder to create new objects (as opposed to copying them), filling in and generating details (as opposed to choosing and recognizing), objects and functions. They find editing easier than programming and interactive working easier than batch.

The designers developed and adhered to the following principles:

(1) familiar user's conceptual model,
(2) seeing and pointing versus remembering and typing,
(3) what you see is what you get (WYSIWYG),
(4) universal commands,
(5) consistency,
(6) simplicity,
(7) modeless interaction,
(8) user tailorability.

For example, the desktop itself is a familiar conceptual model, and the use of icons and windows shows the principle of seeing and pointing versus remembering and typing in operation. A page on the screen was the same as a printed page (the WYSIWYG principle). 'MOVE', 'COPY', 'DELETE' and 'SHOW' were universal commands, consistent throughout the system. Simplicity was provided through the use of keys to optimize the changing of certain character properties, such as bold and italics. Modeless interaction was provided through the use of noun–verb commands for all actions, and the ability to change the icons on the desktop to fit in with the user's working environment provided user tailorability.

'There must be a malfunction on the computer.'

(*Source* Honeysett)

One holistic design approach is 'game-playing'. In a review of a redesign of a newspaper production system, Ehn and Sjögren (1991) describe playing a design 'game' with the users, employing a board game representation (the 'Organizational Kit') of the design space in which '*the semantics and syntax of the game have to be situated*, we do not think of objects and relations as general concepts, but as specific to the domain' (p. 229, authors' italics). They produced cards representing the main functions, objects and artefacts and used these to situate and guide the analysis, as shown in Figure 22.1. One of the important features of the newspaper example is that the design is *situated*. The cards put the designer in the user's shoes and enable users to identify with the characters or to point to significant differences under different circumstances. They also enable designers to think about many levels of the interaction at once, capturing aspects of the whole human–computer system – users, in an environment, trying to achieve goals using a system design. In doing this they avoid the separation inherent in the structured approach.

A similar approach is advocated by Muller (1991) and his colleagues. They also use playing cards with pictures of possible screen shots which users can manipulate to show typical ways of working. Other uses for cards include exploring possible metaphors (Section 22.2 and Chapter 7) to see how well they match tasks. Techniques for drawing or sketching conceptual models, computer-based and 'cardboard' prototypes and the use of other graphical techniques can also be highly effective methods for this kind of design. It is particularly important that the images are quick and easy to produce, otherwise designers can get tempted to commit

Figure 22.1 Using the Organizational Kit in analysis of newspaper production (Ehn and Sjögren, 1991).

themselves to one design too early before exploring possible alternatives thoroughly. (Bill Verplank discusses this point in the interview at the beginning of Part V.) The great advantage of paper, pens and Post-its is that they are flexible and quick to use. The disadvantage is that functionality is difficult to represent. All these techniques enhance communication between users and designers. They are also effective in supporting design teams (Chapter 23).

Although the holistic approach tends to blur distinctions between different design stages, it is possible to incorporate more structured HCI methods into the design process where appropriate. For example, information obtained from task analyses about physical, social, cognitive and attitudinal aspects of users can all be taken into account in holistic design. Following the initial holistic exploration of a user interface, a more detailed task analysis can then be performed. Hence, sketches, prototypes and so on can be useful instruments in task analysis for allowing users to explore the proposed interfaces. They also provide a much more concrete basis for exploring the way potential rather than existing tasks are likely to be carried out by users, because they provide a basis for early user testing (see the interview with Bill Verplank and Part VI). This helps to prevent the focus on existing tasks becoming too strong at the cost of using the computer system to do new tasks or radically changing the form of existing tasks. Even though the design is not layered, awareness of these layers can be helpful in later stages of design when the designer needs to check that all the functionality required has been catered for and that the design is consistent. Consequently, some designers successfully mix and match approaches as appropriate.

22.2 Sketching and metaphor

An increasingly commonly used technique is to design a conceptual model as an explicit interface metaphor (Chapter 7) like the desktop analogy, which we have mentioned several times throughout this book. Metaphors can be used to present a coherent image of the whole system or to deal with specific functions or parts of the system. For example, most word processors use the metaphor of 'cut' and 'paste' to explain how a piece of text can be moved from one place to another. Like many metaphors, after a while they become so much a part of the system that their metaphorical links fade to insignificance.

Sketching techniques can be useful for exploring all kinds of design ideas, and Figure 22.2 shows how they can be used to help one think about the organizing metaphor for a system. As well as facilitating communication, **visual brainstorming** (Verplank, 1989) can be used to explore alternative designs. After producing initial sketches the best ideas can be further developed by constructing cardboard representations of the design, which can be evaluated with users. This can then be followed by developing scenarios (Section 22.3), software or video prototypes (Chapter 27). The type of mock-up that is built will depend on how advanced the idea is. It may be quicker and cheaper to use paper-and-pencil forms at early stages,

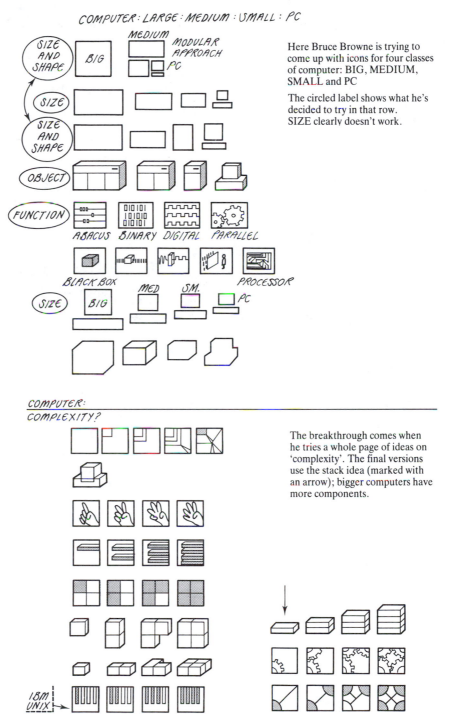

COMPUTER: LARGE : MEDIUM : SMALL : PC

Here Bruce Browne is trying to come up with icons for four classes of computer: BIG, MEDIUM, SMALL and PC

The circled label shows what he's decided to try in that row. SIZE clearly doesn't work.

COMPUTER: COMPLEXITY?

The breakthrough comes when he tries a whole page of ideas on 'complexity'. The final versions use the stack idea (marked with an arrow); bigger computers have more components.

Figure 22.2 An example of structured brainstorming (Verplank, 1989).

whereas computer-based and video prototypes may be important in later stages for exploring and demonstrating interaction and design consistency.

Given that many interface designers do not have artistic and creative flair, however, it may prove to be difficult for them to use sketching methods. To facilitate the process of visual thinking, Verplank (1989) has suggested some training exercises and shortcuts or 'cheating'. Try the following and see what you gain from the experience.

EXERCISE

Try sketching a familiar user interface. Spend no more than five minutes doing it.

COMMENT

From your sketch is it possible to see how the interface works? What problems did you encounter? For example, how easy did you find it to represent the dynamics of the interface and the conceptual model underpinning the system? What graphic techniques did you use (for example, arrows, lines)?

EXERCISE

This exercise is to encourage you to develop your own graphic vocabulary. It is important for designers to have meaningful graphic representations for indicating the elements of an entire system environment. This means having quick ways of representing objects such as the computer system, input and output devices, and people. Look at Figure 22.3 which is taken from Verplank's tutorial notes, and 'cheat' as he suggests.

COMMENT

Although having a natural instinct for doodling and sketching is helpful, Verplank and his colleagues have found from their teaching that it is possible to *learn* to be creative. An important starting point is to develop and practise a 'vocabulary' of simple graphical forms.

EXERCISE

This exercise is to encourage you to use brainstorming as a way of developing visual concepts of all or part of a system. Try to develop simple visual images for a set of icons that represent different sizes of computer systems: large, medium, small and PC. Do this by writing the headings at the top of a clean sheet of paper, and down the

Cheating

Probably more important to the interaction designer is quick tricks for indicating the elements of the system.

Whenever you see a piece of a sketch you like, trace or copy it and then practise using it. With computers and copiers you can use clip art. For free-hand sketches, practise with the simplest and quickest figure indication that will do.

My favourites are the 'star-man' and 'blob-man'. If it's important to know which way he's looking I put a nose on him or bend his arms.

Also useful is a repertoire of arrows and system components like keyboards, screens, boxes and cables.

Trace one you like and then fill a page by trying variations like big or little, looking left or right, standing or sitting, old or young.

Figure 22.3 Collection of graphic images of people (Verplank, 1989).

left-hand side some categories you might use to represent size – like size and shape, size alone, complexity, and so on – to label rows. Then explore different visual forms one row at a time. Try to draw at least five complete rows.

COMMENT

You may have found it easier to draw images for aspects of an interface rather than trying to draw a whole system (as was asked in the first of these exercises).

EXERCISE

Now try to develop visual metaphors for the following programming constructs: 'EDIT', 'DEBUG', 'STRING', 'EXECUTE', 'DECLARE', 'LOOP', 'FIELD'. As these concepts are highly abstract you may alternatively like to consider the use of verbal metaphors.

COMMENT

See Figure 22.4.

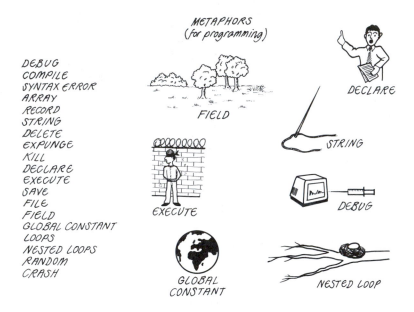

Figure 22.4 Some possible metaphors for programming concepts (Verplank and Kim, 1986).

The visual metaphors that you have just developed may be more helpful for the design of icons (that is, the representational communicative components of the interface). They may not be as helpful in structuring an entire interface unless some theme emerges. If this occurs, then such a theme might be sufficiently powerful to provide a general organizing analogy for an entire interface.

Verplank recommends looking at things that come between us and our environment such as vehicles, clothes, media and tools (see Figure 22.5). Thinking about these things helps to suggest a list of concerns, ideas and inspirations. For example, thinking about vehicles suggests navigation, roads, tracks, moving objects and people. Thinking about tools encourages ideas of direct control, predictability, utility, feedback, tasks, productivity and so on.

The human interface as ...

Here are five analogies for exploring the expressive range of user interfaces; they can provide a means for extending our ideas.

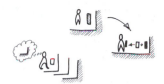

In all the analogies, the interface is seen as an enabler that comes between a human and some environment; quite often it is multi-layered. As users we are more or less aware of these layers, sometimes identifying them as extensions of ourselves (transparency) or the environment (virtuality), at other times seeing the interface as object (tool apparency).

... vehicle

The car is the most obvious vehicle for many city and suburban dwellers. However, there are many vehicles in the environment. They range from children's roller skates through bicycles to stationary vehicles like escalators. Do I want to use my computers to take me to a destination that I decide upon, or do I want them to take me easily to a particular destination? Transport systems, including private cars, trains, buses, trams and bicycles, are interdependent. What does the interface to interdependent systems impose or allow? What are the human interface traffic laws I must obey? What are the traffic reports?

... tool

The layers become obvious in the tool analogy. I only think of the hammer's handle when I have to pick it up, then my focus shifts to its head, then from the hammer head to the nail head to the point of the nail to the board I'm adding to the next row on the fence.

Tools range from precise to crude, from hand to power tools, from multi-purpose to general purpose. A trend is for tools to come with their own tools – adhesives, screwdrivers, and so on. Data can come with its own application interface.

... media

This analogy best captures the information and communication aspects of human–computer interfaces. Some interesting dichotomies might be: active/passive, censored/uncensored, popular press/quality press.

This is also more than simply an analogy. Computers are becoming the medium of the future either because they create a medium (as in desktop publishing) or become the interface to it (teletext).

... clothes

Clothes protect us from our environment (weather) but often they project us into it and help us to fit into it. My computer allows me to present myself to others in the particular role that I am playing. Interfaces can range from uniform to fashion; I may never use the same one two days in a row, or I may use it as a disguise.

Again, there is a literal aspect to this analogy. Datagloves and virtual space helmets raise the spectre of completely cutting me off from the 'real' world; it may be better to think of watches, belts and bow-ties.

... partner

Finally, there are the intriguing yet dangerous notions of anthropomorphism and animism: interface as partner. I can immediately identify with my interface and even create it in my own likeness. Yet it is dangerous because of possible false assumptions and strong feelings.

The term *partner* suggests that the interface cannot only come between me and my environment (act as an agent) but also be on my side, helping me to deal with the environment (as a coach does in sport). This analogy is as rich as the world of human relations; imagine the interface as nag, as fan, as an adviser or an amanuensis.

Figure 22.5 Potential organizing analogies for user interfaces (Verplank, 1989).

Question 22.1

Produce some unifying metaphors for the Eurochange system. Do some sketches of these.

22.3 Scenarios, storyboards and snapshots

A scenario is a personalized, fictional story with characters, events, products and environments. They help the designer to explore ideas and the ramifications of design decisions in particular, concrete situations. Snapshots are single visual – often cartoon-like – images which capture a significant possible interaction. Storyboards are sequences of snapshots which focus on the main actions in a possible situation. By using these techniques designers are able to move from existing to potential interactions and hence to anticipate problems. As with all aspects of system design, you are unlikely to get a scenario 'right' first time. It requires prototyping and evaluating with users in order to achieve a good balance between the various factors. Multiple scenarios will be needed to reflect the different situations and different views that can occur. It is important to stay in character when developing scenarios. The purpose of the representation is to see what happens in specific, concrete situations. Bruce Tognazzini in his entertaining book *Tog on Interface* (Tognazzini, 1992) points out an important link between scenarios and 'brainstorming' (a creative thinking technique): 'Use scenarios to define and develop a sense of user space' (p. 74). By this he means to emphasize that scenarios force designers to consider the range of users who will use the system and the range of activities for which they will use it. The user space is defined by the variety of users, work and environments in which the interaction can take place. Scenarios are used to make concrete particular combinations of these dimensions. They are populated with fictional, but possible, characters, who want to undertake real work. During the detailed design, the scenarios can be revisited with comments such as 'OK, but what would Hillary do?' or 'Deepak won't like that arrangement'. They also provide a useful source of hypothetical cases for evaluation. For example, given the design for the Eurochange system in Chapter 21, we may test the operation of the system with the following scenario.

> Pat Smith has just arrived at Amsterdam Schiphol airport en route to a large conference on Human–Computer Interaction. Pat is carrying a portable computer and a large, heavy suitcase and needs to get to the conference centre quickly. Looking around for a bank in order to get some local currency, Pat sees the Eurochange machine with its blue flag style logo showing a circle of twelve stars.
>
> Pat goes up to the machine. It seems similar to the automatic teller machine that Pat uses regularly. Pat puts down the suitcase, takes out a credit card and inserts it into the slot. A message is displayed on the screen:
>
> Enter your PIN
>
> Pat thinks for a few moments and then types a four-digit number on the numerical pad, listening to the reassuring beep which follows each number pressed. The machine pauses for a few seconds and then displays:

> Select currency required

Pat pauses again. What is the currency in Holland? Pat browses the currencies available, sees 'Dutch Guilder' and presses the key. The machine displays the message:

> Exchange rate is 3.52 DG to £1
>
> Enter amount required in Dutch Guilders in units of [10]
>
> Press <Proceed>

Pat types 253 and presses <Proceed>. A message is displayed:

> Machine deals in bank notes only
>
> Smallest bank note is [10] DG
>
> Enter new amount to obtain DG or press <Cancel>

Pat enters 260 and presses <Proceed>. There is a whirring noise and a few other indeterminate clunks and clicks. The credit card is returned from the card entry slot and the money deposited in the delivery slot, with a printout of the transaction.

Question 22.2

Write down the issues which this scenario has raised in your mind.

Scenarios force the designer to consider the appropriateness of the design, including the type and amount of user support and other aspects of the environment. Snapshots of critical situations and storyboards (pictorial representations of scenarios) are other effective methods. Rather than dealing with abstract representations, this approach provides concrete, situated representations of the design which help the designer to focus on many aspects of a possible interaction at once. Chapter 32 considers many of these approaches from an evaluation perspective.

Key points

- The creativity of design often comes from employing techniques that stimulate thought and encourage consideration of a wide design space.
- Sketching techniques can be effectively taught to and used by designers – you do not have to be an artist to use them.
- Recognizing the social context of design and the importance of particular situations can be revealed through using scenarios, snapshots and storyboards.

Further reading

GREENBAUM J. and KYNG M., eds (1991). *Design at Work*. Hillsdale, NJ: Lawrence Erlbaum Associates.

An excellent book, which emphasizes the situating of designs in real environments. A number of techniques and approaches are explored with the authors providing candid views on their successes and failures.

VERPLANK W. and KIM S. (1986). Graphic invention for user interfaces: an experimental course in user interface design. *SIGCHI Bulletin*, **18**(3), 50–67.

Verplank is perhaps the most accomplished user of the approaches discussed here – particularly the use of metaphor and sketching techniques. This paper outlines the ideas and describes the methods that he uses. There are also SIGCHI Tutorial Notes, which are produced annually.

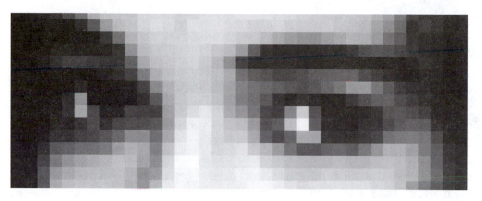

INTERACTION DESIGN: DESIGN SUPPORT

Design is a complicated process and designers need as much support as possible. Although attempts to automate software production are being made, even in the bastions of automatic programming there has been a move away from complete automation towards supporting the human process. In Part V of the book we shall focus on supporting human designers and not replacing them. In Chapter 2 we introduced the theme of people, work, technology and the environment, and it has been a constant theme throughout the book. In this part of the book we shall interpret this quartet slightly differently: the people are designers; technology has the dual role of target (the software that is being designed to run on a computer) and provider (the role of computers in providing design support); the work is the work of the designers in developing the software; and the environment is the context in which the system is being designed and developed.

If we are to support the designers, then, it is important to understand what designers do, in other words 'how they design'. Part V therefore begins by exploring some of the reasons why designers need support. Although much can be learned by observing experienced designers, not all designers can be good at their jobs naturally – even the most experienced of us needs some help and advice sometimes. Interface design guidelines offer that help through principles and rules which capture wisdom distilled from experience over many years. Quality too is an important issue in software development and one way to achieve a certain level of quality is to develop agreed standards against which software can be evaluated. Having striven to produce a quality design, it seems criminal that the experience gained should not be used again. Obviously, the designers involved have learned a lot and others could benefit directly from their experience, if only the rationale for the design were recorded effectively.

Communicating and testing ideas is also an important part of design, which is often done through prototyping and can take many forms depending on the stage of the design. At some point, the software must begin to take shape in the form of implemented code, and at this point software support is unavoidable and very desirable. It may also be useful to have some software support much earlier for prototyping, managing the development, text editing and many other activities. The interview with Deborah Hix discusses some of these issues.

This part begins with an interview with Bill Verplank, a well known interaction designer from California, who has also taught HCI at Stanford for many years. He advocates envisioning techniques, such as those discussed in Chapter 22. One reason why he believes in this approach to design is because it helps designers to avoid commiting themselves to one design before exploring other alternatives.

INTERVIEW WITH **BILL VERPLANK**

Bill Verplank is an interaction designer at Interval Research where he works on a wide variety of industrial and consumer products. Bill was one of the pioneers at Xerox where he worked on the Star user-interface – a precursor of modern day graphical user interfaces. Bill is also a part-time lecturer at Stanford University where he has taught visual thinking, human factors and interaction design for the past twenty years. In this interview Bill discusses the roles of visualization and early exploration of alternative designs.

How important is visualization in design?

There is a big push towards prototyping tools that will lead very directly to the product. Almost every computer-based development that I've been part of has suffered from a lack of consideration of alternatives. I think one of the first things you learn in design is to put forward a number of alternatives so that you can then compare them. Having a lot of display space is important for doing this because you can make them visual. One of the things you can do with visual things is superimpose them, or put them side by side and quite often when you start doing that you like one better than another. Until you've made a comparison, you have no idea why you prefer one over another. The criteria emerge from the comparison.

In other words, what you're describing is the need to avoid evolutionary prototyping of the interface, isn't it?

Yes. I've just spent two years with a firm doing a product based on Smalltalk. Smalltalk is a wonderful, rich environment in which you can construct an elaborate system and keep trying it. What happened was that they set out with some very fixed notions early on, and simply kept refining them, so there was no real comparison of alternatives. There was really only one idea and they refined it and refined it and there were maybe two or three little alternatives. Then one would die and they would pursue the main direction again. No-one was ever very satisfied with the design and what I attribute that to was that they had a working prototype even before they decided what the product was going to be.

What should they have done?

I think that what we needed was more awareness about the importance of considering alternatives. What we should have done, for instance, was get separate groups to work on alternatives. I think it's something that individuals can learn to do. They need to learn to suspend judgement for a while until some of the alternatives take on a life of their own. If you cut down an idea before it's been expressed, it's always a bad idea because you never get a chance to repair it, fix it, to bounce it off someone else. I think we get seduced by the apparent reality of the computer medium. We get sucked into thinking that the design already works and all we have to do is fix it. Sketch ideas, in contrast, assist visual thinking and they are especially well suited to preliminary thinking and brainstorming. The coming of ideas and comparing ideas is one of the important things about visual representations. They allow for side-by-side comparison.

467

So how do you train people to keep alternative ideas open?

One way is to keep 'idea logs', so that you never lose an idea. For instance, you may have gone through an iteration period and you may discover later that there was a seed of an idea which is worth going back to. A problem with computer design is that it happens so quickly, it is transient. Really, the computer ought to be the kind of machine which could keep track of everything but, in fact, one of the advantages of putting ideas down on paper tends to be that you don't lose them as easily.

At Stanford we teach creativity and a lot of it involves playing games so that people get the idea of what it's like to be creative. Students design games for children. Anything where the context is one that's fun. For effective problem-solving, there's four things that are important: motivation – it should be a problem that you really want to solve; information – you should know something about the problem and the potential ways to solve it; and two other things that you can teach – fluency and flexibility. You can teach people to get better at sketching. You can teach people paint skills on PCs, programming skills, writing skills and presentation skills. There is a lot of skill involved. Part of learning these skills is just looking at creative people, seeing the volume of stuff they do, and realizing the role of chance. For example, I'm amazed at photographers who just take picture after picture after picture. You might think taking good pictures is just skill, but even though the photographers have years of experience and knowledge about exactly how to hold the camera, and focus it and aim it, they still take reams of pictures. They capture the right moments but it's a tricky thing, a chancy thing and that's part of what creativity is. It's not just producing the right idea, but recognizing the right idea in all the mess that you produce. Having that rich field of things to compare and contrast that you've either generated or collected, is something that designers need to know how to produce. Evaluation also comes into brainstorming; when you stop generating ideas you have to start evaluating them.

So have you any views about who should contribute to design teams? Do we need more graphical input?

Certainly, I think we'll see a lot of people, either picking up graphics skills, or graphic designers will be brought in. We've found that industrial graphic designers are often more sensitive to where to put a switch so that you can reach it, or how to put a knob or a handle on something so that you can operate it. And that kind of visual design often affords usability.

23

Supporting Design

Aims and objectives

The aim of this chapter is to examine the different kinds of support needed by individual designers and design teams. After studying this chapter you should be:

- able to appreciate the need to provide support for the design activity,
- able to understand what is needed to support design, designers and design teams,
- aware of the wide variety of support available.

Overview

Software systems are very complex entities, often consisting of thousands of procedures, with many calls upon each one. Designing software is therefore a complex task. As with all complex tasks, humans need help to complete the task efficiently: support for managing the complexity, support for expressing and testing ideas and support for ensuring that a quality product is developed. There are many forms that support for design can take, ranging from pencil-and-paper techniques for recording and experimenting with ideas to sophisticated computer-based support environments, from very vague, widely-applicable guidelines to very detailed specific design rules, and from corporate style guides to internationally agreed quality standards.

Throughout the chapter, we do not limit our attention to HCI design. Although this remains our main focus, we also draw on information about software design in general. Firstly, because HCI design is a form of software design, it is reasonable to assume that the kind of support generally needed for software design is likely to be needed for HCI design too. Secondly, it is important to set HCI design in the context of overall software development, as we said in Part IV.

23.1 Supporting the design process

In Chapter 2 we introduced the star life cycle, which we then discussed in more detail in Chapter 18. The effectiveness of each stage of this process can be enhanced by the use of appropriate supporting techniques and tools. However, moving between different stages and having to translate between different representations, such as from a task analysis to an early prototype, can be tricky. Support is needed, therefore, not only for individual tasks, but also for managing the production and coordination of the results and integrating them into a coherent whole. The larger the project and the more people that are involved, then the more important is the support. Although the exercises presented in this book are, of necessity, small problems, you should be able to understand the value of relevant support from your own experiences of design and of working through the earlier parts of this book.

EXERCISE

Refer to the Eurochange design example in Sections 21.2–21.4. Look through these sections again, and identify the kinds of support that you think would help to achieve a quality design more effectively and efficiently. Consider also the consequences for support if the system were many times the size of Eurochange.

Note that the term 'support' is used in this context to cover any kind of help or assistance. Consider the use of paper-based techniques, meetings and discussions with others, software support and so on.

COMMENT

We have identified the following points from considering the Eurochange design exercise. You may have thought of other kinds of support.

- Software support could be very beneficial for handling the various notations and diagramming techniques used. Although it is relatively easy to sketch dataflow diagrams or ER diagrams that contain only a few nodes by hand, designing a system much bigger than Eurochange could be accomplished more quickly and easily if specialized editors with tracing facilities for data dictionary entries were available, for instance.

- Discussion with the users, credit card companies and other interested parties is an important element of user-centred design at all stages of the design process. However, this requires the design to be expressed in a medium that users can understand easily. Prototyping the design, either paper-based or through software, is clearly an effective way of achieving this communication, although not the only way. Prototyping would also have been useful during the discussion about allocating tasks between the human and the machine, since simulating the system's operation may have given a clearer picture of problems and possibilities. Techniques for brainstorming ideas, envisioning designs, exploring alternative metaphors and so on are also important.

- In considering process 2, 'Check Credit', three alternatives for the content of 'Currency Amount' were suggested. Choosing between alternatives is a crucial part of design. Exploring the different ways in which the requirements can be realized helps the designer to understand the requirements themselves better, but also enhances the chances of a better than average design being produced. To help in this process, measurements of quality, support for generating alternative options, and techniques for choosing between alternatives would be useful.

- Software support for designing and producing screen layouts, icons and other screen elements is crucial if a true picture of the design of the final system is to emerge.

- Throughout the exercise, guidance would be useful about how to apply design techniques, when to use which technique, the psychological effect of certain interface decisions, the suitability of certain display elements, which interaction style to use, and so on. This kind of guidance is particularly helpful for inexperienced designers, but can be just as important for experienced developers.

Other areas that do not emerge directly from this example, but that you may have identified include: support for documentation production, programming support, support for moving between different notations, and project management.

23.2 Supporting designers

Thankfully, the days when programmers had to write software directly in machine code have gone. Compilers exist that automatically transform a program written in a high level language such as Modula-2, C + + or LISP into executable machine code. For interface designers, many of the low-level concerns of implementation have been taken away by the introduction of predefined screen elements and palettes that allow a 'pick and choose' approach to design. Figure 23.1 contains a screen from NeXT's Interface Builder, which shows the creation of a button from a palette of predefined options. This allows more attention to be focused on the organization and structure of interfaces, areas where design expertize should rightfully be focused.

Automatic code generation is possible from higher level formal program specifications under certain constraints and research is being conducted into the automation of the whole software development process. Each advance in automation seems to be accompanied by more extensive demands on software, so that the role of the human designers changes but is not lessened. Since designers will remain a crucial element in the design process, providing design support will mean providing help and assistance to them, not replacing them. It is, therefore, important to consider not only what designers need to achieve, but also how they work – what do designers actually do?

A number of observations have been made by researchers studying software designers in action. As with many significant discoveries, none of these observations is particularly surprising – once they have been pointed out! However, they are worth thinking about when you are considering the kind of support that you or any other designer might need.

Designer experience

Novice designers tend to concentrate on the superficial elements of the design, whereas experienced designers have a deeper view of the design and its implications. The designer's level of experience within the particular application domain also affects their performance. This is not particularly surprising. As one researcher puts it, if you want to have good designs, hire good designers!

EXERCISE

How might it be possible to minimize this reliance on experience, so that inexperienced designers can also produce good designs?

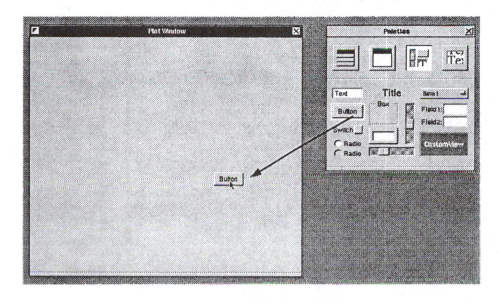

To resize the button:

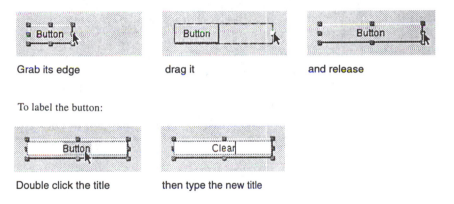

Grab its edge   drag it   and release

To label the button:

Double click the title   then type the new title

Figure 23.1 Positioning and resizing a button using NeXT's Interface Builder (Brest *et al.*, 1991).

COMMENT

Unfortunately, we cannot all be good interface designers naturally, and it can take many years of experience to develop a wide range of skills. However, through the provision of appropriate support, based on the experience that is available, suitable help and guidance can be given to the less experienced.

Previous known solutions

Wherever possible, designers will use their knowledge of previous projects to identify known successful solutions to similar problems, which can be suitably modified and reused.

EXERCISE

A very useful resource for supporting this behaviour would be a library of previous design problems and their solutions, and indeed some libraries of reusable components do exist. However, there is difficulty in using such libraries.

If you were writing a system to play backgammon and were looking for reusable components, what characteristics would you look for in a problem whose solution is in the library?

COMMENT

A good starting point would be to look at any other designs for game-playing software. These are likely to contain the right kind of functions such as 'compute move', 'redraw game board' and so on. However, the rules for playing backgammon are unique to backgammon (this is what makes it a distinctive game). Would you therefore choose to modify components from a chess playing system, a draughts system or some other, non-board game? Characteristics that you might look at include similar number of inputs and outputs, similar type of data, and so on. However, it is not necessarily obvious which designs in the library are 'similar' enough to the current problem for them to be modified easily and reused effectively.

Human designers are able to identify suitable candidates for modification, but capturing this capability either for use in an automatic system, or to offer as guidance for other designers is proving difficult.

Problem decomposition

Designers at all levels of experience decompose large problems into less complex, more well-defined subproblems. In studies of dialogues between designers and their clients, cycles of discussion have been identified, that is, portions of the total problem are taken and addressed as if they were the main problem.

EXERCISE

Why do you think it is common for such decomposition to take place?

COMMENT

Part of the rationale for decomposing large problems into subproblems is to enhance the likelihood of being able to identify known solutions: the subproblem being addressed will be less complex and more well-defined than the main problem, so it is more likely that a known solution will exist. A second reason is simply because of human cognitive limitations: large, complex problems are more difficult to understand than small, simpler ones.

Alternative designs

Alternative designs are explored and evaluated. The number of alternatives explored and the criteria used to evaluate them vary across designer experience, design activity and application domain. For example, if the designer has been involved previously in a very similar project, the number of alternatives considered is likely to be lower since many possibilities were probably considered for the previous design activity. It is not always easy to identify alternatives, especially when one solution has been developed; it is a well-known human trait to gather information that supports an existing idea, rather than try to identify new ones.

EXERCISE

What kind of assistance could be provided to support the consideration of alternatives?

COMMENT

Designers need to explore as many alternatives as possible so that a solution that is close to the optimal one can be identified. Support for this activity could take many forms, including:

- access to previous designs of similar systems,
- well-tested relevant criteria for evaluating alternatives,
- regular design reviews with other designers, who critique the existing design and suggest alternatives or refinements,
- using envisioning techniques like those discussed in the previous chapter to explore alternatives.

A further form of support for this behaviour, called Design Space Analysis, is introduced in Chapter 26.

Design simulation

Designers will try to simulate partial designs and designs in progress so as to determine the correctness and efficiency of the design ideas so far.

EXERCISE

Pen and paper prototyping, rigorous design languages and graphical visualization techniques all provide support for this behaviour. What other kinds of activity could help designers understand their designs more and identify possible faults?

COMMENT

Discussion or simulation sessions with other designers. It is always useful to ask someone else who has not been involved in producing the design. Not only is it possible to get a fresh eye on the problem, but, also, one designer is unlikely to feel reluctant about changing another designer's masterpiece!

Understanding the problem domain

Experienced designers spend a lot of time exploring and understanding the problem before developing a design solution; understanding the 'problem' includes understanding the task environment as well as the task itself. It has been shown that domain knowledge is very important early on in the design process, although its exact use is not clear.

EXERCISE

If you were designing a system for monitoring helicopter flights to and from an oil platform in the North Sea, how would you prefer to gather the necessary information? Would you rather base your design on information given to you from the company's head office in London, or from a telephone conversation with potential users in Scotland, or just by exchanging letters, or would you rather visit the relevant oil platform and helipad yourself?

COMMENT

Although it would be possible to glean some information from head office personnel, they would not be representative of the real end users of the system. Talking or writing to real end users would give a better understanding of the system's requirements, but it would not be possible to gain a real understanding of the conditions (particularly the physical conditions) under which the system must operate without visiting the system site.

Reasoning strategy

A designer's reasoning during the early stages of design is opportunistic and evolutionary. This means that instead of following a fairly structured progression from abstract thinking to more concrete ideas, to yet more concrete issues, a designer jumps about between levels of abstraction as insights emerge and other designs are recalled.

EXERCISE

What implications would the above have for the design of a software design support environment?

COMMENT

A software design environment should not rigidly prescribe the steps needed to complete a software design; the designer should be free to move between design phases and system components.

One of the most difficult elements of design to support is the early design stage where ideas are generated and creativity plays a major role. How can this creativity be supported effectively? A study of interface designers (Rosson *et al.*, 1988) included an investigation into how designers generate and 'flesh out' ideas. The results are reproduced in Table 23.1. The techniques mentioned by the designers have been grouped into six categories, and by studying each it is possible to identify where support would be useful. The first two represent preparatory or information gathering activities, which are more suited to getting initial ideas than to fleshing out ideas. The next three categories involve discussing and analysing the information gathered, and the last one is concerned with trying out ideas and designs. You will notice that, in fact, the first five categories are really concerned with requirements gathering in the broadest sense.

Clearly, informal techniques play a substantial role in ideas generation (remember the interview with Bill Verplank at the beginning of Part V?), and it is not at all obvious how such informality can be supported. In their paper, Rosson *et al.* (1988) suggest that, among others, the following may be considered:

Table 23.1 Techniques for getting and fleshing out design ideas (Rosson *et al.*, 1988).

Get original idea	Flesh out idea
Task/user analysis	
Take user perspective	Take user perspective
Generate task scenario	
Interview, observe users	
Research the problem	
Rely on domain experience	
Key user on design team	
External source	
Other systems	
Literature, trade press	
Current research issues	
Interaction with others	
Discussion/brainstorm	Discussion/brainstorm
	Explain to coders
Meta-strategies	
Distraction	Distraction
Incubation	Incubation
Concentration	
Clear out mind	
Design activities	
Logical analysis	Logical analysis
Notes, charts, diagrams	Notes, charts, diagrams
	Write specifications
Trial and error	
Build prototype	Build prototype
	Make paper mock-ups
	Implement

(1) Generating task scenarios lends itself to software support; environments could include storyboarding facilities (see Chapter 22 for an explanation of storyboarding).

(2) Designers' reliance on other systems could be supported by allowing designers to view as wide a variety of systems as possible. For example, this may be achieved most effectively via a video database service.

(3) Group discussions and brainstorming can be supported to an extent by, for example, providing suitable communication facilities, which we shall discuss more fully in Section 23.3.

(4) Prototyping can be supported quite effectively by paper and pen techniques and by software support (see Chapter 27).

Other aspects of design that could be supported include note taking and the use of charts and diagrams. However, it is important not to stifle creativity by over-formalizing the process.

Question 23.1

Consider the techniques listed on the left-hand side of Table 23.1. What kind of designer behaviour do they illustrate? In your answer, refer to the observations of designer behaviour listed in Section 23.2.

23.3 | Supporting design teams

Designers usually work in teams but often they will have their own tasks so support for both individual and team work is important. Simon (1981) points out that most design problems are only partly decomposable, and consequently individual designers have to interact and negotiate (Strubing, 1992) with others.

EXERCISE

Consider the Eurochange example in Chapter 21. Imagine you are developing this system as one of a team of three people instead of on your own. What kind of support might you need for the team that you would not need on your own?

Now imagine that you are developing a worldwide Eurochange system involving a team of 100 people. What further impact would this have on the team's support needs?

COMMENT

If designers are working in a team, then they have to communicate their ideas to each other so that alternatives can be considered, possible conflicts recognized and resolved, elements integrated, and final decisions taken. Tightly coupled to the goal of good communication is the need for coordination. Designers' efforts must be coordinated so that they work complementarily rather than counterproductively.

The bigger the team, the more difficult it becomes to maintain effective communication, and the more managed the coordination needs to be. For example, in a team of 100 you could not hope for every team member to know details of every part of the system. User involvement also becomes tricky.

Effective communication requires access to each other and each other's ideas and partial designs, use of a common 'language', for instance, a formal specification language, dataflow diagrams or ER diagrams, a way of tracking and recording ideas and decisions, and so on. Most importantly, however, it requires an environment that promotes ease of communication. Software environments that help communication are discussed in Chapter 28, but there are other mechanisms, such as that described in Box 23.1.

Box 23.1   The design room

The 'design room' environment (Karat and Bennett, 1991) is an example of a cooperative approach to working in a design team. This room supports design teams by providing an environment that allows them to explore ideas during the early stages of design. This has proved helpful in facilitating a user-oriented overview and in prompting communication, discussion and generation of alternatives.

The room itself is big enough to hold between two and eight people. A variety of representations of design issues are posted on the walls:

- objectives for the system: goals, usability and so on,
- guidelines for style (see Chapter 24),
- abstract, generic objects and actions: types of object, such as 'containers', and actions, such as 'copy',
- screen pictures: representative images extracted from current documentation, storyboard sequences or design prototypes,
- resources and tools available for system construction: aids for software engineering, prototyping or screen definition (see Chapter 28),
- sample scenarios: sequences illustrating the flow of specific user actions needed for a result, concentrating on what the user will see.

The design process is facilitated because use of the room recognizes the importance of the social context of design, particularly the role of meeting facilitators, that is, people who effect communication between groups of people.

The layout of the design room is shown in Figure 23.2, and the summary of a scenario description is illustrated in Figure 23.3.

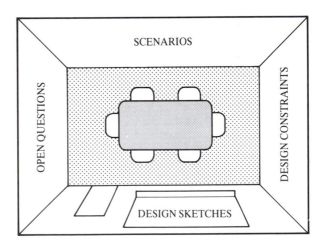

Figure 23.2   The design room layout (Karat and Bennett, 1991).

Scenario Component	Level of Detail
Name	A short label used when referring to a scenario.
Situation Description	Running prose giving a concrete illustration of a situation.
Logical Essentials	With respect to the system, information that must be supplied in order to achieve the desired result within the system. With respect to the user, the representations and actions that must be made available by the system to the user. Information at this level is intended to be implementation-independent, what would be needed regardless of methods used to achieve the result.
Generic Steps	The sequence of user steps (sometimes ordered) that must be performed regardless of implementation method.
Specific Steps	A particular design will presume a series of user steps with particular devices and with system feedback to the user as each step is taken. Error analysis (what happens if a user makes a mistake or if information needed by the system is missing) can also be considered at this level.

Scenario Name	Object 1 (source)	Object 2 (target)	Specific Design: Direct manipulation as a method	Specific Design: Menu dialog as a method
Scenario 1. Between documents link	Text: visible	Text: visible	Select source Context menu Select target Drag	Select link item Select source Select target Close dialog
Scenario 2. Within document link	Point: visible	Point: not visible	Select source Context menu Make target visible Select target Drag	Select link item Select source Make target visible Select target Close dialog
Scenario 3. Future document link	Text: visible	Object: named, not yet existing	Select source Context menu Select handle Property sheet Enter target name Close dialog	Select link item Select source Enter target name Close dialog
Scenario 4: Term indexes another document	Symbol: visible or not	Text: visible	Select source Context menu Select handle Property sheet Select 'all occurrences' Select target Drag	Select link item Select source Cascade to new menu Select 'all occurrences' Select target Close dialog
Scenario 5. Static target data linked direct to document	Data	Point	Select source Context menu Select point Drag Context menu Create inset Make graph from target template	(Not designed)

Figure 23.3 Using scenarios in the design room environment (Karat and Bennett, 1991).

The cost (in all senses of the word) of coordination involved in a team effort was first highlighted by Brooks in the 1970s (Brooks, 1982) and it is now a well-recognized problem, particularly with large development teams: 'the sheer number of minds to be coordinated affects the cost of the effort, for a major part of the cost is communication and correcting the ill effects of miscommunication (system debugging)' (Brooks, 1982, p. 30).

The problem of communication, particularly the inadequacy of written documentation, was highlighted again in a study by Curtis *et al.* (1988): 'The communication needs of teams were poorly served by written documentation since it could not provide the dialectic necessary to resolve misunderstandings about requirements or design decisions among project members. Rather, forging a common understanding of these issues required interaction' (Curtis *et al.*, 1988, pp. 1279–80).

The most common form of team interaction is meetings, which are an important forum for communication. However, a surprising amount of meeting time is taken up with coordination and clarification issues. Studies of small design teams indicate that, even when there are only half a dozen participants, less than half the time in meetings is spent discussing design (Olson *et al.*, 1992), the rest of the time is spent on coordination and clarification issues. This is often particularly true in large projects, in which 200 or more participants may be involved. How can a team of this size be coordinated effectively? The following excerpt from Brooks is referring to the production of the manual for IBM's System/360, a large mainframe computer. Although the project produced hardware, not software, the principles concerning coordination are just as applicable:

'Needless to say, meetings are necessary. The hundreds of man-to-man consultations must be supplemented by larger and more formal gatherings. We found two levels of these to be useful. The first is a weekly half-day conference of all the architects, plus official representatives of the hardware and software implementers, and the market planners. The chief system architect presides.'

'Anyone can propose problems or changes, but proposals are usually distributed in writing before the meeting. A new problem is usually discussed a while. The emphasis is on creativity, rather than merely decision. The group attempts to invent many solutions to problems, then a few solutions are passed to one or more of the architects for detailing into precisely worded manual change proposals.'

'Detailed change proposals then come up for decisions. These have been circulated and carefully considered by implementers and users, and the pros and cons are well delineated. If a consensus emerges, well and good. If not, the chief architect decides. Minutes are kept and decisions are formally, promptly, and widely disseminated.'

'... there builds up a backlog of minor appeals, open issues, or disgruntlements. To settle these we held annual supreme court sessions, lasting typically two weeks. (I would hold them every six months if I were doing it again.)'

(Brooks, 1982, pp. 66–7)

This mammoth effort may seem a long way from the design exercises you have met in this book, but large projects like this do exist, particularly in telecommunications and the space industry, and considering them helps to bring a sobering reality to the importance of communication and coordination support within design teams.

Question 23.2

Apart from electronic communication equipment, what kind of support could help with communication and coordination problems?

Team design complicates the goal of involving the user in the design process and in a large project the problem goes deeper than simply having to have the interactions well planned. Formal chains of communication between the developer and the client have to be established for sound managerial reasons, but this often has the effect of distancing the actual developers from the real users. Difficulties then arise in trying to arrange suitable access to users under these circumstances. One of the main problems is that different people answer to the name user (Curtis *et al.*, 1988). Remember the discussion of stakeholders in Chapter 2? An alternative, but related problem arises when the product is being developed for several customers whose requirements vary. It may be that the requirements of the first customer are delivered and others have to modify theirs.

Question 23.3

Why might formal communication channels via management interfere with communication between designers and users?

23.4 Different kinds of support

From the discussion so far and from Part IV, you should be aware of the kinds of design support that are needed. In the rest of this part we shall discuss the following:

- Guidance, ranging from universal design guidelines to detailed design rules, and from international quality standards to detailed measurements of usability (Chapters 24 and 25).
- Support for communicating and recording design decisions: helping to capture ideas and explore alternatives before the translation into software begins (Chapters 26 and 27).
- Software support: capturing ideas, exploring alternatives, recording decisions in machine-readable form, and translating into executable code (Chapter 28).

Question 23.4

It is very common for 'design support' to be interpreted as being software support. However, this textbook is one form of design support. In which of the above categories might you expect this book to be described?

Key points

- Design support is needed because of the nature of the task: designing software is complex and knowledge-intensive. There is a limit to the amount of information that human designers can process and store.
- Design support is needed at both the individual task level and at the overall process level.
- Designers themselves must be supported as well as design tasks.
- A team structure introduces factors of communication and coordination that affect the kind of support that is appropriate.
- Support for users to be involved in the design process is needed.
- In large projects, the formal communication channels that need to be established for managerial reasons can restrict the feasibility of involving end users in the design process.

Further reading

GUINDON R. (1990). Knowledge exploited by experts during software systems design. *International Journal of Man–Machine Studies*, **33**, 279–304.

This article reports on a study to identify the knowledge requirements of software designers. A good starting point for anyone wishing to investigate this area further.

Human–Computer Interaction, Vol. 7 (1992), Special Issue on CSCW.

The article by Seifert and Hutchins, 'Error as opportunity: Learning in a cooperative task', is particularly relevant to this chapter. Although based on an investigation of navigation teams on board ship, it throws light on some interesting group behaviour.

POOLE M.S. and HIROKAWA R.Y. (1986). *Communication and Group Decision-Making*. New York: Sage.

This book provides useful coverage of this area.

RIESBECK C.K. and SCHANK R.C. (1989). *Inside Case-Based Reasoning*. Hillsdale, NJ: Lawrence Erlbaum Associates.

Case-based reasoning is a technique that can be used to understand further reuse of previous examples.

SCHÖN D.A. (1983). *The Reflective Practitioner: How Professionals Think in Action*. New York: Basic Books.

This book is quite philosophical. It discusses the nature of professional work and in particular the role of reflection as part of actually doing work. Schön's book was mentioned in Chapter 2 and, having studied more of this book, you should now find Schön's work thought-provoking.

VISSER W. (1991). The cognitive psychology viewpoint on design: examples from empirical studies. In *Proceedings of Artificial Intelligence in Design '91* (GERO J., ed.), pp. 505–24. Oxford: Butterworth-Heinemann.

This paper offers an interesting overview of the findings from various cognitive studies of design.

24

Guidelines: Principles and Rules

Aims and objectives

Many guidelines for interface design have been suggested, but unfortunately, they are sometimes misinterpreted or misapplied. There are, in fact, two kinds of guidelines – high level guiding principles and low level detailed rules – and our aim is to help you to use both effectively. After studying this chapter you should be able to:

- appreciate the difference between principles and rules,
- state some of the major HCI guiding principles,
- discuss the various forms of guidance available to HCI designers,
- evaluate guidelines in relation to a specific design,
- decide between conflicting advice.

Overview

Good design results partly from the knowledge and experience of the designers and partly from the way in which they actually apply this knowledge. Design guidelines can help to provide a framework that can

487

guide designers towards making sound decisions. These guidelines can take a variety of forms and may be obtained from several sources. For example, journal articles, general handbooks and company house style guides are common sources. The important thing to remember about guidelines is that they need to be applied very carefully; they provide guidance – no 'cookbook' of HCI design exists, nor is such a thing likely to exist.

24.1 Principles and rules

The word 'guideline' has been misused and many varieties of advice are packaged together as so-called guidelines. The best user interface design guidelines are guidelines in the true sense: high level and widely applicable directing **principles**. For example, the following principles offer high level advice that can be applied widely:

- Know the user population. This can be difficult to achieve, especially when a diverse population of users has to be accommodated or when the user population can only be anticipated in the most general terms. Knowing the user includes being sympathetic to different user needs by, for example, providing program shortcuts for knowledgeable users, promoting the 'personal worth' of the individual user and allowing users to perform tasks in more than one way.
- Reduce cognitive load. This concerns designing so that users do not have to remember large amounts of detail (Chapters 5 and 7).
- Engineer for errors. A common excuse is that a problem occurred because of 'human error'. But people will always make errors and indeed *have* to make errors in order to learn. Engineering for errors includes taking forcing actions that prevent the user from making an error (or at least make it more difficult!), providing good error messages, using reversible actions that allow users to correct their own errors and providing a large number of explicit diagnostics.
- Maintain consistency and clarity. Consistency emerges from standard operations and representations and from using appropriate metaphors that help to build and maintain a user's mental model of a system (Chapters 6 and 7). A designer can only have ideas about what is clear based on initial information about users.

In order to use these principles in practice, they need to be interpreted in relation to the context of use. Simply applying guidelines will not lead to good design. For example, the principle 'reduce cognitive load' may be interpreted as 'minimize learning by being consistent'. This in turn may be put into practice as follows:

(*Source* Microsoft Press)

- always position the trash can in the bottom right-hand corner of the screen,
- always use 'quit' to mean 'abort the command' and 'exit' to mean 'execute the command and continue',
- always require an 'end of input' signal, such as pressing 'enter'.

Unfortunately, because of a perceived demand for 'cookbook-style' HCI design, instructions sometimes result in rules masquerading as principles. However, design rules can be distinguished from principles: a **design rule** is an instruction that can be obeyed with minimal filling out and interpretation by the designer, for example, date fields should be in the form DD–MM–YY or MM–DD–YY in North America. High level principles, on the other hand, must be interpreted and translated into a strategy for producing an unambiguous and clear-cut design rule which is appropriate for the system in question; for example, the input medium should be appropriate for the system's environment.

EXERCISE

Classify the following guidelines as principles or design rules:

- always issue a 'warning' message to the user before deleting a file
- allow query in depth
- provide a 'RESET' command
- design for user growth
- allow input flexibility
- adapt to different user levels and styles
- ensure ease of understanding
- give appropriate quantity of response
- display the 'quit' button in the bottom left-hand quarter of the screen.

COMMENT

There are six principles in the list:

- allow query in depth
- design for user growth
- allow input flexibility
- adapt to different user levels and styles
- ensure ease of understanding
- give appropriate quantity of response

There are three design rules:

- always issue a 'warning' message to the user before deleting a file
- provide a 'RESET' command
- display the 'quit' button in the bottom left-hand quarter of the screen.

Care must be taken to interpret principles appropriately; guidelines can and have been developed which simplify and distort the psychological theory upon which they are based. Take the well-known finding that the capacity of short term memory (STM) is limited to 7 ± 2 items, for example (see Chapter 5). In several sets of guidelines this has been translated into a design principle prescribing the maximum number of items that should be displayed at any one time. For example, in a set of recommendations for using colour displays, Durrett and Trezona (1982) suggest: 'the average user should not be expected to remember [the meaning of] more than 5 to 7 colours. This is the "magic number" usually associated with STM ... Novel displays should have no more than 4 colours since this is well below the average limit of STM' (p. 53). Although it is true that overuse of colours is undesirable the reason for this is not because we can remember the meaning of only a few colours at any time (this will depend on the nature of the information that is being represented by the colours), but because having a multitude of colours on any screen causes problems of distraction and confusion (see Chapter 4). It is therefore a perception and attentional problem, and *not* primarily one of recognition. We may well recognize 250 different animal names (or remember the meaning of 250 different animal names), but we will not be able to memorize more than about seven animal names when they are displayed for a few seconds. The guideline shows a clear misunderstanding of psychological principle. It therefore provides no guarantee of good design and has led many system designers to think in terms of categorizing and displaying items on the screen in 'chunks' of no more than seven. For example, when faced with the decision of how many items to display on a menu, designers may be misled by the guideline into thinking that menus should be constructed with a maximum of seven items. This can be quite inappropriate in terms of optimizing the display of options for the user. The advantage of using a menu is that the user does not need to recall an item from memory but only needs to recognize a particular option from a set.

Guidelines are limited in their use. However, they can be useful in helping designers to focus on what is needed and to deal with trade-offs. In this sense, the best kinds of guidelines are general principles. For example, guidelines like 'write clearly' and 'use consistent terms' may be more useful than guidelines like 'for headings use capital letters, size 14 point and centre the second line' or 'use opposite pairs of words for command names that have reversible actions, such as OPEN and CLOSE'. In addition, it can be helpful to provide examples of how the guideline can be used, what the exceptions are and the psychological data the rule derives from. An illustration of this type of technique, which was used by Smith and Mosier, is given below.

2.3-1 Consistent format

Adopt a consistent organization for the location of various display features, insofar as possible, for all displays.

Example: One location might be used consistently for a display title, another area might be reserved for data output by the computer, and other areas dedicated to display of control options, instructions, error messages, and user command entry.

Exception: It might be desirable to change display formats in some distinctive way to help a user distinguish one task or activity from another, but the displays of any particular type should still be formatted consistently among themselves.

Comment: The objective is to develop display formats that are consistent with accepted usage and existing user habits. Consistent display formats will help establish and preserve user orientation. There is no fixed display format that is optimum for all data handling applications, since applications will vary in their requirements. However, once a suitable format has been devised, it should be maintained as a pattern to ensure consistent design of other displays.

(Smith and Mosier, 1986, p. 881)

EXERCISE

Imagine that you are required to design the interface for an environment supporting several tasks. The system supports five types of task. These are text editing, electronic mail, graphics, networking and access to an on-line reference database. Using the guideline given by Smith and Mosier above, how would you go about designing the interface for the different applications? What underlying psychological principles are of relevance here?

COMMENT

Based on the guideline of consistent format, one approach is to represent the different applications in separate windows that can be readily associated with each application. To achieve this, colour coding could be used so that a window with a red background is used for electronic mail, a blue background is used for text editing, and so on. The format within the windows should be consistent throughout so that, for example, the titles of each window are all in the same location.

The underlying psychological principles are about focused and divided attention. While users cannot perform two or more tasks simultaneously they can carry out multiple tasks by switching between them. A way of allowing users to switch between windows quickly and easily should therefore be provided.

You will find that high level principles are a good guide when doing design. In fact, many experienced designers tend to apply them without even thinking – they become second nature.

24.2 Where do guidelines come from?

Guidelines have two main origins: psychological theory and practical experience. The latter group are often based on years of practitioner practice. As you may remember from Part II, current research cannot usually deliver the prescriptions that many designers seek. These guidelines need to be applied with care. For example, the most efficient human–computer task allocation, from a cognitive standpoint, may be unacceptable in the political or organizational context of a working environment. Often guidelines have to be traded-off against other constraints or against each other. It is also misleading to say that there are 'good' and 'bad' design guidelines. What may be 'good' is the way a guideline is applied in a particular context; what may be 'bad' is its misapplication or failure to apply it. Ultimately, there are only good and bad design decisions, which reflect the way in which guidelines were applied. So you need to choose and apply the right guidelines intelligently at the right time. Attitude, experience, insight and common sense help in this process. Indeed, common sense underlies a number of guidelines. For example, 'An application should be visually, conceptually and linguistically clear' (Microsoft, 1992). It seems hard to believe that anyone would deliberately design an interface which was unclear in any of these respects!

EXERCISE

In 'form-fill' interaction (referred to in Part III) data is entered through predefined fields on a screen, just like the boxes in the paper counterpart from which it derives (see Figure 24.1). For example, screens used by airlines for booking aeroplane tickets usually involve this kind of data entry; systems which deal with customer orders in the retail trade also use this method of entry.

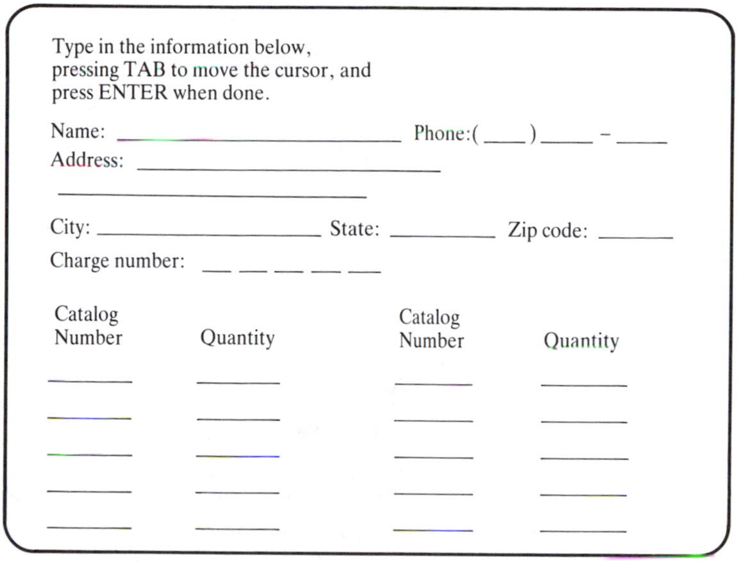
Type in the information below,
pressing TAB to move the cursor, and
press ENTER when done.

Name: ______________ Phone:(___) ___ - ___
Address: ______________
____

City: ______________ State: ________ Zip code: ______
Charge number: __ __ __ __ __

Catalog Number	Quantity	Catalog Number	Quantity
____	____	____	____
____	____	____	____
____	____	____	____
____	____	____	____
____	____	____	____

Figure 24.1 A form-fill design for a department store (Shneiderman, 1992).

By drawing only on your experience and common sense, write down four guidelines that would be applicable to the design of a screen for data entry from a standard order form.

COMMENT

Probably one of the first points which occurred to you is that the screen should reflect the paper form as closely as possible. Others you may have suggested include using meaningful error messages, using an appealing screen layout, using familiar terminology, and so on. A longer list, produced by Shneiderman (1992), is given in Table 24.1.

Many guidelines are less intuitive, as you can see from the list by Brooks (1988) in Table 24.2.

Question 24.1

What are most guidelines based on?

Published guidelines can be found in professional, trade and academic journal articles, house style guides and general handbooks. For example, the guidelines for three-dimensional interfaces in Table 24.2 came from a paper presented at an HCI

Table 24.1 Form-fill design guidelines (Shneiderman, 1992).

Meaningful title: avoid computer terminology

Comprehensible instructions: use familiar language, be brief

Logical grouping and sequencing of fields: related fields should be adjacent; sequencing should reflect common patterns

Visually appealing layout of the form: pay attention to the spacing of entry fields; if users are working from a paper form, ensure that the screen and form match in layout

Familiar field labels: use common terms

Consistent terminology and abbreviations

Visible space and boundaries for data-entry fields: use underscores or other markers to indicate the number of characters in a field

Convenient cursor movement: use a simple and visible mechanism such as tab button or cursor keys

Error correction for individual characters and entire fields: backspacing and overtyping should be allowed

Error messages for unacceptable values: error messages should be displayed on completion of an erroneous field; permissible values should be included in this message

Optional fields clearly marked: optional fields should also follow required fields where possible

Explanatory messages for fields: these should be displayed in a consistent location whenever the cursor is in that field

Completion signal: make it clear to users what action they should take to signify that they have finished form completion

conference. Articles provide a good source of current practice and experience. They tend to draw on application- or designer-specific experiences but present general-purpose advice on interactive systems design.

House style guides are sets of guidelines produced by machine manufacturers and software developers. They are generally mandatory or strongly recommended rules and cover low level detail about interaction and presentation. The aim behind such house styles is to produce suites of products with the same 'look and feel' so

Table 24.2 Guidelines for three-dimensional interfaces (Derived from Brooks, 1988).

Explicit selection of an interface 'metaphor' helps to define issues and make consistent decisions

Users need to spend a long time and require the provision of many cues (depth, shade, light sources, and so on) before they can form an accurate mental model of the virtual world

The user often needs to see both a view of the virtual world and a map of his location

Always move objects realistically, sacrificing image resolution or model complexity if necessary. As soon as the user stops moving objects, automatically invoke resolution improvement and add visual details

Enhance the visual image with illusions to other senses, for example, sound effects when objects collide

Assist the user in the control of many dynamic variables by mapping correlated variables onto a single, separate input device

Two cursors are required to provide distinct control of (a) movement in the viewing area and (b) menu selection and command input. The user should be able to operate both cursors in comfort that users can easily transfer from one system to another, expending minimum effort to learn the new system. A designer's freedom can be greatly reduced by such guidelines. House style guides are discussed in more depth in Chapter 25. General handbooks, on the other hand, offer a coherent and comprehensive coverage of the area, although presentation and level of detail varies. The best known is Smith and Mosier's (1986) *Guidelines for Designing User Interface Software*, from which the 'consistent format' example was taken. This handbook combines experimental evidence, design experiences, opinions and rational evaluations. See Box 24.1 for more about the style of guidelines.

Box 24.1   The style of guidelines varies

The format and presentation of guidelines varies from fairly formal, such as the example from Smith and Mosier (1986), to informal proverbs such as the following advice, taken from *The Art of Computer Conversation* by Gaines and Shaw (1984):

'The sixth proverb is:
> Take into account the possibility that the user's expectations of the computer will affect his interpretation of any dialog with it. The dialog should be designed to minimize confusion arising from these prior expectations.'

(p. 56)

'The nineteenth proverb is:
> Remember that the computer is a tool for simulation and that what is simulated becomes reality for the user. The power of the computer should be used to create worlds that are simple for the user and natural to the task.'

(p. 120)

24.3   Evaluating guidelines

Guidelines inevitably contain some overlapping and contradictory advice. Consistency might, for example, be important for learning to use a particular system but troublesome when a user becomes experienced. Many of these contradictions appear early and then disappear during the design process as high level principles become refined into lower level design rules. Often the constraints imposed by the characteristics of the users, their work and the environment will remove the need to choose between contradictory items of advice, because one refinement of a higher level principle will clearly apply when others do not. The skill that must be acquired in order to accumulate and apply guidelines wisely is the ability to evaluate them critically. So how does one evaluate guidelines?

There is no mechanical technique. Principles have different forms, which affect how one goes about evaluating them. Generalizations such as 'users will treat computer systems as if the latter were human' are based on inductive reasoning from experience. We can see people doing this. Prescriptions such as 'develop a consistent and intuitive conceptual model when designing a system' are based on deduction from the effects of not doing this. To evaluate guidelines based on inductive reasoning, the data on which the principles are based must be available. If, however, these data consist of the undocumented collective experiences of a design community, then inexperienced designers cannot access them easily. For guidelines based on deduction, specialist knowledge may be the basis for many of the inferences that lead to the formulation of a principle. If the authors of a guideline do not present an argument for a guideline, it is easy to reject it, even if it is good. Authors may also present a false argument. A reasonable guideline such as keeping colour coding simple can appear *un*reasonable if it is deduced from the wrong evidence and if it is made too specific (for example, allowing no more than seven colours at once).

Evaluating guidelines requires considerable expertise. So the short answer to 'how does one evaluate guidelines?' is 'become an HCI expert'! This expertise takes two forms: drawing from publicly available knowledge and drawing on private experience. By expanding your knowledge of HCI disciplines further you will be able to know when arguments behind guidelines are wrong and whether better arguments can be made for a poorly presented guideline. Watching users interacting with systems will improve your ability to judge the applicability of guidelines. The best way to check a guideline is to act on it and observe the result, paying particular attention to the context in which it is used.

24.4 An example of applying conflicting guidelines

Although some guidelines offer conflicting advice, many contradictions disappear when you are working on a design. As mentioned in Section 24.3, the constraints imposed by the characteristics of users, their work, their work environment and the available hardware will often eliminate the need to choose between contradictory items of advice because one guideline will clearly apply when others do not. Maguire (1982) advocates an approach to conflict resolution in which guidelines are specialized so that they apply to specific user groups, hardware and applications. However, some conflicts persist until implementation, and others may not be detected until then. Consider the design of a scrolling menu (Figure 24.2) in which the following guidelines apply:

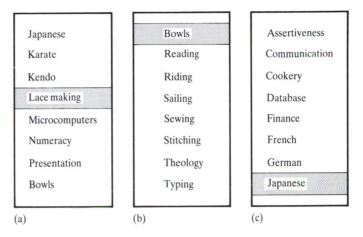

Figure 24.2 Menu scrolling.

- optimize use of output media,
- preserve some context between displays,
- maximize display inertia,
- design for predictability,
- design reversible operations.

In this early 1980s design a list of items is scrolled by operating function keys or using keyboard commands (such as 'FORWARD'), and the current item is highlighted. When scrolling forward or backward, context is preserved by keeping some currently visible items on the next display. The simplest design rule is to move the bottom item on the screen to the top when scrolling forward (Figure 24.2(b)) and to move the top item to the bottom when scrolling backward (Figure 24.2(c)).

In many word processors multiple items (for example, up to three lines of text) may be common to consecutive scrolled screens. However, there are occasions when considerations other than preserving context take precedence. For example, on a scroll forward, when the bottom item is four items from the end of the list, but the window size is five items long, the bottom item becomes the top item, thereby 'wasting' item space in a very limited window. To use the full display space and to let users see as much as possible, we can change the design rules as follows:

Scroll forward: Bottom item becomes top item on next menu.

Exception: (Window size minus 1) less than (difference between numbers of last item and bottom item).

Here: Top item becomes the item with the number equal to (number of last window size minus 1).

Scroll backward: Top item becomes bottom item on next menu.

Exception: Number of bottom item less than (window size minus 1).

Here: Top item becomes first item.

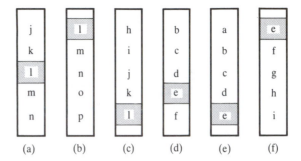

Figure 24.3 Irreversible menu scrolling.

This elaborated design rule preserves context and at the same time optimizes display use with small windows. It shows as much information to the user as possible.

Unfortunately, all the other guidelines are broken. Display animation is maximized, as the highlighted item can appear anywhere at the end of the list. This causes a disconcerting apparent jump in the display. All other scrolls are predictable. With the unoptimized display rule (top to bottom or bottom to top), the user will always be drawn to the top or bottom of the list, whereas with the optimized version the user is drawn unnervingly to an apparently random point in the list. The resulting interaction is not smooth. Similar problems occur when scrolling back to the first item of the list where it may not be possible to move the top item to the bottom of the window.

Most command- or key-driven text and list scrolling systems do not attempt optimal scrolling behaviour. Think of the scrolling systems that you use. Do most of them leave space when you scroll to the end of an object?

Finally, the optimized version is difficult to reverse. In Figure 24.3(b), the user has scrolled forward from the situation in Figure 24.3(a). The last item on the menu is 'p'. In Figure 24.3(c) the user has scrolled back from the situation in Figure 24.3(b). Figure 24.3(a) and (c) are different, although a scroll forward followed by a scroll back *should* have no effect. Figures 24.3(e) and 24.3(f) show a scroll backward followed by a scroll forward from the situation in Figure 24.3(d). Again, Figures 24.3(d) and (f) differ, even though scroll backward then scroll forward should have no effect.

This irreversibility penalizes users who make errors. If a user makes an error and then scrolls forward to the end of the list, the only way to redisplay exactly the same items as appeared on the screen at the time the error was made is to scroll back to the beginning, then scroll forward to where the mistake was made. In certain cases, reversibility, smoothness and predictability (human-oriented concepts) are more important than optimal use of display space (a machine-oriented concept). In such a case, the trade-off is straightforward and an unoptimized design rule should be used. Other trade-offs are less straightforward. Norman (1983b) has tried to model trade-offs with mathematical functions. No usable methods resulted, but the examples are valuable. Difficult trade-offs include:

- adequate menu detail versus a fast response time,
- adequate menu detail versus adequate work space,
- ease of learning versus speed of execution.

Unlike the scrolling list example, the trade-offs here are not clear-cut. Optimization is a function of user preference. Expert users will trade the characteristics on the left-hand side of each pair listed above for those on the right.

Key points

- Principles are high level and widely applicable; design rules are low level instructions.
- Principles must be interpreted and applied in relation to the particular application.
- Guidelines may be based on psychological theory or on practical experience.
- Published guidelines can be found in journals, house style guides and general handbooks.
- Trade-offs often have to be taken into account and conflicts between guidelines need to be resolved by taking account of the context of the application.

Further reading

GAINES B.R. and SHAW M.L.G (1984). *The Art of Computer Conversation: a New Medium for Communication*. Englewood Cliffs, NJ: Prentice-Hall.
Provides an easy-to-read exposition of a number of guidelines, expressed in the form of those in Box 24.1.

GRUDIN J. (1989). The case against user interface consistency. *Comm. ACM*, **32**(10), 1164–73.
This article discusses consistency and provides examples of when consistency may not necessarily be a good thing. The article is interesting reading and thought-provoking.

MAGUIRE M.C. (1990). A review of human factors guidelines and techniques for the design of graphical human–computer interfaces. In *Human–Computer Interaction: Selected Readings* (PREECE J. and KELLER L., eds), pp. 161–84. Hemel Hempstead: Prentice-Hall.
This article discusses guidelines in relation to the design of graphical user interfaces, and argues for the need for guidance.

SHNEIDERMAN B. (1992). *Designing the User Interface: Strategies for Effective Human–Computer Interaction*, 2nd edn. Reading, MA: Addison-Wesley.
Chapter 1 contains a useful annotated list of both specific and general guidelines. Chapter 13 lists a number of guidelines.

25

Standards and Metrics

Aims and objectives

The aim of this chapter is to discuss the role of standards and to introduce you to various kinds of standards. After studying this chapter you should be able to:

- understand the importance of standards,
- discuss the main standards activities in the interface design domain,
- appreciate the significance of house style guides,
- discuss interface metrics and their use.

Overview

Standards concern prescribed ways of discussing, presenting or doing something, which seek to achieve consistency across products of the same type. We are familiar with standards in many walks of life – standard colours for electrical wiring, standard controls on cars, standard shoe and clothing sizes. In Britain, a 'kitemark' appears on products to inform potential buyers that the item in question conforms to a known standard. In many situations this quest for consistency is also related to safety and quality. As yet, there is no comprehensive set of standards for software, but standards are being used and developed for particular aspects of hardware and software design.

25.1 Standards and standardization

Standards exist for most everyday items in our houses. We have standard brick sizes and food labels, standard arrangements for telephones and typewriter keyboards, safety standards for electric kettles and gas ovens, and so on. Standardization generally makes people's lives easier and safer.

Question 25.1

(a)   If you were used to driving a car with the gear stick in the floor and you moved to one where the gear stick was on the steering column, do you think you would find it easier or more difficult to drive?

(b)   The position of foot pedals in cars is standardized: the clutch is on the left, the brake is in the middle and the accelerator is on the right. What would the safety implications be if a car were developed in which the brake and accelerator were in different positions?

In Britain, the first standards committee was set up in 1901 by Sir John Wolfe Barry, a past president of the Institution of Civil Engineers. It was formed as a result of a paper about standardization given to the British Iron Trade Association regarding the many different screw and metal girder sizes. This committee produced agreed recommended sizes of structural steel sections and tramway lines, which led to a saving of £1 million a year. Consequently, the demand for standards mushroomed. Nowadays, proposals for national or international standards still come mainly from industry, although government, consumers and many others also ask for them. Such requests can be prompted by new materials or products, an identified need for safety improvements, government legislation, or any other incident that signals the need for a change in practice, as Box 25.1 shows.

EXERCISE

If you were buying an item such as an electric fire, a cuddly toy or a squash racquet would you be influenced by whether it conformed to the relevant standard or not? Why?

COMMENT

On the whole, standards are about quality. Most people would choose to buy a product that conforms to the relevant standard, all other things being equal. In this way, a potential buyer is assured that the product reaches a certain level of safety, durability and fitness-for-purpose. In other words, it means that it is unnecessary for the customer to test the strength of a hammer, or to throw a plastic toy on the floor to see if it breaks. Standards are a way of reassuring the customer that the product reaches a certain level of quality. It should be stressed, however, that anyone may claim to have conformed to a public standard, but this does not mean that this is confirmed by independent tests. Also, the standard itself may represent only a minimum level of quality.

Box 25.1   Requests for standards come from various sources

During the late 1960s, a disaster in Canning Town, London, led to a review of standards in the construction industry. One corner of a high-rise block of flats, which had been constructed from blocks of concrete, collapsed following a gas explosion on one of the upper floors. Although there were many reasons why this failure occurred, it was realized that a formal standard for this type of construction, which was new at the time, was needed. This standard now states that the structure must be capable of withstanding the removal of a certain proportion of it.

25.2   Software standards

Quality in software is very important. In the past, poor quality software has been implicated in disasters in the worlds of finance, clinical care, air transport and nuclear power. Remember the excerpts in Chapter 1 from Lee's (1992) book, *The Day the Phones Stopped*?

EXERCISE

Can you think of any recent events in which software failure has been implicated?

COMMENT

Events for which software has been blamed include:

- excessive and unwanted share dealing on the world's stock markets,
- errors in the dosages given to patients receiving radiation therapy,
- erratic behaviour of military and civil aircraft,
- difficulties in controlling nuclear power plants during some system failures,
- delays in despatching ambulances to accidents, resulting in the loss of life.

Standards are developed and promoted by a number of different organizations for a number of different reasons. National and international organizations are the most prominent. There are two major international standards bodies: the International Organization for Standardization (ISO) and the International Electrotechnical Commission (IEC). The first covers the field of mechanical standardization, and the second is responsible for standards in the field of electrical standardization. Because computing straddles both camps, they have formed a joint committee to deal with standards in the field of information technology (JTC1). The international standard series ISO 9000 is concerned with general software quality (the British version is BS 5750; the European equivalent is EN29000; the American equivalent is ANSI/ASQC Q90–94). The main standard relevant to HCI design is ISO standard 9241, discussed in Section 25.3. ISO works closely with national standards bodies such as the American National Standards Institute (ANSI) and British Standards Institution (BSI). CEN (Comité européen de normalisation) is the European equivalent of ISO. European standards supersede any national standards in member states that cover the same field. Eventually, therefore, it may be that Europe-wide standards will replace all national standards. This would have a strong impact on trade across Europe.

Standards are drafted by technical committees whose members are nominated by manufacturers, trade and research associations, professional bodies, central and local government, academic bodies, and user and consumer groups. The work is entirely voluntary. At international level, interested countries nominate individuals to take part in the various committees, and to vote on the country's behalf. Ensuring consistency across national boundaries is very important for international trade. In terms of marketing, the producer and the consumer will be more confident about a product if a standard that is recognized by both parties can be used to confirm the product's quality. At the fairly simple level of terminology, consistent definitions can be facilitating.

Other bodies that produce different forms of standard are:

- Governments. The UK's Ministry of Defence (MoD) has produced a variety of standards. For example, all software development commissioned by the MoD must conform to defence standards 00-55 and 00-56, which are concerned with safety-critical systems. In the US, industry standards are developed by many non-government organizations, but the Government OSI Profile (GOSIP) initiative mandates that procurements must conform to the Open Systems Interconnection (OSI) standard.

- Professional bodies such as the British Computer Society (BCS) and the Institute of Electrical and Electronics Engineers (IEEE) also develop and promote standards.
- Industry standards help with transferring knowledge from one system to another and in providing a common identity. For example, the software development company Microsoft uses standard command keys on all of its products.
- *De facto* standards exist. For example, the qwerty keyboard is the standard English-language keyboard layout, but it evolved because of the mechanical limitations of early typewriters. Once a *de facto* standard has evolved and been widely adopted, it is usually too late to change it easily. Industry standards often become *de facto* standards which may subsequently become national or international standards.
- House standards, that is, house style guides, are important in industry, particularly in large organizations where commonality can be vital. House standards apply to diagram notation, documentation style, programming methods and so on. We shall return to house style guides in Section 25.4.

Standards are there to help produce good software. However, just as guidelines can constrain the designer, standards can also curb a designer's creativity. After all, standards are guidelines that have become formalized because they are recognized as being sufficiently important and widely relevant. Constraints that are placed on designers are usually done so for good reasons: to ensure safety, to maintain good interface standards, to ensure compatibility and so on.

Question 25.2

What advantage could a large organization perceive in constraining the creativity of its designers? After all, designers are employed to design.

25.3 | HCI standards

The first section of this chapter explained why standardization is generally useful, and why it is sometimes vital. Standards have been produced for many areas of the computer industry: paper sizes, transmission protocols, compilers, character set representations, language definitions and so on. New standards are being developed all the time, as different needs are identified, or problems occur. The publishing of interface standards started only recently, although they have been a concern for several years.

EXERCISE

Why, do you think, it is important to produce standards for interface design?

COMMENT

Standardization in interface design can provide the benefits discussed above, but in addition, it provides the following:

- A common terminology. For example, standard measures of usability or performance mean that designers and users know that they are discussing the same concept. All systems of the same type can be subjected to a standard benchmark that facilitates comparisons.
- Maintainability and evolvability. Standard implementation techniques facilitate program maintenance because all programs can be expected to have a shared style and structure. Additional facilities can be added to a system if its external interfaces are of a standard form.
- A common identity. An in-house or industry standard for display style or screen layout ensures that all systems have the same 'look and feel' and are easily recognizable.
- Reduction in training. Knowledge can be transferred more easily from one system to another if standard command keys and other interaction techniques are adopted.
- Health and safety. Users are less likely to be surprised by unexpected system behaviour if standard controls and warnings are used. Unfriendly systems can be a source of stress.

The most obvious items that standards could address are the interfaces of specific products.

EXERCISE

List some specific examples of hardware and software commonly in use in office environments.

COMMENT

Examples of hardware are: keyboards, display screens, furniture; examples of software are operating systems, word processors and on-line help facilities.

One of the criticisms levelled at early work on HCI standards was that they were based on product characteristics which were not transferrable to the rapidly changing technology. For instance, if standards for interface design had been developed and agreed before WIMP interfaces appeared, we might never have seen the emergence of a mouse since standards might have precluded their development. Moves are now being made to base standards on usability and performance issues instead of product characteristics, so that they are more generally applicable. However, it is considerably harder to pin down these issues in a suitable form so that they can be measured and checked against the standards required.

User performance measures could include speed, accuracy and the avoidance of discomfort, but how exactly can 'discomfort' be measured? We are beginning to understand something about what is an easy interface to use or what is an aesthetically unpleasing display, but when it comes to specifying precisely how easy or how appealing an interface should be, it is not so easy. The problem with HCI standards is that they have to deal with the multiplicity of human characteristics. There are certain limitations that are applicable to most humans, such as a minimum and maximum hand span, but human capabilities and expectations vary considerably, and expectations and capabilities will continue to change as more and different technology becomes part of our everyday lives.

Question 25.3

What kind of user performance could be measured?

The following two subsections discuss the kinds of issues that are being addressed.

ISO 9241

ISO 9241 addresses the ergonomics requirements for work with Visual Display Terminals (VDTs), both hardware and software. Office tasks including text and data processing are covered by ISO 9241, but CAD and industrial process control tasks are not. Industrial process control is covered by ISO 11064. Issues covered by ISO 9241 include: workstation layout and postural requirements, human–computer dialogue, software aspects of display design, keyboard requirements and user guidance. In recognition of the fact that many problems attributed to poor equipment design stem, in fact, from poor job design, part of the standard provides guidance on the design of VDU tasks.

A full list of all the parts covered by this standard is given in Table 25.1. Part 14, for example, covers menu dialogues.

> 'Interface design depends upon the task, the user, the environment, and the available technology. Consequently, this part of the standard cannot be applied without a knowledge of the design and use context of the interface and it is not intended to be used as a prescriptive set of rules to be applied in their entirety.'
>
> (ISO 9241, Part 14 (Draft International Standard))

Table 25.1 Ergonomic requirements for office work with VDTs (ISO 9241).

Part 1	General introduction
Part 2	Guidance on task requirements
Part 3	Visual display requirements
Part 4	Keyboard requirements
Part 5	Workstation layout and postural requirements
Part 6	Environmental requirements
Part 7	Display requirements with reflections
Part 8	Requirements for displayed colours
Part 9	Requirements for non-keyboard input devices
Part 10	Dialogue principles
Part 11	Guidance on usability specification and measures
Part 12	Presentation of information
Part 13	User guidance
Part 14	Menu dialogues
Part 15	Command dialogues
Part 16	Direct manipulation dialogues
Part 17	Form-filling dialogues

EXERCISE

Most non-trivial systems contain too many options for them all to be included in one single menu; therefore a menu structure must be designed. There are three main aspects to designing a menu structure.

Consider a drawing system in which all actions apart from text input must be performed via menus, that is, there is no palette or icons. The commands needed in the system are: start new drawing, open existing drawing, close file, draw straight line, draw a circle, draw a square, delete object, input text, change typeface of text, change justification of text, duplicate object and paste object.

Define a menu structure for this system. You do not need to consider the presentation of options, that is whether an option should be ticked when activated, or whether boxes should be used to indicate choice and so on, and your only constraint is that the maximum number of options allowed per menu is five.

Using this example, identify three design issues that must be considered when designing a menu structure.

COMMENT

To design the menu structure, you need to consider how many menus to use, that is, the overall structure; which options should go in which menus, that is, the options' grouping; and the ordering or sequencing of the options within each menu. These three aspects are covered in ISO 9241.

For example, the following excerpt from Part 14 (Draft International Standard) of ISO 9241 addresses an element of the overall structure:

> '3.1   Structuring into levels and menus (overall structure)
>
> Menu structures should reflect user expectations and facilitate the user's ability to find and to select menu options relevant for the task. In order to increase the probability of meeting this objective, the following conditional requirements and recommendations shall be evaluated . . .
>
> 3.1.1   Conventional categories
> If options can be arranged into conventional or natural groups known to the users, options shall be organized into levels and menus consistent with that order.
>
> | | |
> |---|---|
> | Example: | Grouping foods into meats, vegetables, fruits. |
> | Dialogue principle: | User expectations. |
> | Conformance: | applicability – documented evidence, analytical evaluation or empirical evaluation compliance – observation' |
>
> Notice that the standard gives examples to clarify the intention of the recommendation, and it also refers to a set of dialogue principles. These principles are in Part 10 of the standard, and are high level principles which apply to the design of dialogues between humans and information systems. Other categories covered under this section are logical groupings, where options have no conventional categories, but they can be grouped in a manner that is unambiguous and easily learned, and arbitrary categories, where options do not have a logical or conventional category grouping.

Question 25.4

What kind of guidance do you think might be given for structuring an arbitrary collection of options?

Part 14 also includes a suggested process for applying the standard, and some documentation which could be used in that process.

EC Council Directive

The Council Directive from the European Community issued on 29 May 1990 addresses the minimum safety and health requirements for work with display screen equipment. It is not a standard as such, but its impact on HCI design practice and standards of the future is quite high. Directives from the EC are part of their legislative action and are binding for member states as regards the result to be achieved. However, it is left to national authorities to determine the methods for achieving these results. It therefore says nothing about penalties and enforcement. The technical annexe to the EC directive contains a number of very general minimum requirements which apply to both the workstation and the task of the user. These points include the following:

'Display screen
- well-defined clear characters
- stable flicker-free image
- adjustable brightness and/or contrast
- easy swivel/tilt
- free of glare and reflections

Keyboard
- tiltable and separate from display
- space in front to support arms and hands
- non-reflective surfaces
- "adequately contrasted symbols"
- ...

Operator/computer interface
- easy to use
- adapted to users' level of knowledge
- no checking of user performance without their knowledge
- system to provide feedback to user
- information to be displayed in format and at pace adapted to operator
- the principles of software ergonomics shall be applied in particular to human data processing'

Question 25.5

Would you classify the above operator/computer interface guidelines as principles or rules? You may wish to refer to Chapter 24.

The Directive obliges employers to keep themselves informed of scientific findings concerning workstation design and stresses that the ergonomic aspects are of particular importance for a workstation with display screen equipment. Interestingly, the Directive only covers employees of the organization, so, for example, temporary self-employed users of a system are exempt. In the UK, this anomaly has been picked up by the Health and Safety Executive Regulations, which include regulations for temporary and self-employed labour. The directive does not apply to the following:

- drivers' cabs or control cabs for vehicles or machinery,
- computer systems on board a means of transport,
- computer systems mainly intended for public use,
- 'portable' systems not in prolonged use at a workstation,
- calculators, cash registers and any equipment having a small data or measurement display required for direct use of the equipment,
- typewriters of traditional design, of the type known as 'typewriter with window'.

The majority of these exemptions are due to lobbying by interested parties.

Question 25.6

What reason might be given for the Directive not covering systems mainly intended for public use?

Employers' obligations include:

- VDU health and safety in the workplace must be evaluated, especially with regard to eyesight, physical problems and mental stress,
- workstations put into service after 31 December 1992 must meet the minimum requirements in the technical annexe,
- workstations already in service on 31 December 1992 must be made to comply within four years, that is, by 31 December 1996,
- worker activities must be planned in such a way that work on the display screen is periodically interrupted by breaks or by changes of activity.

25.4 House style guides

The importance of consistency has been mentioned a number of times. Consistent interfaces can aid usability considerably.

Question 25.7

What problems can be caused by inconsistent interfaces?

One way to ensure consistency across different parts of a system, or across a family of systems, is for the developers to base their designs on one set of principles and rules. It is therefore advantageous for organizations that develop software to produce sets of guidelines for their own developers to follow. These collections are called house style guides, and vary in detail, spirit and intent between companies. There are two main kinds of **style guides**: commercial style guides produced by hardware and software manufacturers, and corporate style guides produced by companies for their own internal use. Obviously, the main advantage of using these guides is that usability can be enhanced through consistency, but there are other reasons. Software developed for Apple Macintosh or IBM PC, for example, maintains its 'look and feel' across several product lines. Users of these systems will then feel comfortable with all the packages running on that platform which, in turn, leads to product loyalty. Although style guides have traditionally been in book form, some organizations are providing a 'soft', interactive version so that third party developers can actually see the styles.

Commercial style guides

Although commercial guides often contain some high level design principles, the majority of the document is usually taken up with low level design rules, which have been developed from those principles. Example sections from each of three commercial guides are shown in Figures 25.1–25.3. These extracts were chosen to give you a flavour of the kinds of guidelines that these books contain. To provide a deep understanding of any one of these would require many more pages than this book contains: IBM's *Common User Access Guide to User Interface Design* (1991) has over 600 pages; Apple's *Inside Macintosh*, Vol. V, also has over 600 pages.

Although it is not possible to illustrate in a book the distinctive 'feel' that a family of applications developed for certain platforms has, the distinctive 'look' of these systems can be illustrated by examining elements of systems designed to conform to

> Searching a remote database, transferring data to the workstation, generating a report, or performing the steps necessary to ensure data integrity could take several minutes. The CUA guidelines recommend displaying a progress indicator whenever the time needed to complete an action exceeds five seconds.

Figure 25.1 An extract from IBM's *Common User Access Guide to User Interface Design* (reproduced courtesy of IBM Corporation).

> In general, the only use of color in menus should be in menus used to choose colors. However, color could be useful for directing the user's choices in training and tutorial materials: one color can lead the user through a lesson.

Figure 25.2 An extract from Apple's *Inside Macintosh*, Vol. V (1985: © Apple Computer, Inc.).

> When data is selected, it appears highlighted. The appearance of highlighted text depends on the abilities of the system and the display. On monochrome displays, reverse video should be used to indicate selected data. On gray-scale displays, the selection should be marked with a shade of gray. On color displays a highlight color should be used. Graphics may be highlighted in these same ways or by the addition of rectangles with resizing handles; these two methods may also be combined.

Figure 25.3 An extract from Microsoft's *The Windows Interface: An Application Design Guide* (reproduced courtesy of Microsoft Press).

two different style guides. The series of pictures in Figure 25.4 shows a sample of screens from the PC version of the Word word processing system, developed using Microsoft's style guide. The screens in Figure 25.5 show the corresponding screens in the Apple Macintosh version of Word, developed using the guidelines in *Inside Macintosh*. Although they look very similar, and indeed contain more or less the same information, you can see that there are distinct differences in style.

EXERCISE

Look at Figures 25.4(a–c) and 25.5(a–c). List at least five differences you can see.

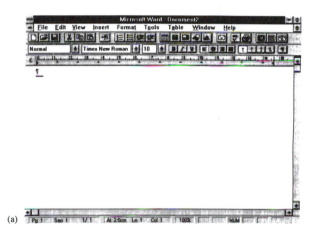

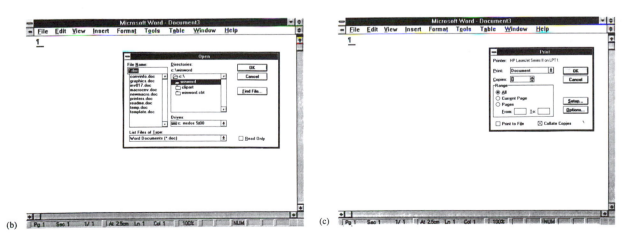

Figure 25.4 Screens from the PC version of Word (courtesy of Microsoft Corporation).

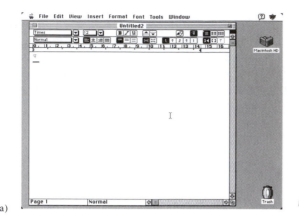

(a)

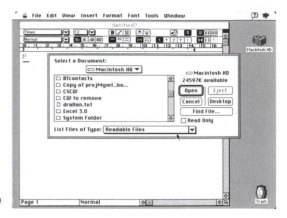

(b)

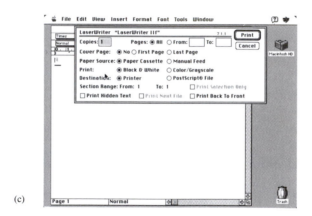

(c)

Figure 25.5 Screens from the Apple Macintosh version of Word (courtesy of Microsoft Corporation and Apple Computer UK Ltd).

COMMENT

The following are some of the points you may have noticed:

- There are different menus across the top of the screen.
- There are different title bars: different in both content and design.
- The icons for enlarging and shrinking the windows are different: on the PC version, there are arrows in the top-right corner, while the Mac version has a 'box' icon.

- The icon in the top-left hand corner for closing a document is an open box in the Mac version, but a box with a bar in the middle on the PC version.
- The size and shape of the buttons is different.
- The way in which a button is highlighted is different: the PC version has a darker outline, while the Mac version has a double outline.
- In the Print dialogue box for the PC version there are more options 'hidden' in further submenus (Setup, Options), while the Mac version has all the information in one box.

Some of these points may seem very minor, but every element of the interface helps to create that particular look which is the Apple look or the Microsoft look. Other elements that distinguish the two include different icons and messages, as shown in Figure 25.6.

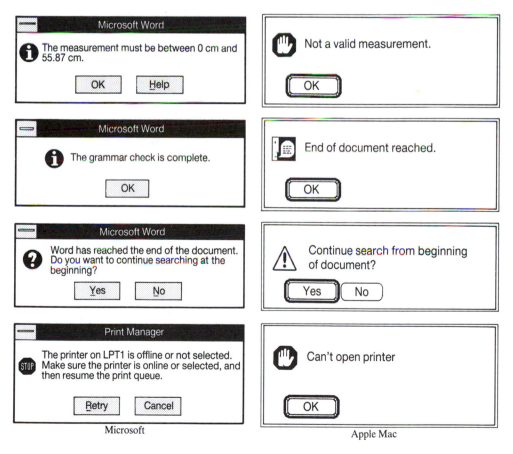

Figure 25.6 Corresponding screen elements from Microsoft and Apple Macintosh (courtesy of Microsoft Corporation and Apple Computer UK Ltd).

EXERCISE

What is the main difference between the Microsoft messages and the Apple Macintosh versions?

COMMENT

The Microsoft messages offer more information than the Apple Macintosh versions. For example, the first box was displayed when the top document margin was changed to −450cm (clearly a ridiculous measure!). The Microsoft message actually says what the legal measurements are; the Apple Macintosh merely says that the measure is invalid.

Corporate style guides

If an organization wishes to develop its own corporate style for software, the chances are that the starting point will be one of the commercial style guides, such as those introduced above. However, many questions have to be addressed when developing such a guide, which are not answered by the commercial guides. For instance, how should optional and mandatory input fields be distinguished? How should dialogue boxes be organized? The first point to consider is what constitutes 'style', that is, what elements have to be addressed in order to begin to produce a coherent image. We have already discussed the role of commercial style guides in providing a distinctive 'look and feel', but for an organization to develop its own style, any commercial style guide it chooses needs to be augmented with further details concerning the style's use. The following exercise is intended to give you an insight into the meaning of 'style'. It is derived from a well-known case study, which you may like to refer to at a later stage (Arent *et al.*, 1989).

EXERCISE

Produce a sketch screen design conforming to the specification given below. Assume that the system will be implemented using a PC-style interface, that is, the detailed designs of screen items such as buttons and error messages are predetermined. Identify two major issues, apart from screen layout, which need to be considered.

The system displays a map of the world. On receiving the name of a city from the user, the system must identify the location of that city on the map. Only one screen is needed in the system; it must display the map, and provide suitable mechanisms for obtaining the name of the city and displaying the city's location.

COMMENT

The point of the exercise was to identify the two major issues that you needed to consider: what input mechanism should be used to obtain the name of the city from the user, and how should its location be displayed on the map. For the former, we decided to allow a simple text input field, but alternatives may have included an alphabetical list of cities known to the system. For the latter issue, we decided to use a coloured shape, but an alternative would have been to use a flashing light.

Thus, the three main elements of style which must be considered when developing a corporate style guide are:

(1) Which commercial style should be used?
(2) Which elements of the commercial style should be used for which purpose; for example, when should a button be used, when a slider, when a check box and so on?
(3) How should colour, graphics or other overlays be used?

25.5 | Metrics

If standards are going to be meaningful, we must have a way of expressing fairly precisely the quality level we expect, and a way of measuring the system's performance against the standards laid down. Informal measurement is better than no measurement, but being able to measure something numerically is a great advantage. When addressing the Institution of Civil Engineers in 1883, Lord Kelvin expressed this point well: 'I often say that when you can measure what you are speaking about, and express it in numbers, you know something about it; but when you cannot express it in numbers, your knowledge is of a meager and unsatisfactory kind' (quoted in DeMarco, 1982).

Numerical measures of the products and processes of software development are called software **metrics**. Within the overall software project, there are many kinds of metrics that may be useful: metrics for the functional complexity of a system, metrics for the inter-module and intra-module connectivity of a system, metrics for the amount of effort required to develop a system and so on. Obviously, the interface of a system is part of that overall development, and code which makes up the interface and determines the form of the human–computer interaction should have metrics like the rest of the system.

Once something can be measured numerically, you move away from the world of opinion and intuition – 'I like using this interface but I don't know why' – to a precise world of facts and figures – 'It took me 5 minutes longer to perform the task using the old system than it does using this new one'. However, we should issue a word of warning: figures can be misleading if not interpreted properly, or if the wrong measurements are taken. In Part VI we will discuss the value of qualitative assessments as well as quantitative ones. Even if the correct measures are taken, they can still be misleading if interpreted incorrectly (an interesting account of this is given in Huff's *How to Lie with Statistics*, 1973).

EXERCISE

Consider each of the following statements, which could be given in response to a question regarding the usability of an interface:

(a)   When using this system, I am 60% more efficient than I was with the old one.
(b)   Using this interface, I have processed 26 more transactions today than my colleague who doesn't have this interface.
(c)   I have been working with this interface for two weeks and I have processed an average of 10 transactions fewer a day.

Which of the above statements tells you most about the quality of the system's interface?

COMMENT

Answer (a) certainly sounds impressive, but what does the user mean by saying that they are 60% more efficient? In simple terms, efficiency in engineering has been stated as the ratio of useful work performed to the total energy expended. To the user, energy expended may be measured in terms of time taken, or the effort required. To the organization, energy expended would probably include other elements such as the labour costs of the user's time, the cost of training, and the cost of the resources used. Efficiency is in the eye of the beholder!

Answer (b) provides more concrete information, since it refers to the number of transactions being processed, and there is a comparison with another worker. However, comparisons are very dangerous. It refers only to one day, and it gives no information about the colleague. Many factors may influence a person's performance on a particular day: tiredness, concentration level, humidity. The user's colleague may be more or less experienced, she may be in a different room, they may be handling different transactions and so on.

Although the third answer may not be giving you the message you want to hear (this interface appears to make the user less efficient!), it nevertheless gives accurate information regarding performance. However, nothing is said about the quality of the work produced. Despite the fact that 10 transactions per day were 'lost', it may be that those that were processed were dealt with more thoroughly.

Before choosing the specific measure, however, it is important to consider what you want to measure and why.

Question 25.8

What might the following measures give you information about?

(a) The number of times on-line help screens are accessed during a session.
(b) The time it takes to access the correct specific record from a database.
(c) The number of employees smiling on Monday morning.

People are keenly affected by their surroundings, both physically and mentally, so it is important to make sure that measurement takes place in a context that is as close as possible to the target environment. Some of these issues are considered further in Part VI. Various kinds of metrics can be devised to measure the design at different stages of development; these include: analytic, performance and psychometrics. Analytic metrics are generally applicable when only a paper-based product specification is available. A well-known example is the keystroke level model, which is discussed in Section 33.4. There are many different performance-related measures that can be taken: how long it takes to modify a sentence, how many errors are made in an hour, how many times the mouse button is clicked to open a file, how many cups of coffee the user drinks in a day, and so on. These kinds of measures are at the heart of usability engineering, which is discussed in Section 31.2, and when systematically recorded in a usability specification they provide designers with information about acceptable levels of usability. There are four main kinds of **performance metrics**: duration measures, count measures, proportion of task completed, and quality of output:

- Duration metrics measure how much time is spent doing a particular thing, for example, how much time is spent looking at on-line help screens.
- Count measures simply count how many times an event happens, or how many discrete activities are performed, for example, how many errors are made.
- It is not easy to measure how much of a task has been completed; however it can be achieved by carefully setting the task goals, and then counting how many have been completed after a certain time. The final result could be expressed as a numerical percentage of the original task goals.
- Again, it is not easy to provide an absolute measure of quality, although it is usually not difficult to identify good or bad quality output.

Box 25.2 contains an example of the use of a performance metric.

EXERCISE

In an evaluation task to measure the usability of a drawing package, a user is asked to replicate a figure that is supplied on paper. Suggest task goals that could be used in this case to measure the proportion of the task completed after an hour.

How might quality be measured?

COMMENT

The goals would include successful replication of each of the features in the original diagram, and successful replication of their relative positions. The final decision on the number of goals achieved may need to rest with an independent assessor.

The quality metric could probably only be obtained by independent subjective evaluation.

Box 25.2 Example use of a performance metric

In an evaluation (Rengger *et al.*, 1993) to measure the usability of a multimedia holiday information system used by the general public in travel agencies, a task requiring a user to identify all the hotels in the database with specified characteristics (such as in a particular country, within a particular price range and with a swimming pool) was chosen. As only four hotels in the database were known to possess all the stated characteristics, the goals of the task were for the user to identify these four hotels. The users were asked to write down on paper the names of the hotels they identified, so this was the tangible output.

The proportion of task completed was measured as the percentage of the four hotels appearing in the user's list, the presence of any one of the four representing 25% of the goals being achieved.

Psychometrics can only be applied once an operational prototype has been built, towards the end of design. Users complete questionnaires designed to ascertain their attitude to the system after using it for a number of hours. These measures include control, helpfulness, likeability, learnability and efficiency. For example, one internationally standardized questionnaire, called SUMI (Porteous, Kirakowski and Corbett, 1993), gives a global usability figure and then readings on five subscales:

(1) **Efficiency** refers to the user's feeling that the software is enabling the task(s) to be performed in a quick, effective and economical manner or is hindering performance.
(2) **Affect** refers to whether the user feels good, warm, happy or disgruntled when using the system.
(3) **Helpfulness** refers to the user's perception that the software communicates in a helpful way and assists in the resolution of operational problems.

(4) **Control**   refers to the user's feeling that the software is responding in a normal and consistent way to commands and input.

(5) **Learnability**   refers to whether users find the software easy to learn, and the documentation easy to use.

There are 50 questions on the SUMI questionnaire, each of which is answered with 'agree', 'undecided' or 'disagree'. The following sample shows the kind of questions that are asked:

(1)   This software responds too slowly to inputs.
(2)   I would recommend this software to my colleagues.
(3)   The instructions and prompts are helpful.
(11)   I sometimes wonder if I am using the right command.
(12)   Working with this software is satisfactory.
(13)   The way that system information is presented is clear and understandable.
(21)   I think this software is inconsistent.
(22)   I would not like to use this software every day.
(23)   I can understand and act on the information provided by this software.

At least ten users should complete the questionnaire if the results are to be significant. In addition, the questionnaire provides an 'item consensual analysis', which is 'an indication of those SUMI items on which the software being assessed differs significantly from the standardization sample data'. The method for determining these measures is too detailed for this book. Further detail can be found in Porteous, Kirakowski and Corbett (1993).

Key points

- Standardization generally makes people's lives easier and safer.
- Standardization is beneficial for trade.
- A key aspect to standardization is quality assurance.
- The main international standards organizations are ISO and IEC.
- Other organizations that produce standards are governments, professional bodies and companies (house style guides).
- HCI standards are important, but difficult to pin down because human beings vary in a number of ways.
- ISO 9241 addresses the ergonomics requirements for work with visual display terminals.
- The Council Directive from the EC addresses the minimum safety and health requirements for work with display screen equipment.
- The EC Directive is a legal requirement; standards are not a legal requirement unless they are specifically quoted in legislation.
- House style guides are used to maintain consistency across a family of products.

- Metrics can be misinterpreted and misused. It is important to be clear about what is being measured and why.
- Analytic metrics can be taken at an early stage in design and are based on design notation.
- Performance metrics can only be taken once a working prototype is available. They measure a user's performance.
- Psychometrics are based on questionnaires used to assess the user's view of the amount of effort needed to complete a task.

Further reading

EDELSTEIN D.V., FUJII R., GUERDAT C. and SULLO P. (1991). Internationalizing software engineering standards. *IEEE Computer*, **24**(3), 74–8.

SALAM A.G. (1989). The new rules for international standardization. *IEEE Standards Bearer*, **3**(5), 1.
Both of these articles provide detailed information on standards.

STEWART T. (1991). *Directory of HCI Standards*. London: DTI.
This provides a comprehensive view of the need for HCI standards, and how they can be used. It also includes a list of relevant standards bodies and working groups.

26

Design Rationale

Aims and objectives

It is important to record design decisions so that they may be reviewed at future meetings. After studying this chapter you should be able to:

- critique the support available for communicating and recording design decisions,
- discuss the importance of properly exploring and then recording design decisions.

Overview

Communicating and recording the decisions made during the course of producing a design is useful and important for a number of different people. Traditionally, system documentation is the main method of communicating about a software system between the relevant parties: developer to customer, analyst to designer, resigning design team member to new member, and so on. Unfortunately, it is common for documentation to be inadequate: 'Most programmers regard documentation as a necessary evil, written as an afterthought only because some bureaucrat requires it. They

523

do not expect it to be useful. This is a self-fulfilling prophecy' (Parnas and Clements, 1986).

Parnas and Clements (1986) go on to say that often documentation is incomplete and inconsistent, poorly organized, written in boring prose and uses confusing and inconsistent terminology. These comments were written in the context of an appeal for the rational recording of design decisions, as the system is developed. Although this is bound to be a time-consuming process, and one which may seem unimportant at the time, the lack of such a record can cause even more time to be wasted and can be frustrating.

Many people involved with software need to know the reasoning or rationale behind the design of that software. For many years, the issue of documentation has been one of the focal points for software engineering. It is clearly important for the maintainers of a system to have access to a coherent description of its structure and purpose, but there are others who also benefit from understanding as much as possible about the product and why it is the way it is; for example, software maintainers, trainers and marketing personnel. If new staff join the development team they need to understand why certain design decisions have been made. Design team members themselves will benefit from an explicit representation of the design's rationale while it is being developed. End users, too, may benefit from understanding how the system is constructed. A further possible advantage of having a design and its decisions recorded is that this could facilitate reuse.

Question 26.1

Why might the lack of good documentation which records design decisions be frustrating and time-wasting?

EXERCISE

Why is it helpful for software maintainers, trainers and marketing personnel to understand the rationale of a system? Suggest one reason for each category.

COMMENT

It is fairly clear that software maintainers need to understand why the design is the way it is so that when modifications have to be made they know how the system can be changed without disrupting its overall stability.

> Marketing personnel need to sell the system to potential customers. In the course of this, they are likely to be asked why the system does certain things, and why it doesn't do other things. Understanding the rationale for the system's design would help them to answer these questions appropriately. They are unlikely to use a record of the detailed design decisions, but a higher level understanding about the system would help.
>
> People training end users should understand why certain functions behave the way they do so that they can help the end users to build a suitable understanding of the system.

Of course, if every design decision and every blind alley were documented in detail, the documentation would quickly become unwieldy. It is therefore only practical to document key decisions in detail, or decisions that were particularly contentious or difficult to make or where an exploration of alternatives is important.

One of the main questions associated with design rationale is how to document it. One could imagine producing a table of some sort, with maybe a date, alternatives considered, reasons for choosing one solution over the others and so on. This would be one step better than narrative text, which in turn is one step better than a transcript of the meeting or meetings at which the decisions were made. However, none of these ways would make the information particularly accessible. Imagine, for example, trying to identify the reasons for a decision made at the beginning of the project during its maintenance phase. If information was categorized by date, you might have an idea of where to find it, but many decisions are made at the beginning of a project, and it could take a long time to find the specific point you need.

We cannot present all approaches that have been developed for documenting design rationale, but we describe three of the more significant: IBIS, Design Space Analysis and Claims Analysis. The first is an early documentation technique that led to the development of many others; the second actively encourages designers to explore alternatives and results in a documented account of the alternatives considered and the reasons for choosing the final design; and the third concentrates on analysing and refining an existing design.

26.1 IBIS

IBIS (Issue-Based Information Systems) (Kuntz and Rittel, 1970) is a technique which was devised in order to capture design decisions as the design progressed; that is, it was to be a by-product of the design process itself. The central activity of IBIS is deliberation, that is, considering the pros and cons of alternative answers to questions. The questions are called *issues*, the answers are called *positions* and the pros and cons are the *arguments* for or against the position. An IBIS discussion begins with a root issue, which is the main question to be addressed; for instance:

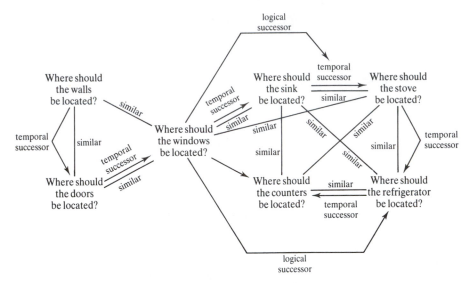

Figure 26.1 An example IBIS issue map (Fischer *et al.*, 1991).

what should this system do? Positions are put forward to answer this question, together with arguments for and against them. Secondary issues can be generated and deliberated in the same way, and these may lead to tertiary issues, and so on until a solution is reached. The issue deliberations are charted by producing a graphical diagram called an issue map, which illustrates the issues and their relationships. An example map is given in Figure 26.1. This shows a set of issues related to the design of a kitchen. As you can see, even this relatively simple problem yields a fairly complex network.

Question 26.2

List as many issues as possible from the issue map in Figure 26.1.

Various relationships between the issues were recognized in the original IBIS technique; these included 'more general than', 'similar to', 'replaces', 'temporal successor of', and 'logical successor of'. In Figure 26.1, only 'similar to' and 'temporal successor' are used. During the 1970s and 1980s, a number of projects tried to use IBIS. Each one failed because there were problems with the approach. Two main problems suggested were:

(1) Dependencies between issues were not catered for; that is, no account was taken of whether the answer to one question relied on the answer to another.
(2) Only questions which become issues, that is, which are deliberated, are represented on the issue map.

Question 26.3

Why should it be a problem if only those questions that become issues are documented?

A number of new versions of IBIS were developed. For example, PHI is a hypertext version of IBIS which takes account of the above aspects (see Box 26.1); gIBIS is a graphical hypertext tool for building IBIS networks.

IBIS broke important ground and was the precursor for other policy decision making recording techniques.

Box 26.1   Procedural Hierarchy of Issues: an enhanced version of IBIS

Procedural Hierarchy of Issues (PHI) (McCall, 1991) is a version of IBIS that addresses the main problems identified with the original method. It differs from IBIS in four main ways.

What constitutes an issue?

In IBIS, issues are only the design questions that are deliberated in any sense; that is, design decisions that are agreed without discussion do not become issues in an IBIS issue map. In PHI, however, all questions related to the design are regarded as issues, whether they are deliberated or not, and are documented as such.

How to relate issues

PHI introduces an element of hierarchy in its relationships, and deals only with two notions: which issues serve the current issue, and which issues does it serve? The serve relationship is defined as follows: issue A serves issue B if resolving A helps to resolve B.

How to resolve issues

Like IBIS, PHI uses deliberation to resolve issues, looking at the arguments for and against each proposed answer and deciding, on that basis, which answer to choose. However, PHI extends this idea with the notion of generality/specificity of answers. PHI also does away with the idea of categorizing arguments as being for or against possible answers, and simply thinks of them all as arguments.

How to raise issues

PHI is more restrictive than IBIS in the order in which issues can be raised. PHI has two rules for identifying issues:

(1) Generate the issue hierarchy in a top-down manner, starting with a Prime Issue and proceeding down a hierarchy of sub-issues until no more sub-issues can be identified.

(2) Perform sub-issue generation breadth first.

26.2 Design space analysis

Design can be viewed as an exploration of a space of alternatives (see Chapter 17 for alternative definitions). That is, there are a host of alternative designs that fulfil the system's specification, and the process of design involves identifying the one, or ones, that satisfy the system's constraints and goals as closely as possible. For example, having a scrolling window for a word processor fulfils the condition of allowing documents larger than the screen to be worked on, but exactly how that scrolling works may be influenced by other factors, such as the use of a mouse, the importance of avoiding screen clutter, speed and so on. In **design space analysis**, the designer is actively encouraged to explore alternative designs, so the final result is not just a detailed description of the 'whys' and 'wherefores' of a design, but also better quality designs since the designer will have explored many more alternatives.

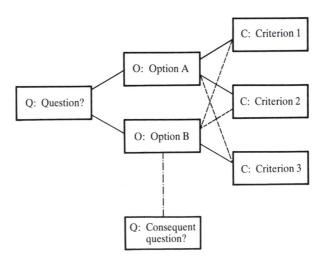

Figure 26.2 The components of the QOC notation (MacLean *et al.*, 1991).

A notation called **QOC** (Questions, Options and Criteria; MacLean *et al.*, 1991) can be used for this purpose. Figure 26.2 contains an example of this notation. Notice that options can be thought of as answers to questions, just as the IBIS notation considered questions and answers. However, the major difference between questions, options and criteria and issues, positions and arguments is that the issues and positions in IBIS are general purpose, whereas the questions and options in design space analysis are specifically for design. The questions addressed highlight important dimensions in the design space; they represent issues that must be considered. Criteria are positive goals, which are used to distinguish between the various options; they argue for or against the various alternatives. Unbroken lines indicate a positive relationship between the criteria and the option whereas dotted lines indicate a relatively negative relationship, that is, that the option is not supported by the criterion. In Figure 26.2, for example, criterion 3 argues against option A, while it argues for option B. Options may spawn new questions, which allow more detailed aspects of the design to be explored.

A fuller example is shown in Figure 26.3. This is concerned with the design of an UNDO facility in a multi-user text editor. The original specification for this facility is as follows:

> A team of designers is designing a multi-user text editor. They are considering two versions of how the UNDO facility should work:
>
> (1) Relative to the individual: individual users can UNDO only their own actions.
> (2) Relative to the document: actions can be undone regardless of who carried out the original action.

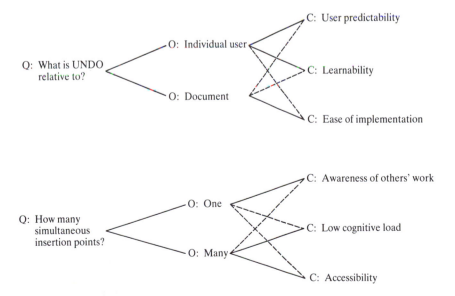

Figure 26.3 A design space analysis of the UNDO scenario (MacLean *et al.*, 1991).

The designers are also considering two versions of the software:

(A)   The first release will have a single insertion point, with control moving between the users by an explicit action.

(B)   The second release will have multiple insertion points, so that each user can make changes simultaneously.

Figure 26.3 represents the initial QOC diagram produced from this specification. In this case, the criteria were derived from principles identified by the design team early in design.

Question 26.4

Identify all of the criteria which do not support the second option in Figure 26.3: designing the undo to be relative to the document.

Although this notation aids in identifying alternative designs and clarifies the options, the criteria to be used and their relationships, it does not in itself identify the best option for you. Deciding which option should be chosen is not a simple matter of counting the positive links, counting the negative links, subtracting them for each option and then choosing the one with the highest score; other factors must be considered. Criteria have different weights or importance depending on the context and usage, and ultimately the skill of a designer is required to choose between options. For example, although the option 'one insertion point' is assessed negatively against the criterion 'low cognitive load', the importance of this varies with context. If there are only two or three users of the system, it does not weigh as heavily against it as if there were 20 or 30. In addition, it may be that awareness of others' work is rated very highly, and on this basis, the option of one insertion point may be chosen.

Representing the design space in this way, using the principles identified by the design team as criteria, can highlight how the different principles interact, indicate whether the principles are being applied consistently, and help to identify priorities between them. This in itself results in the designers examining their decisions very closely, so that the benefits of doing design space analysis are more than just producing design documentation.

EXERCISE

In the exercise on p. 33–4 we discussed the design of a bar code system in a supermarket. Two options for the position of the bar code reader were suggested: at the checkout or on the front of each trolley. Study the comment relating to this exercise and formulate the design question. List the two bar code reader options and suggest some criteria that can be used to choose between them.

Evaluate the options according to the criteria and draw a QOC diagram to represent the analysis.

Note that criteria should be stated as positive goals.

COMMENT

An appropriate question for this system would be: 'Where should the bar code reader be located?' Options would be: at the checkout, on the trolley.

Appropriate criteria should be: easy to use by customer, minimizes discomfort for checkout staff, minimizes customer delay, minimizes number of errors. There are many others, but we shall constrain our discussion to these four. Our QOC diagram is shown in Figure 26.4.

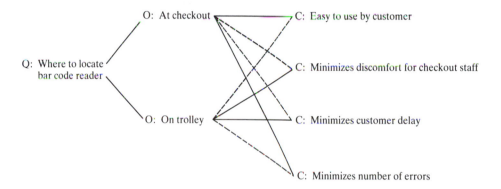

Figure 26.4 QOC diagram for the bar code reader problem.

EXERCISE

The Xerox Common LISP (XCL) environment provides scroll bars to control the views of the objects in the windows; this allows documents larger than the windows to be viewed. The scroll bar differs from many of the more recent window systems in that it is normally invisible and only appears when it is needed for scrolling; it is also fairly wide. It is interesting to explore the possible reasons for choosing this design. Two main questions need to be considered (assuming that a scroll bar of some kind is to be used anyway): 'How wide should the scroll bar be?' and 'How should the scroll bar be displayed?'

Assume that the only two options to consider for the width of the scroll bar are relatively wide and relatively narrow, and that the options for how to display the scroll bar are permanent and appearing. Suggest criteria which might be used to decide between the options, and assess how the criteria support the options. Draw a QOC diagram to represent this.

COMMENT

Allan MacLean, the originator of the QOC notation, and his colleagues produced the QOC diagram shown in Figure 26.5. How does yours compare? You may have been able to identify a different set of criteria against which to judge the options. Note that in MacLean *et al.*'s version, having an appearing scroll bar is only supported by one of the three criteria identified. This indicates the designer's priority to maximize screen compactness.

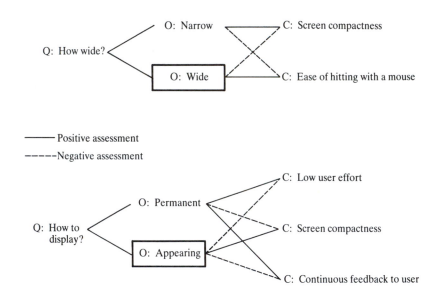

Figure 26.5 A QOC representation for the XCL scroll bar design space (MacLean *et al.*, 1991).

As you may have realized by now, recording design decisions is fairly time-consuming (which is why it usually does not happen). As with other design rationale techniques, design space analysis requires a lot of effort to maintain the QOC diagrams, and a careful balance needs to be struck between taking design decisions and knowing which decisions to document. This technique does, however, result in a thorough coverage of important design issues, and perhaps the advent of appropriate software support tools will support designers using the technique. This could have the added benefit of not only supporting the exploration of alternative designs but also the reuse of designs, in much the same way that code is sometimes reused. This could enable inexperienced designers to learn from more experienced colleagues.

Question 26.5

When using QOC diagrams to record design decisions, designers often raise high-level issues such as 'what are all the criteria we've used?' and 'which questions are particularly related to criterion x?', which are difficult to answer from paper and pencil sketches.

What kind of support would help to resolve these issues relatively easily?

26.3 Claims analysis

An alternative way to identify the rationale of a software design of an existing system is to examine the psychological claims that the designer is making or has made with regard to the use of a system, the user of the system, the environment of use and so on. The range of issues that may be addressed by a claim is very broad. A **claim** relates some aspect of a system's design with an important consequence for the user. In this sense, it represents a rationale for the design, in that it explains why a design decision was made, based on the implications of that decision for the system's use. Training Wheels (Carroll and Kellogg, 1989), for example, is a training environment for a stand-alone text editor in which the available functionality is greatly reduced (see Section 15.1). One of the characteristics of the Training Wheels interface is that it 'blocks' certain commands so that the novice user does not have access to them. For example, a user who has not yet mastered typing and printing documents is blocked from invoking the data merging function; the selection of the print command before the create command is blocked, and so on. The claim that this design embodies is that understanding real-world tasks is facilitated by filtering inappropriate goals, that is, inappropriate functions. It is possible to identify claims at various levels of abstraction. For instance, either of the following two claims would be equally legitimate: 'accomplishing familiar tasks is intrinsically motivating' or 'using a mouse to choose menu options rather than a keyboard requires less effort'. As with all analyses, it is important to have an idea of the kind of information you are looking for.

Claims analysis is done by creating scenarios of the system's use and analysing them for claims. Core tasks that the system is intended to support and key errors that the system must be able to handle should be included. Although the primary purpose is to identify how the system positively supports the user, claims analysis may also identify trade-offs, that is, situations in which the design decision was perhaps not the best for supporting the user. However, it is useful to remember that all designs have to accommodate compromises and that trade-offs can be viewed as the usability gambles taken by designers. In Part VI we shall discuss the issue of trade-offs further.

EXERCISE

Consider the 'hole-in-the-wall' cash machines, sometimes called automatic teller machines, similar to the Eurochange example. There are commonly two designs for these systems. In one design, you are asked for the amount of cash you wish to withdraw first, you enter your PIN number, your card is taken and immediately returned while the cash is being counted, and finally the cash is issued. In the other design, the machine takes the card first and keeps it while you enter your PIN, choose the transaction you wish and the amount, if appropriate; it returns the card after all other interactions are finished apart from collecting the cash.

What claims about the system's use, its users and its environment of use do the designs for these two cash machines embody?

COMMENT

The first machine processes transactions much more quickly than the second. This implies that the user does not want to hang around for too long, maybe because the environment is unpleasant. The second machine, on the other hand takes longer to process the transaction, but gives more functionality and is more secure, since it keeps the card until the transaction is nearly complete. Note that the card is returned before the cash, thus embodying the claim that people are less likely to forget their card if they have to wait for their cash.

Ironically, the second type of machine is usually found outside in the cold where the user is exposed to the elements and is therefore unlikely to want to hang around, whereas the first type is usually inside a warm bank! A further claim relating to the system's environment might be the reason for this: security is unlikely to be such a risk inside the bank.

Claims analysis can be used to guide the redesign of an existing system, or to help in the prototypical development of a new system. The premise of claims analysis is that the system should support the user. By analysing the claims it is making, any inappropriate decisions can be identified and rectified. See Box 26.2 for an example.

Question 26.6

What are the differences between the uses of design space analysis and claims analysis?

Question 26.7

In what ways is the documentation of design rationale useful? What kinds of question does it allow you to answer?

Box 26.2   Example of inappropriate psychological claims

A system was built to help in the diagnosis and prioritization of aircraft maintenance (*Computers in Context*, 1987). Two versions were produced. The first was an expert system which proved to have negative effects on the aircraft workers. This was explained by the fact that the system did too many of the wrong things: making judgements of what should be done, and stipulating the order in which things should be done. The workforce thus experienced a feeling of deskilling. The second version was a system for experts and avoided the mistakes of the first version. If a claims analysis of the first design had been done, such shortcomings could have been identified, since the psychological claims embodied by the first version would have been identified as inappropriate.

Key points

- Design decisions need to be recorded and communicated to many different people.
- Documentation is an inappropriate way to communicate design information to users.
- Documenting design rationale is a time-consuming process.
- Design space analysis encourages designers to explore alternatives.
- Claims analysis concentrates on refining one design.

Further reading

CONKLIN E.J. and BEGEMAN M.L. (1989). gIBIS: A tool for all reasons. *Journal of the American Society for Information Science*, **40**, 200–13.
This paper describes a graphical support tool for IBIS.

MacLEAN A., YOUNG R.M., BELLOTTI V.M.E. and MORAN T.P. (1991). Questions, options and criteria: elements of design space analysis. *Human–Computer Interaction*, **6**, 201–50.
This article describes the background to design space analysis and the QOC notation. It explains how it can be used in the design process, and to study reasoning in design. Other articles of interest on this topic also appear in this issue of the journal.

Prototyping

Aims and objectives

The aim of this chapter is to introduce you to a variety of prototyping techniques. After studying this chapter you should:

- know about a range of different prototyping techniques,
- be able to describe how and when you would use different techniques.

Overview

Users can be involved in testing design ideas by using experimental, incomplete designs known as **prototypes**. Developing prototypes is an integral part of iterative user-centred design (discussed in Chapter 17) because it enables designers to try out their ideas with users and to gather feedback. Traditionally, involving users in system development has been fraught with problems because:

- users often lack the ability to imagine the ramifications of design decisions,
- users are often unable to comment on technical design documents,

- providing a complete, consistent and readable representation of user interaction was virtually impossible.

Broadly speaking, there are two kinds of prototyping: paper-based and computer-based. In Chapter 22 we discussed techniques for producing paper sketches, storyboards and scripts. As Bill Verplank pointed out in his interview, these are quick and inexpensive, and they can provide very valuable insights, but they do not demonstrate functionality. Computer-based prototyping provides a version of the system with limited functionality so that users can actually interact with it. As in other areas of engineering, there is a philosophy that prototypes should be quick and inexpensive to produce and that they can be thrown away after they have served their purpose. The implication, therefore, is that a prototype will concentrate on some aspects of an interactive system and ignore others. Consequently, prototypes differ from final systems in size, reliability, robustness, completeness and construction materials.

Software prototyping is a dynamic simulation. Users can try out operations by interacting with the system in 'real time' but usually the functionality is only partial or is simulated.

A **software prototype**, therefore, is a system that:

- actually works, that is, it is not an idea or a drawing
- will not have a generalized lifetime: at one end of the spectrum it may be thrown away immediately after use, at the other end it may eventually evolve into the final system
- may serve many different purposes
- must be built quickly and cheaply
- is an integral part of iterative user-centred design in which evaluation (see Part VI) and subsequent modification of the design are fundamental concepts.

27.1 Prototyping techniques

Prototyping resolves uncertainty about how well a design suits users' needs. It helps designers to make decisions by eliciting information from users on:

- the necessary functionality of the system
- operation sequences
- user support needs
- required representations
- look and feel of the interface.

'We've used a computer to prototype the structural strength of the project and I'm afraid the results aren't encouraging.'

(*Source* Honeysett)

Ensuring that a proposed system has the necessary functionality for the tasks that users want to do is an important part of requirements gathering and task analysis. Information on operation sequences tells designers how users want to interact with the system: dialogues can be fixed and supportive, yet potentially constraining, or free and flexible, and potentially unsupportive. If designers make the wrong choice, the resulting system may have poor usability despite having adequate functionality. Wherever constraints on operation sequences are introduced, work patterns should not be disrupted. Prototypes have revealed that some ways of operating systems *create* tasks for users that are inappropriate. For example, users may have to search for off-line information at an unsuitable moment. In such cases, prototyping can provide information that enables designers to provide more appropriate operation sequences. Prototyping can also fulfil an important role in testing out how suitable help and other kinds of user support are for proposed users. Information on representation reveals those symbols and displays which users can readily understand and recognize without confusion or regular lapses of memory and those which they find difficult. Icon design, display layout, message content and command or menu item names all require suitable representations. No theoretical analysis can, as yet, determine the adequacy of many representations, so designs have to be tested with users, which is discussed in Part VI.

Various kinds of prototype have been developed to elicit different kinds of information. One form of prototyping is sometimes called **requirements animation**. Possible requirements (usually functional) are demonstrated in a prototype, which can then be assessed by users. **Rapid prototyping** is also used to collect information on requirements and on the adequacy of possible designs. In rapid prototyping, the prototype is thrown away, in the sense that it is not developed into the final product, although it is an important resource during the project's development. In contrast, **incremental prototyping** allows large systems to be installed in phases to avoid delays between specification and delivery. The customer and supplier agree on core features and the implementation is phased to enable an installation of a skeleton system to occur as soon as possible. This allows requirements to be checked in the field so that changes to core features are possible. Extra, less important, features are then added later. **Evolutionary prototyping** is the most extensive form of prototyping; it is a compromise between production and prototyping. The initial prototype is constructed, evaluated and evolved continually until it forms the final system. Some designers believe that more acceptable systems would result if evolutionary prototyping were interspersed with periods of requirements animation or rapid prototyping. However, one problem, identified by Bill Verplank in his interview and by others, is that evolutionary prototyping tends to encourage designers to 'fix' on a particular solution too soon rather than exploring the alternatives more fully. Table 27.1 contains a summary of the key features of these kinds of prototypes.

EXERCISE

Why might more acceptable systems result if evolutionary prototyping were interspersed with requirements animation or rapid prototyping?

COMMENT

Evolutionary prototyping is a cross between full production and rapid prototyping of a system, in that the final product grows in form and size from an initial prototype. Each stage of development could be viewed as a mini-project in its own right. If rapid prototyping were to be used for each stage, the benefits that we have just described would accrue for each stage, and a better product would result. Furthermore, a major problem with evolutionary prototyping is that designers become committed to the prototype because they have invested time in its construction.

Other terms that you may encounter in HCI literature are full, horizontal and vertical prototyping, high fidelity and low fidelity prototyping, chauffeured prototyping and Wizard of Oz prototyping. A **full prototype**, as the name suggests, contains complete functionality although with lower performance. A **horizontal prototype** shows the user interface but has no functionality behind the buttons. A **vertical prototype** contains all of the high level and low level functionality for a restricted part of a system. **High fidelity prototyping** refers to prototyping

Table 27.1 Prototyping methods and tools.

Prototype method	Description	Useful tools
Requirements animation	Allows possible requirements to be demonstrated in a software prototype which can then be assessed by users.	Purpose-built animation packages and screen painters are suitable for animating the representational aspects. Data manipulation languages and other high level languages are suitable for animating the functional aspects. Authoring languages, menu builders and active images tools prototype operational aspects.
Rapid (throw-it-away) prototyping	Aims to collect information on requirements and the adequacy of possible designs. Recognizes that requirements are likely to be inaccurate when first specified. The emphasis is on *evaluating* the prototype before discarding it in favour of some other implementation.	Representational requirements and designs can be created quickly using animators, screen painters, forms systems, report generators and menu systems. Hypermedia and very high level language systems are also particularly suitable.
Evolutionary prototyping	Compromise between production and prototyping. The system can cope with change *during* and *after* development. Helps overcome the traditional gap between specification and implementation.	It is important to prototype using the facilities that will eventually be used to implement the final system. Additions and amendments are made to the model following evaluation and the system is regenerated.
Incremental prototyping	The system is built incrementally, one section at a time. Incremental prototyping is based on one overall design.	Reusable software and highly modular languages can be useful as more pieces are 'bolted on' to produce the final system gradually.

through a medium, such as video, which resembles as closely as possible the final interface. High fidelity video prototypes tend to be popular with commercial organizations because they make the product appear very polished and aesthetically pleasing. **Low fidelity prototyping** involves the use of materials that are further away from the final version and that tend to be cheaper and faster to develop. For example, a software version of the interface with cut down functionality would be higher fidelity than storyboards. **Chauffeured prototyping** involves the user watching while another person, usually a member of the development team, 'drives' the system. It is a way to test whether the interface meets the user's needs without the user actually having to carry out low level actions with the system. This may appear to contradict the intentions behind involving the user, but it can be useful for confirming, for example, the sequence of actions needed to perform a task. **Wizard of Oz** prototyping also involves a third party, but in this case, the user is unaware of it. The user interacts with a screen, but instead of a piece of software responding to the user's requests, a developer is sitting at another screen answering the queries and responding to the real user. This kind of prototyping is likely to be conducted early in development to gain an understanding of the user's expectations. There is an added advantage for the development team in using chauffeured or Wizard of Oz prototyping in that extra understanding can be achieved through being involved so closely with the users.

The use of different kinds of prototype in different stages of a design results in a two-phase view of iterative design. In the first phase, prototypes are developed to gather different forms of information, and radically different alternatives may be tested in parallel. At some point, this prototyping phase ends with a proposal for a single full initial design. One solution is then iterated through design, code and test cycles. Any further radical changes are unlikely, as production standards will now be in force, and major changes will be expensive. This phase can be regarded as a convergent fine-tuning stage with a slow cycle time. The earlier prototyping phase, by contrast, is a divergent, exploratory and bold stage, with fast cycle times and the preservation of alternative designs.

27.2 Prototyping to support design

Prototyping can be useful at different stages of design; for product conceptualization, at the task level and for determining aspects of screen design.

Product conceptualization

In the early stages of system development, prototyping can be used to gain a better understanding of the kind of product required. Several different sketch designs (like those described in Chapter 22) can be presented to users and to members of the development team for comment and improvement. Just as architects produce prototypes, sketches and three-dimensional models to help them explore alternative designs, HCI design can also benefit from similar techniques.

EXERCISE

Why might it be beneficial for members of the development team to see a prototype design?

COMMENT

If design is being carried out by a team, it is important for the team members to communicate effectively and a prototype can help to facilitate communication.

Also, remember from the list of designer activities in Chapter 23 that designers need to simulate their designs-in-progress as an aid in making design decisions. Although it may be possible for designers to perform such simulations in their heads, it is not necessarily desirable: humans have a limit to their cognitive capacity, it is tiring, people are prone to forget or to make errors which they may not realize or remember later on. It may therefore help the designer to see a prototyped version of her design.

Bill Verplank argued in the interview at the beginning of Part V that it is undesirable to convert ideas into working software too early since this gives the idea too much credibility (think how much better a report looks once typed up properly, compared to handwritten script). Once a 'glossy' version of an idea exists it is too easy to get carried away by thinking that this must be the only or the best solution to the problem. In addition, do you really want to throw it away? After all, it looks so good. It may be more beneficial at this stage to consider using some paper-based prototyping such as storyboarding or sketching. This avoids prematurely closing the design space, which may in turn result in a suboptimal system being produced.

There is, however, a counter-argument to this which says that prototyping should be done with a product that is as close to the intended system as possible. After all, the whole purpose of producing a prototype is to give a good picture of what the final system will look like. In addition, there are some aspects of a pictorial representation that you need to see on a screen, such as animation. A compromise would be to produce a computer-based prototype, which may simply involve a sequence of screens controlled from the keyboard, or programmed as a predetermined sequence. Box 27.1 describes MacroMind Director, a software package that can be used for this.

Box 27.1 MacroMind Director and QuickTime

MacroMind Director (MMD) is a Macintosh-based multimedia package for combining text, graphics, animation, music and other sound, and video. The package has been very popular in a wide range of professions: the film industry, engineering, education and business. It is a powerful tool for producing impressive simulations, visualizations, presentations and for prototyping interfaces. Results can be displayed on the Macintosh screen or output to a video channel.

Although producing complex animations requires programming skill, one of MMD's most attractive features is that no programming is needed to create an interface, and it can therefore be used by graphic designers with no programming expertise. The designer can draw example screens and cause a video clip, music, animation, another screen, or other screen movement to occur when the mouse is

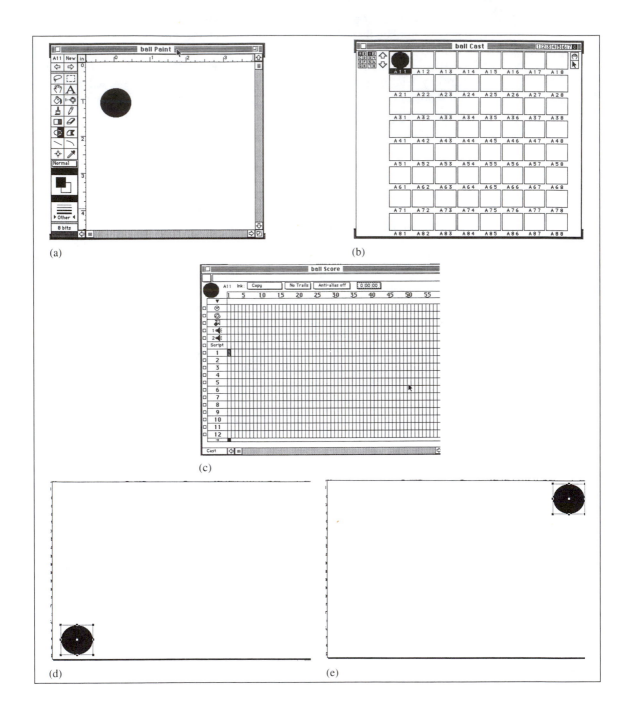

(a)

(b)

(c)

(d)

(e)

Figure 27.1 An example session with MacroMind Director (see text for description).

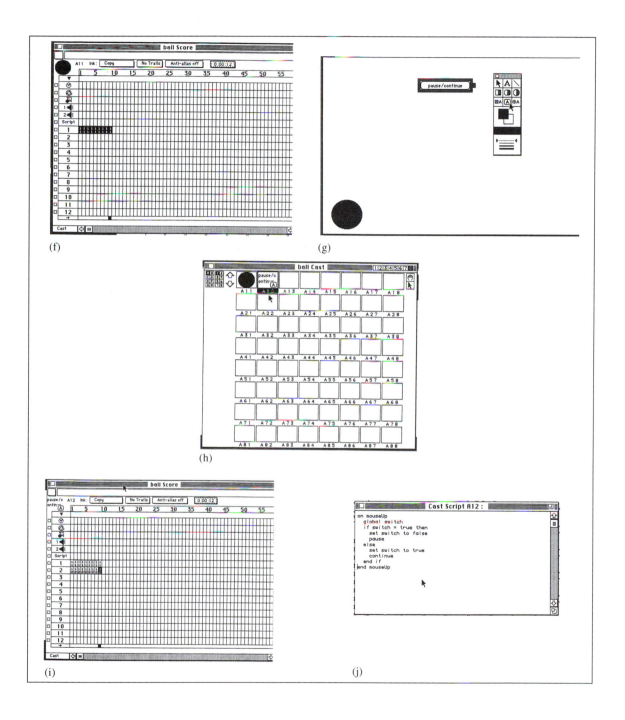

Figure 27.1 *(cont.)* An example session with MacroMind Director (see text for description).

clicked on a certain portion of that screen. Screen elements can be used repeatedly throughout the interaction.

There are three aspects to producing an application in MMD: animating graphics, creating interactive elements and assembling the final movie. Scores written in Lingo, a script language like HyperTalk, are used to define the functionality of the program, and can be attached to a graphic or text object thus giving a 'button' effect. External functions written in a third generation language such as C can be attached to MMD scripts.

The screens given in Figure 27.1 show the production of a simple animation, involving a ball which moves from the bottom left-hand corner of the screen to the top right-hand corner, and is controlled by a button.

The ball is created using a simple graphics editor (Figure 27.1(a)). It automatically becomes part of the cast list, and is named A11 (b). To create the animation, time frame 1 is highlighted (c) and the cast member A11 is dragged to the bottom left of the stage (the screen) (d), and then the ninth time frame is highlighted and the ball dragged to the top right of the stage (e). MMD then allows the user to specify the animation to be performed in the intervening time frames (f). We chose to use a straight line path between the locations in (d) and (e). MMD includes a palette of icons, which allows you to create a button (g). This is added to the cast list automatically, and is named A12 (h). It must then be added to the score, and in this case is included in every time frame, that is, it is always visible (i). In order that the button should do something, we must associate a script with it (j). This script simply starts and stops the ball's movement.

MMD calls on the facilities provided by QuickTime, which can also be used by other animation packages. QuickTime allows dynamic time-based data such as animation, video clips and sound to be incorporated in a document. It facilitates copying, pasting, recording, playing and cutting of dynamic media, which in QuickTime's jargon are called movies. It is an addition to the system's software, which applications such as MMD can access.

QuickTime could be used:

- In educational software, instead of simple hypertext documents for computer aided instruction, special effects such as physics experiments or chemical reactions could be simulated at the click of an icon. Clips of historical speeches or events could be incorporated into history teaching materials.
- In business presentations, sales figures can be shown to creep up (or down) in real time, slide shows including sound and music can be incorporated.
- In science and engineering, data recorded by monitoring equipment can be replayed through QuickTime for scientists to study events of interest such as earthquakes or tidal waves.

Requirements animation, mentioned above, is a useful technique to use during the product conceptualization stage (see Box 27.2). Visualization techniques that also assist with requirements animation are described in Chapter 28.

Box 27.2 An example requirements animation session

The following excerpt (Wulff, Evenson and Rheinfrank, 1990) from a reported session with the 'Animating Interfaces' technique illustrates how paper-based prototyping approaches can be used by a design team to explore the concept of a product. The product in this example is the interface for the collaborative management and use of a large multimedia information base. After some brainstorming, an initial interface has been suggested which consists of a frame containing information tools in a palette-like arrangement (see Figure 27.2).

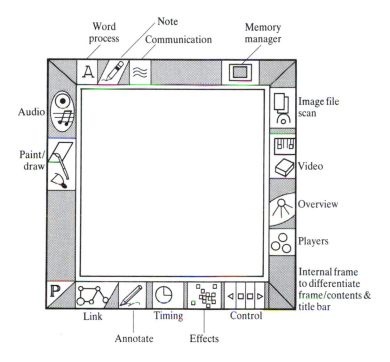

Figure **27.2** An information frame as an interface convention (Wulff, Evenson and Rheinfrank, 1990: © 1990, Association for Computing Machinery, Inc. reprinted by permission).

The two participants are referred to as Chris and Tim.

'The two animators act out collaborating on a first draft of the presentation using the information frame and tools from the intermediate sketch.

> C: *I think we should sort our information by country.*
> T: Hmmm. I think we should sort it by type of occupational craft.

C: I'm going to get a linking tool and link all of our references by county. Why don't you do the same for types of crafts and then we can compare?

T: All right. While I'm at it, I'd like to use an annotating tool to comment on the sources I find.

C: Great. Later we can look at the shapes our individual linked bases have taken. Then we can use the results to talk about "information by county, within type of craft" as a starting point for the presentation.

The graphic interface designer listens to their dialogue, watches how they simulate using her sketches, and uses both of these sources of information to help her redesign and refine the frame and the information-management tools it contains. She reacts to Chris' comment about linking. She refines a "linking tool" so that it can be modified by various descriptors (location, type, media, etc.). She sees that two annotating tools will be needed: one for annotating information from the archives, and one for annotating the presentation. She redesigns the original annotating tool as an "archive annotator" and then uses that one as a basis for designing a new "presentation annotator".

By this time the designer has been pulled into the fictional world that student and teacher have acted out and now begins performing herself. Her performance is enactment, rather than acting, because she explores the Animation from her point of view as an interface designer. She runs through the Animation in her mind and realizes that the users of the system will need to create linked groups of tools. She creates and represents a facility that will allow users to do this.

Finally one of the participants engages the designer in a reflective conversation about the interaction between Chris and Tim. The other participant points out that if Chris and Tim continue linking information tools, they will soon have cluttered screens. The graphic interface designer refines the frame to look like a mosaic, where the information tools can be seen if you look for them, but appear as a pattern if you do not.

After all the participants have had a chance to interact with, comment on and contribute to the intermediate sketch of the frame, the designer creates a carefully hand-crafted, finished version.'

EXERCISE

In the above excerpt, the interface designer becomes 'pulled into' the fictional world created by the animators; from there on, she begins acting herself. Refer back to the list of observed designer behaviour in Chapter 23 and identify the behaviour being exhibited by the designer.

COMMENT

It has been observed that designers will try to simulate partial designs and designs in progress; the designer of the information frame interface was using the animation exercise to simulate her design and to push her understanding of the system further. Involving other imaginary users through the use of group discussion, acting and animation has clearly enhanced the simulation exercise.

Question 27.1

What kinds of prototyping could be useful during the early stages of system development, that is, during product conceptualization?

Task level prototyping

Once the requirements for a system have been determined, and its functionality is clearer, prototyping can help to establish the suitability of the interface at the task level. The aim is to ensure that the user can perform the tasks necessary for the job, and to ensure that a task sequence can be completed easily and efficiently. Generating realistic scenarios is important for all forms of prototyping, but particularly so in this situation. It is not enough for the user to 'play with' the prototype. Tasks need to be chosen and scenarios generated to reflect the system's intended use. System tests and acceptance tests which are generated through standard software engineering practices could be used in these scenarios. Providing and testing early versions of the user documentation can also be useful as the step-by-step nature required to describe the system's operations may unearth usability problems. You may remember, for example, that in the Olympic Message System (Gould *et al.*, 1987) early versions of the user guides were developed, which served to identify issues and problems in system organization. For instance, it was found that the user interface for family and friends required trained intermediaries to work very quickly so as to minimize the expensive long-distance telephone charges for people calling from outside the USA. Furthermore, operators needed to be able to change the language of a message.

An area that has proved critical in the recent past is process control fault diagnosis. At the task level, prototyping the steps needed to identify and correct an error is crucial. Waiting until the system is in place before performing such testing could be fatal so good prototyping is essential. The Ministry of Defence (MoD) has recognized this problem and developed defence standard 00-55: the procurement of safety-critical software in defence equipment. This standard states that an executable prototype must be produced from the functional specification: all software contracts for the MoD must conform to this standard. The kinds of questions that a prototype can be used to answer include: how much information needs to be displayed? If too much information is given, this can result in confusion. On the other hand, there must be enough information available for the operator to be aware of the system's state, and to be able to assess the situation should a fault arise.

Question 27.2

In Chapter 1, poor interface design of the control panels for a nuclear power plant was cited as one cause of the Three Mile Island disaster. What interface problems were identified?

EXERCISE

Users sometimes feel that it is appropriate to gather performance measures during task level prototyping. Would task duration be an appropriate performance metric to measure using a prototype? Explain your answer and also suggest another metric that could be used.

COMMENT

Certain performance metrics could be used with a system developed for task-level prototyping, but, as was emphasized in Chapter 25, you must be clear about what you are measuring.

Measuring task duration would be inappropriate unless a vertical prototype was being used for the functions associated with the task being studied. This is because task duration would depend on the efficiency of the software being used, and efficiency may be one of the compromises made in building the prototype. Even with an appropriate vertical prototype, task duration measures may not be representative of the performance of the final system because the final environment may include factors such as other users which would impact on the speed of the software.

The number of keyboard strokes necessary to complete a task would probably be a more appropriate measure.

Box 27.3 shows an example of using a prototype to help to determine the functionality required for a weather forecasting system.

Question 27.3

What forms of prototyping are likely to be of value in resolving task level uncertainty?

Box 27.3 Using a prototype to identify the functions involved in generating a weather forecast

Figure 27.3 illustrates the screen of a weather forecasting system (Miller-Jacobs, 1991, pp. 278–9). This system is for a weather workstation to be used by meteorologists in developing forecasts. The prototype was used to identify various functions that a meteorologist might use in generating a forecast; it was not the final user interface for the system. It was developed on a Sun workstation using the DataViews graphics software package from VI Corp.

The major portion of the screen is devoted to a graphics map, depicting the area of interest. Across the top, in the rectangular boxes, is a row of major functions that a meteorologist may use in generating the forecast. These include all the steps from the Monitoring of Status to the Distribution and Dissemination of

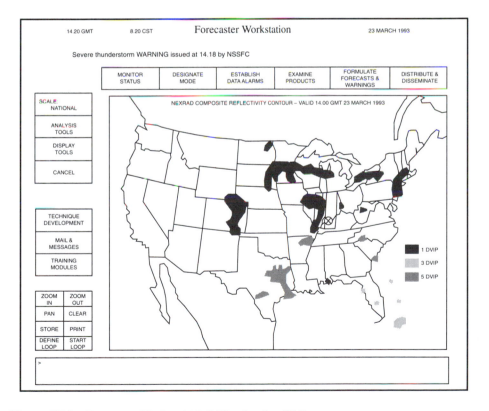

Figure 27.3 Forecaster Workstation (Miller-Jacobs, 1991).

the forecast products, in this case the entire US. These are actually menu buttons that have associated submenus when activated. In the prototype, clicking on one of these buttons opens up its associated submenu.

Down the left side of the screen are more menu buttons for tools that an operator may use in performing the various forecasting functions. In addition, there are tools for manipulating the image, such as Zoom, Pan and Store. In the prototype some of these buttons were functioning.

To verify that the listed functions were the primary ones needed by a meteorologist, a scenario was developed that started with a thunderstorm warning. A message containing the general WARNING, which was issued by the National Severe Storms Center, is listed near the top of the screen. The prototype was designed to enable the meteorologist to perform all the steps needed to verify the extent of the thunderstorm and to issue a local warning. Approximately a dozen subsequent screens were developed that tracked the various functions used and enabled a simulated operation of the system. These were then shown to meteorologists, and their comments were incorporated in the prototype. When working interactively with the prototype it appeared as if it was an actual system with limited functionality. The realism facilitated informative feedback and was an essential part of clarifying the requirements.

The major benefits of this approach were that it incorporated in several screens a representation of what was thought to be the primary functions needed by a meteorologist to perform the required tasks. There were definitely errors and omissions, which were easily corrected. The major benefit, however, was the time saved by using this approach. After a quick analysis was performed to understand the basic functionality, the actual implementation of the prototype took less than a week!

Screen design prototyping

Screen design prototyping concentrates on icons, menus and screen layouts. Issues to be resolved at this level include the suitability of icons and screen layouts, the use of colour, visual and audio effects, and the grouping of commands within menus. Initial ideas can be prototyped using paper-based sketches and drawings, as discussed in Chapter 22, but a true understanding of the effect of these issues requires high fidelity prototyping in the form of a software prototype.

COMMENT

The suitability of interface elements and layouts depends heavily on the context in which the system will be used. For example, the meaningfulness of an icon depends on five aspects (Chapter 5): the context in which the icon is being used; the task for which it is being used; the surface form of the representation; the nature of the underlying concept being represented; and the extent to which it can be discriminated from other icons being displayed.

A second issue is the categorization used for menu dialogues. In ISO 9241 Part 14 (Draft International Standard), which deals with categorization for menu dialogues, it is stated that 'interface design depends on the task, the user, the environment, and the available technology', and that 'if options can be arranged into conventional or natural groups known to the users, options shall be organized into levels and menus consistent with that order' (Chapter 25).

Question 27.4

Name two kinds of prototyping that would be inappropriate for resolving uncertainty at the screen level.

27.3 | Software prototyping tools

One of the skills of the interface developer lies in choosing tools that are appropriate both for the prototyping method chosen and for the purpose to which the prototype is to be put. It is important to establish what a prototyping exercise is intended to achieve, but even the best laid plans may be changed. The developers may intend a prototype to be thrown away, but in reality it may evolve into the final system. Similarly, developers may begin an evolutionary prototype, which is eventually thrown away and replaced by another system. The variety of prototypes and particularly the differences between throw-away prototyping and evolutionary prototyping has implications for the requirements for software tools for prototyping. A desirable feature for any prototyping tool is that it should require only limited programming skills. This will speed up the prototyping cycle and allow designers who are not proficient programmers to design and test with minimal training. Two types of tool are used for prototyping: production tools, which can be used for prototyping as well as for the design itself, and tools that are specifically designed for prototyping.

Prototyping with production tools

Not surprisingly, there can be a problem in using production tools for prototyping. Production tools have to be comprehensive and they impose certain constraints, so that complete, reliable, robust and maintainable software is produced. Such constraints are not compatible with the generality required for prototyping. Thus, the use of production tools can slow prototyping and raise its cost, in some cases to the point of infeasibility, although it is common to use a very high level language, such as Prolog, on a powerful machine to determine the functional requirements of a system that is to be implemented in an efficient language such as C on a less powerful machine; this approach can be quite effective. Other differences between prototyping and production can be viewed as divergences rather than conflicts. Prototyping is enhanced by visual representations in the most appropriate medium for configuring HCI components. Conversely, production tools for computer specialists do not need such representations, as most software tools for code management work only with text files. In contrast, good code management and quality assurance tools are vital to production, but represent an unproductive burden during prototyping. (Code management involves the control of versions of a program and access to a program.) The implication of these conflicts and divergences is that production tools may be unsuitable for prototyping, especially if people with limited technical computing skills are to use the tools directly.

Question 27.5

Which prototyping method, by definition, has to use a production tool?

Prototyping tools

Prototyping tools need speed in carrying out construction of a prototype, which means reducing the standard of quality. Tools may use a different configuration medium from the final product, for example, text as opposed to graphics. They may fully automate code management at the expense of efficient, maintainable code. They may remove enforced quality checks in a compiler, allowing a designer to take risky shortcuts that do not matter in throw-away software. Finally, prototyping tools may limit what can be configured.

Question 27.6

In what way might prototyping tools limit what can be configured?

Different tools may also be appropriate for different levels and kinds of prototyping. For example, MacroMind Director (see Box 27.1) would be more appropriate for horizontal prototyping of screen elements than vertical prototyping of user functions. If the focus is on requirements animation, then special types of programming language may be used. For example, RAPID (see Box 27.4) is a tool that attempts to combine a restricted focus with rapid reconfiguration facilities in a special-purpose language (TDI).

Box 27.4   RAPID

RAPID (Wasserman and Shewmake, 1985) is an early example of a special-purpose interactive information system prototyping tool. It uses visual programming and interpretation of a special-purpose programming language, TDI, to support prototyping. The language is simple, which makes it suitable for designers and users with limited computing skills, but its simplicity also means that complex user interfaces are very difficult, if not impossible, to configure.

A TDI script is a textual equivalent of a set of transition diagrams which describe a user interface. This script is input to an interpreter, which checks the specification of the diagrams. This interpreter (also called TDI) creates an executable program from a syntactically correct script.

Figure 27.4 shows an example transition diagram, and its equivalent TDI script is given in Figure 27.5. Note that the user is not intended to interact with, or even to see, the TDI script. Users would only view the prototype itself or the transition diagrams.

A transition diagram editor to prototype textual interfaces as part of the RAPID/USE method is included in the more recently developed Software through Pictures modular tool set from Interactive Development Environments.

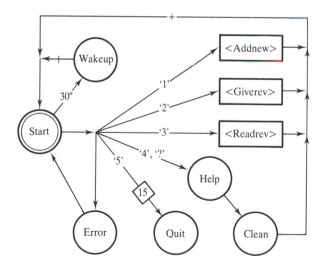

Figure 27.4   A transition diagram (Wasserman and Shewmake, 1985).

```
diagram  irg  entry  start  exit  quit

node start
        cs, r2,rv,c_'Interactive Restaurant Guide',sv,
        r6, c5, 'Please make a choice: ',
        r+2,c10, '1: Add new restaurant to database',
        r+2,c10, '2: Give review of a restaurant ',
        r+2,c10, '3: Read reviews for a given restaurant',
        r+2,c10, '4: Help', r+2,c10, '5: Quit', r+3,c5, 'Your choice: ', mark_A

node help
        cs,  r5,c0, 'This program stores and retrieves information on',
        r+1, c0,'restaurants, with emphasis on San Francisco.',
        r+1, c0, 'You can add or update information about restaurants',
        r+1, c0, 'already in the database, or obtain information about',
        r+1, c0, 'restaurants, including the reviews of the others.',
        r+2, c0, 'To continue, type RETURN.'

node error
        r$-1,rv,'Illegal command.', sv , 'Please type a number from 1 to 5.',
        r$, 'Press RETURN to continue.'

node clean
        r$-1,c1,r$,c1

node wakeup
        r$,c1,rv,'Please make a choice', sv, tomark  A

node quit
        cs, 'Thank you very much.   Please try this program again',
        n1,'and continue to add information on restaurants.'

arc start single_key
        on '1' to <addnew>
        on '2' to <giverev>
        on '3' to <readrev>
        on '4','?' to help
        on '5' to quit
        alarm 30 to wakeup
        else to error
arc error
        else to start

arc help
        skip to clean

arc clean
        else to start

arc <addnew>
        skip to start

arc <readrev>
        skip to start

arc <giverev>
        skip to start
```

Figure 27.5 TDI script for the diagram in Figure 27.4.

Hypermedia systems are computer applications which structure information in a navigable form (as discussed in Sections 15.3 and 15.4). Many help systems on personal computers use some kind of hypertext system (see Chapter 15) to allow users to jump between related subjects at the click of a mouse, rather than having to scroll or search through linear documents. Hypermedia tools are very useful as prototyping tools for interactive systems, because they are common (that is, relatively low cost and easily obtainable) and they reach a high standard of software quality. Consequently, research and development teams have seized on hypermedia tools as a basis for user interface prototyping. The HyperCard system, available for the Apple Macintosh computer since 1987, is a useful and well known example of hypermedia, and it is described in Box 27.5.

Box 27.5 HyperCard

HyperCard applications or documents are called stacks (because they are analogous to a stack of cards). Each stack has one or more backgrounds, which are templates common to several cards (see Figure 27.6). Each background then has associated with it one or more cards. Each background may contain

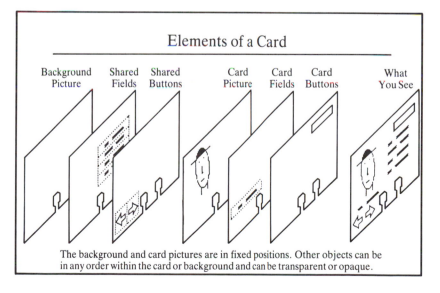

Elements of a Card

Background Picture · Shared Fields · Shared Buttons · Card Picture · Card Fields · Card Buttons · What You See

The background and card pictures are in fixed positions. Other objects can be in any order within the card or background and can be transparent or opaque.

Figure 27.6 A HyperCard stack (courtesy Apple Computer UK, Inc.).

bitmapped artwork, buttons and textfields, as may each card. Cards are HyperCard's basic units of information: a card is what you see on the screen at any one time.

Each HyperCard object (stack, background, card, button or textfield) has associated with it a script. These scripts describe what an object must do in response to particular HyperCard messages. For example, when a user clicks on a button, HyperCard will send the message 'mouseUp' to that button. If the button object needs to do something in response to that click, it must have a message handler called 'mouseUp'. The HyperTalk script for this could be the following sequence of statements:

```
on mouseUp
    visual effect scroll left/refresh the screen with a visual effect then ...
    go to card id 3914/goto (display) another card
end mouseUp
```

In the above example, 'visual effect' is a HyperCard command with the parameter 'scroll left'. Statements can use control constructs (such as loops and conditions) for sequential control within each message handler.

When an object receives a message, it checks its script for a matching message handler. If none is found, it passes on the message to the next object in the order shown:

```
button
or
field script- >  card script- >  background script- >  stack script- >
    home script >
HyperCard.
```

Scripts can also be used to define your own messages:

```
on mouseUp
comment/user-defined message
end mouseUp

on comment
    answer "it's time for lunch"
end comment
```

Scripts can also be used to define your own function handlers:

```
function square x
    return x*x
end square
```

Four screens in Figures 27.7–27.10 show how it is possible to build up a card in an application showing 'film' slides of animals. In Figure 27.7 background artwork has been prepared. The two rectangular windows on the right are 'tear-off' menus. The upper menu contains a palette of patterns. The lower menu contains a set of card tools – browse (hand), button and field, left to right, top row. The remaining tools are paint functions such as shapes, fills and text. The artwork of 'blank film' on the left of the example background was prepared using the menus.

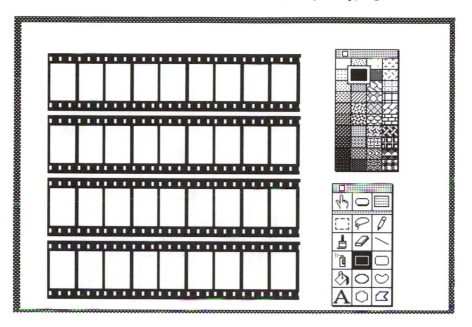

Figure 27.7 Background artwork (courtesy Apple Computer UK Ltd).

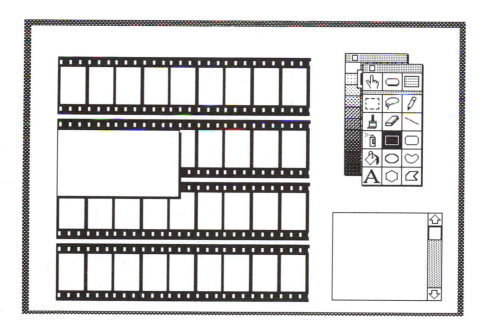

Figure 27.8 Background fields added (courtesy Apple Computer UK Ltd).

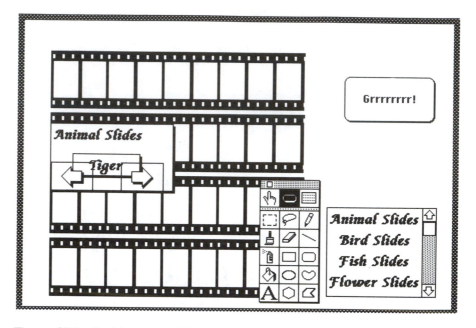

Figure 27.9 Card buttons and fields added (courtesy Apple Computer UK Ltd).

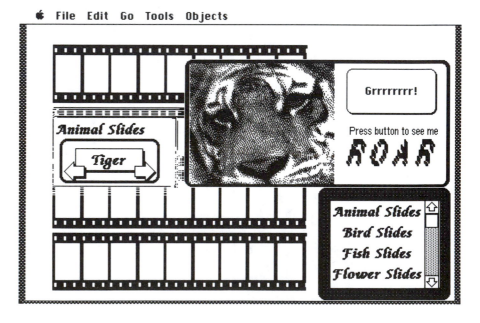

Figure 27.10 Finished card (courtesy Apple Computer UK Ltd).

In Figure 27.8 the tear-off menus have been moved to allow placement of the background text fields. The left text field is a shadowed opaque rectangle, which can display a fixed amount of text. The lower right field is a scrolling field that can display variable (large) amounts of text. This is an example of interactive configuration, which is very important for prototyping. No textual specifications or declarations are required; everything is done with a mouse in this case.

In Figure 27.9 the first card items have been added. These overlay the background. Text has also been typed into the background fields. This text can be 'locked' during user interaction, but during configuration the designer can change it at any time. A simple 'wysiwyg' text editor is active in every text field. This can be used to allow users to enter and change text too, and scripts can respond to these changes. Text fields are thus integrated input–output objects; they encapsulate the simple interaction of user input with graphic output. This simple interaction could be used to provide a range of simulated input objects, but only text fields and buttons are provided in HyperCard. Separate input and output can be used to make new interactive objects using scripts.

A card field has been added in Figure 27.9 to label some artwork (a digitized photograph of a tiger) which will be displayed on the final card. Three buttons have been added (the two arrows and the 'Grrrrrrr!' button). These are outlined because the button tool is active. Each button has a script associated with it which defines part of the behaviour of the card. The arrow buttons will move through the slides. The 'Grrrrrrr!' button's script will generate a roaring sound.

In Figure 27.10, the card is finished by adding artwork. The appearance of the background text fields has been altered with a simple 'coat of paint'. The main card item, a displayed picture with a caption, has been added. The tiger's face was digitized from a photograph, but any images that can be stored as MacPaint files or pasted into the Macintosh clipboard can be used in HyperCard. Further media are provided by the sound commands in scripts, which can generate speech, music or roars. In Figure 27.10 the tear-off menus have been hidden and the menu bar at the top has been redisplayed. All HyperCard commands can be reached from menus.

Extensions to HyperCard can provide facilities not supported within HyperCard. However, they must be programmed in a high-level language. The linkage in HyperCard to the underlying application is a simple, modular interface between scripts and external commands and the functions of the underlying application.

The appearance of an interactive system is very easy to prototype in HyperCard, provided that the structure of the display is simple enough to exploit the two-level model consisting of card and background. More sophisticated display structures that require commonality at a number of levels require a full hierarchical display model to maximize reuse of display components. Graphic displays often have a hierarchical structure that can require more than six levels, rather than the two of HyperCard.

Simple behaviour is easy to prototype. Buttons and text fields are fairly general purpose, integrated input–output objects that are adequate for even relatively complex applications. However, any prototyping that requires dynamic interaction with a graphic display is difficult to prototype in HyperCard. This is because the abstraction for artwork is bit-based and has no support for applying a structure or for naming. So the designer or the end user cannot manipulate part of a picture. For example, it is not possible to structure the digitized picture of the tiger so that, say, an eye can be made an object, named and then changed independently of the rest of the tiger's face. To make the tiger wink, you would need several digitized pictures on several cards and a script to cycle through them.

HyperCard is best suited for rapid changes to structurally simple artwork and simple event-driven behaviour using a small set of interaction techniques. More complex behaviour requires long scripts and highly creative use. Special development tools are available for managing the use of many complex scripts, as normally a HyperCard stack cannot be read like a traditional program. This can make it difficult to track down problems.

HyperCard appears to be very valuable for early prototyping, when much information is uncertain. Designs can be advanced considerably with HyperCard prototypes. Stacks can be left with suitably skilled users to try out and modify, although exploiting this potential requires some forethought and careful structuring of the use of the prototype.

HyperCard's special advantage is that if user representatives are properly trained they can make simple changes to prototypes. This could change the process of early design for interactive systems considerably. Since the development of HyperCard a number of other systems have also been developed which serve a similar purpose.

EXERCISE

How well is HyperCard suited to rapid prototyping and evolutionary prototyping?

COMMENT

HyperCard is best for rapid prototyping, especially in the early stages of a design. Some requirements animation is possible, but detailed semantics cannot be explored. Evolutionary prototyping with HyperCard cannot be recommended except for hypermedia information systems. For most interactive applications, the restriction of HyperCard to the Apple Macintosh computer and the limited set of project and code management tools means that HyperCard is unsuitable for general use in large projects requiring high standards of software engineering.

Question 27.7

There are many other kinds of software support tools which would be useful to an interface designer. List at least four types of support tool that you think would be worth having. You may find it helpful to refer to Chapter 23, where design support was first introduced.

Key points

- Prototyping is an appropriate way to communicate design information to users.
- It is important to be clear about what information a prototype is intended to help to elicit.
- Different kinds of prototyping are appropriate for different stages of design.
- Prototyping can be achieved with the use of production tools, but this can be infeasible as they are not designed to accommodate the kind of compromises which prototyping needs.
- Prototyping tools must compromise on quality in order to produce working systems quickly.

Further reading

HEKMATPOUR S. and INCE D.C. (1988). *Software Prototyping, Formal Methods and VDM*. Wokingham: Addison-Wesley.

The first few chapters of this book, in particular, give a very good introduction to prototyping. The rest of the book concerns prototyping using executable formal specifications and VDM.

HIX D. and HARTSON H.R. (1993). *Developing User Interfaces: Ensuring Usability Through Product and Process*. New York: John Wiley.

This book contains an interesting chapter on rapid prototyping of interface designs (Chapter 9).

IEEE Software, **6**(1) (1990). Special issue on user interfaces.

This special issue includes several papers on prototyping user interfaces.

McDERMID J.A. (1991). *Software Engineer's Reference Book*. Oxford: Butterworth-Heinemann.

Chapter 40, by Darrel Ince, is a useful chapter on prototyping.

28

Software Support

Aims and objectives

Each stage of a system development – planning, requirements analysis and specification, systems design, implementation, evaluation and maintenance (see Part IV) – can be supported and improved by the provision of software tools. After studying this chapter you should be able to:

- describe the different kinds of software support that are available to support designers,
- discuss how these different tools can be used during design.

Overview

General purpose tools that can be used for all kinds of software development include programming languages and tools for editing, compiling and running the programs once written, and text editors and desktop publishing systems that facilitate the production of documentation. We shall consider these only briefly. Other tools have

565

been specifically designed to support HCI, and we shall look at these in more detail.

The focus of this chapter is on implementing interactive systems, which is complex for two reasons:

(1) There are many transformation tasks: a wide range of input and output devices must be configured (function keys, joystick buttons, graphic displays, speech synthesizers and so on); operation sequences and interaction must be programmed (for example, security checks, menu sequences); and computational objects must be linked into the interaction (for example, bar chart formatters and application functions like database query).

(2) There are discrepancies between the way people think about designs and the way they must make programs work. This is known as the gap between specification (what to do) and implementation (how to do it). The extent of the gap is reflected in the amount of rethinking and re-orienting needed to turn design ideas into software.

Help with this process can be provided in two main ways: the range of tasks can be reduced or each task can be simplified. It is possible to reduce the range of tasks by automating some of them, but this is difficult, and often complete technical solutions are elusive or unsatisfactory. Task simplification tends to be easier, as it should always be possible to reduce the complexity of transformations somehow. Even a low degree of automation can result in useful support. Software tools not only make software but they also manage the process, analyse programs and test them. Any program used to design, make, maintain, manage or test a software product can be called a **software tool**. However, the concept of a software tool is not one that can be adequately communicated in a simple definition. A rough working definition is that software tools are programs that support designers and programmers at some point in the development of a software product.

Tools give varying degrees of support for specific tasks: the more specialized the tool, the more support it will offer for the task it is designed to support. For example, a text editor allows great freedom to input text of any shape, whereas a structured editor for inputting Pascal gives less freedom and requires the program to be input in a set form. Tools that give more freedom tend to be helpful early in design, when ideas are just beginning to take shape, but are not far enough advanced to be specific. However, once the system requirements are well understood, tighter controls on what is produced may be useful. Although the aim of this chapter is not to discuss general purpose software tools in detail some information about the main types of programming languages and related tools and text input tools is contained in Tables 28.1 and 28.2. One development paradigm that has had great success in the user interface application area and is therefore worthy of extra note is object-oriented development. In fact, HCI and object-oriented development share much

Table 28.1 Languages and related tools.

Language or tool	Features and uses
Third-generation languages (3GLs) such as COBOL, Pascal, Fortran	Procedural languages. Programmers have to deal with details of the sequence of program operations. Widely available, widely used.
Reusable software	Modules (general limited-purpose programs) are gathered into libraries. Modules from the same or different libraries are linked together into a program and can be reused any number of times. For example, the same module may move the cursor on a number of different video displays. Commercial libraries are available, such as PARTS Workbench from Digitalk Inc.
Fourth-generation languages (4GLs): many proprietary brands available	4GLs provide enhanced screen handling facilities and are easier to write and test than 3GLs, but have limited flexibility. Often capable of generating 3GL code (program generators). Good for prototyping and quick production of working systems. 4GLs can be used by end users.
Fifth generation languages (5GLs)	These incorporate artificial intelligence techniques. Systems now available couple production rule programming, functional programming and/or OOP (see below) with 4GL.
Very high level languages (VHLL) such as APL, LISP and Prolog	Allow complicated operations to be expressed in very little code. Quick to write. May have poor screen handling. Limited for end user use. Expressive, usually interpretive and interactive, and often with good programming environments. All these characteristics contribute to their suitability for prototyping, particularly system functionality. May use a lot of memory and be uneconomic for the implementation of a final system.
Data manipulation languages (DML), for example, SQL	Highly non-procedural languages associated with database systems. Free the programmer from details of navigation. Excellent for prototyping content of reports and displays before layout is considered. Typically little screen handling. May be coupled with 4GLs.
Functional languages, such as SASL, ML, Miranda	Programs are smaller and easier to produce than with 3GLs. Used as a part of 5GL approach
Object-oriented programming (OOP), such as, SmallTalk™	Concentrates on the definition of the attributes and behaviour of objects. An object is a collection of data together with modules (called operations or methods) for accessing these data. Objects group data and operations into a coherent unit. Particularly important in interface design to describe interface objects such as icons, windows and active images (Table 28.3).
Hypermedia systems, for example, HyperCard®, Guide	Useful as prototyping tools for interactive systems. Low cost, easily obtainable and attaining a high standard of software quality. The appearance of an interactive system is very easy to prototype in HyperCard® provided that the structure of the display is fairly simple. Buttons and text fields are fairly general-purpose, integrated input–output objects that are adequate for even relatively complex applications.
Programming by example	Typified by the way that robots are 'taught' (that is, programmed) to perform certain functions. The programmer leads the robot through a typical example procedure, and the robot records the actions taken. Applications are being explored in office systems. May have a big impact particularly for end-user development.
Authoring languages	Provide a number of facilities for describing screen layouts and conditional branching mechanisms. Used to develop Computer-Aided Instruction (CAI) systems. Useful for prototyping operational aspects.
Event–response or rule-based languages	Based on the 'IF condition THEN action' construct. Easy to write but can become complex. Particularly relevant to expert systems, but are also used extensively in programming active images (see Table 28.3).
Access-oriented and data-directed programming	Special data values (called cells, active values or daemons) exist that are constantly active and can notify other parts of a system when they are accessed or changed. Used with active images (see Table 28.3), access-oriented programming offers a very powerful facility for prototyping and implementing graphic interfaces.

Table 28.1 *(cont.)* Languages and related tools.

Language or tool	Features and uses
Browsers	Provide navigation facilities that enable the user to move rapidly through a program, graphic, database or other environment locating specific objects. Browsers often include facilities for moving, copying, opening and closing objects, zooming in on a portion of a graphic or panning out to get a better perspective. Other browsing facilities will show the user's current location in the program and the sequence of objects that have been accessed. This is particularly important in hypermedia systems, where it is very easy to get lost without these navigational aids.
Debugging tools	Provide a variety of facilities for showing traces of a program's behaviour, which pieces of code have been executed, what the values of variables are, and so on. Displays can be made at different points and programs can be altered quickly and re-run immediately.

Table 28.2 Text manipulation tools.

Tool	Features and uses
Text editors	Developed to help with entering and amending program statements. Structured editors are designed to be used with specific programming languages and reflect the particular structure of those languages.
Word processors	Provide a range of facilities for entering, changing and laying out text. Have continually matured and now provide many facilities related to producing text such as spell-checking and outlining.
Desktop publishing systems or document processing systems	Enhanced word processors. Have additional facilities coupled with enhanced quality of printing, variety of font sizes and styles and details of layouts. Facilitate laying out pages and documents. The very advanced systems verge on electronic publishing (EP) systems as used by newspapers and publishing businesses.

common history; the development of the object-oriented language Smalltalk was bound up with the desire to improve the quality of HCI. The key concepts of this approach are outlined in Box 28.1.

Question 28.1

Which of the languages listed in Table 28.1 are particularly useful for prototyping?

Box 28.1   The object-oriented development paradigm

In conventional development, the emphasis is on procedure. The procedural aspects of the application are mixed up with the data being processed. In **object-oriented** development, the emphasis is on defining the attributes and behaviour of objects and is much more closely related to the data-oriented approach to systems development.

Objects group data and operations into a coherent unit. Proponents of the technique have suggested that object-oriented development is 'more natural' since objects in the software can be related directly to objects in the real world.

So, for example, we have a Person object with attributes name, address and date of birth, which corresponds to you, me, your boss, my father, and so on, each of whom has a name, address and date of birth.

Object-oriented development is founded on four basic notions: encapsulation, classification, inheritance and polymorphism.

Encapsulation is another word for information hiding. This refers to the practice of separating the external view of the object (often called the public interface), which is available to other objects, from the internal details (often called the private interface), which are not accessible by other objects. This basically means that objects do not need to be concerned about how another performs a task as long as they know how to ask for the task to be performed.

Each object belongs to a class, and every object within a class has common data structure and behaviour. Therefore a class is an abstraction of interesting behaviour and data. Examples of classes include Aeroplane, Bank account and Tree. The classes within a system form a class hierarchy. This hierarchy is built by considering the generalization/specialization (is-a) relationships between objects. For instance, 'an Alsatian is-a Dog' records the fact that the object Alsatian has behaviour and state which is common to other kinds of dog. Similarly, 'a Pekinese is-a Dog' records the fact that the object Pekinese also has behaviour and state which is common to other dogs, such as Alsatians. The objects Alsatian and Pekinese are said to inherit the properties of class Dog, but note that they can have extra data and behaviour of their own. An Alsatian is brown and black with short straight hair, while a Pekinese is brown with long wavy hair.

For another example, consider Contract employee and Salaried employee, which are both kinds of Employees. They have common state and behaviour (associated with the Employee object), but they also differ from each other, in this case in the way they are paid.

Polymorphism allows the same command to be interpreted according to the recipient of the command. For example, if you were told to 'go home', you would interpret that in one way, which might involve using a car or a bus, or even an aeroplane, and you would make your way to wherever your home is. If, however, I was told to 'go home', I would go to a totally different place, and might well use a different means of transport. The advantage of this in software terms is that an object can give a command to a number of other objects, without worrying about including any control information.

28.1 The user interface and software tooling

User interface functions were originally supported by general input and output modules or programming language features. The advent of graphic output and non-textual input demanded that user interface support be separated from these general modules at the level of module libraries. Special libraries were developed for video displays and graphics workstations and some of these libraries now follow international standards, such as the Graphical Kernel System (GKS) standard (ISO, 1985). For windowing PCs, there are commercial libraries like GEM, Microsoft Windows and the Macintosh toolkit. For windowing workstations, MIT's X11 window system library (Scheifler and Gettys, 1986) is becoming a standard. (Also, see Chapter 14 on windowing systems.) Once libraries are in place, they can be invoked by extensions to a programming language or by special-purpose languages. The screen painters of fourth-generation languages (4GLs), for example, took this concept further and allow interactive construction of screens.

By closing the gap between specification and implementation, it has become easier and quicker to produce user interfaces. Unfortunately, the needs of the end user have not been foremost in this process. The behaviour of modules, language features and 4GL-generated screens can be inflexible, and although consistency does result, it is only a good thing if the ready-made components are suitable. Hence, although 4GLs support the designer in generating systems relatively quickly, they have problems. Poor-quality modules, language features or tools that impose inappropriate interaction and presentation on an end user frustrate good designers. Support must simultaneously balance the needs of the designer and the user; a good balance results in user-centred support in the broadest sense: the designers' design tasks are well supported and so, ultimately, are the needs of the end users. The aim is not merely to close the gap between specification and implementation but to constrain what is specified to prevent poor user interfaces and at the same time to encourage good design. Flexibility is needed for the latter, but restraint is needed to avoid possible poor practice. User-centred support is thus difficult to achieve. An example of poor interaction is auto-tabbing in generated screen forms. Auto-tabbing is a data entry technique which jumps the cursor from one input field to the next for fixed-length fields (for example, a year field consisting of two or four characters). A user only has to make one extra keystroke in a burst of rapid keying and an error will be spread across all subsequent fields until the user notices. The user must then correct all the fields individually. This is an example of a speed-up technique that introduces errors and may thus be unacceptable to many users. It could be an option, but in some forms-producing tools it is a fixed feature of the interaction.

EXERCISE

How do you think developments in software tools will affect the process of iterative design?

COMMENT

Anything that saves time on coding allows more time for user testing and participation. If changes can be made quickly, then more changes can be made in the time allocated for a design. More iterations become possible.

Question 28.2

(a) *How have software tools made it easier and quicker to produce computer applications?*

(b) *Why has the use of software tools not resulted in good user interfaces being developed more easily?*

(c) *How does inflexibility result from current programmer-centred graphics standard libraries?*

28.2 Stand-alone tools

The strength of stand-alone tools is their flexibility; they are not tied in to an environment with other support tools. This is also their weakness, however, since the designer has to ensure that the collection of tools chosen for a project will work easily together.

Graphics tools

Graphics tools allow interface designers to create and manipulate drawings, icons and other graphic images. Designers need to be able to lay out windows and displays composed of display objects such as text, lines, shapes and icons. Designers may also want to create other graphic objects such as buttons, dials, cursors, sliders, scroll bars, bubbles, highlightable menu items and so on. In addition to simply designing the screen layout, that is the representational aspects, an HCI designer must link the screens, images and text to the functions of the system, and sequence the images in order to describe operational aspects of the interface. These determine what it is that makes one interactive session different from another and give interaction its character as much, if not more, than the physical presentation of a display. Some tools are like a sketch pad, allowing free movement of the 'pen' so that designers can literally sketch out their ideas. These are likely to be of use in the early stages of design when the designer might use such a product instead of the back of an envelope. Other graphics tools allow more rigorous drawings to be produced, such as boxes, circles, straight lines and so on, but provide no specific support for interface design. These may be applicable once ideas are slightly clearer. For example, Figure 28.1 shows outputs from a drawing package and a sketching tool. The designer is working on the same screen, but in the first case has only a sketch idea of the layout and contents, while in the second ideas take on a more precise flavour.

There are many kinds of graphics tools that could support interface designers, and Table 28.3 contains brief details of some of them.

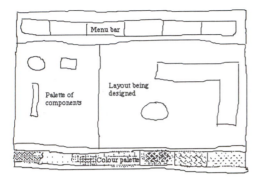 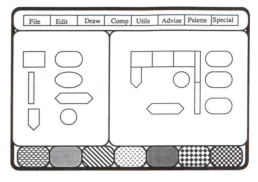

Figure 28.1 Outputs from a sketching tool and a drawing package.

Table 28.3 Graphics tools.

Tool	Features and uses
Icon editors	Facilitate the creation of icons and the manipulation of these through reshaping, resizing, rotating and so on.
Menu builders	Allow the rapid creation of menu structures. Menus may be textual, but can also appear as labelled boxes in a vertical or horizontal layout.
Window managers	Enable the production of windows of varying and variable size and shape. Also support the manipulation of windows by the end user so that they can be moved around the screen, hidden behind one another, overlap each other and so on.
Drawing packages	Group graphic primitives such as circles, rectangles and lines of various dimensions into display objects. Offer other capabilities such as shading in different styles. From these primitives, designers can create intricate drawings which can also be rotated, moved, stretched and shrunk.
Painting packages	Use a bitmap representation of rectangular portions of a display which can be moved over each other, inverted or combined. Similar facilities to drawing packages.
Menu systems	Provide facilities to link menu items together and attach them to system functions.
Screen painters	Enable the designer to lay out an entire screen such as an input 'form'. Fields on the screen can be defined as input and/or output and can have various attributes such as reverse video or highlighting. Fields can also be tailored to accept only particular data types.
Report generators	Provide facilities similar to screen painters for producing printed or displayed reports. Provide additional facilities such as the production of totals, page headings and summaries.
Active processes or active images	Allow images on a screen to be connected to the underlying functions of a system. Used with access-oriented and data-directed programming. For example, a graphic image of a dial will always accurately reflect the value of the datum to which it is attached. Changing the datum will automatically change the appearance of the dial. Similarly, moving the graphic image will change the underlying datum value.

Special-purpose tools for building icons, menus, windows and so on exist, which provide some purpose-built elements that can be used within a new design. If a library of predefined elements is available, this helps to promote the development of a certain 'look and feel' (see Section 25.4 on house style guides).

EXERCISE

(a) If you were designing a set of icons to be used in a familiar domain, such as a university administration system, what kind of assistance might you need?

(b) What support might you like if you were designing icons for a system in an unfamiliar domain, such as agricultural economics?

COMMENT

(a) If you were working in a familiar domain, it is likely that you would require little or no support as to which concepts need to be modelled as icons. For example, for the university administration system, concepts such as student, faculty, examination, course and so on would be needed. Therefore, the support required would be concerned with creating the icons themselves: a set of guidelines for designing icons, a graphics package for drawing icons, and so on.

(b) If you were dealing with an unfamiliar domain, support for creating the icons would still be relevant, but help in identifying appropriate concepts would also be needed. Of course, the system specification will be able to help, but support for identifying the attributes of key domain objects so that they can be translated into the icon design would be of much greater use (Gray *et al.*, 1990).

Question 28.3

What might designers use graphics tools for?

Modelling and diagramming tools

Modelling tools can be either graphically-based or text-based. They differ from simple text and graphics editors because they also check and maintain the syntax and semantics of a model, which can be an advantage. Editors for graphic representations such as dataflow diagrams, state transition diagrams and so on are very popular. Some of these have syntax checkers built in so that the user can be sure that the diagrams are syntactically correct. In a graphics package, drawing a line connecting two boxes has no intrinsic meaning whereas in a modelling tool it may mean that data can flow between objects represented by boxes. If a box is moved on the screen when using a drawing package, the line will move with it only if the box and line have been grouped together. With a modelling tool the line will automatically move (and be shrunk, extended or reshaped as necessary) in order to maintain a semantic link. Some modelling tools also check that a model conforms to any in-house standards or rules of a specific methodology.

'Every now and then I let it do a self-portrait.'

(*Source* Honeysett)

Graphically-based models, or diagrams, tend to be simpler to produce and easier to understand than text-based models. However, complex diagrams are still notoriously difficult to draw and maintain, particularly if they are large. Automating the diagramming process overcomes this problem. Unfortunately, many of the models used for interface design are not graphically-based, but are text-based. Moreover, many of the design techniques discussed in Part IV do not have any software support at all. Although there is limited support for some grammars, formal methods, the specification of dialogues and direct manipulation, it is often complicated and hence liable to error. Table 28.4 describes the principal modelling tools that are available.

Table 28.4 Modelling tools.

Tool	Features and uses
Diagrammers	Allow the production of diagrams such as dataflow diagrams, structure charts and other graphic notations.
Concept modelling tools	Model the concepts or objects in a system and the relationships between them.
Transition network modellers	Represent the methods of moving from one system state to another. Particularly useful for designing dialogue sequencing.
User modelling tools	User modelling has been suggested as both an aid to design and a component in an adaptive system or intelligent interface. Characteristics of the possible users of a system are represented either to assist a designer or to be accessed directly by a system, which eventually builds a model of the preferences, style and knowledge of each individual user.

Visualization tools

Visual programming and **program visualization** are popular techniques for making programming and program understanding more accessible (see also Chapter 12). For instance, in order to program a command for opening a file, instead of writing 'create(my_file)', in visual programming the programmer can take a symbol of a file, name it 'my_file' and add it to the existing file structure. It has been known for some time that a flowgraph representation of a program is easier to understand than the text version; visual programming takes this idea one step further by allowing the programmer to produce running programs from visual representations. Box 28.2 contains information about a visual programming tool called Prograph.

Box 28.2   Prograph

Prograph (from The Gunakara Sun Systems, Ltd) allows object-oriented applications to be built and traced using a graphical language. Figure 28.2 shows a sorting program written in this language which takes a list of names and reproduces it in alphabetical order. The long shaded bars at the top and bottom of the window are the input bar and output bar, respectively. The rectangles named 'sort names' and 'show' are operation icons. They are connected via input and output data links; a small circle against an operation indicates that the

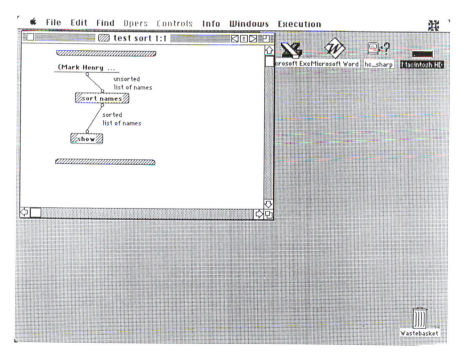

Figure 28.2 Example screen from the visual programming tool Prograph (courtesy Apple Computer UK, Inc.).

operation cannot execute until it has input. This program therefore has two main operations: one that sorts the names and one that lists the results.

The elements of the display are generated automatically. The designer merely specifies that an operation called 'show' is required. When the program is executed, each element of the design is highlighted as control is passed to it; new windows open to show the detailed execution of an operation as it happens.

Program visualization, on the other hand, takes programs that have been written in the traditional way, using a textual notation, and animates them so that the program execution is more visible. Certain analysis and design notations are amenable to these techniques. **Visualization tools** allow you to see your design working before the system has been coded. This capability greatly assists designers in trying to simulate their partial designs, although there are constraints about how complete a design must be before it can be animated. This topic is also raised in Section 12.3.

Question 28.4

What is the difference between visual programming and program visualization?

User interface toolkits

A **user interface toolkit** is a library of interface objects and related information such as buttons, menu bars, scroll bars and icons, error messages and help messages. Figure 28.3 shows the user interface toolkit for the NeXT system. The palette offers a choice of elements which can be 'dragged' across to the screen design: plain buttons, switches, radio buttons, sliders, menu items and so on. In this example, a screen is being created with three buttons: input, output and convert. In order to design an interface using a toolkit, a designer needs to write the control sequence to organize and invoke the relevant interface elements. In this sense, it does not support the actual design of interfaces, but the bringing together of discrete interface objects.

Toolkits are very flexible, on the one hand, in that they provide programmers with 'ready-made' screen items that can be called up by applications as they are needed. However, they are inflexible, on the other, as it is not possible to change the look or behaviour of the items supplied, and if the item you require is not in the library, you may be unable to include it in your system at all. In addition, it is difficult to modify an application built using one toolkit so that it uses another. A **virtual toolkit** is built on top of an existing toolkit and hides the toolkit dependencies, thus making it easier to transfer an application between different toolkits.

Question 28.5

The use of a proprietary toolkit can help to enforce house styles. How?

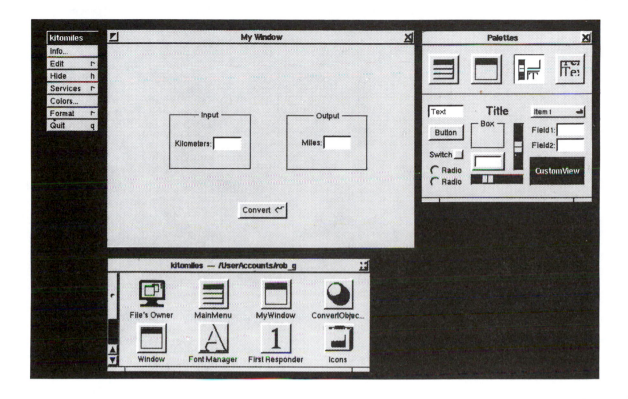

Figure 28.3 Part of the user interface toolkit for the NeXT computer.

An **interface builder** is a more sophisticated type of tool, allowing properties of the interface to be specified. Interface builders allow the designer to place predefined items (from an interface toolkit) on the screen and to specify behavioural aspects of the system. They can generate source code, which can be used further during application development. There are a number of interface builders on the market, including InterfaceBuilder for NeXT. Box 28.3 describes UIM/X, a commercially available interface builder for the OSF/Motif toolkit.

Box 28.3 UIM/X: An example interface builder

UIM/X (Figure 28.4) is an interface builder that supports the development of user interfaces based on the OSF/Motif toolkit. It allows you to create screens using the 'drag and drop' technique; that is, you choose your screen element from a palette, click on a mouse button, drag the item to where you want it on the screen, and

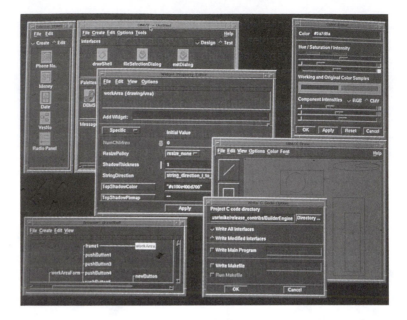

Figure 28.4 UIM/X gives you the tools to simplify the creation of graphical interfaces for new applications and existing character programs (*UNIXWorld*, May 1992). See colour plate 12.

then release the button to 'drop' the element. It also includes an interpreter for the language C, thus enabling screen elements to be linked with specific behaviour in the application, and vice versa. The following description of a session with UIM/X is taken from *UNIXWorld*, May 1992.

'When UIM/X starts, it displays a single main window that is divided into sections for interfaces, palettes, and messages. The interfaces section contains an icon for each top-level window in your application. The palettes area holds commonly used widgets, and the messages section prints system messages and warnings.

You begin an interface by selecting a shell or container widget from the Create menu or palette. You then use the mouse to define the on-screen area for the widget. Next, you fill the container with any other widgets you need, such as the usual fare of push buttons and scrollbars.

For each interface in your project, you can use a browser window that gives you the choice of viewing the interface in tree or outline format. The browser supports the usual editing functions and gives you another opportunity to add widgets to the interface. For each widget – or group of widgets – in the interface, you can also invoke a property editor to change widget resources and attributes.

To help you organize resources, UIM/X imposes some structure on the resource list. You can choose to view core resources, those common to all widgets; resources specific to the widget in question; callback-related, declarative properties, such as widget name and parent; or all of the above. Astutely, UIM/X gives you the choice to define resource values in code to prevent users from changing them, or in the resource file to allow users to customize them.

The dynamic behaviour of an application is called the *dialog component* in UIM/X. The dialog component comprises the link between the interface and application. In UIM/X, you enter C code directly into a callback editor, and the system-integrated C interpreter automatically parses the code and reports errors instantly.

UIM/X has two basic modes: design and test. The design mode is where you build the interface. Test mode uses the C interpreter to test the entire application, including callbacks, which eliminates the compile/link/debug cycle. As a result, you can only compile after you have tested all components in the interpreter. UIM/X also provides an interpreter window in which you can execute code fragments and get instant results.'

(© 1992 McGraw-Hill)

<h1>28.3   Integrated environments</h1>

There are a number of problems with using stand-alone tools, for example:

- Transferring data between tools can be very difficult and time-consuming. Even where tools provide a transfer facility, details of formatting and structuring can be lost in the process.
- One or more facilities may be inadequate. For example, the text processing facilities in a drawing package may not be as good as those in a word processor.
- There may be lack of consistency among tools. There is also likely to be a lack of consistency across interfaces, which means that a 'house style' and internal interface standards cannot easily be enforced.

As a result of these problems, there has been a move away from stand-alone tools to integrated programming environments, which are also referred to as system shells, management systems or environments. Integrated environments that incorporate a collection of facilities such as those described in Section 28.2 can be expected to provide a number of other facilities over and above those offered by their constituent tools. The kinds of facilities that may be included are:

- Configuration management. It should be possible to set up or configure an integrated environment to reflect any in-house standards or methodology.
- Version control. Controlling different versions of designs, including screens and other objects, in a system is vital to ensure good quality (for example, an untested version of a system object cannot replace a well-tested one) and can become very complex.
- A coherent body of knowledge about the system itself, such as a data dictionary. Such a body of knowledge is necessary for version control, but it is also invaluable for ensuring consistency and unambiguous communication between system developers.
- Accommodation of other tools. There is a danger in becoming tied to a single environment and much effort has gone into establishing a standard for common interfaces so that environments can accommodate new tools as they are released or as the organization requires them. This standard is referred to as the Public Tools Interface (PTI) or the public common tools interface (PCTI). PTI has been implemented as the Portable Common Tools Environment (PCTE) (Campbell, 1987).

Not all of these will necessarily be provided by any one environment. Some are oriented towards supporting design, others to implementation and others to operation and maintenance. For example, one kind of integrated environment, called an **Analyst's Workbench** (AWB) is a collection of software tools that support a system analyst's and designer's work. An AWB is usually built around providing support for a particular method, such as SSADM (Longworth and Nichols, 1987), Yourdon (Yourdon and Constantine, 1979) or information engineering (Martin, 1986). Other integrated environments are **Integrated Project Support Environments** (IPSEs), which include tools to cover the complete development process, and **Computer-Aided Software Engineering (CASE) tools**, which support the software engineering process. Box 28.4 contains brief details about an integrated environment for developing interfaces, but we shall not discuss the other environments here as they are not specific to interface design.

Box 28.4 Integrated environment for developing interfaces

'DESIGN/1 is part of a complete set of software tools, FOUNDATION, that supports a proprietary structured methodology SSADM and others, and that covers the entire system development life cycle. As well as a range of CASE facilities, DESIGN/1 includes screen/report designing and prototyping facilities to encourage user involvement in the Systems Analysis process.

> DESIGN/1 includes a central repository for sharing definitions,⋅ etc. among the development team, and a set of facilities for creating various representations of the intended system.
>
> Screen, Report and Window painters are available for the designer to create and modify screen and report layouts using elements stored in the design repository. Previously-defined elements can be selected and painted on the screen or report image.
>
> A prototyping facility is provided so that, using the specifications from the repository, screen navigation of the completed application can be simulated.'
>
> (*Source*   The HCI service for the UK Department of Trade and Industry (DTI), 1991 p. 16.)

Question 28.6

What advantages do integrated environments offer over stand-alone tools?

User interface management systems

Many commercial systems, including interface toolkits and limited interface builders, have claimed to be User Interface Management Systems (UIMSs). This has led to considerable confusion over the meaning of the term, as Deborah Hix points out in her interview at the end of this part. In addition, there is a further group of tools called user interface development environments or systems, which are also often referred to as UIMSs.

In this book, we identify **User Interface Management Systems (UIMSs)** as follows: UIMSs focus on the runtime problems of interface execution. A UIMS is a high-level interactive software application that facilitates the efficient development of high quality user interfaces. A UIMS mediates the interaction between the end user of an application and the application code itself. This results in a separation of the responsibility between the UIMS and the application, with the application being responsible for carrying out the 'work' while the UIMS handles all details of communication with the end user (Coutaz 1989; Hill and Herrmann, 1990; Sibert *et al.*, 1989). A number of different conceptual architectures for UIMSs have been proposed; a discussion of such architectures is given in Dix *et al.* (1993, pp. 353–7). A **User Interface Design Environment** (**UIDE**) is an integrated environment that offers facilities for designing the interface, not necessarily for managing the interaction at runtime. This environment allows application programmers and interface designers to create interfaces without programming and without having to learn details of underlying toolkits. A typical UIMS requires the designer to focus on the syntactic and lexical levels of design, such as command names, screen and icon design, menu organization, sequencing rules, and interaction techniques (Foley *et al.*, 1989). Through UIDEs, the designer creates an interface for an application by

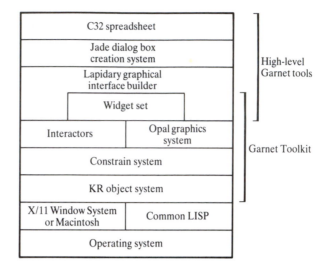

Figure 28.5 The structure of the Garnet system (Myers *et al.*, 1990: © 1990 IEEE).

describing the application at the semantic level, in terms of its functionality, using objects and operations. In practice, a UIDE often offers UIMS facilities, and systems that claim to be UIMSs offer more facilities than simply runtime management.

One system that has been referred to both as a UIMS and as a UIDE is Garnet, developed at Carnegie Mellon University (Myers *et al.*, 1990). Garnet provides an object-oriented approach to user interface design which is intended to ease the development and prototyping of interactive, graphical, direct manipulation user interfaces. Garnet combines facilities for handling runtime issues with higher level facilities for prototyping and designing the look and the behaviour of an interface. Garnet is composed of a number of different components grouped into two layers: the toolkit and high level design aids (Figure 28.5).

The Garnet toolkit has the following components:

(1) A custom-built object-oriented programming system that facilitates prototyping. The object-oriented paradigm supported by this system (called the prototype–instance model) differs from the conventional class–object model in that it does not distinguish between instances and classes, and that it does not distinguish between instance variables containing data and those containing methods. This results in a more dynamic and flexible model than is possible using the class–object approach.

(2) A constraint system, which allows the designer to specify constraints on the graphical interface. For example, one constraint may be that an arrow attached to a box should move when the box is moved.

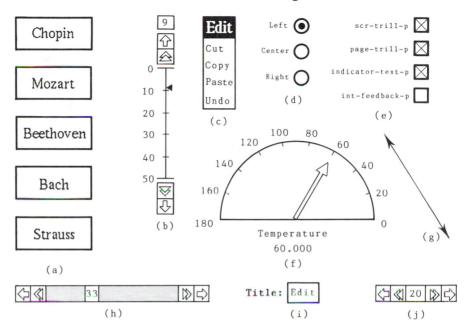

Figure 28.6 Some of Garnet's gadgets. (a) Floating buttons, (b) a number slider, (c) a menu, (d) floating radio buttons, (e) floating check boxes, (f) a semicircular gauge, (g) an arrow-line, (h) a scroll bar, (i) a labelled text entry field and (j) a number entry field (Myers *et al.*, 1990: © 1990 IEEE).

(3) A graphical object system, called Opal, which allows graphical objects to be created and edited. Opal can be used to add interface elements to the environment. So, for instance if a special kind of button is needed, it can be designed through Opal. Multiple copies of it can then be taken and placed in the screen design, as required, and if subsequent changes to the button are needed, all instances of the button will automatically inherit the updated characteristics.

(4) A system for handling input from the variety of devices needed in an interactive system: keyboard, mouse, digitizer and so on. Garnet provides a set of 'interactors' which capture commonly required behaviour, and facilitate their implementation.

(5) A collection of screen items called gadgets or widgets (see Figure 28.6); this is Garnet's tool kit.

There are three high level design aids:

(1) Lapidary, Garnet's interface builder. Lapidary offers the facilities of a conventional interface builder, as described above, but it also allows the behaviour of the objects at runtime to be specified. In particular, it allows the designer to draw pictures of application-specific objects, which the application will create at runtime. These pictures are the prototypes; the application creates instances of the prototype as needed.

(2) Jade, the dialogue box creator. Given a specific look and feel (for example, Macintosh, Garnet, NeXT, and so on), and the contents of the dialogue box, Jade will create a box that conforms to the correct look and feel.

(3) Although some constraints can be added through the constraint system, it is necessary on occasions for the designer to enter LISP expressions directly to specify high level constraints. This is allowed through the C32 spreadsheet (see Figure 28.5).

For more information about Garnet email: garnet@cs.cmu.edu

Question 28.7

Describe the main differences between an interface toolkit, an interface builder, a UIMS and a UIDE.

28.4 | Support tools for group working

Question 28.8

In what ways might the support requirements for group working vary from the requirements for a single designer? Refer to Chapter 23 if necessary.

Support for collaborative work ranges from fairly simple communication styles such as electronic mail to sophisticated workstations which allow two or more designers to work on the same drawing at the same time even if they are hundreds of miles apart. There is support for synchronous communication, that is group members working at the same time, which is necessary for meetings, and support for asynchronous communication, that is group members working at different times, where the participants do not need to be ready to communicate at the same time.

Meetings support

Design meetings often revolve around a whiteboard where various ideas and partial designs are written, so that they can be discussed and modified. In order to keep a record of the session, one member of the team needs to be transferring the information from the whiteboard to paper, or maybe directly into a computer. Electronic whiteboards, with a large screen so that everyone can see it, cut out the transcribing and in addition allow a transcript of the session to be recorded automatically. It is often the case that these whiteboards can be accessed by any member of the team sitting at his or her own terminal. With a large team, arranging meetings where everyone is in one room can be difficult. **Teleconferencing** – holding conferences of three or more people across telephone lines – is a well proven technology. With the advent of more and more sophisticated communications technology, like that discussed in Box 28.5, it is possible for meetings to be held between people who are literally on opposite sides of the globe.

Box 28.5 The ROCOCO project

The ROCOCO (Remote Cooperation and Communication) project investigated the communicational requirements of remotely-sited designers working on a shared problem. The ROCOCO Station, shown in Figure 28.7 is designed to replicate face-to-face working. It enables a pair of geographically separated designers to communicate in real time via an eye-to-eye video link, an audio link and a shared drawing surface.

A central feature of the ROCOCO Station is the ROCOCO Sketchpad, a computer-based distributed shared drawing surface (Scrivener *et al.*, 1993) which allows persons sitting at different computer workstations to share a drawing surface. The surface takes the form of a large 'shared window' which is displayed on each workstation screen. Users have simultaneous access to the drawing surface (the ROCOCO Sketchpad). They are able to draw with a selection of pen-types and can point to existing drawings with a telepointer. The drawing surface can, in principle, be shared by any number of users. The sketchpad is operated via a digitizer and pen. To one side of the workstation screen is a 'video tunnel' video link (incorporating a video camera and monitor). Users have a high-quality headset audio link.

See also Section 16.1 on CSCW.

Figure 28.7 The ROCOCO Station. See colour plate 13.

Technology is available to transmit video, voice, text and images between workstations, such as the Integrated Services Digital Network (ISDN) in the UK, so that meetings can be held in which participants can see and hear each other, and even share a whiteboard display, even though they are hundreds or thousands of miles apart. One of the most successful cooperative meeting support environments is the Colab system (Stefik *et al.*, 1987), which consists of three meeting tools: Cognoter for brainstorming, organizing and evaluating ideas, Argnoter, a tool for proposing, arguing and evaluating arguments, and Boardnoter, a tool for freestyle sketching. These tools are discussed in more detail in Box 28.6.

Box 28.6   Colab

Colab (Stefik *et al.*, 1987) was originally designed for supporting face-to-face meetings, but it has been extended for use between remote sites. Participants have their own computer screens and can broadcast their results to everyone else at the meeting, or view the contents of the common or public window; a large central electronic board also displays the public window. The original design had three systems: Cognoter, Argnoter and Boardnoter.

Cognoter is designed for preparing presentations collectively by supporting the process of producing an outline of a talk or article. Using Cognoter, a meeting is organized broadly into three phases: brainstorming, organizing and evaluation.

In the brainstorming phase, ideas are suggested by the participants by typing in a public window. No organization or evaluation is imposed by the system at this time; the only constraint is that nothing can be deleted. Participants can enter information simultaneously, and can move text around. In the organizing phase, ideas can be placed in order of potential presentation, or grouped with related ideas. Grouped ideas can be placed in a separate window, leaving a bracketed term in the original window. In the evaluation phase, participants review the current structure and are allowed to delete irrelevant items.

Argnoter is designed for presenting and evaluating proposals. An Argnoter meeting comprises three phases: proposing, arguing and evaluating.

Proposals can be put forward by participants in two ways. Either a private copy, which is displayed only at the proposer's screen, is developed completely and then transmitted to others' screens, or the proposal is developed for everyone to see. Many proposals can be considered at any one time; a proposal can consist of text or graphics. Once a proposal has been put forward, arguments for and against it can be written by any participant. Proposals can be modified during this time. During evaluation, Argnoter structures the proposal and its arguments based on 'belief sets', which map the set of arguments into valid (believed) or invalid (not believed) categories, and a set of ranked evaluation criteria. It is possible for participants to explore the effects of different evaluation criteria ranking or belief set mappings.

Boardnoter is a freestyle sketching system that can be shared between meeting participants. It is therefore useful for initial brainstorming sessions.

The Argnoter system is an example of a Group Decision Support System (GDSS), which is designed to facilitate face-to-face meetings by providing tools to help generate, structure, vote on and rank ideas. Such tools are frequently used in conjunction with a 'facilitator', that is, a person who controls the operation of the support tool. Often, the facilitator is charged with inputting ideas. Three levels of GDSS have been suggested: the first provides facilities for messaging, screen viewing, rating or ranking of ideas, meeting agendas and voting. Level 2 includes more sophisticated modelling and group decision techniques, including project management tools such as PERT networks or critical-path models. Level 3 is still to be developed and should include more intelligent support such as meeting rules and counsellors.

Day-to-day support

Support for day-to-day activities includes electronic mail, telephone and teleconferencing, shared access to files and facsimile. At a fairly simple level, access to a directory of shared files provides considerable support; every team member has access to the latest version of every document, without having to deal with piles of waste paper. Diary systems and bulletin boards also help. Box 28.7 contains information about a package called Windows for Workgroups, which contains many of these facilities.

EXERCISE

In what ways could diary systems and bulletin boards support the design team?

COMMENT

Diary systems, if kept up to date, allow each team member to know where other team members can be reached and when important meetings or relevant seminars are being held. Bulletin boards also help to keep team members in touch with the activities of their colleagues.

Box 28.7   Windows for Workgroups

Windows for Workgroups allows between two and twenty PC Windows users to share information via a local area network; it supports Ethernet, Token Ring and ARCnet. PC-based Windows for Workgroups is an update to existing Windows software, that is, Windows is required to run it and if you are not running Windows, you are not connected.

A cut-down version of Microsoft Mail is included with Windows for Workgroups, which allows users to compose, send and forward messages, and to read and reply to those received. This email facility is not sophisticated, but is a useful addition if no email connections currently exist. Real-time messaging is also supported, allowing users to communicate immediately across the network.

It also contains a shared organizer diary, Schedule +, which allows users to see each other's diaries, to share lists of tasks and to maintain schedules. Multiple views of task information are available, arranged by priority, by project or by date. Arranging meetings is particularly easy since Schedule + will, given a list of attendees, automatically pick a day and time, based on the individuals' diaries held by the system. An email message is sent to each meeting participant, allowing them to accept or reject the suggestion.

The problems associated with sharing information and sharing PC access are addressed by having password entry, a monitoring program to check how much time your computer spends executing your own applications, and how much time acting as a server for others, and a logger, which records who accesses which files on your machine and the length of connection.

Collaborative writing

Producing documents collaboratively can take two forms: either each individual works on one section of the final product, accepting comments from and giving comments to other collaborators, or one person can be responsible for the whole product, accepting and acting on comments from others in the group. In practice, bursts of both styles of working are often intermixed. Support for collaborative writing therefore needs to be flexible. It is not unusual to be influenced by several sources when writing something new. You may, for example, get ideas from newspapers, journal articles, overheard conversations, advertisements and so on. It is, therefore, quite difficult to say exactly what facilities are required to support the writing process.

EXERCISE

List the software-based tools that you think could help to support a writer.

COMMENT

As with any team effort, meetings play a central role; therefore, support for meetings, and other team support, discussed earlier, will apply equally for collaborative writing. In particular, group whiteboard access could be beneficial for commenting and sharing ideas.

A writer's performance is affected by experiences and available information. Therefore, software tools that provide access to relevant information would offer appropriate support, for instance, a database of interesting quotations, news articles, journal papers, books, authors, materials, definitions and so on. Tools that allow ideas to be expressed in different ways would also be useful.

Ideas are often generated by group working so the tools discussed earlier would be appropriate. Once the actual writing starts some form of document sharing system would be useful. Even primitive tools such as electronic mail or shared directories could be used. More sophisticated tools include multi-user editors and group authoring systems that support synchronous or asynchronous interaction. In the former case, problems could arise if more than one author tried to modify the same section of the document. Therefore, the system needs to divide the document into separate sections which can be sent out to the individual authors. Asynchronous editors allow many group members to see the document and to make comments on it, but the system keeps a copy of the original document together with reviewers' comments, thus allowing the document's owner to consider all comments before deciding on changes.

See also Chapter 16 for another example of CSCW.

EXERCISE

Which kind of editor would be more suitable for the production of a book such as this one, with different authors writing separate parts – synchronous or asynchronous?

COMMENT

When the authors do not need much contact with each other, maybe they just need to collaborate on a few points but they need to get the first draft of their own material completed, asynchronous communication would be fine – in fact, email was used extensively. When two or more authors are working together to co-author a section or chapter it would have been useful to have had synchronous communication.

Question 28.9

In the design context, what function do you think collaborative writing systems could perform?

Key points

- User interface designers used to use general-purpose drawing and diagramming tools, but more specialist support tools are now available.
- Software tools make software, manage the process, analyse programs and test them.
- Stand-alone tools provide general support, which tends not to be task-specific.
- Examples of stand-alone tools are graphics tools, modelling and diagramming tools, visualization tools and user interface toolkits.
- Integrated environments provide more facilities than their individual tools do. Some examples are user interface management systems, analyst's workbenches, AI toolkits and computer-aided software engineering tools.
- CASE tools support the software engineering process.
- A UIMS is software intended for the development and use of user interfaces. UIMSs help to free interface designers from low-level interface details.
- Design teamwork can be supported by electronic whiteboards, CSCW systems, electronic mail, bulletin boards and teleconferencing.

Further reading

ALEXANDER H. (1987). *Formally Based Tools and Techniques for Human–Computer Dialogues*. Chichester: Ellis Horwood.
A useful source of information on CSP-based user interface prototyping.

COUTAZ J. (1989). UIMS: promises, failures and trends. In *People and Computers V: Proceedings of the Fifth Conference of the British Computer Society on Human–Computer Interaction* (SUTCLIFFE A. and MACAULAY L., eds). Cambridge: Cambridge University Press.
A lucid review of the key issues in the research and development of UIMSs.

DIX A., FINLAY J., ABOWD G. and BEALE R. (1993). *Human–Computer Interaction*. Hemel Hempstead: Prentice-Hall.
This book contains a useful chapter on implementation support (Chapter 10) that covers some of the issues discussed in this chapter and also addresses others.

Human–Computer Interaction, **7** (1992). Special issue on CSCW.

Articles particularly relevant to this chapter are: McLeod P.L. An assessment of the experimental literature on electronic support of group work: Results of a meta-analysis; Heath C. and Luff P. Media space and communicative asymmetries: Preliminary observations of video-mediated interaction; and Kraut *et al.* Task requirements and media choice in collaborative writing.

Johnson P. (1992). *Human–Computer Interaction: Psychology, Task Analysis and Software Engineering*. Maidenhead: McGraw-Hill.

Chapter 8 of this book reviews a collection of user interface development environments.

Myers B.A. (1992). *State of the art in user interface software tools*. Technical report CMU-CS-114. Carnegie Mellon University.

This paper provides a comprehensive review of the subject.

Prime M. (1989). User interface management systems – a current product review. *Computer Graphics Forum*, **9**(1).

Contains a UIMS product analysis and valuable discussion of comparative design and performance features. This paper has dated, but its discussion of many fundamental issues is still valuable.

Shu N.C. (1988). *Visual Programming*. New York: Van Nostrand Reinhold.

This book gives a comprehensive discussion of visual programming and program visualization.

INTERVIEW WITH **DEBORAH HIX**

Deborah Hix is a research computer scientist at Virginia Tech in Blacksburg, Virginia. She has done extensive consulting and training in the area of human–computer interaction for a broad variety of organizations in business, industry and government. At Virginia Tech, she is a principal investigator on one of the nation's pioneering projects in human–computer interaction, investigating how to improve the usability of user interfaces through development of specialized methodologies, techniques and tools. In this interview Debbie discusses issues related to User Interface Management Systems (UIMS).

Will you describe what a User Interface Management System (UIMS) is for us please?

The first thing I'd like to say about a UIMS is that that term is one of the most overused and misunderstood terms in the field. I think everybody thinks it's something different. My own personal perception, and it's the perception of the group that I work with, which has been working with UIMS for ten years now, is that it is an interactive software system or interactive tool to help develop other interactive systems. That means many, many things and we have tried to take a very broad view of what a UIMS is, or rather what an interactive development tool, should be. It should support all phases of the interface development process, beginning with activities like task analysis, user analysis and functional analysis. We don't have tools that support these activities well now, but an ideal UIMS would do all those things and then go all the way through, helping with the design, implementation, and even usability evaluation and refinement of the

user interface. So probably, by my definition, a UIMS doesn't exist today.

What are the key issues in UIMS research?

Well, I've already alluded to it a bit, by saying that the early phases of the development process not supported by UIMS-like tools need to be addressed. There are really two domains that exist in producing an interactive system. One is the behavioural domain, and one is the constructional domain. I think it's in the constructional domain, that is software from the view of the system, where so much of the work has been done, and especially the UIMS work.

The behavioural domain involves looking at the development of the interaction component of the system, that is, what devices are used for input and output, all the things the user sees, hears and does. How we design, develop, evaluate and refine that part of an interactive system is becoming very important and the new buzz phrase in UIMS work is 'usability this', and 'usability that'.

What about usability from the point of view of the designers – those using UIMSs?

An interesting thing that occurred in the history of these tools is that the tool builders, who were producing systems to develop other interactive systems, didn't seem to care how good or how bad the tools were, at least in terms of usability. So UIMSs were notoriously difficult to use for a while. They were often based on grammars and other unreadable notations. There was direct manipulation, they were command-line driven. So it was very, very difficult to use those tools, which is ironic – one of the great ironies of the field. It is only in the last few years that user interface development tools have had any sort of graphical interface of their own.

Let's turn to your own work. Which areas is your laboratory particularly interested in?

We have been building UIMSs since 1984 but now we are looking at the wider issues in the behavioural domain, which is very unusual for computer scientists. Computer scientists are typically in the constructional domain. In fact we often have people say, 'Oh you're a human factors person'. And our answer is, 'No, we're computer scientists who just happen to be interested in the user as well as the computer'. We are looking for ways to write down, to capture the design of the user interaction portion of the interactive system. That includes ideas for icons and how the user is going to manipulate them, what actions a user performs, what the system will do in response, and all those sorts of things. Design starts with a good idea

in the designer's head, and somehow the designer has to capture that, presumably by writing it down somehow. When you ask designers how they do this, they say, 'Oh we do some screen sketches, then we write a little bit of English explanation'. At that point everybody groans because that's only the tip of the iceberg. It doesn't give you a very complete picture of the interaction design.

And it isn't easy to communicate to computer scientists?

That's exactly right. So we are working on a notation to facilitate capturing the interaction design. It is called the 'User Action Notation' or the UAN, and it is exactly that: a notation to write down the actions that the user will perform with the system and system responses, from the user's point of view. A simple example would be when the user moves to an icon and double clicks on that icon. A second topic that we're working on is the development of a tool, not a UIMS, but a tool to help with the usability evaluation process. The tool is called IDEAL, which stands for

Interface Design Environment and Analysis Lattice, and it supports all activities in the usability evaluation process. It provides connections between, for example, user task descriptions written in the User Action Notation, the appropriate benchmark tasks for users to perform during an evaluation session, the usability goals for each task, and then capturing and analysing the results of observing users performing their tasks.

What is it that motivates you in your research?

That's a very easy question for me to answer. And it relates to the same reason I'm in computer science. I think that computer science in general, and human–computer interaction specifically, are areas in which the work that one does can have an impact, can actually make a difference in the world. Having worked in HCI for ten years, it's been really exciting. We have incredibly powerful boxes on our desks – computers – and work in HCI is helping to realize their full potential.

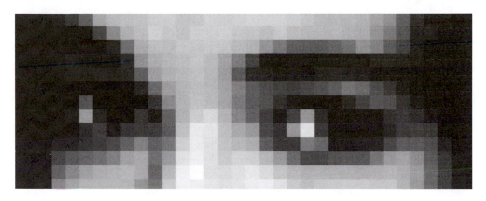

INTERACTION DESIGN: EVALUATION

The general aim of Part VI is to introduce you to some well-known evaluation methods so that you can plan and carry out your own evaluation studies and critically appraise documented studies. When you have worked through Part VI, you will be able to:

- recognize how design and evaluation are intermeshed,
- identify the differences between different evaluation methods,
- select appropriate evaluation methods for different contexts,
- carry out effective and efficient evaluations,
- critique reports of studies done by others.

In Part IV we adopted the star life cycle (Hix and Hartson, 1993) as our model for considering design because of the importance that it gives to evaluation. Evaluation is central as shown in Figure 1, and supports the whole design process by informing the design team about how well the proposed design fits the needs of users in terms of their characteristics, the kind of activities for which the system will be used, the environment of use and the technology that supports it.

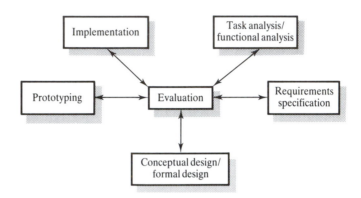

Figure 1 The star life cycle (adapted from Hix and Hartson, 1993).

As you have seen in Part IV, different kinds of evaluation feedback are needed at different stages in the design process. In the early stages ideas are being explored and tried out, and often informal testing is sufficient. For example, after a brainstorming session to explore different metaphors, the initial range of alternatives generated may be reduced as a result of peer discussion. At other times, and particularly later in the design process, more extensive formal user trials may be called for.

This part of the book begins with an interview with Brian Shackel. Brian was professor of ergonomics at the University of Loughborough and founder of the internationally known HUSAT Research Centre. He is well known for his pioneering work on usability and has many years of experience in consulting, research and teaching. One of Brian's contributions to the field has been to operationalize statements about usability so that they can be tested quantitatively. In the interview Brian describes how evaluation has influenced the design of some products with which he has been involved. He also talks about the need for HCI and human factors specialists to gain credibility with industrial development teams and presents some interesting personal anecdotes.

One important message from this part of the book is that, although the array of evaluation techniques may appear daunting, especially when valuable resources such as time are limited, it is always both possible and necessary to do some sort of evaluation. In fact, any time spent watching, working with or talking to users will be time well spent. The scale, formality and techniques that you can use for different kinds of evaluations will depend on:

● the kind of information required,
● the nature of the system or specification that is being evaluated,
● the stage in the life cycle being evaluated,
● whether or not statistical validity is needed (for example, if you are doing a formal experiment or large-scale survey, you may not need this),
● the resources available.

Very early on in Chapter 1 we mentioned the importance of feedback and it has rightly been a recurring theme throughout the book. Designers, too, need feedback and this is the role of evaluation. Brain Shackel also raises this point in his interview.

The aim of this part of the book is not to present all the possible evaluation techniques or to prescribe exactly how and when you should use each. It is to present the main techniques and to discuss the reasons why different approaches to evaluation are needed. In most practical situations you will find that you have to select one or more techniques and adapt them to fit the needs of your own circumstances. The resources that are available, for example, generally have a big impact on the kind of evaluation that you can do. Selecting appropriate evaluation techniques involves 'picking, mixing and adapting' from the range of techniques available.

In Chapter 29 we discuss the role of evaluation in system design, before examining a number of different evaluation techniques in detail. In Chapter 34 we compare these techniques and present some advice about selecting appropriate techniques.

INTERVIEW WITH **BRIAN SHACKEL**

From 1969 until 1992 Brian Shackel was professor of ergonomics at Loughborough University. He was also Founder Director of the HUSAT Research Institute, the largest institute in Europe specializing in human sciences and advanced technology. Prior to this, Brian was Head of the Ergonomics Department at EMI Electronics Ltd, in Britain. He is also Chairman of Technical Committee No. 13 on Human–Computer Interaction of the International Federation for Information Processing. In this interview Brian recounts some of his early experiences at EMI and discusses why usability testing is important.

Brian, What would you say is important when going into a company to do usability testing?

The first thing is that you have to 'earn the right'. Management and particularly the system designers with whom you are going to work have to not merely accept that you've got to be there because management says so, but to welcome you and accept that you're going to make some valuable contributions to the development of their product. I've got two or three anecdotal examples to illustrate this from one of the first computers that I was involved with at EMI in 1959 – an awful long time ago! This was the first of the transistor computers in the world, which was a very large machine that was used eventually to run the National Health Pensions Insurance System. First an engineering prototype was developed and then they scheduled a phase of ergonomic and industrial design. On the very first visit to see the console there were several examples of ways in which one could 'earn the right'. Five engineers were present who said

they would show us how they started up the machine. One man solemnly took a little reminder sheet and set up a row of 32 toggle switches in a particular configuration, 8 times over, which took 5 minutes! Well, they'd already shown us that there was going to be a punch paper tape readout, and eventually punch card readout and printers and so on. At that time, I didn't know much about computing but I thought this process was unnecessary so I asked how it could be simplified to make it easier and quicker. Unfortunately, I didn't know enough to say 'Why not use punch paper tape input?'. A month later when we went back the man

said: 'We thought about the question you asked on your last visit'. Then he pressed the main switch, went over to the punch paper tape reader, pressed the button, and ... 'BRRRR' – the machine was running! My naive question not only helped them to improve their design, it also helped me to 'earn the right'. Another example is provided by a 'check panel' for ensuring that the correct tape reel is mounted on the correct tape unit for any particular application. The operator would see a series of five successive readings in the form of a row of lights, which he'd write down, at the same time converting them from binary to octal. So, for example, the characters might be 2 3 4 5 6. This panel enabled the operator to verify that the correct tape reel was inserted on unit by going back to the list he'd written down, 2 3 4 5 6, and setting the values on a corresponding row of knobs below the indicators. However, because there wasn't enough room on the prototype, the knobs were in the shape of the letter W so what he would naturally do would be to set the top row of the

W as '2, 3, 4' and then the bottom row as '5, 6'. This was wrong because those five knobs in the shape of the W paralleled the row of five lots of lights on the top of the panel. What he should have done was to set the knobs as: top left 2, bottom left 3, centre one 4, bottom right 5 and top right 6. I guessed that this arrangement would probably cause errors and when I asked the operator to read the values he did not read off the knobs in the shape of the letter W: 2, 3, 4, 5, 6, he read them, as anyone would, across the top row first and then across the bottom row.

By demonstrating the problem with this design I was 'earning the right' to have my other recommendations taken into account.

Are there any rules to help people do evaluation?

That's a difficult one, because obviously you might be expecting me to come up with one golden rule or three golden rules, or even eight golden rules for evaluation. But, what I will give you are my recommendations. There are a number of evaluation methods that are suitable for evaluating different stages of product development, as you will see from this book. The issue is 'which do you use?'. There is no single golden rule or overriding guideline. Each product will be different and will be designed for different users with different types of working situations. Furthermore, users differ; for example, naive, first time users have different needs to those who have been using the product for six months or a year. So, if I was forced to provide a guideline, my guideline would be 'do not expect to succeed with just one evaluation method'. Almost certainly you will need to choose several during the course of the development process. Simple easy ones that can be done quickly in the earlier stages and perhaps more rigorous ones in the later stages. You must accept that your choice of method will depend upon the development stage of the product, the type of task, the type of system you're developing, the kinds of users you're aiming at and the funds you have available to carry out the evaluation. You will have to balance all these parameters against one another.

What would you say to people who tell you that they haven't got time to do user testing?

I can never accept that they haven't got time, though I can believe that they might not have the money because the management has not given them enough money and of course, money means time. Nevertheless, that doesn't absolve them from doing some testing. Even if it's just getting colleagues around the laboratory to comment. This can be very useful and it doesn't take long to do. Or you can bring in a few people from outside to try out the product.

It is very difficult if you are desperately short of funds and up against time, and the market people are insisting you get the product out onto the market. I can understand that and I have seen that happen. However, I could quote you examples where they did just that and the product was a 'flop' and the company realized subsequently, how stupid they were to have saved a month, and gone to the market without evaluating the product.

A more general issue behind your question is 'what about the company that just doesn't believe in evaluation?'. This is analogous to a pilot who is flying an aircraft with his eyes closed – he will end up crashing on the nearest hill, very quickly.

Let me challenge any of you reading this to experience what it is like to have no feedback to evaluate your actions. Just consider what it would be like to take your car to a large empty disused airfield where you won't hit anything or hurt anybody, and then, while driving at 30 miles an hour shut your eyes and count five seconds. I am prepared to bet that hardly any of you would be able to drive even counting up to 5 seconds without evaluation. That is without feedback, without opening your eyes. For a company to say 'we don't need evaluation' is just the same as saying 'our system designers don't need to see anything when they are driving; they can drive with their eyes shut and achieve the goal that they want'. You can't possibly produce a good product blindfolded.

29

The Role of Evaluation

Aims and objectives

The aim of this chapter is to raise some issues about what evaluation is, and why, when and how you do evaluations, which we will build on in the chapters that follow. After studying this chapter you should be able to:

- say what evaluation is,
- discuss the interrelationship between design, development and evaluation,
- outline the key differences between different approaches to evaluation,
- understand why pilot studies are important,
- be aware of users' rights and ensure that they are protected in any evaluations you do.

Overview

In Parts IV and V you saw that evaluation is a central part of user-centred system design. Without doing some form of evaluation it is impossible to know whether or not the design or system fulfils the needs of the users and how well it fits the physical, social and organizational context in which it will *be used. This chapter will provide a foundation for learning about the methods that are discussed in the chapters that follow.*

Evaluation is concerned with gathering data about the usability of a design or product by a specified group of users for a particular activity within a specified environment or work context. In this book we are concerned primarily with evaluations that provide answers to questions that inform design in some way and form an integral part of the user-centred design process. We shall take a very broad view of the term 'evaluation'. At one end of the spectrum we are interested in getting quick informal feedback of the 'and what do you think of this idea?' type. At the other end of the spectrum we shall consider evaluations that are much more rigorously planned and controlled, such as those that use laboratory experimentation or large-scale surveys. Regardless of the type of evaluation being done, it is important to consider:

- The characteristics of the users (or the predicted users) of the product who take part in the evaluation (for example, experience, age, gender, psychological and physical characteristics).
- The types of activities or predicted activities that the users will do. These may range from tightly specified tasks, which are defined and controlled by an evaluator, to activities decided by the users.
- The environment of the study, which may range from a controlled laboratory situation to a natural work setting. If it is the latter, the study is known as a **field study**.
- The nature of the artefact being evaluated, which may be anything from a series of sketches to a working software prototype or fully developed product.

Even in predictive evaluations, in which experts attempt to predict the usability of a system without directly involving users, evaluators take these same four aspects into account. They do this by drawing on their knowledge of the kinds of things that typical users would do and the sorts of circumstances in which they know typical users of the system will work. As we hope you will notice, we are again drawing on the same basic model of HCI that was first presented in Chapter 2 and then again throughout the other parts of the book. We are viewing evaluation within the framework of people, their work, the environment in which they work and the technology that they use to do their work.

The kind of evaluation methods that are used in different evaluations will depend on the nature of the different components in our model and why the evaluation is being done. An evaluation in which the aim is to find out how users work with their current systems in their workplace will use quite different methods to an evaluation to compare two different screen layouts in a laboratory.

(*Source* The Washington Post)

29.1   What do you want to know and why?

What do you want to know and why? Why do evaluation? The general answer to this question is: to find out what users want and what problems they experience, because the more understanding designers have about users' needs, then the better designed their products will be. Without evaluation the products reaching consumers would be untried; they would reflect the intentions of the design team but there would be no study of the actual relationship between design and use. (Remember the interview with Brian Shackel at the beginning of this part?) There are many questions that can be addressed by evaluation. Marketing may want to know how a company's product or proposed product compares with the products of key market competitors. For example, is the proposed functionality and 'look and feel' of the product at least as good or better than the other products around? For this reason most large developer organizations test their products against those of their competitors and keep track of exactly what is available in the market-place and how much it costs. Products may also be evaluated to check that they conform to specific standards such as ISO standards or the EC Directive, discussed in Chapter 25. Evaluations are also needed to answer specific questions that arise during design and development, and in this book we regard this as their key role.

There are many times during design when designers need answers to questions in order to check that their ideas really are what users need or want. In this way evaluation meshes closely with design and guides the design by providing feedback. This kind of evaluation helps to form a product that will be usable as well as useful, and for this reason it is said to be **formative**. In contrast, evaluations that take place after the product has been developed are known as **summative** because they are concerned with making judgements about the finished item, such as testing that a product conforms to a particular house style (see Chapter 25). As the focus of this book is on design we shall concentrate primarily on formative types of evaluation.

EXERCISE

From your knowledge of design, list some of the questions that design teams may want answers to during design.

COMMENT

There are many questions that you could list, such as:

- What are the problems with the old system?
- How is the old system being used in the workplace?
- Which metaphor would be the best?
- Which of the five icon designs should I use?
- Do users like this screen layout or that one?
- How well does the prototype support the kind of activities that the users do in their normal work environment?
- Have we used the corporate styles appropriately?
- Does the design of the system conform to legal standards?
- Which specification is likely to be most successful for this task?

Evaluations provide ways of answering questions about how well a design meets users' needs. If we examine questions like these further and try to group them into categories, we can see that four (and perhaps more) reasons for doing evaluations seem to emerge.

Reasons for doing evaluations

Four reasons for doing evaluations that we have identified are:

- **Understanding the real world**.   How do users employ the technology in the workplace? Can designs be improved to fit the work environment better? This kind of activity is particularly important during requirements gathering and then later for checking that prototypes of the system do fulfil users needs.
- **Comparing designs**.   Which is the best? There are various occasions when designers want to compare two or more designs or design ideas. For example, early in the design process there may be debate about exactly which functions are essential and how it is best to represent them on the screen display. On such occasions the designers may run tests that aim to compare two or more designs. Comparisons may also be made of design specifications using techniques, discussed later, that do not involve users.

- **Engineering towards a target**.   Is it good enough? Here the design process can be viewed as a form of engineering. The designers have a target, which is often expressed as some form of metric, and their goal is to make sure that their design produces a product that reaches this goal. There are two commonly occurring occasions when design teams operate in this way. One is to make sure that their product is at least as good as that of a competitor for a particular set of features. The other is when a company is upgrading its product and it is agreed that a particular feature that was not liked by the users of the previous version must be improved or replaced in the upgraded version. The kind of metric against which a prototype or system may be tested could be, for example: 'x % of novice users should be able to print out a document correctly first time'. You will remember from Part IV that this approach is used in usability engineering.
- **Checking conformance to a standard**.   Does this product conform to the standard? For example, is the screen legibility acceptable? Standards bodies have rigorous testing procedures to test that products conform to the standards that they have set.

Different kinds of information are needed for answering these questions, which are asked at different stages of design and development.

29.2   When and how do you do evaluation?

Evaluation in the life cycle

During the early design stages evaluations tend to be done to:

- predict the usability of the product or an aspect of it,
- check the design team's understanding of users' requirements (Chapter 19) by seeing how an already existing system is being used in the field,
- test out ideas quickly and informally (as part of envisioning a possible design, Chapter 22).

Later on in the design process the focus shifts to:

- identifying user difficulties so that the product can be more finely tuned to meet their needs,
- improving an upgrade of the product (as in usability engineering, Chapter 31).

As a general rule, any kind of user testing is better than none. You will learn something valuable from even the most informal evaluations – watching a single user interacting with technology will provide feedback about its design.

Different kinds of evaluations may be carried out at different stages of design and for different reasons, but the role of the evaluation is always to inform the design and to improve it at all stages.

The need for evaluation in the user-centred design has been discussed throughout this book, and in Chapter 17 we presented two brief case studies, which illustrate this point. The first describes the design of the 1984 Olympic Messaging System (OMS) (Gould *et al.*, 1987), which was a novel 'walk-up and use' system for enabling athletes to communicate with each other and with their families and friends by leaving voice mail messages. The second describes the update of the British national air traffic control system (DTI, 1991).

Question 29.1

Look at the description of the user-centred design process used in the development of the Olympic Messaging System and the air traffic control system described in Section 17.3. From the information given:

(a)   What kinds of evaluation were done in the development of the two systems?
(b)   Why were different evaluation methods used to evaluate the two systems?

Forte Travelodge (FT) is a hotel and catering company in the UK. Box 29.1 contains a description of the evaluation that was done by IBM (UK) during the development of a new central booking system for FT. The role of evaluation in this case study is interesting because it illustrates some of the constraints that designers tailoring 'off-the-shelf' software encounter. However, this case study shows that it is still possible to follow user-centred design principles to great advantage. The case study also describes some aspects of usability laboratory testing.

Box 29.1   Evaluation in the development of the Forte Travelodge customer reservation system

The main aim of the Forte Travelodge (FT) system (Department of Trade and Industry (DTI), 1991) was to provide a more efficient central room booking system for customers, so that customers could make several bookings at once and management could keep track of bookings and vacancies more easily. Both managers and users (that is, reception staff) contributed to the specification for the system and the system was developed by Forte programmers using bought 'off-the-shelf' software, which was tailored to the specific needs of the company. During its development both laboratory and field trials were done to ensure that it had good usability. Work at the IBM Usability Evaluation Centre in London had the following aims:

- to identify and eliminate outstanding problems with the system before going live,
- to avoid business difficulties during implementation,
- to ensure that the system was easy to use by inexperienced staff,
- to develop improved training material and documentation.

The IBM usability centre is a typical usability laboratory in that it resembles a TV studio and is equipped with microphones and video recording equipment. It has a large one-way mirror, which allowed Forte Travelodge and IBM staff to watch the FT reception staff trial the new system. The laboratory was set up to *resemble* Forte Travelodge receptions and to be as non-threatening as possible, similar to that shown in Figure 29.1.

The particular aspects of the system and training materials that Forte wanted to evaluate were:

- system navigation, especially how quickly the operators could complete the booking while answering the telephone,
- screen design and its ease of use, clarity and efficiency,
- effectiveness of on-screen help panels and error messages,
- complexity of the keyboard for non-computer literate operators,
- the effectiveness and practicality of the training programme,
- documentation clarity and ease of use.

A set of fifteen common scenarios were developed, which a cross-section of the reception staff enacted. The evaluation consisted of eight half-day sessions with

Figure 29.1 The IBM usability laboratory set up to resemble an FT reception area (DTI, 1991: reproduced courtesy of IBM Corporation). See colour plate 14.

several scenarios being evaluated per session, each lasting two or three hours. The evaluation team consisted entirely of FT personnel: reception staff, management, designers and programmers.

Care was taken to reassure the reception staff that it was the system that was being evaluated and not them. The video cameras were remotely controlled so that the whole team could simultaneously observe what was going on in the scenario and particularly so that they could see which keys were being pressed and how the documentation was used. Debriefing sessions were also held after each testing period, so that the reception staff could tell the evaluators about any problems they had experienced and their feelings about the system and documentation.

By the end of the week, as well as the designers seeing the problems with the system, a valuable by-product of the activity was that the reception staff and managers were conversant with the system and had received useful training. Around 62 usability failures were identified, which enabled the designers to improve the system greatly. Priority was given to the following:

- speed of navigation through the system,
- titles and screen formats causing problems,
- operators unable to find key points in documentation,
- need for redesigned telephone headsets,
- uncomfortable furniture.

As a result of the installation of this new system, FT claim that it has brought the following benefits:

- productivity of staff was increased and higher occupancy rates were achieved,
- bookings were completed more quickly and guest requirements were met more effectively,
- staff turnover rate remained satisfactorily low and morale high,
- the system has been expanded quickly to meet demand,
- operating costs and training times have not been high.

Before its installation, an average of 14 500 calls were recorded per week. After its inception, during the latter part of 1990, call rates rose by 80 % to 27 000 per week.

Question 29.2

(a)   How was the usability laboratory set up in the FT study and why?
(b)   What kind of data did the evaluators collect?

EXERCISE

Only one period of testing seems to have been done during the development of the FT system. Why might this be so? Why might a different approach to that used in the development of OMS (described in Chapter 17) be necessary?

COMMENT

In most cases you would expect there to be more testing at different stages of user-centred design. However, it was probably difficult for the FT design team to arrange this and also maybe it was not so necessary because the system was being tailored from 'off-the-shelf' software, which hopefully would already have been tested, but which in any case, FT would not be able to change. Having involved users and managers in the system specification, one major set of testing and field trials was, therefore, considered adequate. Also, the functionality of this system appears to be quite small. OMS, by comparison, was a novel system and the designers had full control over the design so they could do as much testing as they wished within the time available.

Review of methods discussed in successive chapters

The three case studies mentioned above say only a little about the actual methods used. There are several methods that you can use to collect and analyse data. Choosing what to do will depend not only on the question that you want to answer but also on logistical factors such as the time available to do the evaluation, availability of suitable expertise and equipment, access to users and so on. Often the choice comes down to money: 'How much will it cost and what will we get from doing it?'

Most kinds of evaluations, including those discussed in the three case studies, can be described as one of the following: observing and monitoring users' inter-actions, collecting users' opinions, experiments or benchmark tests, interpreting naturally-occurring interactions or predicting the usability of a product. In the discussion that follows we provide a brief outline of each of these categories of evaluation methods and then we discuss how each relates to the reasons for doing evaluations mentioned in Section 29.1

As you will see, these categories are different but not always totally independent. For example, a benchmark test may include monitoring as do some kinds of interpretive evaluation. They differ, however, in the way data is collected and analysed.

Observing and monitoring usage

In one way or another, several different kinds of evaluation depend on some form of observation or monitoring of the way that users interact with a product or prototype. Observation or monitoring may take place informally in the field or in a laboratory as part of more formal usability testing. Alternatively, it may be done from a participative or ethnographic perspective with the aim of really trying to understand how users themselves interact with technology in natural settings. There are a number of techniques for collecting and analysing data. Data may be collected using direct observation with the observer making notes or some other form of recording such as video may be used. Keystroke logging and interaction logging can also be done and often they are synchronized with video recording. The way the data is analysed will depend on the question that the evaluators want to answer. In Chapter 30 we discuss some data collection and analysis techniques that may be used in their own right or as part of usability engineering, which is discussed in Chapter 31, or interpretive evaluation, which is discussed in Chapter 32.

Collecting users' opinions

As well as examining users' performance, it is important to find out what they think about using the technology. However good users' performance scores are when using technology, if they do not actually like using it for some reason it will not be used. Sometimes, for example, a quite small and seemingly trivial feature (to designers) may be extremely annoying to users (remember the discussion of Donald Norman's examples of designs with poor affordance and transparency in Chapters 1 and 13). Surveys using questionnaires and interviews provide ways of collecting users' attitudes to the system (Chapter 30).

Experiments and benchmarking

Doing well-designed laboratory experiments is not easy. A testable hypothesis needs to be stated and all but the variables of interest need to be controlled. Knowledge of statistics is also necessary to validate the results. Controlling all of the variables in complex interactions involving humans can be difficult and its value is often debatable. Consequently, HCI has developed an engineering approach to testing in which benchmark tests are given to users in semi-scientific conditions. The experimental set-up and procedure roughly follows the scientific paradigm in that the experimenter attempts to control certain variables while examining others. Often the user works in a usability laboratory which is specially created for this kind of work. Although some of the same techniques are used to collect data (for example, video, audio and interaction logging), as when just observing or monitoring usage the evaluation is usually more rigorously controlled because the data that is collected will be analysed quantitatively to produce metrics to guide the design. Experiments, benchmarking and usability engineering are discussed in Chapter 31.

Interpretive evaluation

The purpose of this kind of evaluation is to enable designers to understand better how users use systems in their natural environments and how the use of these systems integrates with other activities. The data is collected in informal and naturalistic ways, with the aim of causing as little disturbance to users as possible.

Furthermore, some form of user participation in collecting, analysing or interpreting the data is quite common. The kinds of methods that belong to this category include participative and contextual evaluation – two evaluation methods specially devised for HCI – and ethnography – a technique borrowed from anthropology. In the latter, researchers attempt to immerse themselves in the environment of study. Notes, video and audio recordings may be made as in other methods. However, the way that the data is collected is much less formal than usage or benchmark data and the way that it is analysed and interpreted is quite different, as you will see in Chapter 32.

Predictive evaluation

The aim of this kind of evaluation is to predict the kind of problems that users will encounter when using a system without actually testing the system with the users. As the term suggests, some kind of prediction is involved. This may be made by employing a psychological modelling technique such as keystroke analysis or by getting experts to review the design to predict the problems that typical users of the system would be likely to experience. These techniques require a specification, mock-up or low level prototype. Predictive evaluation methods are discussed in Chapter 33.

In Table 29.1 we show the possible relationship between the evaluation methods just reviewed, and the reasons for doing evaluation that were identified in Section 29.1. As you can see, for all except standards conformance testing, several methods could be used. The exact choice would depend on the question to be answered and logistical considerations such as time, expertise, availability of users, and equipment and so on. Often, more than one method will be used so that the results from the different kinds of data can be reviewed in conjunction to give a better overall picture of the system's usability. For example, users' opinions are often sought to support results from observing and monitoring interactions. Furthermore, as you will discover,

Table 29.1 A summary of the relationship between the different kinds of evaluations and reasons for doing evaluation (X indicates a very likely choice, x is less likely).

	Observing and monitoring	Users' opinions	Experiments and benchmarks	Interpretive	Predictive
Engineering towards a target	x	X	X		x
Understanding the real world	X	X		X	
Comparing designs	X	X	x		X
Standards conformance			X		

it is usually necessary to adapt methods to meet the needs of particular evaluation circumstances. In Chapters 30–33 we will discuss evaluation methods in more detail, and then in Chapter 34 we return to the issue of selecting different methods. Firstly, however, we address two more issues of general importance: pilot studies and users' rights.

Question 29.3

(a) Which kind of evaluation requires a formal or semi-formal design specification?
(b) Which kind of evaluation requires the greatest degree of preparation and control over the evaluation situation?
(c) Which kinds of evaluation requires the presence of users?

Pilot studies

You need a clear question to answer or hypothesis to test before doing any evaluation. You also need to plan your study carefully, but however carefully you draw up your plans it is unlikely that you will anticipate everything that happens. Although good planning helps to ensure success it is not a substitute for experience, so do a small study, that is a **pilot study**, first before attempting your main study. Pilot studies provide an opportunity for you to learn from your mistakes without ruining your main study. The possible benefits of a pilot study include:

- the main study can be planned better because you will see what kinds of problems occur in the pilot and you can fix them,
- it provides an opportunity to practise a technique so that data collection is consistent,
- you will be more confident.

For example, before giving out a questionnaire to 500 people it would be a good idea to give a draft of it to just 20 people to try out. From this pilot study you would see which questions were ambiguous or poorly worded, enabling you to change the questionnaire before doing the main study. Distributing a poorly designed questionnaire to 500 people could be an expensive mistake if you later decide that the respondents were not able to answer one or two of the most important questions because they were poorly worded. Soliciting the opinions of your peers is also a good idea.

Users' rights

Don't forget that users are people too, and that they have other things to do apart from your tests, and that they have feelings. They may get anxious if they think you are watching what they do and perhaps criticizing them. Everyone feels threatened at the prospect of being thought stupid. Users generally do not have to help you, and, as well as remembering that yourself, it is good to make them aware of their own rights and to let them know that you are sensitive to these rights. In particular, you should guarantee them privacy and assure them that data about their interactions will not be released to anyone else. This means that you should develop some way of labelling transcripts of interviews, questionnaires and other data. For example, you can use numbers instead of names. You should also make sure that your users know what the aim of the test is in advance, the kind of activity that you will ask them to do and that they are free to withdraw from the test at any time.

Key points

- Formative evaluation provides information that contributes to the development of the system whereas summative evaluation is concerned with assessing the finished product.
- Every evaluation takes place within a definite context determined by the characteristics of the users, the activities that they will do, the system being evaluated and the environment in which the study is situated.
- Evaluation can occur at almost any point in the design cycle.
- Four main reasons for doing evaluation were identified: comparing designs, understanding the real world, engineering towards a target and checking conformance to a standard.
- Evaluation methods were classified into five groups: observation and monitoring, experimenting and benchmarking, collecting users' opinions, interpreting situated events and predicting usability.
- Several methods use the same data capture mechanisms (for example, video, audio and interaction logging) but the conditions under which the data is collected and the way that it is analysed are often quite different.
- A pilot study is a small study to test out the procedures to be used in a larger scale study.
- Users should be made aware of their rights, particularly their right to anonymity and to withdraw at any time if they wish.

Further reading

Dix A., Finlay J., Abowd G. and Beale R. (1993). *Human–Computer Interaction*. Hemel Hempstead: Prentice-Hall.
    Chapter 11 provides a good overview of the main evaluation methods and discusses how to select appropriate ones.

PREECE J., ed. (1993). *A Guide to Usability: Human Factors in Computing*. Wokingham: Addison-Wesley.

Part 6 contains a concise overview of the main evaluation methods, which are classified slightly differently from the way in which they are classified in this book.

SHNEIDERMAN B. (1992). *Designing the User Interface: Strategies for Effective Human–Computer Interaction*, 2nd edn. Reading, MA: Addison-Wesley.

Chapter 13 contains a good overview of many important evaluation issues and includes many useful tips for obtaining feedback informally as well as formally.

30

Usage Data: Observations, Monitoring, Users' Opinions

Aims and objectives

The general aim of this chapter is to introduce you to a number of different ways of collecting and analysing usage data and to ways of finding out what users think and feel about a system. After studying this chapter you should be able to:

- discuss the advantages and disadvantages of different ways of collecting and analysing observational data,
- collect and analyse verbal protocols,
- describe different kinds of automatic data logging,
- select between different kinds of interviewing techniques,
- criticize different styles of questionnaires and construct your own,
- recognize issues that need to be addressed when planning a survey.

Overview

Observation can be quite informal, and there are a number of ways of recording your observations. You can observe user behaviour directly, making notes of points of interest, or you can record it on video or audio tape, or you can log it using an automatic software logging tool. The basic trade-off between these techniques is that if you record data using video or logging you can go back and look at it later but you may end up with an overwhelming mass of data to analyse, which can be a problem unless you have a very clear notion of what you are looking for. If, however, you record those things of interest by hand your recording will probably be incomplete because you will miss things and you will have a less complete picture to review later.

As well as observing and measuring users' performance, it is important to find out what aspects of the system users like and what they don't like. Interviews and questionnaires are the main vehicles for obtaining this kind of data. These methods seek to draw out users' attitudes.

30.1 Observing users

Although the idea of observing events may seem very easy, Diaper (1989) points out that it is not as straightforward as it may seem and that we may not really be seeing what we think we are seeing. For various physiological and psychological reasons the eye produces a very poor visual image, which the brain has to interpret (see Gregory, 1966). Therefore, there is some truth in the saying that, to a certain extent, 'you see what you want to see'.

> 'One of the hardest aspects of teaching psychology is to persuade students that their sensory world is a property of the enormously complicated mental processes that operate on the stunningly poor evidence provided by the senses. This is true of all the senses though it is perhaps most pernicious in the visual modality.'
>
> (Diaper, 1989, p. 221)

During design and development there will be many times when you will want to observe users using or reacting to your ideas. Exactly what you ask the users to do and how they do it will depend on the reasons for observing them. You may, for example, want to see how they do a specific task. Alternatively, you may be more interested in seeing how they use the technology in their own work environment totally uninfluenced by you. The reasons for doing the observations coupled with your access to resources, such as equipment, will determine how you record your observations. Direct observation is the cheapest way of recording observations but given the choice most people would usually opt for some form of automatic recording, such as video, because it provides a permanent record to which you can return many times later as necessary. Furthermore, there are various tools that you can use to assist you in your analysis.

Direct observation

Individual users may be directly observed doing specially devised tasks or doing their normal work, with the observer making notes about interesting behaviour or recording their performance in some way, such as by timing sequences of actions. However, direct observation is often an obtrusive method because users may be constantly aware of their performance being monitored, which can alter their behaviour and performance levels. This phenomenon is known as the **Hawthorne effect**, after a 1939 study of workers in the Hawthorne, Illinois, plant of the Western Electric Company. Also, although the observer may take notes, the record of the observation will usually be incomplete.

EXERCISE

Imagine that you are in Oxford Street in London and you are evaluating a prototype of the Eurochange system discussed in Section 21.2. The design team has asked you to find out how long the average transaction takes and to note any problems that users experience. What kinds of problems might you experience?

COMMENT

You would need to find a position from which you could see which keys users press on the Eurochange interface but at the same time you would have to try not to be conspicuous, because people might be disturbed by you watching them, particularly as a financial transaction is involved. It would be quite difficult to time exactly when the transaction started and finished and at the same time note any problems that people appeared to have. We haven't mentioned where the Eurochange system is located. Suppose it is outside in the street and it rains (which is not unusual in England!); your notes would get wet.

Another problem with direct observation is that it only allows a 'single pass' at the data collection, and the evaluator rarely gets a full record of user activity for several passes at the detailed analyses. The evaluator has to make decisions about what is important to record and there is no opportunity to review that decision and look at alternative data later on. In the previous exercise this may not seem to be a problem because the system is quite simple and the objectives of the evaluation are clearly defined but this may not always be the case.

EXERCISE

Now suppose you have been asked to go into a school where a prototype of a new multimedia system (like the Beethoven system described in Section 12.6) is being tried out by groups of 13-year-olds for the first time. The developers have asked you not to interfere with the childrens' activities but to note the kinds of things that they do and what problems they encounter. What problems might you experience using direct observation?

COMMENT

There will be an awful lot of things going on: children talking at once, getting excited, maybe changing groups, maybe taking turns to use the keyboard. Some children may not have listened to the instructions and may be more interested in disrupting the activities of others than of joining in the lesson. You will not be able to record everything. You will have to decide what is important and focus on that, which may mean that you miss some interesting interaction. You may also get distracted and miss things. When you come to analyse your notes you may not understand your own cryptic comments or be able to read your own writing. However, despite these problems, you will undoubtedly have a better idea of how the system can be used than if you had not gone into the school, so even this kind of observation is better than none at all.

Direct observation may also be very useful early in a project when you are looking for informal feedback, and gaining a picture of the kinds of things that users do and what they like or do not like is more important than formal data. You can also improve the quality of your data by developing a specific recording technique such as a shorthand notation. If you know exactly what you are looking for then a checklist may be useful so that you can record each time an event occurs. If you want a permanent record then some sort of recording equipment will be necessary such as video, audio or interaction logging.

'*After another week he should be ready to record his first jump.*'

(*Source*   Honeysett)

Indirect observation: Video recording

Video logging provides an alternative to direct observation, which is much preferred for the reasons mentioned above. Sometimes the video recording may be synchronized with some form of automatic keystroke or interaction logging, which is built into the system software. Collecting several kinds of data obviously has the potential for providing a very complete picture of the HCI being evaluated. However, there are trade-offs. The different kinds of data collection techniques have to be managed and synchronized and there is more data to analyse, which as you will see, can be very time consuming. Indirect observation also creates more distance between evaluators and users.

In many studies several aspects of user activity are monitored by different video cameras. For example, one camera may be focused on the keyboard and screen while another is directed at the user. The second camera can record where the user is looking on the computer screen and her use of secondary material such as manuals. Users' body language can provide useful clues about the way they are feeling about using the system. Although specially mounted equipment that records all the aspects just mentioned is very useful, especially if it supports data analysis too, you will probably be surprised by just how much useful data you can collect using inexpensive video equipment – even the kind of equipment used by home-movie makers is adequate for some kinds of observation. However, there are some important issues to consider. You need to plan the observation, which means thinking about what you want to find out and what kind of data you need. For example, in a study of the way that people use a system in the context of their own workplace it may be useful to collect daily record samples over a period of several days or weeks and then to analyse the activities by categorizing them. A study with quite a different and much finer focus might involve an in-depth analysis of two users interacting over a period of just five minutes.

There can also be practical problems associated with setting up video equipment, which need to be considered. However unobtrusive you try to be, users are likely to be aware that they are being filmed. One way of reducing the impact that this may have on their behaviour is to leave the equipment in place for several days before recording starts so that they get used to it. This should help to reduce the Hawthorne effect. You will also need to decide how and when you will start and stop your recording, how you will label the recording so that you can catalogue it, who will change the cassette, where the equipment will be physically located and so on.

Analysing video data

Although many different kinds of study can be done using video, researchers agree that analysing video data can be very time consuming and that studies should be well planned to avoid wasting time. In less formal studies video can be very useful for informally showing managers or disbelieving designers exactly what problems users encounter. This can provide a strong motivation for redesign. Apart from this informal approach two other types of analysis can be undertaken: task-based analysis and performance-based analysis. **Task-based analysis** attempts to determine how the users tackled the tasks given, where the major difficulties lie and what can be done. **Performance-based analysis** seeks to obtain clearly defined performance measures from the data collected. The most common measures are: frequency of correct task completion, task timing, use of commands, frequency of user errors and time taken up by various cognitive activities, such as pausing within and between commands and reading or inspecting various areas of the screen display. Measuring the frequency of errors requires an error classification scheme. Furthermore, with performance-based analysis the issue of reliability is raised, that is, the measures have to be obtained in a uniform fashion that can be repeated by different evaluators across different groups of users.

An important factor in the use of video or any observational method is the trade-off between time spent and depth of analysis. An informal evaluation can be undertaken in a few days, possibly consisting of direct observation, system logging or video recording typical users undertaking selected tasks. If a more detailed understanding of user actions or task performance is required, the evaluators either have to collect and analyse user protocols or select relevant performance measures and play through any videotape or system log several times to extract all the measures. This greater depth of analysis can be very time consuming, and a ratio of 5:1 (analysis time to recording/logging time) is often cited; that is, one hour of videotape could take five hours or even a day or more to analyse.

Good support tools can help to reduce analysis time and several are now available on the market. For example, the European ESPRIT Project MUSiC has produced a suite of tools to support usability testing, which includes video analysis (see Chapter 31). At the University of Toronto a video analysis tool called VANNA (Video ANNotation and Analysis) has been developed to support real-time annotation and detailed analysis of video. This tool is discussed in Box 30.1.

Box 30.1   The University of Toronto VANNA system

VANNA (Harrison, 1991) runs on Macintosh workstations and PowerBook with an 8 mm Sony VHS recorder. VANNA allows observers to annotate the videotape by synchronizing it with a file on the computer. Observers code the data with index markers by assigning unique names to index buttons. These index buttons are used to label important events on the video and textual comments can be added either to the event or to an interval between buttons. Brief comments of around twenty characters tend to be used for real-time annotation, while lengthy paragraphs may be entered later during more detailed analysis.

All annotations are recorded in a log file, with each item type recorded in a different column, for example, time indexes and interval comments. The log file is then available to be viewed, sorted by any column, edited, searched and played back. Keyword searching is provided and the items retrieved may be played back by pressing a playback button. Built-in data analysis routines calculate the frequency of occurrence for each index label and the variability of duration between intervals. Data can easily be exported to a statistics package for analysis and graphical display.

In Section 31.2 we discuss usability engineering, in which video data forms an important part, so we will return to the issue of analysis again.

30.2   Verbal protocols

Video recording is usually coupled with some form of audio record, which is known as a **verbal protocol** (Ericsson and Simon, 1985). Sometimes this verbal protocol may contain users' spoken observations, and this adds an extra dimension to the information gathered by addressing the cognitive activity underlying the user's physical behaviour. From such a protocol it is possible to obtain a wide range of information such as, for example, the way that the user has planned to do a particular task; her identification of menu names or icons for controlling the system; her reactions when things go wrong and whether or not she understands the error messages provided by the system and so on. You may even get a clue about her subjective feelings about the activity from comments and the tone of her voice.

Sometimes verbal protocols may be collected on their own without video, either because the video added little extra information or because for some logistical reason use of video was not feasible.

A **think aloud protocol** is the term given to a special kind of verbal protocol in which the user says out loud what she is thinking while she is carrying out a task or doing some problem solving. Verbal protocols place added strain on users, who are required to do two things at once – the task itself and talk about their actions or what they are thinking about. Evidence from cognitive psychology (Section 5.1) shows that humans are poor at maintaining divided attention for more than a few minutes so you will need to think of ways to support users if you want to collect this kind of data. How can you prevent the long silences, which will not tell you much?

EXERCISE

Try this thought exercise. Imagine that you are driving your car through town and we ask you to tell us everything that you are doing or thinking about doing. Pretend that the journey starts off being straightforward. There isn't much traffic and you know the route well. However, once in town there is road maintenance and you are directed to take a quite different route, which is poorly signposted. Furthermore, the traffic is now very busy and it is rush hour so many of the other drivers are impatient. What do you think we would notice about your verbal protocol?

COMMENT

To start off it is likely that you will give a fairly full account of your driving actions and plans. You know the route and you don't have to put much thought into what you are doing so talking about it is easy. However, as soon as you reach the area where the diversion is you find that not only do you not know where you are going but that there is a lot of traffic so there is not much room for error – now you have to concentrate much more to try to figure out where to go. During this part of the journey you will probably stop talking because your attention will be needed to do the driving task. If you are prompted by a comment like 'And what are you thinking now?' you may continue your commentary for a while at least. However, if you are asked this question more than a few times you will probably get annoyed, particularly if you feel that the interruptions have caused you to make a mistake which will waste time and make you late.

The kind of experience described in the exercise comment is not unusual. The last thing that anyone wants when trying to sort out a tricky problem is to be interrupted. However, if you are trying to find out why someone cannot use a feature of the system that you thought was quite straightforward you will want to find out what the person is thinking and planning to do so you need to overcome the silence in a way that encourages her to give you this data. One way of doing this is to arrange for two users to work together so that they talk to each other about their thoughts. Allowing users to ask questions if they need to and providing minimal answers, just enough to keep them going, is another variation that you can try. Prompting can also be used.

With pairs of users the dialogue between them forms the protocol. The level of user experience is important for both paired-user and question-asking protocols. In some studies the researchers have arranged the paired-user situation so that a more experienced user has to teach her less experienced partner how to use the interface.

Alternatively, protocols can be obtained after the tasks have been completed. These are known as **post-event protocols**. With this technique, users view videos of their actions and provide a commentary on what they were trying to do. This is often used in situations where the tasks require careful concentration and are time-critical, such as air traffic control rooms, where it may be the only feasible way to collect verbal protocols. However, there is some debate on the extent of the differences between 'think aloud' protocols and those collected after task completion, and it should be noted that the post-event protocols can contain recalled information that was not used during the task sequence: hindsight can produce a rationalization of the user's own actions. Conversely, however, some researchers (such as Monk *et al.*, 1993a) report that when users are invited to participate in data analysis, it is often very beneficial because they are stimulated to recall useful details about their problems. We return to the topic of user participation in Chapter 32.

Analysing an example of a think aloud protocol

An example of the think aloud method is shown in the extract below. In this study, Carroll and Mack (1984) were investigating the learning problems that novice users, who were temporary secretaries, experienced when learning a new word processing system. Although the study is now quite old the excerpt from the transcribed protocol of one of the secretaries illustrates a typical verbal protocol and shows how these researchers interpreted the secretary's comments. Comments are provided in italics; L is the learner (the secretary) and E is the evaluator:

'1 *The learner [L] is trying to delete the underscore from the second of three words "will not change". She is not locating the cursor in a way that identifies the special underscore character.*
L: What happened? The line [*underscore line*] didn't disappear, now what do I do? Was I over too many spaces? I could have been.

Let me try again. I can replace the other one anyway. *Presses character delete, deleting the "c" of the third word "change". Not clear why she did this.*

What's happening?

2 *Positions cursor immediately after the third word and "under" the underscore instruction, so that the character delete operation correctly deletes the underscore from that word.*

It worked on that one. I don't understand. *Here is the problem: Underscore is represented by a special character symbol. To delete, the cursor must be positioned "under" this symbol and then deleted as any other character. The learner did not enter underscore instruction at the correct location for the second word but did so for the third. Therefore her action of locating cursor "under" the underscore character works as per instructions for the third, but not the second word. The learner does not understand what the instructions really mean or she would be able to recognize the discrepancy, and modify the instructions for the second word.*

3   *Presses word delete key, and deletes the third and fourth words.*
E: What did you just press there?
L: I just pressed word delete.
    Moves cursor to the next word and deletes it.
    Oh, wait a minute, that keeps moving all of the ... [*i.e., the line adjusts after material has been deleted*]
    Looks in the manual for information. Checking out something here under [*the topic of*] word delete.
E: What is that you're looking for?
L: I'm just trying to see ...

4   *"Not" is still underlined and every word in the line after "not" has been deleted.*
    I got a little paranoid when I saw everything moving backward. I thought "wait a minute". Now, I realized I wanted to erase the whole thing anyway and retype it and then ... Because I lost a space in there and I couldn't get rid of the line under "not".
E: What were you looking for when you looked under [*the topic of*] word delete?
L: Yes, for some reason I was afraid. I saw this moving over and I saw this moving over and I was afraid that I was going to erase. I don't know I'd ... I'd forgotten that everything was going to move over anyway as you erase, as you delete. So I didn't want to go on to the next word, although actually I may have to erase that also. OK. I'll see. I'll see if I can type this, retype this line ...
    Types in the rest of the sentence, after underscored "not".
    Oh, that's OK, alright.

5   *Moves the cursor back to the space before the underscored word "not".*
E: What are you looking for now?
L: OK, I'm just looking to see what it says here again. [*I want to*] start again with the underscore ... deleting the underscore ... Yes, no I'm just going over what I did before.
    Still trying to delete the underscore line under "not", places the cursor under the space after the "t" and deletes a space.
    Oh, what did I do?

6   *Moves the cursor under the "t" in "not", then moves the cursor to the space after the "t".* I see. OK. I didn't realize that before. I didn't realize it [*the cursor*] has to pass through ... the underscore. It has to pass through the underscore from what I understand.

E: How did you find that?

L: Um, under the, under the delete underscore instructions.

When she moves the cursor under the "t", the message "word under" appears on the screen.

I did that automatically before. It was supposed to be "under" the last letter of the underscore. *Presses a delete function with the cursor "under" the underscore symbol: the underscore is deleted.'*

(Carroll and Mack, 1984, pp. 33–4)

The most notable feature of this extract is the richness of information in the user's protocol. Reading just the italicized comments in this dialogue we see that on one occasion the user is able to delete the underscore character but not able to repeat this action and she has problems with inserting characters. The protocol provides an indication of where the user's misconceptions lie and how problems can become compounded when she tries a particular course of action.

EXERCISE

In analysis of the whole transcript Mack *et al.* (1984) identified the following eight kinds of learning problems:

(1)   Learning is difficult
   (i)   Learners experience frustration and blame themselves
   (ii)   Learning takes longer than expected, and learners have trouble applying what they know after training
(2)   Learners lack basic knowledge
   (i)   Learners are naive about how computers work
   (ii)   Learners do not know what is relevant to understanding and solving problems
(3)   Learners make *ad hoc* interpretations
   (i)   Learners try to construct interpretations of what they do or for what happens to them
   (ii)   Learners' interpretations can prevent them from seeing that they have a problem
(4)   Learners generalize from what they know
   (i)   Learners assume that some aspects of text editors will work like typewriting
   (ii)   Learners assume that text editing operations will work consistently
(5)   Learners have trouble following directions
   (i)   Learners do not always read or follow directions
   (ii)   Learners do not always understand or correctly follow directions even when they do try

(6) Problems interact
    (i)   Learners have trouble understanding that one problem can create another
(7) Interface features may not be obvious
    (i)   Learners can be confused by prerequisites and side effects of procedures
(8) Help facilities do not always help
    (i)   Learners do not always know what to ask for
    (ii) Help information is not always focused on the learner's specific problem

Examine each of the numbered statements in the protocol transcription above and say which kind of learning problem, if any, it supports. You should note that categories like these are devised on the basis of many protocols and should have been agreed by several researchers. For instance, what often happens is that one or two researchers will develop a taxonomy like this one and then give it to at least two other people, who will independently attempt to use it. If these independent users have problems applying the taxonomy or do not agree with some categories then there will be negotiations with the original researchers and the taxonomy may be modified accordingly.

COMMENT

It is more than likely that you have different answers from those below since it is difficult to work out what was going on, which demonstrates one of the problems of this kind of analysis. The answers agreed by the authors are as follows:

1   Could be (1), (2) or (3) or a combination
2   (2)
3   (5), (8)
4   (1), (2), (3), (6)
5   (2)
6   (1)

30.3   Software logging

Software logging has always been popular with some researchers because it does not require the researcher to be present and at least part of the data analysis process can usually be automated. Furthermore, it is unobtrusive, which is an advantage but one that raises ethical issues. You must inform users that they will be logged even though there should be no interference for them.

There are now a number of software logging tools around but most of them fall into two broad categories: those that simply record time-stamped keypresses and those that make a real-time recording of the interaction between users and technology. **Time-stamped keypresses** provide a record of each key that the user presses and also record the exact time of the event. **Interaction logging** is similar except that the recording is made in real time and can be replayed in real time so the observer can see the interaction between the user and the machine exactly as it happened. Very often researchers combine video, audio and keypress or interaction logging. The now famous playback system devised by Neal and Simons (1983) is an example of a combined system. Using the playback system the researcher watches a video screen set up in another room to observe user input at a terminal. The screen shows a log of the user input and system responses. The researcher can then add her own input to the time-stamped log in the form of a code (from a predetermined categorization scheme for user actions) and short comments for each user operation. The interesting feature of the playback system is that the researcher can replay the log of user actions at different speeds and perform further detailed analyses during this run through. The different speeds enable the researcher to pass quickly through sections of the log where the user has no apparent problems. Modern day usability laboratories like those discussed in Chapter 31 provide similar facilities. The advantage of using combinations of data capture techniques is that evaluators can relate revealing data about body language (posture, smiles, scowls and so on) and comments or more detailed audio protocols with records of the actual human–computer interaction. Although this may sound ideal there are two major drawbacks. The first is cost: it can be expensive to buy or build synchronized equipment. The second is that the volume of data collected can be quite daunting.

Question 30.1

Direct observation, think aloud protocols, post-event protocols, video recording (without collecting protocols) and logging are all well suited to different situations. Describe the main features of a situation in which you would use each method. You will need to consider the availability of equipment and users, types of activities, the Hawthorne effect, time needed for the method and so on.

EXERCISE

What determines whether or not the observational data captured is qualitative or quantitative?

COMMENT

The raw stream of data will be a sequence of events (in the case of video), comments (in the case of audio) and times (in the case of a time log). It only makes sense to think of them as being qualitative or quantitative when they have been analysed. For example, snippets of video could be extracted, which would be qualitative, whereas the same video could be analysed to count and categorize different kinds of errors, which would provide quantitative measures.

30.4 | Users' opinions: Interviews and questionnaires

What is lacking with the methods described so far is an indication of the users' subjective opinions about the system or prototype. Users' attitudes can have a strong influence throughout the design and development of products. At the requirements stage of design, for example, users express their opinions of existing work practices while at the implementation stage their attitudes affect the acceptance of the computer system and its effective use in the workplace. Checking users' opinions at various stages of the design is essential and can save a lot of time by ensuring that unusable, unnecessary or unattractive features are avoided. Interviews and surveys provide ways of gathering data on users' preferences, but they differ in the amount of preparation required, their style of presentation and the flexibility of question asking. The data collected from interviews tends to be qualitative but surveys are generally quantitative. Surveys also offer the advantage that large numbers of people can be reached, so there is the possibility of obtaining statistically significant results if required.

Interviews

You will need to plan interviews carefully so that the line of questioning that you follow is relevant to the issues being investigated. There are two main kinds of interviews: structured and unstructured (flexible). **Structured interviews** have predetermined questions that are asked in a set way and there is no exploration of individual attitudes. This fixed structure is often found in public opinion surveys and it is important if you want to compare the responses of different subjects or make statements supported by statistics. For example, you have probably seen statements in papers of the type 'x% of the people interviewed disagreed with the statement that...'. In contrast, **flexible interviews** generally have some set topics but no set sequence and the interviewer is free to follow the interviewees' replies and to find out about personal attitudes. This kind of interview is less formal and may be used early in design for requirements gathering (Chapter 19) and to gauge users' opinions about a particular idea. However, even if you plan to do an unstructured interview you will find it useful to have a rough plan in your head or discreetly written on paper and kept out of view of the kind of things that you want to cover in the interview; particularly if you are inexperienced at interviewing. As you get more experienced you will find the task gets easier. Another thing you will need to consider is how to make the interviewee feel comfortable so that rapport is established between you. This is particularly important if you are trying to gain information that the interviewee may feel threatened or embarrassed about telling you. For example, some people feel embarrassed about criticizing a system, particularly if it involves them in describing their own difficulties in using it. In general people who lack confidence tend to assume that the mistakes they make are due to their own stupidity and not to poor design. Alternatively, they may think that their opinions are trivial and of no interest to you. If you want to obtain this kind of information you will need to create a friendly, unthreatening atmosphere by being casual yourself while being in sufficient control to direct and channel the discussion so that you obtain the data you want. Experienced interviewers are excellent at this.

Intermediate types of interview styles that you may come across include semi-structured and prompted interviewing. In **semi-structured interviews**, the interviewer often has a set of questions that she can draw on to direct the interview if the interviewee either digresses or does not say very much. **Prompted interviewing** is used to draw out more information from the interviewee. Typically, the interviewer may resort to such tactics as saying '...and can you tell me a bit more about that' or '...and what do you mean by...'. Alternatively, prompting may take the form of showing the interviewee an alternative item such as a screen design, in order to promote further discussion or generate new ideas for discussion.

In general, as Welbank (1990) has commented, the more structured the interview the easier it is for the interviewer. This may be an important consideration if you are intending to interview domain specialists, particularly highly technical ones who know the domain better than you do. The trade-off that exists is the less structured the interview, the more scope for picking up relevant issues but the harder it is for the interviewer. You will need to make a judgement about how to balance the trade-off. Another issue to consider is that you need to avoid asking leading questions that beg a particular response. In fact, as with the other methods mentioned, you will gain a lot from doing a small pilot study. Either try out your interview and practise your interviewing skills on one or two users who will not take part in the real study, or, if you have too few subjects, try it out on colleagues.

In HCI research, flexible interviews have been used predominantly to determine users' understanding of interfaces. An example of a semi-structured interview is a study by Nielsen *et al.* (1986) on integrated software packages. Their interviews addressed the users' work procedures and identified the main task goals and reasons for particular task structuring. In this study a checklist of questions was formulated to guide the investigation of tasks undertaken by users of integrated packages. The checklist is shown below.

(1)   Why do you do this? (To get the user's goal.)
(2)   How do you do it? (To get the subtasks and then later ask these questions recursively for each subtask.)

(3) Why do you not do this in the following manner? (Mentioning some alternative way of doing the same thing. This is a 'critique' of the subject's working method and the purpose of doing it is to get a rationale for the choice of method actually used.)

(4) What are the preconditions for doing this?

(5) What are the results of doing this?

(6) May we see your work product?

(7) Do errors ever occur when doing this?

(8) How do you discover and correct these errors? (Nielsen *et al.*, 1986, p. 163)

This checklist provided guidance on the topics that needed to be covered but the interviewer was also free to follow interesting comments made by users if they appeared to offer valuable additional information.

EXERCISE

If you can find an unsuspecting friend or colleague who doesn't mind being interrupted for 10 or 15 minutes, try out Nielsen's list or tailor your own derivative of it and tape record the session. What kinds of problems did you experience and how did you feel about the interview?

COMMENT

You probably had to reword and tailor the list to suit the kind of activity that your friend was doing and also to fit your own style. For example, I would find question 4 rather stilted and I would prefer to word it as follows: 'did you have to do any particular task before doing this?' Similarly, I would replace question 6 with: 'And is it possible for me to see the work that you have been doing, please?' When you replayed the interview, how did you sound and how did your friend sound – nervous or relaxed? If the former, you may need to practise with more friends before interviewing people as part of a more formal study.

Of course data analysis is more difficult with flexible or poorly structured interviews but in general they provide much richer information. As in the case of verbal protocols you should get your interview transcribed so that you can examine it in detail because sometimes it is easy to miss subtle comments. For example, in a study of 14-year-olds interpreting multiple curve graphs of ecological situations, Preece and Janvier (1992) found that some interview transcripts needed to be analysed extremely carefully in order to distinguish between comments that showed formal understanding of the science concepts and those that relied on plausible but scientifically incorrect everyday knowledge.

A number of variations on the themes of structured and unstructured interviews are described by Welbank (1990) and outlined briefly in Box 30.2.

Box 30.2 Variations on interviews

The following methods (Welbank, 1990) are used primarily for eliciting knowledge from experts in order to build expert systems but they are useful for evaluating HCI.

- **Prompted interviews** in which domain items such as charts or equipment may be used to stimulate discussion. For example you could use your sketches of metaphors from Section 22.2 as target material to stimulate an interview about which metaphoric representation a particular group of users prefers and why.
- **Card sorting** in which users are presented with a number of cards and asked to group or classify them to form answers to certain questions. This is a popular technique with professional market researchers. For example, one of the authors of this book was once interviewed in this way about her preferences in airline travel by a company commissioned by British Airways. The interviewer laid a series of cards, usually about six, and then asked her a question and she had to select the card that most closely represented her views on the topic. The interviewer then recorded the number of the card and proceeded to the next question. The answers were recorded on a specially designed data collection sheet, which was then automatically read into a computer for analysis.
- **Twenty questions** in which the expert or the user asks the other person questions to which only a 'yes' or 'no' answer may be given, and in this way information is elicited.

Questionnaires and surveys

Questionnaires take a different approach to interviews. The focus shifts from the style of presentation and the consideration of the flexibility of the data gathering to the preparation of unambiguous questions. Potentially, questionnaires can reach a very large number of people so it is important to ensure that they are well designed by doing at least one pilot study.

Broadly speaking, there are two types of possible question structure: **closed questions**, where the respondent is asked to select an answer from a choice of alternative replies, and **open questions**, where the respondent is free to provide her own answer. Closed questions usually have some form of rating scale associated with them. The simplest rating scales are just checklists consisting of basic alternative responses to a very specific question. For example, a three-point scale of 'yes', 'no' and 'don't know' is often used, as shown in Figure 30.1.

Can you use the following text editing commands?

yes   no   don't know

DUPLICATE ☐   ☐   ☐

PASTE ☐   ☐   ☐

Figure 30.1 A simple checklist.

More complex scales increase the number of points to produce a **multi-point rating scale**, and the meanings of either each individual point or just the end points are given, as shown in Figure 30.2.

Rate the usefulness of the DUPLICATE command on the following scale:

very
useful |___|___|___|___|___|___| of no
use

Figure 30.2 An example of a six-point rating scale.

One variant on the multi-point rating scale is the **Likert scale**, shown in Figure 30.3, where the strength of agreement with a clear statement is measured.

Computers can simplify complex problems

|___|___|___|___|___|___|___|

strongly   agree   slightly   neutral   slightly   disagree   strongly
agree   agree   disagree   disagree

Figure 30.3 An example of a Likert scale.

A popular form of attitude scale used in HCI research is the **semantic differential**, as shown in Figure 30.4, which has bi-polar adjectives (such as easy–difficult, clear–confusing) at the end points of the scale, and respondents rate an interface on a scale between these paired adjectives.

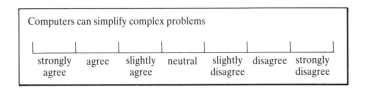

Rate the Beauxarts drawing package on the following dimensions:

|extremely | quite | slightly | neutral | slightly | quite | extremely |

easy   difficult
clear   confusing
fun   boring

Figure 30.4 A semantic differential example.

Finally, a named scale can be dispensed with and particular items can be placed in a specified number order. For example, items can be ranked for their usefulness, as shown in the part of a **ranked order** questionnaire in Figure 30.5. Note that a rank ordering process is most successful for quite limited groups of items as large groups can lead to respondents giving arbitrary rankings.

Place the following commands in order of usefulness:
(use a scale of 1 to 4 where 1 is the most useful)

PASTE ☐ DUPLICATE ☐ GROUP ☐ CLEAR ☐

Figure 30.5 An example of a ranked order questionnaire.

Once the questionnaires have been given to the selected population, the responses obtained on the different rating scales are converted into numerical values and statistical analysis is performed. Usually means and standard deviations from the mean are the main statistics used in the analysis of most survey data. If you think you need more advanced techniques we advise you to consult a statistician while planning your survey. Many statistical packages are available to support data analysis. One well known package is Statistics Package for Social Sciences, more commonly known just as SPSS. If you choose to consult a statistician, make sure you do so with regard to the questionnaire design in advance. Many inexperienced evaluators fall into the trap of collecting data and then trying to decide what statistics they should apply to it.

As well as taking care to make questions unambiguous it is wise to consider any measures that will increase the chance of respondents completing and returning the questionnaire. This means you have to make it as easy as possible for them. One rule of thumb applied by many survey research departments is to try to keep the questionnaire short. Unless absolutely necessary, aim for no more than two sides of paper. Of course there are occasions when you will want to obtain a lot of detailed information so you may decide to break this rule. If this is the case you may want to consider providing an incentive to respondents. A small fee may be used for a particularly long questionnaire if the survey population is small and money is available. A more usual and mutually acceptable inducement is to offer to send the respondent a copy of your report. The inclusion of a stamped addressed envelope also helps to make it easy for people to reply.

EXERCISE

Remember Eurochange from Chapter 21? One of the prime sites for locating this automatic *bureau de change* machine is in British airports and railway stations so that travellers can obtain the main European currencies quickly without having to find the

---

EUROCHANGE QUESTIONNAIRE

Background information

Departure lounge   Flight   Destination

How often do you make European flights?   Do you normally get your foreign currency at?
(please tick one box)   (please tick one box)

- less than once a month
- 2–4 times a month
- 4–8 times a month
- other (please specify)

- own bank
- any convenient bank
- special bureau de change
- airport bank

Please indicate the reasons for using this machine:
(you can tick more than one box)

- did not know where airport bank was
- long queues at airport bank
- last minute need for extra currency
- wanted to try out machine
- shortage of time – had to go directly to departures

The Eurochange machine is a useful addition to airport services:
(please tick one point)

strongly agree   neutral   strongly disagree

The Eurochange machine should be more widely available at European airports:

strongly agree   neutral   strongly disagree

Rate the Eurochange machine on the following dimensions:

	extremely	quite	slightly	neutral	slightly	quite	extremely	
predictable								haphazard
easy								difficult
simple								complicated
clear								confusing
fast								slow

Figure 30.6 The proposed Eurochange questionnaire.

nearest bank. Figure 30.6 contains part of a hypothetical questionnaire that will be given out in selected airport departure lounges where a prototype of the Eurochange machine is being evaluated. The questionnaires will be given to people after they have completed their transactions. Comment on the questionnaire design so far.

COMMENT

It is likely that some people will be confused by the use of three different rating scales one after the other. The semantic differential scale may be particularly foreboding and people may avoid answering the questions associated with it for that reason. The only way to ascertain whether this is true would be to try the questionnaire with a small number of people (that is, do a pilot study), so that such problems are detected and rectified before the questionnaire is put into general use. You may also have anticipated other potential problems concerned with the wording of the questions or the layout of the questionnaire. Readability is particularly important if the questionnaire is to be completed on-line. Notice also that in the first question about the number of European flights, 4 appears in two categories. So if you wanted to answer 4 which category would you tick, 2–4 or 4–8 times a month? This is a common error and one that can be very confusing for respondents.

Another well-known use of questionnaires is in 'before and after' studies of users' performance. Subjects are given a questionnaire to elicit their expectations or test their performance before being given a particular experience. Then, after the experience, they are given the same questionnaire again. This use of questionnaires, known as **pre-** and **post-questionnaires**, enables researchers to see how attitudes and performance change. Root and Draper (1983) took this approach using a combined checklist with open questions in an evaluation of the understanding of text editing commands. For each editing command the users were asked to respond on a three-point scale (yes, no, don't know) as to whether they: (1) knew the command; (2) avoided it; (3) found it awkward to use; (4) found it hard to type; and (5) found it hard to predict its outcome. Users were also asked open-ended questions about complaints and desired changes to the existing text editor. The authors questioned users about their opinions on specific enhancements to the text editor, both before and after they were given the enhanced editor. The results showed little correlation between the before and after responses, which led Root and Draper to suggest that questions concerning future changes are of limited value unless people have some experience with the changed interface. Box 30.3 contains examples of some other uses of questionnaires.

Box 30.3   Some uses of questionniares

Ben Shneiderman (1992) describes the QUIS questionnaire developed by Kent Norman at the University of Maryland, which is used for collecting feedback about a range of applications, including a public library access catalogue. Many of the questions in this questionnaire use a ranking scale and the respondent picks an actual number which corresponds to her ranking of the named feature.

The Open
University

Undergraduate computing survey

> Thank you for your help in completing this questionnaire. Please return it to
> **The Survey Office, IET, Walton Hall** by using the enclosed label.

The questions ask you to indicate your response either by ringing numbers, like this: 1 ② 3 4, or by writing in numbers. * *When you are asked for course codes they must be written in like this:*

	LETTERS	NUMBERS
	Start here	Start here

1   **Which course(s) are you studying <u>this</u> year?**

M205	1	*(1)*
M355	1	*(2)*
M353	1	*(3)*
M357	1	*(4)*
DT200	1	*(5)*
EH232	1	*(6)*
D309	1	*(7)*

2   **Which course(s) did you study <u>last</u> year?**   *(write in course codes)*

	(8-14)
	(15-21)
	(22-28)
	(29-35)

NOTE:

> A "computing course" could mean different things to different people. For this survey please interpret it very widely, as meaning a **course which involves some aspect of computing.**

3   **Are you interested in studying a "computing course"** *(or a further one)* **at <u>3rd</u> or <u>4th</u> level?**

Yes	1	...	Go to Qu 4
No	2	...	Go to Qu 5
I don't know	3	...	Go to Qu 5 *(36)*

4   **Which computing courses** *(only!)* **are you considering studying in the future?**
(Write in course codes)

	(37-43)
	(44-50)
	(51-57)
	(58-64)

Page 1

Figure 30.7   The OU computing survey.

NOTE:

HCI is *Human-Computer Interaction*; it is concerned with the design of computer systems which are safe, efficient, easy and enjoyable to use, as well as functional. This includes designing effective user interfaces, but it also involves understanding the nature of the work which people want to do and the environment in which they will do it. Designers also need knowledge about the psychological capabilities of the users.

5   **Would you be interested in a course on HCI which focuses on the human aspects of computer system design?**

Yes	1	...	Go to Qu 6	
No	2	...	Go to Qu 7	
I don't know	3	...	Go to Qu 7	(65)

6   **Which topics would you like to see included?**

	Very interested	Somewhat interested	A little interested	Not interested	
Programming for Microsoft Windows <u>or</u> Programming for IBM Common User Architecture	1	2	3	4	(66)
Programming for Hypertext systems	1	2	3	4	(67)
Input, output and interaction design	1	2	3	4	(68)
Techniques for evaluating a system's usability	1	2	3	4	(69)
Design methods which ensure the active participation of users in the design process	1	2	3	4	(70)
Use of design support tools	1	2	3	4	(71)
The role of psychology in design	1	2	3	4	(72)
Physiology and ergonomics	1	2	3	4	(73)

7   **Do you consider youself as primarily . .**

A Computing student?	1	
A Psychology student?	2	
An Education student?	3	
None of these	4	(74)

8   **Are there any other points you wish to make?**

Thank you for filling in this questionnaire. Please ensure that you return it to **The Survey Office, IET, Walton Hall** by using the enclosed label.

Page 2

Figure 30.7 *(cont.)*   The OU computing survey.

QUIS also provides a space for respondents to mention any other issues that they consider important. This is a good idea if the questionnaire is intended for just a few people, say under a hundred people, but it would be tedious to analyse for a large population. Shneiderman acknowledges that the time it takes to complete questionnaires can be prohibitive to some people. The developers of QUIS have catered for this problem by providing two versions of the questionnaire. There is a full version and a short version for impatient or very busy respondents.

Figure 30.7 is included to illustrate some aspects of questionnaire design. It was designed by the Open University Survey Office, and will be sent out to 5000 potential HCI students studying related courses to ascertain their interest in an undergraduate HCI course.

First of all, you should notice that this questionnaire is just two pages long, contains only eight questions, is accompanied by a reply paid label and is clearly and formally structured. The numbers at the side of each question indicate that the responses will be entered into a computer for analysis, except the answers to question 8, which requires a free form answer. All the other questions require a clear answer; either an item must be ringed or a course number of a fixed length must be given. This questionnaire has been reviewed by members of our group and prepared by a professional market researcher. This does not mean that it is perfect but does suggest that it should do the required job.

Key points

- Observing can change what is being observed – the Hawthorne effect.
- Verbal protocols help to reveal what the user is thinking.
- The problem with think aloud protocols is that in difficult problem solving situations users usually stop talking.
- Prompting, questions or working with pairs of users are ways of avoiding silences.
- There are two main types of software logging – time-stamped keypresses and interaction logging.
- Users should always be told that they are being recorded.
- Structured interviews are easier to carry out than unstructured ones but they forfeit the opportunity to pick up interesting issues.
- Questions in a questionnaire should be unambiguous and clearly laid out.
- Ranking scales should not overlap.
- Check that the length of the questionnaire is appropriate.
- Always try to carry out a pilot study to test the questionnaire design, particularly if it is being sent to a large population.
- Pre- and post-questionnaires enable researchers to check changes in attitudes or performance.

Further reading

DIAPER D. (1989). Task observation for human–computer interaction. In *Task Analysis for Human–Computer Interaction* (DIAPER D., ed.). Chichester: Ellis Horwood.

This chapter contains a good discussion about why it is difficult to be an objective observer and why observation itself is not easy.

ERICSSON K.A. and SIMON H.A. (1985). *Protocol Analysis: Verbal Reports as Data*. Cambridge, MA: MIT Press.

This book contains a detailed account of how to collect and analyse verbal protocols.

SHNEIDERMAN B. (1992). *Designing the User Interface: Strategies for Effective Human–Computer Interaction*, 2nd edn. Reading, MA: Addison-Wesley.

Chapter 13 contains a discussion of a number of issues related to interviewing, questionnaire design and evaluation techniques in general. Tables 13.2 and 13.3 contain the QUIS questionnaire.

WELBANK M. (1990). An overview of knowledge acquisition methods. *Interacting with Computers*, **2**(1), 83–91.

This paper contains a useful discussion of interviews and other techniques used in knowledge acquisition.

31

Experiments and Benchmarking

Aims and objectives

The aim of this chapter is to describe briefly the main issues involved in planning and carrying out laboratory experiments and then to examine benchmarking and usability engineering. After studying this chapter you should be able to:

- critique experimental design,
- define common experimental terms like 'hypothesis', 'independent variable' and 'dependent variable',
- formulate testable hypotheses,
- recognize how and why benchmarking is different from traditional scientific experimentation,
- understand the scope and role of usability engineering testing methods.

Overview

Considerable skill and scientific knowledge is necessary to do well-designed experiments. A good knowledge of statistics is also important. The introduction to the topic provided in this chapter will enable you to achieve the objectives listed above. Designing your own laboratory experiments will require further study. Studying this chapter will also provide a foundation for understanding usability engineering, which is a key practice in HCI. Usability engineering is derived partly from scientific practice and partly from engineering, as the name suggests. Like engineering its aims are to improve design by applying scientific practices. You should, therefore, not be surprised to discover that usability engineering modifies scientific practice so that it fulfils the practical needs of design and development. As in traditional experiments measurement is important. Unlike traditional behavioural research, however, controlling all the variables except those of direct interest is generally not possible. If you have a background in pure science you will need to get used to the more applied approaches that dominate HCI.

31.1 Traditional experiments

When experiments are used in HCI they tend to have a narrow scope and usually address specific aspects of human–computer interface design. The important feature of experimental studies is that the investigator can manipulate a number of factors associated with the design and study the effect on various aspects of user performance. Before testing, the required level of user experience and the design of the experiment need to be decided. Usually only one or a few factors are manipulated so that the causal relationship between manipulations and user performance can be established. Well-designed experimental studies usually have a clear hypothesis, which predicts the expected performance effects associated with the experiments and concludes with a statistical analysis of the data collected.

During the 1970s and 1980s psychologists did a lot of laboratory experiments in order to establish basic knowledge about such things as how deep menus ought to be for particular contexts, and it is possible that you may wish to do similar narrowly defined studies to investigate a particular aspect of HCI such as, for example, the design of icons. Experiments like these inform design but it is generally not practicable to do them as part of the design process because the amount of resource required in terms of time and expertize to do such studies is prohibitive. Furthermore, their findings tend to be at a micro level compared with the kind of decisions that designers often have to make. However, when very specific information is needed, such as deciding on the best way to select text in the design of the Star Office Workstation (Bewley *et al.*, 1990) experiments can be useful, as you can see from Box 31.1.

Box 31.1 Evolution of the text selection schemes in the Star Workstation

'The goal of the two selection schemes tests was to evaluate methods for selecting text. The schemes are various mappings of one, two or three mouse buttons to the functions needed for indicating what text is to be operated on. The kinds of selection behaviour needed are:

(1) Point: indicating a point between two characters, to be used as the destination of a Move or Copy, or the position where new typed text will be inserted.
(2) Select: selecting some text, possibly in increments of a character, word, sentence, paragraph or the whole document.
(3) Extend: extending the selection to include a whole range of text.

Selection scheme Test 1

The first test compared six selection schemes. These schemes are summarized in Table 31.1, schemes A through F. The six selection schemes differ in the mapping between mouse buttons and the three operations. As one example of the differences among schemes, in two schemes, A and B, different buttons are used for Point and Select, while in the remaining four schemes the first button is used for both Point and Select.

Table 31.1 Description of the selection schemes.

	Scheme A	Scheme B	Scheme C	Scheme D	Scheme E	Scheme F	Scheme G
Button 1	Point	Point	Point C Drawthrough	Point C, W, S, ¶, D Drawthrough	Point C, W, S, ¶, D Drawthrough	Point C Drawthrough	Point C, W, S, ¶, D
Button 2	C Drawthrough	C, W, S, ¶, D Drawthrough	W, S, ¶, D Drawthrough		Adjust	Adjust	Adjust
Button 3	W, S, ¶, D Drawthrough						

Key:
Point: Selects a point, i.e. a position between adjacent characters. Used as destination for Move or Copy. If the button does not also make a text selection, Point is also used to indicate a destination for type-in.
C, W, S, ¶, D: Selects a character, word, sentence, paragraph or whole document by repeatedly clicking the mouse button while pointing at something that is already selected.
Drawthrough: The user holds the button down and moves the mouse. The selection extends from the button-down position to the button-up point. The selection is extended in units of whatever was previously selected.
Adjust: The user clicks the mouse button to extend the selection from the existing selection to the button-up point. The selection is extended in units of whatever was previously selected.

Methodology

Using a between-subjects paradigm, each of six groups (four subjects per group) was assigned one of the six schemes. Two of the subjects in each group were experienced in the use of the mouse, two were not. Each subject was first trained in the use of the mouse and in basic Star editing techniques. Next, the assigned scheme was taught. Each subject then performed ten text-editing tasks, each of which was repeated six times. Dependent variables were selection time and selection errors.

Selection time

Mean selection times are shown in Table 31.2. Among these six schemes, scheme F was significantly better than the others over all six trials ($p < 0.001$).

Table 31.2 Mean selection time (s).

Scheme A	Scheme B	Scheme C	Scheme D	Scheme E	Scheme F	Scheme G
12.25	15.19	13.41	13.44	12.85	9.89	7.96

Selection errors

There was an average of one selection error per four tasks. The majority (65 per cent) were errors in drawthrough: either too far or not far enough. The frequency of drawthrough errors did not vary as a function of selection scheme. "Too many clicks" errors, e.g. the subject clicking to a sentence instead of a word, accounted for 20 per cent of the errors, with schemes which employed less multiple-clicking being better. "Click wrong mouse button" errors accounted for 15 per cent of total errors. These errors also varied across schemes, with schemes having fewer buttons being better.

Selection scheme Test 2

The results of the first test were interpreted as suggesting that the following features of a selection scheme should be avoided:

(1) Drawthrough.
(2) Three buttons.
(3) Multiple-clicking.

The second selection scheme test evaluated a scheme designed with these results in mind. Scheme G is also described in [Table 31.1]. It is essentially Scheme F with the addition of multiple-clicking. It avoids drawthrough and uses only two buttons. Multiple-clicking is used because, although 20 per cent of the errors in the first test were attributable to errors in multiple-clicking, Star's designers felt that a selection scheme must provide for quick selection of standard text units.

The same methodology was used for evaluating the new scheme as was used for the rest, except that only one user was experienced with the mouse and three were not.

Results

The mean selection time for the new scheme was 7.96 s, the lowest time so far. The frequency of "too many clicks" errors in Scheme G was about the same as the frequency observed in the first selection scheme test.

Conclusions

The results of the second test were interpreted as indicating that Scheme G was acceptable for Star, since:

(1) Selection time for Scheme G was shorter than for all other schemes.
(2) The advantage of providing quick selection of standard text units through multiple-clicking was judged sufficiently great to balance the moderate error rate due to multiple-clicking errors.'

(Source   Bewley et al., 1990)

Question 31.1

Read Box 31.1 and then answer the following questions.

(a)   Indicate where in the design cycle tests on the selection scheme could have occurred. Describe how the results of these tests could feed back into the design cycle and cause redesign.

(b)   The selection scheme test used separate groups of subjects for each scheme. Suggest some reasons why this was done instead of giving all the selection schemes to one group of subjects.

(c)   The selection scheme tests contained one manipulation or change that was not reported in the results. What was it?

The testing of the Star interface illustrates two key points about experimental evaluation. Firstly, it is a powerful evaluation method, in that it can be used to study the effects of various changes on user preferences and performance. Secondly, experimental evaluations have high resource demands. Even a simple experiment can be very time-consuming and when there are constraints on the design and development effort, it is often difficult to allocate the time required to do experiments. More often than not if experiments are used in HCI design the procedure is adapted; some scientific rigour is traded for reality while retaining some of the objectivity inherent in the scientific paradigm. Usability engineering falls into this category, as you will see in Section 31.2.

Fundamentals of doing experiments

When you plan an experiment you need to think about three aspects:

- the purpose of the experiment – what is being changed, what is being kept constant and what is being measured,
- a hypothesis, which needs to be stated in a way that can be tested,
- what statistical tests you will apply to the data that you collect and why.

For example, an evaluation of relative user efficiency in using function keys or menus in an industrial process control system would have to be stated in terms of the elements to be compared (that is, function keys versus menus), the constant features of the testing situation (such as the experience of the process operators and their control tasks) and the measures of user performance being studied (such as command execution speed or error rates). In this situation, one possible hypothesis is that function keys are more efficient, that is, they produce faster command execution. Groups of users would be given the two interfaces, and the statistical significance of the differences in command execution times and error rates would be determined.

Variables

The **independent variable** is the variable that the experimenter manipulates. The variable that is dependent upon it is the **dependent variable**. So the independent variable should always remain uninfluenced by the dependent variable, whereas the dependent variable is expected to be influenced by the independent variable.

According to Robinson (1990):

'In psychological experiments the independent variable is almost always either concerned with a property of the people taking part in the experiment or a stimulus variable; that is, in general, the *input* to the organism. Conversely, the dependent variable is almost always a response variable (time taken to make a response, strength of response, number of responses, etc.): that is, in general, the *output* from the organism.'

For example, in an experiment in which we want to measure accuracy of typing in relation to the subject's age, the independent variable would be age and the dependent variable would be some measure of accuracy of typing – most likely the number of typing mistakes. (However, we would need to decide what exactly constituted a mistake – an incorrect letter, an incorrect word or sentence, or something else. Even this is not totally straightforward.)

Selecting subjects

You will need to select your subjects carefully so that you avoid biases. For example, if you were doing an experiment to determine which out of four sets of icon designs were recognized fastest by children between 7 and 10 you would need to select children that covered the total age range so that there was no age bias, equal numbers of boys and girls to avoid gender bias and children with the same level of experience of using computers and whose academic records were similar.

Experimental design

The way that the experiment is designed is important, too, and there are three well-known experimental designs (Robson, 1990): independent, matched subject and repeated-measures designs.

Independent subject design

In this condition a group of subjects is obtained for the experiment as a whole and then subjects are allocated randomly to one of, say, two experimental conditions.

Matched subject design

In this condition subjects are matched in pairs (often a male and a female so that any bias resulting from gender can be eliminated) and then the pairs are allocated randomly to the two conditions.

Repeated measures design

In this design all the subjects appear in both experimental conditions, so halving the number of subjects needed in comparison with the other two designs. Although there are no problems of subject allocation with this design, there are problems to do with the order in which subjects do the task. For example, might learning on the first task influence performance on the second?

A fourth type of design is **single subject design**, in which in-depth experiments are performed with just one subject. While this may be essential for reasons of scale in some studies, there can be problems. It may not be possible to validate the results statistically (although small subject pools also have this problem) and any learning that occurs may bias the results.

Any change in the dependent variable that is caused by a change in the independent variable is called an **experimental effect**. However, there may also be changes in the dependent variable that are brought about by variables other than the independent variable. As we have already said, in a repeated measures design it is possible that order will have an effect on subjects' performance. For example, subjects may be nervous and perform less well on the first task, or learning may influence their performance on the second task. Alternatively, if the task is long, fatigue or boredom could be influential. When such things happen the experimental effect is said to be **confounded**. The effect of order can be reduced by dividing the subjects in the repeated measure design into two groups. One group then does task A followed by task B and the other group does task B followed by A. Who does what first can be randomly determined by tossing a coin, thus eliminating the possibility of the experimenter influencing the selection.

Question 31.2

An experimental study gave a single group of users two sets of simple item selection tasks. The first set required simultaneous use of more than one mouse button and the second set used different buttons. Task completion time and users' preferences were measured. The results showed both faster task completion and greater user preference for the selection scheme using different mouse buttons.

(a) *What are the independent and dependent variables in this study?*
(b) *What type of experimental design was used?*
(c) *The experimental effects may be confounded by another possible effect. What is it and how could it have been avoided?*
(d) *What type of experimental design was used in the testing of the Star workstation described in Box 31.1?*

Critical review of experimental procedure

When critically reviewing an experiment it is important to consider whether the experiment achieved what it set out to do and the applicability of these findings to the design. This can be assessed by examining the experimental procedure and the results obtained. To gain an understanding of an experimental procedure it is useful to view it from the subject's perspective. This can be a valuable exercise, both in planning experiments and for reviewing reports of other people's experiments. There are four key issues to consider:

- **User preparation** whether the instructions given to the users were adequate and whether the amount of practice allowed before starting the experiment was sufficient.
- **Impact of variables** what the changes in the independent variables mean to the users as they undertake the experimental tasks.
- **Structure of the tasks** whether the tasks were complex enough to allow full use of the interface facilities (or at least the ones of interest) and whether the users understood the aims of the tasks.
- **Time taken** whether the length of the task sequence produced any fatigue or boredom in the users.

While an experiment can be very well designed at the technical level, these practical issues can have marked effects on the results. For example, an experiment that involves complex tasks and has few practice tasks may be predisposed to large error scores and poor user performance; an experiment that uses very long sequences of tasks may produce fatigue in the users. These kinds of pitfall can be avoided by carrying out small pilot studies (see Chapter 29) before running the experiment on a larger scale. Although this practice might require more preparation time, it can help to avoid cumbersome or unnecessary data collection and analysis, so saving time and money and avoiding frustration in the longer term.

Critical review of experimental results

Experimental results need to be critically reviewed in order to establish exactly what has been found out, how useful this is and whether it is of practical as well as theoretical significance. There are four main points to consider:

- **Size of effect**   the absolute size of the differences found in the dependent variables is important in assessing the results. For example, performance differences of perhaps a few seconds may be statistically significant, but from a practical point of view they may have little impact when the interface is used in a normal working environment where there are all kinds of distractions and interruptions.
- **Alternative interpretations**   experimental results are interpreted as arising from the manipulation of the independent variables. It is useful to consider whether there are any alternative interpretations of the results, perhaps based on other variables which may not have been controlled in the experiment. For example, this could be done by examining the effects of insufficient practice on complex task performance.
- **Consistency between dependent variables**   when several dependent variables are used in one experiment the relationship between them should be studied. In some cases there may be an inconsistency across variables. For example, task completion rates and error scores may indicate that one interface is better than another but user preferences and learning scores may show the reverse. Such inconsistencies indicate that the situation is complex and further experiments may be needed.
- **Generalization of results**   depending on the nature of an experiment its results may not generalize to other tasks, users or working environments. For example, the results obtained from an experiment using one multimedia learning system may not be applicable to another. It is dangerous to over-generalize experimental results, particularly when the results are given the status of 'guidelines' (see Chapter 24).

Understanding and being able to apply statistical tests to validate experimental findings is important, and you will find references to introductory texts at the end of this chapter.

31.2 Usability engineering

In Chapter 19 we discussed the role of usability engineering in design with particular reference to requirements gathering. In this chapter we will consider the techniques that are used in usability engineering. Usability engineering was defined by Tyldesley as 'a process whereby the usability of a product is specified quantitatively, and in advance. Then as the product is built it can be demonstrated that it does or does not reach the required levels of usability' (1988).

Usability engineering has been well received by a number of companies because its semi-scientific and engineering nature provide a systematic procedure for testing the usability of a product during development. The underlying aim of usability engineering is to engineer for improvement. The design and evaluation components of usability engineering are very closely interrelated in cycles of design–evaluate–redesign. The engineering nature of the process is reflected in this iterative development and in the fact that many characteristics of a product are specified quantitatively and in advance. The process that follows results in the building of a product that demonstrates the planned-for characteristics.

The scientific nature of the process is reflected in the evaluation setting. Testing usually takes place in a purpose-built laboratory, like the IBM laboratory in the Forte Travelodge case study described in Chapter 29, and follows a procedure that is broadly scientific in nature. However, the nature of the testing differs from the scientific experimentation described in Section 31.1 in that it is not usually possible to control variables not directly of interest. If you have done courses in scientific experimentation you may at first be surprised by the comparative lack of rigour in usability testing compared with, say, laboratory experiments in physics or many fields of biology. On the other hand, if you have studied ecology or those topics in psychology that defy the construction of tightly controlled experiments you will realize that when many interrelated variables are involved, it is often impossible to control them all. Furthermore if you were to control all the variables you would end up changing the nature of the system being examined. Interestingly, as you will see later, compared with some forms of evaluation such as contextual evaluation and ethnography (Chapter 32), there is a high level of evaluator control in usability engineering. In fact, it is sometimes criticized for being too scientific in nature and for presenting a distorted impression of the product's real usability in the workplace (Whiteside *et al.*, 1988).

Good *et al.* (1986, p. 241) describe the process of usability engineering as consisting of the following steps:

- defining usability goals through metrics,
- setting planned levels of usability that need to be achieved,
- analysing the impact of possible design solutions,
- incorporating user-derived feedback in product design,
- iterating through the 'design–evaluate–design' loop until the planned levels are achieved.

Metrics and the usability specification

In Chapter 19 you read about the use of metrics in updating products. (Metrics are also discussed in Chapter 25.) These metrics are measures that are used to describe various levels of acceptability of key design features. More often than not they are based on measures such as time to complete a particular task, number of errors and attitude ratings given by users in a questionnaire. Table 31.3 contains part of a usability specification (see also Section 19.3) for a conferencing system (Whiteside *et al.*, 1988). The first column shows the attribute of interest and the other columns the way the data is collected (that is, the measuring concept, in Whiteside *et al.*'s terminology); the method and a series of levels. The first attribute, for example, is concerned with initial use, which is measured by setting users a specific conferencing task, known as a benchmark task, and recording the number of successful interactions that occur during a 30 minute period. The worst case given is 1–2, the best case is 8–10 and the design team have agreed that they will aim at developing a system that enables users to achieve an average of 3–4 successful interactions.

You will also notice that Table 31.3 has a column labelled 'now level' which is empty. The 'now level' is often the value achieved by the previous version of the

Table 31.3 Usability specification for a conferencing system (Whiteside *et al.*, 1988).

Attribute	Measuring concept	Measuring method	Worst case	Planned level	Best case	Now level
Initial use	Conferencing task	Number of successful interactions in 30 minutes	1–2	3–4	8–10	?
Infrequent use	Task after 1–2 weeks disuse	% of errors	Equal to product Z	50% better	0 errors	?
Learning rate	Task	First versus second half score	Two halves equal	Second half better	'Much' better	?
Preference over product Z	Questionnaire score	Ratio of scores	Same as Z		None prefer Z	?
Preference over product Q	Questionnaire score	Ratio of scores	Same as Q		None prefer Q	?
Error recovery	Critical incident analysis	% incidents accounted for	10%	50%	100%	?
Initial evaluation	Attitude questionnaire	Semantic differential score	0 (neutral)	1 (somewhat positive)	2 (highly positive)	?
Casual evaluation	Attitude questionnaire	Semantic differential score	0 (neutral)	1 (somewhat positive)	2 (highly positive)	?
Mastery evaluation	Attitude questionnaire	Semantic differential score	0 (neutral)	1 (somewhat positive)	2 (highly positive)	?
Fear of seeming foolish	Questionnaire	Obstacles related to interface	Many	Few	None	?

system or the present value if the update is under way. Deciding how the different levels should be set can be difficult but initial levels are usually provided by a previous version of the system.

One of the values of usability engineering is that the specification is available for the team to see and it provides a record of the current usability of the system.

Benchmark tasks

The main emphasis in usability testing is on monitoring users' performance on carefully constructed standard tests known as **benchmark tasks**, which they perform in a usability laboratory, like the one shown in Figure 31.1, or similar setting. Video cameras are positioned so that simultaneous film of the VDU screen and the user's hands on the keyboard (or other input device) can be obtained. In addition, keystrokes are usually logged. Typically, these data are used in conjunction to obtain information about such things as the time that it took a user to perform particular tasks and subtasks, error rates and types of errors, usage of the manual and so on.

In order to standardize the experimental method as much as possible, as in the experiments that we discussed in Section 31.1, the basic rules of usability testing are to give a specified set of users specified tasks to complete in a controlled environment – in other words, to control as many of the variables as possible.

Figure 31.1 The usability laboratory at the National Physical Laboratory, showing the evaluators' room and a subject working in the room behind separated by a partition of one-way glass (National Physical Laboratory, 1993). See colour plate 15.

Question 31.3
From your knowledge of the human aspects that influence HCI, what kind of user characteristics would you need to take into account when selecting subjects?

Many companies have a collection of standard benchmark tasks such as: 'select, read and print out a mail message'. In general, benchmark tasks are often longer than the tests used in most scientific experiments but quite short compared to everyday real-life tasks. The way that the data will be analysed is planned in advance and video analysis techniques are used, such as those described in Section 30.1. Data from all the subjects is then converted into metrics, which are entered into the usability specification.

Users' opinions

Users' opinions are also important, and are elicited through questionnaires and interviews (see Chapter 30 for a discussion of questionnaires and interviews). Data from the questionnaires is used to produce attitude metrics, which are recorded on the usability specification, as you can see in Table 31.3.

Making trade-offs

When the design team discusses the usability specification it may be faced with having to make trade-offs which involve accepting lower standards for some attributes in order to achieve others (remember the discussion about trade-offs in window design in Chapter 14?) Priorities, therefore, must be established. One way of doing this is through a process called **impact analysis** (Gilb, 1985). This technique involves listing the usability attributes and, alongside them, listing the proposed design decisions. Next, the percentage impact of each design solution is estimated for each of the attributes and entered into the appropriate part of the table. The individual entries show the strengths and weaknesses of the solutions in relation to particular attributes and sets of attributes as a whole. Although this process is reported to be fairly cumbersome many insights can be gained from doing it (see Whiteside *et al.*, 1988 for further details).

Usability engineering has brought structure to HCI design. It has also been important in getting all contributors to the design process to work towards achieving explicit and agreed goals. In this respect, the usability specification is an important document, which represents a consensus and common goals. Consequently, it provides a communication medium through which employees with technical expertise, such as programmers, and those with less technical knowledge, such as marketing personnel and users, can communicate.

As Nielsen (1992) has pointed out, usability applies to the total life of a product, which may stretch through as many as seven or more upgrades. Usability engineering is reported to produce a measurable improvement in usability of about 30 % (Whiteside *et al.*, 1988). However, it is not totally free of problems. The scientific nature of the testing means that it is a fairly unfriendly environment for users and also quite different from the real world. For example, how many people do you know who work on their own, without interruption, in a small glass chamber doing short tasks that they are told to do without interruption? Not very many, I suspect. Informal field observation may also be conducted to compensate for this, because it provides a way of assessing how users use technology in the workplace and how this pattern of usage relates to the laboratory tests. Interpretive methods, such as contextual enquiry, provide another solution to this problem, which we shall discuss in Chapter 32.

EXERCISE

From the discussion in this chapter and Chapter 19, try to list as many strengths and weaknesses of usability engineering as possible.

COMMENT

Some strengths of usability engineering (Karat, 1993) are:

- agreeing on a definition of usability,
- setting this definition in terms of metrics and usability goals,
- putting usability on a par with other engineering goals,
- providing a method for prioritizing usability problems.

Some weaknesses are:

- the assumption that usability can be operationalized,
- the requirement that the practitioner be familiar with laboratory methods,
- the cost of conducting usability tests,
- the unnaturalness of the testing environment.

Key points

- Experiments enable us to manipulate variables associated with a design and study their effects.
- To plan and design a valid experiment, the experimenter must know the purpose of the experiment, must state hypotheses in a way that can be tested and must consider and then choose statistical analyses that are appropriate.
- There are practical issues to consider, including procedural ones such as user preparation, the impact of variables, the structure of tasks and the time that it will take to do the experiment.

- Pilot studies are important for determining whether the experimental design is suitable before time, effort and money are invested in a full-scale evaluation.
- Usability engineering is based on a form of experimentation known as benchmark tasks. Subjects generally do these tasks in a controlled environment, and sometimes special laboratories are created for the purpose. Recordings of the subject's behaviour are made using video and keystroke logging equipment.
- One of the problems with usability engineering is that the test conditions are rather artificial and not representative of the real world. However, it is good for fine-tuning product upgrades.

Further reading

Experimental design and statistics

DIX A., FINLAY J., ABOWD G. and BEALE R. (1993). *Human–Computer Interaction*. Hemel Hempstead: Prentice-Hall.
Chapter 11 provides a useful overview of evaluation techniques and contains a good section on experimental evaluations.

GREENE J. and D'OLIVEIRA M. (1982). *Learning to Use Statistical Tests in Psychology: A Student's Guide*. Milton Keynes: Open University Press.
This book provides a good introduction to statistics and experimental method. It has been a favourite introductory text with students for many years.

JOHNSON P. (1992). *Human–Computer Interaction: Psychology, Task Analysis and Software Engineeering*. Maidenhead: McGraw-Hill.
Chapter 7, Evaluation of Interactive Systems, provides a good introduction to experimental design.

ROBINSON C. (1990). Designing and interpreting psychological experiments. In *Human–Computer Interaction* (PREECE J. and KELLER L., eds), pp. 357–67. Hemel Hempstead: Prentice-Hall.

ROBINSON C. (1983). *Experiment, Design and Statistics in Psychology*, 2nd edn. Harmondsworth: Penguin.
The original text from which Robinson (1990) is derived. Both provide a good introduction to experimental methods and statistics.

Usability engineering

WHITESIDE J., BENNETT J. and HOLTZBLATT K. (1988). Usability engineering: our experience and evolution. In *Handbook of Human–Computer Interaction* (HELANDER M., ed.). Amsterdam: North-Holland.
This chapter provides an excellent review of the development and practice of usability engineering. It describes the methods used and discusses the strengths and weaknesses of the approach.

32

Interpretive Evaluation

Aims and objectives

The aim of this chapter is to introduce some ways of collecting and analysing data about how people use technology in natural situations like at work, at home, in the shopping mall, at school and so on. After working through this chapter you should be able to:

- identify why interpretive evaluation is valuable and how it differs from more objective forms of evaluation,
- select different methods for collecting and analysing interpretive data.

Overview

So far the methods that we have discussed all rely on the researcher controlling subjects in some way or another. The data collection techniques are fairly formal and there has been a strong 'us and them' distinction between evaluators and users, which precludes access to information about informal and situated use of the technology. For example, if in an interview the evaluator does not ask a particular question because she does *not think of it or does not consider it to be important the user is unlikely to talk about the topic – why should she, if she hasn't been asked? During the late 1980s and early 1990s there has been a trend, by some researchers, to move away from evaluator-controlled forms of evaluation in favour of more informal techniques, some of which are derived from anthropology and sociology. An important distinction between interpretive evaluation and the techniques described in earlier chapters is that the agenda for the evaluation arises out of the context of study and is generally jointly decided by users and evaluators.*

The techniques that are discussed in this chapter vary in the degree to which they can be described as interpretive but they all illustrate a move away from objective evaluation towards more subjective interpretation of the findings in relation to the context of study. Walsham (1993) summarizes the approach as follows:

> '**Interpretive methods** of research start from the position that our knowledge of reality, including the domain of human action, is a social construction by human actors and that this applies equally to researchers. Thus, there is no objective reality which can be discovered by researchers and replicated by others, in contrast to the assumptions of positivist science. Our theories concerning reality are ways of making sense of the world and shared meanings. ... Interpretivism ... [is] concerned with approaches to the understanding of reality and asserting that all such knowledge is necessarily a social construction and thus subjective.'
>
> (Walsham, 1993, p. 5)

A useful distinction between the methods described in the previous chapters and those discussed in this chapter is that 'the former emphasizes the statement of goals, the use of objective tests, and the production of research-type reports; the latter emphasizes the usefulness of findings of the evaluation ... to the people concerned with the programme' (Walsham, 1993, p. 166).

As in other methods, 'the purpose of the evaluation' is a key element that drives the evaluation. Interpretive evaluation is particularly appropriate for understanding the complex interactions that occur in natural environments and this is important if systems like CSCW systems are to be successful. An interpretive evaluation can be valuable at various stages in the development life cycle but particularly for a feasibility study, design feedback or post-implementation review. In all cases it broadens understanding and engenders shared commitment. (See also Chapter 29.)

32.1 | Contextual inquiry

In the laboratory benchmarking that is done in usability engineering (Chapter 31) users have little or no control over what they do and how and when they do it. This kind of setting is unnatural and quite different from the kinds of environments in which most people work. Awareness of these differences has encouraged researchers to explore techniques that provide data that reflects real usage more accurately. **Contextual inquiry** is a form of elicitation which can be used in evaluation. In this approach users and researchers participate to identify and understand usability problems within the normal working environment of the user.

EXERCISE

Reflect for a moment on the discussion of laboratory benchmarking. What are the main differences that subjects would be likely to experience in these tests compared with their normal working environment?

COMMENT

Whiteside *et al.* (1988) have identified the following key differences:

- **Work context**   typically, word processing benchmark tasks are six pages long, whereas Whiteside *et al.* report that most of the people in their studies were, in practice, working with documents 30–50 pages long.
- **Time context**   experiments generally have a prescribed time context, whereas in real work environments people tend to have some choice about the order in which they do tasks and how long they take.
- **Motivational context**   in the experimental context the experimenter controls the situation, whereas usually in the work context there is scope for some negotiation.
- **Social context**   in the work environment there is normally a social network of support which does not exist in the experimental context.

Anecdotes about important usability issues that have gone undetected in laboratory testing only to be discovered in field observations also support the case for unobtrusive context-sensitive methods. For example, John Whiteside, a senior scientist at Digital Equipment Corporation, tells the story of a woman who had been a subject for the company's usability testing for several years. In her normal work the woman was paid according to the number of lines she typed. Consequently, so the story goes, for every eight hours of work, approximately one hour was spent counting up how much typing she had done. This behaviour went totally undetected in usability tests and was spotted only when the human factors team decided to do some field observation and visited her at home. Had they known of her need to count up her work it would have been a simple matter to program the word processing software to perform this onerous task for her. Other examples are provided by Whiteside and Wixon (1987), among which is the case of a usability study on the installation of office systems. In the laboratory the tests started after the equipment had been unpacked. However, observations in real work environments showed that, in fact, the mere unpacking of the equipment was a major problem for many customers because of the design of the packaging. Whiteside *et al.* (1988) summarize the unnatural nature of laboratory testing as follows:

> 'Consider the context of the laboratory experiment, as opposed to an actual workplace situation. The language used to describe the experiments reveals the differing context. Experiments involve an experimenter and a subject. A subject is someone who is under the power of another person. Indeed, experimenters wield considerable power over subjects – they remove them from their accustomed environment, remove them from their usual social context, prescribe what work they are to do during the experiment, prescribe the time available for completing the work, minimize "external variables" such as interruptions (e.g. phone calls from home), and often attempt to conceal the details of why the experiment is being run (for fear of contaminating the data).'

Unlike usability engineering, contextual inquiry has its roots in the ethnographic paradigm (described in Section 32.3) and not in science or engineering. Usability issues of concern are identified by users, or by users and evaluators collaboratively, while users are working in their natural work environments on their own work. The term 'contextual interview' has been used to describe the discussions that drive contextual inquiry. This is an interview between users and evaluators in which any aspect of concern is discussed and recorded on video for re-examination later by users and evaluators together. The kinds of things that are of particular interest to the evaluator (Holtzblatt and Beyer, 1993) are:

- structure and language used in the work,
- individual and group actions and intentions,
- the culture affecting the work,
- explicit and implicit aspects of the work.

Like any protocol data, this analysis may be time-consuming but Holtzblatt and Beyer (1993) recommend that evaluators try to:

- get as close to the work as possible,
- uncover work practice hidden in words,
- create interpretations with customers,
- let customers expand the scope of the discussion.

Unlike usability engineering, there are no metrics to feed back to the design team, although judiciously selected video clips of users struggling with some aspect of their work provide strong and meaningful messages to the design team. The interpretation of the data is also done with reference to the wider work context and the users' general aims. As Whiteside *et al.* (1988) say, 'The important point about contextualism is that it implies that interpretation is primary (rather than data); knowledge lives in practical action (rather than being based on representation) and it is assumed that behaviour is meaningful only in context (rather than that behaviour can be studied scientifically)'.

EXERCISE

Under what kind of circumstances do you think that design teams would want to use:

(a) contextual inquiry
(b) usability engineering

COMMENT

Contextual inquiry and usability engineering are complementary approaches in many respects as they inform design in different ways.

(a) Contextual inquiry will produce data from which we can infer valuable information about the context of work and how the system fits that context. It is a useful technique for obtaining requirements (Chapter 19) for a new product, particularly if the product is some form of groupware like a CSCW system.

(b) Usability engineering is a good technique for refining and fine tuning design and for ensuring that internal user interface standards are upheld. The metrics that are produced enable the design team to compare directly one version of a system with another, which is particularly useful when upgrading products.

Question 32.1

What are the main differences between the philosophy that underlies usability engineering and that underpinning contextual evaluation?

32.2 Cooperative and participative evaluation

At the University of York, Andrew Monk and his colleagues have developed a form of cooperative evaluation in which users are heavily involved in deciding both what the evaluation issues are and techniques for collecting and analysing video protocols. Cooperative evaluation is described as follows:

> '**Co-operative evaluation** is a technique to improve a user interface specification by detecting the possible usability problems in an early prototype or partial simulation. It sets down procedures by which a designer can work with the sort of people who will ultimately use the software in their daily work, so that together they can identify potential problems and their solutions.'
>
> (Monk *et al.*, 1993a, p. ix)

Cooperative evaluation is designed to be a low cost technique that can be used by designers and users without specialist HCI knowledge. Very little training is needed to do cooperative evaluation. Initially, designers identify the evaluation tasks but users are encouraged to comment and to suggest appropriate alternatives and to ask questions. The aim is to make the interaction as natural as possible. Monk and his colleagues place strong emphasis on the need to create a relaxed and informal atmosphere before starting the evaluation. During the evaluation, think aloud protocols (see Chapter 30) are collected using the following procedure:

- One or more users is recruited and care is taken to make sure that the users are typical of the population that will be using the final product.
- Tasks are selected that will be representative of the kinds of things that the users would wish to do when working with the system. (If a very early prototype is being used in the test this can have an important function in helping to restrict the number of functions that are available to be used.)
- As each user works with the system she verbalizes the problems that she experiences and the evaluator makes notes.
- A debriefing session is held at the end of the session so that any misunderstandings that might have occurred can be cleared up and to check for common understanding.
- The designer then summarizes the notes and reports the problems back to the design team.

Variations to the technique may also be used, including post-test surveys to check users' opinions and round table discussions when there is a wide variety of users in the user population.

The protocol analysis is similar to that of Carroll and Mack (1984), described in Section 30.2, except that designers and evaluators intervene with questions and also discuss users' questions, as shown in Box 32.1.

Box 32.1   Excerpt from a cooperative evaluation protocol

'The evaluator decides to find out whether the user has seen the information on the screen that would help her work out what was going on.

[The evaluator points to the status window in the top right hand corner of the screen]

Evaluator's comments are shown in italic and user's comments are in normal text.

> *Yeah. Erm this box over here.*
> no references selected. Ah.
> *This is a message box yeah. What do you think no references selected means?*
> well I would have assumed, that it couldn't find it and one of the reasons that maybe it couldn't find it is because it's not in the library.
> *okay. Well no references selected definitely means it hasn't found it. Erm.*
> And I don't think I spelt it wrongly.

The evaluator draws the user's attention to the status box and the fact that it tells the user that there are no references selected. Then the evaluator asks the user for any ideas about what this box means. For the rest of the extract the user tries to fathom out why there are not any references selected. Instead of telling the user what the problem is, the evaluator decides to ask the user to start the task over again to see whether she'll see what to do next time.'

(*Source*   Monk *et al.*, 1993)

Participative evaluation

Throughout this book we have emphasized the close relation between design and evaluation, which is demonstrated clearly by participative evaluation. **Participative evaluation** differs from cooperative evaluation in that it is more open and subject to greater control by users. Participative design (see Chapter 18) and evaluation share the same philosophy and many of the same techniques, and in practice they are closely interwoven. In fact, to think of them separately would be artificial; they are basically one and the same thing, so in this chapter we will aim only to extend a little what has been said in Chapters 18 and 22, in which we discussed envisioning design. Greenbaum's and Kyng's (1991) book entitled *Design at Work* contains a host of examples of informal evaluations in which such techniques are used. They claim that mock-ups facilitate evaluation because they are not threatening and are accessible to everyone, which encourages user participation. They enable users and designers to trace breakdowns in the interaction by recreating them, trying solutions and discussing issues in users' own language. According to Ehn and Kyng (1991), 'mock-ups become useful when they make sense to the participants ... not because they mirror "real things" but because of the interaction and reflection they support' (p. 177). These authors suggest that cooperative prototyping (not to be confused with Monk *et al.*'s, 1993, cooperative evaluation) can be encouraged by:

- establishing focus groups, which include competent representatives from the whole user group range, who will work with the designers and collaborate in the mutual learning process;
- designers being prepared to coordinate the groups and work on the development of prototypes with users;
- providing prototypes that are sufficiently realistic and stable to enable users to take charge of the evaluation;
- ensuring that communication is maintained;
- using early prototypes to focus on exploring the coupling between the social and political issues in the workplace and the technical ones (remember the discussion of sociotechnology in Section 18.2?);
- highlighting the benefits of cooperative prototyping, particularly early in design, so that the activity is well resourced.

Cooperative prototyping provides a way of inter-meshing evaluation and design so closely that they are virtually a single ongoing process. There is, therefore, a clear testing stage with identifiable data.

Question 32.2

What are the main differences between cooperative evaluation and participative evaluation?

32.3 Ethnography

A number of HCI researchers have recently shown interest in ethnography as a method of collecting data about the real work situation. Not only do they see the limitation of the scientific hypothesis-testing paradigm but they also acknowledge the importance of learning more about the way technology is used *in situ*. Some of the reasons why the experimental approach to HCI is criticized are provided by Monk *et al.* (1993a):

- the laboratory is not like the real world,
- it is not possible to control all of the variables that affect human behaviour,
- no account is taken of context; researchers try to eliminate its influence,
- subjects are given highly constrained artificial tasks, which have to be completed in a very short time frame,
- little or no attention is given to subjects' ideas, thoughts and beliefs about what is studied.

Notice that this list is surprisingly similar to some of the complaints levelled by Whiteside *et al.* (1988) described in Section 32.1. Ethnography will provide an alternative view which is deeply contextual in contrast. Of course, ethnography is not a new method; it has been a standard practice in anthropology for several years. Ethnographic researchers strive to immerse themselves in the situation that they want

IF YOU ENJOYED
THE PROGRAM PRESS
BUTTON 'A'.
IF NOT, THROW THE
CONTROL PANEL
THROUGH THE SCREEN

(*Source* Honeysett)

to learn about. For instance, anthropologists using ethnography to study, say, a remote mountain community, would use whatever means available to help them gain acceptance into the community. For example, they would probably go and live in the community, learn the language and customs, adopt the community's form of dress and so on. Monk *et al.* (1993a) describe the role of the ethnographer as that of 'an uninformed outsider whose job it is to understand as much as possible about the "natives" *from their own point of view*'. According to Monk *et al.* (1993) this implies:

- 'the need to use a range of methods including intensive observation, in-depth interviewing, participation in cultural activities and simply hanging about, watching and learning as events unfold',
- 'the holistic perspective, in which everything – belief systems, rituals, institutions, artefacts, texts etc. – is grist for the analytical mill; and immersion in the field situation'.

From this immersion in the study the ethnographer gradually extracts and makes sense of the key aspects that have an influence on the study. Considerable emphasis is placed on interpreting data in relation to the context.

All kinds of data sources may be collected as part of this practice, including video, annotations in notebooks, snapshots and artefacts from the activity being observed. In HCI video tends to be the primary recording mechanism and, as we said in Chapter 30, a major problem is created by the time-consuming nature of analysis. In fact, in ethnographic studies this problem may be even more severe in that often the same video is rewatched several times in order to identify previously missed subtle insights into the behaviour recorded. The activities are also documented for further analysis. Multiple views of the data can also be developed, which may be juxtaposed. Suchman and Trigg (1991) comment on these activities as follows:

> 'viewing and reviewing video records both individually and in groups, generating activity or "content" logs for each record, conducting detailed sequential analyses of selected portions of the records, integrating multiple records (often in different media) of the same activity, identifying conceptual categories and gathering "collections" of instances and finally, juxtaposing multiple analytic perspectives on the same activity.'

Both manual and automated tools can be used to support the process. Murray and Hewitt (1992) describe a database in which the material is classified under the categories shown in Box 32.2. Suchman and Trigg (1991) use a hypermedia environment for analysing and recording data, which is shown in Figure 32.1. The three windows show text from part of a verbal transcript, a graphics window and a three-paned worksheet window used to control and annotate the video record. Although the methodological basis of ethnography is observation and interviews, the way in which this data is analysed is different from studies discussed in earlier chapters (see, for example, Chapter 30 on usage data and Chapter 31 on usability engineering).

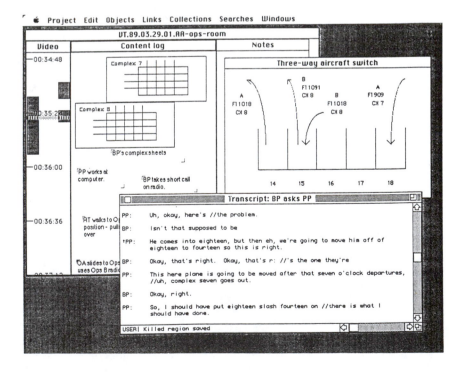

Figure 32.1 A computer-based environment for video analysis (Suchman and Trigg, 1991).

Box 32.2 Classification of activities in a database in a case study of a technical publications unit

- Discussing job specification/quotation
  - meeting around table (public)
  - 2+ people (staff + contractor)
  - duration: long or short
  - content: technical
  - with document/artefact/examples
  - notes taken (informal)
- Discussing work with client
  - meeting around table (public) or client's office (private)
  - 2+ people (staff + client)
  - initial consultation for requirements or checking drafts/new instructions
  - duration: long or short
  - content: technical
  - with document/artefact/examples
  - notes taken (informal)
- Telephone call
  - staff + caller
  - usually at desk
  - duration: usually short, occasionally extended
  - content: technical
  - with document/artefact/examples
  - occasional notes taken (informal)
- General discussion
  - 2+ staff
  - short duration, may be very brief
  - usually acknowledgement given
  - usually at desk, or in passing
  - calling over screens
  - private (but may be overheard)
  - artefacts such as letters, screen views, sometimes to pass onto others

  This can be subdivided into:
    - information seeking
    - information passing
    - position/information checking
    - scheduling/administrative requests
    - working together/teaching
- Dealing with resources: requests, status and return
  - 1+ staff, need artefact/shared resource
  - very brief, acknowledgement given

- Informal 'constructed' communications
  - 1+ staff, hard to quantify, sometimes artefact
- Interaction with ethnographer
  - 1 person, explanatory
- Chat
  - 2+ people, talk, social interactions

(*Source* Murray and Hewitt, 1994.)

This overview of this new and important topic is brief but several references are given in the further reading list for those wanting to follow it further. These techniques are providing useful information for understanding and evaluating the requirements of multi-user systems. Most importantly, they illuminate how systems are used in the cultural, political and social environment of the workplace.

Question 32.3

What is the overall philosophy of interpretive evaluation?

Key points

- Contextual inquiry, cooperative evaluation and participative evaluation are approaches in which users and researchers participate to identify and understand usability problems within the normal working environment of the user.
- Cooperative evaluation, as described by Monk *et al.* (1993a), is designed to be a low cost technique that can be used by designers without specialist HCI knowledge and by users.
- Participative evaluation is closely associated with participative design.
- Ethnographic researchers strive to immerse themselves in the situation that they want to learn about.
- Interpretation of data is always done with strong reference to the context of the study in all these types of evaluation, but particularly in ethnography.
- Video tends to be one of the main data capture techniques, but notebooks, snapshots and artefacts from the activity are also collected.
- Video analysis tends to be even more labour intensive than in other studies using video because it is often reviewed many times to ensure that insights about the activity are not overlooked.
- Video analysis support tools are particularly important for ethnography. Databases also provide a valuable way of categorizing material.

Further reading

Contextual evaluation

HOLTZBLATT K. and BEYER H. (1993). Contextual design: integrating customer data into the design process. In (ASHLUND S., MULLETT K., HENDERSON A., HOLLNAGEL E. and WHITE T., eds) *Bridges Between Worlds*, INTERCHI'93 Tutorial Notes 6. Reading, MA: Addison-Wesley/ACM Press.

These tutorial notes outline the key issues in contextual evaluation and provide pointers for planning evaluations. In many respects, there is much in common between these notes and sociotechnical design, which was discussed in Section 18.2.

WHITESIDE J., BENNETT J. and HOLTZBLATT K. (1988). Usability engineering: our experience and evolution. In *Handbook of Human–Computer Interaction* (HELANDER M., ed.). Amsterdam: North-Holland.

This is a very useful article which discusses usability engineering and explains why researchers at Digital Equipment Corporation and IBM started to develop contextual methods.

Cooperative evaluation

MONK A., WRIGHT P., HABER J. and DAVENPORT L. (1993). *Improving your Human–Computer Interface: A Practical Technique*. New York: Prentice-Hall.

This book describes the cooperative evaluation technique developed at the University of York, UK and provides much practical advice and examples so that others can use the technique.

Ethnographic and related approaches

EASON K. (1988). *Information Technology and Organisational Change* London: Taylor & Francis.

This book discusses the need to develop the organizational structure alongside the technical system. Chapter 10 deals specifically with user evaluation, although it is mentioned frequently throughout the book. You will see that in Chapter 10 many of the techniques discussed in earlier chapters (for example, system logging and questionnaires) are used but with a different philosophy, in which there is more user participation, particularly in data analysis.

GREENBAUM J. and KYNG M., eds (1991). *Design at Work: Cooperative Design of Computer Systems*. Hillsdale, NJ: Lawrence Erlbaum Associates.

This book contains many examples of participative design and evaluation and examples of ethnographic practice. Chapter 4, by Suchman and Trigg, provides an example of the use of ethnographic techniques in the design of an air traffic control system.

WALSHAM G. (1993). *Interpreting Information Systems in Organisations*. Chichester: John Wiley.

Walsham focuses on the integration of systems in organizations. This book provides an excellent and lucid description of the interpretive approach. Chapter 8 is about evaluation. The first two thirds of the chapter discuss evaluation in the field with reference to several case studies; the remainder examines some relevant literature on information systems evaluation.

Predictive Evaluation

Aims and objectives

The aim of this chapter is to introduce you to different kinds of predictive evaluation that do not involve user testing. After studying this chapter you should be able to:

- describe what a review is and say how you could provide feedback,
- critically discuss the positive and negative aspects of expert reviews as an evaluation technique,
- recognize the ways in which evaluation costs can be lowered by using heuristic and discount methods,
- briefly describe how a structured method of simulating usage, like a cognitive walkthrough, can be used to discover problems,
- use a keystroke level analysis to evaluate potential efficiency of performance.

Overview

Usability testing can often incur large costs. The methods described in this chapter attempt to lower the cost of evaluation by predicting aspects of usage rather than observing it directly, as in the methods discussed in

Chapters 30 to 32. Most of the methods that you will learn about in this chapter do not involve users. They involve either some form of inspection (Nielsen, 1992), as in the case of reviews and heuristic evaluation, or modelling, as in the case of the keystroke level analysis. There is no user testing, which makes them comparatively quick to do and low in cost. Furthermore, specialist equipment is not required. These characteristics are an obvious attraction for software developers. The keystroke level model and cognitive walkthroughs do not even require a prototype system; they can be done using just a specification. The exception is discount evaluation in which heuristic evaluation is used in conjunction with limited user testing.

The chapter starts with a description of the way in which a typical review is done. It then goes on to discuss the advantages and problems associated with reviews and how heuristic evaluation (Molich and Nielsen, 1990) and discount usability evaluation can provide useful alternatives in some circumstances. Walkthroughs and the keystroke model are then discussed briefly.

33.1 Inspection methods

Inspection methods, as the name suggests, involve the inspection of aspects of technology by specialists who have knowledge of both the technology and the intended users, which they can bring to bear in the evaluation. Usually, the emphasis is on the interaction dialogue between a single user and a system. Nielsen (1993) describes usability inspection as 'a set of highly cost-effective methods for finding usability problems and improving the usability of user interface design by inspection'. The main goal of all inspection methods is to generate a list of usability problems. Often these problems can be fixed early in the design. Two less obvious goals may be to build a design rationale, as described in Chapter 26, or to evolve an alternative parallel design.

In Sections 33.2 and 33.3 we discuss three of the most well known inspection methods: expert reviews or usage simulations, heuristic evaluation, walkthroughs and a technique known as discount evaluation, which is a hybrid between usability testing and heuristic evaluation. Two other forms of inspection are standards inspection and consistency inspection (Wixon *et al.*, 1990). In **standards inspections** standards experts inspect the interface for compliance with specified standards. Interestingly, according to Nielsen (1993), most of the inspection can often be done with little task knowledge. **Consistency inspections** involve teams of designers, including at least one from each project, inspecting a set of interfaces for a family of products one after another.

Usage simulations

Usage simulations involve reviewing the system to find out usability problems. These reviews are usually done by experts, who simulate the behaviour of less experienced users and try to anticipate the usability problems that they will encounter. For this reason they may also be referred to as **expert reviews** or **expert evaluation**. Ideally, these reviewers will be experts in HCI and will also have a broad experience of different kinds of systems, so they should be able to spot usability problems concerned with inconsistency, poor task structure, confusing screen design and so on. The main reasons for having reviewers pretend to be less experienced users rather than employing typical users in the first place are to do with efficiency and prescriptive feedback. In terms of efficiency, a small number of reviewers can usually identify a whole range of potential problems for users during a single session. Real users would take much longer and require more facilities. Furthermore, experts are often forthcoming with prescriptive feedback about how the system can be improved and how usability problems can be put right. Often little prompting is needed to get reviewers to suggest possible solutions to the problems identified because they have experienced many systems, and the design team may benefit from this additional input. Generally, they provide detailed reports based on their use of the prototype or working system.

An example of a review is a study by Hammond *et al.* (1984) in which the authors used pairs of experts, one role-playing the 'user' and the other taking notes to evaluate the initial lessons of a training course for a text processing system. These reviewers were asked to assess the system and its attendant course from the perspective of both novices and more experienced users. The reports produced by the reviewers consisted of lists of specific difficulties and proposed system modifications to overcome these difficulties.

EXERCISE

Do a review of the Eurochange system described in Section 21.2. Try to role-play typical users and make a note of the kinds of usability problems that you think they might encounter.

COMMENT

One of the authors recently set this exercise on a training session for programmers and analysts from a company in the UK. The comments that were made included:

- The interface is boring, not colourful, no graphics or multimedia.
- It provides a limited range of currencies – not even all European ones.
- Interaction is all in English.
- It is difficult to change your mind about which currency is required.
- Ambiguous button labels, such as 'proceed'.
- The position of the '0' is non-standard (cf. telephones, calculators).

- It is oriented to left-handed people because of the physical layout.
- It limits user choices too much.
- Poor support for inputting the card.
- It is not clear what cards it will accept.
- The dialogue is ambiguous.
- The keyboard is fixed/non-adjustable.
- There is no feedback on the amount of credit left on the card.
- Little flexibility, for example, the ability to specify an amount in your own currency.
- Lack of consistency between dialogue and display.
- Why not offer local currency as a default?
- Limited and unchanging currencies.
- More innovative use of icons needed, for example, map showing relevant currency.
- If it is an EC machine it should offer ECUs.
- Printout should be in a separate slot.
- Should be able to put card in any way up.

While reviews are relatively straightforward, it is necessary to consider the following:

- To ensure an impartial opinion the reviewers should *not* have been involved with previous versions of the system or prototype.
- The reviewers should have suitable experience, both of the application and of HCI. Media and creative design expertise may also be needed for some systems. Finding a small panel of reviewers with the necessary expertise may be difficult and compromises may have to be made.
- The role of the reviewers needs to be clearly defined to ensure that they adopt the required perspective when using the system. While it is relatively easy to assess both the very limited understanding of novice users and the extensive knowledge of very experienced users, intermediate categories of user experience are much more difficult to define and role play.
- The tasks undertaken, the system or prototype used and any accessory materials, such as manuals or tutorials, have to be common to all experts and representative of those intended for the eventual users.

During data collection and analysis the aim is to obtain a common set of factors from the individual reports that address the most important problems. This aim may be achieved in three ways:

- **Structured reporting**   reviewers have to report observations in a set way. For example, they are asked to specify the nature of the problems they encounter, their source, the importance for the user and any possible remedies.
- **Unstructured reporting**   reviewers report their observations and a categorization of common problem areas is then determined.
- **Predefined categorization**   reviewers are given a list of problem categories and they report the occurrence of problems in these categories.

EXERCISE

The final choice of reporting method can depend on the circumstances of the particular evaluation. What do you think the advantages and disadvantages associated with each reporting method might be?

COMMENT

The answer agreed by the authors is shown in Table 33.1.

Table 33.1 Advantages and disadvantages of reporting styles.

Reporting style	Advantages	Disadvantages
Structured	Easy to analyse	Requires time to categorize problems. Inhibits spontaneous suggestions
Unstructured	Invites spontaneous comments and suggestions	More difficult to analyse than structured reporting. More difficult to categorize common problems
Predefined categories	Categories of problems already agreed. Very easy to analyse	Completely inhibits spontaneous comment and advice. May miss problems not already categorized

Reviews appear to be an attractive method in terms of their potential efficiency and prescriptive feedback. However, there are a few problems that need to be noted. These problems are bias, locating suitable reviewers, role playing and the behaviour of real users:

- Experts are often renowned for their strong views and preferences, in other words, biases. They may concentrate on certain features and virtually ignore others. In practice, therefore it is advisable to use several experts so that the effects of individual bias are reduced.
- Finding reviewers with the right experience and expertise can be difficult, particularly for small companies.
- Good role playing requires an extraordinary amount of information about the knowledge level of the users, the kinds of things for which they would use the system and their responses to problems. For example, imagine you were called in to evaluate a computer interface for children and asked to role play 9- or 13-year-olds. The role playing would require quite a lot of detailed information about these two age groups – could you do it?
- Reviews cannot capture the variety of real users' behaviour. Novice users can do some very unexpected things so it is unlikely that all the problems will be found using this technique.

Two issues that should also be addressed are: how can reviewers be supported so that some of these problems are avoided, and when has enough reviewing been done – that is, when have the problems that needed to be found been found? Heuristic and discount usability evaluation are two variations on the theme that try to address these problems.

33.3 Structured expert reviewing

The three methods discussed in this section also use a form of expert reviewing but, unlike those discussed in Section 33.2, these methods are based on reviews of carefully planned and structured tasks. They are, therefore, more prescriptive and focused than the general reviewing of usage simulations discussed previously.

Heuristic evaluation

Molich and Nielsen (1990) devised a method known as heuristic evaluation in response to the need for cheap, cost effective methods that could be used by small companies who could not afford or did not have the facilities, time or expertise necessary to do usability engineering. In **heuristic evaluation** reviewers examine the system or prototype as in a general review or usage simulation, but their inspection is guided by a set of high-level heuristics (Nielsen, 1992), which guide them to focus on key usability issues of concern. The following list is typical of the kind of heuristics that can be used. Notice also that they are surprisingly like the guidelines that you read about in Chapter 24. It obviously makes good sense to evaluate the system directly against the principles used in its design:

- use simple and natural dialogue
- speak the users' language
- minimize user memory load
- be consistent
- provide feedback
- provide clearly marked exits
- provide shortcuts
- provide good error messages
- prevent errors

According to Nielsen (1993) each reviewer normally does two or more passes through the interface in order to:

- inspect the flow of the interface from screen to screen,
- inspect each screen one at a time against the heuristics, examining features such as system messages, dialogue and so on.

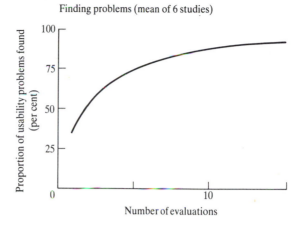

Finding problems (mean of 6 studies)

Figure 33.1 The number of evaluations required in a heuristic evaluation (Nielsen, 1993: ©
1993, Association for Computing Machinery, Inc. reprinted by permission).

A typical session will last between one and two hours but if the interface is large more
time may be needed. When all the evaluators have finished they will aggregate their
lists of problems. Nielsen reports that in a study that he carried out, forty core
usability problems were detected with heuristic evaluation compared with just
seventeen found by four users in usability testing. However, user testing did find other
problems. He, therefore, suggests that the two methods may usefully supplement
each other. A key question for anyone wishing to use heuristic evaluation is 'how
many evaluators are needed?' Figure 33.1 shows the mean of six studies. Perhaps not
surprisingly, the graph shows that the more evaluators used (up to 15), the higher
the proportion of usability problems detected. Notice, however, that on average just
five evaluators detected almost 75% of the usability problems. This suggests that
heuristic evaluation with five evaluators is likely to be very cost effective. This is borne
out by some comparisons between heuristic evaluation and other evaluation
methods (Jeffries *et al.*, 1991), which suggest that heuristic evaluation compares
favourably in that all the major usability problems were detected and the cost of the
study was low. However, some other comparisons have been less favourable (Karat
et al., 1992), as you will see in Chapter 34.

Discount usability evaluation

Discount usability evaluation was also developed by Nielsen (Nielsen, 1989;
Potosnak, 1990). The idea behind this technique is to enable developers with few
resources – in terms of time, money or expertise – to benefit from usability testing
during product design and development. In particular, the method was geared
towards small companies that cannot afford full-scale usability testing like that used
in usability engineering (Chapter 31). In Nielsen's words, 'The discount usability

engineering method consists of scenarios, simplified thinking aloud and heuristic evaluation and is intended to alleviate the current problem where usability work is seen as too expensive and difficult by many developers' (Nielsen, 1989, p. 1).

Discount usability engineering is thus really a hybrid of empirical usability testing and heuristic evaluation. The first part of the method uses usability testing and involves the construction of scenarios (Chapter 22), which are tested using 'think aloud' protocols (Chapter 30). Interestingly, often only one to three subjects take part in this testing phase. On the basis of the results obtained from this test the scenario is changed and tested again. The second part of the method involves testing the scenario using the heuristic evaluation method described above.

The features that result in important discounts include:

- the scenarios are small and so can be changed easily – paper mock-ups are often used or HyperCard simulations of the interface,
- the think aloud method is done informally and does not require psychologists,
- just a few key guidelines are used rather than the large number available – the nine guidelines listed above were found to be ample for the purpose,
- the whole cycle need only involve two or three testers since the number of additional usability problems found by more testers was not worth the extra effort.

Box 33.1 describes an example of discount usability engineering in a Danish bank.

Question 33.1

When might reviews and discount evaluation be used in the design of Eurochange?

Box 33.1   An example of discount usability engineering

A Danish bank (Nielsen, 1989) wished to improve its bank account statements, so it planned to redesign them. At the beginning of the redesign a vocabulary study was performed on the original version of the statements, which identified 26 words, and 30 people were asked to rate these words according to how well they understood their meaning. Of the 26 words, 7 were difficult to understand, as the 'think aloud' method later confirmed. The statements were then redesigned and several iterations of discount design–test–redesign were carried out using well known usability heuristics such as 'be consistent'. In this study a total of 8 different versions of the account statements were tested. However, the whole study was reported to take only 90 person hours, including the design of 7 different versions of 12 different kinds of bank statements.

Walkthroughs

The third structured kind of expert review is a walkthrough. As in software engineering, the goal of a walkthrough in HCI design is to detect problems very early on so that they may be removed. **Walkthroughs** involve constructing carefully defined tasks from a system specification or screen mock-ups. A typical example would be to walk through the activities (cognitive and operational) that are required to get from one screen to another. Before doing the walkthrough experts determine the exact task that will be done, the context in which it will be done and their assumptions about the user population. They then walk through the task, reviewing the actions that are necessary to achieve the task, and attempt to predict how the user population would most likely behave and the problems that they would encounter. In many respects this is similar to a review, except that it requires a more detailed prediction of user behaviour.

HCI researchers tend to adapt methods to fit their needs; Polson *et al.* (1992), for example, take a strongly cognitive stance. They describe their brand of cognitive walkthrough as a 'hand simulation of the cognitive activities of a user'. The focus is cognitive and the underlying aim is to identify potential usability problems. This is a fairly fine-grained approach, which relates closely to cognitive task analysis (see Section 20.3). By structuring the review process around specific questions, psychological theory can be embedded into it, which helps to illuminate how well the interface fulfils the cognitive needs of the intended users. The method is still being developed and more effective versions that can be adopted by companies may emerge. A checklist for doing a cognitive walkthrough is shown in Box 33.2.

Bias (1991), refers to a version used by IBM as a 'pluralistic walkthrough', because three kinds of people take part in the activity: representatives of the expected user population, product developers and human factors specialists. This kind of walkthrough is much less formal than cognitive walkthroughs and can be used to check that an interface design complies with user interface standards. It can also be used as a way of articulating usability issues in the broader decision making framework of formal design reviews (Mack and Nielsen, 1993).

Box 33.2 Checklist for doing a cognitive walkthrough

Cognitive walkthough start-up sheet

Interface _____

Task _____

Evaluator(s) _____ Date _____

Task description: Describe the task from the point of view of the first-time user. Include any special assumptions about the state of the system assumed when the user begins work.

Action sequence: Make a numbered list of the atomic actions that the user should perform to accomplish the task.

Anticipated users: Briefly describe the class of users who will use this system. Note what experience they are expected to have with systems similar to this one, or with earlier versions of this system.

User's initial goals: List the goals the user is *likely to form* when starting a task. If there are other likely goal structures list them, and estimate for each what percentage of users are likely to have them.

Next action #: ____ **Description:** _____

I. Correct goals

II. Problems forming correct goals

A. Failure to add goals. ____ %

B. Failure to drop goals. ____ %

C. Addition of spurious goals. ____ %

No-progress impasse. ____ %

D. Premature loss of goals. ____ %

Supergoal kill-off. ____ %

III. Problems identifying the action

A. Correct action doesn't match goal. ____ %

B. Incorrect actions match goals. ____ %

IV. Problems performing the action

A. Physical difficulties. ____ %

B. Time-outs. ____ %

Cognitive walkthrough form instructions

Start-up form

I. **Task description**   Very briefly describe the task the user needs to perform with the system being analyzed. This description should be from the user's point of view. It generally shouldn't include system-specific operations that a first-time user couldn't perform.

    Example: Check spelling of file 'my.paper'.

II. **Initial goals**   State the goal structure a user with this task can be assumed to have before starting to use the system. Be sure not to include goals or goal structure that you are not confident actual users would have. If the user would have a hierarchy of goals and subgoals, indent the subgoals in an outline-like format. Use the convention that goals at the same indent level are sequential (i.e., 'AND-THEN'), unless specifically marked as 'UNORDERED'.

    Example: A possible goal structure for the 'check spelling' task might look like this:

> Check spelling of the file named 'my.paper'
> > Start the word processor
> > Load the 'my.paper' file
> > Run the spelling checker

Notice that there aren't any detailed, system-specific goals here (e.g., no 'Press Ctrl-S to run the spelling checker'). Also, this initial high-level goal structure isn't even complete: it doesn't include saving the file and exiting the word processing program. These are goals that the interface, and the process of using it, will have to generate in the user.

Action form – top line

Next action number and description   Give a simple description of the next *correct* action needed to complete the task.

    Examples: Type 'my.paper'
                  Press the Return key
                  Pull down the 'Edit' menu
                  Select 'Save' from the 'File' menu
                  Double-click on the word 'time'

Action form – walkthrough questions

I. **Correct goals**   State the appropriate goal structure for choosing the next action. In the 'appropriate' goal structure, the user typically has a goal that matches the effect of the next action. There may also be a more specific goal that describes the action itself.

Example 1: The next action is 'Click on-screen button labelled "Spelling."' An appropriate low-level goal might be to 'start the spelling checker'.

Example 2: The next action is 'Press Ctrl-S,' (which starts the spelling checker). In addition to the goal of 'start the spelling checker', the user will probably need the more specific subgoal of 'press Ctrl-S.'

II. **Problems forming correct goals**   Compare the goal structure you've just entered with the goal structure on the previous form. For each of the questions in this section consider:

- the *current system state*,
- the system's *response to the previous action*,
- the user's *goals and expectations* in performing the previous action.

A. **Failure to add goals**   If the new structure contains new goals, is there a clear indication to the user that these should be added? What percentage of users might fail to add these goals?

Example: The user needs to add the goal 'load local spelling dictionary', but there is no prompt or other information in the interface indicating this step is required before the spelling checker can be used.

B. **Failure to drop goals**   If the old structure contains goals that must be dropped, is there a clear indication to the user that these should be dropped? What percentage of users might fail to drop these goals?

Example: A cautious user has the goals of loading a file into the word processor, saving a backup copy, editing the file, saving the file, and deleting the backup copy. In fact, the word processor automatically creates a backup copy of a file when it is first opened, deleting it when the edited file is closed. But since the interface gives no indication of this activity, the user won't drop the goals of manually creating and deleting the backup.

C. **Addition of spurious goals**   Does the system suggest any extra or incorrect goals to the user? What are they, and what percentage of users might adopt them?

Example: The user tries to save a corrected file, and the system presents a dialog box asking 'Save as . . .' The user may add the goal of entering a file name, even though the next correct action is to click 'OK', which saves the file under its current name.

D. **No-progress impasse**   Does the system's response indicate that progress has been made toward some higher goal? If not, what percentage of users might adopt a goal to undo, quit, confirm, or repeat the last action?

Example 1, no significant response: The user types 'rm my.file' to delete a file, and the system responds with the command-line prompt. The user may add the goal of confirming that the file has been deleted. Notice that there is progress here towards the lower-level goal of typing 'rm my.file', as indicated by the new command line prompt, but there's no obvious progress toward the higher goal of deleting the file.

Example 2, inappropriate response: The user gives the command 'open my.file' in a word processor, with the goal of loading an existing file. The system loads the file and positions the cursor on a blank page following the last page of the existing document. Seeing nothing but the blank screen, the user may decide that the file hasn't been loaded and add the goals of quitting and trying again.

E. **Premature loss of goals** Does the system suggest that any goals should be dropped that are in fact still needed? Which ones, and what percentage of users might drop them?

Example: The user's goal is to send a document to a printer in another room. The user opens the document, pulls down the 'File' menu, and selects 'Print'. The file menu disappears, and the user goes into the other room to pick up the document. After a moment, a dialog box appears on the screen, asking whether the document should be printed draft or letter quality. The delay in showing the dialog box has allowed the user to drop a goal that hadn't yet been achieved.

F. **Supergoal kill-off** Is there a possibility of supergoal kill-off here? That is, is there a subgoal that has just been completed but that is in an 'AND-THEN' structure whose supergoal is similar to the completed subgoal? If so, which supergoal, and what percentage of users might prematurely mark the supergoal complete and drop its trailing subgoals?

Example: The user's goal structure is:

Get a printed copy of my.file
log into the system
print 'my.file' on the local printer
log out of the system

The user logs in, types 'print my.file', and goes to the printer to confirm that the document is printing OK. The 'print "my.file"' subgoal is almost identical to the supergoal of 'Get a printed copy', and as soon as the printout is complete the user drops the entire goal structure, forgetting to log out.

III. **Problems identifying the action** Compare the goals you have listed in the box at the top of the sheet to all available actions.

A. Correct action doesn't match goal   Is there a problem matching a current low-level goal to the correct action? What percentage of users might fail to identify the match and be unsure of the correct action?

Example: The user, working with a word processor, has selected the first column of a table and has the goal 'make the selected column of the table wider'. The correct action is to select the menu item 'Cells', but this is a poor match to the user's goal, which is formulated in terms of a 'column' of a 'table'.

B. Incorrect actions match goals   Are there incorrect actions available that match active user goals? What are they, what goals do they match, and what percentage of users might select one of these actions instead of the correct action?

Example: The user wants to change a section of text to boldface. There are top-level menu items entitled 'Format', 'Font', and 'Style'. The correct action is to pull down the 'Style' menu, but the user may choose one of the other two instead.

IV. Problems performing the action

A. Physical difficulties   Are there any difficulties in performing this action, such as might arise in pressing multiple keys simultaneously, or finding a hidden control? What are they, and what percentage of users might have difficulties?

Example: The cursor-left command in a word processor is Ctrl-B. On a keyboard with a single control key on the far left side, a user with small hands may have difficulty touch-typing Ctrl-B, since the little finger must be on the control key while the index finger stretches to press the B.

B. Time-outs   If the system has time-outs, what percentage of users might have difficulties deciding on the action and performing it before a time-out?

Comment: User response times can vary greatly, and even an experienced user may be interrupted while performing a task. In addition to considering whether time-outs might occur, it's useful to consider whether there is an obvious way to recover from a time-out if one does occur.

(*Source*   Personal communication with Cathleen Wharton, 1994. These forms were developed circa 1991 by Clayton Lewis, Peter Polson, John Rieman and Cathleen Wharton.)

33.4 Modelling: The keystroke level model

Modelling techniques provide a form of evaluation that is even more remote from methods that involve users. All that is required for this kind of evaluation is:

- a specification of the system's functionality or at least that part of it which is to be examined,
- a task analysis, which is basically a list of all the proposed user tasks with a breakdown of each task into its components. Often these components are sequences of subtasks that require further decomposition.

In recent years several analytic evaluation methods have been developed. The differences between these methods revolve around task structure, user operations and the combination of user and system operations. Some examples of these are:

- the task structure can vary from a simple task consisting of a single user command to more complex tasks composed of several commands,
- user operations can be evaluated with analytic methods using either extremely simple memory operations closely linked to physical actions at an interface (such as recall of what is to be typed or selected) or more complex cognitive operations.

Two kinds of models exist: single layer models that can be thought of as having a flat representation and multi-layer models, which are more complex and which will not be considered further in this book. One of the most widely known analytic methods is the keystroke level model developed by Card *et al.* (1980). This is an example of a single-layer model and it deals with short tasks, usually just single commands, and has very simple user operations embedded in the task sequence. The purpose of the keystroke level model is to enable designers to calculate task performance times that can be achieved by experienced users, that is, it gives the designer an idea of the minimum performance time for specified commands.

The keystroke level model asserts that the execution part of a task can be described in terms of four different physical-motor operators – K (keystroking), P (pointing), H (homing), D (drawing) – and one mental operator, M, by the user, plus a response operator, R, by the system. (You should note that the model was developed during the era of command systems, so features (that is, operators) such as dragging and clicking in direct manipulation systems are not included in the original model but they can be added if accurate times for these operators are available.) Execution time is simply the sum of the time for each of the operators:

$$T_{\text{execute}} = T_{\text{K}} + T_{\text{P}} + T_{\text{D}} + T_{\text{M}} + T_{\text{H}} + T_{\text{R}}$$

The estimated times for each operator, which have been calculated from empirical evidence, are:

T_{K} = 0.35 seconds (estimate which varies with typist's skill)
T_{P} = 1.10 seconds
T_{M} = 1.35 seconds

$T_R = 1.2$ seconds
$T_H = 0.4$ seconds
T_D varies with the length of the line and is not relevant to the problem here.

Using the heuristics for the placement of mental operators, these operators may be put into a description of a task and the performance time calculated.

For example, for the task 'save a file' with a new name in a word processor that uses a mouse and menus that pull down from the top of the screen, the following estimate of performance would be produced. The assumptions are: the task starts with a homing action as the user places a hand on the mouse; the time per keystroke is 0.35 seconds; and the system response time is 1.2 seconds.

(1) Initial homing: T_H
(2) Move cursor to file menu at top of screen: T_P plus the mental operator T_M
(3) Select 'save as' in file menu (click on file menu, move down menu and click on 'save as'): $T_M + T_K + T_P + T_K$
(4) Word processor prompts for new file name (system response time 1.2 seconds) and user types 'file-2.4 < return >': $T_R + T_M + T_K$ (file-2.4) + T_K (return)

Inclusion of the mental operators gives:

(1) 0.4
(2) $1.35 + 1.10 = 2.33$
(3) $0.35 + 1.35 + 1.10 + 0.35 = 3.15$
(4) $1.2 + 1.35 + 0.35(8) + 1.35 + 0.35 = 7.05$

Total $= 13.05$ seconds

EXERCISE

Eurochange, which was described in Section 21.2, is intended initially for installation in British airports and railway stations and will allow travellers to obtain the main European currencies quickly without having to find the nearest bank. The bank is interested in how quickly travellers will be able undertake transactions using either their banker's card or a credit card. Figure 21.7 shows the Eurochange interface.

Use the keystroke level model to calculate the transaction times for the current interface specification. Use the times listed in the 'save file example' above. You will have to make a few decisions of your own. For example, our answer will assume that picking up the card and the money from the machine take the same time as a keypress, and that moving between physical operations with the card and pressing keys is the same as moving between the mouse and the keyboard in Question 33.2. You will also have to decide which operators are anticipated and therefore do not have an M value added before them. Assume that pressing < proceed > is not anticipated like pressing < return >.

The Eurochange interface will work as shown in the transaction sequence:

(1) User inserts credit card in Card Entry Slot (takes 3 seconds)
(2) Message displayed on screen: 'Type your PIN code' (display time of LCD screen is constant at 0.2 seconds)
(3) User types four-digit number on numerical pad
(4) Machine checks PIN code (5 seconds to check and display message)
(5) Message displayed: 'Select currency required'
(6) User presses key marked 'Dutch Guilder'
(7) Message displayed: 'Exchange rate is 3.52 DG to £1. Enter amount required in Dutch Guilders in units of [smallest banknote]. Press < Proceed >'
(8) User types 253 and presses < Proceed >
(9) Message displayed 'Machine deals in banknotes only. Smallest banknote is [amount] DG. Enter new amount to obtain DG or press < Cancel >
(10) User enters 255 and presses < Proceed >
(11) Message displayed: 'Do you require any other currency? Select currency or press < Proceed > to finish transaction'
(12) User presses < Proceed >
(13) Credit card returned from Card Entry Slot and money deposited in Delivery Slot with printout of transaction (card return takes 3 seconds)

COMMENT

Our answer is as follows:

(1)	$T_H + T_{CARDI}$	= 0.4 + 3.0
(2)	T_R	= 0.2
(3)	$T_H + T_M + T_K(4)$	= 0.4 + 1.35 + 0.35(4)
(4) (5)	$T_{CHECK + DISPLAY}$	= 5.0
(6)	$T_M + T_K$	= 1.35 + 0.35
(7)	T_R	= 0.2
(8)	$T_M + T_K(3) + T_M + T_K$	= 1.35 + 0.35(3) + 1.35 + 0.35
(9)	T_R	= 0.2
(10)	$T_M + T_K(3) + T_M + T_K$	= 1.35 + 0.35(3) + 1.35 + 0.35
(11)	T_R	= 0.2
(12)	$T_M + T_K$	= 1.35 + 0.35
(13)	$T_{CARDR} + T_H + T_M$	= 3.0 + 0.4 + 1.35
	$+ T_K + T_H + T_M + T_K$	= 0.35 + 0.4 + 1.35 + 0.35

When all these values are added up the total time is 31.15 seconds.

Question 33.2

Based on your own experience, what kind of problems do you think people might experience using this method?

Key points

- It is important to select reviewers who not only have expertise in HCI and the application area being tested but who are also impartial (for example, not involved in the current or past development of the product).
- Three kinds of reporting are often done for reviews: structured, unstructured and predefined. Each has advantages and disadvantages, which need careful consideration.
- Known problems with reviews are that experts may be difficult to find and they may have biases, but heuristics can be used to guide them. When this is done the evaluation is generally known as heuristic evaluation.
- A general problem with evaluations that involve users is that they can be expensive. Discount usability engineering is a particularly cost-effective form of evaluation for improving the usability of products developed by small companies with limited resources.
- Walkthroughs are used to predict the problems that a defined user group will encounter doing a specified task.
- Modelling techniques require a detailed description of the task and some kind of definition of the system.
- Modelling techniques assume expert error-free behaviour. The keystroke level model takes no account of novice learning behaviour.

Further reading

CARD S.K., MORAN T.P. and NEWELL A. (1980). The keystroke-level model for user performance time with interactive systems. *Comm. ACM*, **23**(7), 396–410. Reprinted as Chapter 16 in PREECE J. and KELLER L., eds (1990) *Human–Computer Interaction: Selected Readings*. Hemel Hempstead: Prentice-Hall.
This classic paper contains a detailed description of the keystroke model, which requires close and careful reading.

DIX A., FINLAY J., ABOWD G. and BEALE R. (1993). *Human–Computer Interaction*. Hemel Hempstead: Prentice-Hall.
Chapter 11, on evaluation techniques, contains a general review of evaluation methods and has a good description and worked example of a cognitive walkthrough.

MACK R. and NIELSEN J. (1993). Usability inspection methods: Report on a workshop held at CHI'92, Monterey, CA. *SIGCHI Bulletin*, January, pp. 30–3.
This article provides a discussion of key issues and a comparison of inspection methods.

MOLICH R. and NIELSEN J. (1990). Improving a human–computer dialogue. *Comm. ACM*, **33**(3), 338–48.

NIELSEN J. (1989). Usability engineering at a discount. In *Designing and Using Human–Computer Interfaces and Knowledge Based Systems* (SALVENDY G. and SMITH M.J., eds), pp. 394–401. Amsterdam: Elsevier.

NIELSEN J. (1992). Finding usability problems through heuristic evaluation. In *Human Factors in Computing Systems CHI'92 Conference Proceedings* (BAUERSFIELD P., BENNETT J. and LYNCH G., eds), pp. 373–80. New York: ACM Press.
These three papers provide detailed information about heuristic and discount evaluation methods.

WHARTON C., BRADFORD J., JEFFRIES R. and FRANZKE M. (1992). Applying cognitive walkthroughs to more complex user interfaces: experiences, issues and recommendations. In *Human Factors in Computing Systems CHI'92 Conference Proceedings* (BAUERSFIELD P., BENNETT J. and LYNCH G., eds), pp. 381–8. New York: ACM Press.
This paper focuses on five core issues of concern when carrying out cognitive walkthroughs and offers some practical advice to evaluators.

WHARTON C., RIEMAN J., LEWIS C. and POLSON P. (1994). The cognitive walkthrough method: a practitioner's guide. In *Usability Inspection Methods* (NIELSON J. and MACK R., eds). New York: John Wiley.
This chapter provides much valuable information and advice based on the authors' experience of using the cognitive walkthrough method.

34

Comparing Methods

Aims and objectives

The aim of this chapter is to examine issues that need to be considered when selecting evaluation methods and planning a study and to give you experience of critiquing the studies of others. After studying this chapter you should be able to:

● plan your own evaluations
● constructively criticize plans and studies reported in the evaluation literature.

Overview

Selecting appropriate methods and planning an evaluation are not trivial. Many factors need to be taken into account. Some are concerned with the stage of system development at which feedback is required, the purpose of the evaluation and the kind of information that is needed; others are concerned with the practicalities of doing the actual evaluation such as time, the availability and involvement of users, specialist equipment, the expertise of the evaluators and so on. In Section 34.1 we compare the methods discussed in the previous chapters in terms of the level of interface development required to use them, the involvement of users, the type of data collected and practical issues that influence evaluation practice. Finally, you are invited to comment on some brief accounts of studies that have themselves attempted to compare different evaluation methods.

34.1 Differences between methods

A number of factors need to be taken into account when you are deciding which kind of evaluation methods to use, including the purpose of the evaluation, the stage of system development, the involvement of users, the kind of data collected and how it is analysed, and the practical constraints associated with actually doing the evaluation.

The purpose of the evaluation

The purpose of the evaluation is a key factor, which we have mentioned several times already. In Chapter 29 we identified four main purposes for doing evaluation:

- Engineering towards a target: is it good enough?
- Comparing alternative designs: which is the best?
- Understanding the real world: how well does it work in the real world?
- Checking conformance to a standard: does this product conform to the standard?

The way in which the data is collected and analysed must be suitable for the practical and philosophical nature of the evaluation. For example, laboratory experiments are not suitable for understanding how users work in the real world. Similarly, ethnographic methods are not appropriate for testing conformance to a standard.

Question 34.1

Which evaluation methods might be suitable for evaluations with the purposes listed above?

Stage of system development

Different methods are appropriate for different stages of system development. Some methods, like walkthroughs or keystroke level analysis, can be done on a formal or semi-formal specification very early in design. Other kinds of evaluation, such as benchmarking, observation and monitoring and interpretive studies are usually done later on a prototype or working system. In the case of benchmarking, the evaluation will take place in a laboratory setting, observation may be in a laboratory or field location and interpretive studies will always be natural field settings. Often quick informal evaluations will be done in which ideas are tested out with users and where the setting is not important. For these studies paper and pencil sketches are often adequate. Such studies take place early in design or at the time when decisions about screen design are being made. The important thing is that the ideas are at an early formative stage and the purpose of the evaluation is to get rapid feedback to improve them.

Involvement of users in the evaluation process

You can consider user involvement in three ways: (i) the participation of typical end users, (ii) the control that users have over their own tasks during the evaluation, and (iii) the control that users have in running the evaluation. The more formal and scientific the evaluation the less control users tend to have over both their own tasks and over the evaluation procedure. Maximum user control occurs in interpretive studies where users often work with evaluators, have considerable control over their own activities and work in their normal environments. Predictive evaluations make a number of assumptions about the cognitive operations of users but there is no direct involvement with users except in the discount method, and even here involvement is low. Table 34.1 summarizes user involvement and control in different evaluation methods.

Type of data

The major distinction here is between qualitative and quantitative data. Quantitative data deal with either user performance or attitudes that can be recorded in a

Table 34.1 User involvement and control.

Method	User participation	User control over task	User control over evaluation
Observation and monitoring	Yes	Varies	None
Collecting users' opinions	Yes	Not applicable	None
Experiments and UE	Yes	None	None
Interpretive	Yes	A lot	A lot
Predictive	None	Not applicable	None

Table 34.2 The type of data.

Method	Type of data
Observation and monitoring	The raw data in a stream of video can be analysed either qualitatively or quantitatively Usage logs are quantitative
Collecting users' opinions	Questionnaires produce quantitative data Unstructured interviews produce qualitative data
Experiments and UE	Experiments are quantitative Benchmarking produces mainly quantitative data
Interpretive evaluation	Qualitative data
Predictive evaluation	Quantitative data

numerical form. Qualitative data focus on reports and opinions. Some data is inherently either quantitative or qualitative. For example, ethnographic data is qualitative whereas task completion time is quantitative. Other data, like a stream of video, can be either depending on the purpose of the study and the way that it is analysed. Questionnaire data is typically dealt with quantitatively in order to produce statements of the type: 'x % of the users could not guess the meaning of the first icon'. At the other extreme qualitative data may be treated more holistically as in the case of interpretive studies. Quantitative data have the advantage of allowing consistent, detailed analysis across the users tested, which can be validated statistically, but does not contain qualitative 'richness' as there is no account of individuals' responses, opinions and feelings. Qualitative data are limited to some form of descriptive account of the information gathered. However, in the case of interpretive studies the data may be very rich and may provide new insights into the way the technology is used which will enable designers to produce more appropriate products. Table 34.2 summarizes the kind of data that is collected using different evaluation methods.

Practical considerations

Some important constraints that need to be taken into account are:

- absence of specialist equipment for the evaluation, such as a video recorder or means of logging user interactions,
- lack of specialist skills, for example, for designing experiments, undertaking complex statistical analyses, or doing ethnographic work,
- time constraints concerned with conducting either the evaluation or the data analysis,
- access to users (if required) and the system, for example, restricted access to both the interface software (which means that evaluations involving changes to an interface are ruled out) and users required for the evaluation (who may be completely unavailable or accessible only for a very short period of time).

One way or another, many of these constraints are related to cost. If the evaluation is too expensive, for whatever reasons, it is unlikely to happen, especially in companies that still regard evaluation as an additional luxury to be included if time and cost permit. In order to estimate the cost of an evaluation it will be important to consider both data collection and data analysis.

Two issues affect the ease of data gathering. Firstly, the number of users needed is an important factor for empirical evaluations. These evaluations normally observe or test users individually, and user testing can take from several days up to a few months. The number of users required depends on the technique and the statistical analyses undertaken. Secondly, the size of the task set used, that is, the number of tasks and their complexity, must be considered. The size of the task set directly affects the time taken by each user and therefore the time spent on the whole evaluation. Experimental evaluations and usability benchmarking typically have an organized approach to the control of task structure, usually with a set number of tasks of equal complexity.

Before starting the evaluation consideration needs to be given to the overheads associated with data analysis. Even quite simple evaluations can collect large amounts of data, and analysis can become a very time-consuming process. We have already mentioned video analysis in this connection in Chapter 30. However, support systems are being developed. Large surveys can also generate a huge volume of data but there are now many software packages available to support analysis, statistical testing and report generation.

EXERCISE

Draw up a table summarizing the differences between the five categories of evaluation techniques using the headings: purpose, interface development, user involvement, type of data and practical considerations.

COMMENT

Table 34.3 contains this summary.

As well as differing in the areas described in Table 34.3, each category of techniques also has its own advantages and disadvantages. The choice of evaluation technique depends, in part, on making the most of the potential benefits and being aware of, or possibly reducing, the disadvantages associated with it.

Question 34.2

Table 34.4 is a partially completed table giving some of the advantages and disadvantages of each of the evaluation methods. Complete the table.

Table 34.3 Differences between evaluation methods.

	Observing, monitoring and logging	Experiments and benchmarking	Users' opinions	Interpretive	Predictive
Purpose	Understanding the real world, comparing designs and adapted for engineering towards a target	Standards conformance, comparing designs, adapted for engineering towards a target (that is, benchmarking)	Can be used for many different purposes	Only understanding natural usage	Engineering to a target and conformance testing
Interface development	Any level of development	Likely to be at least working prototype	Any level of development	Likely to be working system	Usually early at specification, or mock-up stage
User involvement	Yes, some control of tasks by users	Yes, little or no control	Yes, often no control	Yes, considerable control	No
Type of data	Quantitative and qualitative	Emphasis on quantitative	Quantitative and qualitative but more emphasis on quantitative	Qualitative	Some qualitative but emphasis on quantitative
Practical considerations	Special equipment useful, but may not be essential	Laboratory conditions preferred	None	Little or no equipment needed Video may be used	No equipment needed

Two other criteria that need to be considered are:

- technical criteria, which deal with the details of using the evaluation method;
- scope of the information needed, which is concerned with the relevance of the data collected.

Table 34.4 Some advantages and disadvantages of evaluation techniques.

Method	Advantages	Disadvantages
Observing and monitoring	Widely applicable, highlights difficulties	Can affect users' behaviour
Experiments and benchmarking	Provides measurements to guide design	Requires expensive facilities
Users' opinions	Inexpensive	May get low response rate
Interpretive	Reveals what really happens in the field	Requires sociological expertise
Predictive	Most forms do not require a working system	Some forms have a narrow focus

Technical criteria are concerned with the type of information produced and issues relating to how that information is collected. Three technical criteria may be identified: validity, reliability and biases in data collection.

Validity

In the present context **validity** refers to whether an evaluation method is measuring what is required given the specified purpose of the evaluation, and it operates at two levels. Firstly, it is necessary to determine whether the method is valid for a particular purpose. For example, if the purpose is to find out users' attitudes to certain interface changes, then opinions gathered in an expert review would be invalid as the real users would not be contacted. Secondly, the validity of the measurements made must be considered. For example, the performance times measured in the keystroke-level model are valid only for expert, error-free user performance.

Reliability

The **reliability** or consistency of the measurement process is important. A reliable evaluation method is one that produces the same results on separate occasions under the same circumstances. Different evaluation methods vary in their reliability. Well-designed experiments in which careful control is made of the tasks that the subjects perform and the selection of subjects, for example, have a high degree of reliability. Observational evaluations tend to have much lower reliability.

Biases

Using an evaluation technique is not a neutral activity; there may be **biases** in data collection and analysis and in the deduction of information from those analyses. Basically, there are two main sources of bias:

- selective data gathering,
- manipulation of the evaluation situation.

In selective data gathering attention is focused only on particular aspects of the information available and this can distort the whole evaluation process. For example, the opinions of the experts used in an expert review may be heavily biased because of previous experience and knowledge. The evaluation can also be manipulated by both users and evaluators. For instance, in any situation where a user is prompted for a response, such as in verbal protocols and interviews, subtle influences can guide the respondent to give particular responses. Users can also respond in a calculated way and give a false impression, so that, for example, responses on questionnaires may not reflect true opinions.

Other criteria that need to be considered are the scope of information needed and the ecological validity of an evaluation.

Scope of the information needed

This refers to the completeness of the data collected in relation to eventual use of the system. There are two issues to consider in this respect: the limitations on the information that result from the evaluation technique, and the extent to which findings can be generalized to other situations. Evaluation methods vary considerably in their scope, depending on the amount of contact with users and the structure of the tasks that users perform. For example, a keystroke-level model has a narrow focus (that is, no users, short tasks and expert, error-free performance) and only limited generalizations can be made to real users and error-prone situations. In contrast, observational evaluations have a broader perspective in that they focus on real users doing typical tasks, and consequently more can be said about actual system use. Furthermore, care is usually taken to ensure that the users in an evaluation are representative of the actual user population. To increase their scope some evaluations use more than one evaluation method.

Ecological validity

Ecological validity refers to the environment in which the evaluation takes place and the degree to which the evaluation may affect the results it obtains. Almost all empirical evaluations affect the situation and working practices they are trying to study. The degree to which this occurs depends on the level of intrusion into users' work and the control exercised over the users' tasks by the evaluator. Obtrusive techniques are those where users are constantly aware that their behaviour is being monitored or where they have to interrupt their work to provide some information. Users' tasks can be restricted to some extent, such as having to be tackled in a set order. Obtrusive techniques and controlled tasks produce a very artificial situation which is unlike normal working conditions. When selecting an evaluation method it is important to consider the artificiality created by the method and its possible effects on the evaluation itself. It is also important to take account of how artificial the test environment is when interpreting the findings of an evaluation. It is because many laboratory tests are so unrealistic that many evaluators and design teams are starting to move away from traditional laboratory testing to unobtrusive forms of observation. They are also trying to develop working practices in which designers and users work together alongside each other so that users' opinions and needs can be taken into account throughout system development.

These changes are taking place because there have been reports of errors and types of usage that do not occur in the laboratory and can only be detected in real working environments. In addition, many evaluators acknowledge that laboratory conditions are not only unrealistic but can also be quite alien. For example, it is rare for most secretaries to work on their own on one task without interruption for long periods of time. It is much more likely that there will be interruptions, such as a colleague needing help or stopping to chat, the boss needing a job done urgently and thus requiring that everything else is put aside until it is done, a photocopier repairer or technician calling, the telephone ringing or numerous other distractions.

Question 34.3

(a) *Consider the problem of validity. Could an evaluator apply results from the keystroke-level model to determine the time to train a naive user to expert level? Give reasons for your answer.*

(b) *List two forms of bias that affect the validity of results.*

EXERCISE

Read the following scenarios and select suitable evaluation methods for each, giving reasons for your selection.

Scenario 1: Tourist information system

The Tourist Board of a large European city is developing a computerized tourist information system that will present, on large, flat touch-screens, a range of information about the city. The Board has produced a full specification and an initial prototype of the system and now wants it evaluated before any further development. The Board is interested in the presentational aspects of the system (that is, the use of graphics, colour and symbols in the system), how easily tourists can access relevant information, the suitability of the input and output devices and the communication style (the tourist points at active areas of the screen and there are a few menus located on the edge of the screen for certain operations), as well as indications of how to improve the kind of information in the system. The limitation on the evaluation is that it has to be completed in four weeks. You have an assistant experienced in interface evaluations; you have the ability to change the structure of the interface; you have access to a team of graphic designers employed by the Tourist Board; and video recording equipment is at your disposal.

Scenario 2: Desktop publishing

A small publishing house wishes to buy a desktop publishing (DTP) system to produce brochures, publicity material and some publications. It has done a requirements analysis and as a result has narrowed down the choice to three DTP systems. The publishing house has obtained copies of the three systems (with relevant manuals and training material) for one week. Your job is to evaluate the systems and present recommendations to the managing director. The limitations on the evaluation are that you are not very experienced in interface evaluation (you do not have skills in experimental design or statistics); video equipment and a separate testing area are not available (the systems have been set up in the publicity department's office); the systems are demonstration copies (there is no access to the software and the systems only save small files corresponding to three to four pages of text and graphics); you have ample access to individual office staff but only for periods of up to one hour.

COMMENT

Your answers may vary from the following, but here are two possible ways of doing the evaluations.

Scenario 1: Tourist information system

This evaluation could be split into several parts. You could start with an expert review in order to obtain some feedback about the basic screen presentation and the communication style. This would be quick and relatively cheap, and any really major problems would most probably be detected by the experts. Depending on the results that you obtained, you could do some short laboratory experiments in order to test the experts' suggestions. You could also pay a number of 'typical' users to come into the laboratory to perform usability tests, in which they would carry out prescribed tasks and you would collect video data and time logs and solicit their attitudes by questionnaire. When you were satisfied that you had improved the system as much as possible you would need to test it in the field. This would involve placing prototypes in a few key sites and observing and recording how they were used by the public. Some form of hidden video recording equipment and key-logging would be best for this. Alternatively, you could have unobtrusive observers stationed at the sites. You might also want to interview some of the users to ask their opinions about the system or you might prefer an ethnographic approach. The results that you would get from the field testing might contain some surprises; people can be very unpredictable!

Scenario 2: Desktop publishing

The constraints in this scenario are severe and the best that could be achieved is a fairly 'quick and dirty' evaluation. Apart from working with the systems yourself as a subject you could try to find a small number of people who were experienced in using DTP systems (that is, experts) and ask them to try out each of the systems, maybe using heuristics to guide them, and report back to you. Before doing this you would have to give them details about the kinds of user who would use the systems and the tasks that they would perform. You could also get some novices to use each of the three systems to perform specified tasks. You could observe them as unobtrusively as possible by being present in the room and then follow up each session with a short questionnaire or interview to elicit their opinions about each system.

Question 34.4

Some important criteria that have been discussed in this part are listed below. Test your understanding of how the methods differ in relation to these criteria by drawing up a table or writing revision notes for each group of methods in relation to each criterion.

- *Relation to design cycle: when in the design cycle is the approach used?*
- *Focus: is the focus of the evaluation narrow (for example, a small task consisting of just a few operations) or broad (for example, users doing their work over a period of days)?*
- *Setting: is a laboratory used, a field setting or is the study predictive?*
- *Users: are users involved and if so how?*
- *Expertise: what kind and how much expertise do the evaluators need?*
- *Perspective: is the study carried out from a predominantly scientific, engineering, predictive or ethnographic perspective?*
- *Data collection: what kind of techniques are used?*
- *Data analysis: what kind of techniques are used?*
- *Communication of results: how are the results of the study communicated back to the design team?*
- *Cost: is the cost high, medium or low?*
- *Advantages: what are the main advantages?*
- *Disadvantages: what are the main disadvantages?*

A full answer to this question would be long and involve too much repetition of the content presented in this part of the book, so no answer is printed. You should treat the question as revision and use it as a way of synthesizing this material.

34.2 Empirical comparison studies

There have been several studies that have compared different evaluation methods with the aim of identifying the most cost effective and reliable ones. Summaries of two such comparisons are presented below. Read through them and evaluate the studies by answering the questions and doing the exercises.

Study 1: A comparison of four techniques

In this study by Jeffries *et al.* (1991), the user interface of a commercial software product was evaluated by four groups prior to release using four different forms of evaluation: heuristic evaluation, software guidelines, cognitive walkthroughs and usability testing. All the evaluations were done by human factors specialists under conditions that were as near to identical as possible and that were subject to normal real-world constraints such as time limitations.

Details of the evaluation studies were as follows:

- The heuristic evaluation was carried out by four evaluators with HCI knowledge during a two-week period.
- The usability tests were conducted by a human factors professional who regularly did this kind of testing. Six subjects took part in the tests. They spent about four hours learning to use the system and two hours doing a set of ten usability tests devised by the usability testing team.
- The guidelines group used a set of 62 guidelines, which had been drawn up for internal use by the company but which were derived from general usability guidelines (Smith and Mosier, 1986).
- The cognitive walkthrough was done by a group of evaluators who adapted it to suit the nature of the system. A pilot study was also carried out to ensure that suitable tasks and procedures were being used, as the exact way that tasks are selected and cognitive walkthroughs are performed is not very obvious from descriptions in the literature.

A usability problem was defined as 'anything that impacts ease of use'. The evaluators recorded all their problems on specially prepared report forms, and 268 of these forms were rigorously analysed and the problems categorized into three main groups:

- problems that arose from applying the technique as intended,
- problems arising as a side effect (for example, while applying a guideline about screen layout, a problem with menu organization might be noted),
- problems arising from previous experience with the system.

The results of the analysis are shown in Table 34.5.

Further analyses were also done to examine the severity of the problems found and the cost in terms of time of performing the evaluation. A summary of conclusions is presented in Table 34.6.

Overall, as applied here, the heuristic evaluation technique produced the best results.

Table 34.5 Core problems found by technique and how the problem was found (Jeffries *et al.*, 1991).

	Heuristic evaluation	Usability	Guidelines	Cognitive walkthrough
Via technique	105 (100%)	30 (97%)	13 (37%)	30 (86%)
Side effect	–	1 (3%)	8 (23%)	5 (14%)
Prior experience	–	0	12 (34%)	0

Table 34.6 Summary of the study's findings (Jeffries *et al.*, 1991).

	Advantages	Disadvantages
Heuristic evaluation	Identifies many more problems Identifies more serious problems Low cost	Requires user interface experience Requires several evaluators
Usability testing	Identifies serious and recurring problems Avoids low-priority problems	Requires user interface experience High cost Misses consistency problems
Guidelines	Identifies recurring and general problems Can be used by software developers	Misses some severe problems
Cognitive walkthrough	Helps define users' goals and assumptions Can be used by software developers	Needs task definition methodology Tedious Misses general and recurring problems

Question 34.5

Take a critical eye to these findings. Why might these results be slightly misleading?

Question 34.6

Name one practical drawback of doing heuristic evaluation.

Study 2: Comparison of empirical testing and walkthrough methods

In this case study by Karat *et al.* (1992), usability testing was compared with individual and team walkthroughs in order to identify usability problems in two graphical user interfaces.

The main issues that were considered in the study were:

- Usability problems: how do the two methods compare in the number of usability problems identified?
- Reliability of differences: if the two methods do differ in terms of their effectiveness in identifying usability problems, do the differences persist across different systems?
- Cost effectiveness: what is the relative cost effectiveness of the two techniques in identifying usability problems?
- Human factors involvement: how much human factors involvement is necessary in the use of the two techniques?

Details of the evaluation studies were as follows:

- Three usability evaluation techniques were compared: individual and group walkthroughs and usability testing.
- Six human factors specialists took part in the individual walkthroughs; six pairs took part in the group walkthroughs and each pair was able to converse between themselves freely; and six users took part in the usability tests. The evaluations were done over a three-hour period.
- In the case of the walkthroughs the evaluators were given guidelines and prescribed tasks and they had to document the usability problems that they identified.
- In the usability tests the users were asked to identify and describe the usability problems that they encountered and these were documented by human factors staff who observed the tests.
- The usability problems identified by each of the three methods were classified using metrics so that comparisons between the techniques could be made. This was done by determining the severity of the problem upon completion of the task. The classification was, therefore, known as the 'problem severity classification'.

Table 34.7 contains a summary of the number and problem severity of the usability problems identified when evaluating the two systems using the three techniques.

Table 34.7   The number and severity of the usability problems identified (Karat *et al.*, 1992).

	Empirical test	Team walk	Individual walk
System 1			
PSC 1	19	9	8
PSC 2	18	13	9
PSC 3	3	1	1
Total SPAs	40	23	18
No action areas	7	24	29
Total problem areas	47	47	47
System 2			
PSC 1	10	3	6
PSC 2	15	10	10
PSC 3	2	1	1
Total SPAs	27	14	17
No action areas	16	29	26
Total problem areas	43	43	43

Table 34.8 Unique usability problems (Karat *et al.*, 1992).

	Empirical test	Team walk	Individual walk
System 1	13	1	0
System 2	8	0	2

Table 34.8 shows the number of unique usability problems that were recorded using each technique and Table 34.9 shows a breakdown of the cost effectiveness data for the three techniques.

The results of the comparison were:

- The empirical usability testing technique identified the largest number of problems, including several severe problems that were missed by the walk-throughs. The authors suggest that this kind of study is important as a baseline study for identifying the full range of usability problems. Walkthroughs may provide good alternatives when resources are limited and may be particularly valuable for deciding between alternative designs early in the design life cycle.

Table 34.9 Cost-effectiveness data for the three methods (Karat *et al.*, 1992).

	Empirical test	Team walk	Individual walk
System 1			
Human factors staff hours	136	72	70
Participant hours	24	48	24
Total hours	160	118	94
Problem types	159	68	49
Hours/type	1.0	1.7	1.9
SPAs	40	23	18
Hours/SPA	4.0	5.1	5.2
System 2			
Human factors staff hours	116	77	76
Participant hours	24	48	24
Total hours	140	125	100
Problem types	130	54	39
Hours/type	1.1	2.3	2.6
SPAs	27	14	17
Hours/SPA	5.2	8.9	5.9

- Although about a third of the significant problems were identified by each of the methods, the authors commented that trade-offs between the techniques need to be considered with care because they tend to be complementary rather than producing exactly the same results.
- Team walkthroughs tended to produce better results than individual walkthroughs.
- The cost–benefit data shows that the usability testing required the same or less time to identify each usability problem compared to walkthroughs.

EXERCISE

The results from the Jeffries *et al.* (1991) study and those of Karat *et al.* (1992) give somewhat different indications about the value of usability testing. Why might this be?

COMMENT

One of the reasons why the second study may have been more positive is that the two studies used different methods of comparison. In particular the first study was considerably longer than the second study, which lasted for only three hours. Had the second study been longer, more trivial usability problems may have been identified, as in the first study.

EXERCISE

The two studies differ in a number of ways. For example, different techniques are compared and the experimental procedures differ too. Despite these differences what tentative conclusions can you draw from the two studies?

COMMENT

The conclusions that can be drawn must be very tentative but some suggestions are:

- Usability testing is quite expensive but reveals a large number of usability problems. However, it may be important to select tasks that are not too long and so avoid being swamped by many minor problems. This may also help to reduce the relatively high cost of usability testing.
- Walkthroughs are useful early in design when there are different designs to consider. Group walkthroughs appear to be more effective than individual walkthroughs. The second study suggests that walkthroughs appear to identify different problems to usability testing.

- Heuristic evaluation was not compared in the second study. However, the results of the first study suggest that it is cheap and effective but, like group walkthroughs, it is more effective when done by several experts.
- Guidelines appear to be useful for focusing experts' attention.

EXERCISE

If you were designing a study to compare a number of different evaluation techniques, what are the key issues that you would take into account?

COMMENT

It would be important to:

- make sure that the conditions for using each technique were as similar as possible,
- select appropriate users or experts, depending on the type of evaluation,
- select tasks of a suitable length and complexity,
- find a meaningful way of comparing the data collected using the different techniques.

Key points

- Five factors point up differences between evaluation methods: the purpose, the stage of development, the amount and way in which users are to be involved in the evaluation process, the nature of the data and the practical considerations that need to be taken into account when planning an evaluation.
- Other issues to consider when planning an evaluation are validity and reliability of data collection and analysis, biases, the scope of the information needed and ecological validity.
- Validity concerns whether the evaluation method is measuring what is intended.
- Biases in data collection may occur due to selective data gathering or manipulation of the evaluation situation.
- It is important that data collection is reliable and that the evaluation can be replicated.
- Ecological validity considers the amount of interference to the study caused by the evaluation itself.
- Care is needed when comparing results from different evaluation studies.

Further reading

MEISTER D. (1986). *Human Factors Testing and Evaluation*. Amsterdam: Elsevier.
This book provides broad and detailed coverage of the area.

WHITESIDE J., BENNETT J. and HOLTZBLATT K. (1988). Usability engineering: our experience and evolution. In *Handbook of Human–Computer Interaction* (HELANDER M., ed.). Amsterdam: North-Holland.
This chapter provides excellent reading. As the title suggests, it traces the development of usability engineering and describes its practice. It then goes on to discuss the shortcomings of many current procedures and the need for contextual approaches.

Glossary

3D trackers measure the absolute position and orientation of a sensor in three dimensions. Used in some virtual reality systems to track gloves, headsets, etc.

abstraction a concept in a person's mind. For example, a high-level abstraction is one in which a machine or part of a machine is thought about in a way that is quite distant from the detail of the actual machine. A low-level abstraction is close to the detail of some aspect of the machine.

access-oriented programming a programming style associated with the use of cells. (*q.v.*).

action a task that involves no problem solving or control structure component.

activity theory a theoretical framework, originating from Soviet psychology, that has been adapted to analyse organizational and users' needs.

affordance an aspect of an object which makes it obvious how the object is to be used; for example, a panel on a door to indicate 'push' and a vertical handle to indicate 'pull'. Sound can also have affordance.

agent (i) a virtual character that initiates action; (ii) an automatic goal-directed system (e.g. a human).

alphanumeric keyboard the most commonly used form of input for HCI consisting of a set of characters, numbers, various symbols and possibly also function keys or a number pad.

analogical representations picture-like images (e.g. an image of an apple).

analysis the process of finding out what a client (or customer) requires from a software system.

analyst's workbench a software development environment that provides support for an analyst's or designer's work; often the support offered is limited to one particular development approach.

analytic metrics measurements that assess a user interface design based on a static analysis of an interface design specification.

application description the document that is produced initially by a client which describes what is wanted from the proposed new system (see also **statement of requirements**).

articulatory directness concerns the relationship between the meanings of expressions and their physical form.

articulatory distance the gap between the semantic representations used at an interface and the physical form of the expressions used in an interaction.

associative stage the second stage of learning a skill in which connections between the various elements of the skill are strengthened.

attention the focusing of perception on a limited range of stimuli, leading to heightened awareness.

attribute a characteristic of an entity; a data element which belongs to an entity.

auralization perceptualization using sound. (See also **perceptualization** and **sonification**.)

automatic cognitive processing a mental activity that is carried out rapidly, with minimal attention and unavailable to consciousness (e.g. the process of perceiving colour).

autonomous stage the final stage of learning a skill in which the skill becomes more and more automated and rapid.

Backus–Naur form a formal grammatical notation often used to specify programming languages.

benchmark task is a standard task that is used to evaluate the design of a system by testing users' performance on the task with different versions of the system.

bitmap a way of describing an image as a bit pattern or series of numbers that gives the shade or colour of each pixel (i.e. each point making up the image).

brain metaphor the conceptualization of human cognition, in terms of networks of interconnected nodes that model the neural activity in the brain.

brightness the perceived illumination of an object; emitting, reflecting or pervaded by much light.

capture errors a type of error that occurs when a sequence of less familiar actions is 'captured by' another, more frequent or better learned sequence, for example, driving to work on a weekend when one intended to go somewhere else.

cells special data values that can notify other parts of a system that they have been changed. They are also known as 'active values'.

chauffeured prototyping a form of prototyping in which the user does not 'drive' the system him or herself, rather the system is 'driven' by a system developer while the user observes the system's behaviour.

chord keyboard an input device in which alphanumeric information is entered by pressing groups of keys.

class-inclusion matching the matching of specific commands with category labels given as titles for high-level menus.

click to focus an arrangement whereby the user's input is not directed to a new window until the user clicks somewhere within the borders of that window (see also **mouse focus**).

closed questions are questions in which the respondent selects from a predetermined set of replies (see also **open questions**).

cocktail party phenomenon the ability to switch attention between competing stimuli.

cognitive aids external representations that are intended to gain our attention at a time relevant to the task that needs to be performed.

cognitive ergonomics a discipline that focuses particularly on human information processing and computer systems. By definition, it aims to develop knowledge about the interaction between human information processing capacities and limitations and technical information processing systems.

cognitive mnemonic a memory strategy devised to help remember the ordering, spatial location or a set of items (e.g. the use of an acronym to represent the first characters of a set of commands that have to be typed in a particular sequence).

cognitive model a representation of some aspect of the mind, involving the acquisition of knowledge (e.g. understanding, remembering, reasoning, learning). These include **connectionist** and **computational models**.

cognitive overload excessive demands made on the cognitive processes, in particular memory.

cognitive psychology the study of how we carry out our everyday tasks and how we cope with the booming, buzzing confusion of stimuli that constantly bombard us during our waking life.

cognitive stage the first stage of learning a skill in which declarative knowledge is acquired.

cognitive system the mental apparatus which translates inputs from the perceptual system into outputs to the motor system through the use of memory processes.

collaborative learning peer group learning through talking and observing with each other.

colour coding uses colour for coding and structuring information at the interface as well as making it pleasant and enjoyable to look at.

colour pollution excessive use of colour at the interface making it difficult to locate information.

colour stereoscopy an illusion created at the interface whereby red and blue words appear to lie in different depth planes.

command a form of communication with a computer system, usually via a keyboard, in which a request is made for action by inputting a short word or abbreviation.

commercial style guide a style guide produced by a company for use outside the organization by people who wish to achieve the company's distinctive 'look and feel', e.g. the Microsoft style, the Macintosh style, etc.

communication style a characterization of a type of interaction that can occur between a user and a computer system.

compiler a program that translates high-level programming languages into machine code that can be stored and subsequently executed.

computational model a simulation of a cognitive activity, in terms of goals, planning and action, through the manipulation of symbols according to a set of fixed rules.

computer-aided software engineering (CASE) tools software tools that support the project life cycle.

computer metaphor the conceptualization of human cognition in terms of computations that take place in a computer that model the processes of the mind.

computer-supported cooperative work (CSCW) the sharing of software and hardware among groups of people working together so as to optimize the shared technology for maximum benefit to all those who use or are affected by it.

concatenation the generation of speech by the re-assembly of pre-recorded digitized human speech fragments.

conceptual consistency consistency in the meaning of objects and in behaviours or forms across similar objects.

conceptual design the part of system design that is concerned with questions about what is required.

conceptual model a generic term that describes the different way computer systems are understood by different people (i.e. users, designers, researchers).

connectionist (or PDP) model a simulation of a cognitive activity through the activation of a network of processing units in a computer system.

connectionists argue that images and propositions can co-exist at a higher level of representation.

constraint reduction in freedom, in particular that caused by poorly designed tools.

constraints restrict the possible operations on an object.

constructivist theorists believe that the process of seeing is an active process in which our view of the world is constructed both from information in the environment and from previously stored knowledge.

context diagram the 'top level' view (i.e. most abstract view) of a system's functions that defines the boundary of the system with the major dataflows shown as inputs and outputs.

contextual evaluation or **inquiry** is a form of elicitation which can be used for evaluation that is based on ethnography. It assumes that knowledge is only meaningful in context and seeks to understand user behaviour in natural settings.

continuous entry device an input device which allows the user to enter infinitely variable (analogue) information (e.g. trackballs, joysticks). (See also **discrete entry devices**.)

continuous speech recognition systems are systems capable of recognizing words from continuous speech without deliberate pauses between each word.

contrast the difference in luminance between an object and its background on a display screen.

controlled processes are processes that are not automatic. An example of a controlled cognitive process is performing mental arithmetic where the person has to consciously work through the different parts of the sum.

controlling task the most primitive and basic task used for manipulating objects (e.g. stretching).

control panels typically consist of a collection of controls and displays in an assembly that show the user the state of some object or objects of interest, and allow parameters to be altered interactively.

controls is a general term for interface components such as sliders, buttons, check boxes and so on.

conversation analysis (CA) has the primary goal of detailing the tacit, organized reasoning procedures which inform the production and recognition of naturally occurring talk.

cooperative evaluation is a low-cost evaluation method that is designed to be used early in product design and that, according to the classification in this book, is interpretive in nature.

corporate style guide a style guide produced by a company for use within the organization so that all applications developed by them have a distinctive 'look and feel'.

cursor control keys arrow keys on a keyboard used to control the position of a cursor.

data dictionary a description of all the objects in the system.

data dictionary system a software system that helps to control the process of defining data and processes and which helps the analyst perform consistency checking.

data elements the most basic pieces of data which are of interest in the application.

dataflow diagram (DFD) a diagrammatic representation which describes a system from the point of view of the data which is passed between processes.

dataflow one or more data elements that are transferred from one process to another.

dataglove wired glove with position and flexion sensors which provide the user with the apparent ability to grasp and manipulate computer-generated objects as though they were in three-dimensional space. (See also **3D trackers**.)

datastore a collection of data elements which is more persistent or more permanent than a dataflow.

declarative knowledge stored information consisting of facts about the world which can be verbalized.

decomposition the process of breaking down goals into subgoals and tasks into subtasks.

dependent variable in an experiment is the variable that depends on the independent variable (see also **independent variable**).

depth cues structures in a visual scene that make objects appear as three-dimensional. There are two types: monocular and binocular. Monocular cues enable us to see objects as near or in the distance through the use of shadow, interposition, contrast, texture and size. Binocular cues enable us to perceive depth through presenting slightly different images of the same object or scene to each eye.

description error a type of slip that occurs when information is misinterpreted, resulting in an incorrect action being performed. These errors tend to occur when different actions have similar descriptions.

design (i) the *process* of developing a product, artefact or system; (ii) a *representation* (simulation or model) of the product.

design model the designers' conception of the system (how it should be represented, what interface it should have and how it should behave, etc.).

design rule low-level design guideline that requires no real interpretation before it can be applied, e.g. a menu that contains more than five items should be divided into sections; such rules should be applied with caution.

design space the amount of freedom or scope that a designer has to produce alternative designs.

design space analysis an approach to design that encourages the designer to explore alternative design solutions.

device simulation a software emulation of a logical device where no suitable physical device exists.

dialog see **dialogue**.

dialogue the exchange of instructions and information that takes place between a user and a computer. (See **interaction**.)

dialogue box an overlaying window that appears on the screen with the purpose of providing a message, a warning or an acknowledgement to which the user must respond before a dialogue (*q.v.*) can proceed.

direct manipulation a communication style in which objects are represented on the computer screen, and can be manipulated by the user in ways analogous to how the user would manipulate the real object.

discount usability evaluation a method for providing low-cost evaluation which is especially suitable for small companies. It generally combines think aloud evaluation of scenarios with the use of heuristics.

discrete entry device an input device in which information is entered in an on–off fashion (e.g. keyboard, mouse button).

display refresh rate the rate at which the images on a screen, which fade with time, are 'refreshed' by impulses of electricity. (See **flicker**.)

distributed cognition a theoretical framework that explains cognitive activities as embodied and situated within the context in which they occur. It accounts for the socially and cognitively distributed work activities of a group of people and their interactional use of artefacts. This includes distributed problem-solving, decision-making and shared memory.

distributed model the theory that people have neither purely functional nor purely structural models of devices but, in fact, have knowledge which is distributed between the mind (where such knowledge may be functional, structural, or a combination of the two) and the world.

distributed representations networks of nodes where knowledge is implicit in the connections between the nodes.

divided attention the ability to attend to more than one stimulus at a time.

Dvorak keyboard a more ergonomic, faster and more efficient alternative to the standard alphanumeric qwerty keyboard layout. Never commercially successful due to the cost of replacing existing keyboards and retraining millions of people familiar with qwerty.

dynamic menus are menus whose entries need not be fixed when the program is coded, but can be adapted by the program (or user) at run time.

ecological theorists believe that perception involves the process of 'picking up' information from the environment and does not require any processes of construction or elaboration.

ecological validity refers to the environment in which an evaluation is done and the degree to which the evaluation process affects the results that are obtained.

entity a thing, abstract or concrete; a group of data elements which are conceived of as belonging together.

entity definition a formal description of an entity in terms of its attributes.

entity match a search for an item on a menu where the user knows the semantic representation she seeks.

entity-relationships (E-R) diagram a diagrammatic representation of the structure of data in a system.

entity type a classification of entities.

envisioning bringing abstract ideas to life in the form of physical representations.

episodic memory the storage of autobiographical experience, for example, the objects, events, and people that have been personally encountered. In psychological experiments episodic memory is tested using sets of words and pictures.

equivalence search a search for an item on a menu in which the user has a vague idea of the operation or item wanted but does not know its semantic representation (e.g. wanting to change text and needing to find an EDIT command).

error see **mistake** and **slip**.

ethnomethodology a method that assumes no *a priori* model of cognitive processes when a person does something but instead analyses behaviour by observing events in their natural context.

evaluation a process through which information about the usability of a system is gathered in order to improve the system or to assess a completed interface.

evaluation method a procedure for collecting relevant data about the operation and usability of a computer system.

event something that happens in the external world which is reflected by the arrival or change of some data in the system.

event-response system an abstraction which controls interaction and which is noteworthy for not using an established notation.

evolutionary prototyping an extensive form of prototyping in which the prototype is gradually developed into the final system.

experimental effect a change in the dependent variable that is caused by a change in the independent variable.

expert review is an evaluation method in which experts role-play less experienced users in order to identify usability problems.

explicit pop-up menus (see also **pop-up menus** and **implicit pop-up menus**.) Explicit pop-up menus are triggered by clicking on appropriate interaction objects such as icons, menu bars, window controls etc.

external task see **goal**.

familiarity the frequency with which a word occurs in everyday language.

field study a study that is done in a natural setting as opposed to a controlled laboratory study.

finite state diagram see **transition diagram**.

fixed-matrix menu a permanently-displayed menu (e.g. the 'palette' displayed on the side of many drawing software packages).

flexible interview an interview in which the interviewer is free to explore the opinions of the interviewee. (See **structured interview**.)

flicker an unstable image which results through either or both the image persistence (*q.v.*) being too short or the display refresh rate (*q.v.*) being too low.

forcing function a specific feature of an interface designed to prevent users making errors by forcing the user to take certain action(s).

formative evaluation an evaluation that takes place before actual implementation and which influences the development of the product.

form-fill a communication style in which the computer elicits information from the user by presenting a form, analogous to a paper form, to be filled in by the user.

form painter an interface design tool which forms part of a fourth generation language (4GL). Also known as screen painter.

fourth generation (programming) language (4GL) a specification language for information systems in which whole objects can be constructed relatively easily at a very high-level of abstraction.

full prototype a prototype which contains the full functionality of the final system but with reduced performance.

functional model a user's mental model which consists of the 'how to do it' knowledge about an object (see **task-action mapping model**).

functional requirements what the system (*both human and computer*) has to be capable of doing.

functional specification   a representation of the system showing the result of analysing and collecting the functional requirements.

function key   an input key which, when pressed alone or in conjunction with another, causes a particular operation to take place.

gestural syntax   in systems such as mouse-based systems, some sequences of gestures will make the computer carry out one or more coordinated actions. Other sequences of actions will not. The differences between such gestures can be described by gestural syntaxes which allow the computer to distinguish between gestural sequences such as 'press-drag-release', and 'click-position-click'.

goal   (also called an **external task**) a state of a system (or of the agent) which the agent wishes to achieve.

graphical coding   the use of colour, alphanumerics, shapes, symbols and icons to represent data and processes at the interface.

groupware   software designed to be used by more than one person, for instance networking and electronic mail software.

guidelines   advice about how to design an interface.

gulf of evaluation   refers to the distance between the system's behaviour and the user's goals.

gulf of execution   refers to the distance between the user's goals and the means of achieving them through the system.

handwriting recognition   translation of handwritten characters (letters, numbers, punctuation marks etc.) into ASCII text which can be displayed instantly on screen as printed characters.

Harmony Space   an interface designed to allow both beginners and experts to explore aspects of musical harmony rapidly and effectively.

Hawthorne effect   changes in behaviour and performance of subjects resulting from them knowing that they are being observed.

heuristic evaluation   an evaluation in which the reviewers are guided by heuristic guidelines.

hierarchical pop-up menus   a menu system whereby selecting or browsing a choice on a menu pops up another menu and so on, in such a way that a single zig-zagging gesture can be used to specify a whole series of related choices. (See also **pop-up menus**.)

hierarchical task analysis (HTA)   aims to describe the task in terms of a hierarchy of operations and plans.

high fidelity prototyping   a form of prototyping that uses a medium as close as possible to that used in the final interface; thus the prototype has a look and feel which is close to the finished product.

horizontal prototype   a prototype that illustrates all of the user interface but has hardly any functionality.

human–computer communication   the dialogue ($q.v.$) between human(s) and computer(s). (See also **human–computer interaction**.)

human–computer interaction (HCI)   the processes, dialogues ($q.v.$), and actions that a user employs to interact with a computer in a given environment.

human–computer interface   often now used synonymously with human–computer interaction but in the past it referred more narrowly to the interface between the system and users; e.g. the dialogue on the screen.

human factors engineering   the US counterpart to ergonomics.

human information processing   see **information processing**.

hypermedia   a collection of non-linearly linked nodes that may include text, video, sound or animation. (See also **hypertext**.) In effect, a database containing large quantities of information which can be browsed and searched using various specially devised navigation tools.

hypertext   a system that is based on the notion of documents being non-linear, with optional pointers from words or points in the text to other words or points in the text. (See also **hypermedia**.)

icons   small pictorial images that are used to represent system objects, application tools such as those for drawing, and utilities and commands.

identify   to distinguish between entities of the same type.

image persistence   the duration of visibility of an object or representation before it fades. (See **display refresh rate**, **flicker**.)

imagery   the ability with which a word can elicit images in the mind.

imaging model   a scheme or language provided by a windowing system for describing graphical images to be displayed; for example, bitmaps and PostScript are both imaging models.

imagists   a school of psychology which proposes that people represent visual information in memory through images which bear a close resemblance to the physical object remembered.

impact analysis is a technique in which the impact of different usability trade-offs is estimated.

implementation the process of programming and creating a software system.

implicit pop-up menus (see also **pop-up menus**, and **explicit pop-up menus**.) Implicit pop-up menus appear when a user clicks anywhere on the screen, or on a particular area of the screen, depending on the system.

incremental prototyping a form of prototyping in which the full application is constructed and supplied to the client in discrete chunks.

independent variable is the variable in an experiment that the experimenter manipulates (see also **dependent variable**).

information flow architecture an architecture in which the components manage different stages of the information transformation in a user interface.

information processing the modelling of sensory input and cognitive transformations as a series of processing stages in which meaning is attributed by the receiver to the signal received.

input device a device that transforms information from the user or outside world into data which a computer system can process.

inspection scrutiny of aspects of technology by specialists.

intelligent tutoring systems (ITSs) these are computer systems that have been designed to tutor the student by deciding what students should learn given their current state of knowledge.

interaction the exchange that occurs between users and computers.

interaction configuration specifying the behaviour of a user interface by linking together media and support objects in a temporal structure.

interaction logging a log of the user and computer interaction that can be replayed in real-time.

interaction styles a generic term to include all the ways that users communicate or interact with computer systems.

interaction task the most basic and primitive action that a user carries out in order to communicate with a computer system.

interface component refers to the components that make up an interface. This is sometimes used to include physical input and output devices, but is more often used to refer to virtual objects and widgets such as on-screen sliders, buttons and check boxes.

interface metaphor a representation of a familiar domain that presents a system model to the user as a physical world of objects (e.g. the desktop metaphor).

internal task see **task**.

interpreter a program that executes programs written in high-level programming languages line by line directly from source code.

IPSEs (integrated project support environments) a software development environment which incorporates many facilities for supporting the whole software development life cycle, such as configuration management, version control, a database of knowledge about the current project, and so on.

isolated word recognition system a computer-based speech system which recognizes a limited vocabulary of single words spoken with pauses between them.

joysticks a computer input device consisting of a little stick you push (much as used by plane pilots). Operates in two dimensions and often used for indicating direction and speed rather than location.

keyboard the primary form of input used on most computers and modern typewriters. More generally: a group of on–off pushbuttons, which are used as an input device either in combination or separately.

knowledge in the head and knowledge in the world one of the most established findings in memory research is that we can recognize material far more easily than we can recall it from memory.

language/action approach views language as a means by which people act. The approach is based on the theory of 'speech acts' derived from the philosophy of language. The basic premise is to assume that when we make an utterance we are performing an action.

learning through analogy the invoking of prior knowledge of an apparently similar object or system as a basis for interpreting new information.

level of processing theory according to this theory, information can be processed at different levels, ranging from a shallow analysis of a stimulus (for example, processing the physical features of a word such as its sound) to a deep or semantic analysis.

lexical–semantic consistency the degree to which the meaning of a lexical item is the same as or as close as possible to its meaning in normal life.

library an organized collection of program modules. (See **modules**.)

Likert scale a multipoint rating scale that measures the strength of a subject's agreement with a clear statement.

linkage configuration unites a user interface with its underlying application.

links in the context of hypertext and hypermedia, links are the relationships linking items. When visualizing a network, links are the lines connecting nodes.

long term memory memory which is effectively unlimited in its capacity which stores anything to be remembered after attention is directed elsewhere. (See **multi-store model of memory**.)

low fidelity prototyping a form of prototyping that does not use the same medium as that used in the final interface; such prototyping would concentrate more on the functionality of the system and the construction of the interface, and less on the look and feel of the interface.

macro-driven document preparation systems document editors where commands which direct formatting and printing are embedded in the text but are invisible in the printed version. An example is the *roff* document preparation system in Unix.

macro ergonomics study of the management of technological innovation in an organizational context.

mandatory the characteristic of a relationship which constrains an entity so that it must always participate in the relationship.

man–machine interface (MMI) an older term for human–computer interface, it included automatic and semi-automatic machinery that was not necessarily a computer or computer-controlled.

mapping how a description at one level of abstraction is translated into a description at another level.

mathematical descriptions of curves systems whereby curves and other graphical objects to be displayed are described internally by mathematical formulae as opposed, for example, to patterns of dots. The best known example is PostScript. (See also **imaging model** and **bitmap**.)

media configuration involves setting up input and output structures, linking them to low-level display objects such as buttons, sliders and pop-up menus and filling in any content which does not have to be computed during interaction.

mental model a mental representation that people use to organize their experience about themselves, others, the environment and the things with which they interact. The functional role of mental models is to provide predictive and explanatory power for understanding these phenomena.

menu a set of options displayed on a screen where the selection and execution of one (or more) of the options results in a change in the state of the interface.

message box a special kind of dialogue box that appears on the screen, overlaying the current window with a specific message to which a response must be made.

metaphor a way of describing a concept in a more accessible and familar form. This can help in understanding an unfamiliar or complex subject. Various metaphors have been used in the context of HCI and cognitive science (e.g. verbal metaphor, interface metaphor, brain metaphor and computer metaphor).

minimalist instruction an approach to learning that can also be applied to the design of training manuals. Aims to reduce the amount of information required, to focus on real work activities, and to emphasize how to recover from errors. (See also **'scenario machine'** and **'training wheels'**.)

mistake an error made by a person due to a failure of intention.

modal dialogue boxes are dialogue boxes which force the user to respond to some question before any other action can be taken.

modality-specific stores separate, very short-term memory stores for visual, auditory and other sensory information. (See also **modeless dialogue boxes**.)

mode error a type of slip which occurs when people think they are in one context but are in fact, in another. For example, they may believe they are in 'type-over' mode when they are actually in 'insert' mode.

model a representation of something, constructed and used for a particular purpose. (See **cognitive model**, **connectionist (or PDP) model**, **computational model**, **conceptual model**, **design model**, **multi-layer model**, **multi-store model of memory**, **user model**, **mental model** and **system model**.)

modeless dialogue boxes offer information and request some action, but do not restrict the actions of the user. Typically they can be moved, resized, dealt with or ignored while other interactions continue. (See also **dialogue boxes**.)

model human processor an idealized model of the user based on the human information processing model of cognition. It was developed to provide a theoretical basis for characterizing the cognitive processes that are assumed to underlie the performance of a task.

module a small part of a program which may be reusable.

motor system the mental apparatus which translates cognitive processes into action by activating patterns of voluntary muscles.

mouse focus in contrast to 'click-to-focus', an arrangement whereby the user's input is directed to the window within whose borders the cursor is currently located (without any need for a preliminary mouse click). (See also **click to focus**.)

multi-layer model a hierarchical model representing the high-level (cognitive) operations and the low-level (physical) operations required to use a computer system.

multimedia the use of several different kinds of input and output media (i.e. carriers of information) in combination, e.g. sound, text and video.

multimodal making use of diverse forms of presentation (e.g. sound, touch, moving pictures) and input (e.g. gesture, sound, body movement), with an emphasis on human aspects as opposed to technological aspects. In other contexts, can have other meanings. (See also **multimedia**.)

multi-point rating scale has a number of points representing a set of values from which the user can select the appropriate point to represent her views (see also **Likert scale**).

multi-store model of memory a model of memory which distinguishes between two types of memory: short term (*q.v.*) and long term (*q.v.*). Short term memory (now known as working memory) provides a working space in which limited information can be held for a short period.

multitasking switching between several different tasks at the interface.

natural language languages such as English, French, etc. used by ordinary people – in contrast to artificial languages used for communicating with computers such as Pascal and SmallTalk.

neural network a system based on an artificial intelligence technique which learns from examples.

Often used in handwriting and speech recognition systems.

nodes in the context of hypertext and hypermedia, nodes are the items of content. When visualizing a network, nodes are the places where links terminate.

numeric keypad a separate keypad consisting of numeric keys, arithmetic functions and an <enter> key.

object-oriented architecture a form of software organization with no necessary connection with HCI but which in practice is very well suited to managing the complexity of user interfaces. In the ideal case, there will be one to one correspondence between interaction objects, e.g. menus and buttons, and software 'objects', which can be combined to form a user interface.

object-oriented development an approach to software production which concentrates on defining the attributes and behaviour of independent elements (objects), rather than on the procedural aspects of the domain.

object-oriented programming a programming approach in which program construction is done by constructing objects (items and their associated actions) such as in the Smalltalk environment.

open questions are questions where the respondent is free to provide her own reply (see also **closed questions**).

operational (aspects) how to package conceptual operations into a physical dialogue. The behaviour of the system as opposed to **representational** (aspects).

optional the characteristic of a relationship which allows for entities not to participate in that relationship.

output devices devices that convert information coming from an electronic, internal representation in a computer system into some form perceptible by a human (terminal, printer, loudspeaker, force feedback joystick etc.).

panning moving quickly up and down or left and right over a whole object, which may be larger than the display.

participative design an approach to system design that acknowledges the importance of working with users in the design process.

participative evaluation is an important component of participative design. Users and designers work together closely to understand design problems within their context or simulated context.

pen systems   typically small, notebook size computers that allow the user to write directly on the screen using a special pen.

perception   the process of becoming aware of objects by way of the sense organs.

perceptual depth cues   visual affordances which provide the means by which to help a viewer perceive as three-dimensional objects their two-dimensional representations.

perceptualization   a general term to cover both visualization and auralization. A well-designed presentation in pictures or sound that can make clear relationships that might otherwise be appreciated only slowly if at all.

perceptual system   the mental apparatus that translates sensations of the physical world as detected by the body's sensory systems into internal representations in the mind.

performance-based analysis   of video data is concerned with establishing clearly defined performance measures. (See **task-based analysis**.)

performance metrics   measurements that assess a user interface design based on user performance.

phoneme   the basic building block of the spoken word. A *phoneme* is defined as the smallest unit of sound such that if a single phoneme is changed in a sentence, the meaning may be changed. For example, the spoken words 'banned' and 'hand' differ only in their initial phoneme.

physical consistency   consistency in the representations of objects and in their behaviour or operation.

physical design   part of system design concerned with questions of how the conceptual design will be represented physically and how it will behave.

pilot study   a small study carried out prior to a large-scale study in order to try out a technique or procedure.

planning   the information processing and knowledge necessary to decide upon a course of action.

pop-up menu   a menu that appears when a particular area of a screen is clicked on. The menu remains in position until the user instructs it to disappear again.

positive transfer   occurs when faced with a task which is similar to one that has been done before.

post event protocol   a spoken, descriptive protocol of what the user has done, which is obtained from the user after she has completed a task.

PostScript   a proprietary system for printing or displaying graphical images using mathematical descriptions of curves (see also **mathematical descriptions of curves**).

pre- and post-questionnaires   are given to users before (i.e. **pre-**) the test experience and then after (i.e. **post-**) the experience so that a comparison can be made. The same questionnaire is used both times.

predictive evaluation   a general term used to describe a group of low-cost evaluation methods which predict the usability of a system from a model, specification or early prototype.

primacy effect   in memory experiments, the tendency for initial words in a list to be recalled more readily than later words on the list.

primary task   the task you wanted to carry out in the first place, as opposed to the tasks you got side-tracked into for purposes of mastering the tools. (See **secondary task**.)

principles   high level design guidelines which require interpretation before they can be applied, e.g. 'know the user'.

procedural knowledge   stored information which consists of knowledge of how to do things.

process   (in data flow diagrams) a transformation of an input dataflow into output dataflow.

production rule   (often abbreviated to **production**)   rule containing a *condition–action pair* of the form: *if* (condition) *then* (action).

program visualization   a technique which uses a graphical language or representation to express the behaviour of a program while it is executing.

prompted interviewing   an interview in which prompting is used to draw out the user's opinions on particular issues.

propositionalists   a school of psychology that proposes that information is processed by being transformed into symbolic structures. (See also **imagists**.)

propositional representations   abstract and language-like statements that make assertions (e.g. 'the book is on the table').

prototype   (*n.*) an experimental incomplete design of an application used for testing design ideas.

prototype   (*vb.*) to construct a version of a system that may be (i) functionally incomplete, (ii) does not cover the whole scope of the system, (iii) lacks the performance of the final system.

prototyping   the act of developing a prototype (often as software but the term is also used to include other forms such as video or paper-based prototypes).

pull-down menu   a menu that 'pulls down' like a roller blind from a title bar at the top of a display and then retracts back to its original title.

QOC   see **Questions, Options and Criteria**.

qualitative data   data which can be categorized in some way but which cannot be reduced to numerical measurements.

quantitative data   data which are comprised of numeric values.

query boxes   are a particular kind of dialogue box initiated by the system rather than the user. Query boxes prompt the user for one or more specific pieces of information (for example yes/no answers, a selection from a set of alternatives, or the typing in of a value or name) and provide any context necessary to make the choice comprehensible.

question and answer dialogue   a communication style in which the computer (usually) initiates questions and the user enters yes/no or menu choices.

Questions, Options and Criteria   a notation for expressing a design space analysis. The notation consists of a set of design decision questions, each of which has associated with it a set of potential solutions and a set of criteria which are used to assess each of the potential solutions.

qwerty   the layout of the standard alphanumeric keyboard – so called after the first letters in the uppermost row from left to centre.

ranked order   a scale on a questionnaire which requires respondents to rank their responses to items in specified numerical order. For example, 'rank the following features in order of their importance to you'.

rapid prototyping   a form of simple, rapidly produced prototyping in which the prototype is used to collect information about both requirements and the adequacy of possible designs; it is not developed into the final product.

raster graphics   a form of graphics programming in which an abstraction is used to represent a grid of small rectangular portions on a display which can be moved over each other, inverted or combined.

recall   the ability to access an item of information from memory.

recency effect   in memory experiments, the tendency for the last (most recent) words on a list to be recalled more readily than other words on the list.

recognition   the ability to remember a previously seen (or heard, touched etc.) stimulus when re-presented.

redundant coding   the use of two or more forms of coding (e.g. colour and shape) at the interface to represent one type of information. An example is the traffic light, where the position of each light is reinforced by being colour coded.

rehearsal   the process of repeating information in working memory. This facilitates the short term recall of information and its transfer to long term memory.

relationship   an association between entities.

relationship description   a natural language elaboration of the meaning of a relationship.

reliability   is concerned with the consistency of the measurement process. A reliable evaluation method is one that produces the same results on separate occasions under the same circumstances.

representational   (aspects) the appearance of things on a screen.

requirements analysis   the investigation of a situation which focuses on what is required but not on how to provide it.

requirements animation   a software prototype used to elicit from users their requirements for a system and to explore possible functions.

requirements gathering   (see also **analysis**) the process of finding out what a client (or customer) requires from a software system.

resolution   the 'fineness' of detail that can be produced in an image; granularity.

rooms   a system that allows various alternative arrangements of windows to be stored and used by users.

rule table   a list of rules in, for example, an expert system.

safety-critical systems   systems, such as those used in nuclear power plants, aircraft cockpits and air traffic control, in which human or environmental safety is of paramount concern.

scenario machine   a word processor for the training of beginners, which gives guidance on how to carry out simple tasks whenever users depart from commonplace sequences of actions.

schema   a mental representation which consists of general knowledge about events, objects or actions (*pl.* **schemata**).

scientific management   the underlying assumption behind this approach was that work obeys scientific laws and therefore can be analysed using scientific methods. The organization was viewed as a rational system that should operate as efficiently as possible towards some goal, typically to maximize profit.

screen painter   see **form painter**.

script   (i) a specific version of a schema consisting of general knowledge about likely outcomes; (ii) a series of instructions which provides control in HyperCard by integrating input and output objects (buttons or text fields) with media structures (cards and backgrounds).

scrolling   the movement of lines of text or larger segments, including whole files, up and down or side to side on a screen by use of cursor keys or the control of a box in a bar appearing on the screen.

secondary task   mastering enough of a tool to accomplish more than the primary task (the task you wanted to carry out in the first place).

selective attention   the ability to attend to one stimulus from among a mass of competing stimuli.

semantic consistency   the degree to which phrases expressing similar semantic concepts are denoted in the same way in an interaction language. (See also **conceptual consistency**.)

semantic differential scale   an attitude scale which requires respondents to rate an item using a scale with bi-polar adjectives at each end of the scale (e.g. easy/difficult).

semantic directness   concerns the relationship between what the user wants to express and the meaning of the expressions available at the interface.

semantic distance   the gap between a user's goals and the representations used at an interface for both input and output.

semantic memory   the large body of general information that we build up in memory throughout our lives.

semantic networks   a computational model of how knowledge is structured in memory. Objects are represented as nodes and the relationships between them as links.

semi-structure interview   a hybrid between a structured and flexible interview. (See **structured interview** and **flexible interview**.)

session object   a program which works 'behind the scenes' of a user interface and which acts like an application object (for example by providing computation to build, say, a bar chart) but which is independent of the application function.

short term memory   now known as working memory, a memory which provides a small working space in which limited information can be held for a short period. (See **multi-store model of memory**.)

shrinking   the reduction of the size of an object on a screen to provide the user with an overall view of it.

single layer model   a flat, non-hierarchical model representing the cognitive and physical operations required to use a computer system.

single subject effect   an experimental design in which just one subject is used.

situated learning   learning that occurs in a particular context, such as a community of practice (e.g. medical school).

slip   an error made by a person by accident. These are usually either mode errors (*q.v.*) or description errors (*q.v*).

social action   the social action approach proposes that technology is enabling rather than deterministic.

social protocols   have been established within formal meetings to enable participants to cope better. These include having a pre-set agenda, hand-raising to take a turn and having a chair to control the conversation. These kinds of formalized procedures impose a structure on the conversation which can improve the efficiency of the multi-party communication.

socio-technical design   an approach to system design that focuses on developing complete and coherent human–machine systems by considering both social and technical alternatives to problems.

socio-technical system   a system concerned with how the social and technical sub-systems of an organization interact with each other.

software engineering   the application of engineering principles and methods of design to the production of software.

software prototype   an experimental incomplete implementation used for testing design ideas.

software psychology   psychologically-based investigation of the way humans interact with software structures and systems.

software tools   programs that support designers and programmers at some point in the development of a software product.

solid-object modelling   graphical representations of three-dimensional objects that attempt to obtain a high level of fidelity through the use of colour, shading and other depth clues, which emphasize surface aspects of objects. (See also **wire-frame modelling**.)

sonification perceptualization using sound. (See also **perceptualization** and **auralization**.)

speaker-dependent system a speech recognition system that requires each user to train a system, usually using a restricted vocabulary.

speaker-independent systems speech recognition systems designed to be used by any user, as opposed to one designed to adapt to the idiosyncrasies of a particular user.

spreadsheet a program for entering and calculating accounting-type data designed to mimic a familiar paper predecessor electronically.

statement of requirements the document that is produced initially by a client which describes what is wanted from the proposed new system (see also **application description**).

state transition diagram see **transition diagram**.

structural model a user's mental model which represents the structure of an object and allows the user to reason about and to predict the object's actions in novel situations. (See also **functional model**.)

structured interview an interview in which all the questions are predetermined and there is no scope for exploring the individual's opinions (see **flexible interview**).

structured walkthrough a verbal description of the system, often constructed with the intended user of the system, based on some diagrammatic representation.

style guides a collection of design principles and rules which can be used to develop consistent user interfaces across a family of applications for a specific platform or platforms.

submenu a secondary menu triggered by selecting or browsing a choice on another menu.

subpanes subpanes are parts of windows that typically occupy a fixed position in their parent window, and cannot be moved independently (although their contents areas may be resizable and scrollable).

summative evaluation an evaluation which takes place after implementation and has the aim of testing the proper functioning of a product.

support configuration involves the selection and design of session objects.

surrogate model a user's mental model that appears to act like a replica of the physical object or world, using which simulations can be run in the mind (see **structural models**).

symbol segmentation in handwriting recognition, the problem of deciding where one character ends and another character begins.

syntactic consistency the consistency, for a whole 'language', of the rules about how to combine simple phrases.

synthesis-by-rule the generation of artificial speech phonemic rules and rules that relate to the context of a sentence.

system something that is considered as a whole from a particular viewpoint.

system feedback information provided by the system to reassure, guide and inform users.

system image the image the system conveys to the user – its interface, behaviour and documentation – which forms the basis of the user's mental model of the system.

system specification a document that clarifies a client's requirements in an unambiguous form by respecifying the requirements and distinguishing between system functions and the constraints that the software developer has to work under.

task (or **internal task)** the activities required, used or believed to be necessary to achieve a goal using a particular device.

task-action mapping the functional mapping between a task and a series of action arenas. Mapping refers to the association of one element from one set to another element from another set; maps knowledge about how to carry out a task to the physical characteristics of the task.

task allocation deciding which activities are to be carried out by humans and which by computers.

task analysis (TA) the process of investigating a problem by breaking down tasks that potential users of a system do or would do into sequences of actions and objects.

task-based analysis of video data is concerned with determining how users tackled the tasks and what problems they encountered. (See **performance-based analysis**.)

technological determinism one school of thought believes that technology is the single most important factor in determining the success of an organization.

teleconferencing holding meetings between three or more people across the telephone network.

testing the process of checking a computer program for errors (see also **validation** and **verification**).

text cursor windows that are specialized to deal with text typically have a cursor known as the text input cursor, which shows where input will be directed from the keyboard. This is in addition to the normal mouse pointer cursor.

text fields   are areas on screen which allow the user to input textual data.

thinking aloud protocol   an oral protocol in which a user speaks aloud what she is thinking while carrying out a task. Also called a **verbal protocol**.

tiling   a form of window management whereby windows can be displayed automatically with no overlapping using all available space. The term is named by analogy with tiles on a wall.

time and motion studies   entail carrying out detailed observational studies and taking precise measurements of the workers performing various tasks. The goal is to determine how the work could be decomposed into the optimal number of small tasks that could be done by one person for which there could be found one best method.

time-stamped key presses   a record of the exact key presses and the time of the event.

title bar   most windows have a title bar at the top or bottom of the window with a name which helps users find the window they want.

touch displays   allow the user to input information into the computer simply by touching an appropriate part of the screen or a nearby pad.

trackball   an input device consisting of a ball that a user can rotate in any direction within a fixed socket.

training wheels word processor   a word processor for beginners, which limits the learner to only simple functions – advanced functions are not made available. (See also **minimalist instruction**.)

transition diagram (also called **finite state** and **state transition diagram**)   a graphic structure indicating possible states of a system and transitions from one state to another.

ubiquitous computing   The ultimate aim of ubiquitous computing is to make the interface metaphor invisible to the user in the same way as computer systems are invisible in home appliances.

usability   a measure of the ease with which a system can be learned or used, its safety, effectiveness and efficiency, and the attitude of its users towards it.

usability engineering   an approach to system design in which levels of usability are specified quantitatively in advance, and the system is engineered towards these measures, which are known as metrics.

usability metrics   measure of the usability of a system.

usability specification   a specification quantifying target levels of usability for a system in terms of attributes such as learnability, throughput, flexibility and the positive attitude to be engendered in users.

usability testing   determines whether a system meets a pre-determined, quantifiable level of usability for specific types of user carrying out specific tasks.

usage simulations   see **expert review**.

user-centred design   an approach which views knowledge about users and their involvement in the design process as a central concern.

user-friendly   an over-used term intended to imply a high degree of usability. Its misuse has made it suspect.

user interface   the totality of surface aspects of a computer system, such as its input and output devices, the information presented to or elicited from the user, feedback presented to the user, the system's behaviour, its documentation and associated training programmes, and the user's actions with respect to these aspects.

user interface design environment (UIDE)   interactive environment which facilitates the development of user interfaces; UIDEs support human–computer interaction design but do not necessarily provide facilities for managing the run-time interaction with the application.

user interface management system (UIMS)   a system which enables designers to manage or develop a user interface using high-level integrated tools with much less effort than programming. Some UIMS will include UIDE.

user model   the researchers' or designer's description of the users and their prediction of how the users will behave and perform tasks.

user modelling   the process of constructing (often computer-based) models of individuals and groups of users.

user support   documentation, help and advice available to users.

validation   the process of checking that a product conforms to the client's requirements. In relation to evaluation, validation is concerned with whether the method used is measuring what is required to fulfill the purpose of the evaluation.

value   an instance of an attribute.

verbal metaphor   when a linguistic comparison is made between a computer or its components and a familiar object (e.g. a computer is like a typewriter).

verbal protocol   see **thinking aloud protocol**.

verification the process of checking that a product is a correct and consistent representation of the product at its previous stage of development.

vertical prototype a prototype which contains both high- and low-level functionality but for a restricted part of the system.

virtual devices are like physical devices, but they have no existence except when some relevant computer system is operating. For example, working versions of buttons, sliders, control panels, calculators, and 'rubber bands' represented on a computer screen are all virtual devices.

virtual environment a term for interfaces constructed using virtual reality technology, including their virtual components (see also **virtual device**).

virtual interface metaphors one of the first computer companies to realize the enormous potential of designing interfaces to be more like the physical concrete world that people are familiar with, was Xerox. Instead of developing verbal metaphors as ways of helping users understand the interface, they went one step further and designed an **interface metaphor**.

virtual reality a state in which the user has the illusion of being in a three-dimensional world created by the computer system.

virtual toolkit a toolkit which protects an application from the dependencies of the underlying commercial toolkit; applications built using a virtual toolkit can be moved across platforms.

visual brainstorming in the context of this book means generating visual ideas of abstract concepts.

visualization tools software support tools which support the development and presentation of a visual representation of a program's structure or behaviour (see **visual programming** and **program visualization**).

visual programming program development which uses a graphical language rather than a traditional text-based language.

visual system the sensory organs, nerves and visual cortex that are responsible for the process of seeing. 'Seeing' is achieved through building a model of the world by constructing, distorting and discarding information from visual stimuli.

walkthroughs involve constructing carefully defined tasks from a system specification or screen mock-up so that they can be used for early evaluation. Experts 'walk through' the system commenting on problems that they foresee.

waterfall model a characterization of the software development process as consisting of a number of processes and representations which are produced in an essentially linear fashion.

widget an interface component such as a check box, slider, menu, button, etc. (See also **virtual device** and **interface component**.)

window an area of a visual display, usually (though not always) rectangular, that has a border and contains a particular independent view of the data in the display.

window working set the set of windows needed to carry out a particular task effectively.

windowing system those parts of a user interface consisting of windows and related controls. In other contexts, can have more technical meanings.

wire-frame modelling graphical representation of three-dimensional objects through the use of schematic line drawings. This type gives emphasis to structural rather than surface aspects of the object. (See also **solid-object modelling**.)

Wizard of Oz prototyping a form of prototyping in which the user appears to be interacting with software when, in fact, a member of the development team is responding to the user's actions.

working memory see **short term memory**.

WYSIWYG What You See Is What You Get. For example, a document is displayed on the screen exactly as it would look in printed form.

zooming the ability to view a display at different levels of granularity by moving in and out of specific aspects of a display.

Solutions to questions

Chapter 1

1.1 Historically, the term 'user interface' has been used to describe the physical aspects of a computer system which the user experiences directly. Chiefly, these include the input and output devices and the dialogue structures. 'Human–computer interaction', however, is a much broader term and refers to all aspects that impinge on the way users interact with computing systems.

1.2 There may often be a conflict between different interests. For example, it may not be possible to have both efficiency and safety in one system. Reducing the number of keystrokes necessary to perform a task may make it more efficient but could mean having to cut back on safety measures. It could, for example, result in not including any fallback measures such as providing confirmation stages in a dialogue to users. As with any engineering problem, the HCI practitioner must constantly be aware of trade-offs and must also design a solution that optimizes the specified criteria for that application.

1.3 There may be changes in: the content of people's jobs, personnel policies, job satisfaction, power and influence in the workplace and physical changes to the work environment.

Chapter 2

2.1 The main factors that need to be considered relate to users, their tasks and their work environments. These include: the nature of the task being considered, user characteristics such as memory, organizational issues, health, comfort, constraints, functionality and productivity factors.

2.2 Cognitive psychologists have applied relevant psychological findings and principles of human performance to HCI. These have included the use of predictive models, guidelines and empirical methods to evaluate and investigate the efficacy of different types of interface. Social psychologists have provided organizational theories which help to explain the structure and function of organizations and the way people work together in groups. This knowledge provides a basis for the design, development, introduction and use of technology in organizations so that both individuals and the organization as a whole benefit. The application of ergonomics to HCI has also been concerned with the capabilities of the user but has paid more specific attention to the effects of the physical aspects of the environment. Computer science has significantly contributed to HCI by developing software support tools and methods for interface and system design.

Chapter 3

3.1 The four stages of the human information processing model are: stage 1 – encoding; stage 2 – comparison; stage 3 – response selection; stage 4 – response execution.

3.2 The main use of the model human processor is as a theoretical framework for making predictions about user performance. The main problem with the model is that it oversimplifies human

725

behaviour and so does not account for many of the more complex cognitive processes.

3.3 The main difference between the information processing approach and the computational approach is that the latter is concerned with modelling what knowledge is involved when information is processed, rather than in terms of processing stages and processing times.

3.4 **(a)** The traditional cognitive view of HCI is of an individual user interacting with a system, carrying out a series of cognitive tasks.
(b) The cognitive framework can be widened to take into account the context of HCI by conceptualizing how 'human actors' rather than individual users carry out their 'work activities' when using information systems in organizational settings.

3.5 The main goals of the distributed cognition approach are to analyse (i) how the different components of the functional system are coordinated, and (ii) what causes the various breakdowns that emerge in work settings.

Chapter 4

4.1 **(a)** The main difference between the two approaches is that the constructivists claim that perception involves the use of prior knowledge in the construction of a model of the world, while the ecologists argue that perception is a direct process, in which information is simply detected by the sensory organs.
(b) The constructivist approach has provided an understanding of how information hitting the retina is decomposed into meaningful parts. Specifically, it has been applied to the design of information displays to make certain information stand out and be readily perceivable. The ecological appproach has provided a way of understanding the visual properties of different objects in terms of the extent to which they 'afford' the actions that are intended to be performed on them. This can be very useful when considering the design of interface objects that need to be acted upon, like scroll bars.

4.2 **(a)** The main perceptual depth cues are size, interposition, contrast, shadow, texture and motion parallax.

(b) Solid-object modelling provides more information about the surface and shape of an object, enabling the viewer to distinguish between the inside and the outside. It is very costly, however, in terms of computing resources. Wireframe modelling needs fewer resources. It is useful for tasks in which the surface structure is not critical and it can also be effective when the internal structure of an object needs to be seen.

4.3 **(a)** Colour, especially for identification tasks, offers no advantages over achromatic coding. Also, too many colours can increase search times. Some users may also be colour-blind.
(b) Colour can aid recognition and detection, and facilitates search tasks when used for segmenting a display.

Chapter 5

5.1 The difference between focused and divided attention is that the former refers to our ability to attend to certain events from what amounts to a mass of competing stimuli while the latter refers to our ability to carry out two or more tasks at the same time.

5.2 **(a)** Information can be structured at the interface by grouping it according to meaningful categories (as raised in Chapter 4).
(b) Other techniques that can be used to guide the user's attention to important information at the interface are the use of spatial and temporal cues, colour and various alerting techniques such as flashing, reverse video and auditory warnings.

5.3 Automatic processes are more efficient and are performed more rapidly. Their main disadvantage is that they are inflexible, in that they are difficult to modify, which can disrupt performance.

5.4 The more meaningful a stimulus is the more it will be processed and the more likely it is to be remembered.

5.5 **(a)** The main factors are: the context in which the icons are being used; the type of task; the form of representation that is used; the nature of the underlying concept that is being represented; and the amount of discriminability in relation to the other icons.
(b) The four main mapping types are: resemblance, exemplar, symbolic and arbitrary.

5.6 **(a)** Knowledge in the head is information that is stored in memory, while knowledge in the world is information in the environment. When we carry out our everyday tasks we generally use a combination of both.

(b) A cognitive aid is an external representation that we use as a reminder to help us carry out a task that needs performing at a later time. A cognitive mnemonic is an internal representation that people develop to help them remember things, especially the ordering of objects, such as the points of the compass.

Chapter 6

6.1 Images are picture-like representations, propositions are abstract language-like representations and distributed representations are networks of nodes where knowledge is implicit in the connections between the nodes. The former two are symbolic and the latter are sub-symbolic.

6.2 A schema is a network of general knowledge based on previous experience that facilitates our understanding of commonplace events. A script is a special subcase of a schema that describes a characteristic scenario of behaviour in a particular setting.

6.3 A mental model is a dynamic mental representation that allows people to make predictions about future states, make inferences and imagine situations that have not been experienced before.

6.4 **(a)** A mental model represents the relative position of a set of objects in an analogical manner that parallels the structure of the state of the objects in the world. An image also does this, but more specifically in terms of one view of a particular model.

(b) Running a mental model is a kind of mental simulation that involves inspecting aspects of the model in order to derive certain predictions.

6.5 The advantages of structural models are that they allow users to work out how to achieve most tasks possible with a device, and if a model breaks down it can help in understanding the problem. The disadvantage is that it is very difficult to construct a structural model of even the simplest of devices.

6.6 A main difference between functional models and structural models is that the former develop from past knowledge of a similar domain while a structural model of how the device works has to be learned. Another difference is that functional models are aimed at answering a set of task-related questions whereas, hypothetically, structural models can be used to answer unexpected questions and make predictions. In addition, functional models are context dependent and hence easier to use, whereas structural models are largely context-free, making them easier to extend and integrate with other knowledge.

Chapter 7

7.1 The main types of knowledge that are mapped between a familiar and unfamiliar domain are elements and their relations to each other.

7.2 Verbal metaphors invite users to see the similarities and differences between the new and familiar domains, whereas virtual interface metaphors actually represent the physical objects from the familiar domain as electronic counterparts in the form of icons and other types of graphical displays.

7.3 A composite metaphor is a combination of interface metaphors allowing the various kinds of functionality to be provided.

7.4 Ubiquitous computing is making computer interfaces invisible to the users such that they can be used unconsciously and effortlessly.

7.5 **(a)** A user model in Norman's terms (1986) is a user's mental model of the system. A design model is the collective representation that the design team have of the system. The design model includes a great deal more information about the system than the user model does.

(b) The system image consists of the interface, its behaviour and the documentation. The system image in part shapes the user's mental model.

(c) Mismatches occur between the user and design model if the design model is ambiguous, inconsistent or obscure, or if it is inappropriate for the tasks the user wants to carry out.

Chapter 8

8.1 Novice users adopt the learning strategy of invoking prior knowledge to help them understand the new system.

8.2 A slip is an unintentional error while a mistake is an incorrect action that is based on an incorrect decision.

8.3 **(a)** The six types of slips are captive errors, description errors, data-driven errors, associative–activation errors, loss-of-activation errors and mode errors.

(b) Techniques that can help users deal with their errors include providing warning and alerting messages when they are about to carry out incorrect or inappropriate actions. System error messages should be designed to be informative and honest.

8.4 Declarative knowledge refers to facts about the world while procedural knowledge refers to how we do things.

8.5 The four main techniques that have been developed to facilitate the development of programming skills are the minimalist approach, software visualization, visual programming languages, and intelligent tutoring systems.

8.6 The main difference between the three types of learning is: individual learning is the acquisition of knowledge structures, collaborative learning is when we learn together by observing and talking with each other, while situated learning is a form of apprenticeship, where novices learn a skill through a gradual process of interacting and watching others who are more experienced in the context of a community.

Chapter 9

9.1 **(a)** The main types of speech acts are requests, promises, rejections and counter-offers (that is, suggesting an alternative).

(b) The Coordinator has proved to be most effective in organizations that are stable, hierarchical and authoritarian, and least effective in organizations where the norm is for conversation to be free-flowing and largely spontaneous.

9.2 **(a)** The main difference between turn-taking in two-way and multi-party conversations is one of control. In two-way conversations there are various established conversation norms, such as turn-taking, which the co-participants orient themselves to. In the latter it appears that the coordination of such norms is much more complex; involving much interrupting and interleaving of

conversations between the participants. In formal meetings social protocols have been established to facilitate turn-taking in multi-party situations.

(b) Computer-mediated communication can facilitate conversation by allowing geographically dispersed people to talk in a virtual room. Another advantage for participants who are face to face is that it can provide facilities to enhance group working by encouraging both talking and doing. Disadvantages of computer-mediated communication include a lack of mutual knowing, whereby one person may be able to see on their video screen the other people in the other location, but these others might not be able to see that person on their screen. As a consequence, it can be difficult to maintain eye contact, make meaningful gestures and coordinate control.

Chapter 10

10.1 An organization is a complex, ambiguous entity consisting of a multitude of interacting factors, including people, artefacts, the work organization and the organizational culture. They have been explained in terms of a number of metaphors, including viewing them as machines, systems and information processors.

10.2 **(a)** The scientific management approach has been highly influential because it has mechanized work to be performed in the most efficient manner, by designing jobs to be an optimal number of small tasks that can be carried out by one person using the best method.

(b) The main problem with the approach is that it assumes people are like machines, failing to recognize the human qualities of people. The outcome is that work can often be dehumanizing and alienating. The method is also inflexible and unable to cope with rapid change.

Chapter 11

11.1 Your table may vary from the one on the next page but it should contain most of the same basic information.

11.2 Touch screens are easy to learn, need no extra workspace, have no moving parts and are durable. They can provide a very direct interaction. However, disadvantages can include: lack of precision, high error rates, arm fatigue from reaching to the

Table for Solution 11.1

Device	Description	Key characteristics
Qwerty keyboard	Uses the most common arrangement of alphabetic keys.	Required when the data to be input are highly variable. Many people are trained for using it. Very slow for those not trained.
Dvorak keyboard	Similar to the qwerty keyboard but the arrangement of the keys allows for more efficient input.	People familiar with the qwerty keyboard need retraining.
Chord keyboard	Various arrangements. To form words (usually in a shorthand type notation), several keys are pressed simultaneously.	Can be extremely fast when used by a trained operator. Used to record transcripts of court proceedings, government debates and so on. Requires training to use. The right type can be suitable for the visually impaired when coupled with a braille or speech output device.

Table for Solution 11.3

Device	Description	Key features
Dataglove	Glove that communicates hand and finger position to a computer.	Used for manipulating virtual objects, specifying paths and positions, and issuing commands in the form of gestures.
3D tracker	Device that relays its position and orientation to a receiver.	Used for tracking hand, head and optionally other parts of the body in a virtual environment.
Joystick	Small stick that can be moved in any direction within a fixed socket.	Often used for tasks where a direction and speed is to be indicated, rather than a location. Can require a high level of concentration to use. Fine control is limited where fine grip is not possible.
Mouse	Continuous input device that has one or more buttons for discrete input. Unlike the trackball or joystick it is not fixed, so the user can move it around on a flat surface.	The most common and popular of these devices. Highly versatile. May work by a rolling ball on its underside, or may be optical (with a light on the underside), in which case a special pad must be used, but less maintenance is required. Objects are manipulated by pressing control button(s) embedded in the mouse.
Touch screen	Special screen that detects the position of a finger touching it.	Relatively 'vandal-proof' and less easily stolen than, say, a mouse. May need frequent cleaning. Good for untrained users, but not pleasant to use for tasks requiring high accuracy.
Trackball	Rotatable ball embedded in a surface in a fixed socket.	Can be moved by drawing the fingers or the palm of the hand over the surface. Fast, and does not require good grip for accurate use.

screen, fingers obscuring detail on the screen, and screen smudging. Ease of learning makes them ideal when use by a particular user may occur only once or twice and users cannot be expected to spend time learning to use the system. Highly accurate touch versions of screen are available (see Section 11.7), but most touch screens are unpleasant to use for tasks that require extreme accuracy.

11.3 See above table.

11.4 **(a)** The mapping between gesture and desired result may be more natural or require less learning for some devices than others. Tasks requiring combinations of operations or simultaneous actions that are awkward to perform on one device may be easily possible in a single gesture using another device. The user may have to exert more force or exercise different muscles to achieve the same output. The devices may have different resolutions, or give different kinds of feedback to the user. On the other hand, physically dissimilar devices may require the same muscles to control them.

(b) (i) Panning is easier with the trackball, as is panning then twisting without drift of x, y position. (ii) Simultaneous zooming and panning is easier with the joystick.

(c) Analysing in isolation only one of the tasks that a system is designed for can be totally misleading, as the Buxton case study demonstrates.

11.5 Handwriting recognition systems are claimed to combine the 'naturalness' of pen and notebook with the power of computers to store and process large quantities of data. They can do the job of keyboard and mouse in a single and much more portable device. It can be easy in principle to input special characters and marks.

Current problems with character recognition can make pen-based systems slow and prone to error. Some systems demand that the writer write in a grid of boxes, one character to a box, or restrict themselves to limited symbol vocabularies (for example, upper case letters only), or are designed to work with one user who must train the system.

They are so far used mainly for filling in forms and other applications requiring relatively small quantities of text input, or input of a restricted kind.

11.6 Speech input can be useful when one or more of the following conditions apply:
- the user's hands must be free to operate another device,
- the visual channels of communication are overloaded,
- the user has physical disabilities,
- the visual environment is poor,
- the user must be free to move around.

11.7 (a) High-precision touch screens. Strengths: little learning required, good for casual users, very fast for pointing, little workspace required, durable, easy to maintain. Limitations: relatively costly, can cause arm fatigue (appropriate screen placement can cure this), hands may obscure screen.

(b) Datagloves. Strengths: little learning required, natural and direct interaction, good for three-dimensional manipulation, ability to use all fingers and hand for control. Limitations: touch and force feedback are not easily provided, expensive, fragile, cabling can be obstructive.

(c) Handwriting recognition. Strengths: useful where system can be trained on one user, useful for form filling, useful where number of discrete symbols make a keyboard inconvenient (such as input of Japanese characters). Limitations: slow and error prone unless limited symbol vocabulary or enforced segmentation (one letter per box) or training on an individual is used.

(d) Footmice. Strength: leaves the hands free for other tasks. Limitation: suitable for 'coarse' movements only.

Chapter 12

12.1 (a) It matters greatly, especially if data is complicated. Poorly chosen mappings are unlikely to lead to the most effective visualization.

(b) Two key principles in visualization are to (i) find a mapping from elements and relationships in the chosen domain into display elements and relationships that will make perceptually prominent those things that we wish to be conceptually prominent, and (ii) make the mapping in a principled, consistent way, rather than in an *ad hoc* manner.

(c) Scaleability: a visualization that works well for a small process or collection of data may not work well for industrial-sized collections of data. Navigational aids: if a system makes use of different views there must be some way for the user to understand where she is and how the views relate to each other.

12.2 Visualizations of new situations can be produced quickly or instantly, provided a mapping has been established between the appropriate computer model and the way in which it is to be displayed. Computer visualization can be controlled interactively by the user. The mappings used in a computer visualization are easy to change (for example, someone who is colour-blind might want to change colour assignments).

12.3 **(a)** A user who has to perform a task in which there is a lot of information displayed on the screen might be more likely to take notice of infrequent and unexpected information if it were auditory. An example might be the use of alarms in a chemical processing or power plant.

(b) If a task involves continuously reading and monitoring visual information then users might not hear detailed spoken messages properly if too much of their attention is already taken up looking at screens. Unlike displayed information, speech is transitory and so operators may have no way of knowing what was said if they fail to hear it or mishear it. Speech output can also be problematic in any case in noisy environments.

12.4 High quality sound and high quality video images on screen can be aesthetically appealing. CD-ROMs are high capacity storage devices that can act as very large databases or storehouses of information. A high density of easy to use cross-referencing and indexing can make such large collections of information easy to explore in an interactive way via a consistent interface.

Chapter 13

13.1 With the command-driven system, users must know which commands can be issued to the system and their exact syntax, otherwise the system will respond with an error message. The system does not provide any information on the screen to help the user.

The menu-based system, however, provides information which suggests what the various options might be (semantic information), and as long as a user has the correct knowledge to make use of this information she can explore the menu options with confidence. Menus also provide an excellent form of external memory. The user just has to decide which option she wants; it is not necessary to remember which letters (that is, the syntactic form) to type to specify the option.

13.2 **(a)** Pull-down categorical menus. Word processing applications generally consist of a large number of commands that can be grouped together in various ways.

(b) Pop-up pie menus. It is likely that the operators of a radar warning system will need to select options very rapidly and accurately.

13.3 The software has been designed to resemble the paper versions of both applications, which allows users familiar with carrying out the tasks to recognize quickly the similarities between the paper and the computerized versions.

13.4 Compared with command line interfaces, direct manipulation interfaces let users employ resources, such as menus, and metaphors they are already familiar with, to allow them to work out what actions are possible and what their likely effects will be. This can enable novices to learn to use basic features very quickly. Because less memorization, training and experience is required for each task, experienced users may be able to perform a wider range of tasks more rapidly. Intermittent users can retain their knowledge of how to use the system more easily. Unintended actions are more easily recovered from, even though error messages are less frequently needed, due to the visibility and easy reversibility of the effects of actions.

Command line interfaces can make it quicker for very experienced users to issue commands. They consume less computing resources, and so may allow some systems to run faster. They are easier to program. If a terminal is connected to a computer by a low quality communications link, a direct manipulation style may be impractically slow.

13.5 See table on next page.

13.6 **(a)** The gulf of execution refers to the distance between the user's goals and the means of achieving them through the system, while the gulf of evaluation refers to the distance between the system's behaviour and the user's goals.

(b) It is important to bridge the gulfs to reduce the mismatch between the user's way of thinking about their tasks and the system's representation of them, thereby making it easier for users to carry out their tasks.

(c) The users can bridge the gulf of execution through changing the way they currently think and carry out the task towards the way the system requires it to be done. They can also bridge the gulf of evaluation by changing their interpretation of the system image and evaluating it with respect to their goals.

(d) The designers can bridge the gulf of execution by designing the input characteristics

Table for Solution 13.5

Communication style	Key features
Command languages	Versatile and quick if the syntax and names are learned. Good for tasks where the user has to carry out operations that require the input of repeated commands. Best for experienced, regular users.
Menus	Visible or easily accessed so that there is no problem remembering options. Navigation through menus and selection of objects can be greatly assisted by organizing the options to suit the task. Good for learners and infrequent users.
Natural language	There are many unresolved research issues concerned with parsing and understanding language. Currently use is limited to specific domains. Experienced typists with knowledge of the systems obtain the most efficient use.
Query language	Flexible and powerful, but the user must be familiar with the syntax. Best suited for retrieval of variable information from databases. Best for experienced, regular users.
Question and answer	System-driven, so suitable for novice users, but can be very frustrating since the system keeps control at all times.
Form-filling	Standard input format. All relevant fields are shown on the screen and are fixed. Forms are designed to resemble paper forms. This makes the system inflexible and limits it to tasks with standard input. It is very widely used for clerical applications and can be used by almost anyone with a minimum of instruction.
Spreadsheet	An increasingly powerful interaction style for applications including business calculations, number crunching, database access and constraint satisfaction. Allows end users to write their own programs.
Direct manipulation	Includes everything from moving pieces of text in word processing to moving icons representing objects such as files. Other manipulations include opening, closing, inserting and dragging. Can be fun to use. It is best in constrained environments such as graphics packages, which have a set number of tools that perform given tasks. Said to be suitable for novices, but also liked by users of all levels of experience.

to match the users' psychological capabilities. They can also bridge the gulf of evaluation by changing the output characteristics of the system.

13.7 Semantic directness refers to the relation between what the user wants to express and the meaning of the expressions available at the interface while articulatory directness refers to the relation between the meanings of expressions and their physical form.

13.8 **(a)** To describe an object as having an affordance means that it has a certain property that enables us to perceptually infer the behaviour that is permitted by the object.

(b) The main types of affordances are perceptual and sequential affordances. An example of an object that affords both is the Macintosh scroll bar.

13.9 Examples of good visual feedback include: displaying the details of the date and time when a file was updated, the per cent bar showing the rate

and progress of a process that the system is currently performing (for example, saving a file), and 'busy' icons (for example, the wristwatch and the egg-timer) showing that the system is busy processing and temporarily unable to respond to other commands. An effective use of sound as a form of feedback is for warning and alerting the user's attention.

Chapter 14

14.1 **(a)** A window working set is defined as the set of windows needed to carry out a particular task effectively.

(b) Both Rooms and HP-VUE effectively allow several window working sets for different tasks to be stored in an icon, and restored by activating the icon.

(c) A Rooms-type approach saves time in rearranging windows when switching between

Table for Solution 15.2

Types of on-line help	Key features
Help messages linked to particular objects	Help messages are linked to features that can be pointed to on the screen, such as menu bar options, icons, buttons, text windows. Good for operational information ('What does this do?'), less good for tactical information ('When to use this rather than that') and strategic information ('How do I achieve this end?').
Context-sensitive help	Help message varies according to the current state of the application program or system, or the currently active dialogue box. Can make it easier to find simple operational information by limiting amount of search required, but this same restriction can hinder if other kinds of information are required, or if the user is lost, or missing several pieces of information.
Generic help text	Usually providing a single relatively short explanatory text, or sometimes an index giving access to other help texts. Similar strengths and weaknesses to screen-object linked help (above).
Extended help screens	A series of screens accessed by an index, a 'more' button or hypertext type links. Similar strengths and weaknesses to screen-object linked help (above).
Extensive written documentation on-line	Good when users need extensive prerequisite information. If there is a lot of information, book-like formats are sometimes a more familiar and helpful way of structuring information than a less structured hypertext approach. It is easy to supply several indexes from different points of view.

window working sets for different tasks. It also allows users to work comfortably with more windows.

14.2 **(a)** Images represented as bitmaps are not easily displayed in magnified or reduced form, or rotated at arbitrary angles (except in certain special cases, or subject to a loss of image quality). On the other hand, they can be rendered rapidly with a speed independent of their content. **(b)** Images represented as mathematical descriptions can be scaled to any size or rotated at arbitrary angles, in principle, without loss of image quality. Imaging systems that depend on mathematical descriptions may take a noticeable time to render a complex image. Rendering time will depend on the complexity of the image.

14.3 A non-modal dialogue box lets the user deal with things other than itself first. A modal dialogue does not let the user deal with anything else on screen until it has been dealt with.

Chapter 15

15.1 It suggests a design flaw such as an inappropriate dialogue style, a missing or inconsistent metaphor or other internal inconsistency. If possible, the

system should be redesigned to avoid the problem.

15.2 See table above.

15.3 **(a)** Conceptual navigation concerns navigation through the ideas represented by the material. Physical navigation concerns navigation between items of information as presented. **(b)** Tools, aids and metaphors provided in the system for physical navigation should fit the users' model of the concepts they are investigating. To realize this goal, the designer must help the user build a mental model of the information being presented that matches the designer's conceptual model. At the same time, appropriate tools must be provided to allow the users to navigate the conceptual space in their preferred way.

Chapter 17

17.1 A: You would initiate the system by deciding that you wanted a room, and produce the application description that broadly described what you wanted. This may be expressed in a letter, a sketch or verbally, and would form the basis of discussions with experts such as builders and architects.

Table for Solution 17.4

Factors	Features
People	
Individual characteristics	Age, physical ability, learning abilities, cognitive capabilities, experience, cultural background, fears, personality characteristics
User groups	Homogeneous versus heterogeneous users, group interests, requirements, skills, discretionary versus committed users
Frequency of usage	Infrequent versus frequent users, level and duration of attention
Work	
Task features	Current task practices, individual versus cooperative work, multitasking versus serial tasks, passive versus active, ordering of tasks, well-understood versus vaguely defined tasks
Time constraints	Quality versus quantity trade-off, length of time on tasks, peaks and troughs of working, need for fast response
Errors	Coping with errors, presentation of error messages, how to deal with them, how the system accommodates them, significance of errors, safety-critical errors
Environment	
General environment factors	Conditions – noisy, cold, wet, dirty; stressful, uses dangerous materials
Organization	Channels of communication, structure, effect on work practices and job content, role, deskilling, job loss, shift in power, centralization versus decentralization
User support	Tuition, manuals, demonstrations; new knowledge and skills needed

B: You would produce a requirements specification detailing what the room was for (for example, a kitchen, a lounge, a bedroom), the amount of money available, how large it was to be, and so on. This 'requirements specification' thus describes the purpose, the uses and the constraints that apply to your room. It would probably be produced in consultation with a builder or an architect and expressed in terms of sketches and a natural language description.

C: An architect would produce a set of blueprints (a detailed, formal 'system design') which represented your requirements.

D: A builder would use the blueprints to build ('implement') the design and produce your room.

E: During the lifetime of the room, you might change its purpose (for example, a bedroom becomes a study) and you would certainly have to maintain it by repainting and so on.

F: During these processes you would be checking that the developing product met your requirements (validation), and was being developed in accordance with the plans (verification). You would also test parts of the product (for example, that a window was at the correct height).

17.2
- user-centred and involve users as much as possible so that they can influence the design,
- integrate knowledge and expertise from the different disciplines that contribute to HCI design,
- highly iterative so that testing can be done to check that the design does indeed meet users' requirements.

17.3 The main representations used were scenarios (written descriptions of possible interactions), user guides (explaining how the system would operate) and simulations of the system. The process was a 'rapid, iterative design', that is, the representations were developed and tested with real users, then defined and tested again.

17.4 See table above.

17.5 The system in the OMS was a completely new, bespoke system, functionally simple, but with complex large-scale hardware. Constraints on the system included a fast response time and the size of the input device.

The CAA air traffic control system was a complex system with high resolution displays and use of colour. Bespoke application initially, but need to generalize to other users later.

Chapter 18

18.1 The stakeholders include teachers, parents, children, educationalists, government officials, prospective parents, employers and anyone interested in the education of school-age children. The declared purpose of the system is to increase efficiency in education and to allow comparisons between the performance of schools.

18.2 Clients – teachers, schoolchildren, parents, government, educationalists

Actors – teachers, schoolchildren, assessment material producers, government

Transformation – from inputs of children and assessment material to produce figures showing scores on the tests for each school in each age group

Weltanschauung – government view that such tests are a feasible and desirable method of improving efficiency by facilitating comparisons

Owner – government

Environment – schools in an education system

18.3 SSM focuses on understanding the situation because any problem may be caused by some aspect of the current system other than that perceived to be the problem by any particular group of users. Thus the design space is kept as wide as possible for as long as possible.

Designers are encouraged to develop conceptual models away from the 'real world' because it stops them simply representing what happens now. Conceptual modelling encourages creative thought.

18.4 General information is collected about the nature of the work environment, the inputs to the system, the social system, the nature of the tasks and the transformation processes on the objects in the system.

One reason for performing the analysis in this order is that OSTA acknowledges the important role people will play in determining the success of any future system. Although it is the tasks that determine the way in which the information is to be manipulated, it is the people who will determine the way in which they will be able, and indeed whether they are willing, to manipulate it.

18.5 **(a)** An existing room in your house that is meant for the same purpose as your new room may form the basis of a redesign. Depending on how effective the current room is, you may proceed straight to a new physical design following an evaluation of existing problems. You may evaluate this new design and proceed directly to a new implementation

(b) You may see a room in someone else's house that gives you the idea of developing a similar room in your own home. You would probably evaluate such a prototype room in the light of your own requirements and proceed to draw up a formal conceptual design, continuing then to follow the 'traditional' approach.

(c) You may see a sketch or blueprint of a room and decide to develop your own. In this case you may go to see the actual building that was produced from that blueprint or sketch, evaluate it in the light of your own house and proceed to develop a formal conceptual model for your own room.

(d) You may see a picture of a room that inspires you to develop your own. In the case of a conservatory or garage, you may see one at a showroom and order it directly, thus going from a physical design, through an evaluation to check that you could fit it in, directly to an implementation.

Chapter 19

19.1 Our solution is shown on the next page. Yours should not be much different. In particular, you should not have shown specific user activities on the dataflow diagram.

19.2 See figure on next page.

19.3 The Monitor Temp process takes in the heat level from the reactors, produces the Temp Display data and produces the data Temp. This data is processed by the Check Hazard process and is also sent to process 2. Check Hazard produces a Hazard Warning by checking Temp against Normal Conditions.

It seems clear that more analysis is required and that the processes will have to be specified in more detail. For example, what checking will Check Hazard do and when would Hazard Warning be displayed?

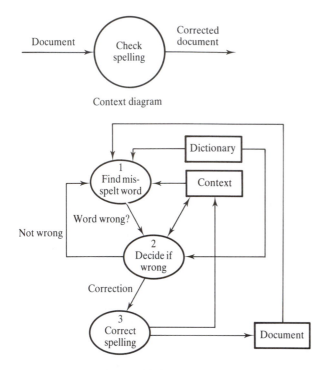

Context diagram

Figure for Solution 19.1

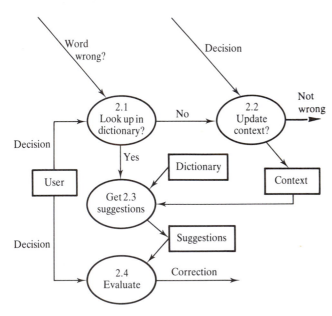

Figure for Solution 19.2

19.4 The system must define the data elements *Heat Level*, *Temp Display* and *Hazard Warning* and must have data stored in the system data concerning Normal Conditions, Clock and Database.

19.5 Here is our solution. Yours should not be much different. We have included the participation constraints (Box 19.3) on the diagram, but they are not strictly necessary at this stage of the analysis.

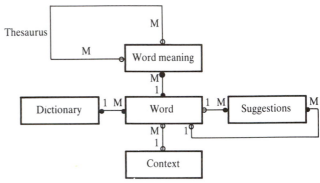

Chapter 20

20.1 Tasks: find the cassette player, select the required tape, insert cassette into player, play tape.
Actions: for task 'Insert cassette into player', press 'Eject', remove cassette from case, insert cassette into player, close cassette player.
Actions: for 'Play tape', press 'play'.

20.2 Tasks: chop, liquidize, put through a sieve, season, serve.
Actions: these will depend on how accomplished you are at cooking. Each of the above tasks is potentially quite complex. 'Chop', for example, might consist of the subtasks/actions: find chopping board, get sharp knife from rack, place vegetable on board and chop with knife. Repeat for all vegetables. However, you may feel that 'season' is an action.
Objects: vegetables, Brie, herbs, sieve, salt, pepper, nutmeg, lemon juice, cream, coriander leaves.

20.3 See figure on next page.

20.4 Here are some possibilities:
Methods
Use CD, Use cassette tape, Use digital cassette, Use LP, Use radio

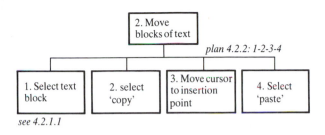

see 4.2.1.1

Figure for Solution 20.3.

Selection rules

IF high quality is required, THEN Use CD or
  Use digital cassette
IF long play is required, THEN Use cassette or
  Use compact disk
IF really old original material is required THEN
  Use LP
IF you can't decide what to listen to THEN
  Use radio

20.5   (adapted from Kieras, 1993)
  (a)   For the goal of cut out text

Step 1 Accomplish goal of select text
Step 2 Remember that the command is CUT
Step 3 Issue CUT command
Step 4 Return with goal accomplished

  (b)   Selection rule set for goal of selecting text

If text is word then accomplish goal of select word
If text is arbitrary then accomplish goal of selecting
arbitrary text.
Return with goal accomplished

  (c)   Method to accomplish goal of select word

Step 1 determine middle position in word
Step 2 move cursor to middle of word
Step 3 Double-click mouse button
Step 4 Verify that correct text is selected
Step 5 Return with goal accomplished.

Method to accomplish goal of selecting arbitrary
text

Step 1 Determine position of beginning of text
Step 2 Move cursor to beginning of text
Step 3 Press mouse button down
Step 4 Determine position of end of text
Step 5 Move cursor to end of text
Step 6 Verify that correct text is selected
Step 7 Release mouse button
Step 8 Return with goal accomplished

20.6   See following figure.

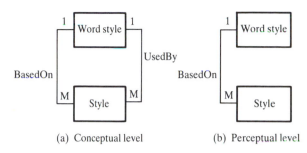

(a) Conceptual level   (b) Perceptual level

Chapter 21

21.1   You may have thought of a number of examples
where you just 'go through the motions' without
knowing why you are doing these things. For
example, in cookery books, you will often find
instructions on how to make a roux, as follows:
(i) melt the butter, (ii) stir in the flour, (iii) pour
in the milk, slowly stirring all the time. It will work,
but do you know *how* it works?

21.2   The conceptual operations are those identified on
the dataflow diagrams in Figures 21.2 and 21.3,
that is, check card, check PIN, check card type,
return card, check stolen, wrong PIN, keep card.
The conceptual objects are the entities in Figure
21.4, that is, currency, exchange rate, amount
owing, amount required, card, card type, PIN,
credit limit.

21.3   A card is of a single card type such as a credit card,
bank card, and so on. A card is associated with a
credit limit and a PIN and uses a currency. A
currency is associated with other currencies
through exchange rates. The amount required
(by the transactor) is expressed in a currency. A
card has an amount owing. The amount required
may relate to a number of amounts owing.

21.4   Some possible attitudes include:
  ● Will it eat my card?
  ● What is my PIN? Which PIN do I need?
  ● Will it accept my card?
  ● What is the exchange rate?
  ● I wish we all used a common currency!
  ● Can I use my bank card on this machine?
  ● I'll beat this one!
  ● Can I press the buttons?
  ● What do I do here?

Some individual differences include:

- Social background
- Language
- Ethnic background
- Educational background
- Experience of using 'walk-up-and-use' systems

21.5 Perceptual aspects such as the clarity of display, using in bright light, affordances of buttons and so on.

Attentional aspects such as ensuring error conditions are highlighted, the next step in the process is obvious, important information is made clear.

Memory aspects such as not requiring the user to remember the exchange rate, ensuring all processes are clearly specified and so on.

Information display aspects such as avoiding clutter on the screen, using display characters that are easy to read and so on.

21.6 In the case of a walk-up-and-use system such as Eurochange there is no opportunity for training users or for having lengthy user manuals or other documentation. The system must be clear and easy to use with all help and information built directly into the interface itself. Part of that interface may be some general instructions. Most importantly, the Eurochange must clearly and accurately reveal its purpose and its limitations to potential users. This will have to be accomplished through signs and other displays forming the overall environment of the system.

Chapter 22

22.1 Some possible metaphors include:

- Eurochange as a bank, or automatic telling machine,
- Eurochange as a slot machine,
- Eurochange as travel agent,
- Eurochange as a transformer,
- Eurochange as a person with bags of money,

We leave you to provide your own sketches!

22.2 Many issues are raised. Here are just a few.

What happens if the user cannot speak English? Currently all the messages are in English and it is difficult to see how they can be provided in all languages. Perhaps there is a need for a question at the start of the interaction which asks which language is required.

Pat remembered the local currency, but what happens if Pat could not? Is there a better way of presenting this information?

Is there a better way of dealing with users who request an amount of money that the machine cannot deliver? Should it check with the user or should it deliver the nearest amount that it can? This is a task allocation question.

Chapter 23

23.1 These techniques are mostly concerned with understanding the problem and exploring alternative solutions. Interestingly, none of the designers seems to have mentioned referring to previous designs they have developed.

23.2 Coordination is a problem for any project involving a number of people. Therefore, good management practice and techniques such as regular meetings and discussions would be useful support. Project management software would also be appropriate.

23.3 The senior management of an organization are likely to be interested in the system being developed, but are unlikely to use the final software. Therefore, relatively senior members of staff from both the developer and the client will be involved in the specification of requirements. Their views of what the software should be like may be listened to at the expense of the users' views.

23.4 This text book contains a set of guidance for potential HCI designers – you – so it should come under 'guidance'.

Chapter 24

24.1 Guidelines may be based on psychological theory but many are formulated from experience.

Chapter 25

25.1 **(a)** It requires extra cognitive effort to perform an action that is somehow different from usual. Therefore, driving a car with the gear stick in a different place from what you are used to would be more difficult.

(b) Driving a car with the foot pedals in a different place would also require more cognitive effort. If a mistake was made with the gear stick, the result is unlikely to be particularly serious, but if a mistake was made with the pedals, there could be a bad accident.

25.2 One reason for wishing to constrain their designers is to ensure consistency across systems within an organization. A second reason might be to speed up the process of design; if fewer design choices are open to designers, it should take less time to produce a good design.

25.3 User performance measures include speed, accuracy, number of keystrokes, use of on-line help and so on.

25.4 Options that do not have logical or conventional grouping could be ordered alphabetically or numerically.

25.5 These guidelines are high level principles since they require interpretation before being applied.

25.6 The Directive is aimed at employers, and covers employees' conditions of work. Members of the public are unlikely to be included in the definition of employee. Also, systems mainly intended for public use are unlikely to involve one person remaining at the system for extended periods of time. However, perhaps their exclusion should be a debatable point?

25.7 Problems for system users caused by inconsistent interfaces are: mistakes (some of which may be safety-critical), cognitive overload and stress. Problems for the organization additionally include increased training costs.

25.8 **(a)** The number of times on-line help is accessed may indicate how easy the system is to use. It may, on the other hand, indicate how easy to use or clear the documentation is. Alternatively, it may mean that the operator has just learned how to access the on-line help facility!

(b) The time to access the correct record from a database may give information about the ease of use of the interface, or it may indicate how efficiently the database is implemented, or, in the case of remote access, it may tell you how busy the telephone lines are.

(c) If a large number of employees are smiling on Monday mornings it may mean that they enjoy using their software systems. It may, however, mean that a pay rise is in the air, or that there was a good party on Saturday night.

Chapter 26

26.1 Designers may need to revisit decisions that they have made because something in the system has changed. If there is no coherent record of the options considered and the reasons for rejecting them, the whole issue may need to be discussed again. Important points may be left out; some options may have been forgotten. The whole exercise could be performed more easily if a record of the previous discussions were available.

26.2 The issues in this map are:
- Where should the walls be located?
- Where should the doors be located?
- Where should the windows be located?
- Where should the counters be located?
- Where should the sink be located?
- Where should the stove be located?
- Where should the refrigerator be located?

26.3 If there is no record of a question being asked, or an aspect of the system being considered at all, then it will not be clear later on whether the question was ever asked.

26.4 User predictability and learnability are both given a negative assessment to the option of having undo relative to the document.

26.5 Software tools that helped to structure the diagrams and allowed global enquiries of the structure would help considerably. We will return to some of these issues in Chapter 28.

26.6 Design space analysis encourages a designer to explore as many alternatives as possible. Claims analysis concentrates on analysing and refining one design.

26.7 Uses for design rationale include documentation, understanding, debugging, verification, analysis, explanation, modification, automation, redesign and reuse of design knowledge.

The questions it allows developers and users to answer include:
- What is the current status of the design?
- What did we discuss last week?
- What do we need to do today?
- What are the alternative designs and their pros and cons?
- How did other people deal with this problem?
- What can we learn from past design cases?
- Why was this first design rejected in favour of this second one?

Chapter 27

27.1 Storyboarding, sketching and other paper-based techniques would be useful. Wizard of Oz prototyping could also yield some interesting results once an idea has been progressed far enough to produce sample screens and dialogues.

27.2 A valve indicator was faulty and another was obscured by a caution tag, but the main problem was the number of alarms that were activated all at once. There were too many lights flashing and alarms sounding all at once, and it was therefore easy to ignore or block out some important warnings. Prototyping this behaviour using suitable task scenarios could have identified the problem before the system went 'live'.

27.3 Most forms of prototyping could be used to answer task level questions, although computer-based prototypes give a more accurate picture of the final design, and should preferably be used. Chauffeured prototyping could also be useful here, and so might the Wizard of Oz technique.

27.4 Chauffeured prototyping: the end user needs to have access to the screen; paper-based prototyping would be inappropriate since the clarity of screen elements, colour and other screen-specific details need to be considered; vertical prototyping might be acceptable provided the system includes a complete screen for the particular aspects being tested.

27.5 Evolutionary prototyping, as the initial prototype will grow into the final product.

27.6 If a prototyping tool allows a user to build a system quickly, it will inevitably be inflexible in some respects in order to save development time.

27.7 Your list may include some of the following (or others): graphics tools, modelling tools, visualization tools, user interface toolkits, integrated environments, tools to support group working. For further details, see Chapter 28.

Chapter 28

28.1 4GLs, very high level languages, data manipulation languages, hypermedia systems, authoring languages, and access-oriented and data-directed languages are all useful for prototyping.

28.2 **(a)** Tools have helped by closing the gap between specification and implementation through automation and by speeding development with code management tools.
(b) User interfaces have not always benefited automatically from these gains, as some tools can enforce poor presentation and interaction on the end user.
(c) Libraries contain ready-made components, which may not be appropriate in some contexts, but may be used anyway.

28.3 Graphics tools would be useful for sketching initial ideas or for producing more precise versions of icons, screen layouts and other graphic elements of the interface.

28.4 Visual programming involves the programmer developing the program using a graphical notation. Program visualization is a visual representation of a traditionally-written program executing; it is an animation of the program.

28.5 If the design of certain elements of the interface is already determined, then the look and feel of the interface will be preserved across the group of interfaces developed using the toolkit. In this sense, toolkits can be used to support the implementation of house styles.

28.6 Integrated environments usually offer facilities for configuration management, version control, a data dictionary and accommodation of other tools.

28.7 An interface toolkit supplies only the screen elements such as buttons, menu bars and so on. An interface builder adds the capability to position the screen elements and to specify some of the behaviour of those elements. A UIMS focuses on providing support for runtime management of the interaction. A UIDE provides the facilities of a UIMS and an interface builder.

28.8 The principal difference between single designer support and group support is in the need for communication and coordination.

28.9 The design activity involves producing many things: models, narrative descriptions, formal definitions, software prototypes, meeting minutes and so on. Most documents need to be seen by at least the majority of the development team, and many team members would wish to add comments for review.

Chapter 29

29.1 **(a)** In the excerpt about the development of the OMS the following kinds of evaluation are mentioned:

- After the first requirements were collected, printed scenarios of the user interface were prepared, which were commented upon by by designers, management and prospective users.
- User guides were tested on the main user groups.
- Early simulations were tested with users.
- Other methods that are mentioned include: interviews with different kinds of users about what they wanted, testing prototypes and inviting passers-by to try to break the system.

The evaluation of the air traffic control system was more formal but the following kinds of evaluation are mentioned:

- An initial system was installed at the London City Airport, a much smaller and less busy airport than Heathrow, and from data collected (we are not told how) of its use many modifications were suggested.
- An upgraded prototype was developed and situated in Heathrow and other airports for use by users.

(b) In both cases user involvement was very important. It is likely, however, that different evaluation methods were used because the two systems have different purposes and in the case of the air traffic control system safety is critical. This, coupled with the fact that the air traffic control system was an upgrade, suggests that more formal methods would be used; probably of the kind used in usability engineering, discussed in Chapter 31.

29.2 **(a)** The usability laboratory was set up to resemble as closely as possible a TF reception area, so that it would be both comfortable and realistic for the users. A one-way mirror, video camera and microphones enabled the evaluators to see and record the users' interaction with the system.

(b) The evaluators collected video records, which showed how the users interacted with the system and recorded any comments that they made. From this the evaluators were able to identify usability problems. At the debriefing sessions at the end of each testing period they discussed the testing with the users and listened to their comments.

29.3 **(a)** Predictive methods
(b) Experiments
(c) All of them, except predictive methods

Chapter 30

30.1 The following can be collected using observational data capture techniques:

- **Direct observation** suitable only for a small number of users doing short tasks because recording is difficult. The data are likely to be incomplete, so this technique is suitable only for informal evaluations and when quantitative data are not required. The presence of the observer may be threatening to novices, which may affect the subjects' performances.
- **Think aloud protocols** relatively easy to administer but can be very time-consuming and difficult to analyse. The data can be collected using audio or video recording equipment. The technique is suitable for any type of user but some users find it difficult to verbalize their thoughts. This can be particularly problematic for users when they are trying to solve tricky problems. Placing pairs of users to work together so that they talk to each other is one way of getting users to externalize their thoughts.
- **Post-event protocols** these are often used when it is important not to interrupt users, for example in the case of air traffic controllers or instructors. Video equipment is required, with some way of recording users' comments while they view the video recording. Users are given the opportunity to explain what they did and why, although a disadvantage of this is that it can encourage post-rationalization.
- **Video recording** this technique is often used with some of the others mentioned. It can be less obtrusive than most other methods. Specialist equipment is needed but it is relatively cheap to use once the equipment has been purchased. The recording can be both difficult and time-consuming to analyse.
- **System logging** the user is often totally unaware that she is being logged. This is a cheap method, which is useful if playback can be in real time. It can be administered by a non-specialist. However, often large amounts of data are collected, which can be difficult to

analyse, particularly if there are no supporting data such as a video or audio recording to help explain what was done and why.

As is obvious from the above answer, many of these techniques are used in combination, as one set of data often helps to explain another.

Chapter 31

31.1 **(a)** The selection scheme tests were carried out on prototypes of the mouse and screen, which would have been devised early in the design. The results of the first selection tests were fed back into the design and resulted in redesign, which was then validated by the second set of selection scheme tests.

(b) Learning might have taken place from one test to the next which would have devalued the results. Using a larger number of subjects would have helped to reduce the effect of any unusual results from particular subjects.

(c) It says in the description of the second selection scheme test that only one of the four users was experienced with the mouse. No reference is made to how this might have affected the results.

31.2 **(a)** The independent variable is the number of mouse buttons and the dependent variable is time.

(b) Repeated measures design: the same group of subjects was asked to do two versions of the task and their performances on each were compared.

(c) The order of presentation of the selection items was the same for both experiments, so subjects may have learned which selection task to expect next and this may have affected their performance times on the second test. The order in which the subjects did each version of the experiment could also have been randomized.

(d) Independent subject design.

31.3 The most important characteristic is likely to be how much experience the subjects have had with the system. Other things to consider include gender and age. Depending on the exact nature of the task, the relative importance of different characteristics will change.

Chapter 32

32.1 **(a)** Usability engineering is based on the theory and practices of science and engineering. Testing is done in laboratory settings and quantitative data is collected from which metrics are derived. These metrics are used to guide the engineering of the improvement of the product.

(b) Usability engineering is most useful in the update of products or for fine-tuning parts of the design. Contextual evaluation is based on ethnography. Contextual evaluation is useful very early on for obtaining requirements by providing information about existing practice. It is also useful for seeing how a working prototype is actually used in the field.

32.2 In all the methods described in this chapter users participate in the evaluation. The context of the evaluation is important.

Chapter 33

33.1 A full review could be carried out to check the usability of the interaction dialogue of a mock-up of the interface. Discount usability engineering could be used to check intermediate designs.

33.2 It is easy for concentration to wander and to leave out steps. Probably the main problem is that you need to remember to be consistent about when you insert mental operators. As with any kind of arithmetic, it is easy to make careless mistakes.

Chapter 34

34.1 Engineering towards a target: usability engineering; benchmark tasks and attitude questionnaires. Comparing designs: experiments could be used if a clear hypothesis can be formed and few confounding variables are involved. Usability engineering and various forms of monitoring might also be appropriate.

Understanding the real world: some form of interpretive evaluation.

Conformance testing: experiments.

34.2 See table on next page.

34.3 **(a)** The keystroke-level model is valid only for users who are already expert and should not be used to extrapolate such measures as the time to train naive users to expert level.

(b) Results can be affected by selective data gathering and manipulation by the evaluator, the subject or both.

34.4 No answer supplied.

34.5 The phrase 'as applied here' provides a clue. There is no indication from either our description or that of the original authors as to whether or not heuristics were provided for the evaluators. Since there is no mention of heuristics, even though the name of the technique implies their use, we must presume that this was basically an expert evaluation. Had heuristics been used the results might have been even better. They would certainly have been different.

34.6 The authors report that the technique depends on having several people with the knowledge and experience necessary to apply the technique. Such people are both scarce and expensive to employ. However, having several people is particularly important as the authors report that no single heuristic evaluator found more than 42 core problems. A second problem that was reported was the number of low-priority problems that occur only once, thus detracting from the main findings of the evaluation.

Table for Solution 34.2

Technique	Advantages	Disadvantages
Observation and monitoring	Quickly highlights difficulties. Verbal protocols valuable source of information on user's conceptual model. Can be used for rapid iterative development. Rich qualitative data	Observation can affect user activity and performance level. Analysis of data can be time- and resource-consuming
Experiments and benchmarking	Powerful methods (dependent effects investigated). Qualitative data for statistical analysis. Can compare between different groups of uses. Reliability and validity good. Replicable	High resource demands. Time spent on experiments can mean evaluation is difficult to integrate into design cycle. Tasks can be artificial and restricted. Cannot always generalize to full system in typical working situation
Users' opinions	Surveys and questionnaires address users' opinions and understanding of system. Can be made to be diagnostic. Can be applied to users and designers. Questions can be tailored to the individual. Rating scales lead to qualitative results. Can be used on a large group of users	User experience is important. Low response rates (especially to mailed questionnaires). Possible interviewer bias. Analysis can be complicated and lengthy. Interviews very time-consuming
Interpretive	Provides feedback about what happens in real-world situations	Requires subjective interpretaion, expertise in social sciences methods. Cannot be replicated
Predictive	Strongly diagnostic. Few resources. High potential return (detects significant problems). Usable early in design. Few resources	Restrictions in role playing. Subject to bias. Problems locating experts. Cannot capture real user behaviour Keystroke-level analyses have a narrow focus (such as error-free tasks). Broad assumptions for user's cognitive operations

References

ACM SIGCHI (1992). *Curricula for Human–computer Interaction*. ACM Special Interest Group on Computer–Human Interaction Curriculum Development Group, New York

ALEXANDER H. (1987). *Formally Based Tools and Techniques for Human–Computer Dialogues*. Chichester: Ellis Horwood

ALTY J. and HOLLAND S. (1993). Human–computer Interaction and Music: Squaring the Circle. Invited talk at INTERCHI, Amsterdam

ANDERSON J.R. (1983). *The Architecture of Cognition*. Cambridge, MA: Harvard University Press

ANDERSON J.R. (1987). Skill acquisition: Compilation of weak-method solutions. *Psychological Review*, **94**, 192–211

ANDERSON J.R. (1990). *Cognitive Psychology and its Implications*, 3rd edn. New York: W.H. Freeman and Co.

ANDERSON J.R., FARRELL R. and SAUERS R. (1984). Learning to program in Lisp. *Cognitive Science*, **8**, 87–129

APPLE COMPUTER INC. (1985). *Inside Macintosh*. Reading, MA: Addison-Wesley

ARENT M., VERTELNY L. and LIEBERMAN H. (1989). Three characters in search of an interface: a case study in interface design process. In *Inventing the Interface* (LAUREL B., ed.). Reading, MA: Addison-Wesley

ATKINSON R.C. and SHIFFRIN R.M. (1968). Human memory: a proposed system and its control processes. In *The Psychology of Learning and Motivation: Advances and Theory* Vol. 2 (SPENCE K.W. and SPENCE J.T., eds). New York: Academic Press

AUSTIN J. (1952). *How to Do Things With Words*. Oxford: Oxford University Press

AVISON D. and WOOD-HARPER T. (1990). *Multiview methodology*. Oxford: Blackwell Scientific Publishers

BADDELEY A. (1992). *Your Memory: A User's Guide*. Harmondsworth: Penguin

BADDELEY A.D. and HITCH G. (1974). Working memory. In *The Psychology of Learning and Motivation* (BOWER G.H., ed.). London: Academic Press

BAECKER R.M. (1981). *Sorting out sorting*. Narrated colour videotape, 30 minutes. Presented at ACM SIGGRAPH'81 and excerpted in ACM SIGGRAPH Video Review 7, 1983. Los Altos, CA: Morgan Kaufmann

BAECKER R.M., ed. (1993). *Readings in Groupware and Computer Supported Cooperative Work*. San Mateo, CA: Morgan Kaufmann

BAECKER R.M. and BUXTON W.A.S., eds (1987). *Readings in Human–Computer: A Multi-disciplinary Approach*. Los Altos, CA: Morgan Kaufmann

BAECKER R., SMALL I. and MANDLER R. (1991). Bringing icons to life. In *Human Factors in Computing Systems, CHI'91 Conference Proceedings* (ROBERTSON S.P., OLSON G.M. and OLSON J.S., eds), pp. 1–6. New York: ACM Press

BAECKER R., GRUDIN J., BUXTON W. and GREENBERG S., eds (1995). *Readings in Human–Computer Interaction: Toward the Year 2000*. San Mateo, CA: Morgan Kaufmann

BAGNARA S. and RIZZO A. (1989). A methodology for the analysis of error processes in human–computer interaction. In *Work With Computers: Organizational, Management, Stress and Health Aspects* (SMITH M.J. and SALVENDY G., eds), pp. 605–12. Amsterdam: Elsevier

BAINBRIDGE L. (1992). Mental models in cognitive skill: the example of industrial process operation. In *Models in the Mind: Theory, Perspective and Application* (ROGERS Y., RUTHERFORD A. and BIBBY P., eds), pp. 119–43. London: Academic Press

BANNON L. (1991). From human factors to human actors: the role of psychology and human–computer interaction studies in system design. In *Design at work: cooperative design of computer systems* (GREENBAUM J. and KYNG M., eds), pp. 25–44. Hillsdale, NJ: Lawrence Erlbaum Associates

BANNON L. and BØDKER, S. (1991). Beyond the interface: encountering artefacts in use. In *Designing Interaction: Psychology at the Human–Computer Interface* (CARROLL J.M., ed.), pp. 227–53. Cambridge, UK: Cambridge University Press

BANNON L., ROBINSON M. and SCHMIDT K., eds (1991). *Proceedings of the Second European Conference on Computer Supported Cooperative Work (EC-CSCW '91)*. Dordrecht: Kluwer

BARBER P. (1988). *Applied Cognitive Psychology*. London: Methuen

BARFIELD W., SANDFORD J. and FOLEY J. (1988). The mental rotation and perceived realism of computer-generated three-dimensional images. *International Journal of Man–Machine Studies*, **29**, 669–84

BARNARD P. (1987). Cognitive resources and the learning of human–computer dialogs. In *Interfacing Thought* (CARROLL J.M., ed.), pp. 112–59, Cambridge, MA: MIT

BARNARD P. (1991). Bridging between basic theories and the artifacts of human–computer interaction. In *Designing Interaction: Psychology at the Human–Computer Interface* (CARROLL J., ed.), pp. 103–27. New York: Cambridge University Press

BASS L. and COUTAZ J. (1991). *Developing Software for the User Interface*. Reading, MA: Addison-Wesley

BENNETT J. (1984). Managing to meet usability requirements. In *Visual Display Terminals: Usability Issues and Health Concerns* (BENNETT J., CASE D., SANDELIN J. and SMITH M., eds). Englewood Cliffs, NJ: Prentice-Hall

BENTLEY R., HUGHES J.A., RANDALL D., RODDEN T., SAWYER P., SOMMERVILLE I. and SHAPIRO D. (1992). Ethnographically-informed systems design for air traffic control. In *CSCW'92 Conference Proceedings* (TURNER J. and KRAUT R., eds), pp. 123–9. New York: ACM

BENYON D.R. (1990). *Information and Data Modelling*. Oxford: Blackwell Scientific Publishers

BENYON D.R. (1992). The role of task analysis and system design. *Interacting with Computers*, **4**(1), 102–23

BENYON D.R. (1992). Task analysis and system design: the discipline of data. *Interacting with Computers*, **4**(2), 246–59

BENYON D.R. and MURRAY D.M. (1993). Applying user modelling for human–computer interaction design. *Artificial Intelligence Review*, **6**, 43–69

BENYON D.R. and SKIDMORE S.R. (1987). Towards a tool-kit for the systems analyst. *The Computer Journal*, **31**(1), 2–9

BENYON D.R. and SKIDMORE S.R. (1988). *Automating Systems Development*. New York: Plenum Press

BEWLEY W.L., ROBERTS T.T., SCHROIT D. and VERPLANK W.L. (1990). Human factors. In *Human–Computer Interaction: Selected Readings* (PREECE J. and KELLER L., eds). Hemel Hempstead: Prentice-Hall

BIAS R. (1991). Walkthroughs: Efficient collaborative testing. *IEEE Software*. September, 94–5

BIEDERMAN I. and JU G. (1988). Surface versus edge-based determinants of visual recognition. *Cognitive Psychology*, **20**, 38–64

BJORN-ANDERSON N. (1986). Understanding the nature of the office for the design of third waver offices. In *People and Computers: Designing for Usability* (HARRISON M.D. and MONK A.F., eds). Proceedings of the BCS HCI Specialist Group. Cambridge: Cambridge University Press

BLACKER F. and BROWN C. (1986). Alternative models to guide the design and introduction of the new information technologies into work organizations. *Journal of Psychology*, **59**, 287–313

BLATTNER M. and GREENBERG R. (1992). Communicating and learning through non-speech audio. In *Multimedia Interface Design in Education* (EDWARDS A. and HOLLAND S., eds). London: Springer Verlag

BLISSMER R.H. (1992). *Introducing Computers*. Chichester, Wiley

BLOIES S.J., GOULD J.D., LEVY S.E., RICHARDS J.T. and SCHOONARD J.W. (1985). The 1984 Olympic Message System – A case study in system design. *IBM Research Report RC–11138*. Yorktown Heights, NY

BLUM T. and CZEISZPERGER M. (1992). Review of 1991 ACM SIGGRAPH convention. *Computer Music Journal*, **16**(1), 77–87

BLY S. and ROSENBERG J. (1986). A comparison of tiled and overlapping windows. In *CHI'86 Conference Proceedings*, pp. 101–6. New York: ACM

BOEHM B. (1988). The spiral model of software development and enhancement. *IEEE Computer*, **21**(5), 61–72

BOISSONNAT J.-D. (1988). *Computer Vision, Graphics and Image Processing*, **44**(1), 1–29

BOOTH P. (1989). *An Introduction to Human–Computer Interaction*. Hove: Lawrence Erlbaum Associates

BORENSTEIN N.S. (1985). The design and evaluation of on-line help systems. *Doctoral dissertation*, Carnegie-Mellon University

BORGMAN C.L. (1986). The user's mental model of an information retrieval system: an experiment on a prototype online catalogue. *International Journal of Man–Machine Studies*, **24**, 47–64

BORNING A. and TRAVERS M. (1991). Two approaches to casual interaction over computer and video networks. In *Human Factors in Computing Systems CHI'91 Conference Proceedings* (ROBERTSON S.P., OLSON G.M. and OLSON J.S., eds), pp. 13–19. New York: ACM Press

BOWERS J. and MIDDLETON D. (1991). Distributed organizational cognition: An innovative idea? Paper presented at the Franco-British Seminar, *Information and Innovation: The Management of Intellectual Resources*. Paris, 16 April

BRAUDES R.E. (1991). Conceptual modelling: A look at system-level user interface issues. In *Taking Software Design Seriously* (KARAT J., ed.). London: Academic Press

BRAYSHAW M. and EISENSTADT M. (1991). A practical tracer for Prolog. *International Journal of Man–Machine Studies*, **35**, 597–631

BREST J., INSCORE J., LARKIN D., MORSE M., STREEPER S. and WALRATH K. (1991). *The NeXTstep Advantage*. Redwood City, CA: NeXT Computer Inc.

BROOKS, Jr. F.P. (1982). *The Mythical Man-Month*. Reading, MA: Addison-Wesley

BROOKS, Jr. F.P. (1986). Walkthrough – A dynamic graphics system for simulating virtual buildings. In *Workshop in Interactive 3-D Graphics*. University of North Carolina, Chapel Hill

BROOKS, Jr. F.P. (1988). Grasping reality through illusion: interactive graphics serving science. In *Human Factors in Computing Systems CHI'88 Conference Proceedings* (SULWAY E., FRYE D. and SHEPPARD S.B., eds). New York: ACM Press

BROOKS, Jr. F.P., OUH-YOUNG M., BATTER J.J. and KILPATRICK P.J. (1990). Project GROPE – Haptic displays for scientific visualisation. *ACM Computer Graphics*, **24**(4), 177–85

BROWN M.H. and HERSHBERGER J. (1991). Color and sound in algorithm animation. *Technical Report No. 76a*, DEC Systems Research Center, Palo Alto, CA

BROWN M.H. and HERSHBERGER J. (1992). Color and sound in algorithm animation. *Computer*, **25**(12), 52–63

BROWN M.H. and SEDGEWICK R. (1984). A system for algorithm animation. *ACM Computer Graphics*, **18**(3), 177–86

BROWN R. and HERRNSTEIN R.J. (1975). *Psychology*. London: Methuen

BUCHANAN D.A. and BODDY D. (1983). *Organizations in the Computer Age*. Hampshire: Gower

BUTTON G., ed. (1993). *Technology in Working Order: Studies of Work, Interaction and Technology*. London: Routledge

BURY K.F., DAVIES S.E. and DARNELL M.J. (1985). Window management: A review of issues and some results from user testing. *IBM Human Factors Centre Report HFC-53*, San Jose, CA, June 1985

BUSH V. (1945). As we may think. *Atlantic Monthly*, **176**(1), 101–8

BUXTON W. (1986). There's more to interaction than meets the eye: some issues in manual input. In *User Centred System Design: New Perspectives in Human–Computer Interaction*. (NORMAN D.A. and DRAPER S.W., eds), pp. 319–38. Hillsdale, NJ: Lawrence Erlbaum Associates

BUXTON W. (1990). There's more to interaction than meets the eye: some issues in manual input. In *Human–Computer Interaction: Selected Readings* (PREECE J. and KELLER L., eds), pp. 122–37. Hemel Hempstead: Prentice-Hall

BUXTON W. (1991). Telepresence: Integrating shared task and personal spaces. *Communications of the ACM*, **34**(12). Special issue on groupware (CSCW)

BUXTON W., GAVER W. and BLY S. (1989). Use of non speech audio at the interface. *CHI'89 Tutorial notes*

CAMPAGNONI F.R. and EHRLICH K. (1990). Information retrieval using a hypertext-based help system. In *ACM Transactions on Office Information Systems*, **8**

CAMPBELL I. (1987). Standardization, availability and the use of PCTE. *Information and Software Technology*, **29**(8), 411–14

CARD S.K., MORAN T.P. and NEWELL A. (1980). The keystroke-level model for user performance time with interactive systems. *Communications of the ACM*, **23**(7), 396–410. Reprinted as Chapter 16 in PREECE J. and KELLER L., eds (1990)

CARD S.K., MORAN T.P. and NEWELL A. (1983). *The Psychology of Human–Computer Interaction*. Hillsdale, NJ: Lawrence Erlbaum Associates

CARD S.K., ROBERTSON G.G. and MACKINLAY J.D. (1991). The Information Visualizer, an information workspace. In *Human Factors in Computing Systems CHI'91 Conference Proceedings* (ROBERTSON S.P., OLSON G.M. and OLSON J.S., eds). New York: ACM Press

CAREY T., McKERLIE D., BUBIE W. and WILSON J. (1991). Communicating human factors expertise through design rationales and scenarios. In *People and Computers VI* (DIAPER D. and HAMMOND N.V., eds), pp. 117–32. Cambridge, England: Cambridge University Press

CARROLL J.M., ed. (1987). *Interfacing Thought*. Cambridge, MA: MIT Press

CARROLL J.M. (1990). Infinite detail and emulation in an ontologically minimized HCI. In *Empowering People, CHI'90 Conference Proceedings* (CHEW J.C. and WHITESIDE J., eds). New York: ACM Press

CARROLL J.M. (1990). *The Nurnberg Funnel: Designing Minimalist Instruction for Practical Computer Skill*. Cambridge, MA: MIT Press

CARROLL J.M., ed. (1991). *Designing Interaction: Psychology at the Human–Computer Interface*. Cambridge: Cambridge University Press

CARROLL J.M. and KAY D.S. (1988). Prompting, feedback and error correction in the design of a scenario machine. *International Journal of Man–Machine Studies*, **28**(1), 11–27

CARROLL J.M. and KELLOGG W.A. (1989). Artifact as theory-nexus: hermeneutics meets theory-based design. In *Wings for the Mind, CHI'89 Conference Proceedings* (BICE K. and LEWIS C.H., eds), pp. 7–14. New York: ACM Press

CARROLL J.M. and MACK R. (1984). Learning to use a word processor: by doing, by thinking and by knowing. In *Human Factors in Computing Systems* (THOMAS J. and SCHNEIDER M., eds), pp. 13–52. Norwood: Ablex

CARROLL J.M. and MORAN T. (1991). Introduction to this special issue on design rationale. *Human–Computer Interaction*, **6**(3/4)

CARROLL J.M. and OLSON J.M. (1988). Mental models in human–computer interaction. In *Handbook of Human–Computer Interaction* (HELANDER M., ed.), pp. 45–65. Amsterdam: North-Holland

CARROLL J.M., KELLOG W.A. and ROSSON M.B. (1991). The task–artifact cycle. In *Designing Interaction: Psychology at the Human–Computer Interface* (CARROLL J.M., ed.). Cambridge: Cambridge University Press

CARROLL J.M., MACK R.L. and KELLOGG W.A. (1988). Interface metaphors and user interface design. In *Handbook of Human–Computer Interaction* (HELANDER M., ed.), pp. 67–85. Amsterdam: North-Holland

CARROLL J.M., SMITH-KERKER P.L., FORD J.R. and MAZUR-RIMETZ S.A. (1988b). The minimal manual. *Human–Computer Interaction*, **3**, 123–53

CATTERALL B.J., TAYLOR B.C. and GALER M.D. (1991). The HUFIT planning, analysis and specification toolset: Human factors as a normal part of the IT product design processing. In *Taking Software Design Seriously* (KARAT J., ed.). London: Academic Press

CHANDRASEKARAN B. (1981). Natural and social system metaphors for distributed problem solving: Introduction to the issue. *IEEE Transactions on Systems, Man and Cybernetics*, **11**(1), 1–5

CHASE W.G. and SIMON H.A. (1973). Perception in chess. *Cognitive Psychology*, **4**, 55–81

CHERNS A. (1976). The principles of socio-technical design. *Human Relations*, **29**, 783–92

CHECKLAND P.B. (1981). *Systems Thinking, Systems Practice*. Chichester: John Wiley

CHECKLAND P. and SCHOLES J. (1990). *Soft Systems Methodology in Action*. Chichester: John Wiley & Sons

CHERRY E.C. (1953). Some experiments on the recognition of speech with one or two ears *Journal of the Acoustical Society of America*, **25**(5), 975–9

CHI H.U. (1985). Formal specification of user interfaces: a comparison and evaluation of four axiomatic approaches. *IEEE Transactions on Software Engineering*, **11**(8), 671–85

CHILD J. (1972). Organizational structure, environment and performance: the role of strategic choice. *Sociology*, **6**(1), 1–22

CHRIST R.E. (1975). Review and analysis of colour coding research for visual displays. *Human Factors*, **17**(6), 542–70

CLARISSE O. and CHANG S.-K. (1986). VICON: A visual icon manager. In *Visual Languages* (CHANG S.-K., ICHIKAWA T. and LIOMENIDES P.A., eds). New York: Plenum Press

CLARK H.H. and BRENNAN S.E. (1991). Grounding in communication. In *Perspectives on Socially Shared Cognition* (RESNICK L.B., LEVINE J.M. and TEASLEY S.D., eds), pp. 127–49. Washington DC: American Psychological Association

CLARKSON M.A. (1991). An easier interface. *Byte*, February, 277–82

CLEGG C. and SYMON G. (1989). A review of human-centred manufacturing technology and a framework for its design and evaluation. *International Review of Ergonomics*, **2**, 15–47

COAD P. and YOURDON E. (1990). *Object-Oriented Analysis*. Englewood Cliffs, NJ: Prentice-Hall

COHILL A.M. and WILLIGES R.C. (1984). Retrieval of HELP information for novice users on interactive computer systems. *Human Factors*, **27**(3), 335–43

COLE M. and ENGESTROM Y. (1993). A cultural-historical approach to distributed cognition. In *Distributed Cognition: Psychological and Educational Implications* (SALOMON G., ed.). New York: Cambridge University Press

COLLINS A.M. and LOFTUS E.F. (1975). A spreading-activation theory of semantic processing. *Psychological Review*, **82**, 407–28

Computers in Context (1987). Videotape published by California Newsreel, 149 9th Street, Suite 420, San Francisco, California, 94103, USA

CONKLIN E.J. and BEGEMAN M.L. (1989). gIBIS: a tool for all reasons. *Journal of the American Society for Information Science*, **40**, 200–13

COUTAZ J. (1989). UIMS: Promises, failures and trends. In *People and Computers V: Proceedings of the Fifth Conference of the British Computer Society on Human–Computer Interaction* (SUTCLIFFE A. and MACAULAY L., eds). Specialist Group. Cambridge: Cambridge University Press

CRAIK F.I.M. and LOCKHART R.S. (1972). Levels of processing: A framework for memory research. *Journal of Verbal Learning and Verbal Behaviour*, **11**, 671–84

CRAIK K.J.W. (1943). *The Nature of Explanation*. Cambridge: Cambridge University Press

CRELLIN J. and PREECE J. (1991). Assessing the usability of different evaluation techniques in a small company. *Information and Software Technology*, **33**(5), 366–82

CROWSTON K. and MALONE T.W. (1988). Information technology and work organization. In *Handbook of Human–Computer Interaction* (HELANDER M., ed.), pp. 1051–70. Amsterdam: North-Holland

CURTIS B., KRASNER H. and ISCOE N. (1988). A field study of the software design process for large systems. *Communications of the ACM*, **31**(11), 1268–87

CYERT R.M and MARCH J.G. (1963). *A Behavioural Theory of the Firm*. Englewood Cliffs, NJ: Prentice-Hall

DAVIDOFF J.B. (1987). The role of colour in visual displays. In *International Review of Ergonomics* (OBORNE D.J., ed.). London: Taylor & Francis

DEMARCO T. (1979). *Structured Analysis and System Specification*. Englewood Cliffs, NJ: Yourdon Press

DEMARCO T. (1982). *Controlling Software Projects*. New York: Yourdon Press

DENNING P.J. (1991). Beyond formalism. *American Scientist*, **79**, 8–10

DENNING P.J., COMER D.E., GRIES D., MULDER M.C., TUCKER A., TURNER A.J. and YOUNG P.R. (1989). Computing as a discipline. *Communications of the ACM*, **22**(1), 9–23

DIAPER D. (1989a). Task observation for human–computer interaction. In *Task Analysis for Human–Computer Interaction*. Chichester: Ellis Horwood

DIAPER D. (1989b). Task analysis for knowledge-based descriptions (TAKD): the method and an example. In *Task Analysis for Human–Computer Interaction* (DIAPER D., ed.). Chichester: Ellis Horwood

DIAPER D. and ADDISON M. (1992). Task analysis and systems analysis for software development. *Interacting with Computers*, **4**(1), 124–39

DiGIANO C.J. and BAECKER R.M. (1992). Program auralization: Sound enhancements to the programming environment. In *Proceedings of Graphics Interface 1992*, pp. 44–53. Palo Alto, CA: Morgan Kaufmann

DiGIANO C.J., BAECKER R.M. and OWEN R.N. (1993). LogoMedia: A sound-enhanced programming environment for monitoring program behaviour. In *INTERCHI'93 Conference Proceedings*, pp. 301–2. New York: ACM Press

diSESSA A. (1991). Local sciences: viewing the design of human–computer systems as a cognitive science. In *Designing Interaction* (CARROLL J., ed.), p. 162. Cambridge: Cambridge University Press

DIX A., FINLAY J., ABOWD G. and BEALE R. (1993). *Human–Computer Interaction*. Hemel Hempstead: Prentice-Hall

DONEY A. and SETON J. (1988). Using colour. In *User Interface Design for Computer Systems* (RUBIN T., ed.). Chichester: Ellis Horwood

DRAPER S. (1985). The nature of expertise in UNIX. In *Human–Computer Interaction, INTERACT'84* (SHACKEL B., ed.), pp. 465–72. Proceedings of the 1st IFIP Conference on Human–Computer Interaction. Amsterdam: North-Holland

DRAPER S. (1993). The notion of task. In *Bridges between Worlds*, INTERCHI'93 Conference Proceedings, adjunct proceedings (ASHLUND S., MULLET K., HENDERSON A., HOLLNAGEL E. and WHITE T., eds), pp. 207–8. Reading, MA: Addison-Wesley

DTI (1991). *Case Studies: Usability Now!* London: DTI

DUNLOP C. and KLING R. (1991). *Computerization and Controversy*. San Diego: Academic Press

DURRETT J. and TREZONA J. (1982). How to use colour display effectively. *Byte*, **7**(4), 50–3

EARNSHAW R.A., GIGANTE M.A. and JONES H., eds (1993). *Virtual Reality Systems*. San Diego: Academic Press

EASON K.D. (1984). Toward the experimental study of usability. *Behaviour and Information Technology*, **3**(2), 133–43

EASON K.D. (1988). *Information Technology and Organisational Change*. London: Taylor & Francis

EASON K.D. (1991). Ergonomic perspectives on advances in human–computer interaction *Ergonomics*, **34**(6), 721–41

EASON K.D. and HARKER S. (1989). An Open Systems Approach to Task Analysis. *Internal Report*, HUSAT Research Centre, Loughborough University of Technology

EASON K.D., POMFRETT S. and OLPHERT W.O. (1984). Work Organisation Implications of Word Processing. *HUSAT Memo No. 313*, HUSAT Research Centre, Loughborough University of Technology

EASTERBY R.S. (1970). The perception of symbols for machine displays. *Ergonomics*, **13**, 149–58

EDELSTEIN D.V., FUJII R., GUERDAT C. and SULLO P. (1991). Internationalizing software engineering standards. *IEEE Computer*, **24**(3), 74–8

EDWARDS A.D.N. and HOLLAND S., eds (1992). *Multimedia Interface Design in Education*. Heidelberg: Springer-Verlag

EDWARDS A.D.N. (1991). *Speech Synthesis: Technology for Disabled People*. London: Paul Chapman

EDWORTHY J. and PATTERSON R.D. (1985). Ergonomic factors in auditory systems. In *Proceedings of the Ergonomics Journal 1985* (BROWN I.D., ed.). London: Taylor & Francis

EGAN D.E., REMDE J.R., LANDAUER T.K., GOMEZ L.M., EBERHARDT J. and LOCHBAUM C.C. (1989a). Formative design-evaluation of 'SuperBook'. *ACM Transactions on Office Information Systems*. New York: ACM Press

EGAN D.E., REMDE J.R., LANDAUER T.K., LOCHBAUM C.C. and GOMEZ L.M. (1989b). Behavioral evaluation and analysis of a hypertext browser. In *Wings for the Mind*, CHI'89 Conference Proceedings (BICE K. and LEWIS C, eds), pp. 205–10. New York: ACM Press

EGAN D.E., REMDE J.R., LANDAUER T.K., LOCHBAUM C.C. and GOMEZ L.M. (1989c). Acquiring information in books and SuperBooks. In *Proceedings of the American Educational Research Association*

EHN P. and KYNG M. (1987). The collective resource approach to systems design. In *Computers and Democracy* (BJERKNES G., EHN P. and KYNG M., eds), pp. 17–57. Aldershot: Avebury

EHN P. and SJÖGREN D. (1991). From system descriptions to scripts for action. In *Design at Work: Cooperative design of computer systems* (GREENBAUM J. and KYNG M., eds). Hillsdale, NJ: Lawrence Erlbaum Associates

EISENSTADT M. and BRAYSHAW M. (1988). The Transparent Prolog Machine (TPM): An execution model and graphical debugger for logic programming. *Journal of Logic Programming*, **5**(4), 1–66

EISENSTADT M., PRICE B.A. and DOMINGUE J. (1993). Software visualization as a pedagogical tool. *Instructional Science*, **21**, 335–64

ENGELBART D. (1988). Toward high-performance knowledge workers. In *Computer-supported Cooperative Work: a Book of Readings* (GRIEF I., ed.), pp. 67–78. Palo Alto, CA: Morgan Kaufmann

ERICKSON T.D. (1990). Working with interface metaphors. In *The Art of Human–Computer Interface Design* (LAUREL B., ed.). Reading, MA: Addison-Wesley

ERICSSON K.A. and SIMON H.A. (1985). *Protocol Analysis: Verbal Reports as Data*. Cambridge, MA: MIT Press

EYSENCK M.W. and KEANE M. (1990). *Cognitive Psychology: A Student's Handbook*. Hove, UK: Lawrence Erlbaum Associates

FEIGENBAUM E. and MCCORDUCK P. (1983). *The Fifth Generation: Artificial Intelligence and Japan's Computer Challenge to the World*. Reading, MA: Addison-Wesley

FISCHER G. (1989). HCI software: lessons learned, challenges ahead. *IEEE Software*, January

FISCHER G., LEMKE A.C., MCCALL R. and MORCH A.I. (1991). Making argumentation serve design. *Human–Computer Interaction*, **6**, 393–419

FISH R.S., KRAUT R.E. and CHALFONTE B.L. (1990). The VideoWindow system in informal communications. In *Proceedings of the Conference on Computer-Supported Cooperative Work (CSCW'90)*, pp. 1–11. New York: ACM Press

FISHER S.F. (1990). Virtual interface environments. In *The Art of Human–Computer Interface Design* (LAUREL B., ed.), pp. 423–38. Reading, MA: Addison-Wesley

FITTS P.M. and POSNER M.I. (1967). *Human Performance*. Belmont, CA: Brooks Cole

FLORES F., GRAVES M., HARTFIELD B. and WINOGRAD T. (1988). Computer systems and the design of organizational interaction. *ACM Transactions on Office Information Systems*, **6**(2), 153–72

FOLEY J., KIM W.C., KOVACEVIC S. and MURRAY K. (1989). Defining interfaces at a high level of abstraction. *IEEE Software*, January, 25–32

FOSS D., SMITH P. and ROSSON M. (1982). The novice at the terminal: Variables affecting understanding and performance. Paper presented at the Psychonomic Society meeting, Minneapolis

FRANCIONI J.M., ALBRIGHT L. and JACKSON J.A. (1992). Debugging parallel programs using sound. *SIGPLAN Notices*, **26**(12), 68–75

GAINES B.R. and SHAW M.L.G. (1984). *The Art of Computer Conversation: a New Medium for Communication*. Englewood Cliffs, NJ: Prentice-Hall

GALBRAITH J.R. (1974). Organization design: An information processing view. *Interfaces*, **4**(5), 28–36

GALEGHER J., KRAUT R.E. and EGIDO C., eds (1990). *Intellectual Teamwork: Social and Technical Bases of Collaborative Work*. Hillsdale, NJ: Lawrence Erlbaum Associates

GARDINER M. and CHRISTIE B., eds (1987). *Applying Cognitive Psychology to User Interface Design*. Chichester: Wiley

GAVER W. (1986). Auditory icons: using sound in computer interfaces. *Human–Computer Interaction*, **2**(2), 167–77

GAVER W. (1989). The sonic finder. *Human–Computer Interaction*, **4**(1). Special issue on non speech audio

GAVER W. (1991). Technology Affordances. In *Human Factors in Computing Systems CHI'91 Conference Proceedings* (ROBERTSON S.P., OLSON G.M. and OLSON J.S., eds), pp. 79–84. Reading, MA: Addison-Wesley

GAVER B., SMITH R.B. and O'SHEA T. (1991). Effective sound in complex systems: the ARKola simulation. In *Human Factors in Computing Systems CHI'91 Conference Proceedings* (ROBERTSON S.P., OLSON G.M. and OLSON J.S., eds), pp. 85–90. Reading, MA: Addison-Wesley

GAVER W., MORAN T., MACLEAN A., *et al.* (1991). Working together in media space: CSCW research at Euro-PARC. In *The Multimedia and Networking Paradigm*, Proceedings of the seminar on CSCW (SCRIVENER S.A.R., ed.), pp. 110–24, Unicom Seminars Ltd, Uxbridge, July

GIBSON J.J. (1979). *The Ecological Approach to Visual Perception*. Boston, MA: Houghton Mifflin

GILB T. (1985). The 'Impact Analysis Table' applied to human factors design. In *Human–Computer Interaction – INTERACT '84, Proceedings of the 1st IFIP Conference on Human–Computer Interaction*

(SHACKEL B., ed.), pp. 655–9. Amsterdam: North-Holland

GLEITMAN H. (1991). *Psychology* 3rd edn. New York: W.W. Norton & Co.

GLINERT E.P. and TANIMOTO L. (1984). Pict: An interactive graphical programming environment. *IEEE Computer*, **17**, 7–25

GOOD M., SPINE T.M., WHITESIDE J. and GEORGE P. (1986). User-derived impact analysis as a tool for usability engineering. In *Human Factors in Computing Systems CHI'86 Conference Proceedings* (MANTEI M. and OBERTON P., eds), pp. 241–6. New York: ACM Press

GOODSTEIN L.P., ANDERSEN H.B. and OLSEN H.E. (1988). Introduction. In *Tasks, Errors and Mental Models* (GOODSTEIN L.P., ANDERSEN H.B. and OLSEN H.E., eds), pp. 1–17. London: Taylor & Francis

GOULD J.D. and LEWIS C. (1985). Designing for usability: Key principles and what designers think. *Communications of the ACM*, **28**, 300–11

GOULD J.D., BOIES S.J., LEVY S., RICHARDS J.T. and SCHOONARD J. (1987). The 1984 Olympic Message System: a test of behavioural principle of system design. *Communications of the ACM*, **30**(9), 758–69. Reprinted in PREECE and KELLER (eds) 1990

GRAY P.D., WAITE K.W. and DRAPER S. (1990). Do-it-yourself iconic displays: reconfigurable iconic representations of application objects. In *Human–Computer Interaction, INTERACT'90* (DIAPER D., GILMORE D., COCKTON G. and SHACKEL B., eds), pp. 639–44. Amsterdam: Elsevier

GREEN T.R.G. (1989). Cognitive dimensions of notations. In *People and Computers IV* (SUTCLIFFE A. and MACAULAY L., eds). Cambridge: Cambridge University Press

GREEN T.R.G. (1991). Describing information artefacts with cognitive dimensions and structure maps. In *People and Computers VI*, Proceedings of the 6th Conference of the British Computer Society Human–Computer Interaction Specialist Group (DIAPER D. and HAMMOND N.V., eds). Cambridge: Cambridge University Press

GREENBAUM J. and KYNG M., eds (1991). *Design at Work: Cooperative Design of Computer Systems*. Hillsdale, NJ: Lawrence Erlbaum Associates

GREENBERG S. (1991). Personalisable groupware: Accommodating individual roles and group differences. In *Proceedings of the Second European Conference on Computer Supported Cooperative Work (EC-*

CSCW'91) (Bannon L., Robinson M. and Schmidt K., eds). Dordrecht: Kluwer

Greenberg S., ed. (1991). *Computer-Supported Cooperative Work and Groupware*. London: Academic Press

Greene J. and D'Oliveira M. (1982). *Learning to Use Statistical tests in Psychology: A Student's Guide*. Milton Keynes: Open University Press

Greenstein J. and Arnaut L. (1988). Input devices. In *Handbook of Human–Computer Interaction* (Helander M., ed.), pp. 495–516. Amsterdam: Elsevier

Gregory R. (1966). *Eye and Brain*. London: World University Library

Gregory R.L. (1970). *The Intelligent Eye*. New York: McGraw-Hill

Gregory R.L. (1978). *Eye and Brain* 3rd edn. New York: McGraw-Hill

Grinstein G. and Smith S. (1990). The perceptualization of scientific data. In Extracting Meaning from Complex Data: Processing Display, Interaction (Farrell E., ed.). *Proceedings of the SPIE*, **1259**, 190–9

Grudin J. (1988). Why CSCW applications fail: problems in the design and evaluation of organizational interfaces. In *Proceedings of the Conference on Computer-Supported Cooperative Work (CSCW'88)*, pp. 85–93. New York: ACM Press

Grudin J. (1989). The case against user interface inconsistency. *Comm ACM*, **32**(10), 1164–73

Grudin J. (1990). The computer reaches out: the historical continuity of interface design. In *Empowering People*, CHI'90 Conference Proceedings (Chew J.C. and Whiteside J., eds), pp. 261–8. New York: ACM

Guetzkow H. and Simon H.A. (1955). The impact of certain communication nets upon organization and performance in task-oriented groups. *Management Science*, **1**, 233–50

Guindon R. (1990). Knowledge exploited by experts during software systems design. *International Journal of Man–Machine Studies*, **33**, 279–304

Halasz F. and Moran T.P. (1982). Analogy considered harmful. In *Human Factors in Computing Systems CHI'92 Conference Proceedings*, pp. 383–6. New York: ACM Press

Halasz F.G. and Moran T.P. (1983). Mental models and problem solving in using a calculator. In *Human Factors in Computing Systems CHI'83 Conference Proceedings* (Janda A., ed.). New York: ACM Press

Hammond N.V., Hinton G., Barnard P., Maclean A., Long J. and Whitefield A. (1984). Evaluating the interface of a document processor: a comparison of expert judgement and user observation. In *Human–Computer Interaction, INTERACT '84* (Shackel B., ed.). Proceedings of the 1st IFIP Conference on Human–Computer Interaction, Vol. 2, pp. 135–9. Amsterdam: North-Holland

Harrison B.L. (1991). Video annotation and multimedia interfaces: from theory to practice. In *Proceedings of the Human Factors Society 35th Annual General Meeting – 1991*, pp. 319–22

Hartson H.R. and Hix D. (1989). Toward empirically derived methodologies and tools for HCI development. In *International Journal of Man–Machine Studies*, **31**, 477–94

Hartson H.R., Siochi A.C. and Hix D. (1990). The UAN: a user-oriented representation for direct manipulation interface designs. *ACM Transactions on Information Systems*, **8**(3), pp. 181–203

Hawkridge D. and Vincent T. (1992). *Learning Difficulties and Computers*. London: Jessica Kingsley Publishers

Hci Service for the Dti (1991). *HCI Tools and Methods Handbook*. London: Impress (Leicester) Ltd

Heath C. and Luff P. (1991a). Disembodied conduct: communication through video in a multimedia office environment. In *Human Factors in Computing Systems CHI'91 Conference Proceedings* (Robertson S.P., Olson G.M. and Olson J.S., eds), pp. 99–103. New York: ACM Press

Heath C. and Luff P. (1991b). Collaborative activity and technological design: Task coordination in London underground control rooms. In *Proceedings of the Second European Conference on Computer-Supported Cooperative Work EC-CSCW'91* (Bannon L., Robinson M. and Schmidt K., eds), pp. 65–80. Dordrecht: Kluwer

Heath C. and Luff P. (1993). Disembodied conduct: Interactional asymmetries in video-mediated communication. In *Technology in Working Order: Studies of Work, Interaction and Technology* (Button G., ed.), pp. 3554. London: Routledge

Hekmatpour S. and Ince D.C. (1988). *Software Prototyping, Formal Methods and VDM*. Wokingham: Addison-Wesley

Helander M., ed. (1988). *Handbook of Human–Computer Interaction*. Amsterdam, North-Holland

Henderson A. and Card S.K. (1987). A multiple virtual-workspace interface to support task switching. In *Human Factors in Computing Systems CHI'87 Conference Proceedings*, pp. 53–9. New York: ACM Press

HEWITT B., GILBERT N., JIROTKA M. and WILBUR S. (1990). Theories of Multi Party Interaction. *TMPI End of Year Report*. British Telecom, Queen Mary and Westfield Colleges and the University of Surrey

HILL R.D. and HERRMANN M. (1990). The composite object user interface architecture. In *User Interface Management and Design*, Proceedings of the Workshop on User Interface Management Systems and Environments (DUCE D.A., GOMES M.R., HOPGOOD F.R.A. and LEE J.R., eds). Berlin: Springer-Verlag

HIRSCHHEIM R.A. (1985). *Office Automation: A Social and Organizational Perspective*. Chichester: John Wiley

HIX D. and HARTSON H.R. (1993). *Developing User Interfaces: Ensuring Usability Through Product and Process*. New York: John Wiley

HOLLAND S. (1991). Virtual machines meet virtual people: the feel of things to come. *AISB Quarterly*, Spring, no. 76

HOLLAND S. (1991b). Two-dimensional visual programming and three-dimensional execution visualization in Prolog. In 'Colloquium Digest of the Institute of Electrical Engineers' *Colloquium on 'Visualisation, Virtual World, Virtual Reality'*, pp. 4/1–4/4. Savoy Place, London: IEE Electronics Division

HOLLAND S. (1992). Interface design for empowerment: A case study from music. In *Multimedia Interface Design in Education* (EDWARDS A. and HOLLAND S., eds). Heidelberg: Springer-Verlag

HOLLAND S. (1994). Learning about harmony with Harmony Space: an overview. In *Music Education: an Artificial Intelligence Approach*. London: Springer Verlag

HOLTZBLATT K. and BEYER H. (1993). Contextual design: Integrating customer data into the design process. In *Bridges Between Worlds*, INTERCHI'93 Tutorial Notes 6 (ASHLUND S., MULLET K., HENDERSON A., HILLNAGEL E. and WHITE T., eds). Reading, MA: Addison-Wesley/ACM Press

HONEYSETT M. (1982). *Microphobia: How to Survive your Computer and the Technological Revolution*. London: Century

HORTON W. (1990). *Designing and Writing On-Line Documentation: Help Files to Hypertext*. New York: John Wiley

HORTON W. (1991). *Illustrating Computer Documentation: The Art of Presenting Information Graphically on Paper On-Line*. Toronto: John Wiley

HUFF D. (1973). *How to Lie with Statistics*. Harmondsworth: Penguin

Human–Computer Interaction (1989). **4**(1)

Human–Computer Interaction (1992). **7**

HUTCHINS E. (1990). The technology of team navigation. In *Intellectual Teamwork* (GALEGHER J., KRAUT R.E. and EDIGO C., eds), pp. 191–220. Hillsdale, NJ: Lawrence Erlbaum Associates

HUTCHINS E. (1991). Organizing work by adaptation. *Organizational Science*. **2**, 14–39

HUTCHINS E. (1995). *Distributed Cognition*. Cambridge, MA: MIT Press

HUTCHINS E. and KLAUSEN T. (1992). Distributed cognition in an airline cockpit. In *Communication and Cognition at Work* (MIDDLETON D. and ENGESTROM Y., eds). Cambridge: Cambridge University Press

HUTCHINS E.L., HOLLAN J.D. and NORMAN D. (1986). Direct manipulation interfaces. In *User Centred System Design* (NORMAN D. and DRAPER S., eds), pp. 87–124. Hillsdale, NJ: Lawrence Erlbaum Associates

IBM (1991). *Common User Access Guide to User Interface Design*. IBM

IEEE Software (1990) **6**(1)

INCE D. and ANDREWS D. (1990). *The Software Life Cycle*. London: Butterworths

Interacting with Computers: The Interdisciplinary Journal of Human–Computer Interaction (1989), **1**(1), 3

ISO (1985). *Information Processing System – Computer Graphics – Graphical Kernel System (GKS) Functional Description*. ISO 7942

IWATA H. (1990). Artificial reality with force feedback: Development of desktop virtual spaces with compact master manipulator. *ACM Computer Graphics*, **24**(4)

JAMES M.G. (1991). PRODUSER: PROcess for Developing USER Interfaces. In *Taking Software Design Seriously* (KARAT J., ed.). London: Academic Press

JAMES W. (1980). *Principles of Psychology*. New York: Holt

JEFFRIES R., MILLER J.R., WHARTON C. and UYEDA K.M. (1991). User interface evaluation in the real world: A comparison of four techniques. In *Human Factors in Computing Systems CHI'91 Conference Proceedings* (ROBERTSON S.P., OLSON G.M. and OLSON J.S., eds), pp. 119–24. New York: ACM Press

JOHN B.E. (1990). Extensions of GOMS analyses to expert performance requiring perception of dynamic visual and auditory information. In *Empowering People*, CHI'90 Conference Proceedings (CHEW J.C. and WHITESIDE J., eds), pp. 107–15. New York: ACM Press

JOHNSON P. (1992). *Human–Computer Interaction: Psychology, Task Analysis and Software Engineering*. Maidenhead: McGraw-Hill

JOHNSON W., JELLINEK H., KLOTZ Jr. L., RAO R. (1993). Bridging the paper and electronic worlds: The paper user interface. In *Bridges between Worlds*, INTERCHI'93 Conference Proceedings (ASHLUND S., MULLET K., HENDERSON A., HOLLNAGEL E. and WHITE T. eds), pp. 507–12. Reading, MA: Addison-Wesley

JOHNSON-LAIRD P.N. (1983). Mental Models. In *Foundations of Cognitive Science* (POSNER M.I., ed.), pp. 469–93. Cambridge: Cambridge University Press

JOHNSON-LAIRD P.N. (1988). *The Computer and the Mind*. Cambridge, MA: Harvard University Press

JONES C.C. (1981). *Design Methods: Seeds of Human Futures* 2nd edn. London: Wiley

JONES S. and DOWNTON A. (1991). Windowing systems: high and low-level design issues. In *Engineering the Human–Computer Interface* (DOWNTON A., ed.). London: McGraw-Hill

KALAWSKY R.S. (1993). *The Science of Virtual Reality and Virtual Environments*. Wokingham: Addison-Wesley

KARAT C.-M. (1993). Cost–benefit and business case analysis of usability engineeering. *Bridges between Worlds*, INTERCHI'93 Tutorial Notes 23 (ASHLUND S., MULLET K., HENDERSON A., HOLLNAGEL E. and WHITE T. eds). Reading, MA: Addison-Wesley

KARAT C.-M., CAMPBELL R. and FIEGEL T. (1992). Comparison of empirical testing and walkthrough methods in user interface evaluation. In *Human Factors in Computing Systems CHI'92 Conference Proceedings* (BAUERSFIELD P., BENNETT J. and LYNCH G., eds), pp. 397–404. New York: ACM Press

KARAT J. and BENNETT J.L. (1991). Using scenarios in design meetings. In *Taking Software Design Seriously* (KARAT J., ed.). London: Academic Press

KAY A. (1990). In *The Art of Human–Computer Interaction Design* (LAUREL B., ed.). Reading, MA: Addison-Wesley

KAY A. and GOLDBERG A. (1977). Personal dynamic media. *IEEE Computer*, **10**(3), 31–44

KEARSLEY G. (1988). *On-Line Help Systems*. Norwood, NJ: Ablex

KIERAS D. (1988). Towards a practical GOMS model methodology for user interface design. In *Handbook of Human–Computer Interaction* (HELANDER M., ed.), pp. 135–58. Amsterdam: North-Holland

KIERAS D. (1991). A guide to GMS task analysis. University of Michigan, Fall, 1991

KIERAS D. (1993). In *Bridges between Worlds*, INTERCHI'93 Tutorial Notes 5 (ASHLUND S., MULLET K., HENDERSON A., HOLLNAGEL E. and WHITE T. eds). Reading, MA: Addison-Wesley

KIERAS D. and BOVAIR S. (1984). The role of a mental model in learning to operate a device. *Cognitive Science*, **8**, 255–73

KIERAS D. and POLSON P.G. (1985). An approach to formal analysis of user complexity. *International Journal of Man–Machine Studies*, **22**, 365–94

KOFFKA K. (1935). *Principles of Gestalt Psychology*. New York: Harcourt Brace

KOHLER (1947). *Gestalt Psychology*. Princeton, NJ: Princeton University Press

KUNTZ W. and RITTEL H. (1970). Issues as elements of information systems. *Working paper no. 131*, University of California, Center for Planning and Development Research, Berkeley

KUUTTI K. (1991). The concept of activity as a basic unit of analysis for CSCW research. In *Proceedings of the Second European Conference on Computer-Supported Co-operative Work: EC-CSCW'91* (BANNON L., ROBINSON M. and SCHMIDT K., eds), pp. 249–64. Dordrecht: Kluwer

LAIRD J., NEWELL A. and ROSENBLOOM P. (1987). SOAR: An architecture for general intelligence. *Artificial Intelligence*, **33**, 1–64

LAKOFF G. and JOHNSON M. (1980). *Metaphors We Live By*. Chicago: The University of Chicago Press

LANDAUER T.K. (1987). Relations between cognitive psychology and computer system design. In *Interfacing Thought: Cognitive Aspects of Human–Computer Interaction* (CARROLL J.M., eds), pp. 1–25. Cambridge, MA: MIT Press

LANDAUER T.K. (1991). Let's get real: a position paper on the role of cognitive psychology in the design of humanly useful and usable systems. In *Designing Interaction: Psychology at the Human–Computer Interface* (CARROLL J., ed.), pp. 60–73. New York: Cambridge University Press

LAUREL B., ed. (1990). *The Art of Human–Computer Interface Design*. Reading, MA: Addison-Wesley

LAVE J. (1988). *Cognition in Practice*. Cambridge: Cambridge University Press

LAVE J. and WENGER E. (1991). *Situated Learning: Legitimate Peripheral Participation*. Cambridge: Cambridge University Press

LEAVITT H.J. (1951). Some effects of certain communication patterns on group performance. *Journal of Abnormal and Social Psychology*, **46**, 38–50

LEE L. (1992). *The Day the Phones Stopped: How People Get Hurt When Computers Go Wrong*. New York: Primus, Donald I Fine, Inc.

LEVY S. (1994). *Insanely Great: The Life and Times of Macintosh, the Computer that Changed Everything*. New York: Viking

LEWIS C. and NORMAN D. (1986). Designing for error. In *User Centred System Design* (NORMAN D. and DRAPER S., eds), pp. 411–32. Hillsdale, NJ: Lawrence Erlbaum Associates

LEWIS C., POLSON P. WHARTON C. and RIEMAN J. (1990). Testing a walkthrough methodology for theory-based design of walk-up-and-use interfaces. In *Empowering People*, CHI'90 Conference Proceedings (CHEW J.C. and WHITESIDE J., eds), pp. 235–41. New York: ACM Press

LICKLIDER J.C.R. (1960). Man–computer symbiosis. *IRE Transactions of Human Factors in Electronics*, **1**, 4–11

LINDSAY P.H. and NORMAN D.A. (1977). *Human Information Processing: An Introduction to Psychology* 2nd edn. New York: Academic Press

LONGWORTH G. and NICHOLS D. (1987). *The SSADM Manual*. Manchester: National Computer Centre

LUDER C.B. and BARBER P.J. (1984). Redundant color coding on airborne CRT displays. *Human Factors*, **26**(1), 19–32

LYONS J. (1970). *New Horizons in Linguistics*. Harmondsworth: Penguin

McCALL R.J. (1991). PHI: A conceptual foundation for design hypermedia. *Design Studies*, **12**, 30–41

McDERMID J.A. (1991). *Software Engineer's Reference Book*. Oxford: Butterworth-Heinemann

MACK R. and NIELSEN J. (1993). Usability inspection methods: Report on a workshop held at CHI'92, Monterey, CA. *SIGCHI Bulletin*, January, 30–3

MACK R.L., LEWIS C. and CARROLL J.M. (1984). *Learning to use word processors: problems and prospects, TOOIS*. New York: ACM Press

MACKINLAY J.D., CARD S.K. and ROBINSON G.G. (1990). A semantic analysis of the design space of input devices. *Human–Computer Interaction*, **5**(2, 3)

McKEITHEN K.B., REITMAN J.S., RUETER H.H. and HIRTLE S.C. (1981). Knowledge organization and skill differences in computer programs. *Cognitive Psychology*, **13**, 307–25

MacLEAN A., YOUNG R.M., BELLOTTI V.M.E. and MORAN T.P. (1991). Questions, options and criteria: elements of design space analysis. *Human–Computer Interaction*, **6**, 201–50

MAGUIRE M.C. (1982). A review of human factors guidelines and techniques for the design of graphical human–computer interfaces. *International Journal of Man–Machine Studies*, **16**(3), 237–61

MAGUIRE M.C. (1990). A review of human factors guidelines and techniques for the design of graphical human–computer interfaces. In *Human–Computer Interaction: Selected Readings* (PREECE J.P. and KELLER L., eds), pp. 161–84. Hemel Hempstead: Prentice-Hall

MALIK R. (1987). *The World's Best Computer Jokes*. London: Angus and Robertson

MANTEI M. (1992). CSCW – What changes for the science of computing. In *Proceedings of Graphic Interface 1992*. Morgan-Kaufmann

MANTEI M., BAECKER R.M., SELLEN A.J., BENTON W.A.S., MILLIGAN T. and WELLMAN B. (1991). Experiences in the use of a media space. In *Human Factors in Computing Systems CHI'91 Conference Proceedings* (ROBERTSON S.P., OLSON G.M. and OLSON J.S., eds), pp. 203–8. New York: ACM Press

MANTEI M., HEWETT T., EASON K. and PREECE J. (1991). Report on the INTERACT'90 workshop on education in HCI: Transcending disciplinary and national boundaries. *Interacting with Computers*, **3**(2), 232–40

MARCUS A. (1992). *Graphic Design for Electronic Documents and User Interfaces*. Reading, MA: Addison-Wesley/ACM Press

MARR D. (1982). *Vision: A computational investigation into the human representation and processing of visual information*. San Francisco, CA: W.H. Freeman

MARTIN J. (1982). *Strategic Data-Planning Methodologies*. Englewood Cliffs, NJ: Prentice-Hall

MARTIN J. (1986). *Information Engineering* Vols 1 and 2. Lancaster: Savant

MAYER R.E. (1988). From novice to expert. In *Handbook of Human–Computer Interaction* (HELANDER M., ed.), pp. 569–80. Amsterdam: North-Holland

MAYES J.T., DRAPER S.W., McGREGOR A.M. and OATLEY K. (1988). Information flow in a user interface: the effect of experience and context on the recall of MacWrite screens. In *People and Computers IV* (JONES D.M. and WINDER R., eds), pp. 257–89. Cambridge: Cambridge University Press

MEISTER D. (1986). *Human Factors Testing Evaluation*. Amsterdam: Elsevier

MICHAELS C.F. and CARELLO C. (1981). *Direct Perception*. Englewood Cliffs, NJ: Prentice-Hall

MICROSOFT (1992). *The Windows Interface: An Application Design Guide*. Microsoft Press

MILLER G.A. (1956). The magic number seven plus or minus two: Some limits of our capacity for information processing. *Psychological Review*, **63**(2), 81–7

MILLER-JACOBS H.H. (1991). Rapid prototyping: an effective technique for system development. In *Taking Software Design Seriously* (KARAT J., ed.). London: Academic Press

MIYAKE N. (1986). Constructive interaction and the iterative process of understanding. *Cognitive Science*, **10**, 151–77

MOLICH R. and NIELSEN J. (1990). Improving a human–computer dialogue. *Communications of the ACM*, **33**(3), 338–48

MOLL T. and SAUTER R. (1987). Do people really use online assistance? In *Human–Computer Interactions, INTERACT'87* (BULLINGER H.J. and SHACKEL B., eds). Proceedings of the IFIP Conference on Human–Computer Interaction, pp.191–4. Amsterdam: North-Holland

MONK A., WRIGHT P., HABER J. and DAVENPORT L. (1993a). *Improving Your Human–Computer Interface: A Practical Technique*. New York: Prentice-Hall

MONK A., NARDIE B., GILBERT N., MANTEIR M. and McCARTHY J. (1993b). Mixing oil and water? Ethnography versus experimental psychology in the study of computer-mediated communication. In *Bridges between Worlds*, INTERCHI'93 Conference Proceedings (ASHLUND S., MULLET K., HENDERSON A., HOLLNAGEL E. and WHITE T. eds), pp. 3–6. Reading: Addison-Wesley

MORAN T.P. (1981). The command language grammar: a representation for the user interface of interactive systems. *International Journal of Man–Machine Studies*, **15**(1), 3–50

MORAN T.P. (1983). Getting into the system: External task internal taskmapping analysis. In *Human Factors in Computing Systems CHI'83 Conference Proceedings* (JANDA A., ed.). New York: ACM Press

MORGAN G. (1986). *Images of Organizations*. Newbury Park, CA: Sage

MUELLER C.G. (1965). *Sensory Psychology*. Englewood Cliffs, NJ: Prentice-Hall

MUMFORD E. (1987). Socio-technical systems design: evolving theory and practice. In *Computers and Democracy* (BJERKNES G., EHN P. and KYNG M., eds), pp. 59–77. Aldershot: Avebury

MURATORE D.A. (1987). Human performance aspects of cursor control devices. *Mitre Working Paper 6321*, Houston, Texas

MURRAY D. and HEWITT B. (1992). Capturing interactions: requirements for CSCW. *TMPI Project Report*, Social and Computer Sciences Research Group, University of Surrey

MURRAY D. and HEWITT B. (1994). Capturing interactions: requirements for CSCW. In *Design Issues in CSCW* (ROSENBERG D. and HUTCHINSON C., eds). Berlin: Springer-Verlag

MURRAY D., HEWITT B., GILBERT N. and ROGERS A. (1993). Suppporting collaboration: A user guide to requirements capture and analysis for computer supported co-operative work. *TMPI Project Report*, Social and Computer Sciences Research Group, University of Surrey

MYERS B.A. (1992). State of the art in user interface software tools. Technical report CMU-CS-114, Carnegie Mellon University

MYERS B.A., GIUSE D.A., DANNENBERG R.B., ZANDEN B.V., KOSBIE D.S., PERVIN E., MICKISH A. and MARCHAL P. (1990). Garnet: Comprehensive support for graphical, highly-interactive user interfaces. *IEEE Computer*, **23**(11), 71–85

NATIONAL ELECTRONICS COUNCIL (1983). *Human Factors and Information Technology: The Inhuman Factors of Information Technology*, Section 2, p. 13

NATIONAL PHYSICAL LABORATORY (1993). *Counting on IT*, Summer, no. 1

NEAL A.S. and SIMONS R.M. (1983). Playback: a method for evaluating the usability of software and its documentation. In *Human Factors in Computing Systems CHI'83 Conference Proceedings* (JANDA A., ed.), pp. 78–82. New York: ACM Press

NEGREPONTE N. (1989). An iconoclastic view beyond the desktop metaphor. *International Journal of Human–Computer Interaction*, **1**, 109–13

NELSON T.H. (1967). Getting it out of our system. In *Information Retrieval: A* (SCHECHTER G., ed.)

NELSON T. (1981). *Literary Machines*. Swathmore, PA (self-published)

NEWMAN W., STEPHENS N. and SWEETMAN D. (1985). A window manager with a modular user interface. *Proc. British Computer Society*, HCI Conference (JOHNSON P. and COOK S., eds), pp. 415–26. Cambridge: Cambridge University Press

NIELSEN J. (1989). Usability engineering at a discount. In *Designing and Using Human–Computer Interfaces and Knowledge Based Systems* (SALVENDY G. and SMITH M.J., eds), pp. 394–401. Amsterdam: Elsevier

NIELSEN J. (1992). Finding usability problems through heuristic evaluation. In *Human Factors in Computing Systems CHI'92 Conference Proceedings* (BAUERSFIELD P., BENNETT J. and LYNCH G., eds), pp. 373–80. New York: ACM Press

NIELSEN J. (1993). Usability evaluation and inspection methods. In *Bridges between Worlds*, INTERCHI'93 Tutorial Notes 22 (ASHLUND S., MULLET K., HENDERSON A., HOLLNAGEL E. and WHITE T. eds). Reading, MA: Addison-Wesley

NIELSEN J., MACK R.B., BERGENDORFF K.H. and GRISCHKOWSKY N.L. (1986). Integrated software usage in the professional work environment: evidence from questionnaires and interviews. In *Human Factors in Computing Systems, CHI'86 Conference Proceedings* (MANTEI M. and OBERTON P., eds), pp. 162–7. New York: ACM Press

NORMAN D.A. (1981). Categorization of action slips *Psychological Review*, **88**, 1–15

NORMAN D.A. (1983). Some observations on mental models. In *Mental Models* (GENTNER D. and STEVENS A.L., eds), pp. 7–14. Hillsdale, NJ: Lawrence Erlbaum Associates

NORMAN D.A. (1983b). Design rules based on analyses of human error. *Communications of the ACM*, **26**(4)

NORMAN D.A. (1986). Cognitive engineering. In *User-Centred System Design* (NORMAN D. and DRAPER S., eds), pp. 31–61. Hillsdale, NJ: Lawrence Erlbaum Associates

NORMAN D.A. (1988). *The Psychology of Everyday Things*. New York: Basic Books

NORMAN D.A. (1992). *Turn Signals are the Facial Expressions of Automobiles*. Reading, MA: Addison-Wesley

NORMAN D.A. (1993). *Things That Make Us Smart*. Reading, MA: Addison-Wesley

NORMAN M.A. and THOMAS P.J. (1990). The very idea: informing HCI design from conversation analysis. In *Computers and Conversation* (LUFF P., GILBERT N. and FROHLICH D., eds), pp. 51–65. London: Academic Press

NOVICK D.G. and WALPOLE J. (1990). Enhancing the efficiency of multiparty interaction through computer mediation. *Interacting with Computers*, **2**, 229–46

OBORNE D.J. (1985). *Computers at Work: A Behavioural Approach*. Chichester: John Wiley

OLSON G.M., OLSON J.S., CARTER M.R. and STORROSTEN M. (1992). Small group design meetings: an analysis of collaboration. *Human–Computer Interaction*, **7**, 347–74

O'MALLEY C.E. (1986). Helping users help themselves. In *User-Centred Systems Design* (NORMAN D. and DRAPER S., eds). Hillsdale, NJ: Lawrence Erlbaum Associates

O'MALLEY C. and DRAPER S. (1992). Representation and interaction: Are mental models all in the mind? In *Models in the Mind: Theory, Perspective and Application* (ROGERS Y., RUTHERFORD A. and BIBBY P., eds), pp. 73–92. London: Academic Press

ORR J.E. (1990). Sharing knowledge, celebrating identity: community memory in a service culture. In *Collective Remembering* (MIDDLETON D. and EDWARDS D., eds). London: Sage

PAAP K.R. and ROSKE-HOFSTRAND R.J. (1988). Design of menus. In *Handbook of Human–Computer Interaction* (HELANDER M., ed.). Amsterdam: North-Holland

PARKIN A.J. (1993). *Memory*. Oxford: Blackwell

PARNAS D. and CLEMENTS P.C. (1986). A rational design process: How and why to fake it. *IEEE Transactions on Software Engineering*, **16**, 251–7

PASSMORE W., FRANCIS C., HALDMAN J. and SHANI A. (1982). Socio-technical systems: a North American reflection on empirical studies of the seventies. *Human Relations*, **36**, 1179–204

PAUSCH R. (1990). Tailor and the UserVers: Two approaches to multimodal input. Technical report, Computer Science Department, University of Virginia

PAUSCH R. (1991). Virtual reality on five dollars a day. *CHI '91 Conference Proceedings*, pp. 265–70. New York: ACM Press

PAYNE S.J. (1987). Complex problem spaces: modelling the knowledge needed to use interactive devices. In *Human Computer Interaction, INTERACT'87* (BULLING H.-J. and SHACKEL B., eds). Proceedings of the IFIP Conference on Human–Computer Interaction. Amsterdam: North-Holland

PAYNE S. (1991). Display-based action at the user interface. *International Journal of Man–Machine Studies*, **35**, 279–89

PAYNE S. and GREEN T.R.G. (1989). Task-action grammar: the model and its developments. In *Task Analysis for Human–Computer Interaction* (DIAPER D., ed.). Chichester: Ellis Horwood

PERROW C. (1984). *Normal Accidents*. New York: Basic Books

POLSON P.G., LEWIS C., RIEMAN J. and WHARTON C. (1992). Cognitive walkthroughs: a method for theory-based evaluation of user interfaces. *International Journal of Man–Machine Studies*, **36**, 741–73

POOLE M.S. and HIROKAWA R.Y. (1986). *Communication and Group Decision-Making*. New York: Sage

PORTEOUS M.A., KIRAKOWSKI J. and CORBETT M. (1993). *Software Usability Measurement Inventory Handbook*. Human Factors Research Group, University College, Cork, Ireland

POSNER M.I., ed. (1989). *Foundations of Cognitive Science*. Cambridge, MA: MIT Press

POTOSNAK K. (1988). Keys and keyboards. In *Handbook of Human–Computer Interaction* (HELANDER M., ed.), pp. 475–94. Amsterdam: Elsevier

POTOSNAK K. (1990). Big paybacks from 'discount' usability engineering. *IEEE Software*, 107–9

PREECE J., ed. (1992). *A Guide to Usability: Human Factors in Computing*. Wokingham: Addison-Wesley

PREECE J. and CROW D. (1994). HalClon: A hypermedia Human–Computer Interaction (HCI) training environment. *Technical Report*, Computing Dept, Milton Keynes: Open University

PREECE J. and JANVIER C. (1992). Interpreting trends in multiple curve graphs of ecological situations – the role of context. *International Journal of Science Education*, **14**, 10

PREECE J. and KELLER L., eds (1990). *Human–Computer Interaction: Selected Readings*. Hemel Hempstead: Prentice-Hall

PRICE B.A., BAECKER R.M. and SMALL I.S. (1993). A principled taxonomy of software visualization. *Journal of Visual Languages and Computing*, **4**(3), 211–66

PRIME M. (1989). User interface management systems – a current product review. *Computer Graphics Forum*, **9**(1)

Proceedings of the Conference on Computer Supported Cooperative Work (CSCW '90). New York: ACM Press

Proceedings of the Conference on Computer Supported Cooperative Work (CSCW '92). New York: ACM Press

Proceedings of the Conference on Computer Supported Cooperative Work (CSCW '88). New York: ACM Press

Proceedings of the First European Conference on Computer Supported Cooperative Work (EC-CSCW '89). Slough: Computer Sciences House

QUAST K.-J. (1993). Plan recognition for context-sensitive help. In *Proceedings of the 1993 International Workshop on Intelligent User Interfaces* (GRAY W.D., HEFLEY W.E. and MURRAY D., eds), pp. 89–96. New York: ACM Press

RASMUSSEN J. (1979). On the Structure of Knowledge – a Morphology of Mental Models in a Man–Machine System Context. *Report M-2192*, Riso National Laboratory, Roskilde, Denmark

RASMUSSEN J. (1986). *On Information Processing and Human–Machine Interaction: An Approach to Cognitive Engineering*. Amsterdam: Elsevier

RASMUSSEN J. and ANDERSEN H.B. (1991). Human–computer interaction: An introduction. In *Human–Computer Interaction* (RASMUSSEN J.R. and ANDERSEN H.B., eds). Hove: Lawrence Erlbaum Associates

RAVDEN S. and JOHNSON G. (1989). *Evaluating Usability of Human–Computer Interfaces: A Practical Method*. Chichester: Ellis Horwood

REISNER P. (1987). Discussion: HCI, what is it and what research is needed? In *Interfacing Thought: Cognitive Aspects of Human–Computer Interaction* (CARROLL J.M., ed.), pp. 350–2. Cambridge, MA: MIT Press

RELLES N. (1979). The design and implementation of user-oriented systems. *Unpublished doctoral dissertation*, University of Wisconsin

REMDE J.R., GOMEZ L.M. and LANDAUER T.K. (1987). SuperBook: An automatic tool for information exploration – Hypertext? In *Hypertext '87 Proceedings*, pp. 175–88

RENGGER R., MACLEOD M., BOWDEN R., DRYNAN A. and BLAYNEY M. (1993). MUSiC Performance Measurement Handbook. *ESPRIT Project 5429*, National Physical Laboratory

RHEINGOLD H.R. (1991). *Virtual Reality*. London: Secker & Warburg

RIESBECK C.K. and SCHANK R.C. (1989). *Inside Case-Based Reasoning*. Hillsdale, NJ: Lawrence Erlbaum Associates

ROBINSON C. (1990). Designing and interpreting psychological experiments. In *Human–Computer Interaction* (PREECE J. and KELLER L., eds), pp. 357–67. Hemel Hempstead: Prentice-Hall

ROBINSON M. (1991). Computer supported cooperative work: cases and concepts. In *Proceedings of Groupware '91*, Software Engineering Research Centre, Utrecht, The Netherlands

ROBSON C. (1990). Designing and interpreting psychological experiments. In *Human–Computer Interaction* (PREECE J. and KELLER L., eds), pp. 357–67. Hemel Hempstead: Prentice-Hall

RODDEN T. (1991). A survey of CSCW systems. *Interacting with Computers*, **3**(3), 319–53

ROGERS Y. (1989). Icon design for the user interface. *International Review of Ergonomics*, **2**, 129–54

ROGERS Y. (1989b). Icons at the interface: their usefulness. *Interacting with Computers*. **1**, 105–18

ROGERS Y. (1993). Coordinating computer-mediated work: A distributed cognition. *Computer supported cooperative work*, **1**, 295–315

ROGERS Y., RUTHERFORD A. and BIBBY P., eds (1992). *Models in the Mind: Theory, Perspective and Application*. London: Academic Press

ROOT R.W. (1988). Design of a multi-media vehicle for social browsing. In *Proceedings of the Conference on Computer Supported Cooperative Work (CSCW'88)*, pp. 25–38. New York: ACM Press

ROOT R.W. and DRAPER S. (1983). Questionnaires as a software evaluation tool. In *Human Factors in Computing Systems CHI'83 Conference Proceedings* (JANDA A., ed.), pp. 78–82. New York: ACM Press

ROSSON M.B., MAASS S. and KELLOGG W.A. (1988). The designer as user: building requirements for design tools from design practice. *Communications of the ACM*, **31**(11), 1288–98

ROSSON M.B., CARROLL J.M. and BELLAMY R.K.E. (1990). Smalltalk scaffolding: A case study of minimalist instruction. In *Empowering People*, CHI'90 Conference Proceedings (CHEW J.C. and WHITESIDE J., eds), pp. 423–30. New York: ACM Press

RUBINSTEIN R. and HERSH H. (1984). *The Human Factor: Designing Computer Systems for People*. Burlington, MA: Digital Press

RUMELHART D.E., McCLELLAND J.L. and the PDP RESEARCH GROUP, eds (1986). *Parallel Distributed Processing*. Cambridge, MA: MIT Press

RUSSO P. and BOOR S. (1993). How fluent is your interface? Designing for international users. In *Bridges between Worlds*, INTERCHI'93 Conference Proceedings (ASHLUND S., MULLET K., HENDERSON A., HOLLNAGEL E. and WHITE T. eds). Reading, MA: Addison-Wesley

SALAM A.G. (1989). The new rules for international standardization. *IEEE Standards Bearer*, **3**(5), 1

SANDERSON P.M. and HARWOOD K. (1988). The skills, rules and knowledge classification: a discussion of its emergence and nature. In *Tasks, Errors and Mental Models* (GOODSTEIN L.P., ANDERSEN H.B. and OLSEN H.E., eds), pp. 21–34. London: Taylor & Francis

SCHANK R.C. and ABELSON R. (1977). *Scripts, Plans, Goals and Understanding*. Hillsdale, NJ: Lawrence Erlbaum Associates

SCHEIFLER R.W. and GETTYS J. (1986). The X Window system. *ACM Transactions on Graphics*, **5**(2), 79–109

SCHMIDT K. (1991). Riding a tiger, or computer-supported cooperative work. In *Proceedings of the Second European Conference on Computer-Supported Cooperative Work (ECSCW'91)* (BANNON L., ROBINSON M. and SCHMIDT K., eds), pp. 1–16. Dordrecht: Kluwer

SCHÖN (1991). *The Reflective Practitioner: How Professionals Think in Action*. New York: Basic Books

SCRIVENER S.A.R., ed. (1991). *Proceedings of CSCW: The Multimedia and Networking Paradigm*. Uxbridge: Unicom Seminars Ltd

SCRIVENER S. (1993). State of the Art Survey: Corelli Multimedia CSCW in Distance Training. Proposal to DTI. *Open University Ref. No. R937/D120*

SCRIVENER S.A.R., HAINS D., CLARK S.M., ROCKOFF T. and SMYTHE M. (1993). Designing at a distance via designer-to-designer interaction. *Design Studies*, **14**(3), 261–82

SEARLE J.R. (1969). Speech acts: An essay on conversation. In *Contemporary Issues in Language and Discourse Processes* (ELLIS D.G. and DONOHUE W.A., eds), pp. 7–19. Hillsdale, NJ: Lawrence Erlbaum Associates

SEARS A. and SHNEIDERMAN B. (1991). High precision touch screens: design strategies and comparisons with a mouse. *International Journal of Man–Machine Studies*, **43**(4), 593–613

SELFRIDGE O.G. (1958). Pattern recognition and modern computers. In *Proceedings of the Western Joint Computer Conference*. New York: IEEE

SELLEN A.J. (1992). Speech patterns in video-mediated conversations. In *Human Factors in Computing Systems CHI'92 Conference Proceedings* (BAUERSFIELD P., BENNETT J. and LYNCH G., eds), pp. 49–59. New York: ACM Press

SELLEN A. and NICOL A. (1990). Building user-centred online help. In *The Art of Human–Computer Interface Design* (LAUREL B., ed.). Reading, MA: Addison-Wesley

SENAY H. and STABLER E. (1987). Online help system usage: An empirical study. In *Proceedings of the 2nd International Conference on Human–Computer Interaction*

SHACKEL B. (1981). The concept of usability. *Proceedings of the IBM Software and Information Usability Symposium*, pp. 1–30

SHACKEL B. (1990). Human factors and usability. In *Human–Computer Interaction: Selected Readings* (PREECE J. and KELLER L., eds). Hemel Hempstead: Prentice-Hall

SHARPLES M. (1993). A study of breakdowns and repairs in a computer-mediated communication system. *Interacting with computers*, **5**(1), 61–77

SHARRATT B. (1987). Top-down interactive systems design: some lessons learnt from using command language grammar. In *Human–Computer Interaction – INTERACT'87* (BULLINGER H.-J. and SHACKEL B., eds), pp. 395–9. Amsterdam: Elsevier Science Publishers B.V.

SHEPARD R. and METZLER J. (1971). Mental rotation of three-dimensional objects. *Science*, **171** (3972), 701–3

SHEPHERD A. (1989). Analysis and training in information tasks. In *Task Analysis for Human–Computer Interaction* (DIAPER D., ed.). Chichester: Ellis Horwood

SHIFFRIN R.M. and SHNEIDER W. (1977). Controlled and automatic human information processing: II. Perceptual learning, automatic attending, and a general theory. *Psychological Review*, **84**, 127–90

SHNEIDERMAN B. (1983). Direct manipulation: a step beyond programming languages, *IEEE Computer*, **16**(8), 57–69

SHNEIDERMAN B. (1986). *Designing the User Interface* 1st edn. Reading, MA: Addison-Wesley

SHNEIDERMAN B. (1992). *Designing the User Interface: Strategies for Effective Human–Computer Interaction* 2nd edn. Reading, MA: Addison-Wesley

SHNEIDERMAN B., ed. (1993). *Sparks of Innovation in Human–Computer Interaction*. Norwood, NJ: Ablex

SHU N.C. (1988). *Visual Programming*. New York: Van Nostrand Reinhold

SIBERT J.L., HURLEY W.D., CHENG Y. and BLESER T.W. (1989). An object centred user interface management systems architecture. In *CAD and CG'89 Beijing: Proceedings of International Conference on Computer-Aided Design and Computer Graphics*. Beijing, China: International Academic

SIMON H.A. (1981). *The sciences of the artificial*. Cambridge, MA: MIT Press

SINGER J., BEHREND S.D. and ROSCHELLE J. (1988). Children's collaborative use of a computer microworld. In *CSCW'88 Conference Proceedings*, pp. 271–81. New York: ACM Press

SMITH D., IRBY C., KIMBALL R., VERPLANK B. and HARSLEM E. (1982). Designing the Star user interface. *Byte*, **7**(4), 242–82. Reprinted in PREECE J. and KELLER L., eds (1990)

SMITH S.L. and MOSIER J.N. (1986). *Guidelines for Designing User Interface Software*. ESD-TR-86-278. Bedford, MA: MITRE Corporation

SOMMERVILLE I. (1992). *Software Engineering* 4th edn. Wokingham, England: Addison-Wesley

STEFIK M., FOSTER G., BOBROW D.G., KAHN K., LANNING S. and SUCHMAN L. (1987). Beyond the chalkboard: Computer support for collaboration and problem solving in meetings. *Communications of the ACM*, **30**(1), 32–47

STEWART T. (1991). *Directory of HCI Standards*. London: DTI

STRUBING J. (1992). Negotiation – a central aspect of collaborative work in software design. In *Proceedings of the Fifth Annual Workshop of the Psychology of Programming Interest Group*, pp. 31–9. Le Chesney, Cedex: INRIA

SUCHMAN L. (1987). *Plans and Situated Actions: The Problem of Human–Machine Communication*. Cambridge: Cambridge University Press

SUCHMAN L.A. and TRIGG R.H. (1991). Understanding practice: video as a medium for reflection and design. In *Design at Work* (GREENBAUM J. and KYNG M., eds), pp. 65–90. Hillsdale, NJ: Lawrence Erlbaum Associates

SUTCLIFFE A.G. (1990). Integrating specification of human–computer interface with Jackson system development. *Information and Software Technology*, **32**(10)

SUTCLIFFE A.G. (1991). Integrating methods of human–computer interface design with structured systems development. *International Journal of Man–Machine Studies*, **34**, 631–55

SUTHERLAND I. (1963). Sketchpad: A man–machine graphical communication system. *Proceedings of the Spring Joint Computer Conference*, **23**, 329–46

TAPPERT C.C., SUEN C.Y. and WAKAHARA T. (1988). Online handwriting recognition, a survey. In *Proceedings 9th International Conference on Pattern Recognition*, 1123–32

TAYLOR F.W. (1911). *Principles of Scientific Management*. New York: Harper and Row

TRAVIS D. (1991). *Effective Colour Displays*. London: Academic Press

TERRANA T., MERLUZZI F. and GIUDICI E. (1980). Electromagnetic radiation emitted by visual display units. In

Ergonomic Aspects of Visual Display Units (GRANDJEAN E. and VIGLIANI E., eds). London: Taylor & Francis

THOMAS C.G. and KROGSOETER M. (1993). An adaptive environment for the user interface of Excel™. In *Proceedings of the 1993 International Workshop on Intelligent User Interfaces* (GRAY W.D., HEFLEY W.E. and MURRAY D., eds), pp. 123–30. New York: ACM Press

TOGNAZZINI B. (1992). *Tog on interface*. Reading, MA: Addison-Wesley

TRAVIS D. (1991). *Effective Colour Displays*. London: Academic Press

TRIST E.L. and BAMFORTH K.W. (1951). Some social and psychological consequences of the longwall method of coal getting. *Human Relations*, **4**, 3–38

TUFTE E.R. (1990). *Envisioning Information*. Cheshire, CT: Graphics Press

TULLIS T.S. (1984). Predicting the Usability of Alphanumeric Displays. *PhD dissertation*, Rice University, Lawrence, KS

TULLIS T.S. (1988). Screen design. In *Handbook of Human–Computer Interaction* (HELANDER M., ed.), pp. 377–41. Amsterdam: North-Holland

TURKLE S. (1984). *The Second Self: Computers and the Human Spirit*. London: Granada

TYLDESLEY D.A. (1988). Employing usability engineering in the development of office products. *Computer Journal*, **31**(5), 431–6

VAN BUREN C. (1992). *Using EXCEL 4 for the Mac*. Carmel, IN: Que Corporation

VASKE J.J. and GRANTHAM C.E. (1990). *Socializing the Human–Computer Environment*. Norwood, NJ: Ablex

VERPLANK W.L. (1988). Graphic challenges in designing object-oriented user interfaces. In *Handbook of Human–Computer Interaction* (HELANDER M., ed.), pp. 365–76. Amsterdam: North-Holland

VERPLANK W.L. (1989). Tutorial notes. In *Human Factors in Computing Systems, CHI'89*. New York: ACM Press

VERPLANK W. and KIM S. (1986). Graphic invention for user interfaces: an experimental course in user interface design. *SIGCHI Bulletin*, **18**(3), 50–67

VISSER W. (1991). The cognitive psychology viewpoint on design: examples from empirical studies. In *Proceedings of Artificial Intelligence in Design '91* (GERO J., ed.), pp. 505–24

VOYAGER COMPANY (1990). *Beethoven's Ninth Symphony*. Santa Monica, CA: Voyager Company CD Companion Series

WALKER J. (1988). Tutorial Notes on online Documentation. *SIGCHI'88*

WALSHAM G. (1993). *Interpreting Information Systems in Organisations*. Chichester: John Wiley

WALTON R.E. (1989). *Up and Running: Integrating Information Technology and the Organization*. Boston, MA: Harvard School Business Press

WASSERMAN A.I. and SHEWMAKE D.T. (1985). The role of prototypes in the user software engineering (USE) methodology. In *Advances in Human–Computer Interaction* (HARTSON H.R., ed.), pp. 191–210. Norwood, NJ: Ablex. Reprinted as Chapter 19 in PREECE J. and KELLER L., eds (1990)

WATABE K., SAKATA S., MAENO K., FUKUOKA H. and OHMORI T. (1990). Distributed multiparty desktop conferencing system: MERMAID. In *Proceedings of the Conference on Computer-Supported Cooperative Work (CSCW '90)*, pp. 27–38. New York: ACM Press

WATERWORTH J.A. (1992). *Multimedia Interaction with Computers: Human Factors Issues*. Chichester: Ellis Horwood

WATT R. (1991). *Understanding Vision*. London: Academic Press

WEBSTER D.E. (1988). Mapping the design information representation terrain. *IEEE Computer*, **21**(12), 8–23

WEISER M. (1991). The computer for the 21st century. *Scientific American*, September, 66–75

WEIZENBAUM J. (1976). *Computer Power and Human Reason*. San Francisco, CA: W.H. Freeman

WELBANK M. (1990). An overview of knowledge acquisition methods. *Interacting with Computers*, **2**(1), 83–91

WENGER E. (1987). *Artificial Intelligence and Tutoring Systems*. Los Altos, CA: Morgan Kaufmann

WENZEL B. (1992). Three dimensional virtual acoustic displays. In *Multimedia Interface Design* (BLATTNER M.M. and DANNENBERG R.M., eds), pp. 279–89. New York: ACM Press

WHARTON C., BRADFORD J., JEFFRIES R. and FRANKE M. (1992). Applying cognitive walkthroughs to more complex user interfaces: experiences, issues and recommendations. In *Human factors in Computing Systems CHI'92 Conference Proceedings* (BAUERSFIELD P., BENNETT J. and LYNCH G., eds), pp. 381–8. New York: ACM Press

WHITELOCK D. and HOLLAND S. (1992). Virtual worlds and their role in investigating change in cognitive models of motion. In Digest of the Institute of Electrical Engineers' (IEE) Colloquium, *Using Virtual Worlds*, pp. 2/1–2/5. London: IEE Electronics Division, Savoy Place

WHITESIDE J. and WIXON D. (1987). Discussion: improving human–computer interaction – a quest for cognitive science. In *Interfacing Thought: Cognitive Aspects of Human–Computer Interaction* (CARROLL J.M., ed.), pp. 353–65. London: Bradford Books and Cambridge, MA: MIT Press

WHITESIDE J., BENNETT J. and HOLTZBLATT K. (1988). Usability engineering: our experience and evolution. In *Handbook of Human–Computer Interaction* (HELANDER M., ed.). Amsterdam: North-Holland

WILSON B. (1984). *Systems: Concepts, Methodologies and Applications*. Chichester: Wiley

WILSON J.R. and RUTHERFORD A. (1989). Mental models: theory and application. *Human Factors*, **31**, 617–34

WILSON P. (1991). Introducing CSCW – what it is and why we need it. In *Proceedings of CSCW: The Multimedia and Networking Paradigm* (SCRIVENER S.A.R., ed.), pp. 1–15. Unicom Seminars Ltd, Uxbridge

WINOGRAD T. (1988a). A language/action perspective on the design of cooperative work. *Human–Computer Interaction*, **3**, 3–30

WINOGRAD T. (1988b). Where the action is. *Byte*, December, 256–8

WINOGRAD T. and FLORES F. (1986). *Understanding Computers and Cognition: A New Foundation for Design*. Norwood, NJ: Ablex

WIXON D. and JONES S. (1991). Usability for fun and profit: A case study of the design of DEC RALLY Version 2. *Internal Report*, Digitial Equipment Corporation

WIXON D., HOLZBLATT K. and KNOX S. (1990). Contextual design: an emergent view of system design. In *Empowering People*, CHI'90 Conference Proceedings (CHEW J.C. and WHITESIDE J., eds), pp. 329–36. New York: ACM Press

WOLTOSZ W. (1988). Stephen Hawking's communications system. *Communications Outlook*, **10**(1), 8–11

WOODHEAD N. (1990). *Hypertext and Hypermedia: Theory and Applications*. Bonn: Addison-Wesley

WOODWARD J. (1965). *Industrial Organization: Theory and Practice*. London: Oxford University Press

WOOFFITT R. (1990). On the analysis of interaction: an introduction to conversation analysis. In *Computers and Conversation* (LUFF P., GILBERT N. and FROHLICH D., eds), pp. 7–38. London: Academic Press

WULFF W., EVENSON S. and RHEINFRANK J. (1990). Animating Interfaces. In *Proceedings of the Conference on Computer Supported Cooperative Work (CSCW'90)*, pp. 241–54. New York: ACM Press

YAVELOW C. (1992). *Macworld Music and Sound Bible*. San Mateo, CA: IDG Books

YOUNG R.M. (1983). Surrogates and mappings: two kinds of conceptual models for interactive devices. In *Mental Models* (GENTNER D. and STEVENS A.L., eds), pp. 35–52. Hillsdale, NJ: Lawrence Erlbaum Associates

YOUNG R.M. and BARNARD P.J. (1991). 'Signature' and 'Paradigm' Tasks: New Wrinkles on the Scenarios Methodology. In *People and Computers VI* (DIAPER D. and HAMMOND N., eds), pp. 91–101. Proceedings of the 6th Conference of the British Computer Society Human–Computer Interaction Specialist Group. Cambridge: Cambridge University Press

YOUNG R.M., HOWES A. and WHITTINGTON J. (1990). A knowledge analysis of interactivity. In *Human–Computer Interaction, Interact'90* (DIAPER D., GILMORE D., COCKTON G. and SHACKEL B., eds), pp. 115–20. Proceedings of the 1st IFIP Conference on Human–Computer Interaction. Amsterdam: North-Holland

YOURDON E. (1989). *Structured Walkthroughs* 4th edn. Englewood Cliffs, NJ: Yourdon Press

YOURDON E. and CONSTANTINE L. (1979). *Structured Design*. Englewood Cliffs, NJ: Prentice-Hall

YUILLE J.C. and STEIGER J.H. (1982). Nonholistic processing in mental rotation: some suggestive evidence. *Perception and Psychophysics*, **31**(3), 201–9

ZIEGLER J.E. and FÄHNRICH K.P. (1988). Direct manipulation interfaces. In *Handbook of Human–Computer Interaction* (HELANDER M., ed.), pp. 123–33. Amsterdam: North-Holland

Index

W

X

Y

Z